NEW PERSPECTIVES ON

Blended HTML and CSS Fundamentals

3rd Edition

NEW PERSPECTIVES ON

Blended HTML and CSS Fundamentals

3rd Edition

INTRODUCTORY

Henry Bojack
Farmingdale State College

Sharon Scollard
Mohawk College

COURSE TECHNOLOGY
CENGAGE Learning·

Australia • Brazil • Japan • Korea • Mexico • Singapore • Spain • United Kingdom • United States

![COURSE TECHNOLOGY CENGAGE Learning]

New Perspectives on Blended HTML and CSS Fundamentals, 3rd Edition, Introductory

Executive Editor: Marie L. Lee

Associate Acquisitions Editor: Amanda Lyons

Senior Product Manager: Kathy Finnegan

Product Manager: Leigh Hefferon

Product Manager: Julia Leroux-Lindsey

Editorial Assistant: Desiree Nattell

Director of Marketing: Elisa Roberts

Developmental Editor: Sasha Vodnik

Senior Content Project Manager: Cathie DiMassa

Composition: GEX Publishing Services

Art Director: Marissa Falco

Text Designer: Althea Chen

Cover Designer: Roycroft Design

Cover Art: © Sandy Jones/iStock Exclusive/
    Getty Images

Copyeditor: Mark Goodin

Proofreader: Vicki Zimmer

Indexer: Alexandra Nickerson

For product information and technology assistance, contact us at
Cengage Learning Customer & Sales Support, 1-800-354-9706
For permission to use material from this text or product, submit all requests online at **www.cengage.com/permissions**
Further permissions questions can be emailed to
permissionrequest@cengage.com

Some of the product names and company names used in this book have been used for identification purposes only and may be trademarks or registered trademarks of their respective manufacturers and sellers.

Microsoft and the Office logo are either registered trademarks or trademarks of Microsoft Corporation in the United States and/or other countries. Course Technology, Cengage Learning is an independent entity from the Microsoft Corporation, and not affiliated with Microsoft in any manner.

Disclaimer: Any fictional data related to persons or companies or URLs used throughout this book is intended for instructional purposes only. At the time this book was printed, any such data was fictional and not belonging to any real persons or companies.

Library of Congress Control Number: 2012940606

ISBN-13: 978-1-133-52610-0

ISBN-10: 1-133-52610-1

Course Technology
20 Channel Center Street
Boston, MA 02210
USA

Cengage Learning is a leading provider of customized learning solutions with office locations around the globe, including Singapore, the United Kingdom, Australia, Mexico, Brazil, and Japan. Locate your local office at:
international.cengage.com/global

Cengage Learning products are represented in Canada by Nelson Education, Ltd.

To learn more about Course Technology, visit **www.cengage.com/course technology**

To learn more about Cengage Learning, visit **www.cengage.com**

Purchase any of our products at your local college store or at our preferred online store **www.cengagebrain.com**

Printed in the United States of America
1 2 3 4 5 6 7 8 9 16 15 14 13 12

Preface

The New Perspectives Series' critical-thinking, problem-solving approach is the ideal way to prepare students to transcend point-and-click skills and take advantage of all that HTML and CSS have to offer.

In developing the New Perspectives Series, our goal was to create books that give students the software concepts and practical skills they need to succeed beyond the classroom. We've updated our proven case-based pedagogy with more practical content to make learning skills more meaningful to students. With the New Perspectives Series, students understand *why* they are learning *what* they are learning, and are fully prepared to apply their skills to real-life situations.

About This Book

This book provides thorough coverage of HTML and CSS, and includes the following:
- Up-to-date coverage of using HTML5 and CSS3 to build real-world Web sites
- Instruction on building interactive Web sites using forms and CSS, and incorporating multi-column designs using both fixed and liquid layouts
- New coverage of Apple OS/X and Safari

New for this edition!
- Each session begins with a Visual Overview, which includes colorful, enlarged figures with numerous callouts and key term definitions, giving students a comprehensive preview of the topics covered in the session, as well as a handy study guide.
- New ProSkills boxes provide guidance for how to use the software in real-world, professional situations, and related ProSkills exercises integrate the technology skills students learn with one or more of the following soft skills: decision making, problem solving, teamwork, verbal communication, and written communication.
- Important steps are highlighted in yellow with attached margin notes to help students pay close attention to completing the steps correctly and avoid time-consuming rework.

System Requirements

This book assumes that students have an Internet connection, a text editor, and a current browser that supports HTML5 and CSS3. The following is a list of the most recent versions of the major browsers at the time this text was published: Internet Explorer 9, Firefox 12, Safari 5.1.5, Opera 12.00 (public beta), and Google Chrome 18.0.1025.168. More recent versions may have come out since the publication of this book. Students should go to the Web browser home page to download the most current version. All browsers interpret HTML and CSS code in slightly different ways. It is highly recommended that students have several different browsers installed on their systems for comparison. Students might also want to run older versions of these browsers to highlight compatibility issues. The screenshots in this book were produced using Internet Explorer 9.0 running on Windows 7 Professional (32-bit), unless otherwise noted. If students are using different browsers or operating systems, their screens will vary slightly from those shown in the book; this should not present any problems in completing the tutorials.

www.cengage.com/ct/newperspectives

The New Perspectives Approach

> "New Perspectives texts provide up-to-date, real-world application of content, making book selection easy. The step-by-step, hands-on approach teaches students concepts they can apply immediately."
>
> —John Taylor
> Southeastern Technical College

Context
Each tutorial begins with a problem presented in a "real-world" case that is meaningful to students. The case sets the scene to help students understand what they will do in the tutorial.

Hands-on Approach
Each tutorial is divided into manageable sessions that combine reading and hands-on, step-by-step work. Colorful screenshots help guide students through the steps. **Trouble?** tips anticipate common mistakes or problems to help students stay on track and continue with the tutorial.

VISUAL OVERVIEW

Visual Overviews
New for this edition! Each session begins with a Visual Overview, a new two-page spread that includes colorful, enlarged figures with numerous callouts and key term definitions, giving students a comprehensive preview of the topics covered in the session, as well as a handy study guide.

PROSKILLS

ProSkills Boxes and Exercises
New for this edition! ProSkills boxes provide guidance for how to use the software in real-world, professional situations, and related ProSkills exercises integrate the technology skills students learn with one or more of the following soft skills: decision making, problem solving, teamwork, verbal communication, and written communication.

KEY STEP

Key Steps
New for this edition! Important steps are highlighted in yellow with attached margin notes to help students pay close attention to completing the steps correctly and avoid time-consuming rework.

INSIGHT

InSight Boxes
InSight boxes offer expert advice and best practices to help students achieve a deeper understanding of the concepts behind the software features and skills.

TIP

Margin Tips
Margin Tips provide helpful hints and shortcuts for more efficient use of the software. The Tips appear in the margin at key points throughout each tutorial, giving students extra information when and where they need it.

REVIEW

APPLY

Assessment
Retention is a key component to learning. At the end of each session, a series of Quick Check questions helps students test their understanding of the material before moving on. Engaging end-of-tutorial Review Assignments and Case Problems have always been a hallmark feature of the New Perspectives Series. Colorful bars and brief descriptions accompany the exercises, making it easy to understand both the goal and level of challenge a particular assignment holds.

REFERENCE

GLOSSARY/INDEX

Reference
Within each tutorial, Reference boxes appear before a set of steps to provide a succinct summary and preview of how to perform a task. In addition, each book includes a combination Glossary/Index to promote easy reference of material.

www.cengage.com/ct/newperspectives

Our Complete System of Instruction

BRIEF

INTRODUCTORY

COMPREHENSIVE

Coverage To Meet Your Needs

Whether you're looking for just a small amount of coverage or enough to fill a semester-long class, we can provide you with a textbook that meets your needs.

- Brief books typically cover the essential skills in just 2 to 4 tutorials.
- Introductory books build and expand on those skills and contain an average of 5 to 8 tutorials.
- Comprehensive books are great for a full-semester class, and contain 9 to 12+ tutorials.

So if the book you're holding does not provide the right amount of coverage for you, there's probably another offering available. Go to our Web site or contact your Course Technology sales representative to find out what else we offer.

COURSECASTS

CourseCasts – Learning on the Go. Always available…always relevant.

Want to keep up with the latest technology trends relevant to you? Visit our site to find a library of podcasts, CourseCasts, featuring a "CourseCast of the Week," and download them to your mp3 player at http://coursecasts.course.com.

Our fast-paced world is driven by technology. You know because you're an active participant—always on the go, always keeping up with technological trends, and always learning new ways to embrace technology to power your life.

Ken Baldauf, host of CourseCasts, is a faculty member of the Florida State University Computer Science Department where he is responsible for teaching technology classes to thousands of FSU students each year. Ken is an expert in the latest technology trends; he gathers and sorts through the most pertinent news and information for CourseCasts so your students can spend their time enjoying technology, rather than trying to figure it out. Open or close your lecture with a discussion based on the latest CourseCast.

Visit us at http://coursecasts.course.com to learn on the go!

Instructor Resources

We offer more than just a book. We have all the tools you need to enhance your lectures, check students' work, and generate exams in a new, easier-to-use and completely revised package. This book's Instructor's Manual, ExamView testbank, PowerPoint presentations, data files, solution files, figure files, and a sample syllabus are all available on a single CD-ROM or for downloading at http://www.cengage.com/coursetechnology.

Content for Online Learning

Course Technology has partnered with the leading distance learning solution providers and class-management platforms today. To access this material, visit www.cengage.com/webtutor and search for your title. Instructor resources include the following: additional case projects, sample syllabi, PowerPoint presentations, and more. For students to access this material, they must have purchased a WebTutor PIN-code specific to this title and your campus platform. The resources for students might include (based on instructor preferences): topic reviews, review questions, practice tests, and more. For additional information, please contact your sales representative.

SAM: Skills Assessment Manager

SAM is designed to help bring students from the classroom to the real world. It allows students to train and test on important computer skills in an active, hands-on environment.

SAM's easy-to-use system includes powerful interactive exams, training, and projects on the most commonly used Microsoft Office applications. SAM simulates the Office application environment, allowing students to demonstrate their knowledge and think through the skills by performing real-world tasks, such as bolding text or setting up slide transitions. Add in live-in-the-application projects, and students are on their way to truly learning and applying skills to business-centric documents.

Designed to be used with the New Perspectives Series, SAM includes handy page references, so students can print helpful study guides that match the New Perspectives textbooks used in class. For instructors, SAM also includes robust scheduling and reporting features.

Acknowledgments

I would like to express my gratitude to the people whose dedication was invaluable in producing this book. Sasha Vodnik, Developmental Editor, set the bar high and constantly surpassed it, motivating me in the process! Kathy Finnegan, Senior Product Manager, kept all the balls in the air, and very calmly let us know which ones needed special attention, with a smile throughout. The rest of the Course Technology team provided stellar support, including Marie Lee, Executive Editor; Michelle Durgerian, Project Manager (GEX); Cathie DiMassa, Senior Content Project Manager; Christian Kunciw, Manuscript Quality Assurance (MQA) Supervisor; and John Freitas, Serge Palladino, Susan Pedicini, Danielle Shaw, and Susan Whalen, MQA Testers. Thanks also to Henry Bojack for creating a strong foundation and input for the revision.

Many thanks also to the reviewers who provided such wonderful feedback and strengthened the outcome: Diana Kokoska, University of Maine at Augusta; Kate Pulling, College of Southern Nevada; and Dennis Roebuck, Delta College.

Finally, thanks to my children, Angela, Robyn and Andrew, and our newest family member, Paul, for your patience, love, and always showing me the humorous side of life. Many thanks to Mom, Linda, Mike, Ann and Dave for your support. Thanks also to dear friends who are always ready to provide a shoulder to lean on: Joe, Paula, Fred, Brenda, Al, Anne, Peggy, Pat, Cheri, Kristin, Fong and Martin.
– Sharon Scollard

BRIEF CONTENTS

TABLE OF CONTENTS

HTML

Using HTML to Create Web Pages

Creating and Formatting a Basic Web Page

OBJECTIVES

Session 1.1
- Explore the history of the Internet and the World Wide Web
- Study the differences between HTML, XHTML, and CSS
- Create a Web page with basic HTML tags
- Apply formatting tags to affect text on a Web page

Session 1.2
- Understand image files and file types
- Add an image to a Web page
- Create ordered, unordered, and description lists
- Create nested lists
- Validate a Web page

Case | *Around the World Music*

Gina D'Angelo loves music from a wide variety of genres and cultures. She recently opened a music store called Around the World Music, located in Saratoga Springs, New York. Around the World Music sells new and used CDs, DVDs, and vinyl records. Gina particularly prides herself on selling music that is not sold in most music stores. Gina wants you to create a Web page so she can advertise her store on the Web. She wants a Web page that is attractive, simple, and provides some basic information about her store. You will create a Web page for Around the World Music that meets Gina's needs.

STARTING DATA FILES

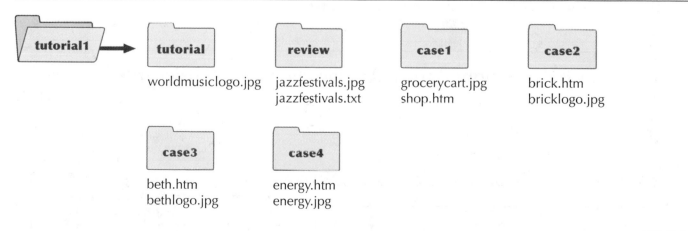

tutorial1 → tutorial

worldmusiclogo.jpg

review

jazzfestivals.jpg
jazzfestivals.txt

case1

grocerycart.jpg
shop.htm

case2

brick.htm
bricklogo.jpg

case3

beth.htm
bethlogo.jpg

case4

energy.htm
energy.jpg

SESSION 1.1 VISUAL OVERVIEW

The h2 heading element is used to indicate a subheading under the h1 heading.

`<h2>Store Information</h2>`

heading elements 1 through 6 identify important parts of the Web page.

Around the World Music

Store Information

`<h1>Around the World Music</h1>`

Gina D'Angelo, owner of Around the World Music, is an avid music fan. She *loves m*
Around the World Music offers a collection of new and used CDs, DVDs, and vinyl r

Around the World Music has a **listening station** so you can listen to CDs before you
for, *we will order it!* Special orders requir— —epayment.

Genres

`has a <strong>listening station</strong> so`

Popular Annual Music Festivals

Contact Information

The strong element is used to represent importance.

Copyright © Around the World Music

`<p>Copyright &copy; Around the World Music</p>`

Special characters not found on the keyboard can be entered using character elements.

`<p>Around the World Music has a ... </p>`

The paragraph element is a block-level element that adds white space above and below.

BASIC WEB PAGE WITH HEADINGS

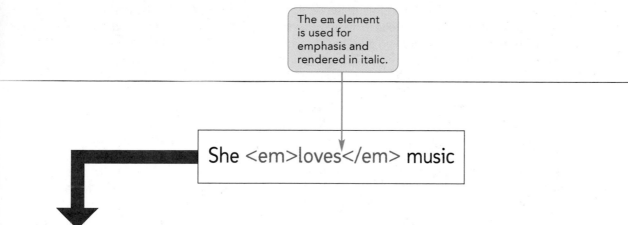

The em element is used for emphasis and rendered in italic.

She loves music

an. She *loves* music from many different cultures and locations around the world.

Ds, and vinyl records.

Ds before you make your purchasing decision. If we don't have what you're looking

The Internet and the World Wide Web

Some people believe the Internet and the World Wide Web refer to the same thing. In fact, there is quite a difference. When two or more computers are connected together, this is called a **network**. When two or more networks are connected together, this is called an **internetwork**. In the 1950s and 1960s there were many networks in development all over the world, but there was no standard method of communication between them. The Cold War era and nuclear threats prompted research in communication systems, and the breakthrough came in 1969 when one of the U.S. Department of Defense networks was connected to a network at the University of California, Berkeley, and a network at the Massachusetts Institute of Technology. This large internetwork became known as the **Internet** and grew quickly, connecting to other networks around the world. Used primarily for research and educational purposes through the 1970s and 1980s, the Internet became a commercial entity in the early 1990s. The Internet includes communications technologies such as email, file transfers, and other data transfers from one network to another. The **World Wide Web** (or simply the **Web**) is the Internet technology that provides the ability to download Web pages. The software application used to download and view Web pages is called a **Web browser**. Current Web browsers include Microsoft Internet Explorer, Apple Safari, Google Chrome, and Mozilla Firefox. Microsoft Windows includes Internet Explorer, and Apple OS X includes Safari.

HTML, XHTML, and CSS

A Web page is just a file that contains some information and formatting instructions. It may include instructions that require Web browsers to download image files or other media files as well. These instructions are written in some version of the **Hypertext Markup Language (HTML)**. When you create a Web page, you consider content, placement, and formatting for each element in the Web page. The content includes the words, images, and other media. The placement is where these items are physically placed in the browser window. The formatting is the look of the items, including styles such as bold, italics, underlining, color, and borders. HTML identifies sections of a Web page and may specify layout placement or formatting. One variant of HTML is **Extensible Hypertext Markup Language (XHTML)**. This is not a version of HTML; rather, it is more like a set of rules applied to HTML to ensure the code conforms to standards. Prior to XHTML, Web developers did not have strict standards and HTML code could be sloppy and difficult to update. HTML has evolved through several versions, and these days most Web developers are using HTML5, the most current proposal for the HTML language at the time this textbook was written. A companion technology, **Cascading Style Sheets (CSS)**, specifies formatting and placement. Throughout this textbook, there will be many examples and explanations using HTML, XHTML, and CSS blended together to create effective Web pages, rather than treating these technologies separately. The focus of this textbook is to use these technologies to understand their capabilities and create effective Web pages, not to undertake an overwhelming comprehensive study of them.

Exploring Hypertext and Markup

A Web browser can interpret a file that contains HTML and CSS and then display the resulting Web page—a process known as **rendering** a Web page. The term *hypertext markup language* is a combination of terms. **Hypertext** is a technology that allows you to click a link that points to a file. If the link points to an HTML file, the HTML file is transferred to your computer and the Web browser renders the Web page. A **markup language** is a system of codes that describes something about the content. Think of editing a document by drawing boxes around different sections of the document and labeling each one, and you get the idea. So HTML is a markup language with the functionality of hypertext.

Most programming languages are owned by a specific company or organization, and when new features are developed, a new version is released. This is not the case with HTML. The standards for HTML are set by the **World Wide Web Consortium (W3C)**, an organization of individuals and member organizations. However, the software companies that develop Web browsers choose which features to support. Although most browsers support most features, sometimes a Web browser does not support a feature that is part of the most recent HTML version standard. The opposite scenario also occurs, where a Web browser supports a proprietary feature, called an **extension**, that is not part of the most current HTML version standard. The end result is that some advanced features work only in specific Web browsers. This issue is called **cross-browser incompatibility**. Although you might be able to predict the problem areas, you should still test Web pages in several of the most popular Web browsers.

INSIGHT

Designing Web Pages for Multiple Browsers

If you open the same Web page in different browsers, you might see slight differences in the left and right margins, whether a vertical scroll bar appears at all times, and what fonts and font sizes are used. You want as many visitors to your Web site as possible, and you do not want them to have problems viewing your Web pages. Therefore, when designing your Web pages, you should always test the pages in several browsers to see if they are displayed in the manner you intend. Test your pages in at least the three most popular browsers, and in both the current and preceding versions of those browsers.

Creating a Web Page with Basic HTML Tags

You meet with Gina to discuss her goals for the Around the World Music store Web page. She wants a logo and the store name at the top of the page. She wants some information that describes the types of products in the store in the center of the page and the store contact information at the bottom of the page. Many Web page developers begin with a hand-drawn sketch during the first meeting with a client, then obtain the detailed content later. Figure 1-1 shows a sketch that outlines the main components of Gina's Web page. Gina will provide the image for the logo and the text content later.

Figure 1-1 **Hand-drawn mock-up**

Figure 1-1 Hand-drawn mock-up

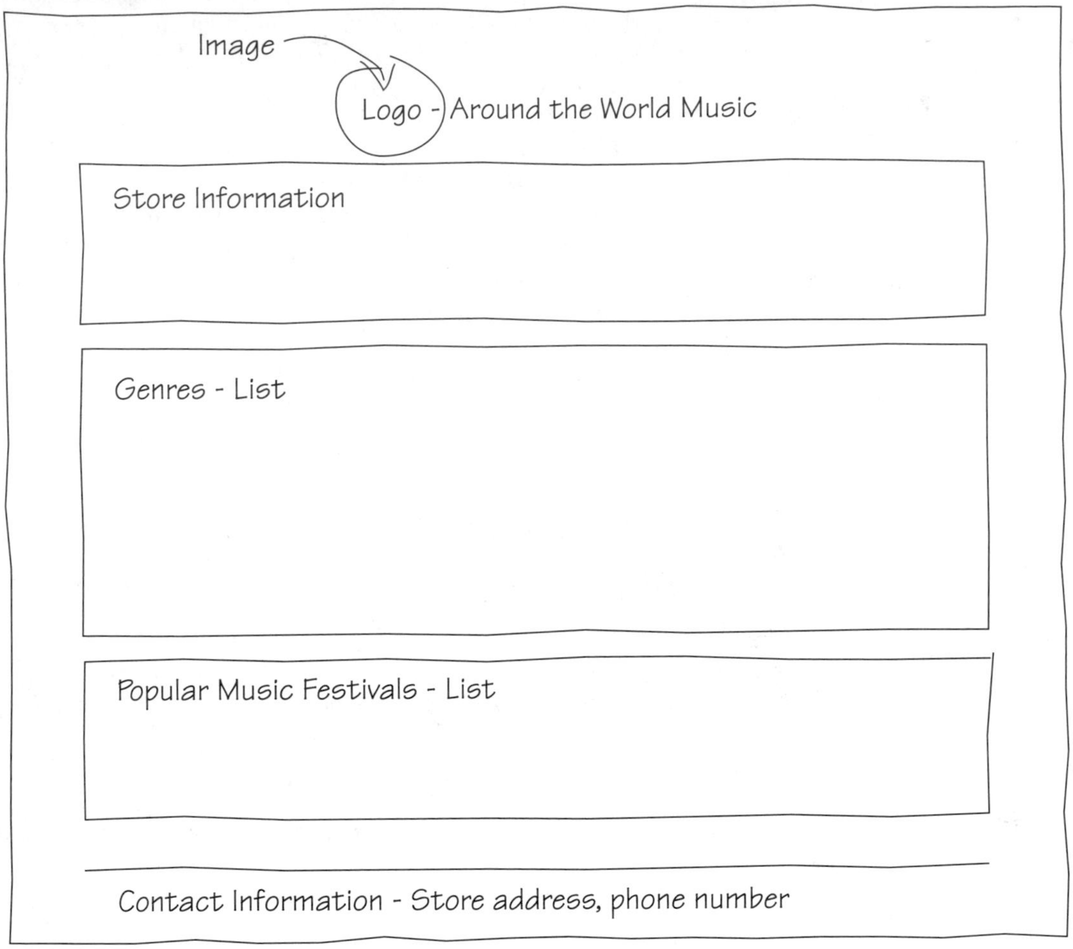

The Structure of a Simple Web Page

HTML and XHTML are tagged markup languages. That is, the language instructions are provided using tags. **Tags** are codes encapsulated in the angle brackets (< >). You probably know these symbols from mathematics as the less-than and greater-than symbols. Most tags are **paired**, with a start tag and end tag occurring as a set, but some tags are **unpaired**, occurring only as single tags. Single tags are also called **empty tags**. A well-formed Web page uses tags to create a structure that identifies the HTML document, the head section, and the body section. Figure 1-2 shows the basic HTML5 code structure, including the head and body sections. The tags `<html>`, `<head>`, and `<body>` are start tags. End tags include the slash (/) after the opening angle bracket, as in the tags `</head>`, `</body>`, and `</html>`. The `<!DOCTYPE html>` tag is a single tag, and does not have a closing tag. It is a special tag that specifies the version of HTML used for this document code. Although this tag begins with an exclamation mark, most HTML tags do not.

| Figure 1-2 | Basic HTML code structure |

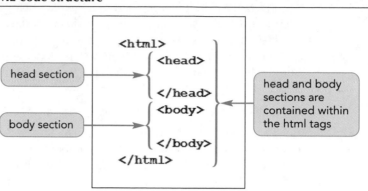

An element consists of the start tag, content, and end tag. Each tag contains the name of an element. Figure 1-2 shows the html, head, and body elements.

The DOCTYPE Tag

Every HTML document should begin with a DOCTYPE tag. This tag identifies the version of HTML used in the document. Web browsers are very forgiving and render HTML documents that do not contain this tag or that do not conform rigorously to HTML standards. An HTML **validator** is software that provides error messages and warnings if the code in a document does not conform to the rules of the specified version of HTML. The validator can be accessed via the Web and can be used by uploading the HTML file or pasting the HTML code into a text box in the validator Web page. The DOCTYPE tag specifies the version of HTML that is used in a Web page, and the validator, in turn, validates the code against that version. Using a DOCTYPE tag and writing HTML code that conforms to current HTML rules is an industry best practice.

Prior to HTML5, the DOCTYPE tag was most often used to point to the rules for XHTML version 1.0, and the tag was very complicated. Web developers could choose to use strict rules, transitional rules, or frames rules. Frames in Web design fell out of favor long ago, and transitional rules allowed the use of tags that are discontinued in practice, so those rules have also fallen out of favor. The DOCTYPE tag used to conform to strict rules is:

```
<!DOCTYPE html PUBLIC "-//W3C//DTD XHTML 1.0 Strict//EN"
  "http://www.w3.org/TR/xhtml1/DTD/xhtml1-strict.dtd">
```

HTML5 greatly simplified the DOCTYPE tag to:

```
<!DOCTYPE html>
```

When using HTML5 it is no longer necessary to specify the version of XHTML. The HTML5 DOCTYPE tag instructs validators to compare the code in the document to the HTML5 rules. You will likely see the older tags in use for quite some time as Web developers migrate to HTML5.

The html, head, and body Elements

The html element is the root element of a Web document, meaning that it is the container for all the other elements on the Web page. The start <html> tag goes immediately below the DOCTYPE tag. Get into the habit of entering the end tag after you enter the start tag, then put the content between the tags. After the start <html> tag, enter the end </html> tag.

After the start <html> tag comes the head section of the document. The **head section** contains HTML code that does not appear in the document window of a browser. You can think of the head section as a container for information about the document. The start `<head>` tag is generally typed on its own line just below the start `<html>` tag. Again, enter the end `</head>` tag before you place content in the head section. The head section usually contains **metadata**—information about the document itself, such as its keywords, its author, and a description of its content.

A head section generally includes start `<title>` and end `</title>` tags, which contain the text for the title of the Web page. It is a common practice to type the `<title>` tags and their content on a separate line:

```
<title>Around the World Music</title>
```

Because the content between the `<title>` tags appears in the title bar or the window tab at the top of the browser window, rather than in the document window of the browser, the page title should be short and should accurately describe the content of the page. Assuming no other code follows the `</title>` tag, an end `</head>` tag follows the title on its own line. Because the title is contained inside the `head` element, you should indent the `title` element by two or more spaces. You can either manually enter the spaces or use the Tab key. Some text editors use up to eight spaces for a tab, though, which stretches out HTML code. You may find that manually indenting two to five spaces makes more sense. Regardless, be consistent in the number of spaces used for indenting. The examples in this textbook use five spaces for indentation, as in the `title` element in the following code:

```
<head>
     <title>Around the World Music</title>
</head>
```

A Web browser interprets and renders text from top to bottom, one line at a time. The tags in the head section are processed before the tags in the body section.

The **body** element is the container for all of the page content that will be rendered in the document window.

The Basic Structure of an HTML5 Document

The basic structure of an HTML5 document contains the `DOCTYPE`, `html`, `head`, and `body` elements as follows:

```
<!DOCTYPE html>
<html>
     <head>
          content for head section
     </head>
     <body>
          content for body section
     </body>
</html>
```

Typing the Code

Creating a file that contains HTML and CSS code does not require specialized software. This code can be written and saved using a very simple text editor such as Notepad, which comes with Microsoft Windows, or TextEdit, which comes with Apple OS X.

You'll continue your work creating the Around The World Web page by entering the basic structuring tags. The page will include a title, which will appear in the title bar of Web browsers that open it. You'll create the `title` element and the `h1` heading element as well.

To create a simple Web page file:

1. Open your text editor. To open the default text editor on a computer running Windows, click the **Start** button, click **All Programs**, click **Accessories**, and then click **Notepad**. To open the default editor on a computer running Apple OS X, click the **Applications** folder, and then click **TextEdit**.

The DOCTYPE tag must include an exclamation character after the opening angle bracket.

2. In your text editor, type the following lines of code, pressing the **Tab** key to increase the indentation of the code when needed and pressing the **Enter** key after each line:

```
<!DOCTYPE html>
<html>
    <head>
        <title>Around the World Music</title>
    </head>
    <body>
        <h1>Around the World Music</h1>
    </body>
</html>
```

Notice the elements that are contained inside other elements are indented. This is an industry convention that helps when it comes to reading and troubleshooting the code. The detailed view is shown in Figure 1-3.

Figure 1-3 ▸ **Web page code for Around the World Music**

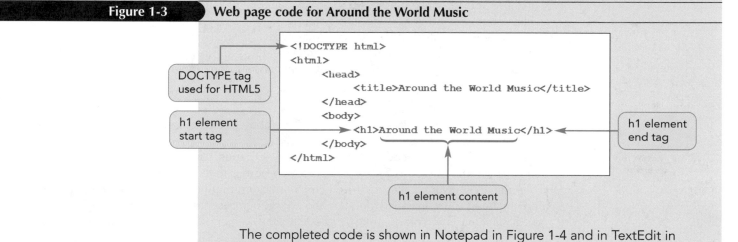

The completed code is shown in Notepad in Figure 1-4 and in TextEdit in Figure 1-5.

Figure 1-4 ▸ **worldmusic.htm in Notepad**

```
Untitled - Notepad
File  Edit  Format  View  Help
<!DOCTYPE html>
<html>
        <head>
                <title>Around the World Music</title>
        </head>
        <body>
                <h1>Around the World Music</h1>
        </body>
</html>
```

Notepad tab indents are eight space characters

Figure 1-5 worldmusic.htm in TextEdit

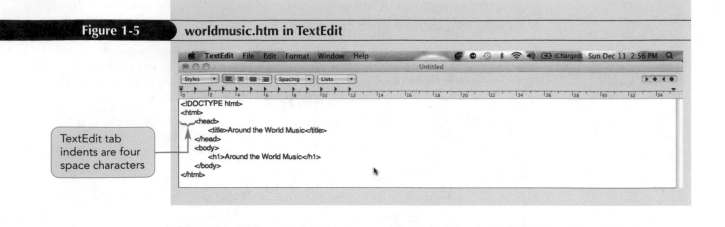

TextEdit tab indents are four space characters

Development Tools

Because HTML files are plain text files, there are many options available for creating HTML files. Here's a list of some of the most popular tools:

- A plain text editor such as Notepad or TextEdit—These are no-frills editors that save plain text files.
- A programmer's text-editing application such as Notepad++ or Context—These editors have some context help for programming languages and provide features such as line numbers and troubleshooting help.
- A sophisticated editor such as Adobe Dreamweaver or Microsoft Expression Web—These development environments have many features for previewing, drag-and-drop editing, and managing an entire Web site that consists of multiple files.

If you are just creating and editing very simple Web pages, a plain text editor or a programmer's editor will do the job. If you are managing and editing multiple Web pages and multiple Web sites, then a robust development environment will make the job much easier.

If there are more advanced tools for creating Web pages, such as Adobe Dreamweaver and Microsoft Expression Web, why bother to learn HTML? While HTML-editing software makes code entry more efficient, there often comes a time when you need to fix an issue by editing the code. Your best strategy is to learn HTML and CSS first, and then graduate to Web-editing software and other Web development languages such as JavaScript.

Saving an HTML File

Before you can see the Web page in a Web browser, you need to save the file. After you save the file, you then open it in the Web browser. The browser will read the file line by line and render the HTML code in its display window.

Most filenames consist of a base filename, a period, and after the period—or dot—is a suffix of three to four characters. The group of characters to the right of the period is known as the **extension**. For instance, an example of a Microsoft Word filename might be resume.doc; in this case, the extension is *doc*. For HTML files, the convention is to use a name with an extension of *htm* or *html*. Web browsers expect HTML code in a file that is named with this extension. If a file is named with a different extension, Web browsers may not read the code or render the Web page. Note that your operating system may not display file extensions by default when displaying lists of files.

Conventions are used when naming files as well. Many Web developers use only lowercase letters, and occasionally numbers. They use lowercase letters because in some instances, the operating system used for the computers that store the files is case sensitive and distinguishes between uppercase and lowercase characters. In this case, an uppercase *M* would not be treated the same as a lowercase *m*. To avoid the confusion caused by this problem, many Web designers use only lowercase characters.

Web designers also often avoid using the space and underscore characters as well as other special characters such as symbols. The reason for this is twofold. First, some special characters are not allowed in filenames at all. Second, the filename becomes part of the **URL**, or Web page address, and it is confusing both to read and to type if there is a space, underscore, or other symbol. For these reasons, you will use mainly lowercase alphabet characters, few numbers, and no special characters when you name your Web page files in this textbook.

You'll name your file worldmusic.htm and store it in the tutorial1\tutorial folder.

The Mac TextEdit application saves files by default in Rich Text Format (RTF), which is a word-processing file type. To save files instead in text-only format, you select a menu item that converts the document to plain text.

> **TIP**
>
> Avoid using the numbers *1* and *0* in a filename. These are too easily mistaken for the lowercase versions of the letters *L* and *O*.

To save your file using Notepad or TextEdit:

1. If you're using TextEdit on a Mac, click **Format**, and then click **Make Plain Text**, as shown in Figure 1-6. You may notice the font changes slightly.

| Figure 1-6 | Making the document contents plain text in TextEdit |

2. In either Notepad or TextEdit, click **File**, and then click **Save**. Figure 1-7 shows the Save As dialog box in Notepad.

Figure 1-7   **Notepad Save As dialog box**

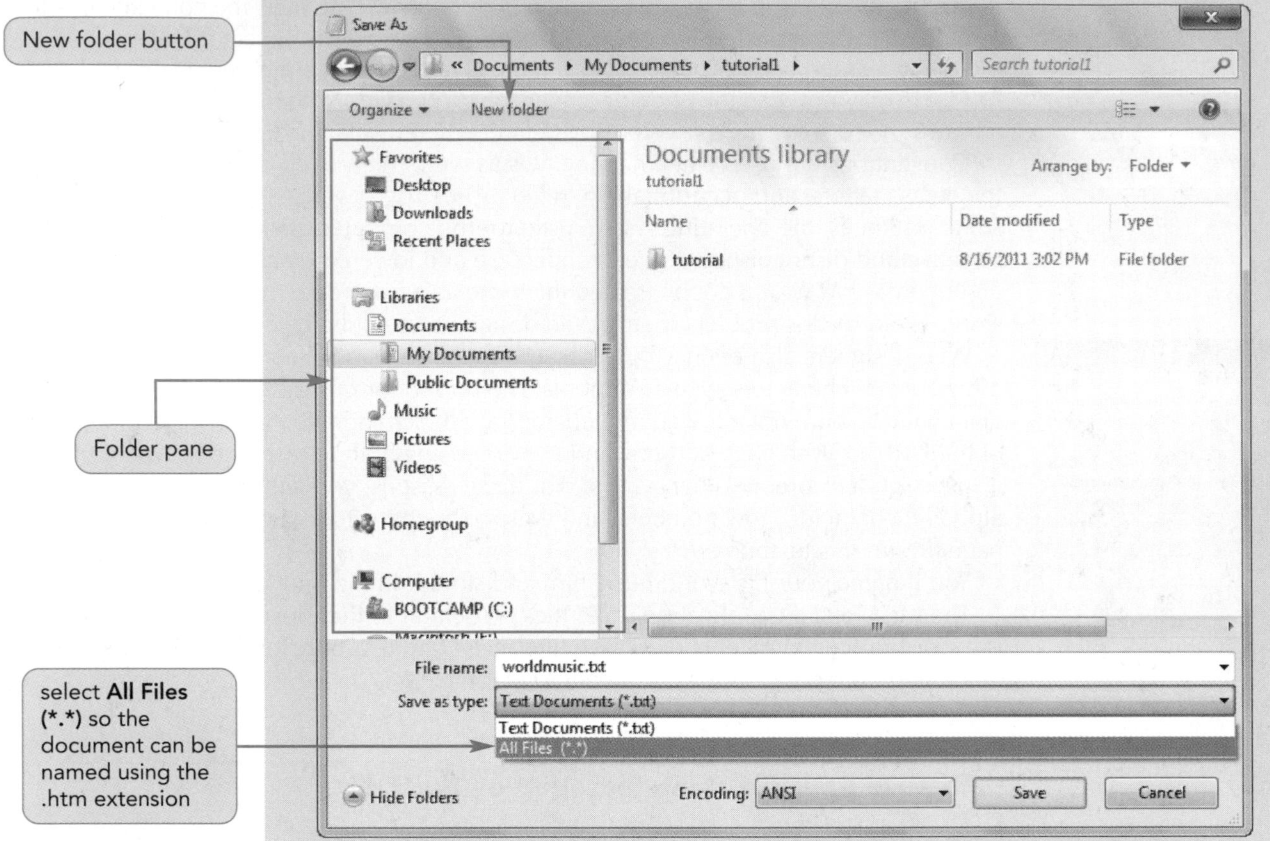

New folder button

Folder pane

select **All Files**
(*.*) so the
document can be
named using the
.htm extension

Save As

« Documents ▸ My Documents ▸ tutorial1 ▸   Search tutorial1

Organize ▾   New folder

☆ Favorites
    🖥 Desktop
    📥 Downloads
    📑 Recent Places

📚 Libraries
    📄 Documents
        📄 My Documents
        📁 Public Documents
    🎵 Music
    🖼 Pictures
    🎬 Videos

🏠 Homegroup

💻 Computer
    💾 BOOTCAMP (C:)

Documents library
tutorial1   Arrange by: Folder ▾

Name   Date modified   Type

📁 tutorial   8/16/2011 3:02 PM   File folder

File name: worldmusic.txt

Save as type: Text Documents (*.txt)
               Text Documents (*.txt)
               All Files (*.*)

Hide Folders   Encoding: ANSI   Save   Cancel

3. Navigate to the tutorial1\tutorial folder.

   Trouble? If you don't have the starting Data Files, you need to get them before you can proceed. Your instructor will either give you the Data Files or ask you to obtain them from a specified location (such as a network drive). In either case, make a backup copy of the Data Files before you start so that you will have the original files available in case you need to start over. If you have any questions about the Data Files, see your instructor or technical support person for assistance.

4. In Notepad, click the **Save as type** list arrow, and then select **All Files**. This allows you to save the file with an .htm or .html extension rather than the default .txt extension.

5. In the Filename box, type **worldmusic.htm**, and then click the **Save** button. In TextEdit, a new dialog box appears that requires you to verify the file extension, as shown in Figure 1-8.

Figure 1-8   **TextEdit Save As dialog box**

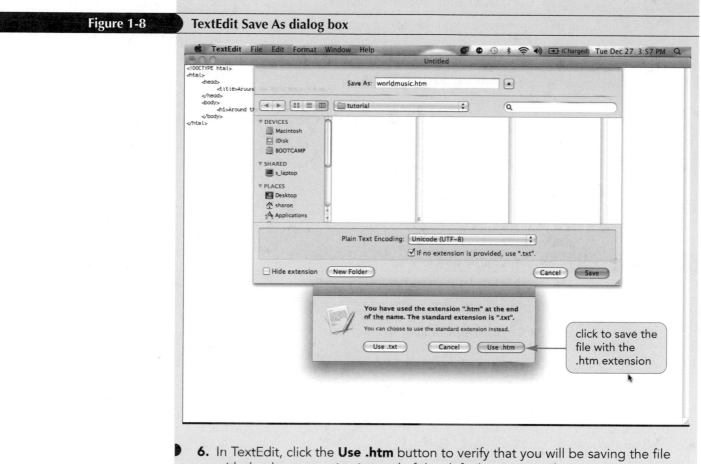

6. In TextEdit, click the **Use .htm** button to verify that you will be saving the file with the .htm extension instead of the default .txt extension.

Now that you've saved the Around The World Web page, you're ready to view it in a Web browser.

To open the Web page in a Web browser:

TIP

If you have more than one Web browser, use the one you like the most.

1. Open a Web browser, such as Internet Explorer or Safari.

2. Click **File**, and then click **Open**.

3. Navigate to the worldmusic.htm file in the tutorial1\tutorial folder.

4. Click the **Open** button, and then click the **OK** button.

The Web page is displayed in the Web browser. Notice the title appears in the title bar or the tab of the Web browser and the text *Around the World Music* is displayed in large, bold font in the browser window. Figure 1-9 shows the Web page in Internet Explorer 9, and Figure 1-10 shows it in Safari 5.

| Figure 1-9 | worldmusic.htm in Internet Explorer |

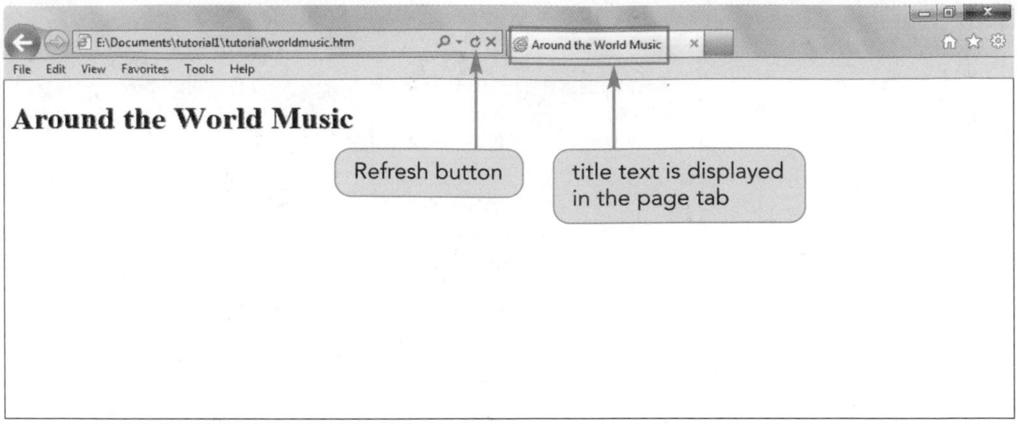

Around the World Music

Refresh button

title text is displayed in the page tab

| Figure 1-10 | worldmusic.htm in Safari |

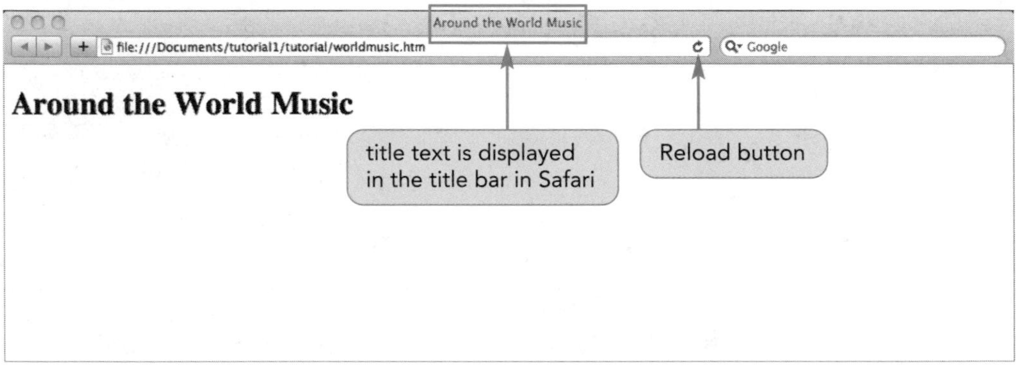

Around the World Music

title text is displayed in the title bar in Safari

Reload button

INSIGHT

Using Multiple Web Browsers

It's important to test your Web pages in more than one browser as you develop the HTML code. Web browsers might render aspects such as colors or the styles of headings slightly differently. Each time you make changes in your text editor, you should save them and then refresh the page in your browser to make sure it displays the current version of the file. Each browser has a Refresh or Reload command or button. In Internet Explorer, for example, you can press the F5 key or click the Refresh button to refresh a page.

As you develop the Around the World Music Web page for Gina, you'll be using tags that apply formatting or affect the position of content. The formatting you can apply with tags includes bold, italic, font sizes, and heading styles. In addition, you can center or right-align content.

An HTML element includes an opening tag, the text content, and the closing tag using the following format: `<tag>content</tag>`. Most tags are paired. The paired tags are used to mark the start and end of some content.

There are some tags that are not paired, called **empty elements**. Empty elements are the exception, rather than the rule, because they do not mark any content. For example, one empty element is used as a line break, to indicate the end of a line of text. An empty element can contain the forward slash at the end of the tag using the format `<tag />`. The forward slash at the end of an empty element tag is optional but used by many Web developers, and you'll use it in this textbook.

Commenting Code

Web developers document their work by adding comments to their code. The comments often include the name and contact information of the developer or any important information about the file. Comments can appear anywhere in HTML code and can also be used to identify sections of the code. Some developers refer to such comments as **internal documentation**. The comment tag is entered as follows:

```
<!-- comments inserted here -->
```

The comment tag begins with the left angle bracket, followed by an exclamation mark and two dashes. Any text after these characters is not rendered in browser windows. After the comment text, the tag ends with two dashes and a right angle bracket. Sometimes Web developers split a comment over several lines, as follows:

```
<!--
    Multiline text for comments that are quite
    long look better indented inside the comment tag like
    this.
-->
```

You'll use a comment to add your author information to the code on Gina's Web page.

To add authorship information in a comment:

▶ **1.** Return to the **worldmusic.htm** file in your text editor.

▶ **2.** Between the start <head> and start <title> tags, type the following comment, as shown in Figure 1-11:

```
<!--
    Tutorial 1
    Author: your name
    Date: today's date
-->
```

Figure 1-11   **Comment added**

```
<!DOCTYPE html>
<html>
    <head>
                       <!--
                           Tutorial 1
                           Author: your name
                           Date: today's date
                       -->

            <title>Around the World Music</title>
        </head>
        <body>
            <h1>Around the World Music</h1>
        </body>
</html>
```

indent inside <html>

indent inside <head>

▶ **3.** Save the file.

▶ **4.** Return to your browser, and then click the **Refresh** or **Reload** button to refresh the Web page.

You will not notice any changes in the appearance of the Web page because the comment appears only in the source code and is not rendered in the browser window.

TIP

If a comment is not properly closed with two hyphens followed by an angle bracket, then it's possible that none of the document will be displayed beyond that comment because the rest of the content will be treated as a comment.

Formatting Text on a Web Page

Word-processing software such as Microsoft Word includes many formatting options to affect the appearance of text. Likewise, when you're creating a Web page with a text editor, you can use HTML codes to add common formatting features such as bold and italic, to change font size, and to customize font color.

Creating Headings

The **heading elements** are used to mark the importance of content as headings and to bring attention to important topics on the page. Each heading element has a style associated with it; however, it's important to think of headings as identifying and organizing content rather than as shortcuts to applying text styles. A heading style might render text in a larger font and bold, or in a smaller font. In HTML5, there are six heading elements: h1, h2, h3, h4, h5, and h6. Each heading changes the text size; h1 headings are the largest text size, and h6 headings are the smallest. The heading tags use the following structure, where *n* is a value from 1 through 6 and *content* is the heading text:

```
<hn>content</hn>
```

Font sizes can be measured in **points** (pt), and there are 72 points in a vertical inch. An h1 heading produces the largest text, and an h6 heading produces the smallest text, as shown in Figure 1-12. In a later tutorial, you will learn about other ways to express text size and use CSS to customize the style to be used for each heading.

Figure 1-12 **Heading styles**

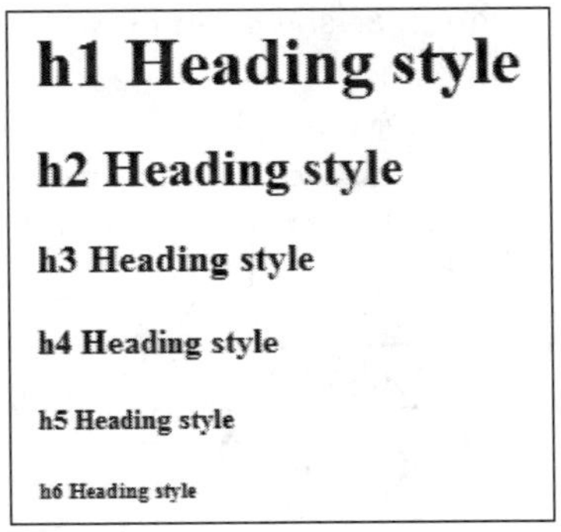

As shown in Figure 1-1, Gina has identified several sections she would like her Web page to contain: she would like a section that contains general information about the store, another section containing information about genres of music, another section for music festivals, and a section for contact information. You'll use the h1 heading to add the name of the store, and then use h2 headings to add the section titles.

To insert headings:

1. Return to the worldmusic.htm file in your text editor.

2. Between the <body> and </body> tags, type the following code to create headings, pressing the **Enter** key twice after each heading, as shown in Figure 1-13:

```
<h2>Store Information</h2>

<h2>Genres</h2>

<h2>Popular Annual Music Festivals</h2>

<h2>Contact Information</h2>
```

Figure 1-13 ▶ **Heading tags in worldmusic.htm**

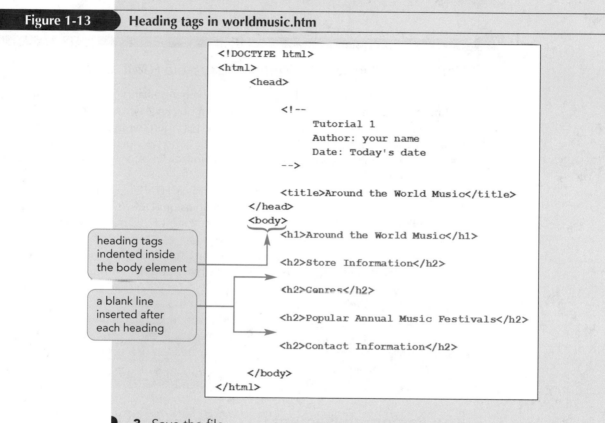

3. Save the file.

4. Return to your browser, and then reload the Web page. See Figure 1-14.

Figure 1-14   **Headings rendered in the Web browser**

Around the World Music

Store Information

Genres

Popular Annual Music Festivals

Contact Information

PROSKILLS

Written Communication: Writing Adaptable HTML Code

The computing industry is well known for rapid changes and growth, and Internet technologies have certainly evolved and grown quickly. With this trend in mind, how can you avoid having to recreate your Web pages when the technologies change? How can you ensure your Web pages will continue to be viewable in a Web browser? Here are a few guidelines that can help to minimize the effort that would be needed to update your Web pages:

- *Keep it simple.* Use a simple design and standard HTML elements.
- *Avoid using the most cutting-edge technologies until they become mainstream.* Using the cutting-edge technologies can also be high maintenance as bugs are found or as the technology falls out of favor.
- *Load your Web page in several Web browsers.* Your Web page should be readable and functional in the current versions of the most popular Web browsers. Know who your target audience is and which Web browsers they are likely to use. You should also load your Web page in several versions of those Web browsers. Don't assume that the Web page will look the same or remain functional in all Web browsers.
- *Pay attention to structure and industry conventions.* Use a code validator to validate your HTML code and fix any errors. Use industry best practices such as indenting content contained within sections.

The Paragraph Element

TIP

You can press the Ctrl+R key combination to refresh the browser in both Internet Explorer and Firefox.

The paragraph element is used to identify a paragraph of text, which can include multiple lines of text or just a single word or character. The structure of the paragraph element is:

```
<p>content</p>
```

You type paragraphs in an HTML document in your text editor the same way you would in a word-processing document—by letting the text wrap as you type if the wrapping feature is on. First, you type the start <p> tag, and then the end </p> tag, and then the paragraph contents between the tags.

One of the biggest differences between a document created in a word-processing application such as Microsoft Word and a Web page is that the default position of text on a Web page can change depending on the size of a user's browser window. If the window is narrow, the text will rewrap to fit the narrow window. Similarly if the window is wider, the text will stretch to the left and right across the page. Depending on the size of the Web browser window, a paragraph may wrap at different points or appear larger or smaller.

The paragraph element and all six heading elements are examples of **block-level elements**. A block-level element has white space around the edge known as **padding**, a border, and an external margin. In a later tutorial about Cascading Style Sheets, you'll use padding, borders, and margins to customize the appearance of your Web pages.

Gina has provided a general description of the store. You'll add it to the Around the World Music Web page now.

To enter the description text:

1. Return to the worldmusic.htm file in your text editor.

2. Click below the h2 heading *Store Information*, and then press the **Enter** key to insert a new blank line.

3. Type the following code. Note that you can press the Enter key at the end of each line within a paragraph, as shown in Figure 1-15, or you can type the text of each paragraph as one very long line.

   Trouble? If the text is scrolling past the right edge of the window and not wrapping, consult the documentation for your text editor for instructions to turn on the word-wrapping feature.

   ```
   <p>Gina D'Angelo, owner of Around the World Music, is an avid
   music fan. She loves music from many different cultures and
   locations around the world. Around the World Music offers a
   collection of new and used CDs, DVDs, and vinyl records.</p>

   <p>Around the World Music has a listening station so you can
   listen to CDs before you make your purchasing decision. If we
   don't have what you're looking for, we will order it! Special
   orders require prepayment.</p>
   ```

Figure 1-15 | Text entered within paragraph tags

```
<h2>Store Information</h2>

<p>Gina D'Angelo, owner of Around the World Music, is an avid
music fan. She loves music from many different cultures and
locations around the world. Around the World Music offers a
collection of new and used CDs, DVDs, and vinyl records.</p>

<p>Around the World Music has a listening station so you can
listen to CDs before you make your purchasing decision. If we
don't have what you're looking for, we will order it! Special
orders require prepayment.</p>

<h2>Genres</h2>
```

4. Save the file.

5. Return to your Web browser, and then click the **Refresh** or **Reload** button to view the changes in the file. The Web page should look similar to Figure 1-16. Recall that the paragraphs may wrap differently if your Web browser window is a different size.

Figure 1-16	Paragraphs rendered in the Web browser

Around the World Music

Store Information

Gina D'Angelo, owner of Around the World Music, is an avid music fan. She loves music from many different cultures and locations around the world. Around the World Music offers a collection of new and used CDs, DVDs, and vinyl records.

Around the World Music has a listening stationso you can listen to CDs before you make your purchasing decision. If we don't have what you're looking for, we will order it! Special orders require prepayment.

Genres

Popular Annual Music Festivals

Contact Information

Text Formatting Tags

TIP

Always switch from the browser to your text editor by using the taskbar (Windows) or Dock (Mac). This is much faster than closing one program to switch to another.

You've used the heading elements to organize content into headings and subheadings. Sometimes you want to draw the reader's attention to text that is not a heading that may be inside a paragraph. The **strong element** marks text to have importance and by default renders text in bold. The **em element** marks text for emphasis and by default renders text in italic. It is very common to mark text with multiple HTML elements. For instance, you can combine both the strong and em elements so text appears as strong and emphasized. Each of these elements is an example of an **inline element**, which is contained within a block-level element and is not surrounded by additional white space.

REFERENCE

Nesting Tags

- To apply two or more effects to content, nest tags using the following format:

```
<tag1><tag2>content</tag2></tag1>
```

TIP

It is good coding practice to type the open and end tags side by side, and *then* type the content between the tags. By typing the tags first, you are less likely to accidentally omit the end tag after typing the content.

Gina really does love music, and you decide to display the word *loves* using the em element for emphasis. You also want to make sure the words *listening station* stand out, so you'll use the strong element to mark those. In addition, you want to make sure readers see that the store can accommodate special orders, so you decide to apply strong and em to the phrase *we will order it!*

To mark text with `strong` and em:

▶ 1. Return to the **worldmusic.htm** file in your text editor.

▶ 2. Edit the first paragraph to add **<em>** just before the *l* in *loves*, and to add the **</em>** tag after the word *loves*, as shown in Figure 1-17.

▶ 3. Using the same technique as in Step 2, add the start **<strong>** tag just before the first letter of the word *listening*, and add the end **</strong>** tag just after the last letter of the word *station*, as shown in Figure 1-17.

▶ 4. Using the same technique as in Step 2, edit the second paragraph to add the **<strong>** and **<em>** tags to the left of the *w* in the word *we*, and the **</em>** and **</strong>** tags just after the exclamation mark after the word *it!*, as shown in Figure 1-17.

| Figure 1-17 | Marking bold and italics in worldmusic.htm |

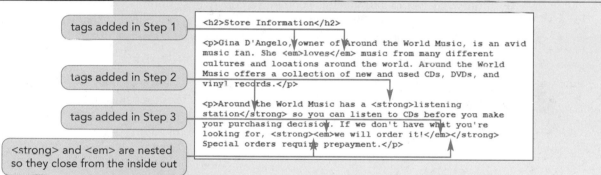

tags added in Step 1

tags added in Step 2

tags added in Step 3

<strong> and <em> are nested so they close from the inside out

```
<h2>Store Information</h2>

<p>Gina D'Angelo, owner of Around the World Music, is an avid
music fan. She <em>loves</em> music from many different
cultures and locations around the world. Around the World
Music offers a collection of new and used CDs, DVDs, and
vinyl records.</p>

<p>Around the World Music has a <strong>listening
station</strong> so you can listen to CDs before you make
your purchasing decision. If we don't have what you're
looking for, <strong><em>we will order it!</em></strong>
Special orders require prepayment.</p>
```

▶ 5. Save the file.

▶ 6. Return to your Web browser, and then click the **Refresh** or **Reload** button to view the changes in the file. The Web page should look similar to Figure 1-18.

| Figure 1-18 | strong (bold) and em (italic) formatting in a Web browser |

Around the World Music

Store Information

Gina D'Angelo, owner of Around the World Music is an avid music fan. She *loves* music from many different cultures and locations around the world. Around the World Music offers a collection of new and used CDs, DVDs, and vinyl records.

Around the World Music has a **listening station** so you can listen to CDs before you make your purchasing decision. If we don't have what you're looking for, ***we will order it!*** Special orders require prepayment.

Genres

Popular Annual Music Festivals

Contact Information

Inserting Special Characters

In most cases, a **special character**, also known as a **character entity**, is one you cannot enter from the keyboard, such as a copyright symbol or a fraction like ½. The left angle bracket (<) can be entered from the keyboard, but in HTML this symbol indicates the beginning of a tag, so you'll need to use the character entity when you need to display this symbol in the browser as well. You can enter a character entity in your code using a name or a number. A name used to enter a character entity is known as a **named character reference** and is generally an abbreviation of the character's name. A named character reference is preceded by an ampersand (&) and followed by a semicolon and has the following form, where *name* is the named character reference:

&*name*;

For example, to render the copyright symbol in browsers, you would enter the following code in your text editor:

©

Browsers would translate this code into a copyright symbol: ©.

A number used to enter a character entity is known as a **numeric character reference** and has the following form, where *number* is the numeric character reference:

&#*number*;

When you refer to a special character by a numeric character reference, you are referring to the special character's position in the character set specified by the International Standards Organization (ISO). The character number is preceded by both the ampersand and pound (#) symbols, and is followed by a semicolon. For example, you could also render the copyright symbol using the numeric character reference:

©

All special characters can be entered into your code by a numeric character reference, but not all special characters can be entered by using a named character reference. In addition, named character references are case sensitive. Figure 1-19 shows the code references and names for some commonly used special characters. See the appendices for the complete list.

Figure 1-19	Character entities

Named Reference	Numeric Reference	Character	Description
&amp;	&#38;	&	Ampersand
&lt;	&#60;	<	Less than or left angle bracket
&gt;	&#62;	>	Greater than or right angle bracket
&dagger;	&#134;	†	Dagger
&Dagger;	&#135;	‡	Double dagger
&bull;	&#149;	•	Raised, large bullet
&ndash;	&#150;	–	En dash
&mdash;	&#151;	—	Em dash
		(a space)	Space
&pound;	&#163;	£	Pound sterling
&cent;	&#162;	¢	Cent sign
&yen;	&#165;	¥	Yen sign
&sect;	&#167;	§	Section sign
&copy;	&#169;	©	Copyright
&reg;	&#174;	®	Registered trademark
&deg;	&#176;	°	Degree
&middot;	&#183;	·	Raised, small bullet
&sup1;	&#185;	^{1}	Superscript 1
&sup2;	&#178;	^{2}	Superscript 2
&sup3;	&#179;	^{3}	Superscript 3
&frac14;	&#188;	¼	one-fourth
&frac12;	&#189;	½	one-half
&frac34;	&#190;	¾	three-fourths
&iquest;	&#191;	¿	inverted question mark

Gina would like you to add a copyright symbol and copyright information at the bottom of the page.

To insert the copyright symbol:

1. Return to the worldmusic.htm file in your text editor.

2. After the Contact Information heading, insert the following code, as shown in Figure 1-20:

```
<p>Copyright &copy; Around the World Music</p>
```

Figure 1-20 Code for copyright symbol

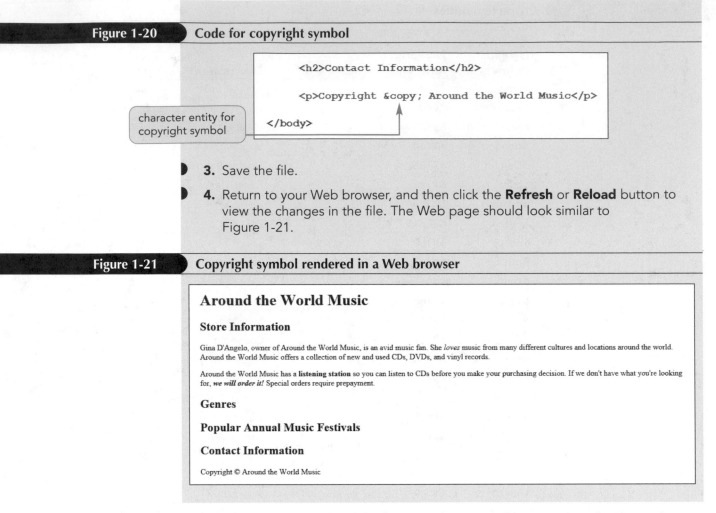

character entity for copyright symbol

```
                    <h2>Contact Information</h2>

                    <p>Copyright &copy; Around the World Music</p>

</body>
```

3. Save the file.

4. Return to your Web browser, and then click the **Refresh** or **Reload** button to view the changes in the file. The Web page should look similar to Figure 1-21.

Figure 1-21 Copyright symbol rendered in a Web browser

Around the World Music

Store Information

Gina D'Angelo, owner of Around the World Music, is an avid music fan. She *loves* music from many different cultures and locations around the world. Around the World Music offers a collection of new and used CDs, DVDs, and vinyl records.

Around the World Music has a **listening station** so you can listen to CDs before you make your purchasing decision. If we don't have what you're looking for, *we will order it!* Special orders require prepayment.

Genres

Popular Annual Music Festivals

Contact Information

Copyright © Around the World Music

Now that you've completed the first part of Gina's Web page and are familiar with the development tools, you're ready to add an image for the logo and add the list of music genres and music festivals. You'll complete these tasks in Session 1.2.

Tips for Typing HTML Code in a Text Editor

The following list contains tips and hints for keeping your HTML code error free:

- *Type all code in lowercase.* Type your HTML code in lowercase, but type content as you normally would.
- *Filenames should also be typed in lowercase, using only letters and numbers.* Avoid using the numbers *1* and *0* in filenames because they are too easily confused with the lowercase versions of the letters *L* and *O*.
- *Paragraph your code by indenting elements that are inside other elements.* Indent tags that are embedded in sections or other containers. You could enter all of the elements and content in a Web page one after the other on a single long line and Web browsers would still render your code. However, paragraphing code neatly is an industry best practice because it ensures that code is easy to read and, as a result, much easier to troubleshoot.
- *Use vertical white space.* A blank line or two separating paragraphs, headings, and other sections of HTML code ensures the code sections are easy to find. This also helps to minimize troubleshooting time.

Session 1.1 Quick Check

1. What element is the root element for a Web page?
2. Where does text typed between `<title>` tags appear in a Web browser?
3. What is the purpose of a comment tag?
4. What is the purpose of the `em` element?
5. What numeric reference would display the fraction ¼ in a Web browser?
6. What named reference would display the fraction ¼ in a Web browser?

SESSION 1.2 VISUAL OVERVIEW

The <img> tag is used to place an image in a Web page.

```
<img src = "images/worldmusiclogo.jpg"
alt = "Around the World Music logo"
title = "Around the World Music logo"
width = "250" height = "188" />
```

An **unordered list** is used to create a list with bullets for each list item.

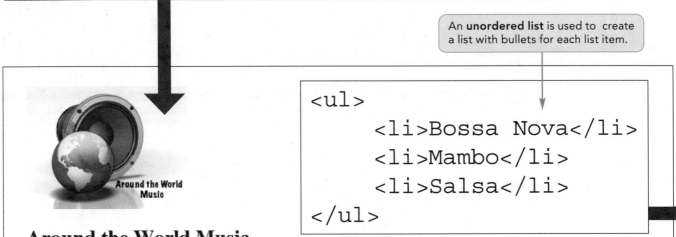

```
<ul>
        <li>Bossa Nova</li>
        <li>Mambo</li>
        <li>Salsa</li>
</ul>
```

Around the World Music

Store Information

Gina D'Angelo, owner of Around the World Music, is an avid music fan. She *loves* music from many different cultures and locations around the world. Around the World Music offers a collection of new and used CDs, DVDs, and vinyl records.

Around the World Music has a **listening station** so you can listen to CDs before you make your purchasing decision. If we don't have what you're looking for, *we will order it!* Special orders require prepayment.

IMAGES AND LISTS

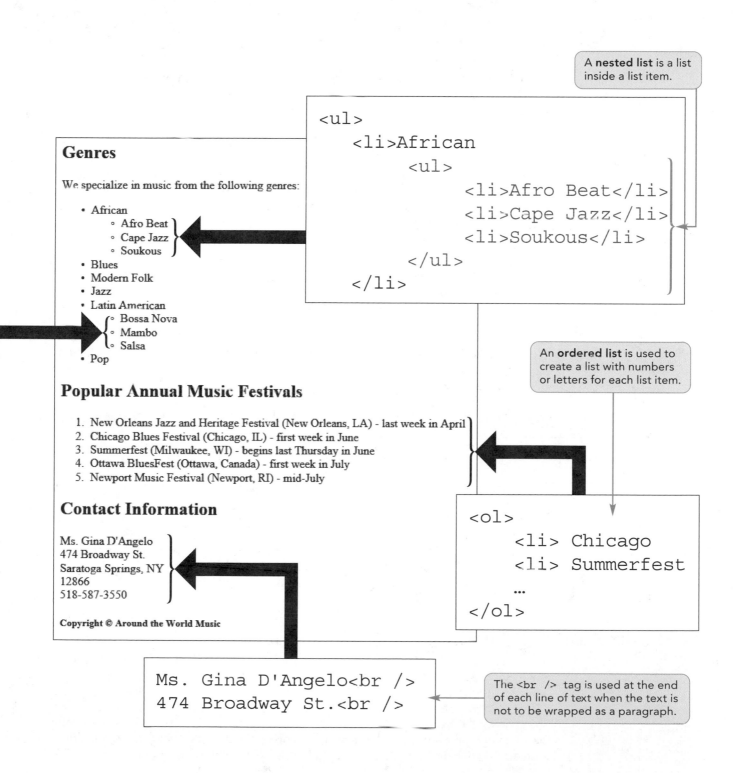

Genres

We specialize in music from the following genres:

- African
  - Afro Beat
  - Cape Jazz
  - Soukous
- Blues
- Modern Folk
- Jazz
- Latin American
  - Bossa Nova
  - Mambo
  - Salsa
- Pop

Popular Annual Music Festivals

1. New Orleans Jazz and Heritage Festival (New Orleans, LA) - last week in April
2. Chicago Blues Festival (Chicago, IL) - first week in June
3. Summerfest (Milwaukee, WI) - begins last Thursday in June
4. Ottawa BluesFest (Ottawa, Canada) - first week in July
5. Newport Music Festival (Newport, RI) - mid-July

Contact Information

Ms. Gina D'Angelo
474 Broadway St.
Saratoga Springs, NY
12866
518-587-3550

Copyright © Around the World Music

A **nested list** is a list inside a list item.

```
<ul>
    <li>African
        <ul>
            <li>Afro Beat</li>
            <li>Cape Jazz</li>
            <li>Soukous</li>
        </ul>
    </li>
```

An **ordered list** is used to create a list with numbers or letters for each list item.

```
<ol>
    <li> Chicago
    <li> Summerfest
    ...
</ol>
```

```
Ms. Gina D'Angelo<br />
474 Broadway St.<br />
```

The <br /> tag is used at the end of each line of text when the text is not to be wrapped as a paragraph.

Using Images on a Web Page

Compared to today, data transmission speeds were very slow in the 1990s when the Internet became accessible to the general public. Because it took quite a while for a Web page to download, many Web pages used only text or included images that had very small file sizes. Today, with the greater use of high-speed broadband transmission, Web pages commonly display many images.

Images can make your Web pages more interesting. However using too many images can be distracting and can look unprofessional. It's also important to be mindful of the fact that many people in the world do not have access to high-speed Internet connections. In addition to people in less affluent countries, many people in industrial countries who live in rural or remote areas also do not have access to high-speed Internet connections. Web pages are also accessed with mobile devices such as cell phones and tablet computers, and Internet connections on these devices can vary in reliability and speed.

Understanding Image Files and File Types

Most images used on the Web today are either photos or drawings. Some people refer to drawn illustrations as **clip art**. There are a few common file formats for storing clip art and photos that are used in Web pages. Clip-art drawings are often stored using the **Graphics Interchange Format (GIF)** format and are identified by the extension .gif. Photos are most often stored as .jpg or .jpeg files. The latter extension is an acronym for **Joint Photographic Experts Group (JPEG)**; the abbreviation is sometimes shortened to **JPG**.

The **Portable Network Graphics (PNG)** image file format is also used, but not as widely as GIF or JPG. GIF, JPG, and PNG files are **compressed**, which means that the amount of data is reduced to shrink the file size. Although a compressed image loses some detail and clarity, the image downloads faster.

Bitmap files, which have a .bmp extension, are uncompressed Windows graphics files. In general, you should avoid using bitmap files on your Web pages because their storage sizes tend to be much larger than other file formats and therefore take longer to download. Bitmap files are not compressed.

Using the Image Element

The **image element** is used to insert an image on a Web page. The image element is an empty element, so the tag ends with a space followed by a forward slash: <img />. An image is an inline element, which must be placed inside a block-level element to be valid HTML5 code. If an image is not already within an existing block-level element, precede the code for the <img /> tag with the code for a block-level element, such as an opening <p> tag, and follow the image code with the appropriate end tag, which is </p> in this instance. By default, an image is aligned at the left edge of the element that contains it, but text does not wrap around the image. In a later tutorial, you will learn how to position an image anywhere on a Web page and how to wrap text around an image.

The `<img />` Tag

To render an image, a Web browser must know the name of the image file. You can specify this information using an attribute. An **attribute** specifies the name of a property related to a Web page element and the value for that property. For instance, the image tag contains a source property called `src`. The `src` property must contain the name of the image file to be rendered, along with the folder where it is located if it is not in the same folder as the HTML file. For instance, to specify a logo image with the filename logo.jpg, you would use the following attribute inside the image tag:

```
src = "logo.jpg"
```

The `src` attribute identifies the image file. If the image file is inside a folder, you must include that as well. For instance, if the logo.jpg file were inside a folder called *images*, the src attribute would be the following:

```
src = "images/logo.jpg"
```

An image element can contain additional attributes as well; you'll learn some of these later in this session.

REFERENCE

Using the `img` element

- To insert an image, use the following code:

```
<img src = "filename"
     alt = "alternate_text"
     width = "widthvalue" height = "heightvalue" />
```

where *filename* is the filename of the image including the file extension; *alternate_text* is a description of the image; *widthvalue* is the width of the image measured in pixels; and *heightvalue* is the height of the image measured in pixels.

TIP

Whenever you type quotation marks in your HTML code, it's a good coding practice to type both quotation marks first so you avoid the mistake of omitting the closing quotation mark. Then type the content between the quotes.

It is a standard industry practice to enclose each attribute value in quotation marks. You type each attribute name followed by an equals sign and then the corresponding attribute value. You can insert a space before and after each equals sign to improve readability. This is a common practice in Web development.

Organizing Image Files

Web developers often organize a Web site's files into folders as soon as there are multiple files. An industry best practice is to create a folder called *images* and store the site's image files inside it. The HTML files would be stored in the main Web site folder, and the images folder would be inside the Web site folder.

Gina has provided the Around the World Music logo in a file called worldmusiclogo.jpg. You will store this file in a folder called *images* inside the main Web site folder. In this case, the main Web site folder is tutorial1\tutorial, and it already contains an *images* folder. You'll create an image tag that points to the worldmusiclogo.jpg file in the tutorial1\tutorial\images folder.

To add the logo image to the Web page:

▶ **1.** Return to the **worldmusic.htm** file in your text editor.

▶ **2.** Place the insertion point after the start `<body>` tag, and press the **Enter** key twice to insert a blank line. Insert the following code as shown in Figure 1-22:

```
<p><img src = "images/worldmusiclogo.jpg" /></p>
```

Figure 1-22   Adding the logo image

images folder is contained inside the folder where the current HTML file is stored

logo image file is stored inside the images folder

```
<body>

        <p><img src = "images/worldmusiclogo.jpg" /></p>

        <h1>Around the World Music</h1>
```

▶ **3.** Save the file.

▶ **4.** Return to your Web browser, and then click the **Refresh** or **Reload** button to view the changes in the file. The Web page should look similar to Figure 1-23.

Figure 1-23   Logo image added to Web page

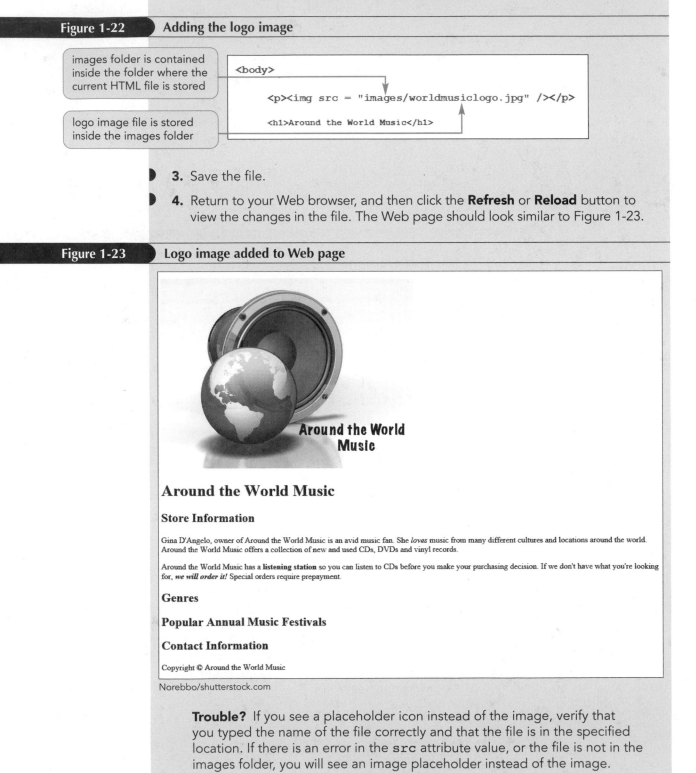

Around the World Music

Store Information

Gina D'Angelo, owner of Around the World Music is an avid music fan. She *loves* music from many different cultures and locations around the world. Around the World Music offers a collection of new and used CDs, DVDs and vinyl records.

Around the World Music has a **listening station** so you can listen to CDs before you make your purchasing decision. If we don't have what you're looking for, *we will order it!* Special orders require prepayment.

Genres

Popular Annual Music Festivals

Contact Information

Copyright © Around the World Music

Norebbo/shutterstock.com

Trouble? If you see a placeholder icon instead of the image, verify that you typed the name of the file correctly and that the file is in the specified location. If there is an error in the `src` attribute value, or the file is not in the images folder, you will see an image placeholder instead of the image.

Using the `alt` and `title` Attributes

TIP

The Web Accessibility Initiative (WAI) at the W3C includes a set of standards and a validator for Web page accessibility. You can find information about WAI on the W3C Web site at http://www.w3.org/WAI/.

Another attribute used with images is the `alt` attribute, which provides a brief description of the image. The words associated with the `alt` attribute may appear with an image placeholder before the image downloads. Also, when a user passes the mouse pointer over the image, the alternate text is displayed in some browsers as a **ScreenTip** or **ToolTip**, a small rectangular box that contains the text. More importantly, people who are visually impaired may be using screen-reading software, and this software will voice the text in the `alt` attribute. You should always include an `alt` attribute in an image. Accessibility is an important consideration when designing a Web page.

Try to use meaningful alternate text so users who rely on it for a description will have the same information as someone who can see the image. For example, instead of using *logo* as alternate text, use a description such as *Around the World Music logo*.

Technically, the order of the attributes and values does not matter, but it's a good coding practice to list the `src` attribute first.

TIP

You must include the end quote after the alt text. Without the end quote, browsers treat all subsequent text in the file as alt text, meaning they won't display the rest of the document.

Recall that cross-browser incompatibility occurs when different browsers don't display HTML code in the same way. For example, the `alt` attribute displays a ScreenTip in Internet Explorer, but not in the Firefox browser. In the Firefox browser, you see the alternate text only if the image fails to download. To display a ScreenTip in all browsers, you must use the `title` attribute as well. The `title` attribute provides some information about the element in which it is included.

To add the `alt` and `title` attributes to the `img` tag:

1. Return to the worldmusic.htm file in your text editor.

2. Position the mouse pointer after the `src` attribute in the `img` element, and click to place the insertion point at that location. Type the following code as shown in Figure 1-24. Let the code word wrap or extend completely. Do not press the Enter key inside the `img` tag to break it to the next line.

   ```
   alt = "Around the World Music logo" title = "Around the World
   Music logo"
   ```

Figure 1-24   Adding the alt and title attributes to the img tag

value of title attribute is displayed as a ScreenTip in most other browsers

value of alt attribute is displayed as a ScreenTip in Internet Explorer

```
<body>

    <p><img src = "images/worldmusiclogo.jpg"
    alt = "Around the World Music logo" title = "Around the World Music logo" /></p>

    <h1>Around the World Music</h1>
```

3. Save the file.

4. Return to your Web browser, and then click the **Refresh** or **Reload** button. The Web page should look the same as before.

5. Hover the mouse pointer slowly over the image to see the ScreenTip appear, as show in Figure 1-25.

Figure 1-25 ScreenTip from the img element

Norebbo/shutterstock.com

Using the `width` and `height` Attributes

The `width` attribute and `height` attribute specify the dimensions of the area of the Web page where the image will be rendered. When you include the `width` and `height` attributes in your code, a user's browser reserves the correct space for the image even before it downloads. You can determine the width and height of an image using image-editing software such as Microsoft Paint or Apple iPhoto. You can also use Windows Explorer or the Mac Finder to find the dimensions of the image.

To determine the dimensions of the logo image using Windows:

▸ 1. Click the **Start** button, and then click **Documents** to open File Explorer.

▸ 2. Navigate to the tutorial1\tutorial\images folder.

▸ 3. Right-click the **worldmusiclogo.jpg** file, and then click **Properties**. The Properties dialog box is displayed.

▸ 4. Click the **Details tab** to view the dimensions of the image, as shown in Figure 1-26.

Figure 1-26   **Image file properties**

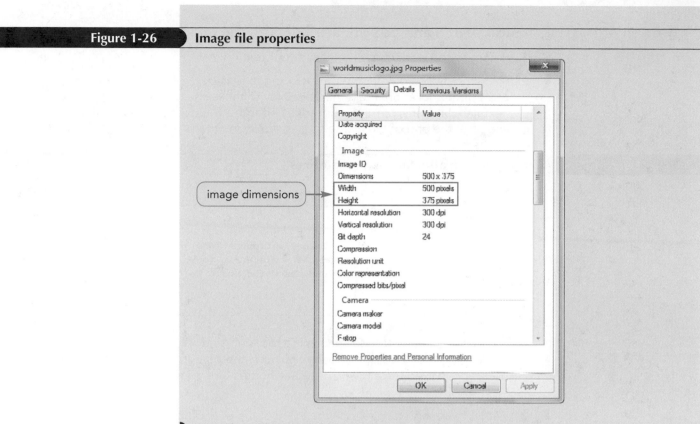

5. Click the **OK** button to close the Properties dialog box.

The best-case scenario is when an image is an appropriate size for the Web page and can be used without alteration. If the image is too large, you must use image-editing software such as Microsoft Paint to reduce the size of the image. Reducing the dimensions will also reduce the file size.

If you omit the `width` and `height` attributes, an image is displayed in its original size. If you include the `width` and `height` attributes, be sure the dimensions match the dimensions of the image. If the dimensions are different than the image, the image will stretch or shrink to match the dimensions. If the proportion of height and width is different, the image could be stretched either horizontally or vertically.

You may have noticed that when some Web pages are loading, the content seems to jump around as the images are loaded. This happens because Web browsers download each image after the image tag is processed. Sometimes a Web browser does not reserve enough space in the document, and the content shifts when the image is downloaded and the browser is able to determine the correct dimensions. By including `height` and `width` attributes in each image tag, you ensure Web browsers reserve the right amount of space in the Web page so when the images load, the rest of the page content will not jump around.

Gina thinks the worldmusiclogo.jpg image is a bit large. One option would be for you to set the `width` and `height` attributes to be smaller, but that only changes the displayed dimensions, leaving the file size larger than it needs to be. Instead, Gina would like you to use a smaller image. She has provided another file, worldmusiclogo_sm.jpg, with a width of 250 pixels and a height of 187 pixels.

To add `width` and `height` attributes to the image tag:

1. Return to the worldmusic.htm file in your text editor.

2. Place the mouse pointer after the `<p>` tag, and click to place the insertion point at that location. Press the **Enter** key to move the rest of the text to the next line. Similarly, press the **Enter** key after the value for the `alt` attribute and after the end of the image tag, as shown in Figure 1-27.

Figure 1-27   **Image tag with attributes on separate lines**

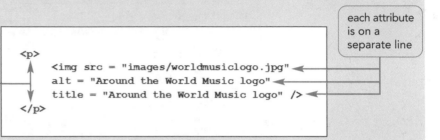

Because the image tag was becoming too long to display as one line of text in the paragraph element, your edits placed the paragraph tags on separate lines, and moved the `alt` and `title` attributes of the image element onto separate lines.

3. Within the image tag, replace the value of the `src` attribute with **images/ worldmusiclogo_sm.jpg**, and then add the attributes **width = "250"** and **height = "187"**, as shown in Figure 1-28.

Figure 1-28   **Image tag with width and height attributes**

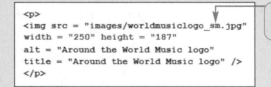

4. Save the file.

5. Return to your Web browser, and click the **Refresh** or **Reload** button to view the changes in the file. The Web page should look similar to Figure 1-29.

Figure 1-29	Smaller logo image

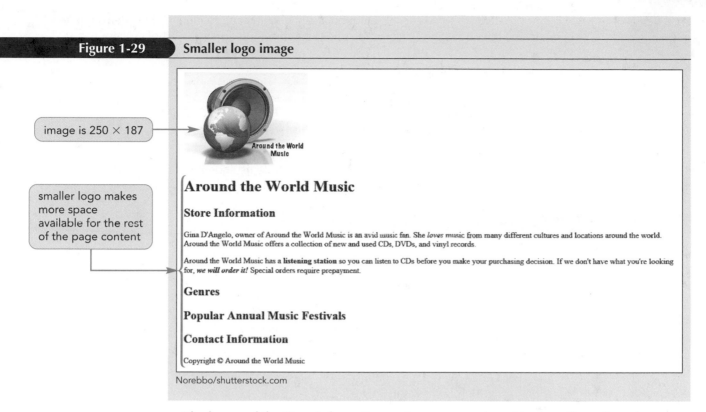

image is 250 × 187

smaller logo makes more space available for the rest of the page content

Around the World Music

Store Information

Gina D'Angelo, owner of Around the World Music is an avid music fan. She *loves* music from many different cultures and locations around the world. Around the World Music offers a collection of new and used CDs, DVDs, and vinyl records.

Around the World Music has a **listening station** so you can listen to CDs before you make your purchasing decision. If we don't have what you're looking for, *we will order it!* Special orders require prepayment.

Genres

Popular Annual Music Festivals

Contact Information

Copyright © Around the World Music

Norebbo/shutterstock.com

The logo and the Store Information section are complete. Next you'll work on the Genres and Music Festivals sections, each of which will contain a list of items.

Creating Lists

HTML has three types of lists available. You can create an **unordered list**, which is a bulleted list; an **ordered list**, which is a list with numbers or letters; or a **description** list, which is a list with a hanging indent format, where the list items are indented. The HTML code for creating unordered and ordered lists is nearly identical, but the code for creating description lists is quite different. Unordered and ordered lists are common on the Web. Definition lists, because they have a special purpose, are less common. Although the lists you will create for Gina's Web page are quite simple, later tutorials will explain how you can style lists to be more visually interesting.

You'll start with the genres list. Gina wants each list item to be preceded by a bullet.

Creating an Unordered List

The structure of the HTML code that renders an unordered list is:

```
<ul>
    <li>first item</li>
    <li>second item</li>
     . . .
</ul>
```

where *first item*, *second item*, and so on are the contents of the list items. An unordered list begins with the open <ul> tag. Each list item begins with the open <li> tag, followed by the text for the actual list item, then the close </li> tag. It's an industry best practice to type each list item on a separate line and to indent all list items one level inside the `<ul>` tags. For example, the following code displays a list of grocery items:

```
<ul>
        <li>apples</li>
        <li>bananas</li>
        <li>apricots</li>
        <li>pears</li>
        <li>oranges</li>
</ul>
```

By default, most Web browsers display the whole list indented slightly, with a bullet symbol to the left of each list item, as shown in Figure 1-30.

Figure 1-30   **Simple unordered list in a browser**

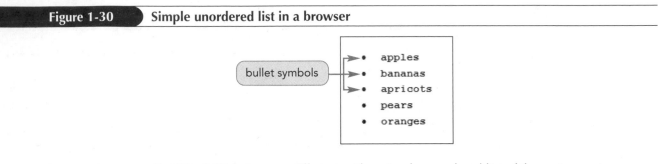

For Gina's Web page, you'll start with a simple unordered list of the main music genres, which is shown in Figure 1-31.

Figure 1-31   **Content for Around the World Music Web page**

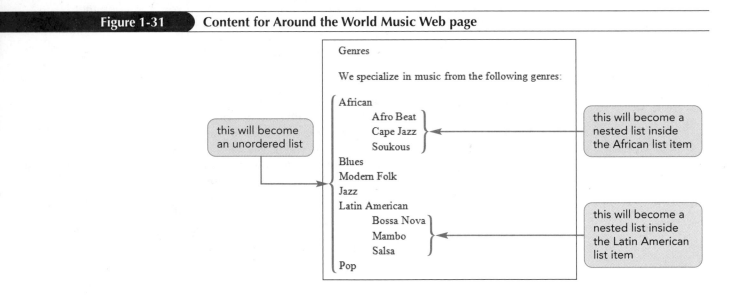

To insert the list of genres:

1. Return to the **worldmusic.htm** file in your text editor.

2. After the Genres heading, insert the following code as shown in Figure 1-32:

```
<p>We specialize in music from the following genres:</p>

<ul>
    <li>African</li>
    <li>Blues</li>
    <li>Modern Folk</li>
    <li>Jazz</li>
    <li>Latin American</li>
    <li>Bossa Nova</li>
    <li>Mambo</li>
    <li>Salsa</li>
    <li>Pop</li>
</ul>
```

Figure 1-32	Code for simple unordered list

```
<h2>Genres</h2>

<p>We specialize in music from the following genres:</p>

<ul>
    <li>African</li>
    <li>Blues</li>
    <li>Modern Folk</li>
    <li>Jazz</li>
    <li>Latin American</li>
    <li>Bossa Nova</li>
    <li>Mambo</li>
    <li>Salsa</li>
    <li>Pop</li>
</ul>

<h2>Popular Annual Music Festivals</h2>
```

3. Save the file.

4. Return to your Web browser, and then click the **Refresh** or **Reload** button to view the changes in the file. The Web page should look similar to Figure 1-33.

Figure 1-33   **Bulleted list of genres in a Web browser**

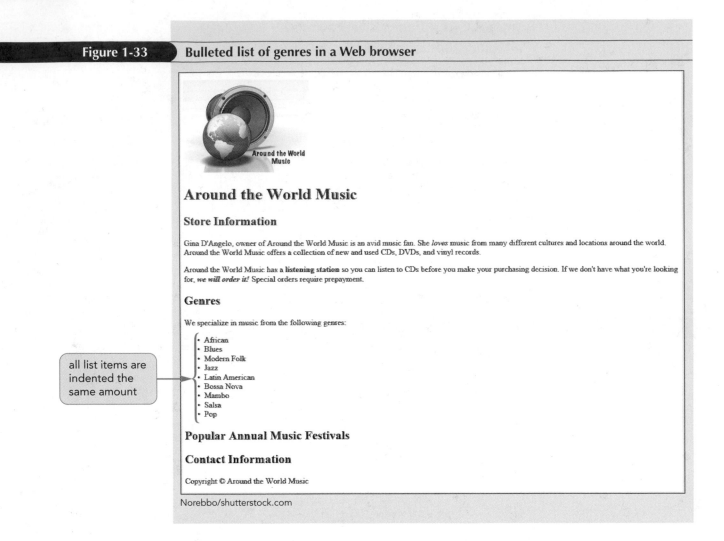

all list items are indented the same amount

Norebbo/shutterstock.com

Nesting Lists

The unordered list for the music genres in Gina's Web page now contains all of the first-level list items. Next you will add the sublists as a second level of bullets. This can be accomplished by nesting an unordered list inside a list item. A **nested** element is an element that is inside another element. You used this technique earlier when you nested an em element inside a strong element. When the nested elements are large, such as lists, you'll indent the elements that are inside. This is an industry best practice and organizes the code. A **sublist**, or **second-level list**, is a list that is nested inside a list item of another list.

The general structure of a nested list is as follows; in this case, the nested list is inside the second item:

```
<ul>
    <li>first item</li>
    <li>second item
        <ul>
            <li>first nested item</li>
            <li>second nested item</li>
            ...
        </ul>
    </li>
    . . .
</ul>
```

Notice that the nested list is entirely contained within the list item tags for the second item.

For example, the following code displays a detailed list of fruits nested within a list of grocery items:

```
<h3>Grocery List</h3>
<ul>
     <li>hamburger</li>
     <li>fruit
          <ul>
                <li>apples</li>
                <li>bananas</li>
                <li>apricots</li>
          </ul>
     </li>
     <li>toilet paper</li>
</ul>
```

This code would be rendered in Web browsers as shown in Figure 1-34.

Figure 1-34   **Nested unordered list**

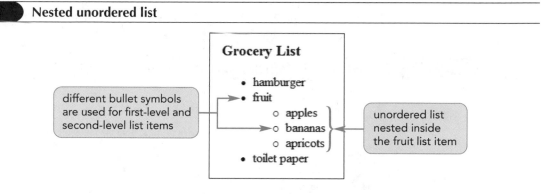

You'll use a nested list to create sublists inside the African and Latin American list items on Gina's Web page.

To create nested lists of music genres:

1. Return to the **worldmusic.htm** file in your text editor.

2. Move the mouse pointer between the letter *n* in *African* and the `</li>` tag. Click to position the insertion point at that location, and then press the **Enter** key twice to add a blank line.

3. Position the insertion point on the blank line you created, and then enter the code for the following unordered list, as shown in Figure 1-35:

```
<ul>
     <li>Afro Beat</li>
     <li>Cape Jazz</li>
     <li>Soukous</li>
</ul>
```

Figure 1-35   **Nested list for African music genre**

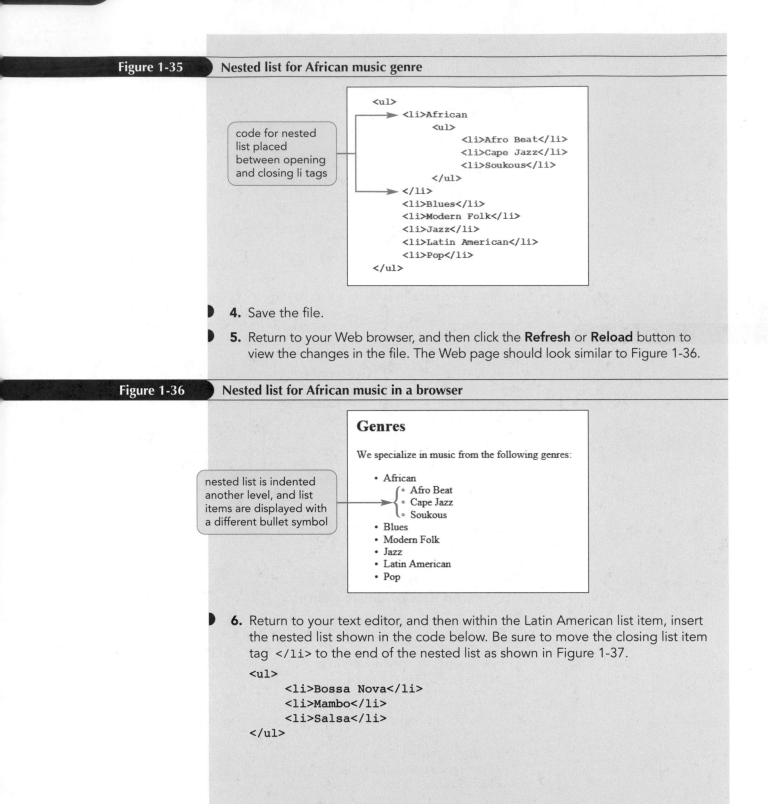

4. Save the file.

5. Return to your Web browser, and then click the **Refresh** or **Reload** button to view the changes in the file. The Web page should look similar to Figure 1-36.

Figure 1-36   **Nested list for African music in a browser**

6. Return to your text editor, and then within the Latin American list item, insert the nested list shown in the code below. Be sure to move the closing list item tag `</li>` to the end of the nested list as shown in Figure 1-37.

```
<ul>
      <li>Bossa Nova</li>
      <li>Mambo</li>
      <li>Salsa</li>
</ul>
```

Figure 1-37   Nested list for Latin American music genre

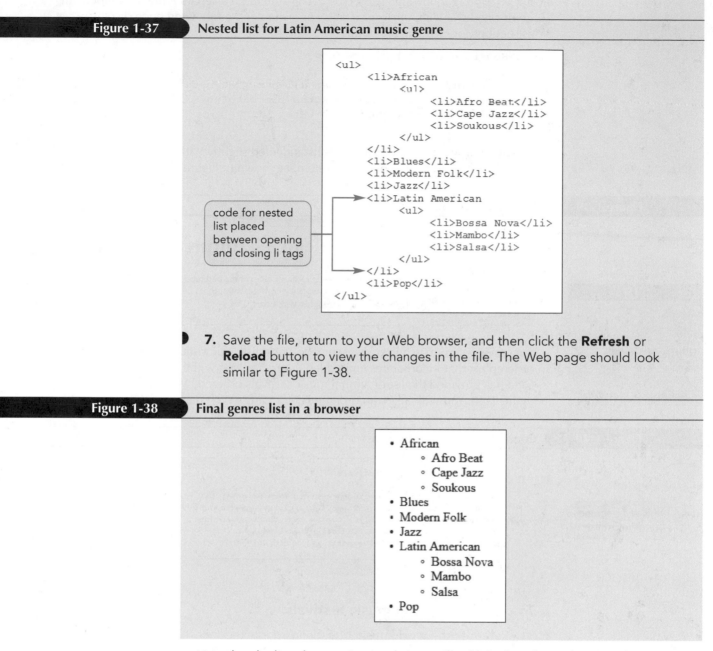

```
<ul>
      <li>African
            <ul>
                  <li>Afro Beat</li>
                  <li>Cape Jazz</li>
                  <li>Soukous</li>
            </ul>
      </li>
      <li>Blues</li>
      <li>Modern Folk</li>
      <li>Jazz</li>
      <li>Latin American
            <ul>
                  <li>Bossa Nova</li>
                  <li>Mambo</li>
                  <li>Salsa</li>
            </ul>
      </li>
      <li>Pop</li>
</ul>
```

code for nested list placed between opening and closing li tags

7. Save the file, return to your Web browser, and then click the **Refresh** or **Reload** button to view the changes in the file. The Web page should look similar to Figure 1-38.

Figure 1-38   Final genres list in a browser

- African
  - Afro Beat
  - Cape Jazz
  - Soukous
- Blues
- Modern Folk
- Jazz
- Latin American
  - Bossa Nova
  - Mambo
  - Salsa
- Pop

Now that the list of genres is complete, you'll add the list of popular annual music festivals to Gina's Web page.

Creating an Ordered List

You use an ordered list when the items in a list have a particular order of importance or should appear in sequence. An ordered list uses the following structure:

```
<ol>
    <li>first item</li>
    <li>second item</li>
    . . .
</ol>
```

where *first item, second item,* and so on are the list items. An ordered list begins with the opening <ol> tag. As in an unordered list, you include each list item on a separate line with an opening <li> tag preceding the text for the actual list item and a closing `</li>` tag following it. You type each list item on a separate line and indent all list items one level within the `<ol>` tags. For example, the following code displays a list of instructions for cleaning a bathtub:

```
<h3>How to clean a bathtub</h3>
<ol>
    <li>Sprinkle some cleanser all over the bathtub.</li>
    <li>Use a wet sponge to scrub the bathtub.</li>
    <li>Rinse thoroughly with water.</li>
</ol>
```

By default, a browser would display this list indented slightly with an automatically generated number to the left of each list item, as shown in Figure 1-39.

Figure 1-39   **Simple ordered list in a browser**

How to clean a bathtub

ordered list is indented and uses a number or letter for each list item

1. Sprinkle some cleanser all over the bathtub.
2. Use a wet sponge to scrub the bathtub.
3. Rinse thoroughly with water.

TIP

Ordered lists are displayed with Arabic numbers (1, 2, 3, etc.) by default, but you can also use Roman numerals, uppercase letters, or lowercase letters.

You can mix and match list types when you nest lists. For instance, you could create an ordered list that incorporates embedded unordered lists within some list items.

Gina has provided the list of annual music festivals ordered by popularity, as shown in Figure 1-40. You will create an ordered list for Gina's Web page using this content.

Figure 1-40   **Content for music festivals list**

```
Popular Annual Music Festivals

New Orleans Jazz and Heritage Festival (New Orleans, LA) - last week in April
Chicago Blues Festival (Chicago, IL) - first week in June
Summerfest (Milwaukee, WI) - begins last Thursday in June
Ottawa BluesFest (Ottawa, Canada) - first week in July
Newport Music Festival (Newport, RI) - mid-July
```

this will become an ordered list

To create the list of music festivals:

1. Return to the **worldmusic.htm** file in your text editor.

2. After the Popular Annual Music Festivals heading, insert the `<ol>` tag, press the **Enter** key twice, and then enter the `</ol>` tag.

3. Position the mouse pointer on the blank line between the `<ol>` and `</ol>` tags, click to place the insertion point at that location, and then enter the list item elements between the `<ol>` and `</ol>` tags, as shown in Figure 1-41. It's all right if the text wraps to the next line.

```
<ol>
        <li>Chicago Blues Festival (Chicago, IL) -
first week in June</li>
        <li>Summerfest (Milwaukee, WI) - begins last
Thursday in June</li>
        <li>Newport Music Festival (Newport, RI) -
mid-July</li>
        <li>New Orleans Jazz and Heritage Festival
(New Orleans, LA) - last week in April</li>
        <li>Ottawa BluesFest (Ottawa, Canada) -
first week in July</li>
</ol>
```

Figure 1-41 | **Code for ordered list of music festivals**

```
<h2>Popular Annual Music Festivals</h2>

    <ol>
        <li>New Orleans Jazz and Heritage Festival (New Orleans, LA) - last week in April</li>
        <li>Chicago Blues Festival (Chicago, IL) - first week in June</li>
        <li>Summerfest (Milwaukee, WI) - begins last Thursday in June</li>
        <li>Ottawa BluesFest (Ottawa, Canada) - first week in July</li>
        <li>Newport Music Festival (Newport, RI) - mid-July</li>
    </ol>

<h2>Contact Information</h2>
```

4. Save the file.

5. Return to your Web browser and then click the **Refresh** or **Reload** button to view the changes in the file. The Web page should look similar to Figure 1-42.

Figure 1-42 | **Music festivals ordered list in a browser**

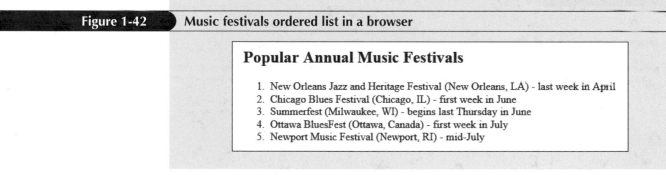

Popular Annual Music Festivals

1. New Orleans Jazz and Heritage Festival (New Orleans, LA) - last week in April
2. Chicago Blues Festival (Chicago, IL) - first week in June
3. Summerfest (Milwaukee, WI) - begins last Thursday in June
4. Ottawa BluesFest (Ottawa, Canada) - first week in July
5. Newport Music Festival (Newport, RI) - mid-July

The Description List

A third type of HTML list is the **description list**, formerly known as the definition list, which is formatted with a hanging indent. A common use of the description list is to create a **chronology**, which is a list of events in time order, or a **glossary**, which is an alphabetic list of terms and their definitions. Description lists can also be used to create a page of works cited that lists author names and citations in alphabetic order, or to create a question-and-answer layout in which a question is entered on one line and the answer is entered on the next line.

A description list uses the structure:

```
<dl>
    <dt>term1</dt>
    <dd>description1</dd>
    <dt>term2</dt>
    <dd>description2</dd>
        . . .
</dl>
```

where *term1*, *term2*, and so on are the described terms and *description1*, *description2*, and so on are the description data.

An example of a description list containing glossary entries follows:

```
<dl>
    <dt>Los Angeles Dodgers</dt>
    <dd>Moved from Brooklyn in 1958. Celebrated their 50th
    anniversary several years ago by winning the National
    League Western Division title.</dd>

    <dt>New York Yankees</dt>
    <dd>The storied franchise recently replaced their
    legendary stadium, often called "The house that Ruth
    built," with a new stadium that cost more than
    $1.5 billion to construct.</dd>
</dl>
```

In the HTML code, a description list element is marked with the start <dl> and end </dl> tags. The dt and dd elements are nested inside the dl element. The dt element contains a term to be described, and the dd element contains the description. Web browsers render the description list using a hanging indent, as shown in Figure 1-43.

Figure 1-43	Sample definition list in a browser

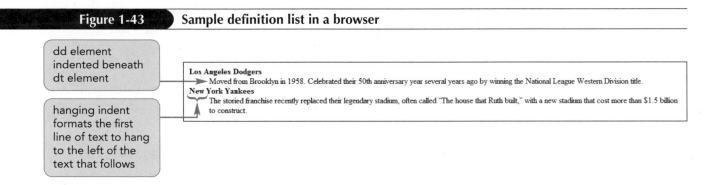

dd element
indented beneath
dt element

hanging indent
formats the first
line of text to hang
to the left of the
text that follows

Written Communication: Writing for the Web

Writing for the Web is quite different than writing a report or an essay; it's closer to writing for advertising. Writing for an essay or article is descriptive, and people expect to take time to read a longer passage. Web users want short text that is easy to read and straight to the point. Here are a few guidelines for writing content for the Web:

- Use a heading to identify each section of text.
- Avoid using long paragraphs.
- Use bulleted lists rather than longer descriptions.
- Use vertical space to visually separate sections of content.
- If the amount of content exceeds the length of a maximized Web browser window, consider using multiple Web pages.

Keep in mind that most people do not want to spend a long period of time reading content online. Many people use the Web for consumer research, online shopping, or finding information quickly. If you want to keep readers interested, aim to provide a content-rich Web site that is easy to read quickly.

Using the Break Element

Now that you've created the music festival list, Gina would like you to include her contact information. She's given you her contact information as follows:

Ms. Gina D'Angelo
474 Broadway St.
Saratoga Springs, NY 12866
518-587-3550

Gina would like her contact information to be displayed with her name on the first line, street address on the next line, and so on. If you placed all of the contact information in a paragraph element as it is, the information would be displayed as one long line, as line breaks are ignored in HTML. This is because of the way HTML works with white space.

Blank lines and indenting are examples of **white space**. In your text editor, you create white space by pressing the spacebar, the Tab key, or the Enter key. Generally, you enter white space to make code and content easier to read. However, when you create white space in a text editor, you are not creating white space that will appear in browsers. Of course, a single space you enter between words in your text editor will appear in browsers, but if you type two or more spaces one after the other, Web browsers will collapse them and display only one space. Similarly, when you enter text on multiple lines, Web browsers will wrap the text differently, ignoring the way the code was wrapped in the text editor.

If you put each line of text in a separate paragraph element, there will be a lot of white space between each line of text, as if it were double spaced. However, ending a line with the `break` element creates the same effect as when you press the Enter key when composing a document in a word-processing application, moving text that follows it onto a new line. The `break` element is an empty element, like the `img` element; it doesn't have any content. As with the `img` element, you end the tag for the `break` element with a space and forward slash:

```
<br />
```

Because the `break` element is an inline element, you can use it only inside block-level element tags, such as the `<p>` tags. You'll add Gina's contact information within a paragraph at the bottom of the Web page. Some Web developers put the `<br />` tag at the beginning of a line of text, and others put it at the end; it's really a matter of personal preference. For Gina's Web page, you'll put it at the end of the line of each line of text.

To enter Gina's contact information:

 1. Return to the **worldmusic.htm** file in your text editor.

 2. After the Contact Information heading, type a start <p> tag, press the **Enter** key twice, and then type the end </p> tag.

 3. Position the insertion point on the blank line between the start <p> and end </p> tags, and then enter the following contact information code, as shown in Figure 1-44:

```
Ms. Gina D'Angelo<br />
474 Broadway St.<br />
Saratoga Springs, NY<br />
12866<br />
518-587-3550<br />
```

Figure 1-44 **Contact information with break elements**

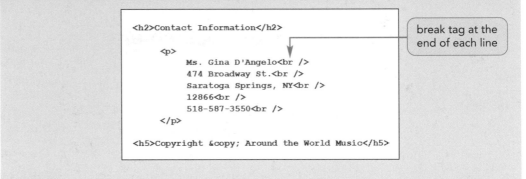

```
<h2>Contact Information</h2>

    <p>
            Ms. Gina D'Angelo<br />
            474 Broadway St.<br />
            Saratoga Springs, NY<br />
            12866<br />
            518-587-3550<br />
    </p>

<h5>Copyright &copy; Around the World Music</h5>
```

break tag at the end of each line

 4. Save the file.

 5. Return to your Web browser and then click the **Refresh** or **Reload** button to view the changes in the file. The Web page should look similar to Figure 1-45.

Figure 1-45 **Contact information incorporating the break element**

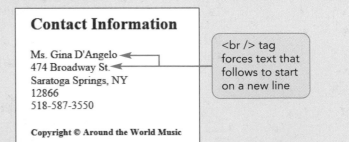

Contact Information

Ms. Gina D'Angelo
474 Broadway St.
Saratoga Springs, NY
12866
518-587-3550

Copyright © Around the World Music

 tag forces text that follows to start on a new line

You've finished creating the code for the content that will be visible on the Web page, and Gina is pleased with the results. She would also like to improve the chances that her Web page will be ranked higher in a search engine result. You'll include metadata to provide more information to the search engines and possibly increase the search engine ranking.

The meta Element

One of the most useful aspects of the Web is the ability to quickly find Web pages about any topic. **Metadata** is data that provides information about other data. In this case, metadata could be a description of Gina's Web page, which is a description about the Around the World Music store. To add metadata to a Web page, you use the meta element.

One use of the meta element is to provide information to search engines. Although search engines do not divulge the details of the rules they use to rank search results, many Web developers use as many reasonable techniques as possible to improve the search engine rankings. The addition of metadata to HTML code is a simple technique that may make a difference in search engine rankings.

The meta element is placed in the head section of a Web page. Like the other content of the head section, the meta element content is not displayed in the Web browser.

The meta element is used to specify metadata such as **keywords**—words that best identify the content of a site—or a description of the topic, store, or service that is the focus of the content of the Web page. When you view the source code for an HTML page, you often see one or more <meta /> tags in the head section. The meta element is an empty element, so it ends with the space and forward slash combination. The <meta /> tag includes the name of a category and its content. The structure of the <meta /> tag is as follows:

```
<meta name="name of category" content="content data" />
```

You can help search engines find your site by including a <meta /> tag that includes the keyword category and lists an effective set of keywords for your Web pages. Some Web developers also include common misspellings and a variety of capitalization options to anticipate the ways users might enter the keywords. You can list the keywords on one line or several lines within a <meta /> tag, as shown in the following example:

```
<meta name="keywords" content="music, DVD, CD, hip hop, rock and
roll" />
```

You might see other categories for the <meta /> tag, including author, which identifies the author of the Web page; description, which includes a description of the Web page written in sentence form; and copyright, which identifies the copyright information. The description and its content value may appear in search engine results if the Web page appears in the search listing. For instance, a description <meta /> tag for Around the World Music might look like this:

```
<meta name="description" content="Around the World
Music offers a diverse selection of new and used CDs
and DVDs. It is located in Saratoga Springs, NY." />
```

Like comment tags, the contents of <meta /> tags are not displayed in the document windows of browsers. However, <meta /> tag code is available for search engines to use.

You will include <meta /> tags for the keywords and description categories in Gina's Web page. You look through the Web page and decide that people who are looking for this Web page, or other music stores, might use any of the following search terms: *music, CD, DVD, Saratoga Springs, African, blues, modern folk, jazz, Latin American, pop, festivals*. You'll include these terms as the value for a keyword <meta /> tag. Gina also provided a short description, which you'll include as a value for the description <meta /> tag.

To insert metadata into the head section:

▶ 1. Return to the **worldmusic.htm** file in your text editor.

▶ 2. After the comment tag in the head section, insert the following code as shown in Figure 1-46:

```
<meta name = "description" content = "Around the World
Music offers a diverse selection of new and used CDs and
DVDs. It is located in Saratoga Springs, NY." />

<meta name = "keywords" content = "music, CD, DVD, Saratoga
Springs, African, blues, modern folk, jazz, Latin American,
pop, festivals" />
```

Figure 1-46   Adding <meta /> tags to Gina's Web page

```
<!--
    Tutorial 1
    Author: your name
    Date: Today's date
-->

<meta name = "description" content = "Around the World Music offers a diverse
selection of new and used CDs and DVDs. It is located in Saratoga Springs, NY." />

<meta name = "keywords" content = "music, CD, DVD, Saratoga Springs, African,
blues, modern folk, jazz, latin American, pop, festivals" />

<title>Around the World Music</title>
```

▶ 3. Save the file.

▶ 4. Return to your Web browser, and then click the **Refresh** or **Reload** button to view the file. Verify that the Web page still looks like Figure 1-45

TIP

If you want, you can press the Enter key to split a long meta tag into multiple lines. If you choose to do this, split in place of a space.

Tips for Working with HTML Documents

The following list will help you speed up the development process and avoid making some common errors:

- Save your file frequently in your text editor, and preview it frequently in your browser. Don't wait until you've entered the code for an entire Web page before you view it in your browser. If you save and preview often, you're more likely to catch errors when they occur, and you won't have to debug an entire page of code at a time.
- Proofread your code and content carefully. Check for typographical errors and misspellings. A Web page should be error free. Errors, such as spelling errors, are distracting and unprofessional.
- Check for syntax errors. Are any angle brackets missing? Are any quotation marks missing? Are any end tags missing?
- If your document is not displayed at all in your browser, check for missing or misspelled end tags such as `</title>` and `</head>`.
- If part of your document is not displayed in your browser, you might be missing the end comment code (`-->`) at the point where the text or images stop appearing.
- If your Web page is not displayed as you intended, you can convert a suspect line of code in the document to a comment by inserting a begin comment code (`<!--`) before the code you are trying to debug and inserting an end comment code (`-->`) after the code. This technique is known as *commenting out* the code. You can then open the page in your browser to check the effect of hiding that code. Commenting out code is a good way to isolate an area that might contain errors. If the error disappears, you've isolated it to the code that was commented.

With work now completed on the Around the World Music Web page, you're ready to verify that the code complies with W3C rules. You'll use a free service available from the World Wide Web Consortium to do this.

Validating a Completed File

Now that your document is complete, you are ready to validate the file, which is the process of checking the file for syntax and compliance errors. Validating a file does not check for spelling, typographical, or grammar errors; it checks only to see if the code complies with the HTML or XHTML standard identified in the DOCTYPE tag. Many Web developers write code that conforms to specific standards as a matter of good practice. Coding standards are generally developed to provide guidance for best practices that organize code and make it more likely to work well in most Web browsers. In addition to checking for conformance with these coding standards, validation also saves time because it generates a list of errors that might otherwise take considerable time to find.

In addition to the HTML and XHTML standards, there is also a Web Accessibility Initiative (WAI) standard, as well as other standards. There are free validators available that will validate code and provide error messages for code that does not conform to a specified standard. Validating a file is optional, but you decide to go through the process because you would like Gina's Web page to be the best it can be.

Validating a File for HTML5

A code validator is generally a Web site that provides a mechanism to submit your code, and provides an error report. You can submit HTML or XHTML code to the W3C validator by either specifying the URL where the code is located, uploading the file containing the code, or pasting the code directly into the Web page for the validator.

You'll submit the code for Gina's Web page by pasting it to the direct input location of the validator.

To validate Gina's file for HTML5 compliance:

1. In your browser, navigate to **http://validator.w3.org**. The W3C Markup Validation Web site opens, as shown in Figure 1-47.

Figure 1-47   **W3C validator Web page**

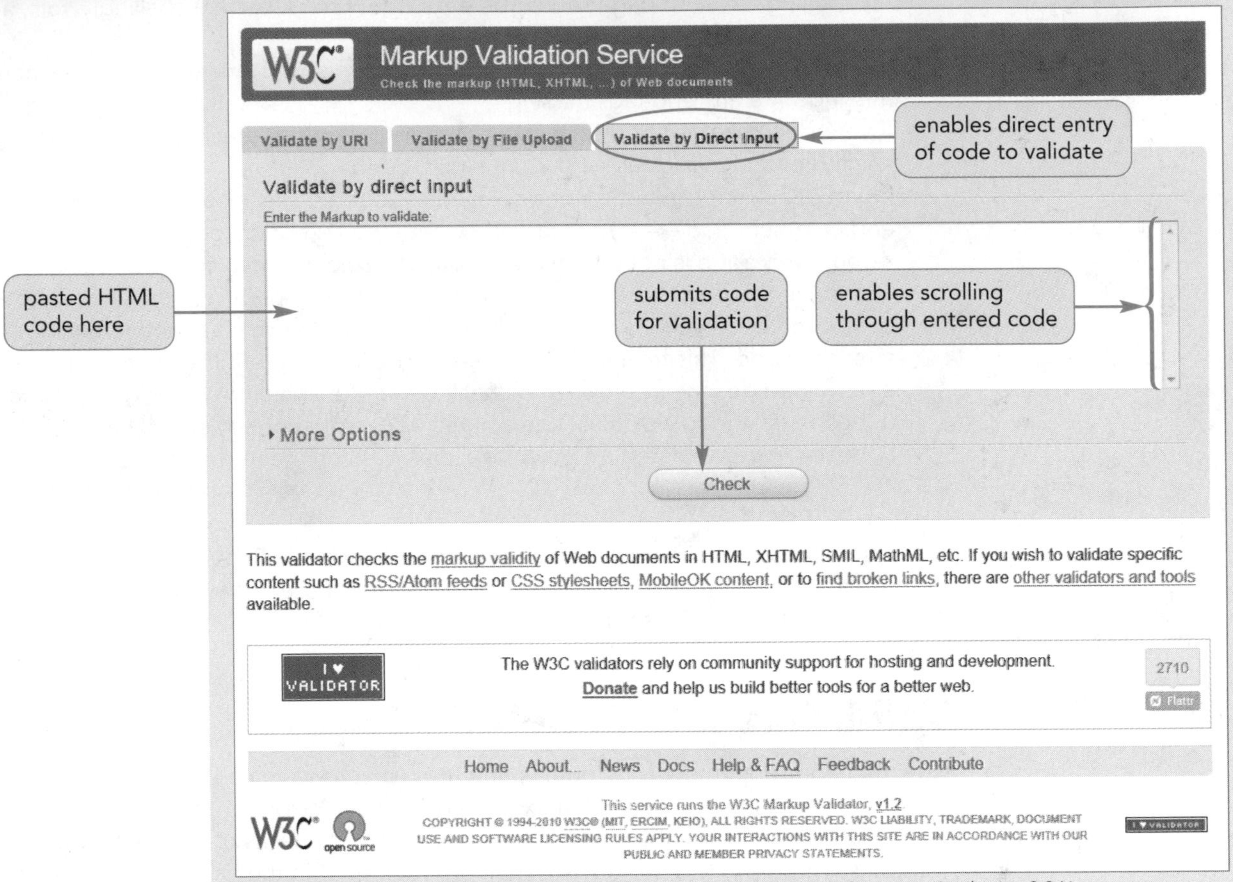

Copyright © 2012 W3C ® (MIT, ERCIM, Keio). Licensed under a Creative Commons Attribution 3.0 License.

2. If necessary, click the **Validate by Direct Input tab**.

3. Return to the **worldmusic.htm** file in your text editor.

4. Press **Ctrl+A** (Windows) or **command+A** (Mac) to select all of the code in the file.

5. Press **Ctrl+C** (Windows) or **command+C** (Mac) to copy the code to the Clipboard.

6. Return to your Web browser, and click in the **Enter the Markup to validate** box to select it, as shown in Figure 1-48.

7. Press **Ctrl+V** (Windows) or **command+V** (Mac) to paste the code into the box, as shown in Figure 1-48.

| Figure 1-48 | W3C validator showing HTML code in the Direct Input box |

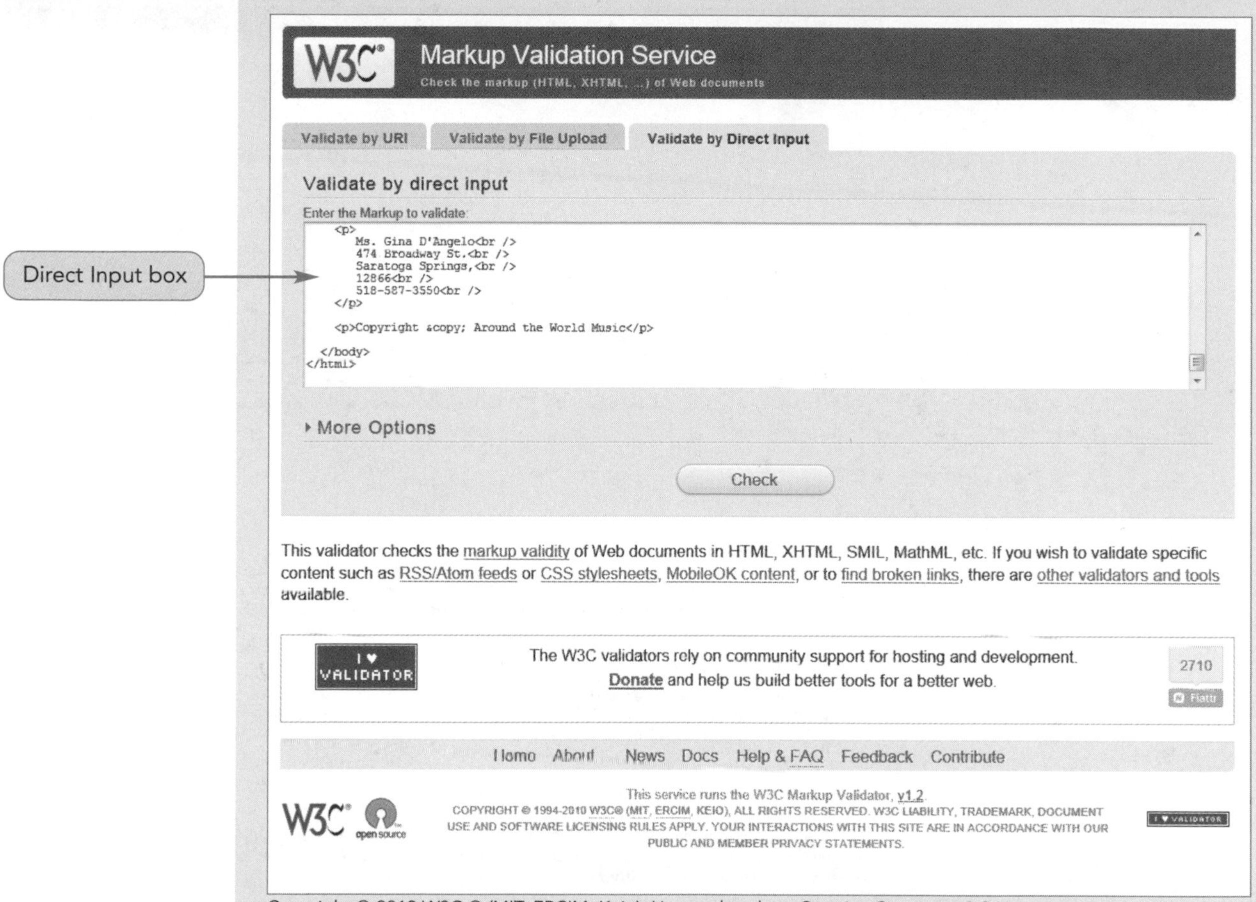

Copyright © 2012 W3C ® (MIT, ERCIM, Keio). Licensed under a Creative Commons 3.0 License.

8. Click the **Check** button on the Web page to submit the code to the validator. The results from the validation check appear in the Web browser, as shown in Figure 1-49.

Trouble?   If the document does not pass validation, note the errors and debug your document accordingly.

Figure 1-49 Validation results

W3C Markup Validation Service
Check the markup (HTML, XHTML, ...) of Web documents

Jump To: Notes and Potential Issues   Congratulations · Icons

This document was successfully checked as HTML5!

Result: Passed, 3 warning(s)

Source :
```
<!DOCTYPE html>
<head>
        <!--
                Tutorial 1
                Author: your name
                Date: Today's date
        -->
        <meta name="description" content="Around the World Music offers a diverse
selection of new and used CDs and DVDs.
        It is located in Saratoga Falls, NY." />
        <meta name = "keywords" content = "music, CD, DVD, Saratoga Falls, African,
blues, modern folk, jazz, Latin American, pop, festivals">
```

Encoding : utf-8   (detect automatically)

Doctype : HTML5   (detect automatically)

Root Element: html

Options

☐ Show Source   ☐ Show Outline   ⦿ List Messages Sequentially ○ Group Error Messages by Type

☐ Validate error pages ☐ Verbose Output   ☐ Clean up Markup with HTML-Tidy

Help on the options is available.   [Revalidate]

Notes and Potential Issues

The following notes and warnings highlight missing or conflicting information which caused the validator to perform some guesswork prior to validation, or other things affecting the output below. If the guess or fallback is incorrect, it could make validation results entirely incoherent. It is *highly recommended* to check these potential issues, and, if necessary, fix them and re-validate the document.

◈ **Using experimental feature: *HTML5 Conformance Checker*.**

The validator checked your document with an experimental feature: *HTML5 Conformance Checker*. This feature has been made available for your convenience, but be aware that it may be unreliable, or not perfectly up to date with the latest development of some cutting-edge technologies. If you find any issues with this feature, please report them. Thank you.

◈ No Character encoding declared at document level

No character encoding information was found within the document, either in an HTML meta element or an XML declaration. It is often recommended to declare the character encoding in the document itself, especially if there is a chance that the document will be read from or saved to disk, CD, etc.

See this tutorial on character encoding for techniques and explanations.

◈ Using Direct Input mode: UTF-8 character encoding assumed

Unlike the "by URI" and "by File Upload" modes, the "Direct Input" mode of the validator provides validated content in the form of characters pasted or typed in the validator's form field. This will automatically make the data UTF-8, and therefore the validator does not need to determine the character encoding of your document, and will ignore any charset information specified.

If you notice a discrepancy in detected character encoding between the "Direct Input" mode and other validator modes, this is likely to be the reason. It is neither a bug in the validator, nor in your document.

Congratulations

The uploaded document was successfully checked as HTML5. This means that the resource in question identified itself as "HTML5" and that we successfully performed a formal validation of it. The parser implementations we used for this check are based on validator.nu (HTML5).

Validating CSS Style Sheets

If you use CSS in your document, you can check it using the W3C CSS Validation Service.

↑ TOP

Home About... News Docs Help & FAQ Feedback Contribute

The validation results in Figure 1-49 show a successful result. There are some warnings listed; however, the code conforms to the standards. Warnings are issued when there is something about the code that is not specified, and the validator makes an assumption. You decide to experiment with the validator to see what error messages might look like. You'll intentionally edit the code in the source window of the validator to introduce an error in the <head> tag; this will let you see what sorts of error messages the W3C validator generates.

To see error messages produced by the W3C validator:

1. In your Web browser, delete the right angle bracket from the <head> tag in the Enter the Markup to validate box so the tag is displayed as <head instead of <head>, as shown in Figure 1-50.

2. Click the **Revalidate** button, as shown in Figure 1-50.

| Figure 1-50 | Code edited to introduce an error |

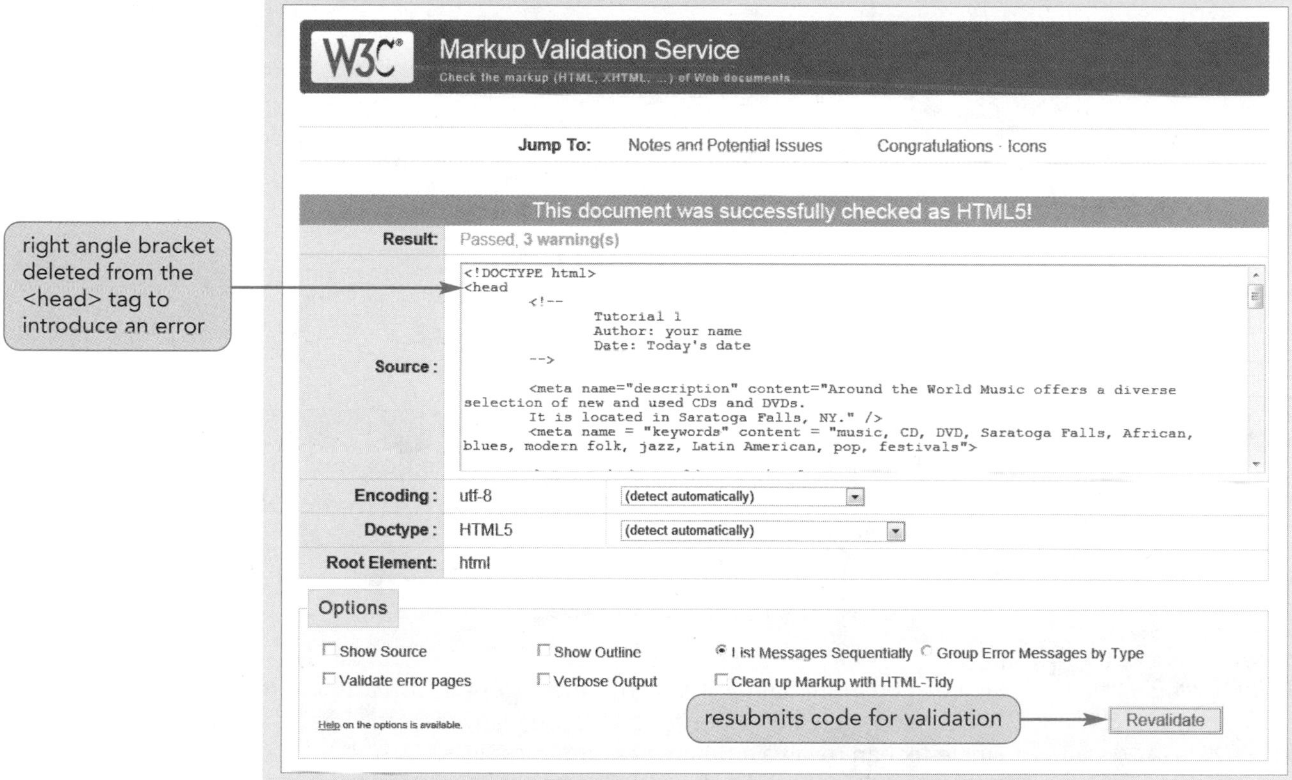

Copyright © 2012 W3C ® (MIT, ERCIM, Keio). Licensed under a Creative Commons 3.0 License.

3. View the error messages listed in the Web page. There are 12 error messages and several warnings generated by this one missing character in the code. Figure 1-51 shows a selection of these messages.

Figure 1-51   W3C validator errors

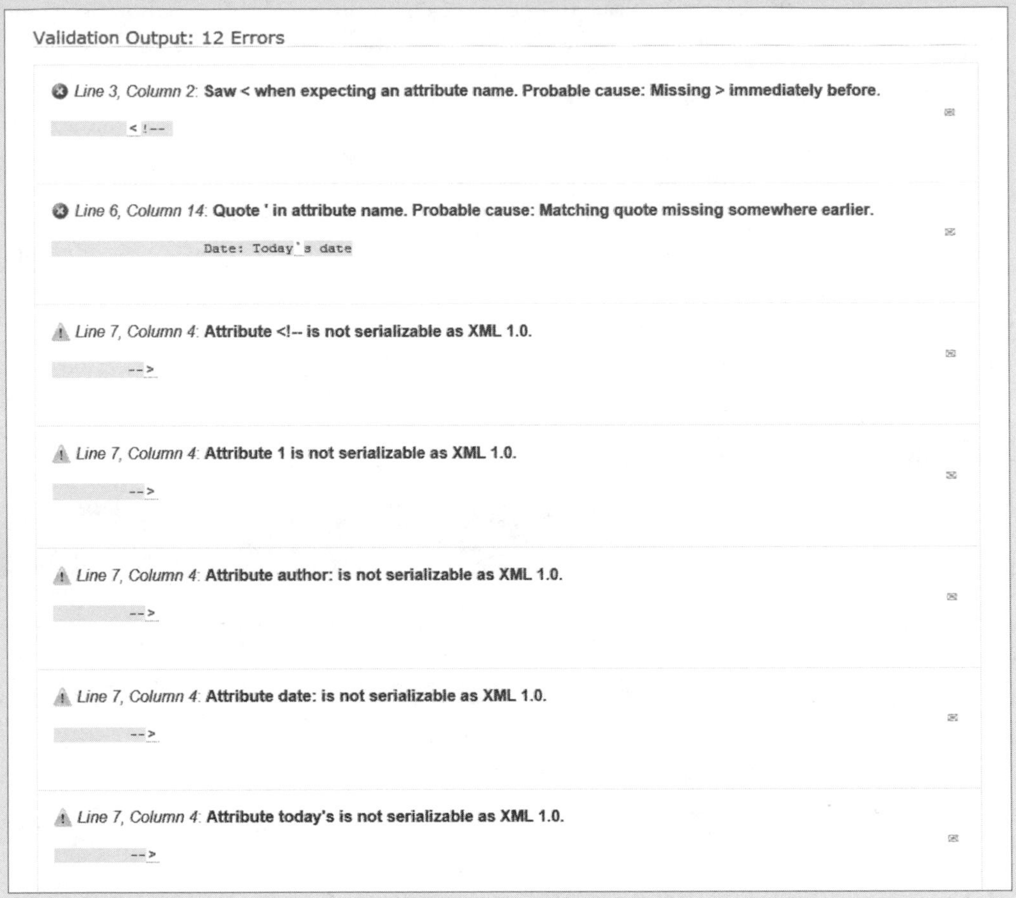

Validation Output: 12 Errors

❌ *Line 3, Column 2:* **Saw < when expecting an attribute name. Probable cause: Missing > immediately before.**

    `< !--`

❌ *Line 6, Column 14:* **Quote ' in attribute name. Probable cause: Matching quote missing somewhere earlier.**

    `Date: Today's date`

⚠️ *Line 7, Column 4:* **Attribute <!-- is not serializable as XML 1.0.**

    `-->`

⚠️ *Line 7, Column 4:* **Attribute 1 is not serializable as XML 1.0.**

    `-->`

⚠️ *Line 7, Column 4:* **Attribute author: is not serializable as XML 1.0.**

    `-->`

⚠️ *Line 7, Column 4:* **Attribute date: is not serializable as XML 1.0.**

    `-->`

⚠️ *Line 7, Column 4:* **Attribute today's is not serializable as XML 1.0.**

    `-->`

4. Return to the Enter the Markup to validate box, and then correct the error in the code by entering the missing right angle bracket in the opening <head> tag.

5. Click the **Revalidate** button to resubmit the code for validation. The code should be error free, as previously.

TIP

If many messages appear when you validate a Web page, start by fixing the most obvious error, and then resubmit the code for validation. A single fix often resolves many error messages.

It can be intimidating when error messages are displayed in the validator. However, because one missing character can cause many error messages, as you just saw, a single fix can resolve a number of error messages.

Session 1.2 Quick Check

REVIEW

1. Why is an image tag considered to be an empty tag?
2. What is the purpose of the `src` attribute in the `img` element?
3. What is the aspect ratio?
4. What does the `<br />` tag do?
5. What is the difference between an unordered list and an ordered list?
6. What is the purpose of using the W3C validator?

Practice the skills you learned in the tutorial using the same case scenario.

PRACTICE

Review Assignments

Data Files needed for the Review Assignments: jazzfestivals.txt, jazzfestivals.jpg

Gina would like you to develop a Web page that lists some of the best jazz festivals. She has provided the content in the file jazzfestivals.txt. A preview of the Web page you'll create is shown in Figure 1-52.

Figure 1-52   **Jazz Festivals Web page**

Jazz Festivals Around the World

Jazz music is celebrated *all around the world* and all through the year. Here is a small list of some of the best festivals:

United States

- Jazz in July Festival, at 92nd Street Y in New York City
- Newport Jazz Festival, in Newport, Rhode Island
- Stanford Jazz Festival, Palo Alto, California
- Atlanta Jazz Festival, Atlanta, Georgia
- Satchmo Summer Fest, in New Orleans, Louisiana

Canada

- Montreal International Jazz Festival in Montreal, Quebec
- Ottawa Jazz Festival, in Ottawa, Ontario
- Toronto Downtown Jazz Festival in Toronto, Ontario
- Vancouver International Jazz Festival in Vancouver, British Columbia

Europe

- France
  - Jazz aux Remparts in Bayonne
  - Uzeste Musical in Uzeste
  - Jazz sous les pommiers in Coutances
  - Banlieues Bleues in Seine-Saint-Denis
  - Festival International Django Reinhardt in Samois sur Seine
  - CareFusion Jazz Festival in Paris
  - Paris Jazz Festival in the Bois de Vincennes
  - Sons d'hiver in Val-de-Marne
  - La Villette Jazz Festival in Paris
- Ireland
  - Bray Jazz Festival in Bray, Co.Wicklow
  - Cork Jazz Festival in Cork City, Co.Cork
  - Galway Jazz Festival in Galway City, Co.Galway

Copyright © Around the World Music

grynold/shutterstock.com

Remember to save and view the HTML file frequently as you progress, reloading it in the Web browser each time.

Complete the following:

1. Use your text editor to create a new file named **jazzfestivals.htm**, and save it in the tutorial1\review folder.

2. Enter the following tags to create the Web page structure:

```
<!DOCTYPE html>
<html>
      <head>

      </head>
      <body>

      </body>
</html>
```

3. In the head section, insert a `title` element that contains the title **Jazz Festivals**.

4. In the head section below the page title, create a comment containing *your first and last name*, the text **Tutorial 1, Review Assignment**, and *today's date*.

5. In the head section below the comment, include an appropriate `<meta />` tag that contains the description **List of jazz festivals around the world**.

6. In the head section below the `<meta />` tag, include an appropriate `<meta />` tag that contains the keywords **music, jazz, festivals, canada, united states, europe, france, ireland**.

7. In the body section, insert an image tag that displays the image jazzfestivals.jpg, which is contained in the images folder. Do not move the file from the images folder. Be sure to place the image tag within a paragraph element. The jazzfestivals.jpg image is 400 pixels wide and 177 pixels tall; add the appropriate `height` and `width` attributes. Using both the `alt` and `title` attributes, add code so when a user hovers the mouse pointer over the image in the browser, a ScreenTip appears that says *Jazz Festivals logo*.

8. Save your work, and then in your text editor open **jazzfestivals.txt** from the tutorial1\review folder.

9. Copy the text from jazzfestivals.txt to the jazzfestivals.htm file, inserting it after the image tag.

10. Add code that renders the words *Jazz Festivals Around the World* as an `h1` heading.

11. Add code that renders the words *Jazz music is celebrated all around the world and all through the year. Here is a small list of some of the best festivals.* within a paragraph element.

12. Add code that renders the words *all around the world* as emphasized.

13. Add code that renders *United States*, *Canada*, and *Europe* as `h2` headings.

14. Format the jazz festivals in the United States as an unordered list. The name of each festival should be a separate list item.

15. Format the jazz festivals in Canada as an unordered list. Each festival should be a separate list item.

16. Format the jazz festivals in Europe as a nested list, with France as one list item and its jazz festivals nested within it, and Ireland as another list item and its jazz festivals nested within it.

17. Add code that renders the words *Copyright Around the World Music* as strong, inside a paragraph element.

18. Insert the copyright symbol after the word *Copyright*.

19. In your browser, open **http://validator.w3.org**, and then validate your code. Correct any errors, and then revalidate until the code is error-free.

20. Save your work, and then submit the completed files to your instructor, in either printed or electronic form, as requested.

Use the skills you learned to update a basic Web page for a small grocery store.

Case Problem 1

Data Files needed for this Case Problem: shop.htm, grocerycart.jpg

Food Store The Food Store supermarket is a small grocery store featuring local produce. Marketing director Janet Ruiz wants your help in creating a Web page that lists the top sale items. A preview of the Web page appears in Figure 1-53.

Figure 1-53 Food Store Web page

Food Store Sales This Week

This week, we have plenty of your favorite summer vegetables on sale. All the vegetables we sell at the Food Store are grown right here, so you know our vegetables are always fresh and delicious. Although our produce is always on sale, just check below to see the savings compared to last week.

Here's just a few of the items on sale this week:

- *potatoes reduced by 50¢ per bag*
- *carrots reduced by 40¢ per pound*
- *iceberg lettuce reduced by 30¢ less per head*
- *string beans reduced by 35¢ per pound*

Although we love to see you spend time at the Food Store, we know that you have other places to be. We've introduced new self-checkout registers at all our Food Stores. Just swipe your Food Sture savings card and you are ready to start saving on everything that's on sale in the store. If you want to really zip in and out of our stores, just grab a price scanner on the way in and take a few paper shopping bags as well. Scan the item before you place it in a bag. As you travel through the store, the price scanner will alert you to what's on sale in that aisle. You'll get **discounts on items** you have in your purchase history, and you will get coupons for items that are not on sale.

Contact Us

Food Store
25 Rocky Mountain Drive
Suite 345
Boulder, CO 80333

877 345-4566

photostudio 7/shutterstock.com

Complete the following.

1. Use your text editor to open the file **shop.htm** from the tutorial1\case1 folder, and then save the file as **shopsolution.htm** in the same folder.
2. Within the `<title>` tags, type **Food Store Sale Items**.
3. Within the head section, enter a comment containing *your first and last name*, the text **Tutorial 1, Case Problem 1**, and *today's date*.
4. In the body section, insert an image element to display the image grocerycart.jpg, which is contained in the images folder. Do not move the file from the images folder. Be sure to place the image element within a paragraph element. The grocerycart.jpg image is 250 pixels wide and 245 pixels tall; add appropriate `height` and `width` attributes. Using both the `alt` and `title` attributes, add code so when a user hovers the mouse pointer over the image, a ScreenTip appears that says *Food Store cart*.
5. In the body section, create the code to mark the text *Food Store Sales This Week* as an `h1` heading.
6. Create code to mark the four sales items as an unordered list, with each list item formatted in bold and italic.

7. In each line in the unordered list, replace the word *cents* with the code for the cents symbol (¢) using a named character reference.

8. In the last paragraph, mark the words *discounts on items* as strong.

9. Create the code to mark the words *Contact Us* using the h3 element.

10. Add break tags where appropriate so the address appears as shown in Figure 1-53.

11. In your browser, open **http://validator.w3.org**, and then validate your code. Fix any errors, and revalidate until the code is error free.

12. Submit the completed files to your instructor, in either printed or electronic form, as requested.

Use the skills you learned to create a Web page for a supplier of masonry materials.

APPLY

Case Problem 2

Data Files needed for this Case Problem: brick.htm and bricklogo.jpg

Bent Brick and Stone   Bent Brick and Stone has sold masonry supplies in the greater Atlanta area for more than 75 years. The name of the company comes from its specialty of producing rounded brick in a variety of colors that are not extensively sold in the southern United States. Until now, the store has relied on in-person business as its only source of revenue. Ben Provo, the owner of Bent Brick and Stone, has asked you to develop a Web site that he hopes will attract more customers. A preview of the Web page appears in Figure 1-54.

Figure 1-54	Bent Brick and Stone Web page

mangiurea/shutterstock.com

Complete the following:

1. Use your text editor to open the file **brick.htm** from the tutorial1\case2 folder, and then save it as **bricksolution.htm** in the same folder.

2. Enter **Bent Brick and Stone** as the title.

3. Within the head section, enter a comment containing *your first and last name*, the text **Tutorial 1, Case Problem 2**, and *today's date*.

4. In the body section, insert an image tag to display the image bricklogo.jpg, which is contained in the images folder. Do not move the file from the images folder. The bricklogo.jpg image is 120 pixels wide and 97 pixels tall; add appropriate height

and `width` attributes. Be sure to place the image tag within a paragraph element. Using both the `alt` and `title` attributes, add code so when a user hovers the mouse pointer over the image, a ScreenTip appears that says *Bent Brick and Stone logo*.

5. Create code to mark the words *Bent Brick Welcomes You* as an `h1` heading.

6. Create code to mark the words *Welcome to Our New Web Site* as an `h2` heading.

7. Create code to mark the words *New Product Offered* as an `h3` heading.

🜚 **EXPLORE** 8. In the first sentence of the second paragraph, insert the registered trademark symbol (™) after the word *QwikStone*. Use a named character reference.

🜚 **EXPLORE** 9. Following the second paragraph, create code to apply both emphasis and strong to the text *Subject to availability*.

10. In your browser, open **http://validator.w3.org**, and then validate your code. Fix any errors, and revalidate until the code is error free.

11. Submit the completed files to your instructor, in either printed or electronic form, as requested.

Use what you've learned to create a Web page for a bridal shop.

APPLY

Case Problem 3

Data Files needed for this Case Problem: beth.htm and bethlogo.jpg

Beth's Budget Bridal   Beth's Budget Bridal is a small bridal shop in London, England. Beth's has achieved its success by giving customers what they want during tough economic times: a great gown at a great price. Over the last year, Beth's Budget Bridal has also begun offering wedding planning services that focus on creating a happy event that does not place a steep financial burden on the bride and groom. Beth Windsor, the owner of the shop, has asked for your assistance in creating a Web site for her shop. A preview of the Web page appears in Figure 1-55.

Figure 1-55   **Beth's Budget Bridal Web page**

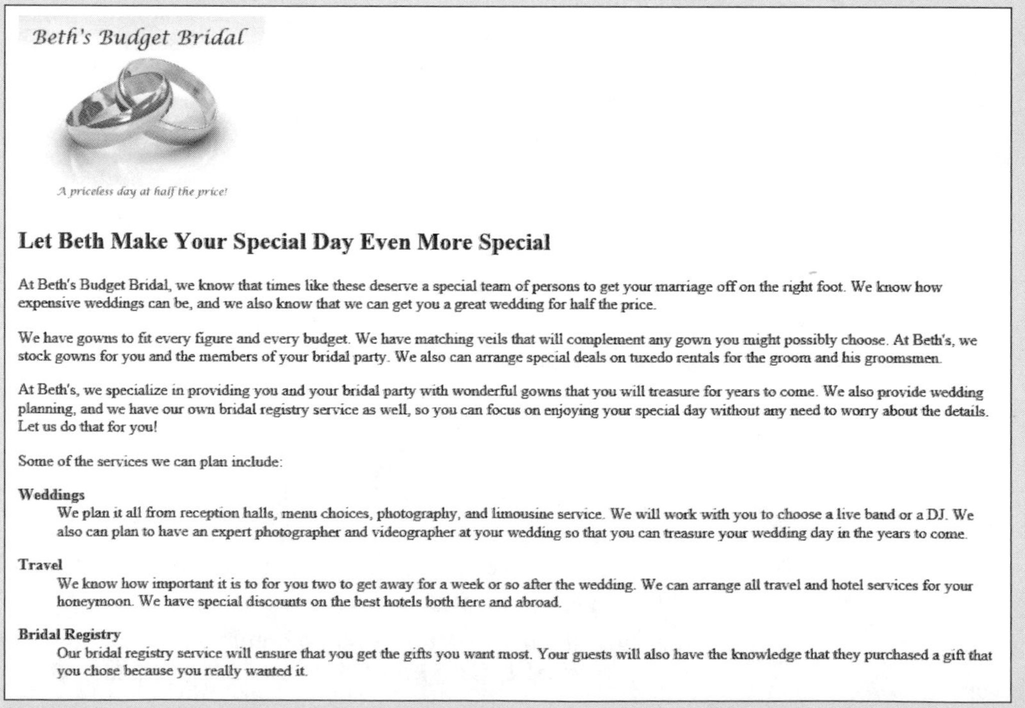

Tristan3D/shutterstock.com

Complete the following:

1. Use your text editor to open the file **beth.htm** from the case3 folder, and then save it as **bethsolution.htm** in the same folder.

2. Enter **Beth's Budget Bridal** as the title.

3. Within the head section, enter a comment containing *your first and last name*, the text **Tutorial 1, Case Problem 3**, and *today's date*.

4. In the body section, insert an image tag to display the image bethlogo.jpg, which is located in the images folder. Do not move the file from the images folder. Be sure to place the image tag within a paragraph element. The bethlogo.jpg image is 250 pixels wide and 187 pixels tall; add appropriate `height` and `width` attributes. Using both the `alt` and `title` attributes, add code so when a user hovers the mouse pointer over the image, a ScreenTip appears that says *Beth's Budget Bridal logo*.

5. In the head section, insert a `<meta />` tag that provides the following description of the Web site: **Beth's Budget Bridal is the only stop you have to make on the way to the altar.**

⊕EXPLORE

6. Create a description list using *Weddings*, *Travel*, and *Bridal Registry* as described terms. Each of the defined terms should be displayed in bold. Format the text below each of the defined terms as description data.

7. In your browser, open **http://validator.w3.org**, and then validate your code. Fix any errors, and revalidate until the code is error free.

8. Submit the completed files to your instructor, in either printed or electronic form, as requested.

Use the Internet to research renewable energy sources and create an informational Web page.

RESEARCH

Case Problem 4

Data Files needed for this Case Problem: energy.htm and energy.jpg

Renewable Energy Research Raj Singh founded Renewable Energy Research in Ottawa, Canada, to study renewable energy sources and their costs and environmental impacts. He recently hired you to assist him in his research and to produce Web pages that educate and inform interested users. Use the Web or other resources to research the topic of renewable energy sources, and create an informational Web page for Renewable Energy Research. In this Case Problem, you will create a new file.

Complete the following:

1. Use your favorite search engine to find and read at least three Web sites or online articles about renewable energy sources. Consider searching for information on solar, wind, hydro, or biofuel energy.

2. Prepare to create the Renewable Energy Research Web page by developing or finding the following material:

   a. At least four paragraphs about renewable energy sources. Describe what they are and what the cost might be.

   b. Headings that will precede each paragraph

   c. A quote from your research that you can use on the Web page and cite using a footnote reference

   d. A list of at least four types of renewable energy sources

3. In your text editor, open the **energy.htm** file from the tutorial1\case4 folder, and then save it as **energysolution.htm**.

4. Within the `<title></title>` tags, give your page a descriptive page title.

5. Within the head section, enter a comment containing *your first and last name*, the text **Tutorial 1, Case Problem 4**, and *today's date*.

6. In the body section, include examples (in any order) of the following:

   a. A comment
   b. Bold text
   c. Italic text
   d. An image, including at least one attribute. You can use the energy.jpg file from the case4\images folder if you wish; the file dimensions are 500 pixels wide and 334 pixels in height. Add the `alt` and `title` attributes to the image tag code, entering an appropriate description of the image. Be sure to place the image tag within a paragraph element. If you choose to use an image that you find online, remember to save it in the images folder.
   e. An ordered or unordered list
   f. Four or more paragraphs of text
   g. Headings
   h. The break tag
   i. A special character

7. In your browser, use the W3C HTML validator to validate the energysolution.htm document. Fix any errors, and revalidate until the code is error free.

8. Submit the completed files to your instructor, in either printed or electronic form, as requested.

ENDING DATA FILES

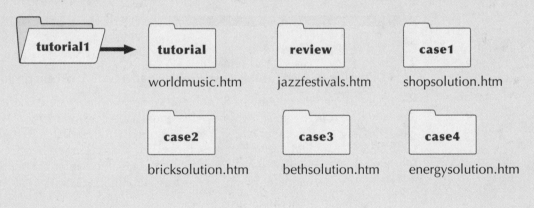

| tutorial | review | case1 |
| worldmusic.htm | jazzfestivals.htm | shopsolution.htm |

| case2 | case3 | case4 |
| bricksolution.htm | bethsolution.htm | energysolution.htm |

Creating Links

Using Links to Navigate Documents on the Web

OBJECTIVES

Session 2.1
- Create a link to another Web site on the Internet
- Create a link to download a file
- Create an email link
- Link to a specific section on the same page
- Create a link to another Web page on the same site

Session 2.2
- Use an image as a link
- Create thumbnail links to larger images
- Create image maps
- Create rectangle, circle, and polygon hotspots

Case | *Australia Information*

Tony Abbott is an Australian expatriate, living in Dublin, Ireland. He will be delivering a presentation to a group of people at Trinity College in Dublin who are interested in travelling to Australia. He wants to create a small Web site that can be accessed by the people who will be attending his presentation. He would like to provide information and pictures for each of the states and territories, in addition to links to some Web resources. He would really like a clickable map of Australia so the users could click each state or territory on the map to see more information. He would also like people to be able to download his presentation, and would like to provide an email contact for the Australian tourism organization. Tony would like you to create the Australia Web site. He will provide the text information and has hired a graphic artist who will provide you with the images as well.

STARTING DATA FILES

 →

tutorial2 → **tutorial**

australia.pdf
australia_states_and_territories.txt
modernizr-2.js
+18 image files

review

australia_logo.jpg
koala_lg.jpg
koala_sm.jpg
koala_T2.htm
modernizr-2.js

case1

barker_logo.jpg
barker_T2.htm
modernizr-2.js
week_lg.jpg
week_sm.jpg
week_T2.htm

 case2

club_logo.jpg
club_T2.htm
modernizr-2.js

 case3

floor_plan_T2.htm
modernizr-2.js
rooms_T2.htm
+9 image files

case4

modernizr-2.js
+6 image files

SESSION 2.1 VISUAL OVERVIEW

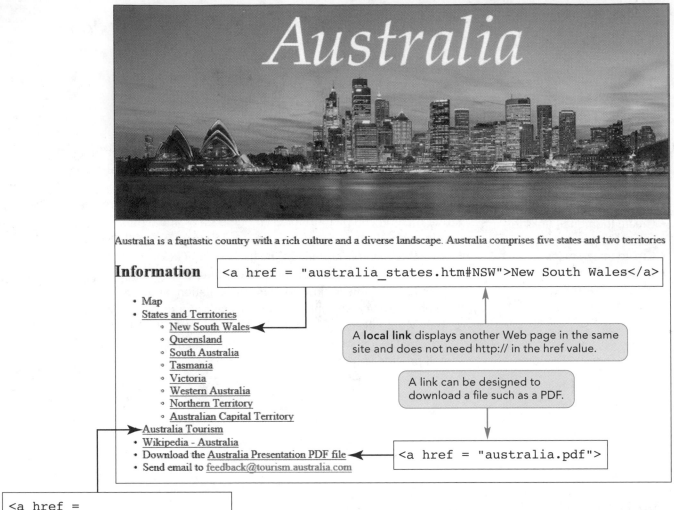

Australia is a fantastic country with a rich culture and a diverse landscape. Australia comprises five states and two territories

Information

<a href = "australia_states.htm#NSW">New South Wales</a>

- Map
- States and Territories
  - New South Wales
  - Queensland
  - South Australia
  - Tasmania
  - Victoria
  - Western Australia
  - Northern Territory
  - Australian Capital Territory
- Australia Tourism
- Wikipedia - Australia
- Download the Australia Presentation PDF file
- Send email to feedback@tourism.australia.com

A **local link** displays another Web page in the same site and does not need http:// in the href value.

A link can be designed to download a file such as a PDF.

<a href = "australia.pdf">

```
<a href =
"http://www.australia.com/"
title = "Australia Tourism">
Australia Tourism</a>
```

An **external link** displays a Web page on a different server.

CREATING LINKS

A link to another section on the same page doesn't need http:// or the filename in the href value.

A **navigation bar** is used to navigate easily from one section to another.

```
<a href = "#NSW">New South Wales</a>
```

Australia - States and Territories

New South Wales | Queensland | South Australia | Tasmania | Victoria | Western Australia | Northern Territories | Australian Capital Territory

States

New South Wales

New South Wales (NSW) is Australia's most populous state. Sydney is located in NSW on the eastern coast, and home to the Sydney Symphony Orchestra. National parks include the Royal National Park, Wollemi National Park and the Mutawintji National Park in western New South Wales.

Top of Page

```
<section id = "NSW">
New South Wales
….
</section>
```

A **section tag** is used to define a section of text and/or images that belong together.

Understanding Communications Technology

The popularity that the World Wide Web enjoys today is due largely to its ability to let you locate and view information in a nonlinear manner—that is, you do not have to read one page after another in a specific order. Many people use the terms *Internet* and *World Wide Web* interchangeably, but they are not the same. The ability to view documents on the World Wide Web is just one of several services provided by the Internet. Other Internet services include transferring files and sending email.

You've likely had some experience accessing the Web already. Perhaps you've searched for some information about a product you wanted to buy or read articles on a news site. To make information accessible in a nonlinear manner, Web pages use hyperlinks. A **hyperlink** (or **link**) is text or an image that, when clicked, displays another part of the same Web page, another Web page in the same site (a local link), or another Web page from a different site (an external link). After a link has been clicked, the page to where the link points becomes a **visited link**. Using links, visitors can choose the topics that interest them and can view those topics in any order.

TIP

The link style—especially color and underline—is determined by Web page settings, but you'll learn to customize this in later tutorials when you learn about CSS.

Introducing Protocols

A **protocol** is a standard for sending and receiving data. Protocols are important. If every company that made transmission media had its own protocol for communicating data, it would be much more difficult to send and receive data, because one company's set of rules would inevitably be incompatible with another company's. Using a protocol sets a single set of rules, and everyone benefits by following the rules for that protocol.

The protocol used to access the Web is **Hypertext Transfer Protocol**, or **HTTP**. HTTP establishes standards for communications between **file servers**—the computers that contain or direct information—and **client software applications**, or simply **clients**, which include Web browsers, email applications, and FTP applications. Another set of protocols, **Transmission Control Protocol/Internet Protocol** or **TCP/IP**, is used to send small bursts of information called **packets** across communication lines. TCP and IP work in tandem. TCP is responsible for ensuring that data is correctly delivered from the client computer to the server. IP moves packets of information from one computer to another.

Understanding Web Site Addresses

TIP

Many domain names may include a two-letter suffix that identifies the country, such as .uk, which stands for United Kingdom.

Every computer that is connected to the Internet is assigned an Internet Protocol address (IP address). Just as your home street address uniquely identifies the location of your home (no two homes have the same street address), the IP address identifies a specific computer. The IP address is composed of a series of four numbers (from 0 to 255) separated by periods, such as 12.34.222.111. A Web site is stored on a computer, and thus the Web site computer also has an IP address. A Web site could be accessed using the IP address, but obviously, it is not easy to remember Web site addresses based on IP addresses. To make the Web more user friendly, the Domain Name System was introduced. The **Domain Name System** refers to Web sites by Web server names rather than IP addresses. The domain name is followed by a **suffix**, a two- to four-letter abbreviation that groups domain names based on their category, such as .com, .net, .org, .edu, .mil, and .info. A suffix is also called a **top-level domain name**.

A **Uniform Resource Locator**, or **URL**, is the complete address of a Web site and page, such as http://www.cengage.com/contact/. Most Web browsers automatically add *http* in the URL, so usually you don't have to type it in the address bar or location bar.

INSIGHT

Understanding the Parts of a URL

A URL for a Web page has the following structure:

protocol://servername.domainname.suffix/path/filename

For example, the URL http://www.cengage.com/contact/ has the following components:

- *http* is the protocol.
- *www* is the name of the server that contains the file that is requested.
- *cengage.com* is the domain name—the name of the domain where the Web server resides.
- *.com* is the suffix (the top-level domain name).
- *contact* is the path (a file folder or folders on the server).

   Often, a filename isn't specified in a URL. In that case the server looks for a default filename such as index.htm, default.htm, index.html, or default.html as the name of the Web page to be sent to the Web browser. Both .htm and .html are used widely as file extensions. Choosing to use .htm or .html is a matter of personal preference. It is a good idea to name the first page of your Web site index.htm so viewers don't need to know the filename of the page.

   Many organizations make it easier for people to remember their URLs by using the default filename such as index.htm for the top-level Web page and configuring their servers to direct traffic to the *www* server by default. That way, people just have to remember the domain name for the organization and can use a shortened URL, such as http://cengage.com.

Creating Links

Tony wants the main page of his Web site to contain links to the following:

- A map Web page showing a map of Australia
- A states and territories Web page describing each of the states and territories of Australia
- The Australian tourism Web page
- The Wikipedia Australia Web page
- The email address for Australian tourism
- A file containing Tony's presentation

   In addition to the main Web page, you'll need to create a page on the Australia Web site that shows a map of Australia and another page that contains information about Australia's five states and three territories. For the states and territories, you could create eight pages, but each would be quite small. Instead, you'd rather create a single states and territories Web page that contains all of this information. Tony would also like the map on the map page to be clickable; he wants users to be able to click a state or territory on the map to view its description on the states and territories Web page.

   You use the information that Tony has provided to sketch a storyboard of the Australia Web site, shown in Figure 2-1. A **storyboard** is a visual representation, such as a sketch, that shows how Web pages are linked to each other. A storyboard could be created using software, or pen and paper.

TIP

It's worth the time to sketch a storyboard of any Web site that will contain more than two Web pages.

Figure 2-1 **Storyboard for the Australia Web site**

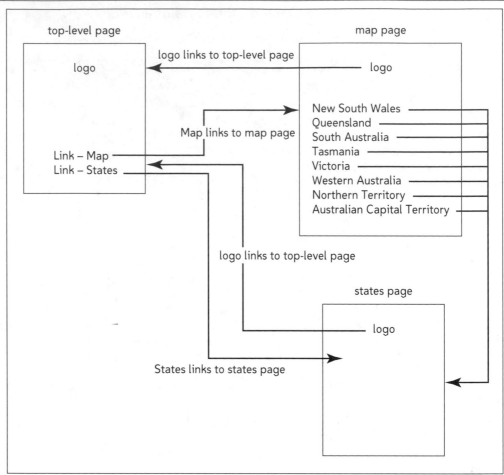

Allowing readers to quickly find topics of interest is critical to the success of any Web site. Your goal as a Web page author is to provide a navigation system that allows readers to select those places, pages, and sites of interest efficiently. When the content on a Web page becomes quite long, you can either break it up into smaller pages or create named sections on the page so users can jump from one section to another. To create Tony's Web site you need to create links to each of the following four types of destinations:

- A named section on the same page
- Another page on the same Web site
- A named section of another page on the same Web site
- A page on a different Web site

To visit each of these destinations, a user would click a link, which could be text or an image. To create Tony's Web site, you also need to create an **image map**, which is a single image that's divided into clickable areas, each of which links to a different destination. Links can also be used to send email and to access other resources, such as downloading a Microsoft Word or Adobe PDF file stored on a file server. You'll create a link to Tony's presentation document so people can download it afterwards.

Written Communication: Using a Storyboard to Describe a Web Site

The Web site design process usually begins with some brainstorming to clarify the purpose of the Web site and to determine exactly what information or functionality should be available on the Web site. At the end of the brainstorming process, you will have some sort of list of functionality and information for the Web site. The next step is to organize the Web site into Web pages. Professional Web developers might use pen and paper or a large white board and markers when speaking with a client to start the storyboarding process. Alternatively, they may use an application such as Visio or the drawing functions in another software application. A storyboard is often composed of several boxes, each representing a Web page, with lines or arrows drawn between the boxes to represent links to Web pages.

The storyboard is your Web site design plan, just as an outline is a plan for writing an essay. The storyboard is also used as a communication tool to discuss the functionality of the Web site with the client. You could use it to explain how the Web pages would link to each other, and how the Web site information would be divided into individual Web pages. It also becomes your development plan, which will guide you in creating the links on each of the Web pages. The storyboard is a planning tool and will help you to communicate clearly to the client.

You begin the Web site development process with the top-level Web page, which will contain the logo and several links. Even though you won't be creating the other Web pages until later, you'll include the navigation structure for the entire Web site now, and you'll add the links to the map page and the states and territories page later.

The storyboard sketch shown in Figure 2-1 is a good start, but it would quickly become unworkable for a large Web site. Another method that could be used to organize a Web site during the development phase is a **hierarchy chart**, which is more structured with rows of boxes, each representing a Web page. The storyboard is a bit more free-flowing and may show links to multiple Web pages more clearly. This small Web site could be represented using the hierarchy chart shown in Figure 2-2.

| Figure 2-2 | Hierarchy chart storyboard |

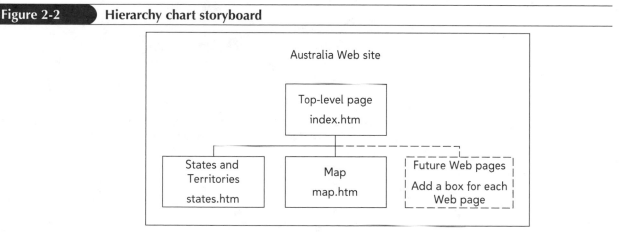

Tony has provided the logo and other images for the Australia Web site and placed them in the images folder.

People who load the Web page will use different Web browsers, and different versions of Web browsers. Older Web browsers do not support some HTML5 elements. However, you can ensure that users of these browsers can still view your Web pages by incorporating a JavaScript file. JavaScript is a programming language that all Web browsers can interpret. To overcome the problem that older browsers pose, you'll add the code for a small JavaScript program called *modernizr-2.js*, which interprets the HTML5 tags that older Web browsers might not be able to interpret.

To link a Web page to a JavaScript file, you add the `script` element. The `script` element can include the `src` attribute to point to an external JavaScript file. For your Web pages, you'll add a `script` element that points to the *modernizr-2.js* JavaScript file.

When you load a Web page that contains a JavaScript, some Web browsers such as Internet Explorer may pop up a dialog box asking if you want to run the script. If this happens, click the OK button to run the JavaScript.

To create the top-level Web page:

1. Open a new document in your text editor (Notepad or TextEdit), and enter the following code. Some of the HTML code in this tutorial is wide, so a two-character indent is used instead of a five-character indent:

```html
<!DOCTYPE html>
<html>
  <head>
    <!--
        Tutorial 2
        Author: your name
        Date: today's date
    -->

    <script src="modernizr-2.js"></script>
    <title>Australia</title>
  </head>
  <body>
    <p>
      <img src="images/australia_logo.jpg"
      width = "800" height = "307"
      alt="Australia logo" />
    </p>

    <p>Australia is a fantastic country with a rich culture and
    a diverse landscape. Australia comprises five states and
    two territories.</p>

    <h2>Information</h2>
    <ul>
      <li>Map</li>
      <li>States and Territories</li>
      <li>Australia Tourism</li>
      <li>Wikipedia - Australia</li>
      <li>Download the Australia Presentation</li>
      <li>Send email to feedback@tourism.australia.com</li>
    </ul>
  </body>
</html>
```

> **2.** Save the file as **index.htm** in the tutorial2\tutorial folder included with your Data Files. If you're using a Mac, you may have to click the **Use .htm** button after the **Save** button.

> **3.** Open the **index.htm** file in a Web browser to view the Web page. The page should look similar to Figure 2-3.

Figure 2-3	Australia index.htm Web page

Australia is a fantastic country with a rich culture and a diverse landscape. Australia comprises five states and two territories.

Information

- Map
- States and Territories
- Australia Tourism
- Wikipedia - Australia
- Download the Australia Presentation
- Send email to feedback@tourism.australia.com

David Iliff/Shutterstock.com

The Anchor Element

The **anchor element** is used to create a link. The anchor element is an inline element, so it must occur inside a block-level element such as the paragraph element (`<p></p>`). In HTML code, the anchor element is represented by the letter **a**. It is a paired tag with the open tag `<a>` and closing tag `</a>` encapsulating the text or image that is clickable. The `href` attribute is included in the anchor element to specify the Web resource that is loaded when the link is clicked. The value of the `title` attribute is displayed as a ScreenTip. For instance, the following code would create a link:

```
<a href = "http://www.google.com/" title = "Google Search
Engine">Search Google</a>
```

The phrase *Search Google* is the linked text in this case; by default, a browser would render it as blue and underlined. If a user hovered the mouse pointer over the Search Google link, the ScreenTip *Google Search Engine* would appear. The `href` attribute value must include the protocol (http://) if the link is referencing an external Web page or email address. Although the `title` attribute is not required, its use with links is common for accessibility reasons, as the value of the `title` attribute is read aloud by screen readers.

REFERENCE

Creating a Link

To create a link, use the format

```
<a href = "protocol://domainname.suffix" title = "popup
text">clickable linked text</a>
```

where
- a is the anchor tag name.
- href is the hypertext reference source.
- protocol is the data transfer method, such as http.
- popup text is the text that appears when the mouse pointer hovers over the link.
- clickable linked text is the text that becomes the link that can be clicked.

Linking to an External Web Page

To create a link to a page at a different Web site, you must include the complete URL of the Web page as the value for the href attribute. It is very important that you include the http:// protocol in the value for the href attribute. If you do not include the protocol, the link will not work.

The site plan you created with Tony includes external links to the Australia tourism site at http://www.australia.com and the Wikipedia article about Australia at http://en.wikipedia.org/wiki/Australia. You'll add those to the main Web page now.

To create a link to an external Web site:

1. Return to the **index.htm** file in your text editor.

2. In the third list item in the unordered list, select the words *Australia tourism* and then replace them with the following code, as shown in Figure 2-4:

```
<a href = "http://www.australia.com/" title = "Official
Australia Tourism Web site">Australia Tourism</a>
```

Figure 2-4	External Web page link

anchor tags are inside the <li> and </li> tags

entire URL is enclosed in quotes

```
<ul>
   <li>Map</li>
   <li>States and Territories</li>
   <li><a href = "http://www.australia.com/" title = "Official Australia Tourism Web
site">Australia Tourism</a></li>
   <li>Wikipedia - Australia</li>
   <li>Download the Australia Presentation</li>
   <li>Send email to feedback@tourism.australia.com</li>
</ul>
```

3. Save the file, return to your Web browser, and then click the **Refresh** or **Reload** button to view the changes in the file. The Web page should look similar to Figure 2-5. Notice the link has been created, and the text *Australia Tourism* is rendered blue and underlined.

Figure 2-5   **Adding an external link**

text link is displayed underlined and in blue by default

David Iliff/Shutterstock.com

4. Move the mouse pointer over the Australia Tourism link, and wait a moment to verify the `title` value is displayed as a ScreenTip. In some Web browsers, the `href` value may appear in the status area at the bottom of the browser window.

5. Click the **Australia Tourism** link to test it. Australia's official tourism Web page should load.

   Trouble? If the Web browser displays an error message or the Australia Tourism Web site doesn't load, return to your text editor and double-check the spelling of the URL in the `href` attribute in the anchor element. Make any corrections necessary, and then save and reload the index.htm Web page.

6. Click the **Back** button in your Web browser to return to the index.htm Web page. In some Web browsers, the link color changes to purple, indicating the Web site referenced in the `href` value has been visited.

Next you'll add a link to the Wikipedia page on Australia. Although many Web page URLs begin with *www*, there are also many that do not. It's important to double-check the spelling of the URL.

TIP

Load the Web page you want to link to in your Web browser, and use the copy feature to copy the entire URL. Then paste the URL into your HTML code.

To create a link to Wikipedia:

1. Return to the **index.htm** file in your text editor.

2. In the fourth list item of the unordered list, select the words *Wikipedia - Australia* and then replace them with the following code, as shown in Figure 2-6. Notice the server name is *en* rather than *www*:

```
<a href = "http://en.wikipedia.org/wiki/
Australia" title = "Wikipedia Australia general
information">Wikipedia - Australia</a>
```

Figure 2-6 Code for Wikipedia link

anchor tags are inside the <li> and </li> tags

```
<h2>Information</h2>
<ul>
 <li>Map</li>
 <li>States and Territories</li>
 <li><a href = "http://www.australia.com/" title = "Official Australia Tourism Web
site">Australia Tourism</a></li>
 <li><a href = "http://en.wikipedia.org/wiki/Australia" title = "Wikipedia Australia
general information">Wikipedia - Australia</a> </li>
 <li>Download the Australia Presentation</li>
 <li>Send email to feedback@tourism.australia.com</li>
 </ul>
```

3. Save the file, return to your Web browser, and then click the **Refresh** or **Reload** button to view the changes in the file. The Web page should look similar to Figure 2-7. Notice that a second link has been created beneath the first, and the text *Wikipedia - Australia* is rendered blue and underlined.

Figure 2-7 Australia top-level page with Wikipedia link

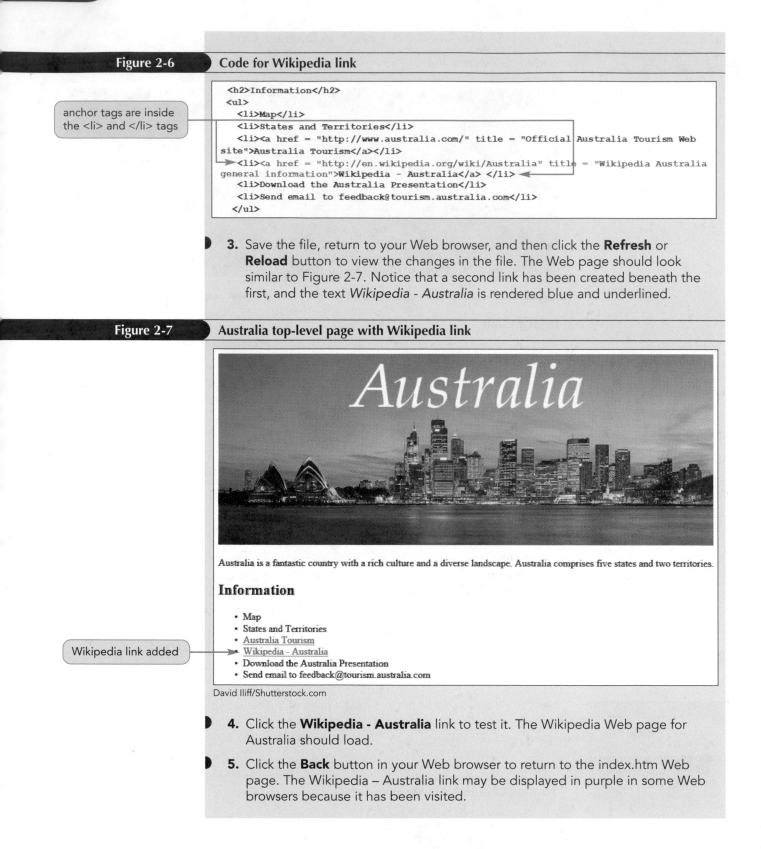

David Iliff/Shutterstock.com

Wikipedia link added

4. Click the **Wikipedia - Australia** link to test it. The Wikipedia Web page for Australia should load.

5. Click the **Back** button in your Web browser to return to the index.htm Web page. The Wikipedia – Australia link may be displayed in purple in some Web browsers because it has been visited.

Linking to Other Web Resources

In addition to linking to other Web pages, links are used to access Web resources such as documents, audio files, video files, and email. Some documents or other files require specific software in order to use or view the contents. Because you can't rely on users to have specialized software, it's wise to use the most common file types that can be viewed on most devices. For this reason, one of the most common file types on the Web is the **Portable Document Format (PDF)**, which is a file format created by Adobe to enable distribution of a document with a consistent appearance. For example, if you wanted to give visitors to your Web site access to a Microsoft Excel file, you could provide a PDF file that shows the contents of your document as it appears in Excel. To open a file stored as a PDF, you need to have the companion viewing software, Adobe Reader, installed on your computer. Adobe Reader is commonly installed on most computers, but if necessary, you can download the free Adobe Reader software at http://www.adobe.com.

Linking to Non-HTML Files

You can use an anchor element to link to any type of non-HTML file, such as a Microsoft Word file or a PDF file. You should always include some text on your page that identifies the file type, or indicates that a file will be downloaded. With this information, users are alerted to the fact that clicking the link initiates downloading a file rather than loading another Web page. Users who have slower Internet connections or simply prefer not to download files can then choose not to download the file.

The HTML code for a link to a file is the same as that for a link to another Web page, except that a link to a file doesn't use the http:// protocol. For instance, to link to a PDF file called birthday.pdf, you could use the following code:

```
<p>Download the PDF file: <a href="birthday.pdf">birthday.pdf</a></p>
```

When a user clicks the link, most browsers open a dialog box that prompts the user to open or save the file.

Tony has provided you with the file australia.pdf, which contains the presentation he would like users to be able to download. You'll add a link to this file from the Web page now.

To create a link to the presentation file:

▶ **1.** Return to the **index.htm** file in your text editor.

▶ **2.** In the fifth list item for the unordered list, select just the words *Australia Presentation* and then replace them with the following code, as shown in Figure 2-8:

```
<a href = "australia.pdf" title = "Australia
Presentation"/>Australia Presentation PDF file</a>
```

Figure 2-8	Adding a link to the presentation PDF document

```
<h2>Information</h2>
    <ul>
        <li>Map</li>
        <li>States and Territories</li>
        <li><a href = "http://www.australia.com/" title = "Official Australia Tourism Web
site">Australia Tourism</a></li>
        <li><a href = "http://en.wikipedia.org/wiki/Australia" title = "Wikipedia Australia general
information">Wikipedia - Australia</a></li>
        <li>Download the <a href = "australia.pdf" title = "Australia Presentation"/>Australia
Presentation PDF file</a></li>
        <li>Send email to feedback@tourism.australia.com</li>
    </ul>
```

the http:// protocol is not necessary since the resource is a local file, not a Web page

3. Save the file, return to your Web browser, and then click the **Refresh** or **Reload** button to view the changes in the file. The Web page should look similar to Figure 2-9. Notice the link has been created, and the text *Australia Presentation PDF file* is rendered blue and underlined.

| Figure 2-9 | Creating the Australia Presentation link |

David Iliff/Shutterstock.com

4. Click the **Australia Presentation PDF file** link to test it. The file may download and open automatically in a PDF viewer, or your Web browser may prompt you to save the file. If so, save the file on the desktop or in a folder such as Documents or My Documents. When you want to view the file, you can navigate to the location where the file is saved and double-click the file to view it.

Trouble? If the Web browser displays an error message, double-check the spelling of the file name in the `href` attribute in the anchor element. Also, ensure the australia.pdf file is saved in the same folder as the index.htm file. Make any corrections necessary, save and reload the index.htm Web page, and then retest the presentation link. If you're using a Mac, you may have to right-click and select *Open Link in New Window*.

File Associations

When a software application is installed on a computer, the data file types used by that software application are associated with it. For instance, when the Microsoft Excel application is installed, the Excel data file type is associated with Microsoft Excel. Excel data files have an extension of .xls or .xlsx. When a file ending in .xls is double-clicked, the Excel application opens and the file is loaded into it. This is the case regardless of whether the computer is running Windows or OS X.

When a Web page contains a link that points to a file that is not an HTML file, the browser downloads the file. If there is a file association with that data file to an application, the browser may also launch that application, which then loads the data file. For instance, if a link points to a file named Q1.xls, then the Q1.xls file is downloaded. When the user clicks on the downloaded file, Microsoft Excel is launched and the Q1.xls file opens in Microsoft Excel. On some computers or mobile devices, the file may open automatically in the software application that is associated with it.

If there is no file association for a specific file, the computer may display a dialog box that prompts you to save the file or to search for an application on the Web.

Creating an Email Link

You have probably seen a link at the bottom of a Web page that lets you send email to someone. An email link does not link to another location on a Web page. Instead, an email link opens email messaging software, such as Microsoft Outlook, so you can compose and send an email message. If the computer or mobile device used to view the Web page does not have an email application set up, the user may not be able to send email using the email link. An email link is created by using the mailto: protocol.

To create a link to an email address, you use the following format:

```
<a href="mailto:addressname@domainname.suffix">linktext</a>
```

In this code for an anchor element, `mailto:` is the protocol, *addressname@domainname.suffix* is the email address of the recipient, and *linktext* is the text that users click to activate the link.

As with the `href` attribute that contains the http:// protocol, it is important that you not include a space between the colon in the mailto: protocol and the email address; if you include a space, the link will not work. For instance, the code to send email to the email address webmaster@mysite.com might look like this:

```
<p><a href = "mailto:webmaster@mysite.com" title =
"webmaster@mysite.com">Send email to the webmaster</a> at
webmaster@mysite.com</p>
```

Spam can be a concern when using an email link. **Spam** is any unsolicited and unwanted email. Some unscrupulous companies use an **email harvester**, which is software that looks for and collects email addresses for the purpose of sending spam. Having said that, Internet service providers and corporate IT departments use excellent antispam software that filters spam and deletes it or stores it in a separate folder. There are advanced techniques that can be used to thwart email harvesters. These techniques include using JavaScript code in HTML documents to scramble email addresses, or running a program on the Web server that allows the user to fill in a form and send email from the server. You'll learn more about forms in a later tutorial. You should be aware that this vulnerability exists and, as a precaution, provide an email address only when you're comfortable with the likelihood that it will receive some spam messages. In the past, Web developers were using techniques to avoid placing email addresses on Web pages; however, with the prevalence of effective antispam software this has become less of a concern, and the trend is to include email addresses on Web pages once again.

When creating a mailto: link, you can also include a default subject for the email. To do this, you add a question mark (?) after the email address followed by the word *subject*, an equals sign, and the subject line for the email. For example, if the email dealt with customer service, the code for the email link might appear like this:

```
<a href = "mailto:webmaster@mysite.com?subject=Web question" title
= "webmaster@mysite.com">
```

Next, you'll create an email link to Australia Tourism. The email address for Australia Tourism is `feedback@tourism.australia.com`. The email link will not include a subject.

To create an email link to Australia Tourism:

1. Return to the **index.htm** file in your text editor.

2. In the sixth item in the unordered list, replace the email address with the following code, as shown in Figure 2-10:

   ```
   <a href = "mailto:feedback@tourism.australia.com" title =
   "feedback@tourism.australia.com">feedback@tourism.australia.
   com</a>
   ```

Figure 2-10	Creating the mailto: link

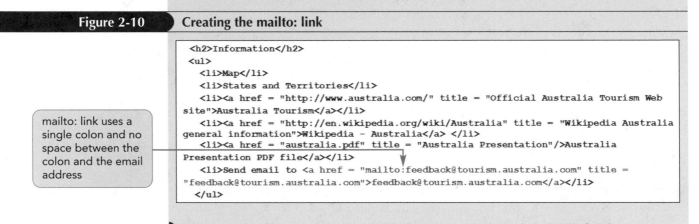

mailto: link uses a single colon and no space between the colon and the email address

```
<h2>Information</h2>
<ul>
  <li>Map</li>
  <li>States and Territories</li>
  <li><a href = "http://www.australia.com/" title = "Official Australia Tourism Web
site">Australia Tourism</a></li>
  <li><a href = "http://en.wikipedia.org/wiki/Australia" title = "Wikipedia Australia
general information">Wikipedia - Australia</a> </li>
  <li><a href = "australia.pdf" title = "Australia Presentation"/>Australia
Presentation PDF file</a></li>
  <li>Send email to <a href = "mailto:feedback@tourism.australia.com" title =
"feedback@tourism.australia.com">feedback@tourism.australia.com</a></li>
  </ul>
```

3. Save the file, return to your Web browser, and then click the **Refresh** or **Reload** button to view the changes in the file. The Web page should look similar to Figure 2-11. Notice the link has been created, and the text *feedback@tourism.australia.com* is rendered blue and underlined.

Figure 2-11	Creating a mailto: email link

David Iliff/Shutterstock.com

> **4.** Click the **feedback@tourism.australia.com** link to test it. If you have an email application installed, it opens and the email address appears in the *To* box.

> **5.** Close the new email window without sending the email message.

Creating a Link to a Specific Section on the Same Web Page

Most visitors to a Web page like to find what they're looking for right away. If your Web page is longer than one screen, you need to assist your readers to view the remainder of the page quickly and easily. Creating a link to an individual section on a Web page is a way to do that. HTML5 includes the new `<section>` tag. The `<section>` tag is used to identify content that belongs together as one section of information. You use the **id attribute** to identify an individual section by assigning it a unique name. Links to sections are also known as **anchor links** or **bookmark links**. The value for the `id` attribute should be a descriptive name based on the location or purpose of the `id`, or the surrounding text.

Creating a Section with an `id`

TIP

Use a descriptive name for an id value. Try to keep it short, and do not use special characters such as the ampersand (&) and punctuation.

To create a section with an `id`, use the syntax

```
<section id = "idvalue">content</section>
```

where `section` is the name of the element, `id` is the `id` attribute, *idvalue* is the value for the `id`, and *content* is the content of the element. The content in the section could be a paragraph of text or additional HTML code. For instance, to create a section called Top, you'd use the following code:

```
<section id = "Top">content</section>
```

Creating a Link to a Section on the Same Page

To create a link to a section id on the same page, enter the following code:

```
<a href = "#idname">linktext</a>
```

where a is the element name, href is the hypertext reference attribute, *idname* is the name of the id you are linking to (preceded by the (#) character), and *linktext* is the text that users click to activate the link. The (#) character is required when the value of *linktext* is defined by the Web developer. For example, you might use the following code to create a link to a section called Top:

```
<a href = "#top">Go to Top</a>
```

Tony would like you to create a Web page that contains some information about each state and territory in Australia. You decide to create a single large Web page rather than individual Web pages for each of the regions. In your Web page, each state or territory will be a separate section of the document. You will create a link to each section so the user can navigate to each section. You will also create a link to the top of the Web page in each section so the user can navigate back to the top. Tony has provided the text information for the states and territories Web page in the file australia_states_and_ territories.txt. Figure 2-12 shows the contents of this file.

Figure 2-12   **Contents of australia_states_and_territories.txt**

```
Australia - States and Territories

States

New South Wales

New South Wales (NSW) is Australia's most populous state. Sydney is located in NSW on the eastern
coast and is home to the Sydney Symphony Orchestra. National parks include the Royal National Park,
Wollemi National Park and the Mutawintji National Park in western New South Wales.


Queensland

Queensland, named after Queen Victoria, is located in the northeast portion of Australia. It is
home to the famous Gold Coast and to the Great Barrier Reef. The state capital is Brisbane. In
addition to the Great Barrier Reef, it is home to other World Heritage preservation areas including
the Gondwana Rainforests and Fraser Island.


South Australia

The state of South Australia is located in the south central part of Australia. The terrain
consists of low mountain ranges and semi-arid and arid rangelands. The state possesses the single
largest deposit of uranium in the world.


Tasmania

Tasmania is an island state 240 kilometers south of the mainland. Its geography consists mainly of
rounded smooth mountains, and it is the most mountainous state in Australia. It is known for its
unique flora and fauna. It has diverse vegetation ranging from grasslands to temperate rainforests.
It is home to the famous Tasmanian devil.


Victoria

Victoria is the second most populous state in Australia, and the smallest mainland state. The state
capital is Melbourne. The terrain includes the Victorian Alps in the northeast and an extensive
series of river systems.


Western Australia

The state of Western Australia occupies the entire western third of the Australian mainland. Its
capital city is Perth. The southwest coast has a Mediterranean climate. It is home to the Western
Australian Academy of Performing Arts (WAAPA) and the West Australian Symphony Orchestra (WASO).


Territories

Northern Territory

The Northern Territory is a federal territory of Australia, occupying the north central part of the
mainland. It is home to two natural rock formations, Uluru (Ayers Rock) and Kata Tjuta (The Olgas).
These locations are sacred to the local Aboriginal peoples and have become major tourist
attractions.


Australian Capital Territory

The Australian Capital Territory (ACT) is located entirely within New South Wales. It is home to
Australia's capital city, Canberra. Canberra is a planned city and the major roads follow a wheel-
and-spoke pattern.
```

First you will need to convert the text file to an HTML file with formatted headings and paragraphs.

To add HTML tags to a text file:

1. In your text editor, open the file **australia_states_and_territories.txt**, and then save it as **australia_states.htm**.

   Trouble? If you're using TextEdit on a Mac and don't have a Save As option, click File, and then click Duplicate. In the window containing the new copy of the file, click File, click Save, change the filename to australia_states.htm, click Save, and then click Use .htm.

2. Insert the following code at the top of the file, as shown in Figure 2-13. If you wish, you can copy this code from the index.htm file, but be sure to edit the `title` element to include *Australia States and Territories*:

```
<!DOCTYPE html>
<html>
  <head>
    <!--

         Tutorial 2
         Author: your name
         Date: today's date
    -->

    <title>Australia States and Territories</title>
  </head>

  <body>
    <p>
    <img src="images/australia_logo.jpg" alt="Sydney,
    Australia skyline" />
    </p>
```

Figure 2-13   Adding HTML code to start the australia_states.htm file

same code as index.htm except for the title element content

```
<!DOCTYPE html>
<html>
<head>
  <!--
     Tutorial 2
     Author: your name
     Date: today's date
  -->

  <title>Australia</title>
</head>
<body>
  <p>
    <img src="images/australia_logo.jpg" alt="Sydney, Australia skyline" />
  </p>

Australia - States and Territories

States
```

title element should include *Australia States and Territories*

3. Scroll down to the end of the file and then insert the following code, as shown in Figure 2-14:

```
</body>
</html>
```

| Figure 2-14 | Adding HTML code to the end of the australia_states.htm file |

```
Australian Capital Territory

The Australian Capital Territory (ACT) is located entirely within New
South Wales. It is home to Australia's capital city, Canberra. Canberra
is a planned city and the major roads follow a wheel-and-spoke pattern.

</body>
</html>
```

4. Save the file and then open the **australia_states.htm** file in your Web browser. The Web page should look similar to Figure 2-15.

| Figure 2-15 | Unformatted Web page |

text without HTML tags is unformatted

Australia - States and Territories States New South Wales New South Wales (NSW) is Australia's most populous state. Sydney is located in NSW on the eastern coast, and home to the Sydney Symphony Orchestra. National parks include the Royal National Park, Wollemi National Park and the Mutawintji National Park in western New South Wales. Queensland Queensland, named after Queen Victoria, is located in the North East portion of Australia. It is home to the famous Gold Coast and the Great Barrier Reef. The captial city is Brisbane. In addition to the Great Barrier Reef, it is also home to other World Heritage preservation areas including the Gondwana Rainforests of Australia, and Fraser Island. South Australia The state of South Australia is located in the south central part of Australia. The terrain consists of low mountain ranges, semi-arid and arid rangelands. It also posesses the single largest deposit of Uranium in the world. Tasmania Tasmania is an island and state, 240 kilometers south of the mainland. Its geography consists of mainly rounded smooth mountains, and is the most mountainous state in Australia. It is known for its unique flora and fauna. It has diverse vegetation ranging from grasslands to temperate rainforests. It is home to the famous Tasmanian devil. Victoria Victoria is the second most populous state in Australia, and the smallest mainland state. The state capital is Melbourne. The terraine includes the Victorian Alps in the northeast and an extensive series of river systems. Western Australia The state of Western Australia occupies the entire western third of the Australian mainland. Its capital city is Perth. The southwest coast has a Mediterranian climate. It is home to the Western Australian Academy of Performing Arts (WAAPA) and the West Australian Symphony Orchestra (WASO). Territories Northern Territory The Northern Territory is a federal territory of Australia, occupying the north central part of the mainland. It is home to two natural rock formations, Uluru (Ayers Rock) and Kata Tjuta (The Olgas). These locations are sacred to the local Aboriginal peoples and have become major tourist attractions. Australian Capital Territory The Australian Capital Territory (ACT) is located entirely within New South Wales. It is home to Australia's capital city, Canberra. Canberra is a planned city and the major roads follow a wheel and spoke pattern.

David Iliff/Shutterstock.com

The text file provided by Tony did not include HTML tags to format the headings and paragraphs for each state and territory. Web browsers display the text as a single block of text, regardless of the fact there is whitespace between the names of states and territories. Without HTML tags that identify headings and paragraphs, Web browsers treat the text as one long unit of text. You will add the heading and paragraph tags to identify the content in the Web page. The main title, *Australia – States and Territories*, will be formatted with an h1 element. The subtitles, *States* and *Territories*, will be formatted with h2 elements. The names of the states and territories will be formatted with h3 elements. The description paragraphs will be contained in p elements.

To add HTML tags to the descriptions of states and territories:

1. Return to the **australia_states.htm** file in your text editor.

2. Locate the *Australia-States and Territories* heading, add the tag <h1> before the first word, and then add the tag </h1> after the last word. Your code should appear as follows:

   ```
   <h1>Australia - States and Territories</h1>
   ```

3. Repeat Step 2 to insert the tags as follows:

   <h2> and </h2> tags around the *States* heading

   <h3> and </h3> tags around the *New South Wales* heading

   <p> and </p> tags around the paragraph after the *New South Wales* heading

   The code is shown in Figure 2-16.

Figure 2-16	Adding the HTML heading and paragraph tags

first-level heading

second-level heading

third-level heading

paragraph

```
<h1>Australia - States and Territories</h1>

<h2>States</h2>

<h3>New South Wales</h3>

<p>New South Wales (NSW) is Australia's most populous state. Sydney is
located in NSW on the eastern coast and is home to the Sydney Symphony
Orchestra. National parks include the Royal National Park, Wollemi
National Park and the Mutawintji National Park in western New South
Wales.</p>
```

4. Insert the following tags as shown in Figure 2-17:

   <h3> and </h3> tags around the *Queensland* heading

   <p> and </p> tags around the paragraph after the Queensland heading

   <h3> and </h3> tags around the *South Australia* heading

   <p> and </p> tags around the paragraph after the South Australia heading

   <h3> and </h3> tags around the *Tasmania* heading

   <p> and </p> tags around the paragraph after the Tasmania heading

   <h3> and </h3> tags around the *Victoria* heading

   <p> and </p> tags around the paragraph after the Victoria heading

   <h3> and </h3> tags around the *Western Australia* heading

   <p> and </p> tags around the paragraph after the Western Australia heading

Figure 2-17 **Formatting headings and paragraphs for states**

```
<h3>Queensland</h3>

<p>Queensland, named after Queen Victoria, is located in the North East
portion of Australia. It is home to the famous Gold Coast and the
Great Barrier Reef. The captial city is Brisbane. In addition to the
Great Barier Reef, it is also home to other World Heritage
preservation areas including the Gondwana Rainforests of Australia,
and Fraser Island.</p>

<h3>South Australia</h3>

<p>The state of South Australia is located in the south central part of
Australia. The terrain consists of low mountain ranges, semi-arid and
arid rangelands. It also posesses the single largest deposit of
Uranium in the world.</p>

<h3>Tasmania</h3>

<p>Tasmania is an island and state, 240 kilometers south of the mainland.
Its geography consists of mainly rounded smooth mountains, and is the
most mountainous state in Australia. It is known for its unique flora
and fauna. It has diverse vegetation ranging from grasslands to
temperate rainforests. It is home to the famous Tasmanian devil.</p>

<h3>Victoria</h3>

<p>Victoria is the second most populous state in Australia, and the
smallest mainland state. The state capital is Melbourne. The terraine
includes the Victorian Alps in the northeast and an extensive series
of river systems.</p>

<h3>Western Australia</h3>

<p>The state of Western Australia occupies the entire western third of
the Australian mainland. Its capital city is Perth. The southwest
coast has a Mediterranian climate. It is home to the Western
Australian Academy of Performing Arts (WAAPA) and the West Australian
Symphony Orchestra (WASO).</p>
```

5. Similarly, as shown below and in Figure 2-18, insert the tags as follows:

   <h2> and **</h2>** tags around the *Territories* heading

   <h3> and **</h3>** tags around the *Northern Territory* heading

   <p> and **</p>** tags around the paragraph after the Northern Territory heading

   <h3> and **</h3>** tags around the *Australian Capital Territory* heading

   <p> and **</p>** tags around the paragraph after the Australian Capital Territory heading

Figure 2-18 **Formatting headings and paragraphs for territories**

```
<h2>Territories</h2>

<h3>Northern Territory</h3>

<p>The Northern Territory is a federal territory of Australia, occupying
the north central part of the mainland. It is home to two natural rock
formations, Uluru (Ayers Rock) and Kata Tjuta (The Olgas). These
locations are sacred to the local Aboriginal peoples and have become
major tourist attractions.</p>


<h3>Australian Capital Territory</h3>

<p>The Australian Capital Territory (ACT) is located entirely within New
South Wales. It is home to Australia's capital city, Canberra.
Canberra is a planned city and the major roads follow a wheel and
spoke pattern.</p>
```

6. Save the file.

7. Return to your Web browser, and click the **Refresh** or **Reload** button to view the changes in the file. The Web page should look similar to Figure 2-19. The tags you've entered have transformed the text file into an HTML file that identifies the headings and paragraphs, which are then rendered in a more readable format by the Web browser.

Figure 2-19   **States and territories page with heading and paragraph elements**

Australia - States and Territories

States

New South Wales

New South Wales (NSW) is Australia's most populous state. Sydney is located in NSW on the eastern coast, and home to the Sydney Symphony Orchestra. National parks include the Royal National Park, Wollemi National Park and the Mutawintji National Park in western New South Wales.

Queensland

Queensland, named after Queen Victoria, is located in the North East portion of Australia. It is home to the famous Gold Coast and the Great Barrier Reef. The captial city is Brisbane. In addition to the Great Barier Reef, it is also home to other World Heritage preservation areas including the Gondwana Rainforests of Australia, and Fraser Island.

South Australia

The state of South Australia is located in the south central part of Australia. The terrain consists of low mountain ranges, semi-arid and arid rangelands. It also posesses the single largest deposit of Uranium in the world.

Tasmania

Tasmania is an island and state, 240 kilometers south of the mainland. Its geography consists of mainly rounded smooth mountains, and is the most mountainous state in Australia. It is known for its unique flora and fauna. It has diverse vegetation ranging from grasslands to temperate rainforests. It is home to the famous Tasmanian devil.

Victoria

Victoria is the second most populous state in Australia, and the smallest mainland state. The state capital is Melbourne. The terraine includes the Victorian Alps in the northeast and an extensive series of river systems.

Western Australia

The state of Western Australia occupies the entire western third of the Australian mainland. Its capital city is Perth. The southwest coast has a Mediterranian climate. It is home to the Western Australian Academy of Performing Arts (WAAPA) and the West Australian Symphony Orchestra (WASO).

Territories

Northern Territory

The Northern Territory is a federal territory of Australia, occupying the north central part of the mainland. It is home to two natural rock formations, Uluru (Ayers Rock) and Kata Tjuta (The Olgas). These locations are sacred to the local Aboriginal peoples and have become major tourist attractions.

Australian Capital Territory

The Australian Capital Territory (ACT) is located entirely within New South Wales. It is home to Australia's capital city, Canberra. Canberra is a planned city and the major roads follow a wheel and spoke pattern.

This Web page is rather long. Fortunately, the content easily lends itself to creating sections. You'll mark each state or territory as a separate section of the Web page; then you'll add links to give users the ability to navigate from the top of the page to a specific section, and to navigate from any section to the top of the page. You'll start this process by identifying the top of the page using a `section` element with an `id` attribute; then you'll add a Top of Page link at the end of every paragraph.

To create a `section` element at the top of the page:

1. Return to the **australia_states.htm** file in your text editor.

2. Above the *Australia – States and Territories* heading insert the opening section tag **`<section id = "top">`**.

3. After the *Australia – States and Territories* heading insert the closing section tag **`</section>`**. Your code should match Figure 2-20.

Figure 2-20   **Section element with the id attribute**

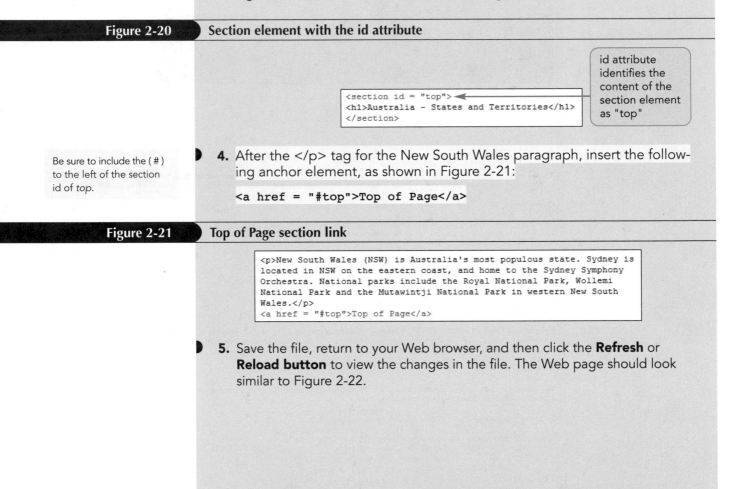

id attribute identifies the content of the section element as "top"

```
<section id = "top">
<h1>Australia - States and Territories</h1>
</section>
```

Be sure to include the (#) to the left of the section id of top.

4. After the `</p>` tag for the New South Wales paragraph, insert the following anchor element, as shown in Figure 2-21:

   `<a href = "#top">Top of Page</a>`

Figure 2-21   **Top of Page section link**

```
<p>New South Wales (NSW) is Australia's most populous state. Sydney is
located in NSW on the eastern coast, and home to the Sydney Symphony
Orchestra. National parks include the Royal National Park, Wollemi
National Park and the Mutawintji National Park in western New South
Wales.</p>
<a href = "#top">Top of Page</a>
```

5. Save the file, return to your Web browser, and then click the **Refresh** or **Reload button** to view the changes in the file. The Web page should look similar to Figure 2-22.

Figure 2-22   Creating the Top of Page navigation link

Australia - States and Territories

States

New South Wales

New South Wales (NSW) is Australia's most populous state. Sydney is located in NSW on the eastern coast, and home to the Sydney Symphony Orchestra. National parks include the Royal National Park, Wollemi National Park and the Mutawintji National Park in western New South Wales.

Top of Page

Top of Page link takes users up to the main heading

Queensland

Queensland, named after Queen Victoria, is located in the North East portion of Australia. It is home to the famous Gold Coast and the Great Barrier Reef. The captial city is Brisbane. In addition to the Great Barrier Reef, it is also home to other World Heritage preservation areas including the Gondwana Rainforests of Australia, and Fraser Island.

South Australia

The state of South Australia is located in the south central part of Australia. The terrain consists of low mountain ranges, semi-arid and arid rangelands. It also posesses the single largest deposit of Uranium in the world.

Tasmania

Tasmania is an island and state, 240 kilometers south of the mainland. Its geography consists of mainly rounded smooth mountains, and is the most mountainous state in Australia. It is known for its unique flora and fauna. It has diverse vegetation ranging from grasslands to temperate rainforests. It is home to the famous Tasmanian devil.

Victoria

Victoria is the second most populous state in Australia, and the smallest mainland state. The state capital is Melbourne. The terraine includes the Victorian Alps in the northeast and an extensive series of river systems.

Western Australia

The state of Western Australia occupies the entire western third of the Australian mainland. Its capital city is Perth. The southwest coast has a Mediterranian climate. It is home to the Western Australian Academy of Performing Arts (WAAPA) and the West Australian Symphony Orchestra (WASO).

Territories

Northern Territory

The Northern Territory is a federal territory of Australia, occupying the north central part of the mainland. It is home to two natural rock formations, Uluru (Ayers Rock) and Kata Tjuta (The Olgas). These locations are sacred to the local Aboriginal peoples and have become major tourist attractions.

Australian Capital Territory

The Australian Capital Territory (ACT) is located entirely within New South Wales. It is home to Australia's capital city, Canberra. Canberra is a planned city and the major roads follow a wheel and spoke pattern.

David Iliff/Shutterstock.com

6. Click on the *Top of Page* link. The position of the Web page in the browser should shift to place the *Australia – States and Territories* heading at the top of the browser window as shown in Figure 2-23.

Figure 2-23 **Top section is scrolled to the top of the Web browser window**

Australia - States and Territories ◄

> Australia – States and Territories section is at the top of the Web browser window

States

New South Wales

New South Wales (NSW) is Australia's most populous state. Sydney is located in NSW on the eastern coast, and home to the Sydney Symphony Orchestra. National parks include the Royal National Park, Wollemi National Park and the Mutawintji National Park in western New South Wales.

Top of Page

Queensland

Queensland, named after Queen Victoria, is located in the North East portion of Australia. It is home to the famous Gold Coast and the Great Barrier Reef. The captial city is Brisbane. In addition to the Great Barier Reef, it is also home to other World Heritage preservation areas including the Gondwana Rainforests of Australia, and Fraser Island.

South Australia

The state of South Australia is located in the south central part of Australia. The terrain consists of low mountain ranges, semi-arid and arid rangelands. It also posesses the single largest deposit of Uranium in the world.

Tasmania

Tasmania is an island and state, 240 kilometers south of the mainland. Its geography consists of mainly rounded smooth mountains, and is the most mountainous state in Australia. It is known for its unique flora and fauna. It has diverse vegetation ranging from grasslands to temperate rainforests. It is home to the famous Tasmanian devil.

Victoria

Victoria is the second most populous state in Australia, and the smallest mainland state. The state capital is Melbourne. The terraine includes the Victorian Alps in the northeast and an extensive series of river systems.

Western Australia

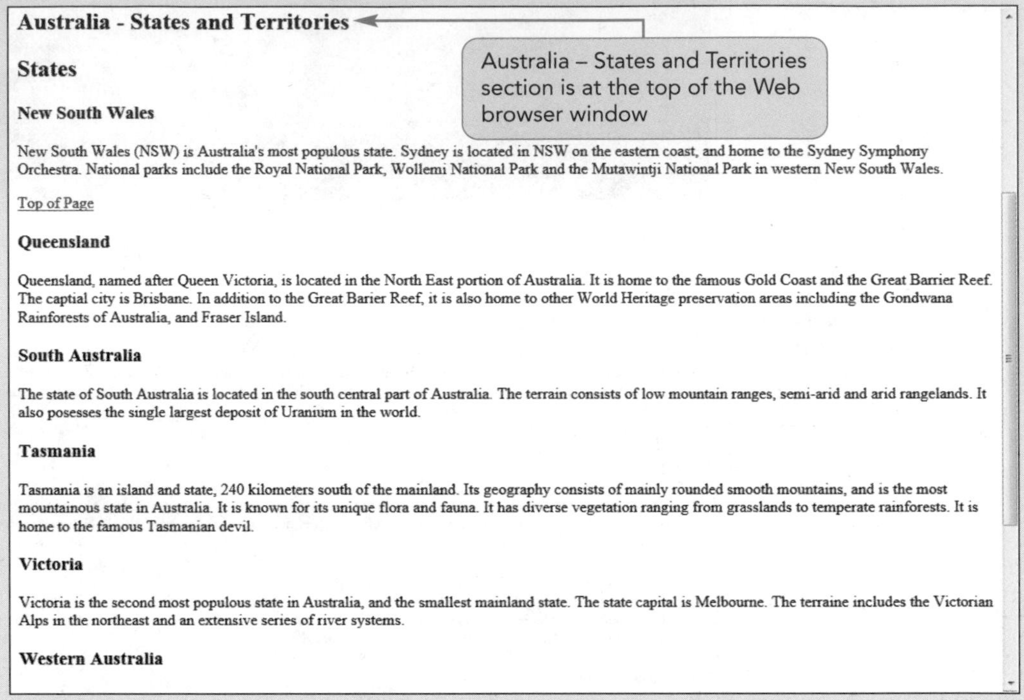

7. Repeat Step 4 to add the anchor element `<a href = "#top">Top of Page</a>` after each of the `</p>` tags in the australia_states.htm file, as shown in Figure 2-24.

Figure 2-24   Adding Top of Page anchor elements

```
<h3>Queensland</h3>

<p>Queensland, named after Queen Victoria, is located in the North East
portion of Australia. It is home to the famous Gold Coast and the
Great Barrier Reef. The captial city is Brisbane. In addition to the
Great Barrier Reef, it is also home to other World Heritage
preservation areas including the Gondwana Rainforests of Australia,
and Fraser Island.</p>
<a href = "#top">Top of Page</a>

<h3>South Australia</h3>

<p>The state of South Australia is located in the south central part of
Australia. The terrain consists of low mountain ranges, semi-arid and
arid rangelands. It also posesses the single largest deposit of
Uranium in the world.</p>
<a href = "#top">Top of Page</a>

<h3>Tasmania</h3>

<p>Tasmania is an island and state, 240 kilometers south of the mainland.
Its geography consists of mainly rounded smooth mountains, and is the
most mountainous state in Australia. It is known for its unique flora
and fauna. It has diverse vegetation ranging from grasslands to
temperate rainforests. It is home to the famous Tasmanian devil.</p>
<a href = "#top">Top of Page</a>

<h3>Victoria</h3>

<p>Victoria is the second most populous state in Australia, and the
smallest mainland state. The state capital is Melbourne. The terraine
includes the Victorian Alps in the northeast and an extensive series
of river systems.</p>
<a href = "#top">Top of Page</a>

<h3>Western Australia</h3>

<p>The state of Western Australia occupies the entire western third of
the Australian mainland. Its capital city is Perth. The southwest
coast has a Mediterranian climate. It is home to the Western
Australian Academy of Performing Arts (WAAPA) and the West Australian
Symphony Orchestra (WASO).</p>
<a href = "#top">Top of Page</a>

<h2>Territories</h2>

<h3>Northern Territory</h3>

<p>The Northern Territory is a federal territory of Australia, occupying
the north central part of the mainland. It is home to two natural rock
formations, Uluru (Ayers Rock) and Kata Tjuta (The Olgas). These
locations are sacred to the local Aboriginal peoples and have become
major tourist attractions.</p>
<a href = "#top">Top of Page</a>

<h3>Australian Capital Territory</h3>

<p>The Australian Capital Territory (ACT) is located entirely within New
South Wales. It is home to Australia's capital city, Canberra.
Canberra is a planned city and the major roads follow a wheel and
spoke pattern.</p>
<a href = "#top">Top of Page</a>
```

Top of Page anchor elements create links to the top section

8. Save the file, return to your Web browser, and then click the **Refresh** or **Reload** button to view the changes in the file. The Web page should look similar to Figure 2-25.

Figure 2-25   **Top of Page links added**

Australia - States and Territories

States

New South Wales

New South Wales (NSW) is Australia's most populous state. Sydney is located in NSW on the eastern coast, and home to the Sydney Symphony Orchestra. National parks include the Royal National Park, Wollemi National Park and the Mutawintji National Park in western New South Wales.

Top of Page

Queensland

Queensland, named after Queen Victoria, is located in the North East portion of Australia. It is home to the famous Gold Coast and the Great Barrier Reef. The captial city is Brisbane. In addition to the Great Barier Reef, it is also home to other World Heritage preservation areas including the Gondwana Rainforests of Australia, and Fraser Island.

Top of Page

South Australia

The state of South Australia is located in the south central part of Australia. The terrain consists of low mountain ranges, semi-arid and arid rangelands. It also posesses the single largest deposit of Uranium in the world.

Top of Page

Tasmania

Tasmania is an island and state, 240 kilometers south of the mainland. Its geography consists of mainly rounded smooth mountains, and is the most mountainous state in Australia. It is known for its unique flora and fauna. It has diverse vegetation ranging from grasslands to temperate rainforests. It is home to the famous Tasmanian devil.

Top of Page

Victoria

Victoria is the second most populous state in Australia, and the smallest mainland state. The state capital is Melbourne. The terraine includes the Victorian Alps in the northeast and an extensive series of river systems.

Top of Page

Western Australia

The state of Western Australia occupies the entire western third of the Australian mainland. Its capital city is Perth. The southwest coast has a Mediterranian climate. It is home to the Western Australian Academy of Performing Arts (WAAPA) and the West Australian Symphony Orchestra (WASO).

Top of Page

Territories

Northern Territory

The Northern Territory is a federal territory of Australia, occupying the north central part of the mainland. It is home to two natural rock formations, Uluru (Ayers Rock) and Kata Tjuta (The Olgas). These locations are sacred to the local Aboriginal peoples and have become major tourist attractions.

Top of Page

Australian Capital Territory

The Australian Capital Territory (ACT) is located entirely within New South Wales. It is home to Australia's capital city, Canberra. Canberra is a planned city and the major roads follow a wheel and spoke pattern.

Top of Page

9. Scroll down the page, and then click on a few of the **Top of Page** links to test them.

   Trouble? If you click on the Top of Page link when the Web page already displays the top of the page, there may not be any change. The page navigation links are useful when the content in the Web page is long or when the Web browser window is small. You may be able to see the change by resizing your Web browser window to shrink its size and then clicking the links again.

TIP

Web developers often refer to a navigation bar as a *nav bar*.

Users are now able to navigate to the top of the page from any of the descriptions of states and territories. The next step is to create a section for each state and territory and to create a navigation bar at the top of the Web page so users can jump to any state or territory.

To create the state and territory sections:

1. Return to the **australia_states.htm** file in your text editor.

2. Above the *New South Wales* heading, insert the section tag `<section id = "NSW">`. This tag assigns the `id` NSW to the New South Wales section.

3. After the *Top of Page* anchor element at the end of the `New South Wales` paragraph, insert the `</section>` tag, and then compare your code to Figure 2-26.

Figure 2-26   **Creating the NSW Section**

all of the content between the <section> and </section> tags is identified as the NSW section

```
<section id = "NSW">
<h3>New South Wales</h3>

<p>New South Wales (NSW) is Australia's most populous state. Sydney is
located in NSW on the eastern coast, and home to the Sydney Symphony
Orchestra. National parks include the Royal National Park, Wollemi
National Park and the Mutawintji National Park in western New South
Wales.</p>
<a href = "#top">Top of Page</a>
</section>
```

4. Repeat Steps 2 and 3 to add `<section>` and `</section>` tags around the content for each state and territory, using the following `id` values. Place each opening `<section>` tag above the `<h3>` heading for the state or territory, and place each closing `</section>` tag after the corresponding *Top of Page* anchor element. Since you're using proper state and territory names, you'll also capitalize the first letter of each word. The Australian Capital Territory is known by its abbreviation ACT, and you'll use that as well. Even though the user will not see the section names, you'll use the proper names rather than creating your own or using all lowercase. Your code should look like Figures 2-27, 2-28, and 2-29.

   ```
   <section id = "Queensland"> </section>
   <section id = "South Australia"> </section>
   ```

Figure 2-27 Creating sections for the remaining territories

```
<section id = "Queensland">
<h3>Queensland</h3>

<p>Queensland, named after Queen Victoria, is located in the North East
portion of Australia. It is home to the famous Gold Coast and the
Great Barrier Reef. The captial city is Brisbane. In addition to the
Great Barier Reef, it is also home to other World Heritage
preservation areas including the Gondwana Rainforests of Australia,
and Fraser Island.</p>
<a href = "#top">Top of Page</a>
</section>

<section id = "South Australia">
<h3>South Australia</h3>

<p>The state of South Australia is located in the south central part of
Australia. The terrain consists of low mountain ranges, semi-arid and
arid rangelands. It also posesses the single largest deposit of
Uranium in the world.</p>
<a href = "#top">Top of Page</a>
</section>
```

```
<section id = "Tasmania"> </section>
<section id = "Victoria"> </section>
<section id = "Western Australia"> </section>
```

Figure 2-28 Tasmania, Victoria, and Western Australia sections

```
<section id = "Tasmania">
<h3>Tasmania</h3>

<p>Tasmania is an island and state, 240 kilometers south of the mainland.
Its geography consists of mainly rounded smooth mountains, and is the
most mountainous state in Australia. It is known for its unique flora
and fauna. It has diverse vegetation ranging from grasslands to
temperate rainforests. It is home to the famous Tasmanian devil.</p>
<a href = "#top">Top of Page</a>
</section>

<section id = "Victoria">
<h3>Victoria</h3>

<p>Victoria is the second most populous state in Australia, and the
smallest mainland state. The state capital is Melbourne. The terraine
includes the Victorian Alps in the northeast and an extensive series
of river systems.</p>
<a href = "#top">Top of Page</a>
</section>

<section id = "Western Australia">
<h3>Western Australia</h3>

<p>The state of Western Australia occupies the entire western third of
the Australian mainland. Its capital city is Perth. The southwest
coast has a Mediterranian climate. It is home to the Western
Australian Academy of Performing Arts (WAAPA) and the West Australian
Symphony Orchestra (WASO).</p>
<a href = "#top">Top of Page</a>
</section>
```

```
<section id = "Northern Territory"> </section>
<section id = "ACT"> </section>
```

Figure 2-29 **Territories sections**

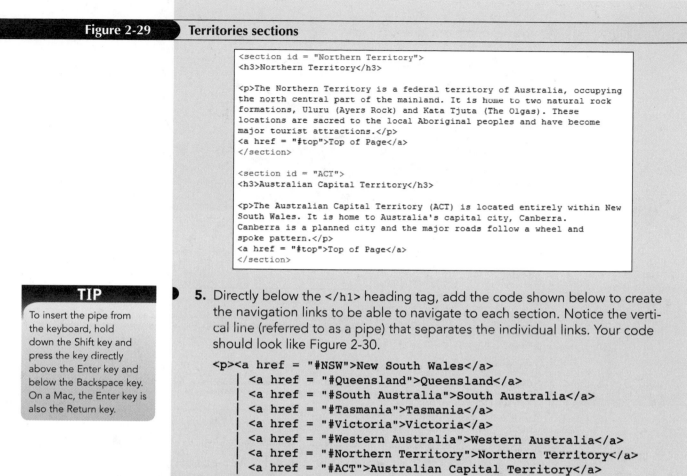

Figure 2-29 **Territories sections**

```
<section id = "Northern Territory">
<h3>Northern Territory</h3>

<p>The Northern Territory is a federal territory of Australia, occupying
the north central part of the mainland. It is home to two natural rock
formations, Uluru (Ayers Rock) and Kata Tjuta (The Olgas). These
locations are sacred to the local Aboriginal peoples and have become
major tourist attractions.</p>
<a href = "#top">Top of Page</a>
</section>

<section id = "ACT">
<h3>Australian Capital Territory</h3>

<p>The Australian Capital Territory (ACT) is located entirely within New
South Wales. It is home to Australia's capital city, Canberra.
Canberra is a planned city and the major roads follow a wheel and
spoke pattern.</p>
<a href = "#top">Top of Page</a>
</section>
```

TIP

To insert the pipe from the keyboard, hold down the Shift key and press the key directly above the Enter key and below the Backspace key. On a Mac, the Enter key is also the Return key.

5. Directly below the `</h1>` heading tag, add the code shown below to create the navigation links to be able to navigate to each section. Notice the vertical line (referred to as a pipe) that separates the individual links. Your code should look like Figure 2-30.

```
<p><a href = "#NSW">New South Wales</a>
| <a href = "#Queensland">Queensland</a>
| <a href = "#South Australia">South Australia</a>
| <a href = "#Tasmania">Tasmania</a>
| <a href = "#Victoria">Victoria</a>
| <a href = "#Western Australia">Western Australia</a>
| <a href = "#Northern Territory">Northern Territory</a>
| <a href = "#ACT">Australian Capital Territory</a>
</p>
```

Figure 2-30 **Creating the navigation menu**

code for each link placed on a separate line for improved readability

```
<h1>Australia - States and Territories</h1>
</section>

<p><a href = "#NSW">New South Wales</a>
| <a href = "#Queensland">Queensland</a>
| <a href = "#South Australia">South Australia</a>
| <a href = "#Tasmania">Tasmania</a>
| <a href = "#Victoria">Victoria</a>
| <a href = "#Western Australia">Western Australia</a>
| <a href = "#Northern Territory">Northern Territory</a>
| <a href = "#ACT">Australian Capital Territory</a>
</p>

<h2>States</h2>
```

vertical bar is a separator between each link

6. Save the file, return to your Web browser, and then click the **Refresh** or **Reload** button to view the changes in the file. The Web page should look similar to Figure 2-31.

Figure 2-31   **Navigation bar with section links**

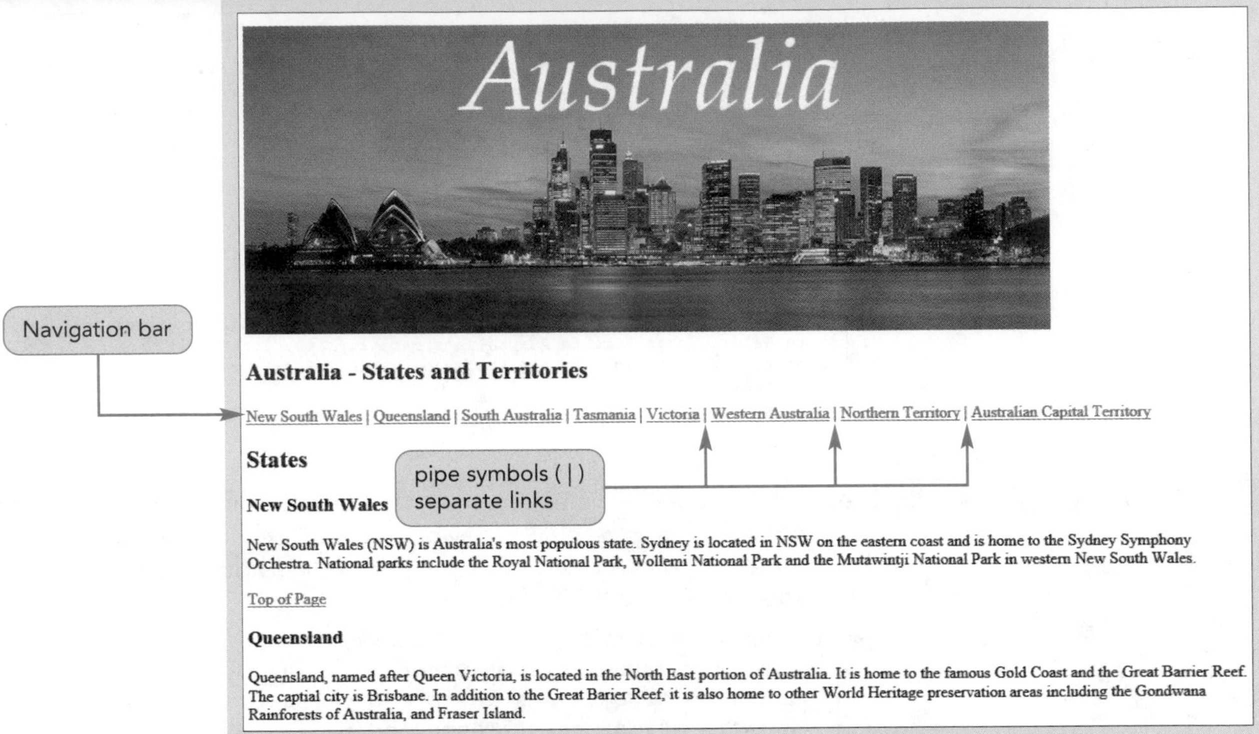

Navigation bar

pipe symbols (|)
separate links

David Iliff/Shutterstock.com

> **7.** Click all of the **state** and **territory** links to test them. When you click the ter-
> ritory links that are near the bottom of the Web page, you may not notice the
> Web page scroll if the content is already visible in the Web browser.
>
>   **Trouble?** If a section link is not working correctly, ensure there is a (#) sym-
>   bol in the `href` value for the link. Also ensure that the corresponding section
>   `id` value matches, character for character. Make any corrections necessary,
>   then save and reload the Web page.

Creating a Link to Another Web Page on the Same Site

You've created an external link to another Web page (Wikipedia – Australia), and
you've created section links to sections on the same Web page. When your Web site
contains multiple Web pages, it's also useful to create links that allow users to navigate
from one Web page to another. When Web developers create a Web site, they create
links to the individual Web pages as they are developing them. Web pages do not have
to be stored on a Web server in order for links between them to function; while creating a Web site, Web developers can store all of the Web pages on the hard drive of
their computer, and still be able to test the links between the Web pages.

A link that points to a Web page on the same site is referred to as a **local link**. A link
that points to a Web page on a different Web server is referred to as an **external link**.
You've created a local link already, but it was a link to download a document, not a link
to another Web page (Australia presentation PDF file). The local link does not contain
the http:// protocol information. Without http:// and domain in the `href` attribute, the
Web browser expects the file to be on the local computer. This feature allows you to test
your Web page links without having to upload the Web pages to a server.

To create a link to another Web page on the same site, you once again use the anchor element, with the following syntax:

```
<a href = "filename">linktext</a>
```

where *filename* is the name of the file you are linking to. For example, to create the link to a Web page file called cities.htm in the same folder as the Web page file that contains the link, you could use the following code :

```
<a href = "cities.htm">Cities Information</a>
```

If the target Web page is stored in a different folder, that folder information would need to be included in the `href` value as well. For instance, if the cities.htm file were stored in a subfolder called *locations*, you might use the following code instead:

```
<a href = "locations/cities.htm">Cities Information</a>
```

This is the same concept as storing images in a subfolder and including this information in the `src` value for the `<img>` tag.

Now that you have developed the index.htm and australia_states.htm Web pages, you'll create a link on index.htm that points to australia_states.htm.

To create a link to the States and Territories page:

▶ **1.** Return to the **index.htm** file in your text editor.

▶ **2.** In the second list item in the unordered list, click before the word *States*, and then insert the anchor element to link the text *States and Territories* to the australia_states.htm Web page, as shown in Figure 2-32.

Figure 2-32 **Creating a local link**

code for a local link

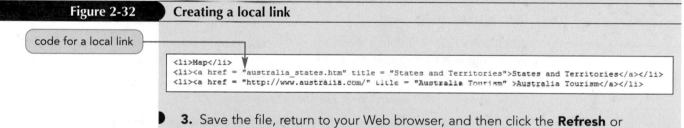

```
<li>Map</li>
<li><a href = "australia_states.htm" title = "States and Territories">States and Territories</a></li>
<li><a href = "http://www.australia.com/" title = "Australia Tourism" >Australia Tourism</a></li>
```

▶ **3.** Save the file, return to your Web browser, and then click the **Refresh** or **Reload** button to view the changes in the file. The Web page should look similar to Figure 2-33.

Figure 2-33   **Creating the States and Territories link**

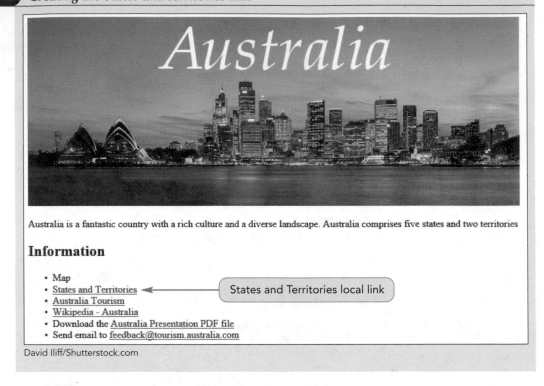

David Iliff/Shutterstock.com

Creating a Link to a Section on Another Web Page on the Same Site

When you create a link to a Web page with sections, you can save users some clicking by linking directly to a specific section. To create a link to a section `id` on another Web page on the same site, you use the following syntax:

```
<a href = "filename#section_id">linktext</a>
```

where *filename* is the name of the Web page you are linking to, and *section_id* is the `id` of the section on the Web page you are linking to. Note that the filename and section `id` are separated by the (#) symbol. For example, to create the link to a section whose `id` is *Montreal* on a Web page file called *cities.htm* in the same folder as the Web page file that contains the link, you could use the following code:

```
<a href = "cities.htm#Montreal">Montreal Information</a>
```

Next you'll create an unordered sublist on the index.htm Web page that includes individual links to the descriptions of the states and territories. For these links to work, you'll need to include the Web page file name in the link code.

To create links to the sections of the States and Territories page:

1. Return to the **index.htm** file in your text editor.

2. In the second item in the unordered list, between the </a> tag and the </li> tag, click and then press **Enter** twice to add a blank line. Type the <ul> tag to begin the unordered list, and then insert the rest of the code that follows for the unordered list of links, as shown in Figure 2-34.

```
<ul>
  <li><a href = "australia_states.htm#NSW">New South Wales
  </a></li>
  <li><a href = "australia_states.htm#Queensland">Queensland
  </a></li>
  <li><a href = "australia_states.htm#South Australia">South
  Australia</a></li>
  <li><a href = "australia_states.htm#Tasmania">Tasmania</a>
  </li>
  <li><a href = "australia_states.htm#Victoria">Victoria</a>
  </li>
  <li><a href = "australia_states.htm#Western
  Australia">Western Australia</a></li>
  <li><a href = "australia_states.htm#Northern
  Territory">Northern Territory</a></li>
  <li><a href = "australia_states.htm#ACT">Australian Capital
  Territory</a></li>
</ul>
```

Figure 2-34	Linking to an id on another Web page on the same site

filename and section id are separated by the (#) symbol

</li> tag ends the States and Territories list item

```
<h2>Information</h2>
  <ul>
    <li><a href = "australia_map.htm">Map</a></li>
    <li><a href = "australia_states.htm" title = "States and Territories">States and
Territories</a>
      <ul>
        <li><a href = "australia_states.htm#NSW">New South Wales</a></li>
        <li><a href = "australia_states.htm#Queensland">Queensland</a></li>
        <li><a href = "australia_states.htm#South Australia">South Australia</a></li>
        <li><a href = "australia_states.htm#Tasmania">Tasmania</a></li>
        <li><a href = "australia_states.htm#Victoria">Victoria</a></li>
        <li><a href = "australia_states.htm#Western Australia">Western Australia</a></li>
        <li><a href = "australia_states.htm#Northern Territory">Northern Territory</a></li>
        <li><a href = "australia_states.htm#ACT">Australian Capital Territory</a></li>
      </ul>
    </li>
    <li><a href = "http://www.australia.com/" title = "Official Australia Tourism Web site">Australia
Tourism</a></li>
```

3. Save the file, return to your Web browser, and then click the **Refresh** or **Reload** button to view the changes to the file. The Web page should look similar to Figure 2-35.

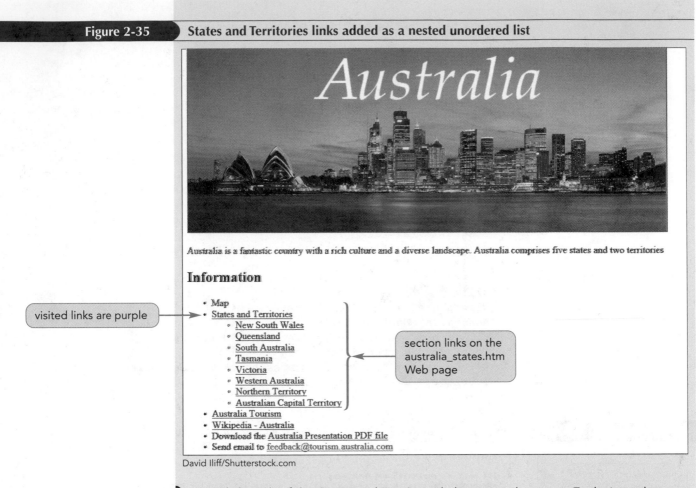

visited links are purple

section links on the australia_states.htm Web page

David Iliff/Shutterstock.com

> **4.** Click each of the **State** and **Territory** links to test them out. Each time, the australia_states.htm Web page should load in the browser, with the appropriate state or territory section at the top of the browser window. The states and territories on the lower part of the Web page will not be at the top of the browser window because the length of the Web page does not extend beyond the last territory content. Then use the **Back** button to return to the index.htm Web page after testing each link.

You can also link to an `id` on a page at another Web site, but doing so can be problematic. You have no control over that page, and if the code for the page is revised and the `id` is moved, renamed, or eliminated, your link to the `id` on that Web site would no longer work. Any link to an external Web page can become a broken link if the Web page is renamed or deleted. Likewise, an external Web page can still exist, but with section links that have been removed or changed.

You've created many different types of links for the Australia Web site. You've created an external link, local links, section links, a link to download a document, and a link to send email to an email address. Now that you've created the index.htm Web page and the australia_states.htm Web page, you're ready to add images that showcase each state and territory, and you'll add a clickable map of Australia. You'll complete these tasks in Session 2.2.

REVIEW

Session 2.1 Quick Check

1. What is an external link?
2. What protocol is used to link to an external Web page?
3. What protocol is used to link to an email address?
4. What is an `id` attribute used for?
5. What is a local link?
6. What symbol is used in a link to specify an `id` on a Web page?

SESSION 2.2 VISUAL OVERVIEW

An image map is an image with clickable hotspots.

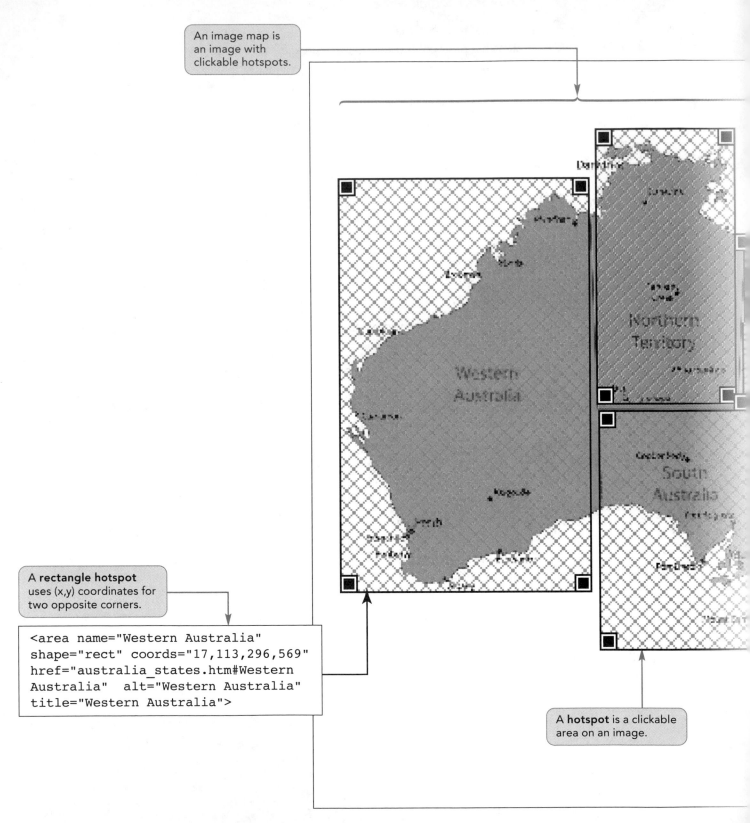

A **rectangle hotspot** uses (x,y) coordinates for two opposite corners.

```
<area name="Western Australia"
shape="rect" coords="17,113,296,569"
href="australia_states.htm#Western
Australia"  alt="Western Australia"
title="Western Australia">
```

A **hotspot** is a clickable area on an image.

IMAGE MAPS

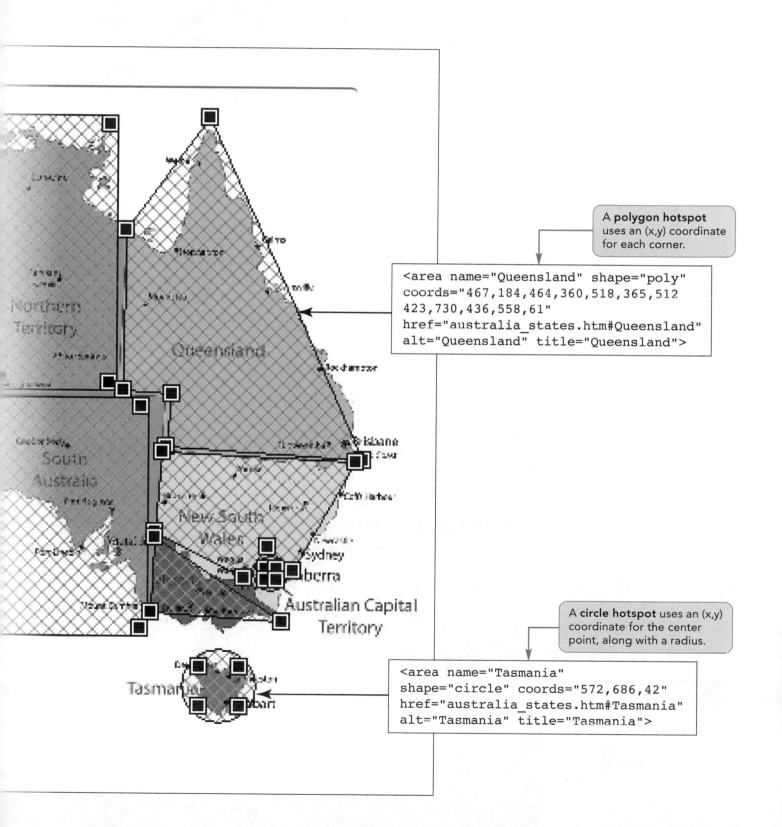

A **polygon hotspot** uses an (x,y) coordinate for each corner.

```
<area name="Queensland" shape="poly"
coords="467,184,464,360,518,365,512
423,730,436,558,61"
href="australia_states.htm#Queensland"
alt="Queensland" title="Queensland">
```

A **circle hotspot** uses an (x,y) coordinate for the center point, along with a radius.

```
<area name="Tasmania"
shape="circle" coords="572,686,42"
href="australia_states.htm#Tasmania"
alt="Tasmania" title="Tasmania">
```

Using Images as Links

In addition to using text as a link, you can use an image as a link as well, allowing users to click on an image to navigate to your Web page or Web site. One common practice is to place a logo at the top of a Web page, or place a small logo at the top-left corner of a Web page, and use it as a link to the top-level page of the Web site.

Sometimes the purpose of a Web page is to make images available to the user, and in this case a small image called a **thumbnail** image can be used to link to another page that contains a larger instance of that same image. Any text or image code that is placed between the start and end anchor tags can be clicked and used as a link in the browser. Whenever you use an image as a hyperlink, you should also provide a `title` attribute value for screen readers and for visually impaired viewers, or a separate text link.

To use an image as a link, you use the following syntax:

```
<a href="filename">
    <img src = "imagename" alt = "alternatetext"
    title = "titlevalue"
    width = "widthvalue" height = "heightvalue">
</a>
```

where *filename* is the name of the file you are linking to, *imagename* is the filename of the image being used as a link, *alternatetext* is the description of the image, *titlevalue* is the description of the image to be used as a ScreenTip, *widthvalue* is the width of the image in pixels, and `heightvalue` is the height of the image in pixels.

For example, to create a link using an image that would link to the index.htm Web page, you might use the following code:

```
<a href="index.htm">
    <img src="images/logo.jpg" alt = "Go to the Home page" title =
    "Go to the Home page" width="40" height="40" />
</a>
```

A widely used convention is to link the logo image on each page of a Web site to the top-level page of the site. You'll link the Australia logo on the australia_states.htm Web page to the index.htm Web page.

To link the logo image to the main Web page:

1. If you took a break after the previous session, make sure that the **australia_states.htm** file is open in your text editor.

2. After the <p> tag that follows the <body> tag, insert the following code as shown in Figure 2-36:

   ```
   <a href = "index.htm" title = "Australia">
   ```

3. After the <img> tag, insert the **</a>** tag as shown in Figure 2-36.

Figure 2-36   **Linking the logo image to the index.htm Web page**

```
<p>
    <a href = "index.htm" title = "Australia">
        <img src="images/australia_logo.jpg" alt="Sydney, Australia skyline" />
    </a>
</p>
```

anchor element makes the image a link

4. Save the file, return to your Web browser, and then open the **australia_ states.htm** file to view the changes. In some browsers you may notice the blue or purple border around the logo. The Web page should look similar to Figure 2-37.

Figure 2-37   **An image as a link**

purple or blue border surrounds the image in some Web browsers when it is a link

Australia - States and Territories

New South Wales | Queensland | South Australia | Tasmania | Victoria | Western Australia | Northern Territory | Australian Capital Territory

States

New South Wales

New South Wales (NSW) is Australia's most populous state. Sydney is located in NSW on the eastern coast and is home to the Sydney Symphony Orchestra. National parks include the Royal National Park, Wollemi National Park and the Mutawintji National Park in western New South Wales.

Top of Page

David Iliff/Shutterstock.com

5. Move the mouse pointer over the large Australia logo image, and notice the pointer changes to a hand symbol. Click the logo to verify the link is working.

In some Web browsers, by default, the image used as a link also has a border around the image. In later tutorials, you will learn how to change the appearance of—or hide— the image border, as well as to create space around an image, position an image both horizontally and vertically, and wrap text around an image.

Creating Thumbnail Links

When one of the purposes of a Web page is to showcase images, a useful technique is to display a thumbnail of the image that is also a link to a larger version of that same image. This technique offers two advantages. First, large images on a Web page can make the content cluttered and unusable, so a thumbnail image enables the developer to organize the content better. Second, larger images are also larger in file size, and it can take a long time to download them if a user does not have a high-speed connection.

Using Consistent Naming Conventions

It's a good idea to use consistent naming conventions for images and files when possible to help you and other developers easily identify the contents of files. For example, when saving images that are larger and smaller versions, consider using the same base file name for both versions and adding something to each name that indicates the difference. In this instance, large files are often named with *lg* at the end of the name and small files are named with *sm* at the end of the name. There may not be concrete rules to cover all cases, so you will find yourself adopting your own naming conventions. The key is to be consistent across all the files in the Web site.

When linking a thumbnail to a full-sized version, the code on the referring page would be similar to the following.

```
<a href = "sydney_opera_house.htm" title = "Sydney Opera House">
   <img src = "images/sydney_opera_house_sm.jpg"
   alt = "Sydney Opera House" />
</a>
```

Note that when an image is small or its placement does not affect the placement of subsequent content on a Web page, the `height` and `width` attributes can be omitted without adversely affecting the function of the Web page. On the page with the full-size image, you should include a link back to the referring page—and the home page—so you don't strand users.

Tony has provided you with thumbnail and larger images for each of the states and territories. You'll display each thumbnail image under the corresponding paragraph description for the states and territories. The thumbnail image will link to a separate Web page that contains a larger version of the image. The images that have been provided are listed in the table in Figure 2-38.

Figure 2-38   **Images for states and territories**

Region	Images
New South Wales	sydney_opera_house_sm.jpg
	sydney_opera_house_lg.jpg
Queensland	gold_coast_queensland_sm.jpg
	gold_coast_queensland_lg.jpg
South Australia	south_australia_outback_sm.jpg
	south_australia_outback_lg.jpg
Tasmania	russell_falls_tasmania_sm.jpg
	russell_falls_tasmania_lg.jpg
Victoria	twelve_apostles_victoria_sm.jpg
	twelve_apostles_victoria_lg.jpg
Western Australia	perth_western_australia_sm.jpg
	perth_western_australia_lg.jpg
Northern Territory	devils_marbles_northern_territories_sm.jpg
	devils_marbles_northern_territories_lg.jpg
Australia Capital Territory	canberra_australian_capital_territory_sm.jpg
	canberra_australian_capital_territory_lg.jpg

You will add a thumbnail image at the end of each state and territory description that links to a Web page displaying the larger image. You'll develop a separate Web page for each state and territory that contains the large image, the Australia logo, and a link back to the australia_states.htm Web page.

To add and link the thumbnails:

1. Return to the **australia_states.htm** file in your text editor.

2. After the </p> tag that ends the paragraph for New South Wales, insert the following code to display a thumbnail image link as shown below and in Figure 2-39:

```
<a href = "sydney_opera_house.htm"
   title = "Sydney Opera House">
  <img src = "images/sydney_opera_house_sm.jpg"
   alt = "Sydney Opera House" />
</a>
<br />
```

Figure 2-39	Adding a linked thumbnail

```
<p>New South Wales (NSW) is Australia's most populous state. Sydney is
located in NSW on the eastern coast, and home to the Sydney Symphony
Orchestra. National parks include the Royal National Park, Wollemi
National Park and the Mutawintji National Park in western New South
Wales.</p>

<a href = "sydney_opera_house.htm" title = "Sydney Opera House">
 <img src = "images/sydney_opera_house_sm.jpg" alt = "Sydney Opera House" />
</a>
<br />

<a href = "#top">Top of Page</a>
```

3. Save the file, return to your Web browser, and then open the **australia_states.htm** file to view the changes in the file. The Web page should look similar to Figure 2-40.

Figure 2-40 **Thumbnail image in the Web browser**

Australia – States and Territories

New South Wales | Queensland | South Australia | Tasmania | Victoria | Western Australia | Northern Territory | Australian Capital Territory

States

New South Wales

New South Wales (NSW) is Australia's most populous state. Sydney is located in NSW on the eastern coast and is home to the Sydney Symphony Orchestra. National parks include the Royal National Park, Wollemi National Park and the Mutawintji National Park in western New South Wales.

Top of Page

Queensland

Queensland, named after Queen Victoria, is located in the North East portion of Australia. It is home to the famous Gold Coast and the Great Barrier Reef. The captial city is Brisbane. In addition to the Great Barier Reef, it is also home to other World Heritage preservation areas including the Gondwana Rainforests of Australia, and Fraser Island.

David Iliff/Shutterstock.com; Jan Kratochvila/Shutterstock.com

in some Web browsers the thumbnail image will be displayed with a blue or purple border

4. Repeat Steps 1 and 2 to add HTML code after each state and territory paragraph to display the appropriate thumbnail image and point to the appropriate Web page, using the filenames listed in Figure 2-41. Use a suitable `alt` attribute to describe each image.

Figure 2-41 **Thumbnail image and Web page file names**

Region	Thumbnail Image	Link to
New South Wales	sydney_opera_house_sm.jpg	sydney_opera_house.htm
Queensland	gold_coast_queensland_sm.jpg	gold_coast.htm
South Australia	south_australia_outback_sm.jpg	south_australia_outback.htm
Tasmania	russell_falls_tasmania_sm.jpg	russell_falls.htm
Victoria	twelve_apostles_victoria_sm.jpg	twelve_apostles.htm
Western Australia	perth_western_australia_sm.jpg	perth.htm
Northern Territory	devils_marbles_northern_territories_sm.jpg	devils_marbles.htm
Australia Capital Territory	canberra_australian_capital_territory_sm.jpg	canberra.htm

The code to insert for each region is shown in Figure 2-42.

Figure 2-42   **HTML code for thumbnail links for each state and territory**

```
Queensland

<a href = "gold_coast.htm" title = "Gold Coast">
 <img src = "images/gold_coast_queensland_sm.jpg" alt = "Gold Coast" />
</a>
<br />

South Australia

<a href = "south_australia_outback.htm" title = "South Australia Outback">
 <img src = "images/south_australia_outback_sm.jpg" alt = "South Australia Outback" />
</a>
<br />

Tasmania

<a href = "russell_falls.htm" title = "Russell Falls">
 <img src = "images/russell_falls_tasmania_sm.jpg" alt = "Russell Falls" />
</a>
<br />

Victoria

<a href = "twelve_apostles.htm" title = "Twelve Apostles">
 <img src = "images/twelve_apostles_victoria_sm.jpg" alt = "Twelve Apostles" />
</a>
<br />

Western Australia

<a href = "perth.htm" title = "Perth">
 <img src = "images/perth_western_australia_sm.jpg" alt = "Perth" />
</a>
<br />

Northern Territory

<a href = "devils_marbles.htm" title = "Devils Marbles">
 <img src = "images/devils_marbles_northern_territories_sm.jpg" alt = "Devils Marbles" />
</a>
<br />

Australian Capital Territory

<a href = "canberra.htm" title = "Canberra">
 <img src = "images/canberra_australian_capital_territory_sm.jpg" alt = "Canberra" />
</a>
<br />
```

5. Save the file. Return to your Web browser, and then reload or refresh the **australia_states.htm** file to view the changes in the file. The Web page should look similar to Figure 2-43.

Figure 2-43 **Linked thumbnails for the states and territories**

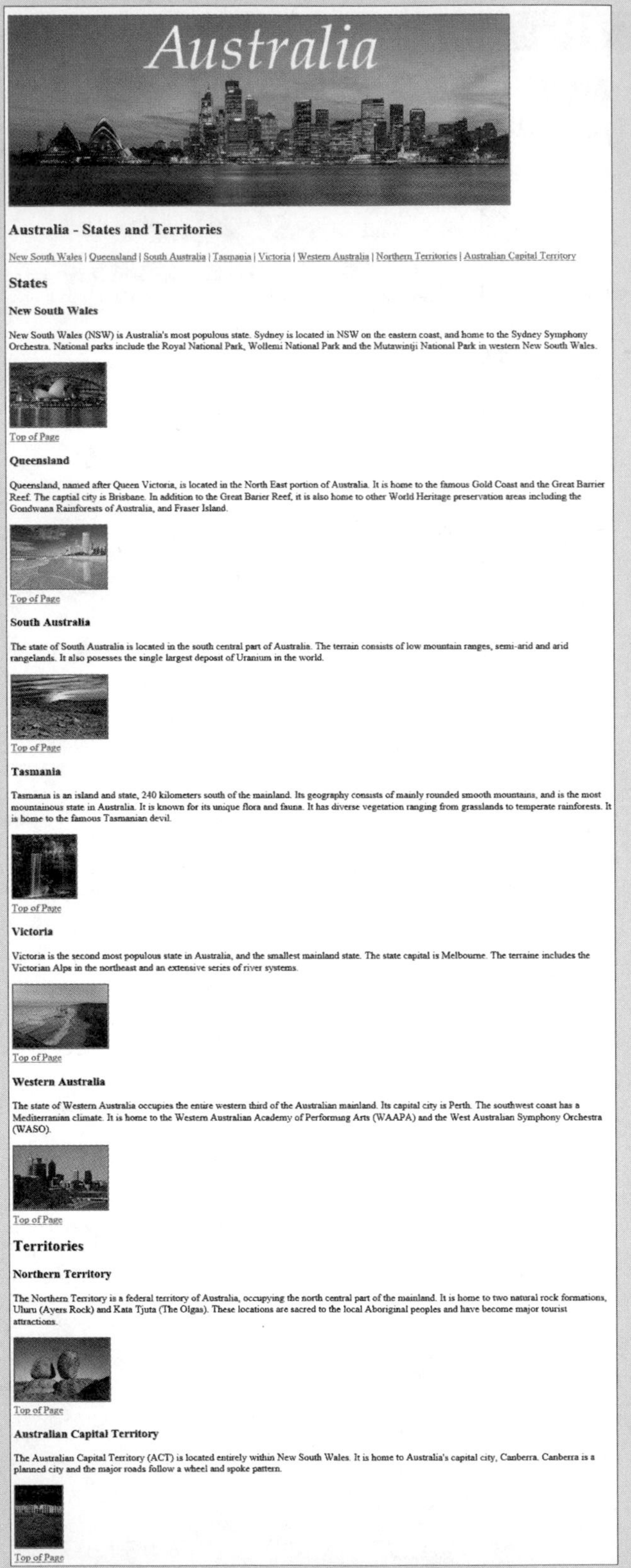

David Iliff/Shutterstock.com; Oskar/Shutterstock.com; Les Scholz/
Shutterstock.com; Ashley Whitworth/Shutterstock.com; Janelle Lugge/
Shutterstock.com; Dan Breckwoldt/Shutterstock.com; Jan Kratochvila/
Shutterstock.com; Simon Krzic/Shutterstock.com; Jiri Foltyn/Shutterstock.
com; tororo reaction/Shutterstock.com

Now that you've created the thumbnail links, you'll create the target Web pages.

PROSKILLS

Written Communication: Using Templates

Consistency is a very effective technique for making a Web site easy to use. When all the pages on a Web site employ the same general look and feel, users can more quickly find the content they seek. This look and feel includes the layout of the content, the language, and the placement of the logo and other content.

A common technique for creating consistency across the pages of a Web site is to use a **template**, which is an HTML document that contains the code for the elements that are the same on every Web page. A developer uses a template to generate the pages for a Web site, and then adds the unique content to each page. Using Web development tools such as Dreamweaver and Expression Web, you can make changes to a template and automatically see those changes reflected on all pages that were built from that template.

You realize that each of the Web pages that displays the large state and territory images uses almost identical HTML code, with the exception of the name of the large image file, the `alt` attribute value, and the title of the Web page. To simplify your task, you'll create the Web page for the large Sydney Opera House image, and then you'll take advantage of the Save As feature of your text editor to create copies of that Web page in which you'll substitute the unique information for the other images.

To create Web pages to display the large images:

1. Return to your text editor, and then open a new file.

2. Enter the following code to create the Web page that will display the Sydney Opera House image, adding your name and today's date where indicated, as shown in Figure 2-44:

```
<!DOCTYPE html>
<html>
  <head>
    <!--
         Tutorial 2
         Author: your name
         Date: today's date
    -->

    <script src = "modernizr-2.js"></script>
    <title>Sydney Opera House</title>
  </head>

  <body>
    <p>
      <a href = "index.htm" title = "Australia">
       <img src = "images/australia_logo.jpg"
       alt = "Sydney, Australia skyline" />
      </a>
      <br />
      <a href = "australia_states.htm"
        title = "Australia States and Territories">
             Back to Australia States and Territories
      </a>
    </p>
```

```
      <h1>Sydney Opera House</h1>

      <p>
        <img src = "images/sydney_opera_house_lg.jpg"
        alt = "Sydney Opera House" />
      </p>

      </body>
    </html>
```

Figure 2-44	HTML code for the sydney_opera_house.htm Web page

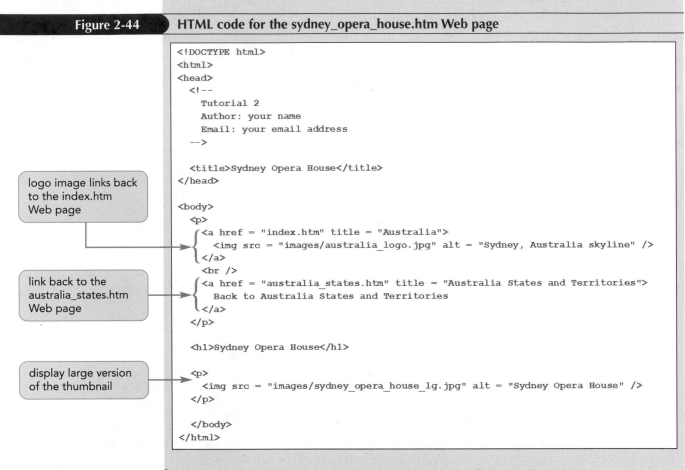

logo image links back
to the index.htm
Web page

link back to the
australia_states.htm
Web page

display large version
of the thumbnail

```
<!DOCTYPE html>
<html>
<head>
  <!--
    Tutorial 2
    Author: your name
    Email: your email address
  -->

  <title>Sydney Opera House</title>
</head>

<body>
  <p>
    <a href = "index.htm" title = "Australia">
      <img src = "images/australia_logo.jpg" alt = "Sydney, Australia skyline" />
    </a>
    <br />
    <a href = "australia_states.htm" title = "Australia States and Territories">
      Back to Australia States and Territories
    </a>
  </p>

  <h1>Sydney Opera House</h1>

  <p>
    <img src = "images/sydney_opera_house_lg.jpg" alt = "Sydney Opera House" />
  </p>

  </body>
</html>
```

3. Save the file as **sydney_opera_house.htm**.

4. In your Web browser, open the **sydney_opera_house.htm** file. The Web page should look similar to Figure 2-45.

Figure 2-45   **Sydney Opera House Web page**

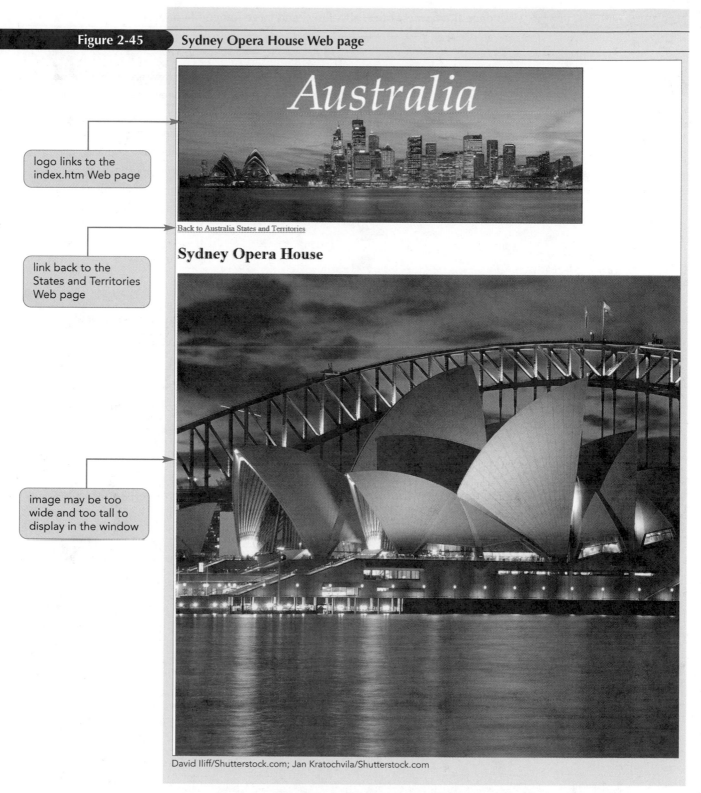

logo links to the index.htm Web page

link back to the States and Territories Web page

image may be too wide and too tall to display in the window

David Iliff/Shutterstock.com; Jan Kratochvila/Shutterstock.com

Now that you've created the first Web page for the large images, you'll create the rest of the Web pages by customizing the code with the unique information for the new page and using the Save As feature to save the new Web page using the appropriate name. If you're using TextEdit on a Mac and don't have a Save As feature, you can use the Duplicate command first, followed by the Save command. You'll use the information in Figure 2-46 to substitute text between the `<title>` and `</title>` tags, between the `<h1>` and `</h1>` tags, and for the `alt` and `src` attributes in the `<img>` tag.

Figure 2-46 **Web page file names, titles, alt values, and large image file names**

Web File Name	Title, Heading, and Alt Values	Large Image File Name
sydney_opera_house.htm	Sydney Opera House	sydney_opera_house_lg.jpg
gold_coast.htm	Gold Coast	gold_coast_queensland_lg.jpg
south_australia_outback.htm	South Australia Outback	south_australia_outback_lg.jpg
russell_falls.htm	Russell Falls	russell_falls_tasmania_lg.jpg
twelve_apostles.htm	Twelve Apostles	twelve_apostles_victoria_lg.jpg
perth.htm	Perth	perth_western_australia_lg.jpg
devils_marbles.htm	Devils Marbles	devils_marbles_northern_territories_lg.jpg
canberra.htm	Canberra	canberra_australian_capital_territory_lg.jpg

To create the remaining Web pages manually with a template:

1. Return to the **sydney_opera_house.htm** file in your text editor.

2. Use the Save As feature to save the file as **gold_coast.htm**.

   You'll create the gold_coast.htm Web page by substituting the unique text for the `title`, `h1`, and `img` information, as shown below and in Figure 2-47.

3. First, in the `title` element, delete *Sydney Opera House*, and then enter **Gold Coast**, as shown below:

   ```
   <title>Gold Coast</title>
   ```

4. Similarly, replace *Sydney Opera House* in the `h1` element with **Gold Coast**, as shown below:

   ```
   <h1>Gold Coast</h1>
   ```

5. Finally, edit the `img` element to replace the Sydney Opera House image with the Gold Coast image as follows, and then save the file:

   ```
   <img src = "images/gold_coast_queensland_lg.jpg"
   alt = "Gold Coast" />
   ```

Figure 2-47 Creating the gold_coast.htm file

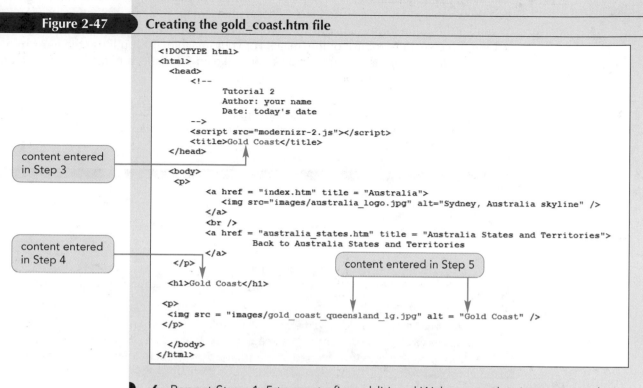

content entered in Step 3

content entered in Step 4

content entered in Step 5

6. Repeat Steps 1–5 to create five additional Web pages that incorporate the content from Figure 2-46. You'll substitute the content for each of the other pages (south_australia_outback.htm, russell_falls.htm, twelve_apostles.htm, perth.htm, devils_marbles.htm, and canberra.htm) and use the **Save As** feature to save the appropriate .htm file.

7. Return to your Web browser, refresh or reload the **australia_states.htm** file, and then test each of the thumbnail links. When you click on each thumbnail link, the corresponding Web page should load.

   Trouble? If the corresponding Web page does not load, check the thumbnail link `href` value in the australia_states.htm Web page.

Now that you've created the thumbnail links and the Web pages showing the large images, you're ready to work on the final feature that Tony requested: adding a clickable map of Australia. To do this, you'll implement an image map.

Creating Image Maps

An image map is an image that is divided into sections that serve as links. The areas of the image designated to be used as links are called hotspots. Any image can be used as an image map—it doesn't have to be an image of a map, although that is commonly the case. Tony has provided you with an image file named australia_map.jpg. You will use this image to create an image map so users can click on a state or territory to open the appropriate section of the australia_states.htm Web page.

Almost any image can be used as the foundation for an image map. An image map is created by adding HTML code that identifies clickable hotspots on an image. Your first step is to enter the code for the image. Because many Web pages include several images, you need a way to specify that a particular image will have a special purpose, namely, that it will be used as an image map. The `usemap` attribute and its value signal to browsers that an image is to be used as an image map. You can use any value you want as the value for the `usemap` attribute, but it's a good coding practice for the value to be somewhat descriptive of the image. For your image map, you'll use the `usemap` value *australia_map*. This value behaves much like an `id` name, and the identifier value begins with the (#) symbol.

```
<p>
 <img src="images/australia_map.jpg"
  alt="map of australia" usemap = "#australia_map"/>
</p>
```

You'll begin work on your image map by creating the australia_map.htm file that contains the map image and the Australia logo.

To create the Web page that will contain the image map:

1. In your text editor, create a new document and enter the following code:

```
<!DOCTYPE html>
<html>
  <head>
    <!--
         Tutorial 2
         Author: your name
         Email: your email address
    -->

    <script src="modernizr-2.js"></script>
    <title>Australia Map</title>
  </head>
  <body>

    <p><img src="images/australia_logo.jpg"
       alt="Australia logo" /></p>

    <p>
    <img src="images/australia_map.jpg" alt="map of
       australia" usemap = "#australia_map"/>
    </p>

  </body>
</html>
```

2. Save the file as **australia_map.htm**.

3. Open the **australia_map.htm** file in your Web browser. The Web page should look similar to Figure 2-48.

Figure 2-48   australia_map.htm Web page

some Web browsers display a blue or purple border around an image that is a link

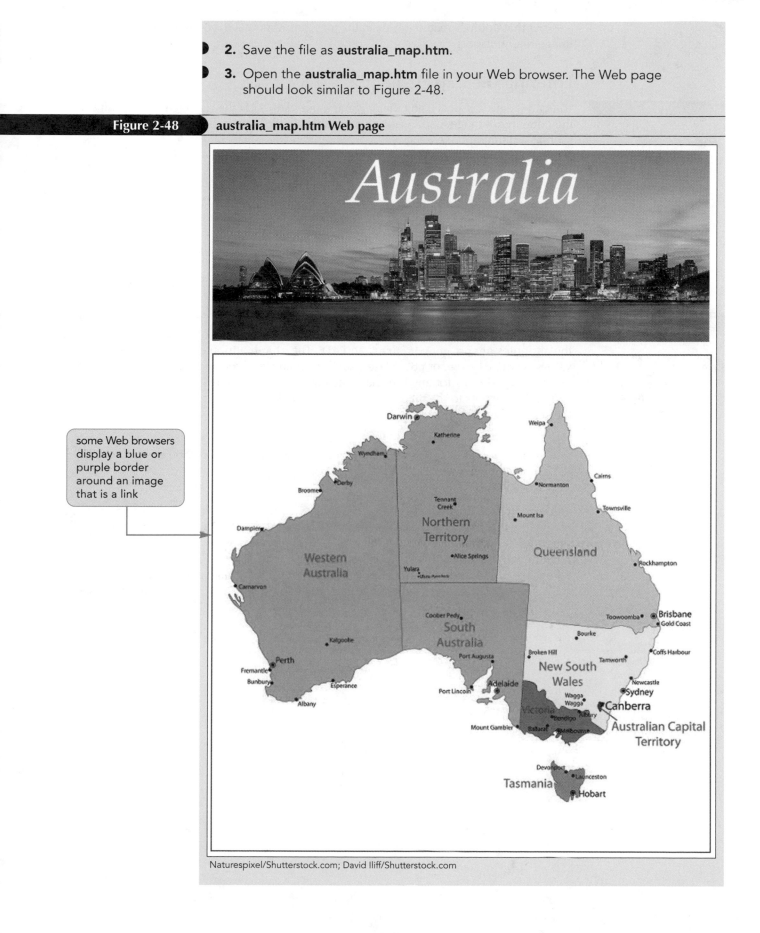

Naturespixel/Shutterstock.com; David Iliff/Shutterstock.com

Now that you've created the australia_map.htm Web page, you'll add code for the image map hotspots.

Entering the map Element

You can create hotspots using the `map` and `area` elements. The `map` element contains all the code in an image map. A `map` element should itself be within a block-level element, such as a paragraph element:

```
<p>
   <map name="mapname">
     <!--Tags defining hotspots will go here-->
   </map>
</p>
```

where *mapname* is the same value assigned to the `usemap` attribute in the `img` element.

Entering area Elements

The `area` element is used to create the hotspots that users click. You can have as many `area` elements as are feasible given the size of an image. The `<area>` tag must include the attributes `shape`, `coords`, `href`, and `alt`. The `shape` attribute takes one of three values: `rect`, `circle`, or `poly`. Use `rect` for squares and rectangles, `circle` for circles and ovals, and `poly` for any irregular shape (basically, any other shape).

To add hotspots to the map, you insert the code for one or more hotspots between the start and end `<map>` tags:

```
<map name="mapname">
  <area shape="areashape" coords="coordinates" href="reference"
  alt="alternatetext" title = "titletext" />
</map>
```

where *areashape* is `rect` to create a rectangle, `circle` to create a circle, or `poly` to create a polygon; *coordinates* is the coordinates for the shape; *reference* is the file or location the hotspot is linked to; *alternatetext* is a description of the file or location the hotspot is linked to; and *titletext* is the description that appears in the ScreenTip. The coordinates refer to pixel positions on the image map using the format (x, y). The top-left corner of the image map has coordinates $(0,0)$. The x value increases horizontally toward the right and the y value increases vertically downward.

INSIGHT

Close Is "Good Enough" for Hotspots

There's an old saying that "Close is only good enough in horseshoes." The game of horseshoes involves throwing a horseshoe at a metal stake. The player whose horseshoe lands closest to the stake wins a point. The horseshoe does not have to directly touch the stake; it just has to be closest to the stake. In the game, then, being "close is good enough."

What does this have to do with hotspots on an image map? The same guideline applies to defining hotspots. Because users click "in a general area" on an image map, a hotspot has to cover most of the area and in particular, the most likely spot where the user will click. It is not necessary to cover every pixel of the image or for the hotspots to be touching each other. So, when you're creating hotspots, "close is good enough." Sometimes it also makes sense to extend a hotspot beyond the shape on an image, particularly if the shape is intricate and the user would reasonably be expected to click beyond the exact location on the image. For instance, if the image map is a map of Europe and one of the hotspots should indicate the country of Italy, the user could click on the Mediterranean Sea west of Italy. It might also make sense to use a larger rectangle as the hotspot for Italy, to include the islands as well.

TIP

For image maps, use an image that contains simple visuals. If the image contains too much detail it may be difficult for the user to determine where to click.

The states and territories on the Australia map can be covered using the basic shapes—circle, rectangle, and polygon. You'll use rectangle shapes to define hotspots for Western Australia, South Australia, and the Northern Territory. You'll use circle shapes to define hotspots for Tasmania and the Australia Capital Territory. Finally, you'll use polygon shapes to define hotspots for Queensland, New South Wales, and Victoria.

Creating Rectangle Hotspots

The `area` element that defines a rectangle hotspot uses the following code:

```
<area shape = "rect" coords = "x1, y1, x2, y2"
href = "reference" alt = "alternatetext"
title = "titletext"/>
```

The coordinates *x1, y1* and *x2, y2* refer to the opposite corners of a rectangle. An (x,y) coordinate pair refers to a pixel position on an image where the x value is the horizontal position and the y value is the vertical position. The code that would define a rectangular hotspot on the Australia map for Western Australia might be the following:

```
<area name="Western Australia" shape="rect" coords="17,113,296,569"
href="australia_states.htm#Western Australia"
alt="Western Australia" title="Western Australia" />
```

The coordinates of the opposite corners of the rectangle are (17, 113) and (296,569). These are the coordinates for the top-left and bottom-right corners, as shown in Figure 2-49.

Figure 2-49 **Coordinates for opposite corners of a rectangle hotspot**

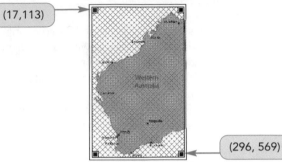

Naturespixel/Shutterstock.com

It doesn't matter which two opposite corners you choose. Use either the top-left and bottom-right as opposite corners or the top-right and bottom-left as opposite corners.

You can find coordinates of a particular point on an image by using an image-editing application such as Paint for Windows or Preview for Mac. As you position your mouse pointer on an image, you see the coordinates listed in the status bar at the bottom of the window.

REFERENCE

Creating Image Map Areas

To create an image map use the following code:

```
<img src = "filename" usemap = "#imagemapname">
<map name="imagemapname">
  <area shape = "circle"
    coords = "x, y, radius"
    href = "url"
    alt = "alternatetext"
    title = "titletext" />
  <area shape = "rect"
    coords = "x1, y1, x2, y2"
    href = "url"
    alt = "alternatetext"
    title = "titletext" />
  <area shape = "poly"
    coords = "x1, y1, x2, y2, x3, y3"
    href = "url"
    alt = "alternatetext"
    title = "titletext" />
  <area shape = "default" href = "url" />
</map>
```

- Values for the shape attribute are `circle`, `rect` (rectangle), `poly` (polygon), and `default` (used when the user clicks on part of the image that does not have a hotspot).
- x, y, x1, y1, x2, y2, x3, y3 are (x,y) coordinates.
- `radius` is the radius of a circle.

You'll be defining the hotspots shown on the Australia map in Figure 2-50.

| Figure 2-50 | Hotspot areas on the Australia maps |

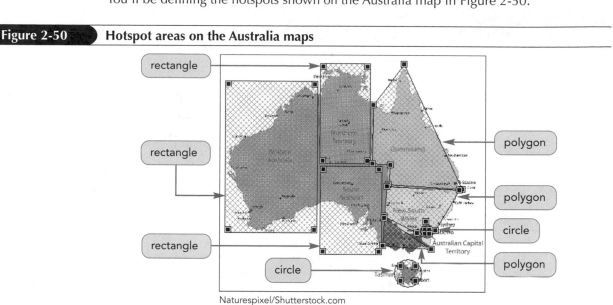

Naturespixel/Shutterstock.com

You'll start by creating rectangle hotspots for South Australia, Western Australia, and the Northern Territory.

To create rectangle hotspots on the image map:

1. Return to the **australia_map.htm** file in your text editor.

2. After the `</p>` tag and before the `</body>` tag, insert the following code:

```
<p>
  <map name="australia_map">
    <area name="South Australia" shape="rect"
      coords="305,368,495,633"
      href="australia_states.htm#South Australia"
      alt="South Australia" title="South Australia" />
    <area name="Western Australia" shape="rect"
      coords="17,113,296,569"
      href="australia_states.htm#Western Australia"
      alt="Western Australia" title="Western Australia" />
    <area name="Northern Territories" shape="rect"
      coords="302,58,459,363"
      href="australia_states.htm#Northern Territory"
      alt="Northern Territory" title="Northern Territory" />

    <area shape="default" href="index.htm" />
  </map>
</p>
```

Compare your document to Figure 2-51.

Figure 2-51	Adding code for rectangle hotspots

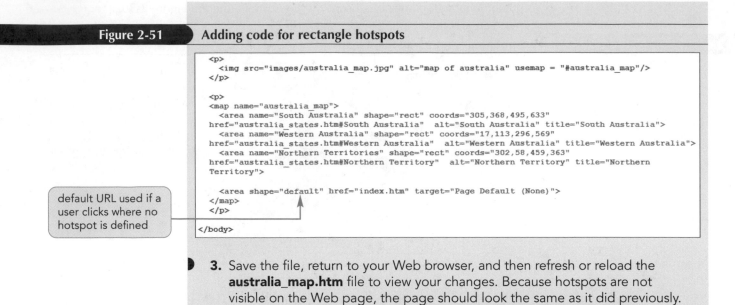

default URL used if a user clicks where no hotspot is defined

```
<p>
  <img src="images/australia_map.jpg" alt="map of australia" usemap = "#australia_map"/>
</p>

<p>
<map name="australia_map">
  <area name="South Australia" shape="rect" coords="305,368,495,633"
href="australia_states.htm#South Australia"  alt="South Australia" title="South Australia">
  <area name="Western Australia" shape="rect" coords="17,113,296,569"
href="australia_states.htm#Western Australia"  alt="Western Australia" title="Western Australia">
  <area name="Northern Territories" shape="rect" coords="302,58,459,363"
href="australia_states.htm#Northern Territory"  alt="Northern Territory" title="Northern
Territory">

  <area shape="default" href="index.htm" target="Page Default (None)">
</map>
</p>

</body>
```

3. Save the file, return to your Web browser, and then refresh or reload the **australia_map.htm** file to view your changes. Because hotspots are not visible on the Web page, the page should look the same as it did previously.

4. Hover the mouse pointer over the South Australia hotspot until the pointer changes to a hand, indicating there is a link or hotspot on the image, and then click the hotspot to test it. The **australia_states.htm** Web page should load, with the South Australia content near the top of the Web browser.

5. Return to the Australia Map page, and click the **Western Australia** and **Northern Territory** hotspots to test them.

Creating Circle Hotspots

The **area** element that defines a circle hotspot uses the following code:

```
<area shape = "rect" coords = "x, y, r"
href = "reference" alt = "alternate_text"
title = "title_text" />
```

The coordinates *x, y, r* refer to the center of the circle (*x, y*) and the length of the radius (*r*) measured in pixels. The code that would define a circle hotspot on an image might be the following:

```
<area name="basketball" shape="circle" coords="114,592,64"
   href="http://en.wikipedia.org/wiki/Basketball"
   alt="Wikipedia - Basketball"
   title="Wikipedia - Basketball" />
```

This code creates a circle centered at (114,592) with a radius of 64.

Next you'll create the circle hotspots for Tasmania and the Australia Capital Territory (ACT).

To create circle hotspots on the image map:

▶ **1.** Return to the **australia_map.htm** file in your text editor.

▶ **2.** After the <area> tag for the Northern Territory rectangle hotspot and above the <area> tag for *index.htm*, insert the following code:

```
<area name="Tasmania" shape="circle" coords="572,686,42"
  href="australia_states.htm#Tasmania"  alt="Tasmania"
  title="Tasmania" />
<area name="Australia Capital Territory" shape="circle"
  coords="628,562,20" href="australia_states.htm#ACT"
  alt="Australia Capital Territory"
  title="Australia Capital Territory" />
```

Compare your document to Figure 2-52.

Figure 2-52	Area elements for circle hotspots

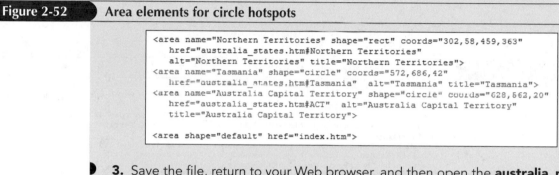

```
<area name="Northern Territories" shape="rect" coords="302,58,459,363"
   href="australia_states.htm#Northern Territories"
   alt="Northern Territories" title="Northern Territories">
<area name="Tasmania" shape="circle" coords="572,686,42"
   href="australia_states.htm#Tasmania"  alt="Tasmania" title="Tasmania">
<area name="Australia Capital Territory" shape="circle" coords="628,562,20"
   href="australia_states.htm#ACT"  alt="Australia Capital Territory"
   title="Australia Capital Territory">

<area shape="default" href="index.htm">
```

▶ **3.** Save the file, return to your Web browser, and then open the **australia_map. htm** file to view your changes.

▶ **4.** Click the new hotspots to test them.

Creating Polygon Hotspots

A polygon is a multisided shape. A polygon could be a three-sided shape (triangle) or have additional sides. You specify a polygon hotspot by specifying coordinate pairs of *x,y* values, with each pair identifying a corner of the shape. An area element for a polygon hotspot uses the following code:

```
<area shape = "poly" coords = "x1, y1, x2, y2, x3, y3, …"
href = "reference" alt = "alternate_text"
title = "title_text" />
```

where *x1, y1*, etc., are (*x,y*) pairs that define the corners of the shape. For instance, the code to define a polygon hotspot on the Australia map for Victoria might look as follows:

```
<area name="Victoria" shape="poly"
coords="501,522,497,605,641,614"
href="australia_states.htm#Victoria"
alt="Victoria" title="Victoria" />
```

The coordinates of the corners of the shape in this case are (501,522), (497,605) and (641,614).

You'll create polygon hotspots for Queensland, New South Wales, and Victoria.

To create polygon hotspots on the image map:

1. Return to the **australia_map.htm** file in your text editor.

2. After the `<area>` tags for the circle hotspots, insert the following code:

```
<area name="Queensland" shape="poly"
  coords="467,184,464,360,518,365,512,423,730,436,558,61"
  href="australia_states.htm#Queensland"  alt="Queensland"
  title="Queensland" />
<area name="New South Wales" shape="poly"
  coords="508,428,722,439,652,558,625,532,598,567,500,516"
  href="australia_states.htm#NSW"
  alt="New South Wales" title="New South Wales" />
<area name="Victoria" shape="poly"
  coords="501,522,497,605,641,614"
  href="australia_states.htm#Victoria"
  alt="Victoria" title="Victoria" />
```

Compare your document to Figure 2-53.

TIP

Polygon `<area>` tag coordinates are always in pairs. If your code contains an odd number of polygon coordinates, you can be certain that one is missing.

Figure 2-53	Area elements for polygon hotspots

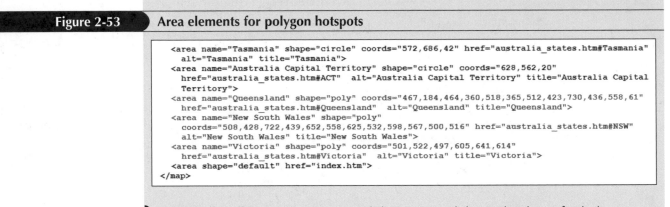

```
<area name="Tasmania" shape="circle" coords="572,686,42" href="australia_states.htm#Tasmania"
  alt="Tasmania" title="Tasmania">
<area name="Australia Capital Territory" shape="circle" coords="628,562,20"
  href="australia_states.htm#ACT"  alt="Australia Capital Territory" title="Australia Capital
  Territory">
<area name="Queensland" shape="poly" coords="467,184,464,360,518,365,512,423,730,436,558,61"
  href="australia_states.htm#Queensland"  alt="Queensland" title="Queensland">
<area name="New South Wales" shape="poly"
  coords="508,428,722,439,652,558,625,532,598,567,500,516" href="australia_states.htm#NSW"
  alt="New South Wales" title="New South Wales">
<area name="Victoria" shape="poly" coords="501,522,497,605,641,614"
  href="australia_states.htm#Victoria"  alt="Victoria" title="Victoria">
<area shape="default" href="index.htm">
</map>
```

3. Save the file, return to your Web browser, and then reload or refresh the **australia_map.htm** file. Click the new hotspots to test them.

Now that the map Web page is complete, you'll link the *index.htm* Web page to the *australia_map.htm* Web page.

To link to the *australia_map.htm* Web page:

1. Open the **index.htm** file in your text editor.

2. In the first item in the unordered list, replace the text *Map* with the following code, as shown in Figure 2-54:

```
<a href = "australia_map.htm">Map</a>
```

Figure 2-54	HTML code for the map link

```
<ul>
  <li><a href = "australia_map.htm">Map</a></li>
  <li><a href = "australia_states.htm" title = "States and Territories">States and Territories</a>
```

3. Save the file. Return to your Web browser, and then reload or refresh the **index.htm** file to view the changes in the file. The Web page should look similar to Figure 2-55.

Figure 2-55   **The completed Web page showing the map link**

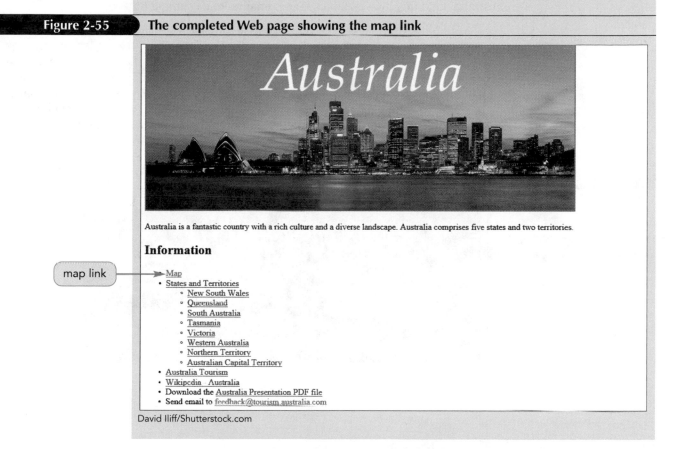

David Iliff/Shutterstock.com

Tony is pleased with the work you've done for the entire Web site. He'll look over your work and is confident that the audience for his presentation will enjoy referring to the information in the Web site you've created.

REVIEW

Session 2.2 Quick Check

1. What is an image map?
2. What is a thumbnail link?
3. How can you determine the coordinates for an image map shape?
4. If the area you want to define as a hotspot is a square, which value would you use for the `shape` attribute?
5. If the area you want to define as a hotspot is irregular, which value would you use for the `shape` attribute?
6. If the area you want to define as a hotspot is a circle, which value would you use for the `shape` attribute?

PRACTICE

Practice the skills you learned in the tutorial using the same case scenario.

Review Assignments

Data Files needed for the Review Assignments: koala_T2.htm, modernizr-2.js, images/australia_logo.jpg, images/koala_lg.jpg, images/koala_sm.jpg

Tony would like you to create a Web page that contains information about koalas, which are animals native to Australia. Tony has provided you with a starter file, koala_T2.htm, along with a thumbnail image, koala_sm.jpg, and a full-size image, koala_lg.jpg. You will create a Web page, koala.htm, that contains information about koalas along with the thumbnail. You will also create a Web page named koala_image. htm that contains the larger version of the koala image. A preview of the koala.htm page is shown in Figure 2-56, and a preview of the koala_image.htm page is shown in Figure 2-57.

| Figure 2-56 | Koala Bear Web page |

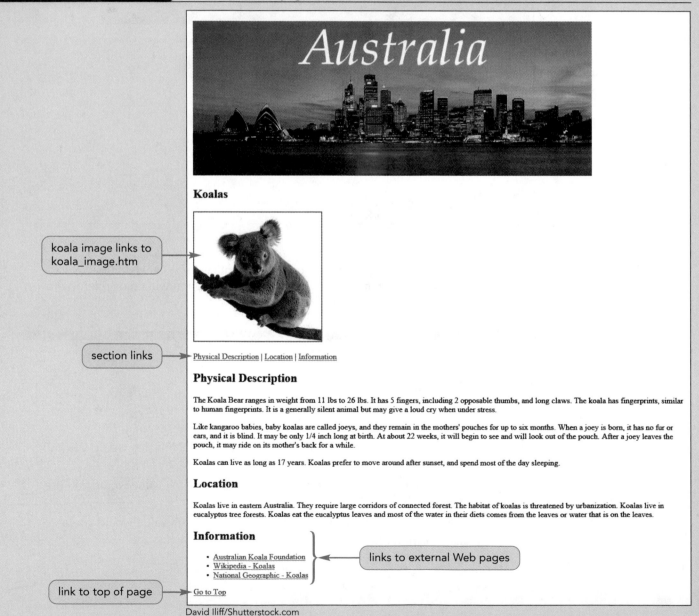

David Iliff/Shutterstock.com
Eric Isselée/Shutterstock.com

Figure 2-57   The koala_image.htm Web page

David Iliff/Shutterstock.com; Eric Isselée/Shutterstock.com

Complete the following:

1. Use your text editor to open the **koala_T2.htm** file from the tutorial2\review folder included with your Data Files. Save the file as **koala.htm** in the same folder. Between the `<title>` and `</title>` tags, type **Koalas**.

2. In the head section and above the page title, create a three-line comment with the following information, substituting your name and the date where indicated:
   Your First and Last Name
   Tutorial 2, Review Assignment
   Today's Date

3. Below the `<body>` tag, insert code that adds the australia_logo.jpg image.

4. Insert the code that defines the `h1` element as a section named top.

5. At the bottom of the page, link the phrase *Go to Top* to the section named top.

6. Insert code to create a section called *Physical* that includes the `h2` element *Physical Description* and the three paragraphs below it.

7. Insert code to create a section called *Location* that includes the *Location* `h2` element and the paragraph below it.

8. Insert code to create a section called *Information* that includes the *Information* `h2` element and the unordered list below it.

9. Near the top of the Web page insert code to convert the text *Physical Description | Location | Information* to three links, each linking to the corresponding section in the Web page.

10. In the unordered list at the bottom of the page, add code to convert each item to a link. The URL for the Australia Koala Foundation is http://www.savethekoala.com. The URL for the Wikipedia koala page is http://en.wikipedia.org/wiki/koala. The URL for the National Geographic koala page is http://animals.nationalgeographic.com/animals/mammals/koala/.

11. Save the **koala.htm** file.

12. Create a new Web page file called **koala_image.htm**.

13. Add the `DOCTYPE` tag, `html`, `head`, and `body` elements to the koala_image.htm file.

14. In the `head` element, add a `title` element that contains the text *Koala*.

15. In the head section and above the page title, create a three-line comment with the following information, substituting your name and the date where indicated:
   Your First and Last Name
   Tutorial 2, Review Assignment
   Today's Date

16. In the `body` element, add an `h1` element that contains the text *Koala*.

17. In the koala_image.htm file, add a paragraph containing the text *Back to Koala page*, and add code that links the text *Back to Koala page* to the koala.htm file.

18. In the koala_image.htm file, add code to display the koala_lg.jpg image.

19. Save the **koala_image.htm** file, and then close the file.

20. In the koala.htm file, link the koala_sm.jpg image to the koala_image.htm file, using the title value *Go to large image*.

21. Open the **koala.htm** file in the Web browser, and test all the links. Repeat to test the link in the koala_image.htm file.

22. Submit your completed files to your instructor, in either printed or electronic form, as requested.

Case Problem 1

Data Files needed for this Case Problem: barker_T2.htm, week_T2.htm, modernizr-2.js, images/barker_logo.jpg, images/week_lg.jpg, images/week_sm.jpg

Barker Bread and Roll   Barker Bread and Roll is a bakery located in Aberdeen, Scotland, that's renowned for its fresh bread and pastry products. Sandra Barker, the owner, describes her company's success in one word: freshness. All of the bread is baked on the premises and in limited quantities all day long. Because of the frequency of baking and high turnaround, products generally stay on the shelves for only a short time each day. Sandra has approached you about creating a Web page for her company. A preview of the Web page you'll create appears in Figure 2-58.

Figure 2-58   **Barker Bakery Web page**

Barker Bread and Roll

Fresh Baked Goods All Day Long

What makes Barker better? We never take a break when it comes to giving you the freshest products on the market. We bake our products on demand. You will never purchase anything that has been sitting on the shelves for days or even for a few hours. We know our customers and we know precisely how to meet demand. All our ordering and scheduling is computerized, and we use those computer models to predict demand based upon the day of the week and the time of the year. We even factor the day's weather into our computerized modeling. If the forecast is for heavy snow or rain, we know not to bake as many of our products on that day. If there's a holiday approaching, we use our historical data to project sales for each product based on past performance. When we receive special orders, we factor in those sales figures as well so that we can always meet our customers' regular demand.

Fresh, Fresh, Fresh!

In real estate, they say the top three rules are location, location, and location. At Barker Bread and Roll, we feel that it's freshness, freshness, and freshness. We want our customers to be satisfied whenever they make a purchase at any of our stores. We never sell anything that isn't fresh. You always walk out of one of our stores with warm bread products that will make your mouth water for more.

Let Them Eat Cake

We carry over our business principles to our pastry products as well. We bake only on demand, and we rely on orders from our customers to determine that demand. We can craft a specialty cake of any kind for you. If you need a birthday or anniversary cake, we can bake a cake that you will be proud to serve. If you need a large sheet cake with specialty decorations, please sit down with one of our cake designers so that we can design just the right cake for your occasion. We are experts at pleasing our customers with our specialty cake designs. Do not worry about freshness here, too. We will bake your specialty cake only several hours before the scheduled pick up time. We do not bake our specialty cakes a day or two in advance. We wait until we are ready to meet your needs, not ours.

Let Them Eat Croissants

Okay, it's not the easiest word to pronounce, but it's one of our tastiest new products. Our croissants are full of buttery, flaky goodness. Eat them plain or with cream cheese or fruit, but eat them! You might know croissants as crescent rolls, but they are delicious no matter what you call them. For those new to this treat, croissants are a puff pastry with layers of dough rolled to perfection. Around lunch time, we also make croissants filled with American or Swiss cheese, ham, pepperoni, and other cold cuts. Check out our picture of the **croissant of the week** below.

The Cake of the Week

Complete the following:

1. Use your text editor to open the file named **barker_T2.htm,** which is provided in your Data Files in the tutorial2\case1 folder. Save the file as **barker.htm** in the same folder. Between the `<title>` and `</title>` tags, type **Barker Bread and Roll**.

2. In the head section and below the page title, create a three-line comment with the following information, substituting your name and the date where indicated:
   Your First and Last Name
   Tutorial 2, Case Problem 1
   Today's Date

3. In the body section and between the first set of `<p></p>` tags, add the barker_logo.jpg image. The images are located in the images folder. Use *Barker Bread and Roll* as the alternate text. The image has a width of 400 pixels and a height of 260 pixels.

4. Near the bottom of the document, within the paragraph element below the comment that indicates the location to insert a thumbnail link, insert an image element that will display the week_sm.jpg image and then link it to week.htm. Use *chocolate cake* as the alternate text for the image, the title *The Cake of the Week* for the thumbnail's link. The thumbnail image has a width of 200 pixels and a height of 150 pixels.

5. Below the thumbnail link that uses the week_sm.jpg image, link the text *The Cake of the Week* to week.htm.

6. Save the **barker.htm** file, and then open the file in your browser.

7. Open the **week_T2.htm** page in your text editor, and then save a copy of the file as **week.htm** in the same folder.

8. In the head section and below the page title, create a three-line comment with the following information, substituting your name and the date where indicated:
   Your First and Last Name
   Tutorial 2, Case Problem 1
   Today's Date

9. Link the text *Back to Home Page* to the barker.htm page.

10. Save your work, and then open the file in your browser.

11. Test all of the links in both the barker.htm and week.htm files.

12. Submit your completed files to your instructor, in either printed or electronic form, as requested.

Use what you've learned to create a Web page for a college business club.

APPLY

Case Problem 2

Data Files needed for this Case Problem: club_T2.htm, modernizr-2.js, images/club_logo.jpg

Byron Pond College Business Club   Professor Sandra Windsor, advisor to the Byron Pond College Business Club in Manchester, England, is preparing a list of Web sites that she has been researching. She wants your assistance in creating a Web page that links to several external Web sites that would be of interest to the club members. She has provided you with the Web site URLs, but she needs your help in creating the Web page, which will be posted on the campus Web site that will publish her research. A preview of the Web page appears in Figure 2-59.

Figure 2-59   **Byron Pond College Business Club Web site**

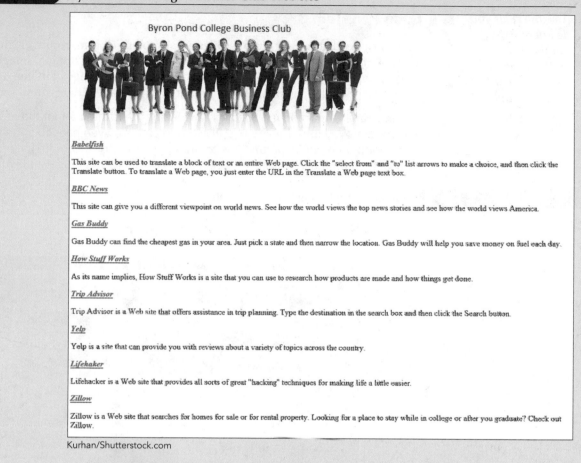

Kurhan/Shutterstock.com

Complete the following:

1. Use your text editor to open the file **club_T2.htm**, which is provided in your Data Files in the tutorial2\case2 folder. Save the file as **club.htm** in the same folder. Between the `<title>` and `</title>` tags, type **Business Web Sites**.

2. In the head section and below the page title, create a three-line comment with the following information, substituting your name and the date where indicated:

    Your First and Last Name

    Tutorial 2, Case Problem 2

    Today's Date

3. Below each comment containing a URL, create an external link to the site noted within the comment. (*Hint*: You can copy and paste the URL from the comment into the code for the link.)

4. Save the **club.htm** file, and then open the file in your browser.

5. Test each of the links on the Web page.

6. Submit your completed files to your instructor, in either printed or electronic form, as requested.

Use the skills you learned in the tutorial to create a Web page to view the rooms in an apartment.

APPLY

Case Problem 3

Data Files needed for this Case Problem: floor_plan_T2.htm, rooms_T2.htm, modernizr-2.js, images/bathroom_lg.jpg, images/bathroom_sm.jpg, images/bedroom_lg.jpg, images/bedroom_sm.jpg, images/floor_plan.jpg, images/kitchen_lg.jpg, images/kitchen_sm.jpg, images/livingroom_lg.jpg, images/livingroom_sm.jpg

Sue and Yang's Apartment Sue and Yang Wong are excited about the new apartment they have moved into. They would like you to create a Web page that includes a click-able floor plan of their apartment with links to pictures of several of the rooms. A pre-view of the Web page with the image map you will create appears in Figure 2-60.

Figure 2-60 Sue and Yang's apartment floor plan

Sue and Yang's Apartment

Tananda/Shutterstock.com

An image showing the hotspots for the floor plan appears in Figure 2-61.

Figure 2-61 Floor plan hotspots

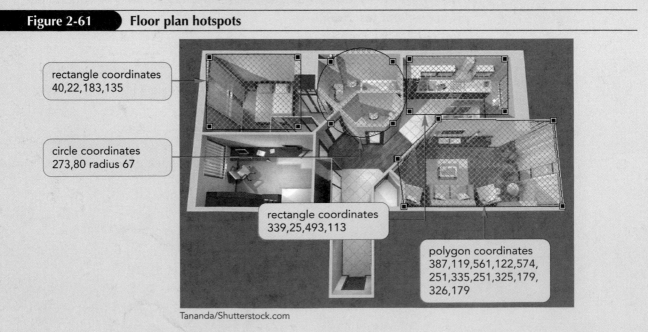

rectangle coordinates
40,22,183,135

circle coordinates
273,80 radius 67

rectangle coordinates
339,25,493,113

polygon coordinates
387,119,561,122,574,
251,335,251,325,179,
326,179

Tananda/Shutterstock.com

A preview of the Rooms Web page appears in Figure 2-62.

Figure 2-62	Rooms Web page

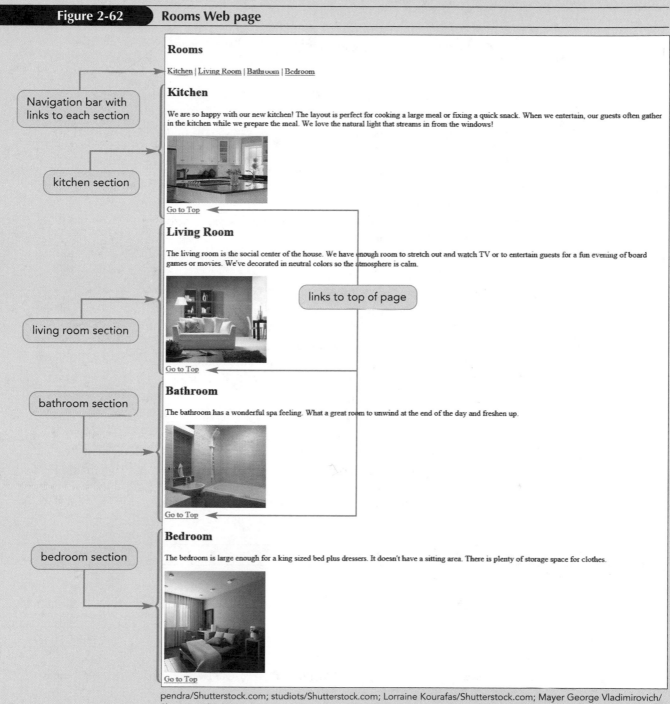

Navigation bar with links to each section

kitchen section

living room section

bathroom section

bedroom section

links to top of page

pendra/Shutterstock.com; studiots/Shutterstock.com; Lorraine Kourafas/Shutterstock.com; Mayer George Vladimirovich/
Shutterstock.com

Complete the following:

1. In your text editor, open the file named **rooms_T2.htm**, which is provided in your Data Files in the tutorial2\case3 folder. Save the file as **rooms.htm** in the same folder. In the head section and below the page title, create a three-line comment with the following information, substituting your name and the date where indicated:

   Your First and Last Name

   Tutorial 2, Case Problem 3

   Today's Date

2. Insert the four images specified by the comment tags in the document. Include appropriate `alt` attributes.

3. Use the `section` element to create sections called **top**, **kitchen**, **livingroom**, **bathroom**, and **bedroom**. For each section, include the related heading and paragraph in the `section` element.

4. Link each word in the text *Kitchen | Living Room | Bathroom | Bedroom* to the corresponding section.

5. At the bottom of each section, add a link to the *top* section where indicated by a comment tag.

6. Save the file, and view it in your Web browser. Test the links.

7. Without closing the rooms.htm file in your text editor, open the file **floor_plan_T2.htm** in new window or tab. Save the file as **floor_plan.htm** in the same folder.

8. In the head section and below the page title, create a three-line comment with the following information, substituting your name and the date where indicated:

   Your First and Last Name

   Tutorial 2, Case Problem 3

   Today's Date

9. Insert the image floor_plan.jpg where indicated by the comment in the floor_plan.htm file. Add the `usemap` attribute, and then set its value to **#floor_plan**.

10. Insert the code required to use the floor_plan.jpg image as an image map. Hotspot shapes and coordinates are indicated in Figure 2-63. The `href` value for each hotspot should point to the corresponding section in the rooms.htm file. Values for the `alt` and `title` attributes are indicated in Figure 2-63.

Figure 2-63 Table of hotspots and coordinates

Shape	Coordinates	Alt	Title
Rectangle	40,22,183,135	Our Bedroom	Bedroom
Circle	273,80, Radius 67	Our Bathroom	Bathroom
Rectangle	339,25,493,113	Our Kitchen	Kitchen
Polygon	387,119,561,122, 574,251,335,251, 325,179,326,179	Our Living Room	Living Room

11. Add a default hotspot that links to the rooms.htm file.

12. Save the file, open it in your Web browser, and then test each of the hotspot links.

13. Create an individual Web page for the large image for each room. In the rooms.htm file, link each room image to the Web page that contains the larger image of the room. Refresh or reload the rooms.htm file, and test each of the new links.

14. Submit your completed files to your instructor, in either printed or electronic form, as requested.

Create a Web page about Web sites that you think would interest college students.

RESEARCH

Case Problem 4

Data Files needed for this Case Problem: modernizr-2.js, images/airplane.jpg, images/email.jpg, images/graduate.jpg, images/search.jpg, images/social_media.jpg, images/students.jpg

College Student Web Resources   Connor Robinson is a college student. He often looks for Web resources to help him with his research and study skills. He would like you to create a Web page that lists Web sites that would be helpful to college students. You might want to include Web sites such as a search engine, dictionary, thesaurus, or Web sites that contain information about internships, job-hunting tips, resume writing, and interview strategies. For each Web site you list, write several sentences describing the resource.

Complete the following:

1. Create a new HTML file called **college.htm** that contains the DOCTYPE, html, head, title, and body elements. Save this file in the tutorial2\case4 folder.

2. Add the text **College Student Web Resources** as the Web page title.

3. In the head section and above the page title, create a three-line comment with the following information, substituting your name and the date where indicated:
   Your First and Last Name
   Tutorial 2, Case Problem 4
   Today's Date

4. In the body section, create the following:
   a. At least five links to external Web sites (including the title attribute in the code for each external link)
   b. A section
   c. A link to a section on the same Web page
   d. An image used as a link; use at least one of the images provided in the data files for this or any other case, or use your own images.

5. Save your file, and then open the file in your browser.

6. Validate your file at http://validator.w3.org using the Validate by Direct Input method. Correct any errors noted by the validator.

7. Submit your completed files to your instructor, in either printed or electronic form, as requested.

ENDING DATA FILES

tutorial2 → **tutorial**

australia_map.htm
australia_states.htm
canberra.htm
devils_marbles.htm
gold_coast.htm
index.htm
perth.htm
russell_falls.htm
south_australia_outback.htm
sydney_opera_house.htm
twelve_apostles.htm

review

koala.htm
koala_image.htm

case1

barker.htm
week.htm

case2

club.htm

case3

floor_plan.htm
rooms.htm
+4 HTML files

case4

college.htm

TUTORIAL 3

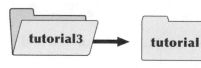

OBJECTIVES

Session 3.1
- Understand the advantages of using CSS
- Define a style rule
- Apply color using CSS
- Create internal and external style sheets
- Change the appearance of a link using CSS

Session 3.2
- Explore the five generic fonts
- Understand the importance of using Web-safe fonts
- Change the size and decoration properties of text
- Manipulate the letter spacing, word spacing, and line height of text
- Set the first line indentation and change text to uppercase using CSS
- Set alignment to center text horizontally

Introducing Cascading Style Sheets

Using CSS to Format Text on a Web Page

Case | *Classic Taxi*

Classic Taxi is owned and operated by the Diefenbaker family in Toronto, Ontario, Canada. It began in 1988 with a fleet of 2 classic cars and has expanded to 30 cars. It offers taxi services throughout the city of Toronto and the surrounding area as an affordable luxury for people who would like to travel short distances in a classic car. Emily Diefenbaker handles marketing for Classic Taxi and would like you to update the current Web site. Emily wants the Web site updated to have a visual style that provides a consistent look on each Web page. She's asking for your help in creating the styles that could be used for every Web page on the Classic Taxi Web site.

STARTING DATA FILES

tutorial

classic_taxi_logo.jpg
extended_colors.htm
faq_T3.htm
index_T3.htm
modernizr-2.js
services_T3.htm
toronto_T3.htm

review

modernizr-2.js
planner.jpg
planner_T3.htm

case1

modernizr-2.js
wireless_T3.htm
wirelesslogo.jpg

case2

modernizr-2.js
record_T3.htm
recordlogo.jpg

case3

contact_T3.htm
gild_T3.htm
gildlogo.jpg
modernizr-2.js

case4

modernizr-2.js
slake_T3.htm
slakelogo.jpg

SESSION 3.1 VISUAL OVERVIEW

The **selector** identifies the element you are applying a style to, such as h1 or body.

The **property** is the name of a specific feature such as color, text-align, or font-size.

```
h1 {
        background-color: orange;
        color: black;
}
```

A **style rule** is the combination of a selector, a property, and a value.

The property value provides a setting for the associated feature.

Classic Taxi

24 Hour Service
(905) 555 - 5555

Home | F

CLASSIC T

Classic Taxi is an owner-operated company serving the residents
Toronto and surrounding area. Our fleet of unique classic cars is a luxu

About Us

Established in 1988, Classic Taxi has been owned and operated b
cars. The Diefenbaker family takes pride in providing friendly, prompt s

Service Area

We service the Toronto and Greater Toronto Area. We provide se
Special pricing is available on request for trips to areas outside of Toro

Reservations

Contact us at (905) 555-5555 for reservations and special pricin

Classic Taxi • 123 Parliament St. • Toronto • Ont

ADDING COLOR TO ELEMENTS USING CSS

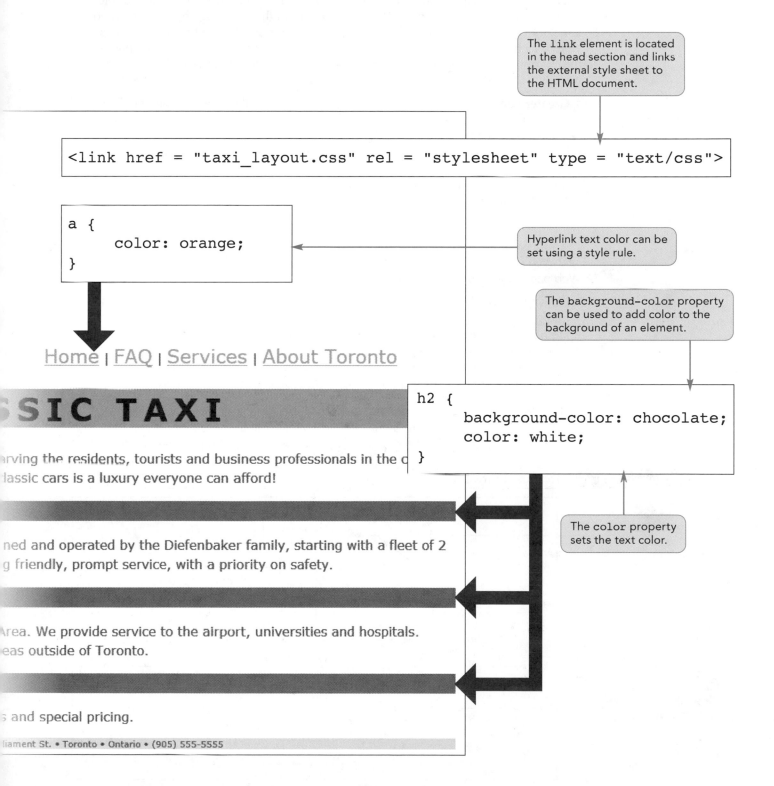

The `link` element is located in the head section and links the external style sheet to the HTML document.

```
<link href = "taxi_layout.css" rel = "stylesheet" type = "text/css">
```

```
a {
      color: orange;
}
```

Hyperlink text color can be set using a style rule.

The background-color property can be used to add color to the background of an element.

Home ı FAQ ı Services ı About Toronto

SSIC TAXI

arving the residents, tourists and business professionals in the c
Jassic cars is a luxury everyone can afford!

```
h2 {
      background-color: chocolate;
      color: white;
}
```

ned and operated by the Diefenbaker family, starting with a fleet of 2
g friendly, prompt service, with a priority on safety.

Area. We provide service to the airport, universities and hospitals.
eas outside of Toronto.

The color property sets the text color.

s and special pricing.

liament St. • Toronto • Ontario • (905) 555-5555

Introducing CSS

In Tutorial 1, you entered HTML elements and content on your Web page. The purpose of HTML is to create structure for the page content and to describe the content as elements. **Cascading Style Sheets (CSS)** is used to format the Web page by applying bold, italic, font style, font size, outlining, highlighting, and positioning of elements. CSS provides a technique to easily and efficiently format an unlimited number of Web pages so they have the same appearance. CSS offers many advantages over using HTML alone, including the following:

- **Greater consistency in your Web site**—You can create all of the styles in one document and link it to some or all of the other pages in your Web site to apply the styles to each document.
- **Easily modified code**—When you modify the linked style sheet code, all of the pages in your Web site can change. This helps you maintain a consistent design and easily update the style to all Web pages at once.
- **More flexible formatting**—You can format and position text in ways that you cannot with HTML.

Emily would like a consistent color theme and layout used throughout the Classic Taxi Web site. You'll be able to use CSS to achieve this. Emily has provided the current Web pages and a logo image, which include:

- *index.htm*—The home page for the Classic Taxi Web site, containing some general information
- *faq.htm*—Some frequently asked questions (FAQ) and answers
- *services.htm*—A description of the services provided
- *toronto.htm*—Some general information about the city of Toronto
- *classic_taxi_logo.jpg*—The corporate logo that should appear on each Web page

The storyboard for the Classic Taxi Web site is shown in Figure 3-1. An arrow indicates that a Web page contains a link to the Web page the arrow is pointing to. The double-arrows indicate that there is a link on each Web page that points to the other.

| Figure 3-1 | Storyboard for Classic Taxi |

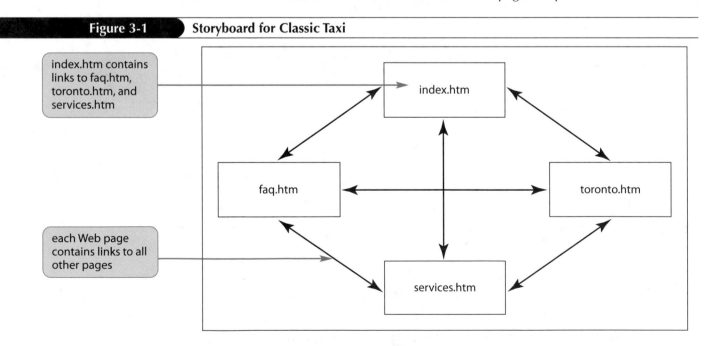

You'll begin your work by opening each of the HTML files in your text editor and in your browser.

To view the Classic Taxi Web site in your text editor and browser:

▶ 1. In your text editor, open the files **index_T3.htm**, **faq_T3.htm**, **services_ T3.htm**, and **toronto_T3.htm** from the tutorial3\tutorial folder. Within each file, edit the comment section to include your name and the date. Save the files as **index.htm**, **faq.htm**, **services.htm**, and **toronto.htm**, respectively.

▶ 2. In your Web browser, open the **index.htm** file. Figure 3-2 shows the current layout and content.

Figure 3-2	Classic Taxi index.htm

Daniel Padavona/Shutterstock.com

▶ 3. Click the **FAQ**, **Services**, and **About Toronto** links to view the corresponding Web pages.

While the content is included on each Web page, the Web pages themselves look very bland. You'd like to incorporate colors similar to the ones in the logo to add a professional look to the Web site. You decide to keep the same general layout in your update, but you'll use CSS to add color to the headings and the footer elements.

A Brief History of CSS

In 1989 when Tim Berners-Lee invented the World Wide Web and began developing HTML, all formatting and positioning of elements was achieved using HTML tags and attributes. Each Web browser would format and position these elements using its own default settings, and developers had very little control over the styling of elements.

Elements such as em and strong were used to style text as italic and bold. In 1996, the first version of CSS, called **CSS1**, was developed. It enabled users to set font size; align text center, left, or right; set body margins; and apply background and foreground colors to page elements. The second version of CSS, called **CSS2**, was introduced in 1998. It included features such as design styles for different output devices such as print media and aural devices, and controlling the appearance and behavior of browser features including the scroll bars and mouse cursors. In 2005, **CSS3** was introduced; features of CSS3 include text effects such as drop shadows and Web fonts, semitransparent colors, box outlines, and rotating page elements. At the time of this writing, CSS3 is a working draft of the World Wide Web Consortium (W3C), which manages and approves the standards for CSS. A set of standards is proposed by the W3C and published as a working draft until it's approved. Information and tutorials can be found at http://www.w3.org/Style/CSS/.

INSIGHT

Browser Extensions

Although the W3C oversees and approves specifications for HTML and CSS, the manufacturers of Web browsers often create their own proprietary extensions. They also often incorporate the draft specifications that have not yet become official. This means that some CSS3 functionality may already be implemented in some Web browsers. This is the nature of HTML and CSS development. Just as the W3C proposes functionality, Web browser makers both incorporate proposed functionality and anticipate functionality that has not yet been proposed. The net result is that Web browsers generally support older standards well, but support for the most recent standards is unreliable. Similarly, older versions of Web browsers do not support the most recent elements, attributes, and styles. When a CSS feature appears in all major browsers without any significant differences, the feature is said to have **cross-browser support**. For critical components and functionality, you should always test HTML and CSS in Web browsers that are at least 2 years old.

Defining a Style Rule

Using CSS, you can change how an HTML element appears in browsers. For example, the HTML strong element renders text as bold, but the strong element does not change the font, size, or color of the text. Using CSS, you can change many properties of an element, including font, font size, color, and positioning. You could create a style rule for the strong element so it always appears in Arial font, in a larger type size, and in red. A style rule is the combination of a selector, a property, and a value. The property is the name of a specific feature such as color, text-align, or font-size. The property value provides a setting for the associated feature. For instance, a property value for the color property could be *yellow*, thus setting the color of text to yellow. The selector identifies the element to which you are applying a style. A selector could be h1 or body, for instance. Combining these components, the structure of a style rule is as follows:

```
selector {
    property1: value1;
    property2: value2;
    property3: value3;
    ...
}
```

The indentation of the style rule is intentional. The properties are indented inside the curly brackets to make the style rule easier to read and edit later. The following example shows a style rule that centers h1 headings and renders them in yellow:

```
h1 {
      color: yellow;
      text-align: center;
}
```

A **style sheet** is a collection of one or more style rules, either within an HTML document, or in a separate CSS document. You'll learn more about style sheets later in this session.

Defining Color in CSS

There are many instances where you want to define the color of an element. For instance, you may want to set the text color of a heading or the background color of an entire Web page. Colors are identified in CSS by a color name or a color value. Particularly if you are not planning to be a Web developer, you may find it easier to use color names rather than values. Some Web developers use values instead of names, however.

There are 16 color names that are standard in CSS2, shown in Figure 3-3. The color values in two different systems—hexadecimal (or hex) and RGB (red, green, blue)—are also shown in this figure. You'll see values like these from time to time in CSS code. Note that when you use a CSS validator, color names don't always validate. In that case, you should substitute hex color values instead. You'll learn more about this later in the tutorial.

A more extensive list of color names was incorporated in CSS3. Even prior to CSS3, most Web browsers were already supporting the extended list of more than 140 color names.

> **TIP**
>
> The full list of color names and values can be found at http://www.w3.org/TR/css3-color/#svg-color.

Figure 3-3   Basic CSS2 Colors

Color	Color Name	Hex Code	RGB Triplet
	black	#000000	(0,0,0)
	silver	#C0C0C0	(192,192,192)
	gray	#808080	(128,128,128)
	white	#FFFFFF	(255,255,255)
	maroon	#800000	(128,0,0)
	red	#FF0000	(255,0,0)
	purple	#800080	(128,0,128)
	fuchsia	#FF00FF	(255,0,255)
	green	#008000	(0,128,0)
	lime	#00FF00	(0,255,0)
	olive	#808000	(128,128,0)
	yellow	#FFFF00	(255,255,0)
	navy	#000080	(0,0,128)
	blue	#0000FF	(0,0,255)
	teal	#008080	(0,128,128)
	aqua	#00FFFF	(0,255,255)

To view the extended list of color names:

▶ **1.** In your Web browser, open the **extended_colors.htm** file from the tutorial3\
tutorial folder. As Figure 3-4 shows, the Web page displays the list of information for more than 140 colors, including sample swatches, CSS names, hex
codes, and RGB triplets.

Figure 3-4 **Partial list of extended colors**

Color	Color name	Hex Code	RGB Triplet
	aliceblue	#F0F8FF	(240,248,255)
	antiquewhite	#FAEBD7	(250,235,215)
	aqua	#00FFFF	(0,255,255)
	aquamarine	#7FFFD4	(127,255,212)
	azure	#F0FFFF	(240,255,255)
	beige	#F5F5DC	(245,245,220)
	bisque	#FFE4C4	(255,228,196)
	black	#000000	(0,0,0)
	blanchedalmond	#FFEBCD	(255,235,205)
	blue	#0000FF	(0,0,255)
	blueviolet	#8A2BE2	(138,43,226)

▶ **2.** Look through the colors, and then close the Web page.

Text Color

Now that you've seen the large selection of colors that are available, you can begin to
use color to add interest and professionalism to the Classic Taxi Web site. The color of
text can be defined using the `color` property as follows:

```
color: color_value;
```

The color value could be the CSS color name, or it could also be the hex code or RGB
triplet. You'll use color names for the Classic Taxi Web site.

INSIGHT

Understanding Hex Codes and RGB Triplets for Defining Color

Graphic artists and other professionals who work with color use color theory to blend colors to make just the right shade. The three primary colors are red, green, and blue. Mixing all three colors together at their maximum intensities produces white. Black is the result of an absence of color. Blending two or more colors with varying intensities produces other colors. The color yellow, for instance, can be produced by blending the maximum intensity of red and green.

Color intensity can be defined as an **RGB triplet**, where each color intensity is represented by a decimal number from 0 to 255. Color as an RGB triplet is defined as follows:

```
rgb(rrr, ggg, bbb)
```

where *rrr* is a decimal value for red intensity, *ggg* is a decimal value for green intensity, and *bbb* is a decimal value for blue intensity. Under this system, the color yellow could be defined as follows:

```
rgb(255, 255, 0)
```

Look at the extended colors chart and notice the RGB values for red (255,0,0), lime (0,255,0), and blue (0,0,255). The named color of green is less intense (0,128,0) than lime, and maroon is less intense than red, with half the red value (128,0,0). Yellow is produced by combining red and green (255,255,0).

Another method to indicate color is by using a **hexadecimal value**, or **hex code**, which specifies color intensity values for red, green, and blue using a different system. A hexadecimal value is a base 16 value. In everyday life, we use the base 10 system, also called the decimal number system, where the numbers 0–9 are used for digits. In the base 16 system, the numbers 0–9 and characters *A–F* are used to represent digits. It's not necessary to know how to convert from one system to another. The important thing to know is that the hex code for a style color really represents the intensity of color for red, green, and blue.

Each color intensity is represented by a pair of digits in the following form:

```
#RRGGBB
```

where the first two digits represent the intensity for red, the next two digits represent the intensity for green, and the last two digits represent the intensity for blue. The least intense is 00, and the most intense is FF. The pound symbol is required as part of the CSS language. Thus, the color red would be defined as #FF0000, and yellow would be defined as #FFFF00.

Even though these systems may seem complex, they provide developers with much more variety and control in color selection. Many image-editing tools also provide color values, so a developer can create an image, and then use the hex or RGB color value from the image editor to match one of the image colors and use it as a background color, for instance.

Implementing Inline Styles

An **inline style rule** is a style rule that is embedded inside an HTML start tag. It includes the style attribute, followed by equal signs (=) and then the property and value. There is a semicolon included after the value. If there is more than one property, the next property and value can be included after the semicolon, and so forth.

For instance, the following inline style rule displays the text of the h1 heading in orange:

```
<h1 style = "color: orange;">Classic Taxi</h1>
```

You'll apply an inline style to the h1 heading on the index.htm Web page.

To apply an inline style:

▶ 1. Return to the **index.htm** file in your text editor.

▶ 2. Position the insertion point after the 1 in the `<h1>` start tag, insert a space, and then type the following, as shown in Figure 3-5:

```
style = "color: orange;"
```

Figure 3-5	Inline style

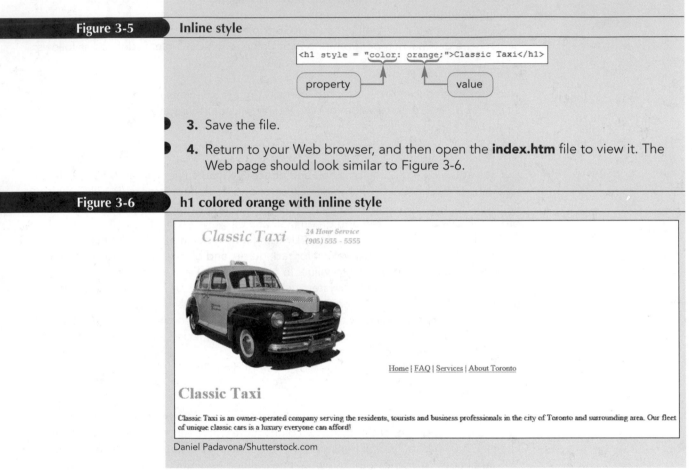

```
<h1 style = "color: orange;">Classic Taxi</h1>
```
property ⎯⎯ value

▶ 3. Save the file.

▶ 4. Return to your Web browser, and then open the **index.htm** file to view it. The Web page should look similar to Figure 3-6.

Figure 3-6	h1 colored orange with inline style

Daniel Padavona/Shutterstock.com

The inline style method is discouraged because the power of CSS is the ability to separate the presentation (styles) from the content. Embedding styles inside an HTML tag makes it more difficult to find the styles when a change is required. Separating styles from the content makes it easy to find styles and make changes when changes are required for the layout and design of Web pages. A more efficient method that separates the style from the content is to create a style sheet. Any style rule contained in a style sheet is applied to all instances of the element in the Web page. A style sheet can be embedded in a document, or it can be a separate style document that is linked to an HTML document.

Embedded Style Sheets

An **embedded style sheet** is a set of style rules contained between the `<style>` start tag and `</style>` end tag in the head section of an HTML document. The structure of an embedded style sheet is as follows:

```
<style type = "text/css">
    style rules
</style>
```

The style rules are placed between the `<style>` and `</style>` tags. For instance, the following style sheet contains style rules that render `h1` headings in orange text and centered, and `h2` headings in green text:

```
<style type = "text/css">
    h1 {
        color: orange;
        text-align: center;
    }
    h2 {
        color: green;
    }
</style>
```

TIP

To reduce the chance of forgetting to type a close bracket, type the close bracket (}) immediately after typing the open bracket ({), and then enter the properties and values between them.

The curly brackets ({ and }) mark the beginning and end of the group of properties and values for each selector. A selector can be the name of an HTML element or a group of elements.

You'll explore using an embedded style sheet for the Classic Taxi Web page.

To create an embedded style sheet:

1. Return to the **index.htm** file in your text editor.

2. Delete the inline style to restore the previous `<h1>` element as follows:

   ```
   <h1>Classic Taxi</h1>
   ```

3. Enter the following code in the head section after the `</title>` tag, as shown in Figure 3-7:

   ```
   <style type = "text/css">
       h1 {
           color: orange;
           text-align: center;
       }

       h2 {
           color: green;
       }
   </style>
   ```

Figure 3-7   Embedded style sheet

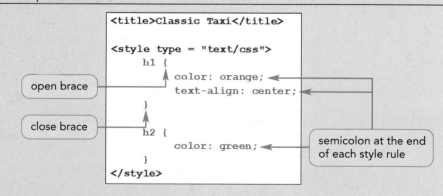

> 4. Save the file.
>
> 5. Return to your Web browser, and then refresh the **index.htm** file to view the changes. The Web page should look similar to Figure 3-8.

Figure 3-8   **Embedded styles applied to Web page**

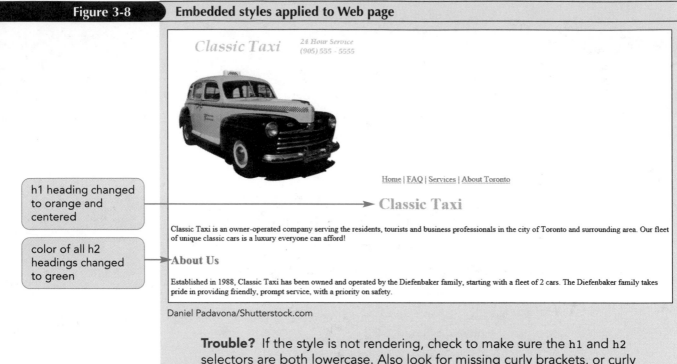

h1 heading changed to orange and centered

color of all h2 headings changed to green

Daniel Padavona/Shutterstock.com

Trouble? If the style is not rendering, check to make sure the h1 and h2 selectors are both lowercase. Also look for missing curly brackets, or curly brackets that are in the wrong place. Compare your code with the code above, looking at every character.

An embedded style sheet is useful for including styles that are used only on an individual Web page. However, Emily would like the styles applied to every Web page in the Classic Taxi Web site. You decide to explore ways of making the same styles available to multiple Web pages.

External Style Sheets

When styles are to be used across several pages in a Web site, it's much more efficient to create a separate document that contains the styles, known as an **external style sheet**, and use the link element to link the external style sheet to the Web pages.

Style Comments

Comments are used in an HTML document to include information about the document or to identify sections of the document. Similarly, comments can and should be used in style sheets for similar purposes. Style sheets can become long and complicated, and comments can help you find and edit sections quickly.

A comment begins with the /* symbols and ends with the */ symbols. A comment can be a single line, or a block of lines. A single-line style sheet comment uses the following syntax:

```
/* comment */
```

Sometimes you'll need to create multiline comments. In that case, you can use a technique such as the following:

```
/*
        Classic Taxi
        Layout Style sheet
*/
```

You decide to create an external style sheet for the Classic Taxi Web site because several Web pages will use the same style sheet. You'll begin your new external style sheet with a comment that identifies the purpose and author.

To create an external style sheet:

1. In the text editor, open a new file.

2. At the top of the file, type the following style comment, as shown in Figure 3-9, replacing *Your Name* with your name:

```
/*
        Classic Taxi
        Layout Style sheet

        Author: Your Name
*/
```

Figure 3-9   **Style sheet comment block**

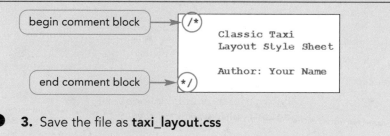

3. Save the file as **taxi_layout.css**

Background Color

You can define a background color for most elements. The background color for heading elements extends across the Web browser window. The effect is like highlighting the entire line containing the heading, because the heading elements are block-level elements. The background color can be defined as follows:

```
background-color: color_value;
```

The color value could be the CSS color name, or it could also be the hex code or RGB triplet.

Inspired by the colors in the Classic Taxi logo, you'll use `orange` as the background color for the `h1` element and `chocolate` as the background color for the `h2` elements. You'll also define the `h1` element text color as `black` and the `h2` text color as `white`. You want to be sure that you choose contrasting colors for the text and background, so the text is easy to read. Also, be aware that the most common color blindness is red-green color blindness, so it's best to avoid using this pair of colors together as text and background. People with red-green color blindness will not be able to read the text if you use one of these colors for text and the other for background.

Even though the default text color might be black, you can't guarantee this will be the case for all users. Sometimes a user may set default colors to be other than black. Setting the text color as black in a CSS rule ensures the text will be displayed as black. You'll use the following style rules to apply these changes:

```
h1 {
    background-color: orange;
    color: black;
}
h2 {
    background-color: chocolate;
    color: white;
}
```

You'll add these style rules to the taxi_layout.css style sheet, and then you'll link the style sheet to the index.htm Web page. Some Web developers use comments to identify each section of the CSS style sheet, and some use comments only to clarify code that might not be self-explanatory. You'll use comments to identify each section of your CSS code. This will make it easier to find and maintain style rules when it's time to edit them.

To define the background and text color for heading elements:

▶ **1.** Return to the **taxi_layout.css** file in your text editor.

▶ **2.** After the comment block, insert the comment and code as shown in Figure 3-10:

```
/* Heading styles */

h1 {
    background-color: orange;
    color: black;
}

h2 {
    background-color: chocolate;
    color: white;
}
```

Figure 3-10 Creating the external style sheet

```
/*
    Classic Taxi
    Layout Style Sheet

    Author: Your Name
*/

/* Heading styles */

h1 {
    background-color: orange;
    color: black;
}

h2 {
    background-color: chocolate;
    color: white;
}
```

3. Save the **taxi_layout.css** file.

4. Return to the **index.htm** file in your text editor, and then delete the embedded style sheet to restore the file to the previous HTML code.

5. Save the file.

The `link` Element

Once the external style sheet has been created, you're ready to link it to the Web page. After linking the two, the styles in the external style sheet are applied to the elements in the Web page. An external style sheet is powerful because you can link one style sheet to many Web pages. When you change the styles in an external style sheet, all the Web pages that link to that style sheet are affected. You can also link more than one style sheet to a Web page, and all of the styles in the linked style sheets are applied.

The `link` element is used to link an external style sheet to a Web page. The `link` element is placed in the head section of the HTML code and has the following structure:

```
<link href = "url" rel = "stylesheet" type = "text/css" />
```

where `url` refers to the URL of the external style sheet file, including the folder if it is not in the same folder as the HTML file and the full name of the file. The attribute `rel = "stylesheet"` identifies this link item as a style sheet, and the attribute `type = "text/css"` further identifies it as a CSS text file.

You'll use the following `link` element to link the taxi_layout.css file to the index.htm Web page:

```
<link ref = "taxi_layout.css" rel - "stylesheet" type = "text/css />
```

To link the external style sheet:

1. Return to the **index.htm** file in your text editor.

2. In the head section, add the following code, as shown in Figure 3-11:

```
<link href = "taxi_layout.css" rel = "stylesheet"
type = "text/css" />
```

Figure 3-11   Adding the link element

```
<!--
      Tutorial 3
      Author: Your name
      Date: Today's date

-->
<script src = "modernizr-2.js"></script>

<link href = "taxi_layout.css" rel = "stylesheet" type = "text/css" />

<title>Classic Taxi</title>
```

3. Save the file.

4. Return to your Web browser, and refresh or reload the **index.htm** file to view the style changes in the file. The Web page should look similar to Figure 3-12.

Figure 3-12 **Styles applied from external style sheet**

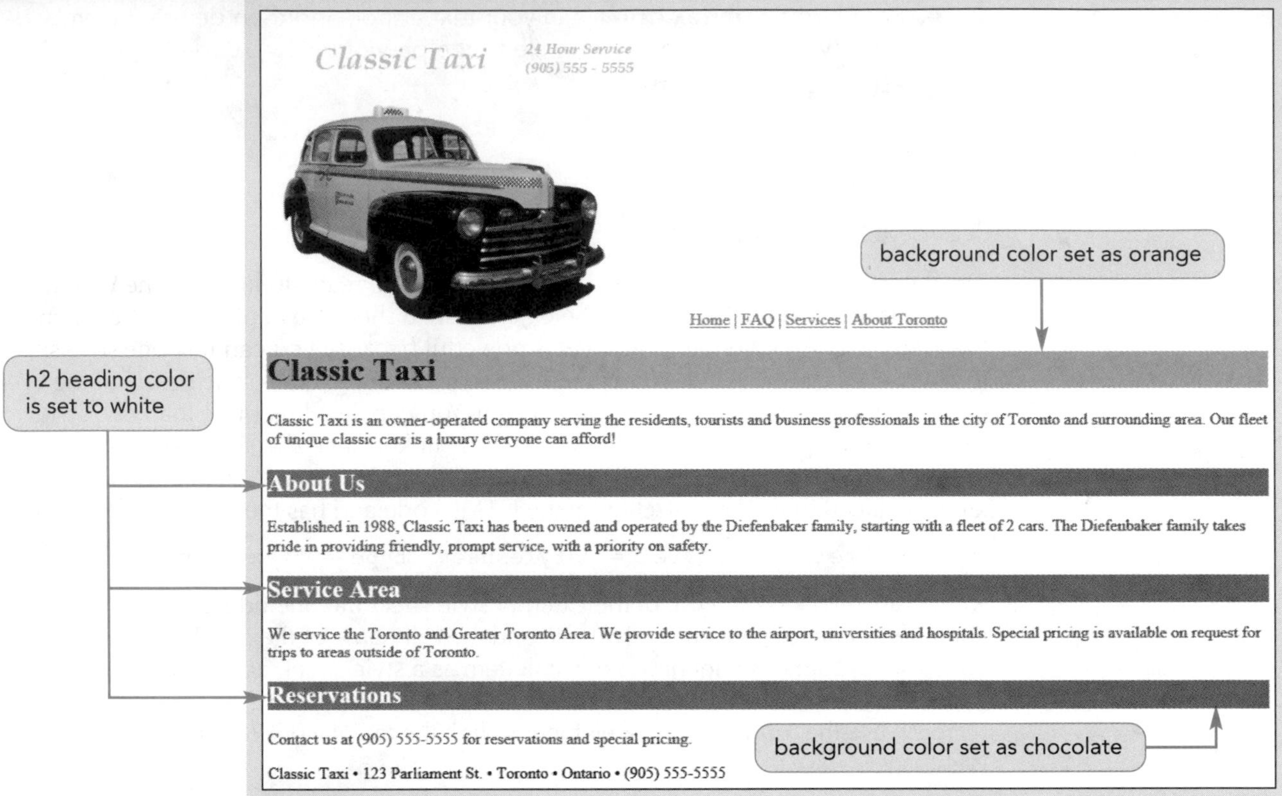

Daniel Padavona/Shutterstock.com

Emily loves the way the background colors of the heading elements coordinate with the color of the taxi on the logo. She would like the text for the paragraphs and the contact information to coordinate a bit better as well. You can change the text color for other elements just as you did for the h1 and h2 elements. You decide to use saddlebrown for the text in the paragraphs and in the footer section. You'd also like to use a slightly lighter color for the background for the footer section, and you select the color palegoldenrod.

To define the color for the paragraph and footer elements:

1. Return to the **taxi_layout.css** file in your text editor.

2. After the h2 style rule, add the following CSS style rules, as shown in Figure 3-13:

```
/* paragraph */
p {
     color: saddlebrown;
}

/* footer */

footer {
     color: saddlebrown;
     background-color: palegoldenrod;
}
```

Figure 3-13   **Paragraph and footer styles**

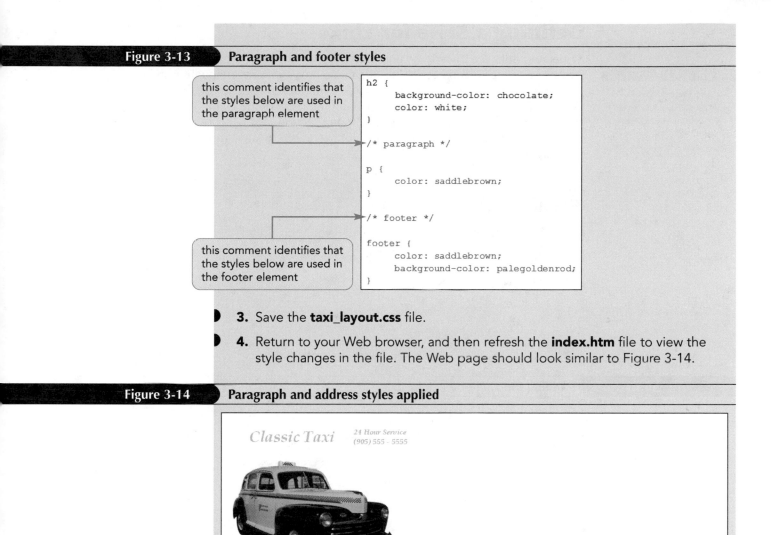

this comment identifies that the styles below are used in the paragraph element

this comment identifies that the styles below are used in the footer element

```
h2 {
        background-color: chocolate;
        color: white;
}

/* paragraph */

p {
        color: saddlebrown;
}

/* footer */

footer {
        color: saddlebrown;
        background-color: palegoldenrod;
}
```

 3. Save the **taxi_layout.css** file.

 4. Return to your Web browser, and then refresh the **index.htm** file to view the style changes in the file. The Web page should look similar to Figure 3-14.

Figure 3-14   **Paragraph and address styles applied**

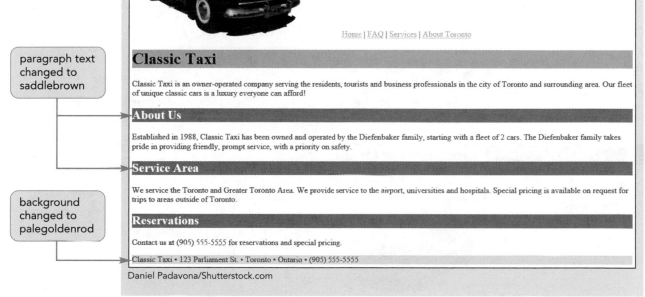

paragraph text changed to saddlebrown

background changed to palegoldenrod

Daniel Padavona/Shutterstock.com

Now that the headings, text, and footer styles are defined, you notice the color of the links looks out of place. You can change the style of the links by applying a style to the element that creates them, which is the **a** element.

Defining a Style for Links

TIP

Be sure the link color is not the same as the text color; otherwise, the link will seem like regular text instead of a link.

By default, links are underlined and blue. You can change the color of the links using the `color` property. You need to be sure that a link is different enough in style that it would not be confused with text that is not a link. You decide to use the color orange for the links. This will coordinate nicely with the color of the taxi in the logo and the background colors for the headings and footer section. Applying a color to the anchor element affects only the links that have not been visited; later, you will apply color and other styles to visited links.

To define the color for links:

1. Return to the **taxi_layout.css** file in your text editor.

2. After the first comment block, insert the following code, as shown in Figure 3-15:

```
/* links */


a {
        color: orange;
}
```

Figure 3-15	Adding the anchor element style

```
/*
        Classic Taxi
        Layout Style Sheet

        Author: Your Name
*/

/* links */

a {
        color: orange;
}

/* Heading Styles */
```

3. Save the file.

4. Return to your Web browser, and then click the **Refresh** or **Reload** button to view the changes in the file. The Web page should look similar to Figure 3-16.

Figure 3-16	Links with color applied

link color changed to orange

Daniel Padavona/Shutterstock.com

PROSKILLS

Written Communication: Color and Culture

You may be familiar with color associated with different moods or emotion, but did you know that colors can have different meanings from one culture to another? Here are some examples of common meaning of colors in a variety of cultures:

Red
- China—Good luck, celebration
- India—Purity
- South Africa—Mourning
- Asia—Worn by brides
- Europe and North America—Love, danger, Christmas (especially with green)

Yellow
- China—Nourishing
- Egypt—Mourning
- Germany—Envy
- Japan—Courage
- India—Merchants
- Europe and North America—Hope, hazards, cowardice

Blue
- Africa—Happiness
- China—Immortality
- Israel—Holiness
- Europe and North America—Masculine

White
- China—Mourning, humility
- Asia—Funerals
- Europe and North America—Purity, peace

If you are developing a Web site for an international audience, it's a good idea to be aware of the meanings of color in a variety of cultures. Consider testing your Web site with a diverse group of people from a variety of ethnic backgrounds.

Emily thinks it might be nice to change the background color.

You've already defined a background color for headings, and you can use the same technique to create a style rule that defines the background color for the entire Web page. The `background-color` property can be placed in a style rule using the `body` selector as follows:

```
body {
     background-color: color;
}
```

You look through the extended color list and decide that khaki might be a nice background color.

To define the background color for the body:

▶ **1.** Return to the **taxi_layout.css** file in your text editor.

▶ **2.** After the first comment block, insert the following code, as shown in Figure 3-17:

```
/* body */
body {
        background-color: khaki;
}
```

Figure 3-17	Body selector with background-color

```
/*
        Classic Taxi
        Layout Style Sheet

        Author: Your Name
*/


/* body */

body {
        background-color: white;
}

/* links */

a {
        color: orange;
}
```

▶ **3.** Save the file.

▶ **4.** Return to your Web browser, and then refresh or reload **index.htm** to view the changes. The Web page should look similar to Figure 3-18.

Figure 3-18	Khaki color background applied

logo image has a white background

Web page background color is khaki

Classic Taxi

Classic Taxi 24 Hour Service (905) 555 - 5555

Home | FAQ | Services | About Toronto

Classic Taxi

Classic Taxi is an owner-operated company serving the residents, tourists and business professionals in the city of Toronto and surrounding area. Our fleet of unique classic cars is a luxury everyone can afford!

About Us

Established in 1988, Classic Taxi has been owned and operated by the Diefenbaker family, starting with a fleet of 2 cars. The Diefenbaker family takes pride in providing friendly, prompt service, with a priority on safety.

Daniel Padavona/Shutterstock.com

The khaki color has been applied as a background on the entire Web page. Emily does not like it because it makes the logo, with its white background, stand out. When the background color of the Web page was white, the logo looked like it was floating on the page because the logo background color matched the Web page background color, which was a more professional look. It's possible for users to change their Web browser settings to specify a default background color for Web pages that do not have a background color specified. For this reason, many Web page designers specify the background color of a Web page in a CSS style rule, even if the color is white.

Emily prefers the Web page with a white background, so you'll change it back.

To change the background color for the body:

1. Return to the **taxi_layout.css** file in your text editor.

2. Edit the color for the `background-color` property for the body selector to delete *khaki* and insert **white**, as shown in Figure 3-19:

   `background-color: white;`

Figure 3-19 Body selector with background-color property value white

```
/* body */

body {
        background-color: white;
}
```

3. Save the file.

4. Return to your Web browser, and then refresh or reload **index.htm** to view the changes. The Web page should look similar to Figure 3-20.

Figure 3-20 Web page with background color white

background color set as white

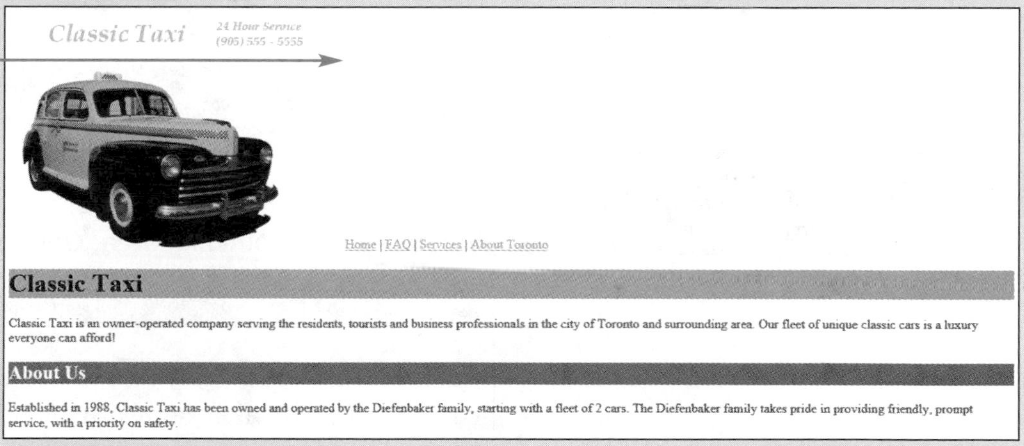

Daniel Padavona/Shutterstock.com

You've added some interest to the Classic Taxi Web site by adding color to the text, and using background color to separate sections of information. In the next session, you'll explore how to align some of the text and stylize the font.

REVIEW

Session 3.1 Quick Check

1. What is the difference between an inline style, an embedded style sheet, and an external style sheet?

2. Specify the code that would be used in a style sheet to add a comment that contains today's date.

3. Specify the CSS code that would be used to display the `h6` headings in `green` with a `greenyellow` background.

4. Where should the `link` element be placed in an HTML document?

SESSION 3.2 VISUAL OVERVIEW

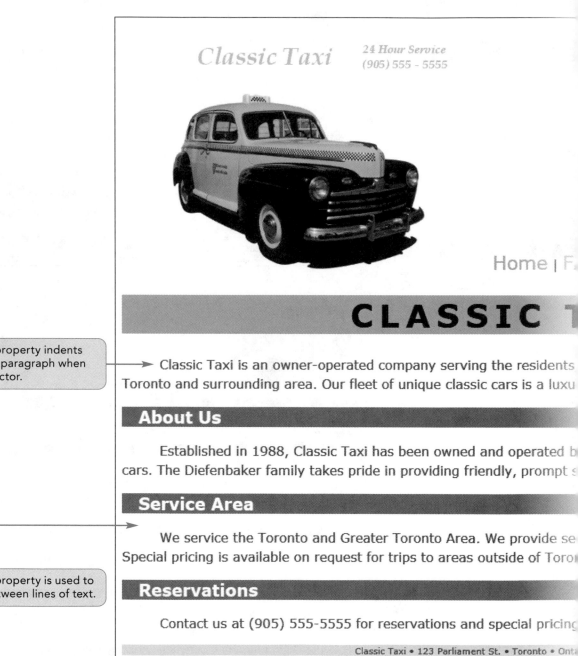

The `text-indent` property indents the first line of each paragraph when used with the p selector.

The `line-height` property is used to add white space between lines of text.

STYLIZING TEXT USING CSS

Specifying the value none for the `text-decoration` property removes the underline from hyperlinks.

A **spread heading** has letters of one word or several words that are spaced apart.

Home | FAQ | Services | About Toronto

SSIC TAXI

The `letter-spacing` and `word-spacing` properties let you adjust the space between characters, which is known as **kerning**.

rving the residents, tourists and business professionals in the city of
assic cars is a luxury everyone can afford!

The value uppercase for the `text-transform` property adjusts characters to all uppercase without changing the actual text in the HTML code.

ned and operated by the Diefenbaker family, starting with a fleet of 2
g friendly, prompt service, with a priority on safety.

rea. We provide service to the airport, universities and hospitals.
eas outside of Toronto.

and special pricing.

ament St. • Toronto • Ontario • (905) 555-5555

The `text-align` property is used to center text horizontally.

Font Families and Web-safe Fonts

Emily loves the color you've added to the Classic Taxi Web page. She would like the font to be a bit more modern looking as well.

A **font** is the recognizable, distinct design of a collection of characters in a particular typeface, such as Arial. A **font family** is a set of fonts that have similar characteristics, such as Arial, Arial Narrow, and Arial Black; the fonts in a font family are designed to be used together. Although thousands of fonts are available for printed text, only certain fonts are commonly used on Web pages. Because it is quite a challenge to install and use all of the available fonts, and because you can't be sure which fonts will be supported by a given user's computer, a group of nonspecific, generic fonts are used in Web page design. A **generic font** attempts to duplicate as many features of a specific font as possible. Five generic fonts are used in Web page design: serif, sans-serif, monospace, cursive, and fantasy. Samples of these fonts are shown in Figure 3-21.

Figure 3-21 **Some common fonts**

Sans-Serif	Serif	Monospace	Cursive	Fantasy
Arial	Georgia	Courier New	*Lucida Handwriting*	Jokerman
Tahoma	Times New Roman	Lucida Console	*Bradley Hand IT*	Old English Text MT

These five generic fonts are designed to be **cross-platform**, meaning that they will be displayed on any computer regardless of the platform. The letters in a **serif font** have finishing strokes—hooks and tails. Because of their detail, serif fonts are very easy to read in print. For example, Century Schoolbook, a font used in primary-grade reading books, is a familiar serif font. A **sans-serif font**, such as Arial, lacks finishing strokes. Sans-serif fonts are considered to have a more contemporary appearance. A **monospace font** has a fixed letter width, meaning that every letter takes up the same amount of space. For example, in a monospace font, the letter *i* takes up as much space as the letter *w*. Computer programming code is often illustrated in a monospace font such as Courier or Courier New. A **fantasy font**, such as Broadway, is artistic and decorative. **Cursive fonts**, such as Lucida Calligraphy or Edwardian Script, are designed to resemble handwritten letters or handwritten script. The five generic fonts are shown in Figure 3-22.

Figure 3-22 **Generic fonts**

Generic Font	Description	Sample
serif	Letters have finishing serifs (hooks and tails) at the top or bottom	Times New Roman Georgia
sans-serif	Letters do not have finishing strokes	Arial Calibri
monospace	Letters have a fixed width	Courier New Miriam Fixed
fantasy	Letters are decorative or artistic	Jokerman **Broadway**
cursive	Letters are designed to look like handwriting or script	*Brush Script* *Lucida Calligraphy*

Because there is a wide variety of Web browsers, operating systems (Windows, OS X), devices (computer, cell phone, tablet), and other variables, the challenge is to choose fonts that will be displayed reliably on most computers. Fonts known as **Web-safe fonts** are displayed reliably in most Web browsers on most devices. Some commonly used Web-safe fonts are shown in Figure 3-23.

| Figure 3-23 | Web-safe fonts |

Generic Font Family	Web-Safe Fonts
serif	Georgia
	Times New Roman
sans-serif	Arial
	Tahoma
	Trebuchet
monospace	Courier New
fantasy	No fantasy fonts are displayed reliably
cursive	Comic Sans MS

The `font-family` Property

The **font-family property** is used to change the typeface of text. When using the `font-family` property, it's common practice to provide a list of the fonts you prefer to be used to display the text, followed by a generic font. Any font name that contains spaces must have quotes around it. Font names are separated by commas, and the generic font is listed last. An example is shown below.

```
font-family: "Times New Roman", Times, serif;
```

While there may appear to be some repetition in these lists, the idea is to capture the most common fonts on the most common devices. A computer with a Windows operating system likely has a Times New Roman font, and a computer running OS X likely has a Times font. If the computer or device opening the Web page does not have either of those fonts, then the computer's default serif font will be used.

REFERENCE

Setting the Font Face

- To set the font face, use the `font-family` property:

  ```
  font-family: Font1, Font2, …, GenericFont;
  ```

  where `Font1`, `Font2`, and so on, are font families, and `GenericFont` is a generic font.
- Include a font that is common on computers running Windows, a font that is common on computers running OS X, and then a generic font.
- Do not include fantasy fonts.
- Use one of the most common `font-family` style properties as follows:

  ```
  font-family: Verdana, Geneva, Arial, Helvetica, sans-serif;
  font-family: "Times New Roman", Times, serif;
  font-family: "Courier New", Courier, monospace;
  font-family: "Comic Sans MS", cursive;
  ```

- If the value of `font-family` has a space, the value must be enclosed in either single or double quotation marks.

Emily would like a font that looks a bit modern, and she would like the same font used for all text on the Web page. She likes the look of the sans-serif fonts. Rather than placing a font-family property in the h1, h2, p, and footer selectors, you decide to place it in the style rule for the body element. This way, the font-family property will apply to all text on the Web page.

To apply the font-family property to the body:

1. If you took a break after the previous session, make sure that the **taxi_layout. css** file is open in your text editor.

2. Position the mouse pointer after the semicolon in the body style, press the **Enter** key, and then type the following CSS code, as shown in Figure 3-24:

   ```
   font-family: Verdana, Geneva, Arial, Helvetica, sans-serif;
   ```

Figure 3-24 Specify the default font for the Web page body

```
body {
    background-color: white;
    font-family: Verdana, Geneva, Arial, Helvetica, sans-serif;
}
```

3. Save the file.

4. Return to your Web browser, and then refresh or reload **index.htm** to view the changes in the styles. The Web page should look similar to Figure 3-25.

Figure 3-25 Displaying the page text in a sans-serif font

sans-serif font applied to all text

Daniel Padavona/Shutterstock.com

Setting the Font Size

Emily would like you to make some adjustments to the font size. She'd like the hyperlinks to be a little larger, the `h1` heading to be larger, and the text in the footer section to be smaller. The style used to change the font size is:

```
font-size: size;
```

The font size can be expressed using the following systems of measurement:

- Centimeters (cm)
- Inches (in)
- Millimeters (mm)
- Points (pt), equal to 1/72 of one inch
- Picas (pc), equal to 1/6 of one inch
- Pixels (px)
- x-Height (ex)
- em, roughly equal to the size of the letter *M* in the font used to display the element
- Percentage

The measurement units fall into two categories: absolute units and relative units. **Absolute units** are a fixed size, regardless of the Web browser or device used to view the Web page. **Relative units** are expressed as a size relative to some other object. The most common relative units are percentage and em. A percentage is relative to the size of the font size used for the element that contains this element. For now think of this as relative to the body font. You'll learn more about elements contained within other elements in a later tutorial. If the size 200% were used, for instance, then the font would be twice as large as it would have been normally. If the size 50% were used, the font would be half the size it would have been normally. The em unit is roughly equivalent to the size of the letter *M* in the font used to display the element. The measurement 1em is 100% of the font size. If the size 2em were used, the font would be twice as large as it would have been normally. If the size .5em were used, the font would be half the size it would have been normally.

Absolute units include pixels (px) and points (pt). One point is 1/72 of one inch, so there are 72 points in an inch. Although pixels were a very common measurement for print media, absolute measurements do not work well with electronic media because they do not scale. For instance, someone with a visual impairment might set the Web browser default font to be larger, but an absolute measurement would override their settings. A relative unit can scale, either increasing or decreasing proportionately to the default font.

Emily would like the hyperlinks to be displayed about 50% larger—or 1.5 times as large—compared to the normal text size. You'll set the font size for the hyperlinks to 1.5em.

> **TIP**
>
> Always use relative units for font sizes to give readers maximum flexibility for viewing the Web page.

To set the font size for the hyperlinks:

▶ **1.** Return to the **taxi_layout.css** file in your text editor.

▶ **2.** Add the following CSS property for the **a** selector, as shown in Figure 3-26.

```
font-size: 1.5em;
```

Do not type a space character between 1.5 and em.

Figure 3-26 **Setting the font-size property for the hyperlinks**

```
a {
        color: orange;
        font-size: 1.5em;
}
```

▶ **3.** Save the file.

▶ **4.** Return to your Web browser, and then refresh or reload **index.htm** to view the style changes. The Web page should look similar to Figure 3-27.

Figure 3-27 **Font size property set for the links**

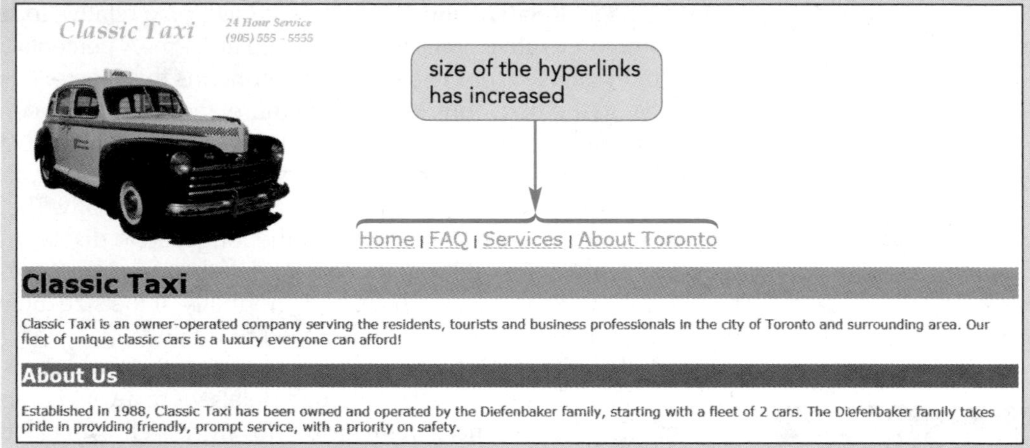

Classic Taxi   24 Hour Service
                (905) 555 - 5555

size of the hyperlinks has increased

Home | FAQ | Services | About Toronto

Classic Taxi

Classic Taxi is an owner-operated company serving the residents, tourists and business professionals in the city of Toronto and surrounding area. Our fleet of unique classic cars is a luxury everyone can afford!

About Us

Established in 1988, Classic Taxi has been owned and operated by the Diefenbaker family, starting with a fleet of 2 cars. The Diefenbaker family takes pride in providing friendly, prompt service, with a priority on safety.

Daniel Padavona/Shutterstock.com

You'll use the same property to set the size of the font for the **h1** and **footer** text. Emily would like the **h1** text size to be 2.5 times larger than the normal text size, regardless of how the **h1** element is displayed in various Web browsers. You'll accomplish this by setting the font size for the **h1** text to 2.5em. Emily would like the **footer** text to be a bit smaller, about 70% of the size of the normal text, so you'll set the font size for the footer text to .7em.

To set the font size for the h1 and footer text:

▶ **1.** Return to the **taxi_layout.css** file in your text editor.

▶ **2.** Add the following CSS property for the font size to the **h1** style rule, as shown in Figure 3-28:

```
font-size: 2.5em;
```

3. Add the following CSS property for the font size to the `footer` style rule, as shown in Figure 3-28:

```
font-size: .7em;
```

Figure 3-28 Setting the font size for h1 and footer text

```
h1 {
        background-color: orange;
        color: black;
        font-size: 2.5em;
}

. . . .

footer {
        color: saddlebrown;
        background-color: palegoldenrod;
        font-size: .7em;
}
```

4. Save the file.

5. Return to your Web browser, and then refresh or reload **index.htm** to view the style changes. The Web page should look similar to Figure 3-29.

Figure 3-29 Font-size property applied to h1 and footer text

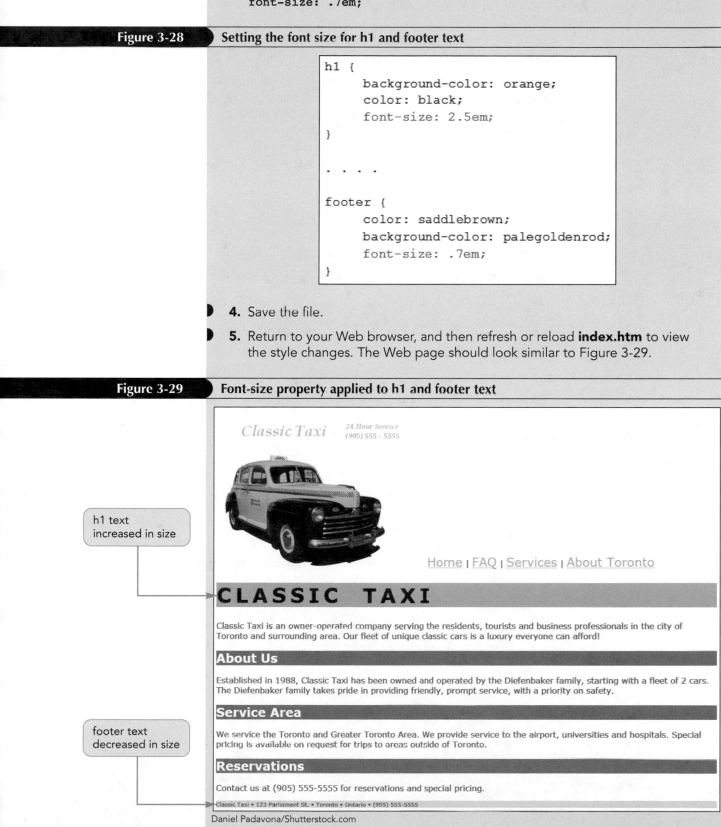

Daniel Padavona/Shutterstock.com

Incorporating Text Effects

CSS provides several ways to style text. You've already used the color and font properties to style text. CSS also provides properties that will transform the text to all uppercase or all lowercase. Emily would like you to use some of these techniques on her Web page.

Transforming Text

While Emily likes the changes you've made so far, she'd also like the `h1` heading to be displayed in all uppercase characters. You could retype the text in the Web page in uppercase, but it's possible that you'd want to apply a different style later and you'd have to retype the text again. Instead, many Web browsers can transform text to all uppercase characters using the **text-transform property**. Some older Web browsers may not recognize this property. This property has several values for changing the case of text, as follows:

- `capitalize` (Text Appears With The First Letter Of Each Word Capitalized)
- `lowercase` (text appears in lowercase)
- `uppercase` (TEXT APPEARS IN ALL CAPS)
- `none` (removes any of the preceding values)

You'll use the `text-transform` property to style the `h1` element as uppercase.

To set the text for the `h1` text to all uppercase:

▶ **1.** Return to the **taxi_layout.css** file in your text editor.

▶ **2.** Add the following CSS property to the `h1` selector, as shown in Figure 3-30:

```
text-transform: uppercase;
```

Figure 3-30   Setting all uppercase for the h1 headings

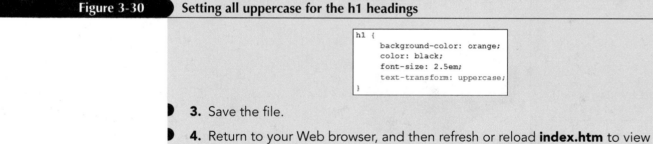

```
h1 {
    background-color: orange;
    color: black;
    font-size: 2.5em;
    text-transform: uppercase;
}
```

▶ **3.** Save the file.

▶ **4.** Return to your Web browser, and then refresh or reload **index.htm** to view the style changes. The Web page should look similar to Figure 3-31.

Figure 3-31   **Uppercase h1 heading**

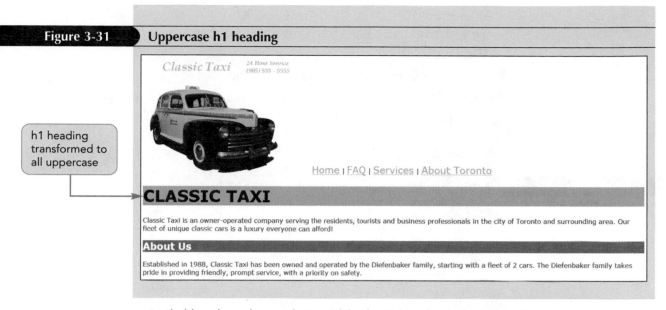

h1 heading transformed to all uppercase

Emily likes the colors and sizes of the fonts, but she feels that the letters are a bit too close to each other in the h1 heading now that the letters are all uppercase, giving the text a cramped feel. She would like you to increase the space between each letter in the h1 heading. You can do this using the letter-spacing and word-spacing properties.

Creating a Spread Heading

The **letter-spacing property** controls the amount of white space between letters. Similarly, the **word-spacing property** controls the amount of white space between words. Letter spacing is also known as kerning. Letter spacing and word spacing are commonly used together to create a spread heading, in which the letters of one word or several words are spaced apart.

REFERENCE

Creating a Spread Heading

To create a style for a spread heading use the letter-spacing and word-spacing properties:

- letter-spacing: *letter_spacing_value*;
- word-spacing: *word_spacing_value*;

The *letter_spacing_value* and *word_spacing_value* can be expressed as absolute (pixel, point) or relative units of measurement (em, percentage)

Emily would like you to add .2em between letters and an additional .5em between words. You'll accomplish this by setting the letter-spacing and word-spacing properties for the h1 selector.

To set the `letter-spacing` and `word-spacing` properties for the `h1` heading:

1. Return to the **taxi_layout.css** file in your text editor.

2. Add the following CSS properties to the h1 style rule as shown in Figure 3-32:

   ```
   letter-spacing: .2em;
   word-spacing: .5em;
   ```

Figure 3-32 Setting the letter and word spacing for the h1 heading

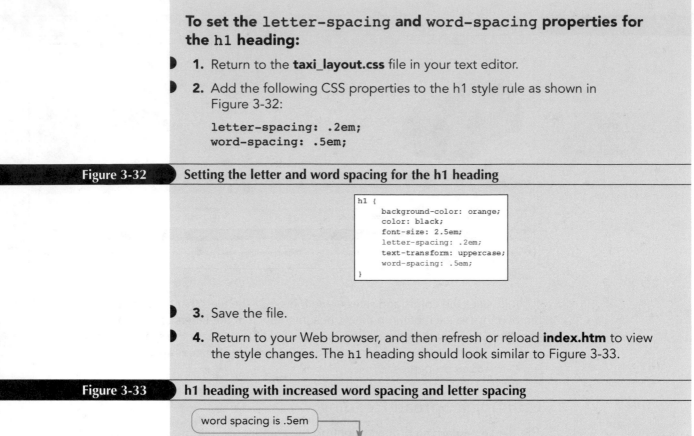

```
h1 {
       background-color: orange;
       color: black;
       font-size: 2.5em;
       letter-spacing: .2em;
       text-transform: uppercase;
       word-spacing: .5em;
}
```

3. Save the file.

4. Return to your Web browser, and then refresh or reload **index.htm** to view the style changes. The `h1` heading should look similar to Figure 3-33.

Figure 3-33 h1 heading with increased word spacing and letter spacing

word spacing is .5em

CLASSIC TAXI

letter spacing is .2em

Emily is happy with the `h1` heading text, but she notices that the beginning of each paragraph is flush with the left margin. She would instead like the first line of each paragraph to be indented. This can be accomplished using the `text-indent` property.

Indenting Text

You can use the **`text-indent` property** to indent the first line of paragraph text, similar to pressing the Tab key on a keyboard. The style used to set the amount of space to indent text is:

```
text-indent: value;
```

where *value* is a value in ems or pixels, or a percentage.

You'll apply the `text-indent` property to the `p` selector to set the text indent to 3em for all paragraphs in the Web page.

To set the text indent for paragraphs:

▶ **1.** Return to the **taxi_layout.css** file in your text editor.

▶ **2.** Add the following CSS property to the **p** selector, as shown in Figure 3-34:

   `text-indent: 3em;`

Figure 3-34 | Setting the text indent for the paragraph style

```
p {
      color: saddlebrown;
      text-indent: 3em;
}
```

▶ **3.** Save the file.

▶ **4.** Return to your Web browser, and then refresh or reload **index.htm** to view the style changes. The Web page should look similar to Figure 3-35.

Figure 3-35 | Paragraphs with text-indent increased

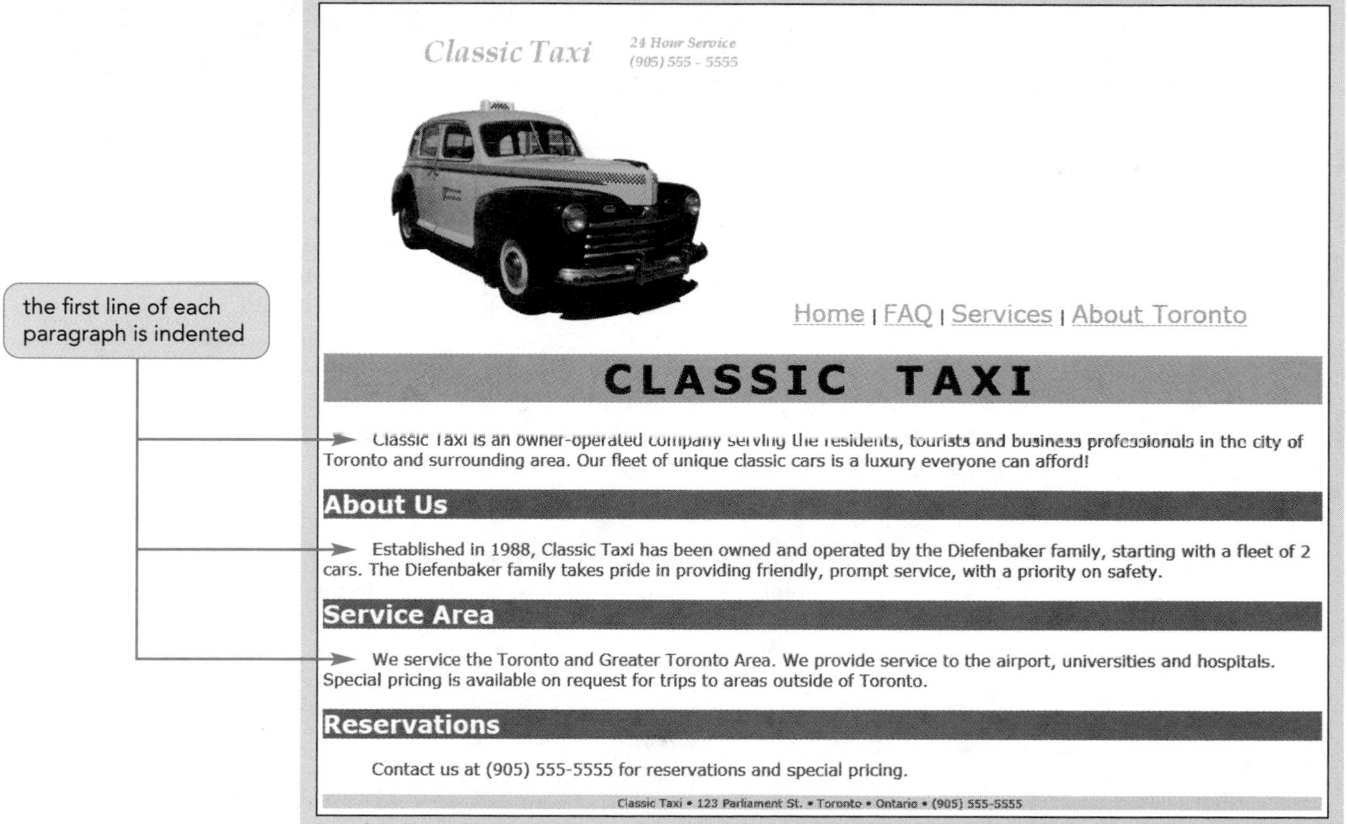

the first line of each paragraph is indented

Classic Taxi   24 Hour Service (905) 555 - 5555

Home | FAQ | Services | About Toronto

CLASSIC TAXI

Classic Taxi is an owner-operated company serving the residents, tourists and business professionals in the city of Toronto and surrounding area. Our fleet of unique classic cars is a luxury everyone can afford!

About Us

Established in 1988, Classic Taxi has been owned and operated by the Diefenbaker family, starting with a fleet of 2 cars. The Diefenbaker family takes pride in providing friendly, prompt service, with a priority on safety.

Service Area

We service the Toronto and Greater Toronto Area. We provide service to the airport, universities and hospitals. Special pricing is available on request for trips to areas outside of Toronto.

Reservations

Contact us at (905) 555-5555 for reservations and special pricing.

Classic Taxi • 123 Parliament St. • Toronto • Ontario • (905) 555-5555

Daniel Padavona/Shutterstock.com

Emily likes the first line indent in the paragraphs, and she's thinking the vertical spacing between each line in the paragraphs is a little small. She'd rather see some space between each line in the paragraphs. You can adjust this spacing using the `line-height` property.

PROSKILLS

Written Communication: Designing Printer-Friendly Web Pages

There are many reasons why someone might want to print a Web page. For instance, a Web page can contain the contact information for a business, including the phone number and a map. A Web page might also contain a coupon or a ticket to a show. Therefore, as you design your Web pages, you should keep in mind the fact that users might want to print them. The following considerations can help make your Web pages printer-friendly:

- Use a white or light background, and dark or black text.
- Use a scalable font, so viewers can increase the size of the font if necessary for printing.
- If there is an email address hyperlink on the Web page, make sure the email address is displayed on the Web page.
- Include contact information on the Web page, perhaps in the footer area.
- Avoid animated images, and any other images that are not essential.
- Use the Web browser's print preview feature to see what the printed Web page will look like. This can help you quickly identify any other elements that might need to change in order to be able to read the document.

It's also possible to use the `media` attribute of the `link` element to specify a style sheet that's applied only when a viewer prints the Web page. This is worth looking into if you are designing a Web page that you know the viewers will want to print. In the meantime, design your Web pages with printing in mind.

Adjusting the Line Height

TIP

Many people with cognitive disabilities have trouble reading text that is single spaced. Always use line height of 1.5em or 2.0em so text is easy to read for everyone.

Single-spaced paragraphs can be more difficult to read than paragraphs that are double-spaced. Single and double spacing are examples of **line height**, which is the vertical spacing between lines of text. By default, Web browsers use 1.0em or 1.2em line height. The 1.0em line height spacing is equivalent to single-spaced, and the 2em line height spacing is equivalent to double-spaced. Actually, the optimal spacing for easy reading is 1.5em or 2.0em (double spaced) line height.

The style used to set the space between lines is:

```
line-height: value;
```

where `value` is a value in ems or pixels, or a percentage.

You'll use a line height of 1.5em for the paragraphs so the text is easier to read for most people.

To set the line height for paragraphs:

1. Return to the **taxi_layout.css** file in your text editor.

2. Add the following CSS property to the p style rule, as shown in Figure 3-36:

```
line-height: 1.5em;
```

Figure 3-36   Setting the line-height property

```
p {
      color: saddlebrown;
      line-height: 1.5em;
      text-indent: 3em;
}
```

3. Save the file.

4. Return to your Web browser, and then reload or refresh **index.htm** to view the style changes. The Web page should look similar to Figure 3-37.

Figure 3-37   Paragraphs with increased line spacing

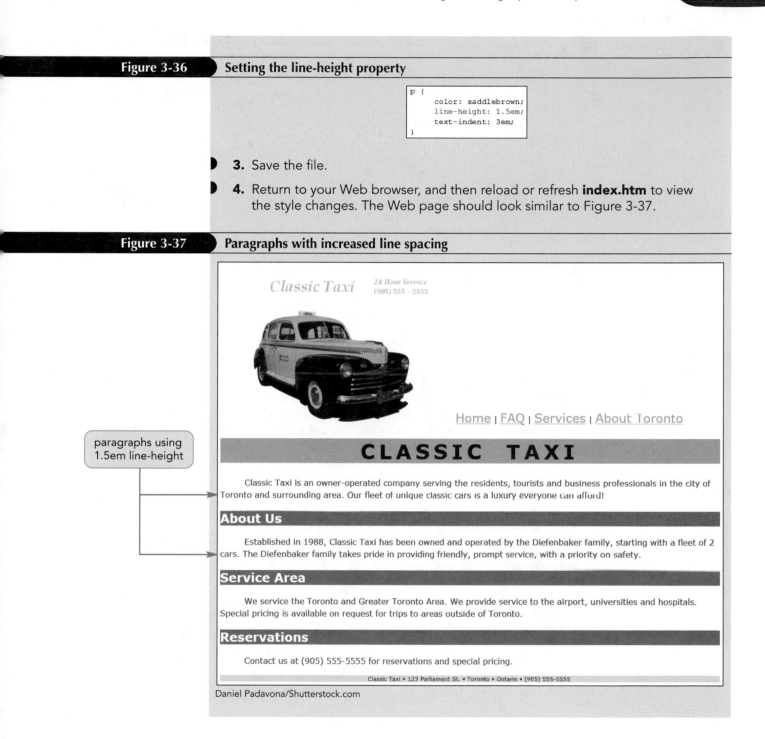

paragraphs using 1.5em line-height

Daniel Padavona/Shutterstock.com

INSIGHT

Using the *font* Shorthand Property

The `font` property is one of several CSS shorthand properties. A **shorthand property** is used to set a related group of properties in one declaration. In this instance, you can set some or all of the font properties in one declaration. For example, you could use the following code to style the `h3` element with a particular font style, weight, size, and family:

```
h3 {
      font-style: italic;
      font-weight: normal;
      font-size: 1.2em;
      font-family: Arial, Helvetica, sans-serif;
}
```

Compare the preceding code to the following, which uses the `font` shorthand property to achieve the same result, but using far less code:

```
h3 {
      font: italic normal 1.2em Arial, Helvetica, sans-serif;
}
```

Here's how the font shorthand property works. You begin by specifying an element as a selector, as you normally would. For the declarations, however, you type the word `font` followed by a colon. Next, you type only the values for font style, font weight, font variant, font size, and font family. You can list as few (or as many) values for the font properties as you want. Property values are separated by spaces, although font list properties are still separated by commas. Using the `font` shorthand property, you can write values for multiple properties with a single declaration, which lets you type substantially less code.

Although you do not have to list values for all five font properties, if you use the font shorthand property, you *must* specify values for both the font size and font family. You must also list the values for the font properties in the following order:

- font style
- font weight
- font variant
- font size
- font family

For example, to specify that an `h3` element should have only a different font style and font weight, you still would have to enter values for the font size and font family, as in the following code:

```
h3 {
      font: italic bold 1em Courier, monospace;
}
```

Text Alignment

Emily would like the text in the h1 heading and in the footer section to be centered horizontally on the Web page. You can use the text-align property to change the alignment of the text, setting the value to one of the following:

- left—Each line of text is flush with the left margin and may be staggered at the right margin.
- right—Each line of text is flush with the right margin and may be staggered at the left margin.
- center—Each line of text is centered horizontally.
- justify—Each line of text is flush with the left and right margins; the Web browser makes adjustments in the word spacing to achieve this effect.

You'll add the text-align property to the h1 and footer style rules to center the text in the h1 heading and the footer area.

To center align the h1 heading and footer text:

1. Return to the **taxi_layout.css** file in your text editor.

2. Add the following CSS property to the h1 and footer style rules, as shown in Figure 3-38:

   ```
   text-align: center;
   ```

| **Figure 3-38** | **Setting the text-align property to center text** |

```
h1 {
        background-color: orange;
        color: black;
        font-size: 2.5em;
        letter-spacing: .2em;
        text-align: center;
        text-transform: uppercase;
        word-spacing: .5em;
}

. . . .

footer {
        color: saddlebrown;
        background-color: palegoldenrod;
        font-size: .7em;
        text-align: center;
}
```

3. Save the file.

4. Return to your Web browser, and then refresh or reload **index.htm** to view the style changes. The Web page should look similar to Figure 3-39.

Figure 3-39 | Displaying the h1 and address text centered horizontally

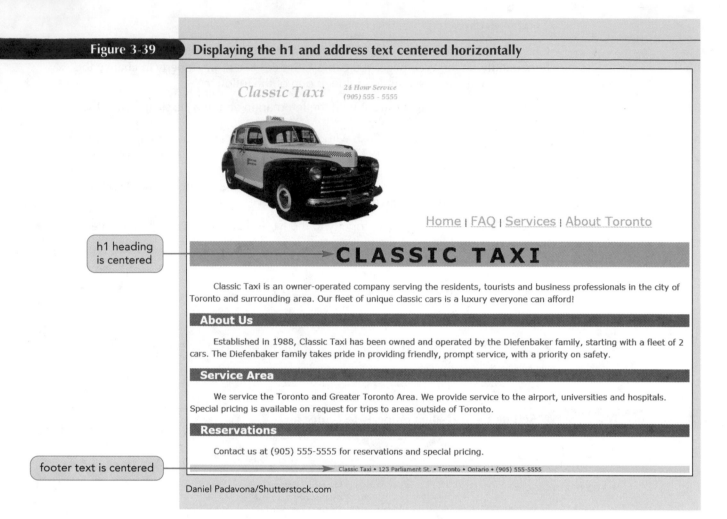

Daniel Padavona/Shutterstock.com

Depending on the Web browser you're using, the footer may not center correctly. Firefox and Internet Explorer 8 may not center the text in the footer correctly.

Removing the Underlines on Links

By default, hyperlinks are underlined. It's important to differentiate links from other text, and the underline does a good job of that. However, these days it's more popular to remove the underline from links and find other ways to make the links stand out from other text. Emily likes the orange color of the links, but she would like you to remove the underline to give the Web site a more current look.

Underline is a text decoration and can be added or removed using the `text-decoration` property. The style used to set the text decoration is:

```
text-decoration: value;
```

where *value* is `none`, `underline`, `overline`, or `line-through`. The following style rule removes underlines from links:

```
a {
    text-decoration: none;
}
```

You've used several different font and text properties including `text-transform` and `font-style`. There are other properties that allow you to apply bold, italic, or small caps. The `font-weight` property sets the heaviness of the text using the values `normal`, `bold`, or `light`. The `font-style` property sets the style to `italic` or removes italic using the value `normal`.

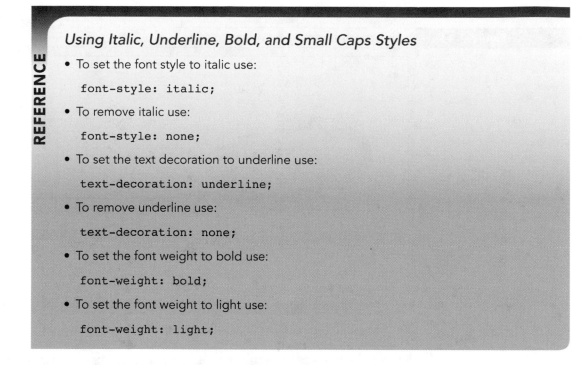

REFERENCE

Using Italic, Underline, Bold, and Small Caps Styles

- To set the font style to italic use:

  `font-style: italic;`

- To remove italic use:

  `font-style: none;`

- To set the text decoration to underline use:

  `text-decoration: underline;`

- To remove underline use:

  `text-decoration: none;`

- To set the font weight to bold use:

  `font-weight: bold;`

- To set the font weight to light use:

  `font-weight: light;`

You'll add the text-decoration property to the **a** style rule to remove the underlines from hyperlinks.

To remove the underlines from links:

1. Return to the **taxi_layout.css** file in your text editor.

2. Add the following CSS property to the **a** style rule, as shown in Figure 3-40:

   `text-decoration: none;`

Figure 3-40	Setting the text-decoration property to none for hyperlinks

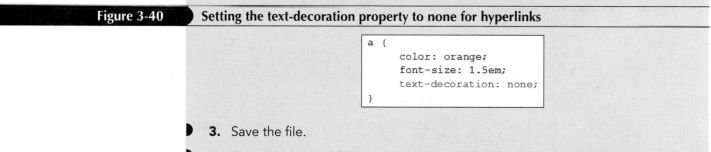

```
a {
        color: orange;
        font-size: 1.5em;
        text-decoration: none;
}
```

3. Save the file.

4. Return to your Web browser, and then refresh or reload **index.htm** to view the style changes. The Web page should look similar to Figure 3-41.

Figure 3-41	Links with text-decoration set to none

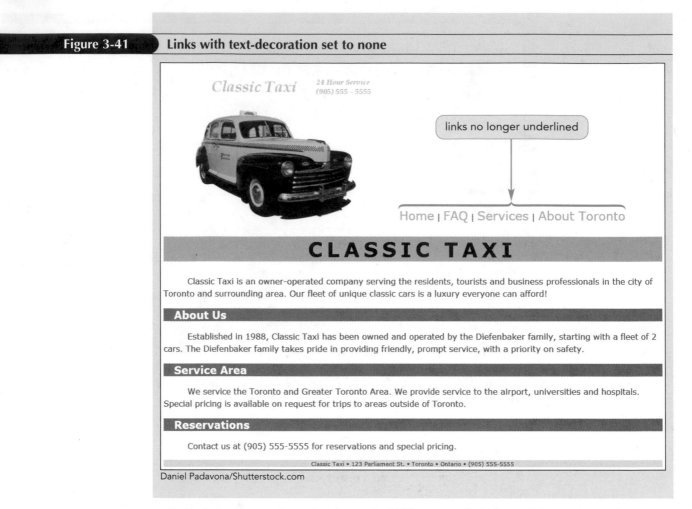

Daniel Padavona/Shutterstock.com

Emily loves the work you've done. She'd like you to link the taxi_layout.css style sheet to all the other Web pages in the Classic Taxi Web site. You'll use the `link` element to link the external style sheet to the Web page and apply all the styles to the Web page.

To link the external style sheet:

▶ 1. Open the **faq.htm** file in your text editor.

▶ 2. Above the `title` element, insert the following `link` element as shown in Figure 3-42:

```
<link href = "taxi_layout.css" rel = "stylesheet" type =
"text/css" />
```

Figure 3-42   Inserting the link element in each Web page

```
<!--
      Tutorial 3
      Author: Your Name
      Date: Today's date
-->
<script src="modernizr-2.js"></script>

<link href = "taxi_layout.css" rel = "stylesheet" type = "text/css" />

<title>Classic Taxi - FAQ</title>
</head>
```

3. Save the file.

4. Repeat Steps 2 and 3 for the files **services.htm** and **toronto.htm**.

5. Return to **index.htm** in your Web browser, and then navigate through Emily's Classic Taxi Web site. Verify that the styles from the style sheet have been applied to the other Web pages in the site. Figure 3-43 shows the faq.htm Web page.

Figure 3-43   FAQ Web page displaying styles

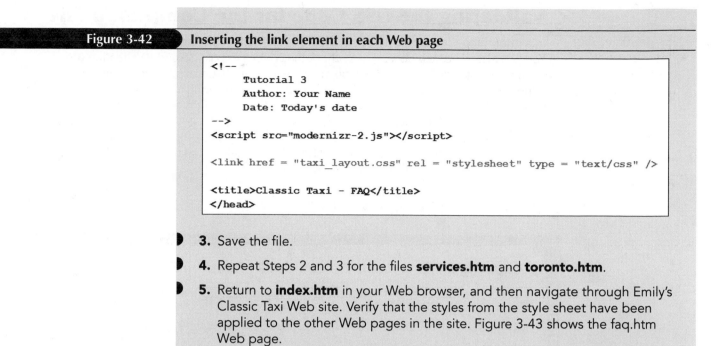

Daniel Padavona/Shutterstock.com

Validating the CSS Code for the Completed File

In a prior tutorial, you validated a document to check the correctness of the HTML code. You can also validate a document to check the correctness of CSS code. Validating CSS code does not check for spelling, typographical, or grammar errors; it checks only to see if the code complies with a given CSS standard. While validating a file for CSS code is optional, it can help to point out errors in the CSS that you might not catch by looking at the code. Note that extended color names may not validate, and you may need to use hex values instead if you want your code to validate. The validating service to check CSS code is not the same one used to check HTML code. The W3C maintains a free CSS code validator service at http://jigsaw.w3.org/css-validator.

Validating a File for CSS Code

REFERENCE

Validating a File to See if the CSS Code Meets the Standard

- Open your browser and navigate to http://jigsaw.w3.org/css-validator.
- If necessary, click the By file upload tab.
- Click the Browse button or the Choose File button, and then navigate to the storage location of the file to be validated.
- Double-click the filename to enter it in the Local CSS file text box.
- Click the Check button.

On the W3C CSS validation page, you'll see two methods for validating a document that has not been posted to a Web server: *By file upload* and *By direct input*. When you choose *By file upload*, you navigate to the storage location of the file you want to validate and then you click the Check button. If you choose *By direct input*, you copy and paste (or type) the code into the text box on the validation page, and then click the Check button. The *By direct input* method is generally used when you want to check just a few lines of code—often called a **code snippet**—rather than an entire document. You'll validate the tax_layout.htm file by using the By file upload method.

To validate the taxi_layout.css file:

1. Open your browser, and navigate to **http://jigsaw.w3.org/css-validator**.

The W3C CSS Validation Service site opens, as shown in Figure 3-44.

Figure 3-44 W3C CSS Validator Web page

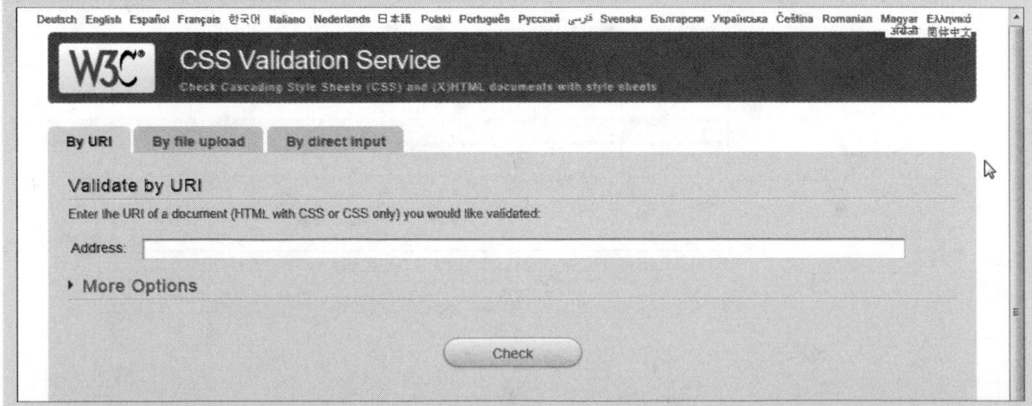

2. If necessary, click the **By file upload** tab.

3. Click the **Browse** or **Choose File** button.

4. Navigate to the storage location of your taxi_layout.css file.

5. Double-click the **taxi_layout.css** filename to insert it in the Local CSS file box.

6. Click the **Check** button. The document validation results are shown in Figure 3-45.

Figure 3-45   **CSS validation results**

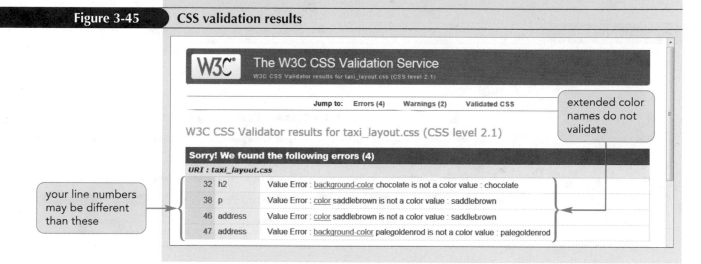

The extended color names do not validate, but other than that, the CSS code is valid. CSS extended color names are not officially recognized by the W3C as part of the CSS3 standard. They are adopted widely by Web browsers, but not part of the official standard.

Emily loves the work you've done with the Classic Taxi Web site. She particularly likes the external style sheet because in the future she'll be able to change styles in the external style sheet and see them reflected on all Web pages that are linked to it.

Session 3.2 Quick Check

REVIEW

1. What's the difference between an absolute unit of measurement and a relative unit of measurement? Provide an example of each.
2. What property can be used to add or remove underlining?
3. What property can be used to change the font?
4. What property can be used to apply bold to text?
5. What are the five generic fonts?

Review Assignments

**Data Files needed for the Review Assignments: planner_T3.htm, modernizr-2.js,
images\planner.jpg**

Emily has asked you to make another page for her Web site. She'd like a different style
rather than using the same external style sheet. Classic Taxi has been aggressively marketing its expanding travel services, and Emily would like you to create a page that describes
the features of these services. A preview of the Web page appears in Figure 3-46.

Figure 3-46	Completed Planner Web page

Get the Classic Taxi Planner

Classic Taxi is proud to announce its new travel planning service. Let Classic Taxi plan your next personal, family, or business trip anywhere throughout the nation or the world.
We have access to thousands of hotel reviews and research. We know when you should visit these hotels to get the best price. We know what rooms to stay based on your
travel needs. If you need just a place to sleep and don't care much about the room amenities, we've got the complete list of rooms in each hotel that will match even the tightest
budget. If you are looking for a hotel that will provide you with the pampering you need, we'll let you know where to stay on your next trip.

Attractions

Once you've arrived at your destination, do you want to know what the most popular attractions are? Of course, you do, but we'll give you the traveler's edge and get you into
those popular attractions at the lowest possible cost. Not sure if an attraction is right for you?; Let our travel planners walk you through the full itinerary of activities so you can
decide for yourself how best to spend your travel time and travel dollars. **Get the best vacation or travel experience you can at the lowest price possible**.

Car Rentals

Need a car to get around? We'll get you the best rates on car rentals. You'll never pay for unnecessary booking or insurance fees. We'll get you the right car at the perfect price
so that you can spend your time at your destination driving in comfort and with ease. Looking just for transportation to and from an airport at your travel destination? We'll get
you from the airport to your business meeting or your hotel swiftly, safely, and economically. If you need a van for several passengers in your group, we can arrange for that as
well. There will be plenty of room for you and your passengers as you make your debut in your destination city.

Travel Advice

Are you new to the travel scene? We'll give you the advice that others won't. We can advise you on what to eat and drink and also what foods to avoid at your travel destination,
especially if you are traveling to foreign lands. We will get you U.S. Passport services and give you travel warnings and consulate information for your destination country. We'll
also tell you where to find and get medical help if you need to should an emergency arise. We have travel guides for every business traveler so that your business trip is a
successful one.

Restaurant Finder and Guide

Of course, no trip would be complete without visiting the restaurants of the region. We'll tell you which restaurants give you the best value and best price so that you can have
an enjoyable dining experience no matter what region or what country you are visiting.

Most Popular Destinations from Toronto

1. Montreal
2. New York City
3. Vancouver
4. Chicago
5. Quebec City
6. Calgary
7. Dallas
8. Los Angeles
9. Orlando
10. Myrtle Beach

Call 905 555-TRIP

iQoncept/Shutterstock.com

Although you will not be instructed to do so after each step, you should do the following whenever you enter code to create a style in your text editor: Save the file, switch to your browser, refresh or reload the page, verify that you entered the style code correctly, and then switch back to your text editor to continue with the next step.

Complete the following:

1. Use your text editor to open the file **planner_T3.htm**, which is provided in your Data Files in the tutorial3\review folder. Save the file as **planner.htm** in the same folder.

2. Between the `<title></title>` tags, type **Classic Taxi Planner**.

3. In the head section below the page title, enter *your name* and *today's date* in the comment section where noted.

4. In the head section, below the comment, enter the start `<style>` tag, along with the required attribute and its value, and then enter the end `</style>` tag on a separate line.

5. Between the start and end `<style>` tags, press the **Enter** key three times to create some white space.

6. In the embedded style sheet code, create a style for the `h1` element so h1 text appears in **navy** and is centered horizontally.

7. Style the `h2` element so the text is **teal** and the background color is **orange**.

8. Style the `h2` element so the text is centered horizontally.

9. Specify a style so the `ol` element text appears in **green**.

10. Specify a style so the `strong` element text appears in **maroon**.

11. Specify a `body` style rule so all text on the Web page is in an **Arial**, **Helvetica**, or other **sans-serif** font and double-spaced.

12. Save the **planner.htm** file, and then open the file in your browser.

13. Submit the completed file to your instructor in either printed or electronic form, as requested.

APPLY

Case Problem 1

Data Files needed for this Case Problem: wireless_T3.htm, modernizr-2.js, images\ wirelesslogo.jpg

Take It Away Wireless   Take It Away Wireless is a small startup company near Mexico City, Mexico. They provide general network solutions for wireless home and commercial networks. They also sell Bluetooth devices for hands-free data entry or mobile device use. You will create a Web page that introduces their wireless services. Because this is the first Web page of a Web site that will be expanding the number of total Web pages, you'll create a document with an external style sheet and link this style sheet to the Web page. A preview of the Web page appears in Figure 3-47.

Figure 3-47   Completed Take It Away Wireless Web page

Take It Away Wireless for Your Office

Take It Away Wireless is your best place for your wireless needs. Need a wireless network installed in your home or business? We can do that. Need a GPS system for a fleet of company cars or just need one for your own personal automobile? We can do that, too. Take It Away Wireless *offers the lowest prices* of *anyone* in the Mexico City area. We won't be beat.

Take It Away Wireless for Your Home

Take It Away Wireless specializes in residential wireless networks. We'll take care of all your wireless connections, including choosing the best *Bluetooth products* for your home office. We will keep you connected and we will do so at the lowest cost in town.

Take It Away Security for Your Network

Take It Away Wireless will install a secure network for your home office. No need to worry about someone accessing your personal or work files without your permission. We will secure your network.

There's no need to worry about viruses or unauthorized people accessing your network. Let us do the worrying for you. We will monitor and log all traffic and provide weekly reports.

**CONTACT US RIGHT NOW
1-800-764-WIRE**

iconmonstr/Shutterstock.com

Although you will not be instructed to do so after each step, you should do the following whenever you enter code to create a style in your text editor: Save the file, switch to your browser, refresh or reload the page, verify that you entered the style code correctly, and then switch back to your text editor to continue with the next step.

Complete the following:

1. Use your text editor to open the file named **wireless_T3.htm**, which is provided in your Data Files in the tutorial3\case1 folder. Save the file as **wireless.htm** in the same folder.
2. Between the `<title></title>` tags, type **Take It Away Wireless**.
3. In the head section, below the page title, enter *your name* and *today's date* in the comment section where noted.
4. In the head section, below the comment, enter the code to link to a style sheet named **wireless_layout.css**.
5. Save the **wireless.htm** file, and open it in your Web browser.
6. Open a new file in the text editor, and save it as **wireless_layout.css**.
7. Create an appropriate comment block in the wireless_layout.css file that contains *your name* and *the date*.

8. Create a style for the `body` element so text on the Web page appears in a font size of **1.2em** and in **Arial**, which is a sans-serif font. Also format the `body` element to have a background color of **#e6e6fa**.

9. Add a style to make emphasized text appear in **green** and **bold**.

10. Add a style to make `h3` headings appear in **maroon**, with all **uppercase** letters, aligned to the **right**, and a font size of **1.3em**, and in the **Times** or **Times New Roman** font, which are serif fonts.

11. Save the **wireless.htm** and **wireless_layout.css** files.

12. In your Web browser, open the wireless.htm Web page to ensure the styles have been rendered.

13. Submit the completed file to your instructor in either printed or electronic form, as requested.

Use the skills you learned in the tutorial to create a Web page for a record company.

APPLY

Case Problem 2

Data Files needed for this Case Problem: record_T3.htm, modernizr-2.js, images\recordlogo.jpg

Bremtone Vinyl Records   Bremtone Vinyl Records is a Duluth, Minnesota, company that is capitalizing on the resurgence of the popularity of vinyl records. With tens of thousands of vinyl records in stock, Bremtone has a wide variety of titles to offer its customers. Bremtone also sells phonographs, record needles, speakers, and other vinyl record accessories. You have been asked to design a Web page for Bremtone records. A preview of the Web page appears in Figure 3-48.

Although you will not be instructed to do so after each step, you should do the following whenever you enter code to create a style in your text editor: Save the file, switch to your browser, refresh or reload the page, verify that you entered the style code correctly, and then switch back to your text editor to continue with the next step.

Complete the following:

1. Use your text editor to open the file **record_T3.htm**, which is provided in your Data Files in the tutorial3\case2 folder. Save the file as **record.htm** in the same folder.

2. Between the `<title></title>` tags, type **Bremtone Vinyl Records**.

3. In the head section, below the page title, enter ***your name*** and ***today's date*** in the comment section where noted.

4. In the head section, below the comment, enter code to link to a style sheet named **record_layout.css**.

5. Save the **record.htm** file, and open it in your Web browser.

6. Open a new file in your text editor, and then save it as **record_layout.css**.

7. Create an appropriate comment block in the *record_layout.css* file that contains ***your name*** and ***the date***.

8. Create a style for the `body` element so text on the Web page appears in **Verdana**, which is a sans-serif font. Also format the `body` element to have a background color of **#c0e59b**.

9. Add a style to center the text in the `h1` element horizontally.

10. Add a style to make the `h2` text appear in **navy**.

11. Add a style to make the `h3` element appear in **bold**, **navy** text.

12. Add a style to indent all paragraph text **5em** and use **1.5em** line height.

13. Add a style to make the `h4` element appear in all **uppercase**, **italic**, **maroon**.

14. Save the **record_layout.css** files.

Figure 3-48 **Completed Bremtone Records Web page**

Welcome to Bremtone Records

Your One Stop for All Things Vinyl

Bremtone is your one stop if you are seeking the pure, true sound of recordings etched on vinyl. There's nothing like the experience of hearing your favorite artists perform in their authentic sound. If you like the sound of music the way it was and the way it can be today, we urge you to contact us today.

POPULAR FORMATS WE STOCK

- 12" (30 cm) / 33 1/3 rpm LP
- 7" (17.5 cm) / 45 rpm EP or Single
- 10" (25 cm)/ 45 rpm LP and 12" (30 cm) / 33 1/3 rpm LP
- 12" (30 cm) / 33 or 45 rpm Maxi Single

Genres We Stock

We have many formats for you to choose from.

- Blues
- Big Band
- Classical
- Country
- Rap
- Dance
- Techno
- Eurosynth
- R&B (especially from the 1950's and 60's)
- Pop (dating back to the 1940's to the present date)

Accessories

We have all types of accessories for you to purchase to enhance your listening experience. We carry a full line of turntables, speakers, woofers, and tweeters. We have every type of cable you will need. We also have an exhaustive collection of turntable cartridges and needles. We carry a full line of protective sleeve jackets and vertical racks so that you can properly store your recordings. We also have an extensive selection of books and magazines about the vinyl listening experience. We also service and repair turntables.

Handling

You'll get the most enjoyment from your vinyl recordings if you use the proper care. Avoid touching the playing surface of any record. Handle the record on its side edges only. Don't leave your records in a horizontal position. When you are not playing a record, store the record in a vertical position in a record rack in its protective sleeve. Don't use a plastic or metal rack to store your records unless you have placed the record first in its protective sleeve.

Cleaning

Clean your disks frequently, particularly after you have played a recording. You want to ensure there is no damage from dust and static, and you want to make sure that you will be storing your disks safely as well. We stock a wide variety of cleaning materials and cloths for eliminating dust and static from your records. Above all, do not use tap water, which might contain harmful minerals and chemicals, to clean your records. Use either spring water or a water-based solution that contains not more than 20% isopropyl alcohol. Cleaning solutions are very effective at removing dust, dirt, and other contaminants that the record may have encountered, especially during the handling process. Clean the disk in the direction of the grooves, never against the direction of the grooves, which might cause tiny particles from the cleaning cloth to collect on the recording surface.

Storage

You want to get the longest life from your records, so the proper storage of your records is key to maintaining the enjoyment of your records for years to come. Consider the temperature and humidity of the room where you will be storing your records. Store your records in an environment that will be heated in winter and cooled during the summer. Don't store your records in an attic or a garage, where temperature extremes might cause warping or other damage to the record. An environment of 60-70 degrees is best, and humidity in the range of 33-50%. You don't want your records being damaged by heat or humidity. Never store your records where there is any exposure to sunlight. Also be mindful of other room factors that might affect the heat level next to the disks, such as heaters, vents, air conditioners, and lighting. Avoid dusty environments such as an attic or basement. Keep your recordings (vertically) in an airtight container, a cabinet with doors, or a sealable box. If your home or apartment has an open-floor layout, be mindful that smoke and cooking greases from the kitchen or outdoor barbeques can affect your records as well.

Special Artists in Vinyl This Month

1964

The Four Seasons, the Beach Boys, the Four Tops, the Supremes, the Beatles, the Rolling Stones, Gerry and the Pacemakers, the Searchers, Little Anthony and the Imperials, Martha and the Vandellas, Dusty Springfield, the Animals, Herman's Hermits, Manfred Mann, and Neil Diamond.

1967

The Doors, Sly and the Family Stone, the Beatles, the Rolling Stones, the Lovin' Spoonful, the Young Rascals, Jefferson Airplane, Pink Floyd, the Who, Chicago, the Jimi Hendrix Experience, the Monkees, the Mommas and the Poppas, Nancy Sinatra, the Turtles, Mitch Ryder and the Detroit Wheels, Sonny and Cher, the Spencer Davis Group, and Donovan.

This represents only a partial list of genres.

15. Return to your Web browser, and refresh or reload the record.htm Web page to ensure the styles have been rendered.

16. Submit the completed file to your instructor in either printed or electronic form, as requested.

Use what you've learned to create a Web site for a global shipping company

APPLY

Case Problem 3

Data Files needed for this Case Problem: contact_T3.htm, gild_T3.htm, modernizr-2. js, images\gildlogo.jpg

Gild Shipping   Gild Shipping is one of the world's largest container freight shipping companies. With its corporate headquarters in San Diego, California, Gild Shipping transports container freight to every country in the Pacific Rim region. Gild Shipping does much of its business with companies in India and along the east coast of Africa. Phillip Green, the marketing director, has approached you to redesign the Gild Shipping home page. Phillip wants a simple page that will download quickly and explain what Gild Shipping can do for its customers. A preview of the Web page appears in Figure 3-49.

Figure 3-49   **Gild Shipping Web page displaying styles**

Gild Shipping -- Your Global Source for Supply

Japan / Pacific Rim / China / Australia / India / East Africa

Thank you for visiting the Gild Shipping Web site. We offer our customers the best service at competitive rates. We have over 45 years of experience in shipping to all areas within the Pacific region. We ship to Japan, China, Korea, the Philippines, Indonesia, Singapore, Australia, New Zealand, India, and to most nations on the eastern coast of Africa. We serve the needs of both business and individual customers. We also ship to Hawaii from all of the western United States, western Canada and Alaska. We specialize in overseas shipping of all types of personal effects, household goods, and commercial cargos to and from the United States. We do not ship hazardous materials or oil. Our minimum shipment charge for individuals is $500. We can handle almost any size shipment. We specialize in moving personal items to and from the continental United States and Hawaii and to all areas of the Pacific Rim, including American Samoa and Guam.

Before You Ship

1. Complete the Instruction Sheet, print and sign it.
2. Send the completed and signed Instruction Sheet to us as an e-mail attachment or fax it to 918 455-3455.
3. For personal items, list all items that are being shipped.
4. For personal items, list an approximate value for each item.
5. For commercial shipments, provide the commercial invoice.
6. Upon receipt of all necessary documents, we will contact you by e-mail or phone to make shipping arrangements.

We Keep You Afloat

Our GildPak system can handle almost any size shipment from small boxes to full container loads. We handle all the details. We book your cargo, make the arrangements for pick up and delivery, and we take care of all necessary paperwork. Our GPS system uses RFID technology to keep track of where your cargo is at all times. We will alert you if conditions change because of inclement weather at sea that might result in a shipping delay. We handle all of the shipping requirements and documentation for both the import and export countries; you don't have to worry about any of the paperwork. We handle all the details from the smallest to the largest.

We Keep You on Time

Our fleet is comprised of both midsize and supersize vessels that can match the size of your cargo and the degree to which you need your shipment expedited. You won't pay extra for a service that you don't need. If you need your shipment expedited, and assuming your cargo is capable of being transported by air, we can arrange for an expedited delivery by combining sea cargo with air freight to produce a delivery mechanism that is not cost prohibitive. Let the largest leg of your journey take place at sea, and then call for expedited jet service once your cargo had been unloaded at its port of call.

We Offer the Following Competitive Features

- Frequent and reliable cargo schedules from major Pacific and Indian Ocean ports
- Advanced GPS cargo tracking
- Secure storage
- Unparalleled safety
- Port-to-Port or door-to-door service
- Alerts -- should your cargo be delayed in transit for any reason
- Competitive pricing

FOR MORE INFORMATION, CALL 1 877 223-SHIP.

Contact Us

mmaxer/Shutterstock.com

Although you will not be instructed to do so after each step, you should do the following whenever you enter code to create a style in your text editor: Save the file, switch to your browser, refresh or reload the page, verify that you entered the style code correctly, and then switch back to your text editor to continue with the next step.

Complete the following:

1. Use your text editor to open the file **gild_T3.htm**, which is provided in your Data Files in the tutorial3\case3 folder. Save the file as **gild.htm** in the same folder.

2. In the head section, below the page title, enter *your name* and *today's date* in the comment section where noted.

3. In the head section, below the comment, enter the code to link to a style sheet named **shipping_layout.css**.

4. Save the **gild.htm** file, and open it in your Web browser.

5. Open a new file in the text editor, and save it as **shipping_layout.css**.

6. Create an appropriate comment block in the shipping_layout.css file that contains *your name* and *the date*.

7. Style the `body` element so text on the Web page appears in a font size of **1.1em** and in **Arial** or **Helvetica**, which are sans-serif fonts. Also format the `body` element to have a background color of **#c19b76**.

8. Create a style for the `h1` element so the text appears in **italic**, does not appear in bold, has a font size of **150%**, and is in **Cooper Black**, which is a serif font.

9. Style both the `h2` and `h3` heading text to appear in **white** with a background color of **teal**.

10. Style the `h4` element so text is styled in small caps.

11. Style the **em** element so the text will appear in **green** and **boldest**. The `em` text should not appear in italics.

12. In your text editor, open the **contact_T3.htm** file, which is provided in your Data Files in the tutorial3/case3 folder. Save the file as **contact.htm** in the same folder.

13. Return to the **gild.htm** file in your text editor. At the bottom of the page and between the `<p></p>` tags, type **Contact Us**, and create a link to the Web page **contact.htm**.

14. Style the link so the text is **1.5em**, **bold**, **teal** color, without an underline.

15. Return to the **contact.htm** file in your text editor. In the head section, below the page title, enter *your name* and *today's date* in the comment section where noted.

16. In the head section, below the comment, enter the code to link to the **shipping_layout.css** style sheet.

17. Open the **contact.htm** file in the Web browser to see the styles displayed.

18. Return to your Web browser and refresh or reload the **gild.htm** Web page to ensure the styles have been rendered. Click the link for the **contact.htm** file to ensure it works properly.

19. Submit the completed file to your instructor in either printed or electronic form, as requested.

Create a file for a campus library that will be a center for international education.

Case Problem 4

Data Files needed for this Case Problem: slake_T3.htm, modernizr-2.js, images\ slakelogo.jpg

Slake College Library of International Education   Slake College is located near Chicago, Illinois, a city that prides itself as being culturally diverse. Slake College wants to construct a new campus library of international education that celebrates the ethnic mosaic that exists in Chicago. Slake College has been gathering ideas from its student body about what type of building to construct and what the library should offer its students and the city in general. Write at least five paragraphs about what books, DVDs, computers, and periodicals you think the library should have. What types of multimedia should the library have? What types of events should be held in the library? What sort of dining facilities or shops should it have? Should it have special rooms such as classrooms, a concert hall, a theatre, lecture halls, a conference center, or a ballroom? Complete the following:

1. Use your text editor to open the file named **slake_T3.htm** that is provided in your Data Files in the tutorial3\case4 folder. Save the file as **slake.htm** in the same folder.

2. Within the title tags, type **Slake College Library of International Education**.

3. In the head section, below the page title, enter ***your name*** and ***today's date*** in the comment section where noted.

4. In the head section, enter the code to create an embedded style sheet.

5. In the body section, enter the code for the following:
    * A comment
    * The h1, h2, and h3 headings
    * The slakelogo.jpg image (available in the images folder)
    * Four paragraphs of content
    * At least one special character
    * The em element
    * The strong element
    * An unordered or ordered list
    * A superscript or subscript
    * An abbreviation (create a ScreenTip for this abbreviation)
    * A link to an external Web site that has information about studying abroad

6. In the embedded style sheet, create styles for your Web page. The styles are up to you, but at a minimum, you should include a style rule to set one or more properties for each of the following elements:
    * p
    * h1, h2, and h3 (change the color and background color for at least one of the headings)
    * em
    * strong
    * li

7. Save **slake.htm**, and then open the file in your browser.

8. Submit the completed file to your instructor in either printed or electronic form, as requested.

ENDING DATA FILES

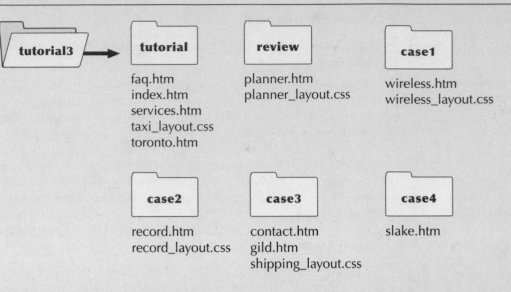

tutorial3 → tutorial

faq.htm
index.htm
services.htm
taxi_layout.css
toronto.htm

review

planner.htm
planner_layout.css

case1

wireless.htm
wireless_layout.css

case2

record.htm
record_layout.css

case3

contact.htm
gild.htm
shipping_layout.css

case4

slake.htm

OBJECTIVES

Session 4.1
- Specify the vertical alignment of an element
- Define list styles
- Implement grouped selectors
- Incorporate descendant selectors
- Style a list as a navigation bar

Session 4.2
- Work with dependent and independent classes
- Set an image as a list marker
- Create dynamic pseudo-classes

Formatting Text and Links

Creating a Career Fair Web Page

Case | *Joseph Brant Community College Job Fair*

Jeff Cooper works in the job center at Joseph Brant Community College (JBCC) and is organizing a career fair. JBCC is located in Toledo, Ohio, and offers a mixture of technology, business, and apprenticeship programs. Jeff has been working at JBCC for 5 years. He has been establishing relationships with the employers in Toledo and the surrounding area, including eastern Michigan. The first Career Fair at JBCC was held last year, and it was a tremendous success. Jeff would like to improve the marketing for the Career Fair this year by using a Web page to advertise the event and to offer tips for students who plan to attend. He has created the Career Fair Web page and would like you to add CSS to stylize it. The JBCC main Web site is outdated, and Jeff hopes that your style sheet for the Career Fair Web page could potentially be used for the rest of the JBCC Web site as well.

STARTING DATA FILES

tutorial

career_T4.htm
college_logo_sm.jpg
green_checkmark_sm.jpg
modernizr-2.js

review

josephbrant_T4.htm
modernizr-2.js
red_square.jpg

case1

berger_T4.htm
bergerlogo.jpg
modernizr-2.js

case2

modernizr-2.js
womensweb_T4.htm
wwlogo.jpg

case3

diamond.gif
energy.jpg
modernizr-2.js
power_T4.htm

case4

donate_T4.htm
modernizr-2.js

SESSION 4.1 VISUAL OVERVIEW

```
nav li {
    display: inline;
    list-style-type: none;
    padding-right: 40px;
}
```

Setting the display property to inline places li elements beside each other.

Setting padding-right to 40px adds space after each li.

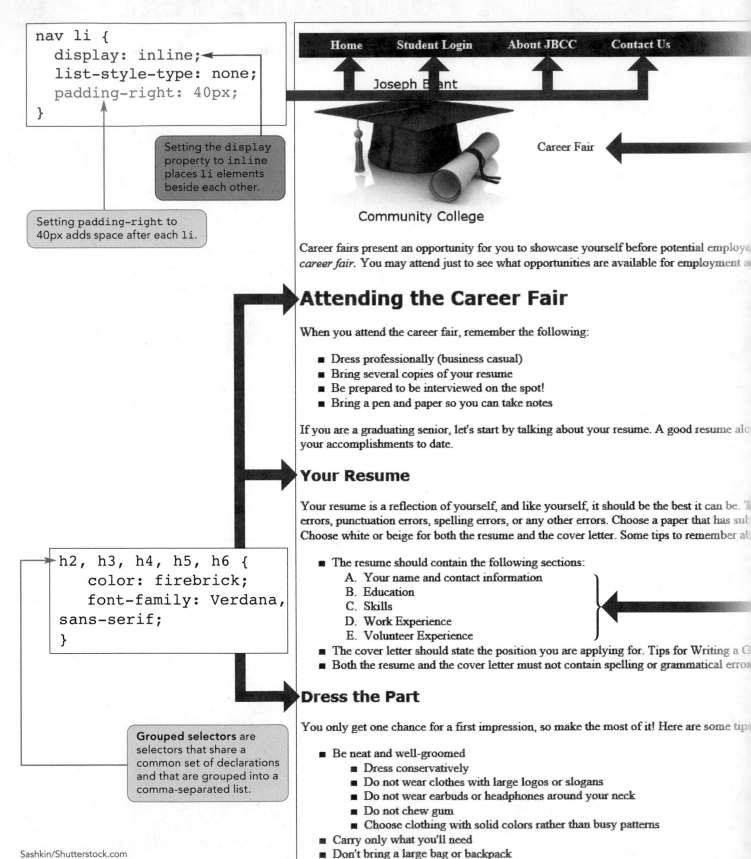

Home   Student Login   About JBCC   Contact Us

Joseph Brant

Community College

Career Fair

Career fairs present an opportunity for you to showcase yourself before potential employe *career fair*. You may attend just to see what opportunities are available for employment a

Attending the Career Fair

When you attend the career fair, remember the following:

- Dress professionally (business casual)
- Bring several copies of your resume
- Be prepared to be interviewed on the spot!
- Bring a pen and paper so you can take notes

If you are a graduating senior, let's start by talking about your resume. A good resume alc your accomplishments to date.

Your Resume

Your resume is a reflection of yourself, and like yourself, it should be the best it can be. T errors, punctuation errors, spelling errors, or any other errors. Choose a paper that has sul Choose white or beige for both the resume and the cover letter. Some tips to remember at

- The resume should contain the following sections:
  - A. Your name and contact information
  - B. Education
  - C. Skills
  - D. Work Experience
  - E. Volunteer Experience
- The cover letter should state the position you are applying for. Tips for Writing a G
- Both the resume and the cover letter must not contain spelling or grammatical error

```
h2, h3, h4, h5, h6 {
    color: firebrick;
    font-family: Verdana,
sans-serif;
}
```

Grouped selectors are selectors that share a common set of declarations and that are grouped into a comma-separated list.

Dress the Part

You only get one chance for a first impression, so make the most of it! Here are some tip

- Be neat and well-groomed
  - Dress conservatively
  - Do not wear clothes with large logos or slogans
  - Do not wear earbuds or headphones around your neck
  - Do not chew gum
  - Choose clothing with solid colors rather than busy patterns
- Carry only what you'll need
- Don't bring a large bag or backpack

GROUPED AND DEPENDENT SELECTORS

ntact Us

The vertical-align property aligns the image with the text.

```
img {
    vertical-align: middle;
}
```

A **descendant selector** is a selector nested within another selector.

before potential employers. *You do not have to be in your graduating year to attend the* ilable for employment after you graduate.

```
p em {
    color: firebrick;
}
```

ume. A good resume alone won't get you the job, but it should – in one page – sum up

d be the best it can be. There is absolutely no room in your resume for typographical oose a paper that has substantial weight; don't type your resume on copying paper. ome tips to remember about the resume and the cover letter:

The list-style-type property sets the marker type for the list.

```
ol {
    list-style-type: upper-alpha;
}
```

for. Tips for Writing a Good Cover Letter ing or grammatical errors.

of it! Here are some tips for a great first impression:

k

tterns

Aligning an Image with Text

You meet with Jeff to discuss the design of the Career Fair Web page. Jeff would like a simple design that uses the colors from the JBCC logo for a professional look. He would also like the JBCC links to appear horizontally as a navigation bar at the top of the Web page. He really likes the look of a white hyperlink on a black background, and he has seen this style on many Web pages. He gives you the Career Fair Web page he has created, along with the JBCC logo. You'll view Jeff's Web page in your Web browser now, recognizing that it will be displayed using the Web browser's default styles.

To open the Career Fair Web page:

▶ **1.** Open the **career_T4.htm** file in your text editor. Enter **your name** and **today's date** in the comment section of the file, and save it as **career.htm**.

▶ **2.** Take a few minutes to view the content and structure of the career.htm file in your text editor.

▶ **3.** Open the **career.htm** file in your Web browser. Figure 4-1 shows the current layout and content.

Figure 4-1	Part of the Career Fair Web page

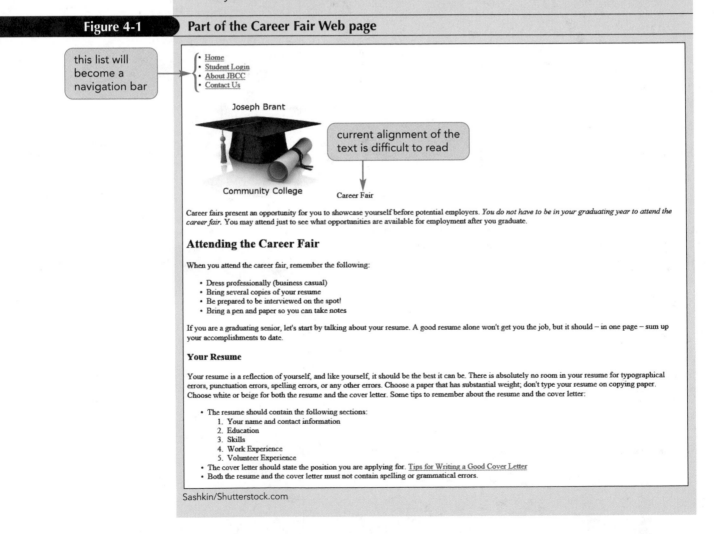

Sashkin/Shutterstock.com

Using the `vertical-align` Property

Jeff would like to make a few changes to the words *Career Fair* beside the logo, starting with aligning it vertically in the middle of the logo. At the moment, the text aligns with the lower edge of the logo.

You can use the `vertical-align` property to position images and other elements vertically with text. The `vertical-align` property has several possible values, but the following are the most common:

- **top**—The top of the image is aligned with the text.
- **middle**—The image is aligned vertically centered with the text.
- **bottom**—The bottom of the image is aligned with the text.

The effects of these values for the `vertical-align` property are shown in Figure 4-2.

Figure 4-2	Vertical alignment

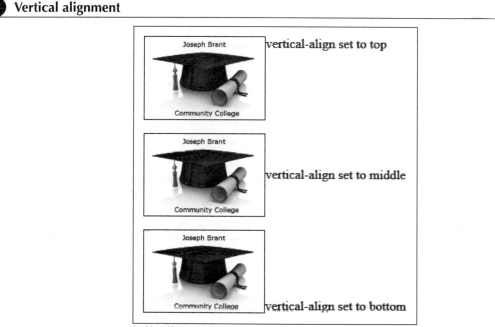

Sashkin/Shutterstock.com

If you want to vertically align the text in the middle of the image, you use the `img` selector and define a rule for vertical alignment as follows:

```
img {
    vertical-align: middle;
}
```

Some additional values for the `vertical-align` property are listed in the table in Figure 4-3.

Figure 4-3	Vertical-align property values

Value	Description
percent%	Raises or lowers an element by a percent of the line-height property, specified by *percent*; negative values are allowed.
baseline	The default value; places the element on the baseline (the bottom) of the parent element.
bottom	Aligns the bottom of the element with the lowest element on the line.
length	Raises or lowers an element by *length*; negative values are allowed.
middle	Places the element in the middle of the parent element.
sub	Aligns the element as a subscript.
super	Aligns the element as a superscript.
text-bottom	Aligns the bottom of the element with the bottom of the parent element's font.
text-top	Aligns the top of the element with the top of the parent element's font.

You'll start adding styles to the Career Fair Web page by adding a style rule that will align the *Career Fair* text vertically in the middle, next to the JBCC logo image. Since you're not planning on applying these styles to additional Web pages at this time, you'll create the style rules in an embedded style sheet.

To vertically align text beside an image:

1. Return to the **career.htm** file in your text editor.

2. After the comment block that contains your name and the date, insert the following code as shown in Figure 4-4:

```
<style type = "text/css">

        img {
                vertical--align: middle;
        }

</style>
```

Figure 4-4	Style rule for the img selector

```
<!--
        Tutorial 4
        Author: Your Name
        Date: Today's date
-->

<style type = "text/css">

        img {
                vertical-align: middle;
        }

</style>
```

3. Save the file.

4. Return to your Web browser, and then click the **Refresh** or **Reload** button to view the style changes in the file. The Web page should look similar to Figure 4-5.

| **Figure 4-5** | **Career Fair text aligned to the middle of the logo image** |

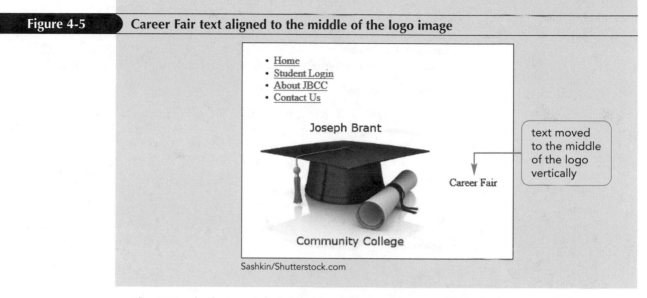

Sashkin/Shutterstock.com

The CSS rule that you've defined for the `img` selector will apply the vertical alignment value to all `img` elements in the Web page. In this case, you have only one image.

Changing the Appearance of Lists

Jeff would like the lists to stand out a bit more. He would like you to change the symbol used for the bullet in the unordered lists from a filled-in circle to a square. He would also like you to change the numbering system for the ordered list. He doesn't like the numeric style and would prefer to use alphabetic characters (A, B, C) instead.

Lists can also be enhanced by graphics and images, using the `list-style-type`, `list-style-position`, and `list-style-image` properties.

Setting List Properties

- To specify the format of a list, enter the following code:

```
ul {
        list-style-property: value;
}
```

where *list-style-property* is list-style-type, list-style-position, or list-style-image.

- To change the bullet type, the numbering, or the lettering for a list, use the code:

```
list-style-type: stylevalue;
```

where *stylevalue* is disc, circle, square, decimal, decimal-leading-zero, lower-roman, upper-roman, lower-alpha, upper-alpha, or none. Numbering systems from other languages are also supported, including Greek and Hebrew.

- To insert an image as an image marker instead of one of the list style types, use the code:

```
list-style-image: url(imagename);
```

where *imagename* is the filename of an image. Do not enclose the filename in quotes.

- To position the bullet either inside or outside the indented text for a list item, use the code:

```
list-style-position: positionvalue;
```

where *positionvalue* is inside or outside (the default).

- To use the shorthand property rather than specifying each list property individually, use the following code:

```
list-style: stylevalue url(imagename) positionvalue;
```

Using the `list-style-type` Property

You use the `list-style-type` property to change the appearance of the default solid bullet for unordered lists. Unordered lists can use only four `list-style-type` values:

- `disc`—A filled circle (the default)
- `circle`—A hollow circle
- `square`—A filled square
- `none`—No bullet is shown

For instance, to create a style that generates a filled square instead of a solid bullet, you use the `list-style-type` property shown in the following code:

```
ul {
     list-style-type: square;
}
```

For ordered lists, you can set the style of the `ol` selector to create the following list style types:

- `decimal`—Arabic numbers (the default)
- `decimal-leading-zero`—Arabic numbers preceded by zeroes (01, 02, 03, and so forth)
- `lower-roman`—Lowercase Roman numerals (i, ii, iii, and so forth)
- `upper-roman`—Uppercase Roman numerals (I, II, III, and so forth)
- `lower-alpha`—Lowercase letters (a, b, c, and so forth)
- `upper-alpha`—Uppercase letters (A, B, C, and so forth)
- `none`—No list markers

TIP

View the Web page in different browsers if you are setting the `list-style-type` for numbering in other languages. Not all browsers support this.

For example, to create a style that numbers a list using lowercase Roman numerals, you use code similar to the following:

```
ol {
        list-style-type: lower-roman;
}
```

Figure 4-6 shows samples of some of the common list style types.

Figure 4-6   **Values for the list-style-type property**

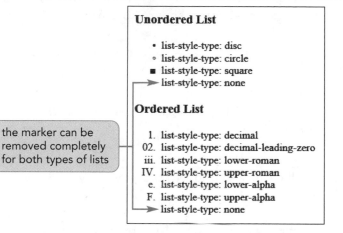

Unordered List

- • list-style-type: disc
- ◦ list-style-type: circle
- ▪ list-style-type: square
- list-style-type: none

Ordered List

1. list-style-type: decimal
02. list-style-type: decimal-leading-zero
iii. list-style-type: lower-roman
IV. list-style-type: upper-roman
e. list-style-type: lower-alpha
F. list-style-type: upper-alpha
    list-style-type: none

the marker can be removed completely for both types of lists

Using the `list-style-position` Property

You use the `list-style-position` property to change the position of the marker or bullet included with a list. You can have unordered lists with markers or bullets inside the element, such as a paragraph indent, or outside the element, which is the default.

Figure 4-7 shows an example of a list styled with the `list-style-position` value `inside` and an example of a list styled with the `list-style-position` value `outside`. The default value for the list-style-position is `outside`.

Figure 4-7   **Lists demonstrating the list-style-position values**

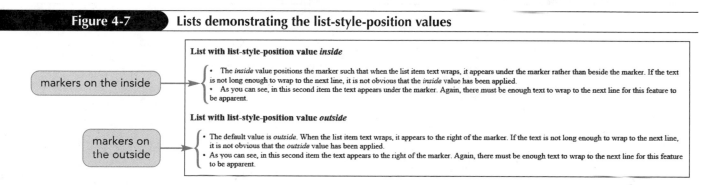

List with list-style-position value *inside*

- The *inside* value positions the marker such that when the list item text wraps, it appears under the marker rather than beside the marker. If the text is not long enough to wrap to the next line, it is not obvious that the *inside* value has been applied.
- As you can see, in this second item the text appears under the marker. Again, there must be enough text to wrap to the next line for this feature to be apparent.

List with list-style-position value *outside*

- The default value is *outside*. When the list item text wraps, it appears to the right of the marker. If the text is not long enough to wrap to the next line, it is not obvious that the *outside* value has been applied.
- As you can see, in this second item the text appears to the right of the marker. Again, there must be enough text to wrap to the next line for this feature to be apparent.

markers on the inside

markers on the outside

INSIGHT

Using the `list-style` Shorthand Property

The `list-style` property is the shorthand property for list styles. You use this property to set values for `list-style-type`, `list-style-image` (if you are using one), and `list-style-position` all at the same time. For example, if you wanted to style an unordered list with square markers positioned inside, you would use the following code:

```
ul {
    list-style: square inside;
}
```

If you wanted to style an ordered list with uppercase roman numerals positioned inside, you would use the following code:

```
ol {
    list-style: upper-roman inside;
}
```

You'll create a style to set `list-style-type` to `square` for all unordered lists.

To display square bullets for unordered lists:

1. Return to **career.htm** file in your text editor.

2. After the `img` style rule, insert the following code as shown in Figure 4-8:

```
ul {
    list-style-type: square;
}
```

Figure 4-8   **Square list style type for an unordered list**

```
<style type = "text/css">

    img {
        vertical-align: middle;
    }

    ul {
        list-style-type: square;
    }

</style>
```

3. Save the file.

4. Return to your Web browser, and then click the **Refresh** or **Reload** button to view the style changes in the file. The Web page should look similar to Figure 4-9.

| Figure 4-9 | Displaying the square list markers in the Web page |

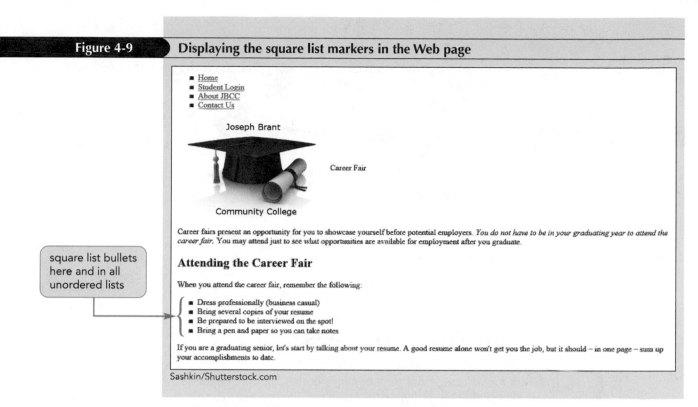

square list bullets here and in all unordered lists

Sashkin/Shutterstock.com

Jeff would also like you to change the numbers in the ordered list. Given the options you've shown him, he would like the values displayed as uppercase alphabetic characters.

To display ordered list markers using the `upper-alpha` list style type:

1. Return to the **career.htm** file in your text editor.

2. After the `ul` style rule, insert the following code as shown in Figure 4-10:

```
ol {
     list-style-type: upper-alpha;
}
```

| Figure 4-10 | CSS style rule for uppercase alphabetic ordered list markers |

```
<style type = "text/css">

    img {
         vertical-align: middle;
    }

    ul {
         list-style-type: square;
    }

    ol {
         list-style-type: upper-alpha;
    }

</style>
```

3. Save the file.

4. Return to your Web browser, and then click the **Refresh** or **Reload** button to view the style changes in the file. The Web page should look similar to Figure 4-11.

Figure 4-11   Displaying the upper-alpha list markers

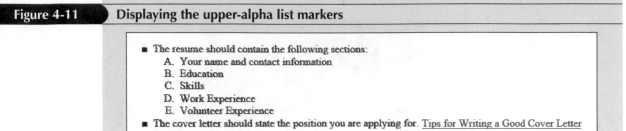

- The resume should contain the following sections:
  - A. Your name and contact information
  - B. Education
  - C. Skills
  - D. Work Experience
  - E. Volunteer Experience
- The cover letter should state the position you are applying for. Tips for Writing a Good Cover Letter
- Both the resume and the cover letter must not contain spelling or grammatical errors.

Using Groups of Selectors

Jeff would like you to change the color of the headings and change their font to a sans-serif font. Because the page contains both h1 and h2 headings, you could define styles for each element individually. However, if you want to apply the same style to more than one element so they have the same appearance, you can group several selectors together. **Grouped selectors** are selectors that share a common set of declarations and that are grouped into a comma-separated list.

Without grouping, if you wanted text in both paragraph elements and list item elements to appear in navy blue, for instance, you would enter the following code in your style sheet:

```
p {
    color: navy;
}

li {
    color: navy;
}
```

TIP

While you must insert a comma after each element in a list of grouped selectors, it doesn't matter if you insert a space after the comma or not.

However, it is not necessary to create a separate style for each selector if the selectors have the same styles. To group selectors, you type the element selectors separated by commas, like this:

```
p, li {
    color: navy;
}
```

TIP

The extended list of CSS color names will validate if you use CSS3 validation. You may have to select the More Options feature and select CSS3 as the Profile option.

The JBCC logo has only a few colors in it. To add some color, yet tie in with the logo, you'll color each of the headings a shade of red called firebrick. You'll also set the font to a sans-serif font to match the font style in the logo. These two styles will be applied to all headings, `h1` through `h6`.

To define styles using grouped selectors:

1. Return to the **career.htm** file in your text editor.
2. After the `<style>` start tag, insert the following code as shown in Figure 4-12:

Be sure to include a comma after each heading selector.

```
h1, h2, h3, h4, h5, h6 {
     color: firebrick;
     font-family: Verdana, Geneva, Arial, Helvetica,
sans-serif;
}
```

Figure 4-12 Style rule using grouped selectors

```
<style type = "text/css">

     h1, h2, h3, h4, h5, h6 {
          color: firebrick;
          font-family: Verdana, Geneva, Arial, Helvetica, sans-serif;
     }

     img {
          vertical-align: middle;
     }
```

3. Save the file.
4. Return to your Web browser, and then click the **Refresh** or **Reload** button to view the style changes in the file. The Web page should look similar to Figure 4-13.

Figure 4-13 | **Headings styled with grouped selectors**

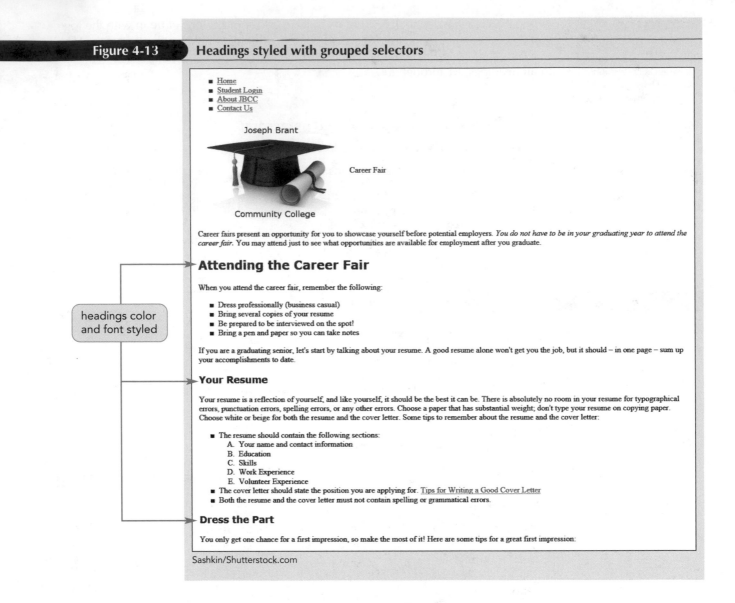

headings color and font styled

Sashkin/Shutterstock.com

Using Descendant Selectors

In HTML, you can nest elements to apply multiple formatting features to their content. For example, if you wanted text to appear using the formatting for both emphasis and strong (bold and italic), you could nest elements as follows:

```
<strong><em>sample text</em></strong>
```

As a result of this code, the text *sample text* would appear in a browser in both bold and italic.

TIP

Descendant selectors are also referred to as contextual selectors.

A **descendant selector** is a selector nested within another selector. For example, suppose that you want text that is contained in the nested elements from the previous paragraph to appear as maroon. To achieve this effect you could create a rule for either the `strong` selector or the `em` selector. However, there may be a case when you want to apply a style to only the `em` element that is nested inside a `strong` element. In that case, you would create the following style:

```
strong em {
    color: maroon;
}
```

There is only a space separating the selectors. The comma is used between selectors when the style applies to all selectors in the group. The space is used, without a comma, to indicate descendant selectors. This descendant selector specifies that whenever the code for an `em` element is nested within a `strong` element, the text appears in maroon. In all other instances where the `em` element is used by itself, the `em` text would continue to appear only in italics, as it normally would, unless you created a different style for the `em` element. Similarly, `strong` text by itself would continue to appear only as bold text, but not in maroon.

Jeff would like you to change the color of any text that is nested inside the `em` element within a `p` element. He would like the color of this text to be firebrick, the same color as the headings.

To define styles using descendant selectors:

1. Return to the **career.htm** file in your text editor.

2. After the `img` style, insert the following code as shown in Figure 4-14:

```
p em {
    color: firebrick;
}
```

Figure 4-14   Style rule for descendant selectors

```
img {
    vertical-align: middle;
}

p em {
    color: firebrick;
}

ul {
    list-style-type: square;
}
```

3. Save the file.

4. Return to your Web browser, and then click the **Refresh** button to view the style changes in the file. The Web page should look similar to Figure 4-15.

Figure 4-15   **Style for the descendant selector p em applied**

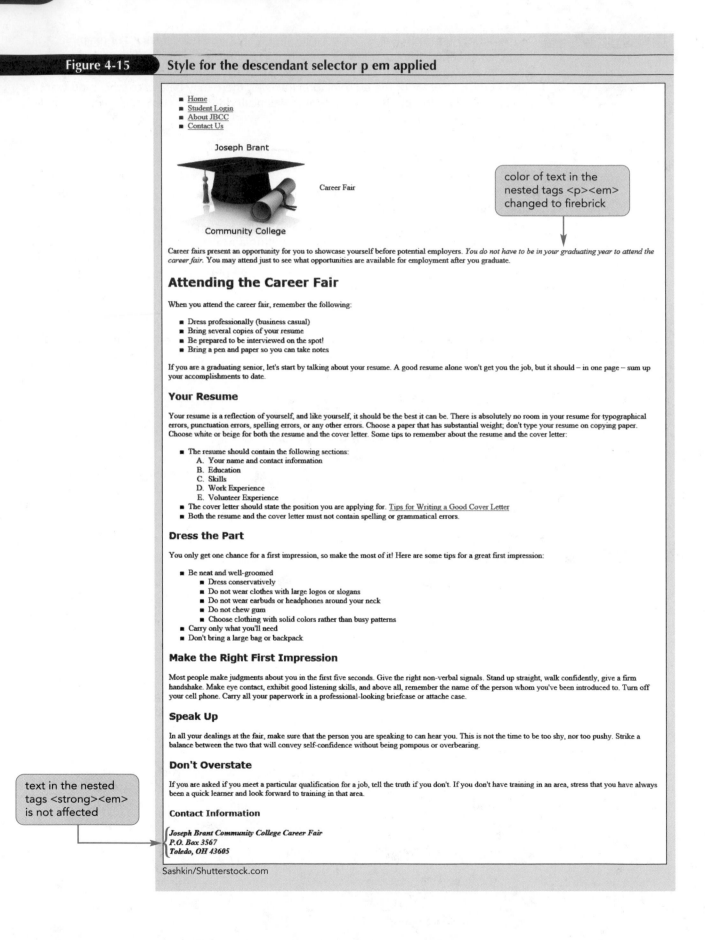

Sashkin/Shutterstock.com

Styling a List of Hyperlinks as a Navigation Bar

Jeff has seen many Web pages that have navigation links at the top of the Web page horizontally, and he has asked you to design the Career Fair styles to incorporate this. The hyperlinks are currently included in an unordered list nested inside a `nav` element.

The nav Element

The `nav` element is used to contain a block of navigation links. The links could point to parts of the same Web page or to other parts of the same Web site. Like the `footer` element, `nav` is a semantic element that does not apply formatting or serve any other functional purpose. The `nav` element simply identifies a block of navigation links.

The nav element included in the Career Fair Web site is as follows:

```
<nav>
    <ul>
        <li>
            <a href = "index.htm" title = "JBCC Home">
            Home</a>
        </li>
        <li>
            <a href = "login.htm" title = "Student
            Login">Student Login</a>
        </li>
        <li>
            <a href = "about.htm" title = "About JBCC">
            About JBCC</a>
        </li>
        <li>
            <a href = "contactus.htm" title = "Contact Us">
            Contact Us</a>
        </li>
    </ul>
</nav>
```

Placing navigation links in an unordered list nested within a `nav` element is a common technique used in Web design. CSS styles are used to style the list as a navigation bar. To achieve this effect, you will include two style rules. One rule will apply a background color to the `nav` element, set the line height twice as high as normal, and display the element as a block so the background color will be applied in older Web browsers. This style will provide a black background with a little room above and below the hyperlinks. The `nav` style will be as follows:

```
nav {
    background-color: black;
    line-height: 200%;
    display: block;
}
```

The second style will affect the list items inside the `nav` element. This style rule will display the list items on one line instead of on separate lines, and will change the element from a block-level element to an inline element. The bullets will be removed, and there will be a 40-pixel space added to the right of each item, which will spread the hyperlinks a bit. You'll use the descendant selector technique because this style will apply only to `li` elements contained within a `nav` element. All other `li` elements in the document will be unaffected by this style. The style rule will be as follows:

```
nav li {
    display: inline;
    list-style-type: none;
    padding-right: 40px;
}
```

You'll edit the Career Fair Web page to include these styles.

To create a navigation bar from an unordered list:

1. Return to the **career.htm** file in your text editor.

2. After the `img` style, insert the following code as shown in Figure 4-16:

```
nav {
    background-color: black;
    line-height: 200%;
    display: block;
}

nav li {
    display: inline;
    list-style-type: none;
    padding-right: 40px;
}
```

Be sure to type only a space, not a comma, between the `nav` and `li` selectors.

| Figure 4-16 | CSS to style an unordered list as a navigation bar |

```
img {
    vertical-align: middle;
}

nav {
    background-color: black;
    line-height: 200%;
    display: block;
}

nav li {
    display: inline;
    list-style-type: none;
    padding-right: 40px;
}

p em {
    color: firebrick;
}
```

3. Save the file.

4. Return to your Web browser, and then click the **Refresh** or **Reload** button to view the style changes in the file. The Web page should look similar to Figure 4-17.

Figure 4-17   **Unordered list displayed as a horizontal navigation bar**

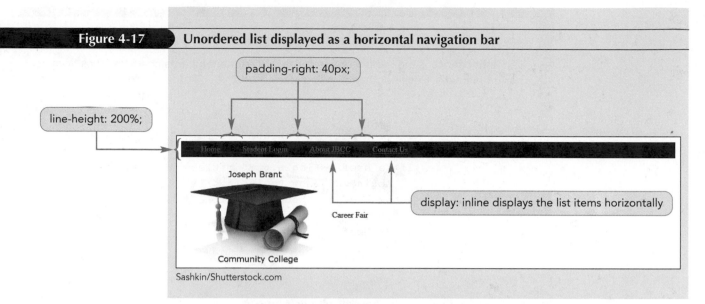

Sashkin/Shutterstock.com

The blue hyperlinks are a bit difficult to read on the black background. Jeff has asked you to change the color of the hyperlinks to white. Only the hyperlinks that are in the navigation bar should be white, though. Other hyperlinks in the Web page cannot be white because the background of the rest of the page is white. To change the color of only the hyperlinks in the navigation element to white, you'll use another descendant selector as follows:

```
nav a {
    color: white;
    font-weight: bold;
}
```

This style rule will apply the color white to the text of each anchor element that's inside a nav element.

You would also like to remove the underlining from all hyperlinks. Hyperlinks that are not in the navigation bar will remain blue, so they'll stand out as hyperlinks and won't be confused with paragraph text. You'll use the following CSS to apply blue color to the hyperlinks and to remove their underlining:

```
a {
    color: blue;
    text-decoration: none;
}
```

The blue color and lack of text decoration defined for the anchor selector will be applied to all anchor elements. In addition, the white color and bold font weight styles will apply only to anchor elements within nav elements. The color defined in the descendant selector will always take precedence over the color defined with the more global anchor selector, meaning that anchors within nav elements will always appear white.

Understanding Inheritance

CSS **inheritance** is the method whereby a child element inherits characteristics from its parent element. Consider the following HTML code:

```
<nav>
    <ul>
        <li><a href = "index.htm" title = "JBCC Home">Home
            </a></li>
        <li><a href = "login.htm" title = "Student
            Login">Student Login</a></li>
        <li><a href = "about.htm" title = "About JBCC">About
            JBCC</a></li>
        <li><a href = "contactus.htm" title = "Contact
            Us">Contact Us</a></li>
    </ul>
</nav>
```

In this case, the `li` elements are children of the `ul` element, and the `ul` element is a child of the `nav` element. You could think of the `nav` element as a grandparent, the `ul` element as the child, and the `li` elements as grandchildren of the `nav` element. Looking at this another way, the `ul` element is the parent of the `li` elements, and the `nav` element is the parent of the `ul` element.

Each child element inherits the properties of its parent element. For instance, if the `nav` element is styled with the text color red, then the `ul` and `li` elements will also be styled with the text color red.

To style the hyperlinks:

1. Return to the **career.htm** file in your text editor.

2. After the `<style>` start tag, insert the following code as shown in Figure 4-18:

```
a {
    color: blue;
    text-decoration: none;
}
```

Be sure to type only a space and not a comma between the nav and a selectors.

3. After the `nav` style, insert the following code as shown in Figure 4-18:

```
nav a {
    color: white;
    font-weight: bold;
}
```

Figure 4-18   **Style rules for the anchor elements**

```
<style type = "text/css">

    a {
        color: blue;
        text-decoration: none;
    }

    h1, h2, h3, h4, h5, h6 {
        color: firebrick;
        font-family: Verdana, Geneva, Arial, Helvetica, sans-serif;
    }

    img {
        vertical-align: middle;
    }

    nav {
        background-color: black;
        line-height: 200%;
    }

    nav a {
        color: white;
        font-weight: bold;
    }

    nav li {
        display: inline;
        list-style-type: none;
        padding-right: 40px;
    }
```

4. Save the file.

5. Return to your Web browser, and then click the **Refresh** or **Reload** button to view the style changes in the file. The Web page should look similar to Figure 4-19.

Figure 4-19   Display hyperlink styles applied

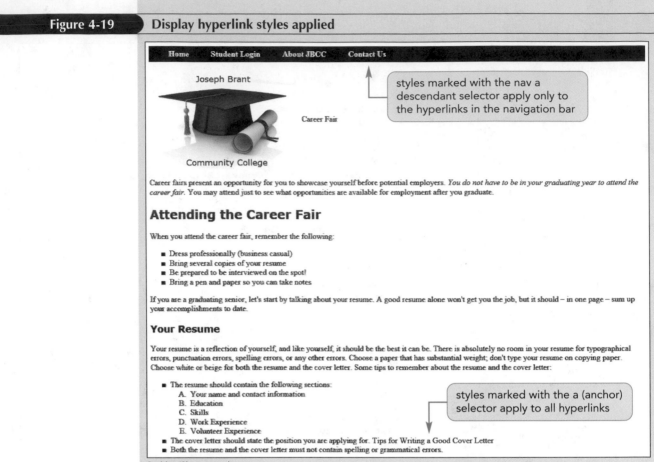

Sashkin/Shutterstock.com

PROSKILLS

Teamwork: Separating Presentation and Content

Separating the presentation from the content facilitates teamwork in Web design. Content refers to the actual information that is presented. There's a saying in media that "Content is king." Without good content, people will not return to view the Web site. But some would also say that "Presentation is queen." If you can't find the content, or if it's not clearly displayed, you won't return to the Web site either.

Using external CSS style sheets, the overall presentation of a Web site can be designed separately while the content is still being developed. Individual Web pages may need some specific styles, which can be addressed using embedded style sheets.

Imagine a large Web design project that has dozens of Web pages. It could be a Web site for a small retail store, a high school, or a non-profit organization. Perhaps there are several people who would like to help develop the Web site, all with different skills and talents. One way to divide the development into tasks that could be done separately would be to assign roles like the following to individual team members:

- **Project manager**—Oversees development of the entire project, including storyboard and development timeline
- **Content developer**—Creates the content and some basic Web pages that are not stylized
- **Graphic artist**—Creates the images, buttons, logos, and other art
- **CSS developer**—Develops the CSS style sheets that will be linked to the individual Web pages; might design the layout and style individually, or may work with the graphic artist to design the "look" together

REVIEW

Session 4.1 Quick Check

1. Write a CSS style rule that sets the text in either an ordered list (ol) or an unordered list (ul) to be green and bold.
2. Write a CSS style rule that sets the text in a strong element that is inside a paragraph element (p) to be orange.
3. What does the `display: inline` property do?
4. What property would you use to ensure the text following an image appears aligned at the top of the image rather than at the bottom?
5. What is a descendant selector?
6. What is a grouped selector?

SESSION 4.2 VISUAL OVERVIEW

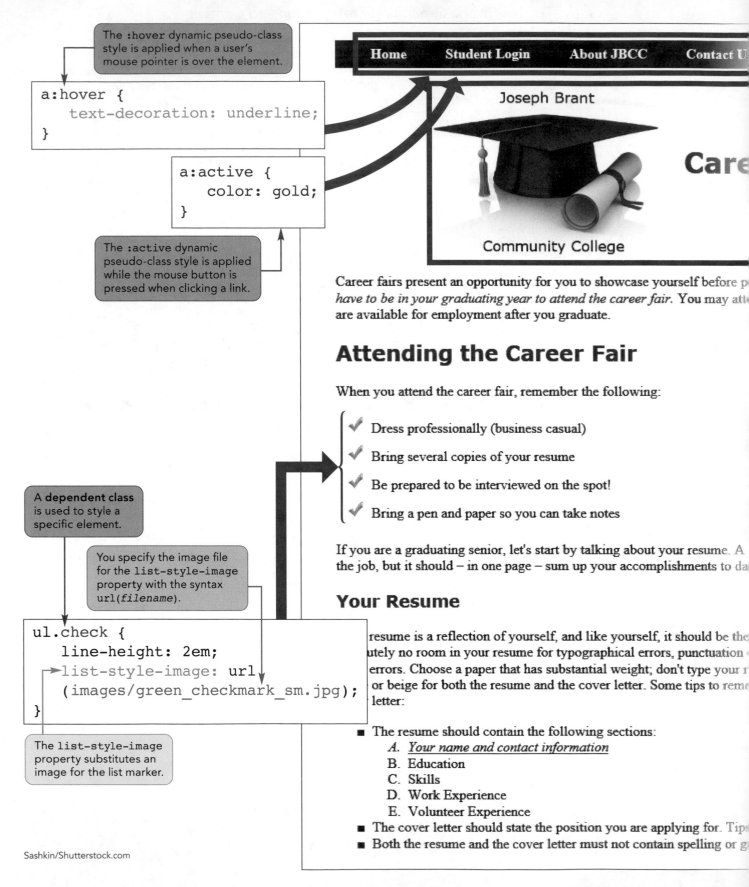

The :hover dynamic pseudo-class style is applied when a user's mouse pointer is over the element.

```
a:hover {
    text-decoration: underline;
}
```

```
a:active {
    color: gold;
}
```

The :active dynamic pseudo-class style is applied while the mouse button is pressed when clicking a link.

A **dependent class** is used to style a specific element.

You specify the image file for the list-style-image property with the syntax url(*filename*).

```
ul.check {
    line-height: 2em;
    list-style-image: url
    (images/green_checkmark_sm.jpg);
}
```

The list-style-image property substitutes an image for the list marker.

Sashkin/Shutterstock.com

Home   Student Login   About JBCC   Contact U

Joseph Brant

Care

Community College

Career fairs present an opportunity for you to showcase yourself before p *have to be in your graduating year to attend the career fair.* You may att are available for employment after you graduate.

Attending the Career Fair

When you attend the career fair, remember the following:

- ✔ Dress professionally (business casual)
- ✔ Bring several copies of your resume
- ✔ Be prepared to be interviewed on the spot!
- ✔ Bring a pen and paper so you can take notes

If you are a graduating senior, let's start by talking about your resume. A the job, but it should – in one page – sum up your accomplishments to da

Your Resume

resume is a reflection of yourself, and like yourself, it should be the utely no room in your resume for typographical errors, punctuation errors. Choose a paper that has substantial weight; don't type your r or beige for both the resume and the cover letter. Some tips to reme letter:

- The resume should contain the following sections:
  - A. *Your name and contact information*
  - B. Education
  - C. Skills
  - D. Work Experience
  - E. Volunteer Experience
- The cover letter should state the position you are applying for. Tip
- Both the resume and the cover letter must not contain spelling or g

USING CLASSES

About JBCC   **Contact Us**

eph Brant

nunity College

ty for you to showcase yourself before potential employers. *You do not ur to attend the career fair.* You may attend just to see what opportunities r you graduate.

areer Fair

emember the following:

ess casual)

ir resume

ved on the spot!

ou can take notes

's start by talking about your resume. A good resume alone won't get you e — sum up your accomplishments to date.

urself, and like yourself, it should be the best it can be. There is e for typographical errors, punctuation errors, spelling errors, or any has substantial weight; don't type your resume on copying paper. Choose e and the cover letter. Some tips to remember about the resume and the

the following sections:
ict information

e the position you are applying for. Tips for Writing a Good Cover Letter ver letter **must** not contain spelling or grammatical errors.

Career Fair

An **independent class** starts with a dot and can be used to style any element.

```
.center {
    text-align: center;
}
```

```
<p class = "center">
```

The **span element** is used to identify inline content.

You can specify a class with the span element to apply styles.

```
<span class = "title">
Career Fair
</span>
```

The `:hover` and `:active` styles apply to all links.

Creating and Using Classes

While Jeff worked on the Career Fair Web page, he was faced with a common Web design problem: What do you do if you want to style different instances of an element in different ways? For example, what if you want to single-space some paragraphs and double-space others? You only have *one* paragraph element selector to style. If you create a style rule for the p selector, it will style all p elements in the Web page.

The solution is to use CSS class selectors. A **class selector** is a name preceded by a period; this name can then be applied to any HTML element. An example of a class selector is *.center*. You could apply this class to an HTML element using the class keyword as follows:

```
<h1 class = "center">Community College</h1>
```

Class selectors can format one or more instances of an element. Using class selectors, you can modify the appearance of any HTML element in a virtually unlimited number of ways. However, unlike element selectors, once you create a style for a class selector, you must apply a class to the start tag of one or more elements on a Web page in order for the style to apply to those elements. Classes can either be dependent or independent. A dependent class styles a particular element, such as the p, ul, or em element. An independent class styles any element.

Applying Dependent and Independent Classes

- To create a dependent class style rule, use the code:

```
selector.dependentclass {
     property1:value;
     property2:value;
}
```

where *selector* is the name of the element and *dependentclass* is the name of the dependent class.

- To apply the dependent class to an element whose name is the same as the selector, use the code:

```
<element class = "dependentclass">
```

- To create an independent class style rule, use the code:

```
.independentclass {
     property1:value;
     property2:value;
}
```

where *independentclass* is the name of the independent class.

- To apply an independent class to any element, use the code:

```
<element class = "independentclass">
```

Creating and Applying a Dependent Class

Each class must have a name that you create. Here are some rules for class names:

- A class name can contain only alphabetic or numeric characters.
- A class name must be one word (no spaces).
- A class name should describe the purpose of the class.
- A class name should not begin with a number because not all browsers will recognize it.

Jeff would like to draw readers' attention to some particularly important tips. One tip is to include the name and contact information in the resume; the other tip, in the *Dress the Part* section, is to not wear headphones and earbuds. He would like these tips to be underlined and italicized. This style is to be used only for list items. Information in other elements that Jeff would like the reader to notice might be stylized differently.

You'll create a class called `attention` and use it to style `li` elements with the selector:

```
li.attention {
```

Note that a period serves as a flag character and separates the element selector (`li`) from the name of the dependent class (`attention`). Next, you'll enter the declarations as you normally would. The code for the `attention` dependent class for the `li` element will look like this:

```
li.attention {
    text-decoration: underline;
    font-style: italic;
}
```

Jeff can then use the `attention` class whenever he has text in a list on a Web page that he wants to make sure the reader notices.

After you've entered the style rule in the style sheet, there's still more work to do. You'll also have to enter code in the body section to specify which element or elements will use the class. Using the class in the body section is called **applying** a class. You apply the class in the start tag of an element—in this instance, the `<li>` tag. The code to apply the *attention* class would look like this:

```
<li class = "attention">Your name and contact information</li>
```

You'll apply the *attention* class to the list items that Jeff has specified.

To create and apply a dependent class:

1. If you took a break after the previous session, make sure that the **career.htm** file is open in your text editor.

2. After the `img` style rule, insert the following code as shown in Figure 4-20:

```
li.attention {
    text-decoration: underline;
    font-style: italic;
}
```

Figure 4-20   **Dependent selector code**

```
img {
    vertical-align: middle;
}

li.attention {
    text-decoration: underline;
    font-style: italic;
}

nav {
    background-color: black;
    line-height: 200%;
}
```

3. Position the insertion point to the left of the > in the open `<li>` tag for the *Your name and contact information* list element. Apply the *attention* class to the list item as shown in Figure 4-21.

```
class = "attention"
```

4. Position the insertion point to the left of the > in the open `<li>` tag for the *Do not wear earbuds or headphones around your neck* list element. Apply the *attention* class to the list item as shown in Figure 4-21.

```
class = "attention"
```

Figure 4-21   **Code to apply the attention class to specific li elements**

```
<ul>
 <li>The resume should contain the following sections:</li>
<ol>
    <li class = "attention">Your name and contact information</li>
    <li>Education</li>
    <li>Skills</li>
    <li>Work Experience</li>
    <li>Volunteer Experience</li>
</ol>

------------------------------------------------------------------------

<ul>
 <li>Be neat and well-groomed</li>
    <ul>
        <li>Dress conservatively</li>
        <li>Do not wear clothes with large logos or slogans</li>
        <li class = "attention">Do not wear earbuds or headphones around your neck</li>
        <li>Do not chew gum</li>
        <li>Choose clothing with solid colors rather than busy patterns</li>
    </ul>
 <li>Carry only what you'll need</li>
 <li>Don't bring a large bag or backpack</li>
</ul>
```

5. Save the file.

6. Return to Web browser, and then click the **Refresh** button to view the style changes in the file. The Web page should look similar to Figure 4-22.

Figure 4-22   **Displaying the dependent style**

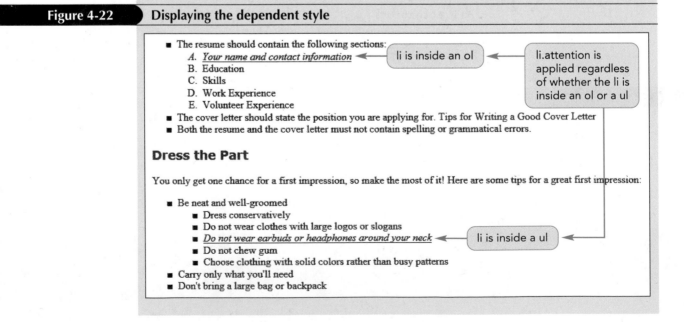

Jeff would also like you to change the bullets for the first list in the Career Fair Web page, which provides students tips for attending the Career Fair. He would prefer checkmarks instead of bullets so students will take notice of these points as things they should do. To do this, you'll need to use an image for the bullet marker.

Using the `list-style-image` Property

You use the `list-style-image` property to specify a graphic image instead of a bullet marker for a list. For example, to use an image named *star.gif* for each bullet in a list, you type the following code:

```
ul {
    list-style-image: url(star.gif);
}
```

TIP

Use a very small image for a bullet marker.

Note that you do not enclose the filename in quotes.

Because you'll use this technique for only one list, you'll need to create a class and apply it to the list. You'll create a dependent class called *check* for the `ul` element and you'll define a `list-style-image` url that will point to the green_checkmark_sm.jpg file. This image file is in the images folder, so you'll need to include that folder name in the path. You'll also set the line height to 2em so the list items don't look crowded.

To use an image as a list marker:

1. Return to the **career.htm** file in your text editor.

2. After the `ul` style rule, insert the following code as shown in Figure 4-23:

```
ul.check {
    line-height: 2em;
    list-style-image: url(images/green_checkmark_sm.jpg);
}
```

Figure 4-23 **Style rule for the check dependent class for the ul selector**

```
ul {
    list-style-type: square;
}

ul.check {
    line-height: 2em;
    list-style-image: url(images/green_checkmark_sm.jpg);
}

ol {
    list-style-type: upper-alpha;
}
</style>
```

3. Position the insertion point to the left of the > in the start `<ul>` tag for the unordered list after the paragraph that discusses first impressions. Apply the *check* class to the unordered list as shown in Figure 4-24.

```
class = "check"
```

Figure 4-24   **Code to apply the class to the ul element**

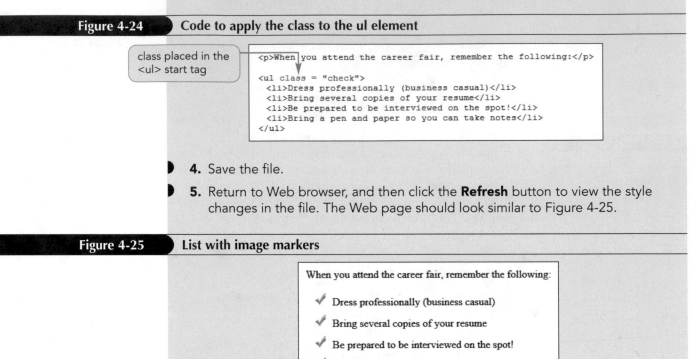

class placed in the `<ul>` start tag

```
<p>When you attend the career fair, remember the following:</p>

<ul class = "check">
  <li>Dress professionally (business casual)</li>
  <li>Bring several copies of your resume</li>
  <li>Be prepared to be interviewed on the spot!</li>
  <li>Bring a pen and paper so you can take notes</li>
</ul>
```

4. Save the file.

5. Return to Web browser, and then click the **Refresh** button to view the style changes in the file. The Web page should look similar to Figure 4-25.

Figure 4-25   **List with image markers**

When you attend the career fair, remember the following:

✔ Dress professionally (business casual)

✔ Bring several copies of your resume

✔ Be prepared to be interviewed on the spot!

✔ Bring a pen and paper so you can take notes

Arcady/Shutterstock.com

Creating and Applying an Independent Class

While you can use a dependent class to format individual instances of a common element, you might also want to use a particular style to format instances of several different elements in the same way. For example, you may want to center several blocks of text in your document, including paragraphs and different heading types. Independent classes can format any element. An independent class selector is preceded by the period flag character, like this:

```
.center
```

You then enter the code for the declarations, just as you would for any other style:

```
.center {
    text-align: center;
}
```

TIP

Choose meaningful names for class selectors rather than class1, class2, and so forth.

Next, you enter the class name in the start tag for each element to where you want it to apply, just as you do with dependent classes:

```
<h1 class = "center">Joseph Brant Community College</h1>
<p class = "center">Joseph Brant Community College is having a
Career Fair!</p>
```

Jeff would like you to center the logo and the Career Fair text beside the logo, as well as the footer section at the bottom of the Career Fair Web page. You'll create an independent class called *center*, and you'll use the `text-align` property with the value `center`. You'll also create a style for the footer selector that will contain the `display` property with the `block` value in order to center the footer correctly in older versions of Web browsers. Then you'll apply the class to the paragraph element at the top of the Web page and to the footer section. You'll place the independent class style rules at the top of the style section, before the element selectors.

To create and apply an independent class:

1. Return to the **career.htm** file in your text editor.

The class name begins with a period; do not type any characters to the left of the period.

2. After the start `<style>` tag, insert the following code as shown in Figure 4-26:

```
.center {
     text-align: center;
}

footer {
     display: block;
}
```

Figure 4-26 CSS code for an independent class

```
<style type = "text/css">

     .center {
          text-align: center;
     }

     footer {
          display: block;
     }

     a {
          color: blue;
          text-decoration: none;
     }
```

3. Position the insertion point to the left of the > in the start `<p>` tag after the end `</nav>` tag, and apply the center class to the first paragraph element as shown in Figure 4-27:

```
<p class = "center">
```

4. Position the insertion point to the left of the > in the start `<footer>` tag, and apply the center class to the footer element as shown in Figure 4-27:

```
<footer class = "center">
```

Figure 4-27 **CSS code to apply the center class to different elements**

```
<nav>

<p class = "center">
<img src = "images/college_logo_sm.jpg" alt = "career fair logo image" />
Career Fair
</p>


. . . .


in that area.</p>

<footer class = "center">
<h4>Contact Information</h4>
```

▶ **5.** Save the file.

▶ **6.** Return to your Web browser, and then click the **Refresh** or **Reload** button to view the style changes in the file. The top of the Web page should look similar to Figure 4-28.

Figure 4-28 **Displaying the logo and text centered**

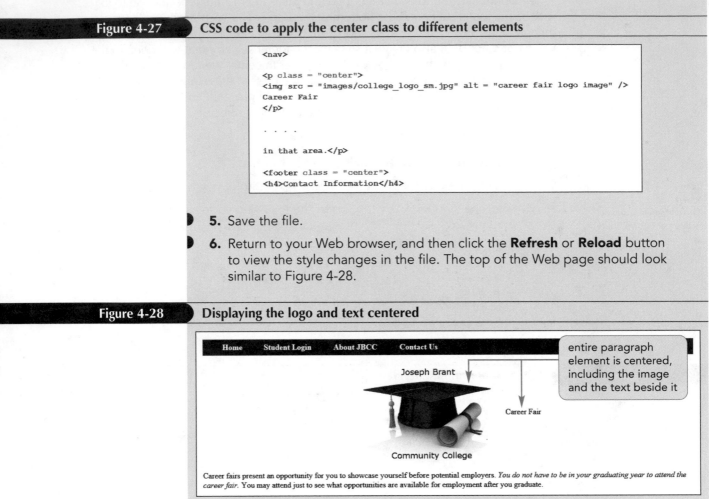

entire paragraph element is centered, including the image and the text beside it

Sashkin/Shutterstock.com

Jeff would like you to change the size of the words *Career Fair* and set their color to firebrick, like the headings. This text is currently inside a paragraph element. If you were to take the text out of the paragraph and place it in a heading element, it would become a block-level element and would appear below the image. Jeff likes the text beside the logo and does not want it to appear below the logo. You need to apply a style to text that is inline, rather than block level.

Using the span Element

All of the HTML elements you've used so far have had specific meanings. They have identified sections, headings, or paragraphs, indicated emphasis, and so forth. The span element is a generic element that does not have any specific meaning, but it allows you to mark inline content. You use the span element as follows:

```
<span>content</span>
```

If you were to include this element as it is above, you would see no effect at all in your browser. The purpose of the span element is to mark, or identify, content that is inline without affecting the position by adding white space above and below. You'll use the span element to mark the *Career Fair* text beside the logo image. You'll create an independent class called *title* and apply it to the span element.

To use the span element with an independent class:

1. Return to the **career.htm** file in your text editor.

2. After the .center style rule, insert the following code as shown in Figure 4-29:

```
.title {
     color: firebrick;
     font-family: Verdana, Geneva, Arial, Helvetica,
sans-serif;
     font-size: 200%;
     font-weight: bold;
}
```

3. Position the insertion point to the left of the text *Career Fair* in the body section, and then insert the following HTML code for the open span tag with the *title* class, shown in Figure 4-29:

```
<span class = "title">
```

4. Position the insertion point to the right of *Career Fair*, and then insert the close **</span>** tag, as shown in Figure 4-29.

Figure 4-29   Code for the .title class and span element

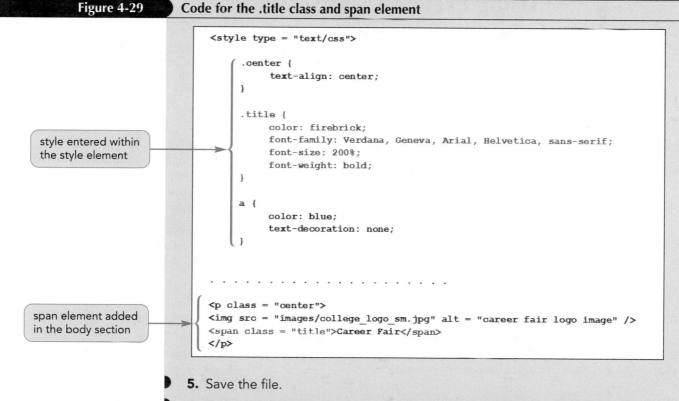

5. Save the file.

6. Return to your Web browser, and then click the **Refresh** or **Reload** button to view the style changes in the file. The top of the Web page should look similar to Figure 4-30.

Figure 4-30 | **Career Fair text with .title class applied**

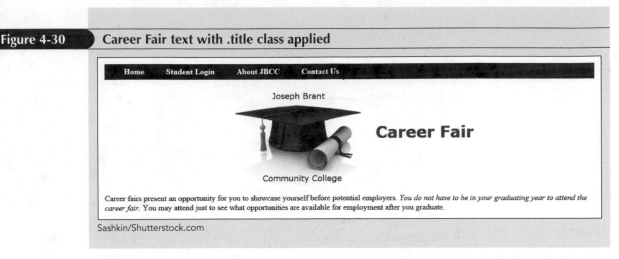

Sashkin/Shutterstock.com

Jeff has noticed an effect on some Web pages where the appearance of a hyperlink changes when the mouse pointer is over it. He likes this effect and would like you to add an underline under each link in the navigation bar when the mouse pointer moves over the link. He also wants you to use this style for all other hyperlinks on the Web page.

Using Pseudo-Class Selectors

The word *pseudo* means "not genuine." You might be familiar with the term *pseudonym*, which is an alias. For example, the famous author Samuel Clemens used the pseudonym of Mark Twain. A **pseudo-class** is a class that exists in CSS but is not directly defined in HTML. You'll be using the pseudo-classes that are associated with the anchor element to achieve the mouse-over effect.

In an earlier tutorial, you created links and formatted the link text. When testing your links, you knew that if the text of a link was blue, you had not yet clicked the link. Similarly, if link text was purple, you knew you had clicked the link. Both of these details give information about the **link state**, which is whether a hyperlink has been clicked or not. The **anchor pseudo-class selectors** expand on the concept so that visitors to your Web site benefit from such visual cues about the link state. By using the anchor pseudo-class selectors, you can style hyperlinks based on the following four states:

- `a:link` is the selector for normal links (links that haven't been clicked).
- `a:visited` is the selector for visited links (links that have been clicked).
- `a:hover` is the selector for the hover state (when the mouse pointer passes over the link).
- `a:active` is the selector for active links (when a user holds down the mouse button to click a link).

Note the colon between the `a` element and each pseudo-class selector, and note that the colon does not have spaces before or after it. A style rule can be created for any or all of the anchor pseudo-classes.

REFERENCE

Creating Styles for Links

- To style the text of a link, create a style for the `a:link` selector.
- To style the text of a visited link, create a style rule for the `a:visited` selector.
- To style the text of a link when the mouse hovers over it, create a style rule for the `a:hover` selector.
- To style the text of a link when the user clicks on it, create a style rule for the `a:active` selector.

TIP

Test your hyperlink styles in all major Web browsers; some Web browsers do not support the `visited` or `active` pseudo-classes.

By using the `a:link` pseudo-class selector, you can make unvisited link text stand out from the surrounding text. Visited links, in contrast, should not stand out; they should have a more subdued color. For the hover state, you might want to change the foreground color and background color, or add underlining to the link text, in order to draw the visitor's attention to the link and provide visual confirmation of the link selection. For the brief moment that a hyperlink is clicked, you might want to style the `a:active` link pseudo-class selector to have the link text appear in an attention-getting color, such as orange or yellow, to verify for the user that the link has been clicked.

TIP

You can also create a separate style rule for the anchor selector in addition to style rules for any of the anchor pseudo-classes.

The order in which you enter code for the link pseudo-class selectors in your style sheets does matter. You don't have to use all of the pseudo-class selectors in your code, but if you do use more than one, you must enter the selectors in this order: `a:link`, `a:visited`, `a:hover`, and then `a:active`.

Jeff would like you to add the hover effect so each hyperlink is displayed with an underline when the mouse pointer is over it.

To use the `a:hover` pseudo-class:

Be sure to type a colon (`:`) between the `a` selector and the `hover` pseudo-class.

1. Return to the **career.htm** file in your text editor.

2. After the a (anchor) style rule, insert the following code as shown in Figure 4-31:

```
a:hover {
    text-decoration: underline;
}
```

Figure 4-31   The code for the a:hover pseudo-class style

```
a {
    color: blue;
    text-decoration: none;
}

a:hover {
    text-decoration: underline;
}

h1, h2, h3, h4, h5, h6 {
    color: firebrick;
    font-family: Verdana, Geneva, Arial, Helvetica, sans-serif;
}
```

3. Save the file.

4. Return to your Web browser, and then click the **Refresh** or **Reload** button. Move the mouse pointer over each of the hyperlinks in the navigation bar and hover over each for a few seconds to view the style changes in the file. The top of the Web page should look similar to Figure 4-32.

Figure 4-32 Mouse pointer hovering over the Student Login hyperlink

link with underline as mouse pointer hovers over it

Sashkin/Shutterstock.com

Jeff would also like you to add the functionality that changes the color of a hyperlink when the user clicks it. He would like the color of the hyperlink to be gold in this situation, to match the tassel on the logo. You'll use the `active` pseudo-class to achieve this. You'll place the style rule for this pseudo-class after the `:hover` CSS rule because some older Web browsers don't recognize the `:active` rule otherwise.

To use the `a:active` pseudo-class:

Be sure to type a colon (:) between the a selector and `active` pseudo-class.

1. Return to the **career.htm** file in your text editor.

2. After the `a:hover` style rule, insert the following code as shown in Figure 4-33:

```
a:active {
    color: gold;
}
```

Figure 4-33 The code for the a:active pseudo-class rule

```
a:hover {
    text-decoration: underline;
}

a:active {
    color: gold;
}

h1, h2, h3, h4, h5, h6 {
    color: firebrick;
    font-family: Verdana, Geneva, Arial, Helvetica, sans-serif;
}
```

3. Save the file.

4. Return to your Web browser, and then click the **Refresh** or **Reload** button. Click the first link in the navigation bar and as you do this, hold the mouse button down for a few seconds to view the style changes in the file. The top of the Web page should look similar to Figure 4-34. Click your browser's Back button to return to the **career.htm** Web page, then repeat for the remaining links in the navigation bar.

Figure 4-34   **Rendering the a:active pseudo-class**

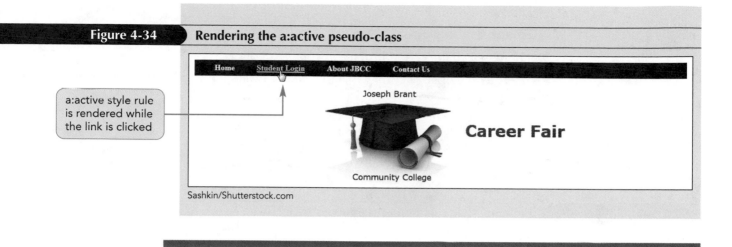

a:active style rule is rendered while the link is clicked

Sashkin/Shutterstock.com

Understanding Browser Styles

Not all browsers display Web pages the same way. Each browser has its own default, built-in styles that control the page margins, the font size, the background color, and the font family. Although the styles are fairly consistent from browser to browser, it's still a good idea to view your Web pages in the current and previous version of every contemporary browser to see how your pages appear. Another good strategy is to create a style for the `body` element to ensure that, regardless of the browser, your Web page will appear with *your* choices for the font, font size, font color, background color, and page margins. At a minimum, always style the `body` element with declarations for the color and the background color, even if your choices are standard black text on a white background.

Setting Margins

The Career Fair Web page is almost complete. As a finishing touch, Jeff would like you to add a style rule that changes the margins so the text and background do not extend to the left and right sides of the browser window. He would like some white space on the left and right sides, as well as at the bottom of the Web page. This effect can be achieved a number of ways, but you'll achieve it by using CSS properties for margins. In later tutorials, you'll learn more about margins, padding, and other properties that affect the placement of elements on a Web page; for now, suffice it to say that the margin is the white space along the edge of a document. A document has top, right, bottom, and left margins. The system measurement used to set the margins is the same as the one for setting the line height and font size. For margins, the measurement is from the corresponding edge of the document. Thus, a left margin of 24px is 24 pixels from the left edge, for instance.

You set margins using the following properties:

- `margin-top`
- `margin-right`
- `margin-bottom`
- `margin-left`

The order of these margin properties is not important.

On the Career Fair Web page, you'll set the left margin to 10em, the right margin to 10em, and the bottom margin to 3em. You'll set the margins in the `body` selector. Note that even if you set the `margin-top` property to 0, the white space above the navigation bar would not disappear completely. You'll look at the properties that affect white space in the next tutorial.

To set the margins:

1. Return to the **career.htm** file in your text editor.

2. After the open `<style>` tag, insert the following code as shown in Figure 4-35:

```
body {
    margin-top: 0em;
    margin-right: 10em;
    margin-bottom: 3em;
    margin-left: 10em;
}
```

Figure 4-35   The body style rule setting margins

```
<style type = "text/css">

    body {
        margin-top: 0em;
        margin-right: 10em;
        margin-bottom: 3em;
        margin-left: 10em;
    }

    .center {
        text-align: center;
    }
```

3. Save the file.

4. Return to your Web browser, and then click the **Refresh** or **Reload** button to view the style changes in the file. The bottom of the Web page should look similar to Figure 4-36.

Figure 4-36   Displaying the lower part of the Career Fair Web page

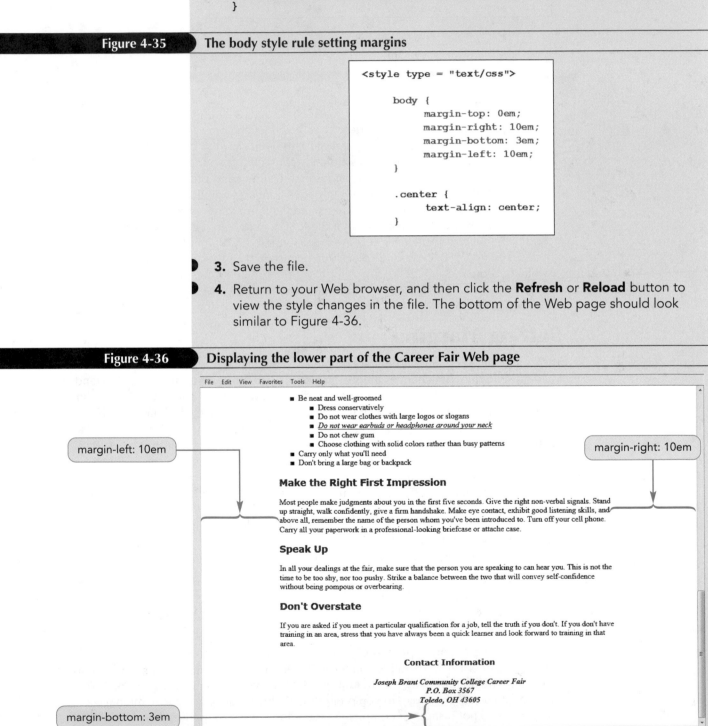

margin-left: 10em

margin-right: 10em

margin-bottom: 3em

Jeff is thrilled with the work you've done on the new stylized Career Fair Web page. He'll continue to examine your work and will get back to you with future projects or design changes.

PROSKILLS

Written Communication: Typography

If a Web page is difficult to read, users are likely to move on to a different Web page pretty quickly. The choice of color is important in making a Web page readable, and ensuring that the text and background colors contrast is an obvious consideration. Also important is the typeface of the font and the space between characters.

Typography is the art and technique of choosing a font and arranging the characters. This is not a new concept. The term *typography* originated with the very first printing presses, referring to the placement of blocks of wood or metal that each contained an individual letter, character, or space.

A Web page generally includes some specific content that is more important and should be emphasized. Good typography dictates that less is more; that is, if you want something to stand out, isolate it visually, and unclutter the page. An extreme example would be a single word printed on a page; regardless of the size of the font, readers will notice the word because it's isolated.

The following are a few additional techniques that can be used to emphasize content:

- *Italics:* One or two words in a sentence that are displayed in italics can disrupt readers just long enough to cause them to slow down and notice the words.
- **Bold:** Type rendered in bold makes a strong statement. This is a stronger emphasis than italic.
- Size: It may seem obvious that enlarging type adds emphasis. At the same time, the drawback is that the characters can look cramped as well. Consider changing the line height or adding some white space around enlarged characters.
- Color: It can be tempting to use color liberally for emphasis. The trick is that less is more; the less color you use, the more valuable it becomes. Consider using color very sparingly.
- Typeset changes: Using a sans-serif font in a document that is predominantly set in a serif font can draw readers' attention to the sans-serif text. Similarly, using a serif font in a document that is predominantly set in a sans-serif font can draw readers' attention to the serif font.

The key is to use each of these methods sparingly. Think of it this way: If you were to use a highlighter to highlight most of the text on a page, which text would stand out? The nonhighlighted text would stand out because it is different. However, if you instead used the highlighter sparingly, then the highlighted text would stand out. In short, less is more.

REVIEW

Session 4.2 Quick Check

1. Describe the difference between a dependent class and an independent class.
2. Write the code for an independent class called *highlight* that changes the font color to green and the background color to yellow and is displayed inline.
3. Write the code for a dependent class called *graybg* that's associated with the p element and that changes the background color to gray.
4. Describe the procedure used to apply a class to an HTML element.
5. What is the purpose of the span element?

Practice the skills you learned in the tutorial using the same case scenario.

PRACTICE

Review Assignments

Data Files needed for the Review Assignments: josephbrant_T4.htm, images/red_square.jpg

Jeff is satisfied with the styling you did for the Career Fair Web page, and he would like your help with another project. He has created a new Web page that describes the life of Joseph Brant, for whom JBCC was named. Rather than applying the same CSS styles, though, Jeff would like you to apply new styles so he can offer some choices to his colleagues as potential new styles for the JBCC Web site. Jeff has already created the HTML file, which he named josephbrant_T4.htm. He would like your help in formatting it.

Although you will not be instructed to do so after each step, you should do the following whenever you enter code to create a style in your text editor: Save the file, switch to your browser, refresh or reload the page, verify that you entered the style code correctly, switch back to your text editor, and then complete the next step. A preview of the Web page you will stylize appears in Figure 4-37.

Figure 4-37   **Completed Joseph Brant Biography page**

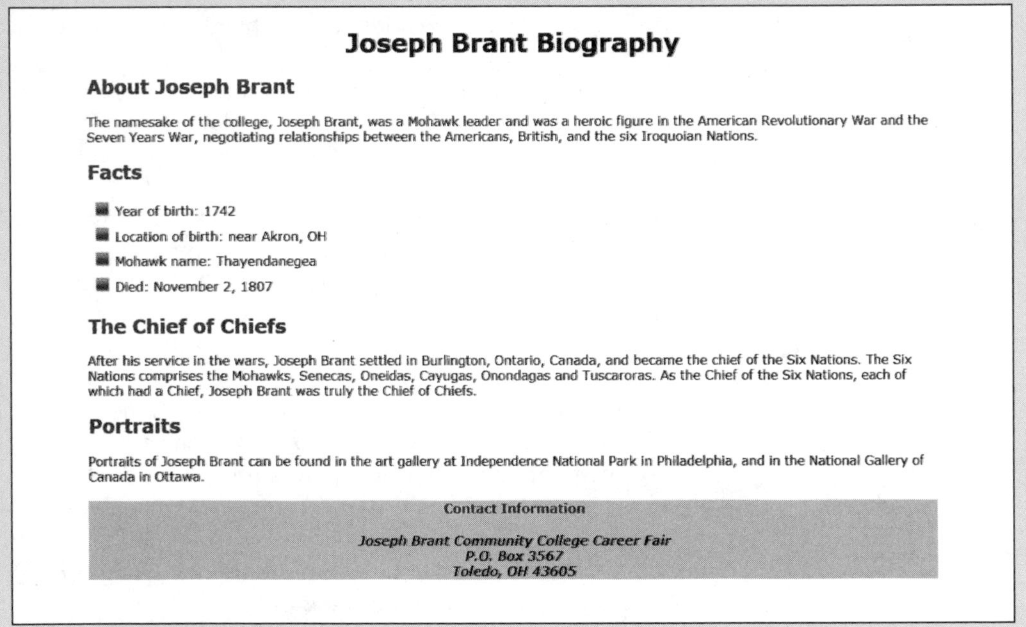

Joseph Brant Biography

About Joseph Brant

The namesake of the college, Joseph Brant, was a Mohawk leader and was a heroic figure in the American Revolutionary War and the Seven Years War, negotiating relationships between the Americans, British, and the six Iroquoian Nations.

Facts

- Year of birth: 1742
- Location of birth: near Akron, OH
- Mohawk name: Thayendanegea
- Died: November 2, 1807

The Chief of Chiefs

After his service in the wars, Joseph Brant settled in Burlington, Ontario, Canada, and became the chief of the Six Nations. The Six Nations comprises the Mohawks, Senecas, Oneidas, Cayugas, Onondagas and Tuscaroras. As the Chief of the Six Nations, each of which had a Chief, Joseph Brant was truly the Chief of Chiefs.

Portraits

Portraits of Joseph Brant can be found in the art gallery at Independence National Park in Philadelphia, and in the National Gallery of Canada in Ottawa.

Contact Information

Joseph Brant Community College Career Fair
P.O. Box 3567
Toledo, OH 43605

artizarus/Shutterstock.com

Complete the following:

1. Use your text editor to open the **josephbrant_T4.htm** file, which is provided in your Data Files in the tutorial4\review folder.

2. Save the file as **josephbrant.htm** in the same folder. Open the file in your browser, and observe the appearance of the original file.

3. Switch back to your text editor. In the head section, enter **Joseph Brant** as the page title.

4. In the head section and above the page title, enter *your name* and *today's date* in the comment section where noted.

5. Below the comment and in the head section, insert the start and end tags necessary to create an embedded style sheet.

6. Within the tags for the embedded style sheet, style the `body` element to have text appear in a font size of **1.1em** and in the **Verdana** font (a sans-serif font), with a text color of **black** and a background color of **white**. Set the left and right margins at **6em** and the bottom margin at **3em**.

7. Save the **josephbrant.htm** file. Refresh or reload the file in your browser, and then verify that the `body` element style appears correctly.

8. Switch back to your text editor. In the embedded style sheet and below the `body` style, create a style for the `h1` element to have text appear **black** and have the heading centered horizontally.

9. Create a style for the grouped elements `h2` through `h6` to have text appear **crimson**.

10. Create a style for the `footer` element to have the background color appear **lightgray**.

11. Create a dependent class for the `ul` element called **redsquare** that displays the list markers using the **images/red_square.jpg** file and sets the line height to **2em**. Apply this class to the unordered list.

12. Create an independent class called **center** that sets the `text-align` property to **center**. Apply this class to the `footer` element.

13. Save the **josephbrant.htm** file. Switch to your browser, and then refresh or reload the page. Compare your file to Figure 4-37 to verify that your file is correct.

14. Submit your completed file to your instructor, in either printed or electronic form, as requested.

Use the skills you learned in the tutorial to create a Web page for a popular restaurant.

APPLY

Case Problem 1

Data Files needed for this Case Problem: berger_T4.htm and images/bergerlogo.jpg

The Berger Street Grille   The town of Chesapeake Haven, Maryland, is home to a local landmark restaurant, the Berger Street Grille. The restaurant offers casual dining in a spacious waterfront setting and serves several hundred diners on any given evening. Although the restaurant is famous for its grilled meat dishes, its location near the Chesapeake River and the Atlantic Ocean makes the restaurant a favorite for seafood lovers as well. Ben O'Brien, the owner of the restaurant, has asked for your assistance in creating a Web page for the Berger Street Grille.

Although you will not be instructed to do so after each step, you should do the following whenever you enter code to create a style in your text editor: Save the file, switch to your browser, refresh or reload the page, verify that you entered the style code correctly, and then switch back to your text editor and complete the next step. A preview of the Web page appears in Figure 4-38.

Figure 4-38 **Berger Street Grille Web Page**

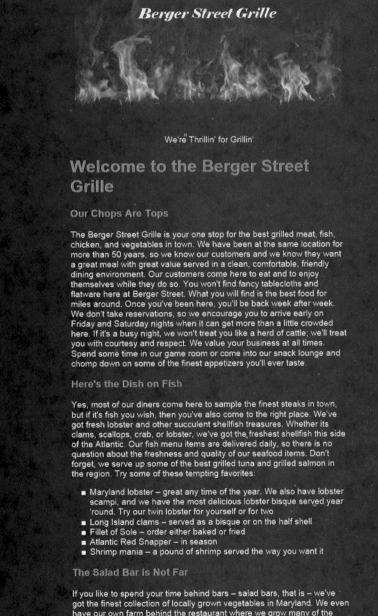

Krasowit/Shutterstock.com

Complete the following:

1. Use your text editor to open the **berger_T4.htm** file, which is provided in your Data Files in the tutorial4\case1 folder.
2. Save the file as **berger.htm** in the same folder. Open the file in your browser, and observe the appearance of the original file.
3. Switch back to your text editor. In the head section and above the page title, enter *your name* and *today's date* in the comment section where noted.
4. Create the HTML `style` element for the embedded style sheet, and then style the `body` element to have text appear in a font size of **1.2em** and in the **Arial** font (a sans-serif font), with a text color of **white** and a background color of **black**. Set the left and right margins at **10em**.
5. Save the **berger.htm** file. Switch back to your browser, and refresh or reload the page. Verify that the `body` element style appears correctly in your file.
6. Switch back to your text editor. In the embedded style sheet and below the `body` style, style the `h1` through `h6` and `footer` elements with the text color **orange**.
7. Create an independent class called **center** that will set the `text-align` property to **center**. Apply this class to the `footer` element and to the first two paragraph elements, which contain the logo and the text *We're Thrillin' for Grillin'*.
8. Style the unordered list items to appear with a **square** marker rather than a circle.
9. Save the **berger.htm** file. Switch to your browser, and then refresh or reload the page. Compare your file to Figure 4-38 to verify that your file is correct.
10. Submit your completed file to your instructor, in either printed or electronic form, as requested.

Use the skills you learned in the tutorial to create and style a Web page for a women's entrepreneurial organization.

APPLY

Case Problem 2

Data Files needed for this Case Problem: womensweb_T4.htm and images/wwlogo.jpg

Women's Web Entrepreneurs   Women's Web Entrepreneurs is an organization in Wilmington, Delaware, dedicated to helping women start their own businesses on the Web. Lynda Fong, an associate at Women's Web Entrepreneurs, has contacted you about creating a Web page that offers some tips for women thinking of creating online businesses. She has asked you to tap into your own experience in creating visitor-friendly Web pages. In the Web page, she wants you to highlight important facts that people need to remember when starting a business online.

After you complete a step to create a style or a set of steps to create and apply a class, verify in your browser that the style code has been entered correctly, and then switch back to your text editor. A preview of the Web page appears in Figure 4-39.

Figure 4-39 Women's Web Entrepreneurs Web page

Women's Web Entrepreneurs

Let Your Web Site Do Your Work

You want to run a business out of your home or a storefront, but you need a sales and marketing plan. The Web can be your most effective, tireless 24x7 salesperson. Here are some tips to turn your Web site into an effective marketing tool:

Looks Matter

Avoid using blinking, flashing, scrolling, and crawling text. These are only suitable for a whimsical Web site. Choose a readable font in a size that's easy to read. Stick to one font face and not more than three font sizes. It may be interesting to have 10 different font faces on your site, but having too many font faces tends to detract from your site, not enhance it. Your Web site should not look like a the Web Designer couldn't decide which font size to use! Use neutral tones or colors that complement each other. Avoid red and green color combinations — 5% of the population is color blind and may have trouble reading such text. Red is also associated with danger and financial loss.

Get Their Attention

At the top of your page, state what your company can do for the customer. Why are you the best? Why should the customer use your services? What makes you so special? Why should the customer buy your goods or use your services? Make these reasons clear from the start and at the top.

Let's Make Contact

Don't make the customer have to search for contact information. That's a great way to kill a sale, not create one. Make sure your contact information is easy to find. Have your address, phone number, fax number, email address and link at the top and the bottom of every page.

Get the Picture

Photos should be the right size (not more than 3 inches by 3 inches) and not be distorted. Your photos should not look like a fun house mirror. Background graphics should contrast with, not compete with, text. If you have a lot of photos, create thumbnail images (about 1 - 1 1/2 inches square) that link to larger-size images. Having the large images on separate pages means your home page will download faster.

How Will You Compete?

Decide early on how you will differentiate yourself from others. Price, selection, expertise, market niche, uniqueness, speed of delivery, and unique knowledge of the subject matter are all important aspects in starting a business and staying in business. For more information, we invite you to visit our office Monday through Friday from 8 a.m. to 4 p.m.

Women's Council on Entrepreneurship in the Americas
23 Butler Blvd.
Suite 400B
Hamilton Creek, NJ 35688

Back to Top

Complete the following:

1. Use your text editor to open the **womensweb_T4.htm** file, which is provided in your Data Files in the tutorial4\case2 folder.

2. Save the file as **womensweb.htm** in the same folder. Open the file in your browser, and observe the appearance of the original file.

3. Switch back to your text editor. In the head section and below the page title, enter *your name* and *today's date* in the comment section where noted.

4. Create the tags for an embedded style sheet, and then style the body element to have text appear with a font size of **1.1em**, in the **Verdana** font (a sans-serif font), in **black**, and with a background color of **wheat**. Set the left and right margins to **6em**.

5. Save the **womensweb.htm** file. Switch back to your browser, and then refresh or reload the page. Verify that the body element style appears correctly in your file.

6. Switch back to your text editor. In the head section and in the embedded style sheet code, create a style for an independent class named **center**. This class should center text.

7. Apply the *center* independent class to the paragraph element that contains the logo image, to the h1 and h2 elements at the top of the page, and to the h4 element at the bottom of the page. In the start <h1> tag, insert the class code to the left of the *id = "top"* code.

8. Create a dependent class named **opening** for the paragraph element. Create a style that sets the first line indent at **6em** and sets the text to appear in the color **maroon**.

9. Apply the *opening* dependent class to the p element for the first paragraph of the document.

10. Style the h2 element selector to display text as **italic**.

11. Create a grouped style for the h3 and h4 element selectors to have text appear in **italic** and indented **6em**.

12. Create two pseudo-class selectors as follows:
    - Normal (unvisited) link text should appear as **black** text and in a font size of **1.4em**.
    - When the mouse hovers over a link, the link text should appear as **wheat** text on a **black** background.

13. Save the **womensweb.htm** file. Switch to your browser, and refresh or reload the page. Compare your file to Figure 4-39 to verify that your file is correct.

14. Pass the mouse pointer over the *Back to Top* link text at the bottom of the page. Click the link. Scroll to the bottom of the page and view the now-visited link.

15. Submit your completed file to your instructor, in either printed or electronic form, as requested.

Use what you've learned and expand your skills to create and style a Web page for an alternative energy power company.

CHALLENGE

Case Problem 3

Data Files needed for this Case Problem: power_T4.htm, images/diamond.gif, images/ energy.jpg.

Sierra Desert Power Solutions   A new alternative energy power company, Sierra Desert Power Solutions, serves customers in Arizona and New Mexico. Eventually, the company hopes to expand its energy services throughout the United States. Sierra Desert Power Solutions specializes in solar energy, but it also has expertise in several other types of alternative energy resources. None of the energy the company produces comes from fossil or nuclear fuels. Sierra Desert Power Solutions hopes to offer cheap, abundant, nonpolluting sources of renewable energy at an affordable cost to consumers. You've been asked to create a Web page that highlights the benefits of the new company and the services it offers to its customers. After you complete a step to create a style or a set of steps to create and apply a class, verify in your browser that the style code has been entered correctly, and then switch back to your text editor. A preview of the Web page appears in Figure 4-40.

Figure 4-40 Sierra Desert Power Solutions Web page

Sierra Desert Power Solutions

Renewable Energy

Here at Sierra Desert Power Solutions, we are dedicated to supplying the Southwest with "green" energy – energy that is clean, reliable, abundant, inexpensive, renewable, and environmentally friendly. It's energy with a "zero-carbon footprint." There is no use of fossil or nuclear fuels. In today's uncertain times, it is imperative that new solutions for today's – and tomorrow's – energy needs be implemented. When you factor in global warming and national security concerns, green energy supplied by Sierra Desert Power Solutions is the right choice at the right time. Don't delay in getting started now.

We offer consulting services for all of the following alternative energy sources:

- Wind Turbine Power
- Ocean Wave and Tidal Energy
- Hydrogen Fuel Cell
- Solar Energy
- Geothermal Energy
- Hydroelectric Energy
- Biofuels

Although we specialize in solar energy, we provide consulting services for all types of alternative energy resources. We are now offering consulting services for those companies interested in employing biofuel technology such as municipal and agricultural waste, algae, specialized energy crops such as switchgrass and miscanthus, ethanol, butanol, biological enzymes and microbes to produce energy. We provide additional consulting services if you need information about feedstocks and biorefineries. If you are a startup alternative energy company or if you are considering creating a startup company in alternative energy, we can get your business up and running within a short time. We also provide you with information about the regulatory and tax issues that startup companies in this business will encounter.

Presently, Sierra Desert Power Solutions operates exclusively in Arizona and New Mexico, but by the end of this year, we will be expanding our power-generating services into Colorado and California. Please check this Web site in the coming months to see when our services will begin to be offered in those areas. Our consulting services, however, are available nationwide. Call 1 800 456-9912 to arrange for a free consultation with one of our specialists in this emerging field.

Contact Sierra Desert Power Solutions today for a free evaluation of your alternative energy needs.

220 Energy Row • Suite 400 • Mt. Marrone, Washington 98101

Back to Top

Massimo Cavallo/Shutterstock.com

Complete the following:

1. Use your text editor to open the **power_T4.htm** file, which is provided in your Data Files in the Tutorial.04\Case3 folder.
2. Save the file as **power.htm** in the same folder. Open the file in your browser, and observe the appearance of the original file.
3. Switch back to your text editor. In the head section and above the page title, enter *your name* and *today's date* in the comment section where noted.
4. In the head section and below the page title, create the `style` element.
5. Create a style for an independent class named **center**. This class should center text. Apply this class to the h1 element and the paragraph element that contains the logo image.
6. Create a style for the `body` element to have text appear in **1.3em** in the **Arial** font (a sans-serif font), with a text color of **black** and a background color of **lavender**, and left and right margins of **12em**.
7. Save the **power.htm** file. Switch back to your browser, and refresh or reload the page. Verify that the `body` element style appears correctly in your file.
8. Switch back to your text editor. In the embedded style sheet and below the `body` element style, style the p element to have a line height of **1.4em**.
9. Create an independent class named **spreadheading** that formats text to have letter spacing of **6px** and word spacing of **6px**.
10. Apply the *spreadheading* independent class to the h2 element before the words *Renewable Energy*.
11. Create a dependent class named **listheading** for the p element selector. The class should format the paragraph to be displayed in **italic** and **navy**.
12. Apply the dependent *listheading* class to the p element of paragraph that precedes the unordered list.
13. Create a dependent class named **contact** for the p element selector. The class should format paragraphs with a font size of **1.1em** and a color of **navy**.
14. In the next-to-last paragraph, apply the *contact* dependent class to the p element before the word *Contact*.
15. Using a descendant selector for the ul element, create a style for the li element to have text appear in a font size of **1.2em** and in **navy**. The style should use the **diamond.gif** image as the list marker.
16. Create a style for the `strong` element selector to have text appear in the color **#808000** (grayish color).
17. Format the h1 element selector to appear with a text decoration of **underline** and **overline**.
18. Using a group selector, format h2 and h4 heading text to be centered and **navy**.
19. Format normal (unvisited) links to appear in **slategray**, without an underline.
20. Format the hover effect so when the mouse passes over a link, the link text appears in **lavender** and has a background color of **navy**. The link text should be underlined.
21. Save the **power.htm** file. Switch to your browser, and refresh or reload the page. Compare your file to Figure 4-40 to verify that your file is correct. Note that depending on your browser and browser version, the spread heading in your file may look different from that shown in Figure 4-40.
22. At the bottom of the page, pass the mouse over the link back to the top of the page to verify the hover effect works as described in Step 20.
23. Submit your completed file to your instructor, in either printed or electronic form, as requested.

RESEARCH

Case Problem 4

Data File needed for this Case Problem: donate_T4.htm

Leigh Taylor Philanthropies Although you were hired at Leigh Taylor Philanthropies a little more than a year ago, your work at the Pittsfield, Virginia, agency has not gone unnoticed. In your brief period of service, you have identified several individuals, agencies, and community organizations worthy of receiving donations. Ms. Taylor has decided to entrust you with $250 million to donate to the worthy causes of your choice. Although you do not have to donate the money equally, you must donate the sum to at least five separate entities. Create a Web page that announces how you intend to donate the money. For each individual, agency, or organization to which you plan to donate money, state the amount of the donation and the reason for it.

Complete the following:

1. Use your text editor to open the **donate_T4.htm** file, which is provided in your Data Files in the tutorial4\case4 folder.
2. Save the file as **donate.htm** in the same folder.
3. In the head section, give your page an appropriate title. In the head section and above the page title, enter ***your name*** and ***today's date*** in the comment section where noted.
4. Within the tags for the embedded style sheet, format the `body` element for the text size, font, color, and background color of your choice. Ensure that the text is readable, attractive, and professional.
5. In the body section, enter at least five paragraphs of text (one paragraph for each of the five entities to which you will donate money). Ensure that the text is informative and pleasant to read.
6. In the embedded style sheet, style one dependent class and one independent class. Use at least three of the text properties.
7. Create an unordered list. Use the list style properties to change the list marker. Use the unordered list to create links to the Web site for each agency you recommend for a donation.
8. Apply the dependent class and the independent class to elements in the body section. Do not clutter your Web page, but highlight important words or phrases for your readers.
9. Save the **donate.htm** file, and then open the page in your browser. Verify that all styles work correctly and that your page is pleasant to read.
10. Submit your completed file to your instructor, in either printed or electronic form, as requested.

ENDING DATA FILES

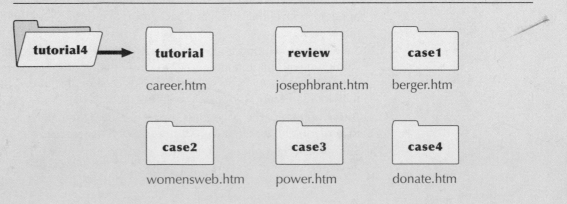

tutorial4 → tutorial — career.htm
review — josephbrant.htm
case1 — berger.htm
case2 — womensweb.htm
case3 — power.htm
case4 — donate.htm

OBJECTIVES

Session 5.1
- Understand the box model
- Create padding, margins, and borders
- Wrap text around an image
- Float a block-level element

Session 5.2
- Use the background properties
- Create a background image for a list
- Create an external style sheet
- Link to an external style sheet

Working with the Box Model

Creating a Conservation Web Page

Case | *African Elephant Facts*

Jackie Selebi lives in Cape Town, South Africa, and is a conservationist. He feels strongly that people should do what they can do to preserve natural habitats and protect wild animals. South Africa is home to many species of wild animals including lions, leopards, giraffes, elephants, and buffalos. Jackie is concerned about the survival of the African elephant, in particular. Jackie believes that the first step in conservation is to provide information about the animals and their habitat. He has created an information Web page that contains facts about the African elephant along with a few pictures. He hopes that people who see his Web page will learn some new facts about the African elephant and will appreciate what a fascinating animal it is. He would like you to stylize the Web page so that it is eye-catching and fun.

STARTING DATA FILES

tutorial

elephant_sunset.jpg
elephant_T5.htm
elephants_drinking.jpg
green_linen.jpg
grey_texture.jpg
modernizr-2.js
small_elephant.jpg

review

consult_T5.htm
JackieSelebilogo.jpg
modernizr-2.js

case1

modernizr-2.js
planetarium_T5.htm
planetariumlogo.jpg
planets.jpg

case2

eventplanner_T5.htm
eventplannerlogo.jpg
modernizr-2.js
parchment.jpg

case3

bio_teal_button.jpg
books_T5.htm
grey_texture.jpg
modernizr-2.js
science_teal_button.jpg
spiralbound.jpg
teal_square_bullet.jpg
travel_teal_button.jpg

case4

hope_T5.htm
modernizr-2.js

SESSION 5.1 VISUAL OVERVIEW

The border-bottom property applies only to the border at the bottom of the box that contains the element.

The border-*side* shorthand properties list border properties as follows: border-*side*: *style weight color*.

```
h3 {
    border-bottom: solid thick darkkhaki;
    padding-bottom: 0.5em;
}
```

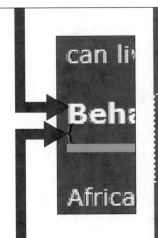

padding-bottom: 0.5em;

The padding-bottom property specifies the amount of white space between the bottom of the content and the bottom of the box that contains the element.

clear:both

The clear property specifies the sides of an element where float elements cannot be placed.

Habitat and Characteristics

African elephants live in the wild in Africa, south of the Sahara Desert. They ɛ fruit. An adult African elephant can be up to 11 feet tall at the shoulder. They can live to be 60 - 70 years old.

Behavior

African elephants are very social animals. They have a complex society that is based on a family unit. Each family unit has approximately 10 individual elephants, composed of closely related females (cows) and their calves. Separate family units join together to form a group. After male elephants reach puberty, they tend to form alliances with other males. Elephants are also very nurturing animals. Two elephants will wrap their trunks together to give each other a hug.

African elephants are very intelligent. They communicate with deep growling or rumbling noises. Elephants also communicate using noises that are too low for humans to hear, yet very loud. Their noises can be heard 5 or 6 miles away. Smell is their most highly developed sense.

Tusks

- Elephant tusks are ivory teeth that grow throughout their lives.
- Elephants are right- or left-tusked, using the favored tusk more often, thus shortening it from constant wear.
- Elephants use their tusks to dig up roots and pry bark from trees to fin food.

Quick Facts

Here are a few interesting facts:

Quick Facts

ALIGN, FLOAT, AND CLEAR PROPERTIES

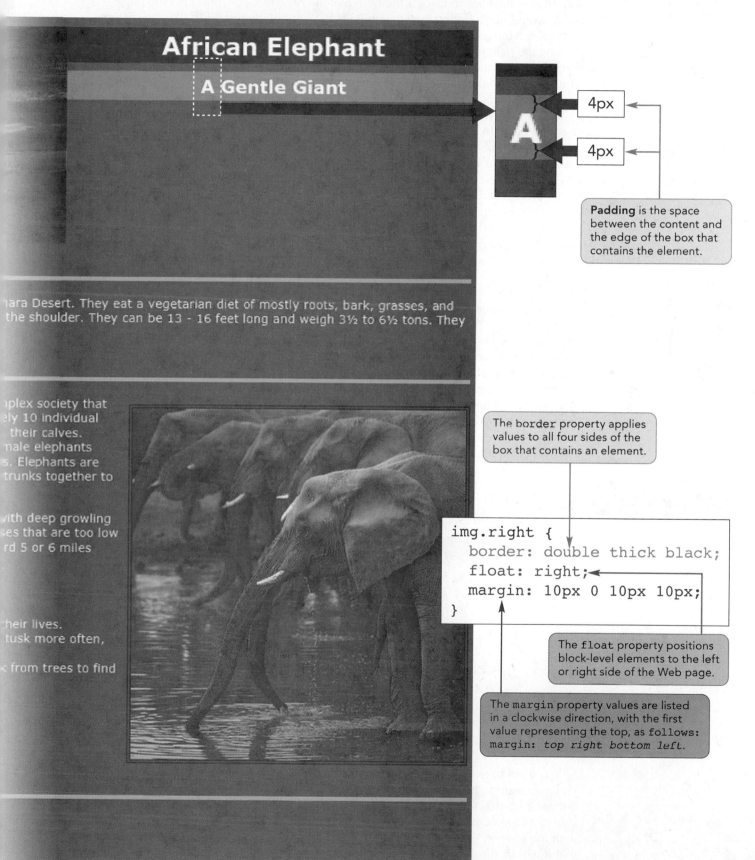

African Elephant

A Gentle Giant

4px

4px

Padding is the space between the content and the edge of the box that contains the element.

...ara Desert. They eat a vegetarian diet of mostly roots, bark, grasses, and ...the shoulder. They can be 13 - 16 feet long and weigh 3½ to 6½ tons. They

...plex society that
...ely 10 individual
...their calves.
...nale elephants
...s. Elephants are
...trunks together to

...ith deep growling
...es that are too low
...rd 5 or 6 miles

...heir lives.
...tusk more often,

...k from trees to find

The **border** property applies values to all four sides of the box that contains an element.

```
img.right {
    border: double thick black;
    float: right;
    margin: 10px 0 10px 10px;
}
```

The **float** property positions block-level elements to the left or right side of the Web page.

The **margin** property values are listed in a clockwise direction, with the first value representing the top, as follows: margin: *top right bottom left.*

Understanding the Box Model

You meet with Jackie to discuss the design of the African Elephant Facts Web page. Jackie would like a design that is simple yet has a bit of interest. He'd like the pictures of the elephants to be staggered so one picture is in the top left, and the other picture is along the right edge, further down the page. He knows there's quite a bit of information, and sometimes a Web page can look too crowded when this is the case. He'd like a bit of space around some of the elements so the content doesn't look too cramped. Creating the layout Jackie wants requires an understanding of the CSS box model.

The CSS **box model** describes the imaginary boxes that are formed around elements in a Web page. In HTML, every element is treated as though it were a box. The box model consists of four parts: a content area, padding, borders, and margins. Because the elements you've created so far haven't had borders, you haven't seen the boxes, but they've been there. The **content area** is the area that contains the box content, such as text or an image. By default, the content just barely fits into the box; there is no white space surrounding the content. The **box properties** are used to add white space and a border around the content. The three most commonly used CSS box properties are `padding`, `border`, and `margin`. Two other box properties you've already used with the `img` element are `width` and `height`. You've also specified margins for the `body` element in a previous tutorial. The `padding`, `border`, and `margin` properties all affect placement of the content inside an element.

Padding is white space that surrounds the box content. It is the space between the content and the edge of the box that contains the element. A **border**, which is a visible solid or decorative ruled line, can be placed around the padding. Borders are useful because they can separate the content of one box from another or call attention to a box. Optionally, you can change a border's color, style, and width. The **margin** is white space outside the border. The margin creates **breathing room**—separation between the boxes so they aren't crowded on the page. To some extent, you've already seen margin space around block-level elements, such as headings. For example, you've seen that headings are preceded and followed by what appears to be a blank line. However, the browser is actually using its own default settings to create the top and bottom margins for the heading. The relationship among the padding, the border, and the margins is shown in Figure 5-1.

Figure 5-1 The box model

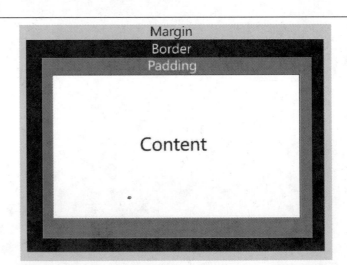

You don't have to use all three of these box properties at the same time. For example, you may want to have padding and margin space around the contents of an element, but not a border. You could even set the padding, margin, and a border to each specific side of an element individually. Jackie has provided the Web page he created, along with the images. You'll view Jackie's Web page in your Web browser now, recognizing that it will be displayed using the Web browser's default styles.

To open the African Elephant Facts Web page:

1. Open the **elephant_T5.htm** file in your text editor. Enter **your name** and **today's date** in the comment section of the file, and then save it as **elephant.htm**.

2. Take a few minutes to view the content and structure of the elephant.htm file in your text editor.

3. Open the **elephant.htm** file in your Web browser. Figure 5-2 shows the current layout and content.

Figure 5-2   African Elephant Facts Web page

African Elephant

A Gentle Giant

Habitat and Characteristics

African elephants live in the wild in Africa, south of the Sahara Desert. They eat a vegetarian diet of mostly roots, bark, grasses, and fruit. An adult African elephant can be up to 11 feet tall at the shoulder. They can be 13 - 16 feet long and weight 3½ to 6½ tons. They can live to be 60 - 70 years old.

Behavior

African elephants are very social animals. They have a complex society that is based on a family unit. Each family unit has approximately 10 individual elephants, composed of closely related females (cows) and their calves. Separate family units join together to form a group. After male elephants reach puberty, they tend to form alliances with other males. Elephants are also very nurturing animals. Two elephants will wrap their trunks together to give each other a hug.

African elephants are very intelligent. They communicate with deep growling or rumbling noises. Elephants also communicate using noises that are too low for humans to hear, yet very loud. Their noises can be heard 5 or 6 miles away. Smell is their most highly developed sense.

Tusks

- Elephant tusks are ivory teeth that grow throughout their lives.
- Elephants are right- or left-tusked, using the favored tusk more often, thus shortening it from constant wear.
- Elephants use their tusks to dig up roots and pry bark from trees to find food.

Quick Facts

Here are a few interesting facts:

Quick Facts

- The scientific name for the African elephant is *Loxodonta Africana*.
- A baby elephant is called a calf.
- A female elephant is called a cow.
- A male elephant is called a bull.
- At birth, a baby elephant weighs approximately 200 pounds and stands approximately 3 feet tall.
- An African elephant can grow to be 3½ to 6½ tons (7,000 - 13,200 pounds), reach a height of 11 feet tall, and grow 13 to 16 feet long.
- An elephant can eat 300 pounds (136 kilograms) of food in one day.
- Elephants have the longest pregnancy of any animal on earth. It lasts 22 months!
- Adult African elephants have only one natural enemy: humans.
- African elephants eat mainly roots, leaves, fruit, grasses, and bark.
- The African elephant's ears are over twice as large as those of the Asian elephant.
- African elephants are slightly larger than Asian elephants.

Elephant Trunk Facts

- The average length of an African elephant's trunk is approximately 7 feet (2 meters).
- An elephant's trunk can hold approximately 2 gallons of water.
- Elephants use their trunks as snorkels when they wade in deep water.
- Two finger-like parts on the tip of an elephant's trunk can be used to delicately pick up a small berry.

Unfortunately, the African elephant and other species of elephants are hunted and killed for their ivory tusks. There are several wildlife organizations that focus their efforts on conservation of elephants.

Elephant Facts • P O Box 3 • Plumstead • Cape Town • South Africa • 7800

Back to Top

Johan Swanepoel/ Shutterstock.com; Pichugin Dmitry/Shutterstock.com

Jackie would like a sans-serif font for the text. He'd also like the text to be white on a dark background, and in a larger font size than normal. You'll use the CSS3 color darkslategray, font Verdana or sans-serif, and the size 1.1em.

To style the body element selector:

1. Return to the **elephant.htm** file in your text editor.

2. After the `title` element, insert the following code as shown in Figure 5-3. In this example, you'll use some comments to identify some of the styles:

```
<style type = "text/css">

/* body */

body {
  background-color: darkslategray;
  color: white;
  font-size: 1.1em;
  font-family: Verdana, sans-serif;
}

</style>
```

Figure 5-3 ▶ Style code for the body element

```
<title>African Elephant</title>

<style type = "text/css">

/* body */

body {
  background-color: darkslategray;
  color: white;
  font-size: 1.1em;
  font-family: Verdana, sans-serif;
}

</style>

</head>
```

3. Save the file.

4. Return to your Web browser, and then click the **Refresh** button to view the style changes in the file. The Web page should look similar to Figure 5-4.

Figure 5-4   African Elephant Fact Web page with body style applied

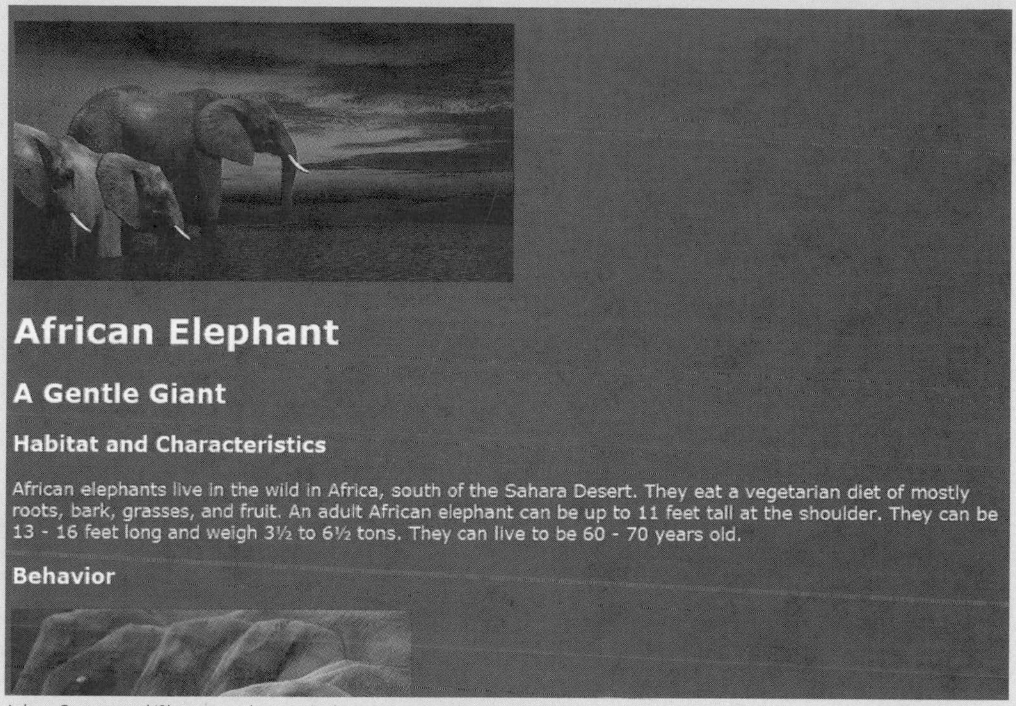

Johan Swanepoel/Shutterstock.com; Pichugin Dmitry/Shutterstock.com

The page already looks much better than Jackie's original. Jackie has noticed that text sometimes appears too close to an image, however, and that images often have too much space around them. You'll use the CSS `padding` and `margin` properties to improve this situation.

Understanding the Padding and Margin Properties

As explained earlier, padding is the internal white space that surrounds the contents of an element; the **padding properties** control this internal white space. By default, the content of an element does not have padding, but all major Web browsers add varying amounts of padding by default. Values for both the padding and the margin properties can be expressed using any of the following measurements:

- em (em values)
- px (pixels)
- mm (millimeters)
- cm (centimeters)
- in (inches)
- % (percentage of the container element)

You set the padding for an element using the `padding` property, which has the syntax:

    padding: width;

where `width` sets the size of the padding on all four sides of the element using one of the CSS units of measure.

You can set the padding for each side individually by using the following four properties:

- `padding-top`
- `padding-right`
- `padding-bottom`
- `padding-left`

For example, to set the padding on the left side of images using em values, you could use the following code:

```
img {
    padding-left: 1em;
}
```

Setting Padding

- To set the padding within an element, use:

  `padding: width;`

  where `width` sets the size of the padding on all four sides of the element using one of the CSS units of measure.
- Use individual padding properties as follows:
  - `padding-top` is used to set only the padding along the top edge of an element.
  - `padding-right` is used to set only the padding along the right edge of an element.
  - `padding-bottom` is used to set only the padding along the bottom edge of an element.
  - `padding-left` is used to set only the padding along the left edge of an element.
- To set the padding within an element using the shorthand property, use:

  `padding: top right bottom left`

  where `top` is the size of the padding on the top edge, `right` is the size of the padding on the right edge, `bottom` is the size of the padding on the bottom edge, and `left` is the size of the padding on the left edge.

TIP

Padding and margin settings are preserved even when the size of the browser window changes.

The **margin properties** control the external white space, which is the white space outside the border. You've used the margin properties in the body element previously. It's intuitive to think that the body element has margins, much like the page of a document in a word-processing application. In fact, every element has margins. The margin properties are often used to create white space around images. Without customization, images may appear too close to their surrounding text.

You can set the margin for each side individually by using the following four properties:

- `margin-top`
- `margin-right`
- `margin-bottom`
- `margin-left`

Setting Margins

- To set the margin space around an element, use:

  margin: *width*;

  where *width* is the size of the margin using one of the CSS units of measure.
- Use individual margin properties as follows:
  - margin-top is used to set only the margin along the top edge of an element.
  - margin-right is used to set only the margin along the right edge of an element.
  - margin-bottom is used to set only the margin along the bottom edge of an element.
  - margin-left is used to set only the margin along the left edge of an element.
- To set the margin for an element using the shorthand property use:

  margin: *top right bottom left*

  where *top* is the size of the margin on the top edge, *right* is the size of the margin on the right edge, *bottom* is the size of the margin on the bottom edge, and *left* is the size of the margin on the left edge.

Using the padding and margin Shorthand Properties

You can declare the top, right, bottom, and left margins for a selector separately as shown in the following code:

```
img {
    margin-top: 4px;
    margin-right: 4px;
    margin-bottom: 4px;
    margin-left: 4px;
}
```

However, you can make your code more compact and easier to write by taking advantage of shorthand properties for padding and margins. The **padding property** is a shorthand property that sets the padding on all four sides. The following code would create the same amount of padding on all four sides of an h1 element:

```
h1 {
    padding: 4px;
}
```

Similarly, the **margin property** is a shorthand property that sets the margin on all four sides. The following code would create the same amount of margin space on all four sides of an h2 element:

```
h2 {
    margin: 1em;
}
```

You can also use the padding and margin properties to be more specific than declaring the same value for all four sides at once. Here's how these shorthand properties work:

- If one value is listed, the value is used for all four sides equally.
- If two values are listed, the first value is applied to the top and bottom equally, and the second value is applied to the left and right sides equally.
- If three values are listed, the first value is applied to the top, the second value is applied to the left and right sides equally, and the third value is applied to the bottom.
- If four values are listed, the values are applied clockwise starting from the top, in the following order: top, right, bottom, left.

Every value except for 0 must have an accompanying measurement, with no space between the value and the measurement—in other words, *1em*, not *1 em*. For values that are less than 1, it's a good coding practice to precede the value with a leading zero (for example, 0.2em), so anyone reading your code can easily recognize that the value is less than 1.

Figure 5-5 summarizes how to set values for the `padding` and `margin` shorthand properties.

Figure 5-5 **Setting values for the padding and margin shorthand properties**

Values	Applies to these sides, in this order	Example
1	All sides equally	padding: 4px;
2	Top and bottom equally, left and right equally	margin: 10px 4px;
3	Top, left and right equally, bottom	padding: 4px 10px 4px;
4	Top, right, bottom, left	margin: 0 0 0 4px;

Understanding How Margins Collapse

When designing a Web page, you could have two adjacent vertical boxes on the page. For example, it's quite common to place an image above or below another image to create an image gallery. In such a case, it can be difficult to determine the top and bottom of the images because of **margin collapse**, which occurs when two adjoining top and bottom margins combine to form a single margin. Browsers render the greater of the two adjacent margins, not the sum of both. For example, let's say that you had two images on your Web page, with one image positioned directly below the other. If the top image had a bottom margin of 25px and the bottom image had a top margin of 20px, you might expect the distance between the two images to be 45px because 25 + 20 = 45. However, the actual distance would be 25px, which is the larger of the two margins. Margin collapse occurs only when two vertical margins come in contact. The margins of two images that are side by side do not collapse. In later tutorials on CSS layouts, you will learn how to correct margin collapse problems.

Jackie would like the `h1` and `h2` heading text centered horizontally and the headings styled with a background color. He would like the headings to be a bit further apart than the default. You'll set the left margin for the `h1` element to be 10px, and you'll set the top and left margins for the h2 element to 10px. You'll use the `margin` and `padding` properties to style these elements.

To style the h1 and h2 elements:

1. Return to the **elephant.htm** file in your text editor.

2. Within the embedded style sheet, insert the following code as shown in Figure 5-6:

Be sure to separate each value of the margin property with a space only. Do not type a comma separator after each value.

```
/* headings */

h1  {
  background-color: black;
  margin: 0 0 0 10px;
  padding: 4px;
  text-align: center;
}

h2  {
  background-color: gray;
  margin: 10px 0 0 10px;
  padding: 4px;
  text-align: center;
}
```

| Figure 5-6 | Margin and padding CSS code |

```
body {
  background-color: darkslategray;
  color: white;
  font-size: 1.1em;
  font-family: Verdana, sans-serif;
}

/* headings */

h1  {
  background-color: black;
  margin: 0 0 0 10px;
  padding: 4px;
  text-align: center;
}

h2  {
  background-color: gray;
  margin: 10px 0 0 10px;
  padding: 4px;
  text-align: center;
}

</style>
```

the margin property has four values separated by spaces

the single value for padding applies to all sides (top, right, bottom, and left)

3. Save the file.

4. Return to your Web browser, and then click the **Refresh** or **Reload** button to view the style changes in the file. The Web page should look similar to Figure 5-7.

Figure 5-7   **Web page rendered with padding and margins**

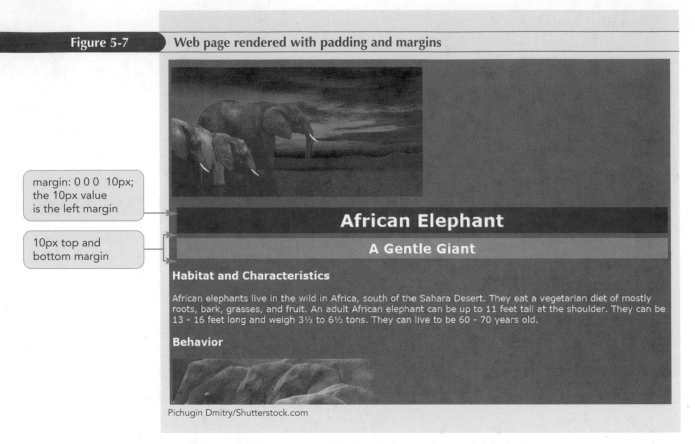

margin: 0 0 0 10px;
the 10px value
is the left margin

10px top and
bottom margin

Pichugin Dmitry/Shutterstock.com

Jackie would like you to add a border around one of the elephant images so it stands out a bit more. You'll use the border properties to do this.

Using the Border Properties

You use the **border properties** to place a decorative border around the contents and padding of an element. Recall that in the box model, the border is located between the padding and the margin. You can change a border's style, color, and width.

Setting Border Styles

The border style value can be any one of the following:

- solid
- double
- dotted
- dashed
- groove
- ridge
- inset
- outset
- none (no border; the default)

Border styles, unfortunately, can look different in each browser. Figure 5-8 illustrates the border styles as they appear in Internet Explorer.

Figure 5-8   **Borders rendered in Internet Explorer**

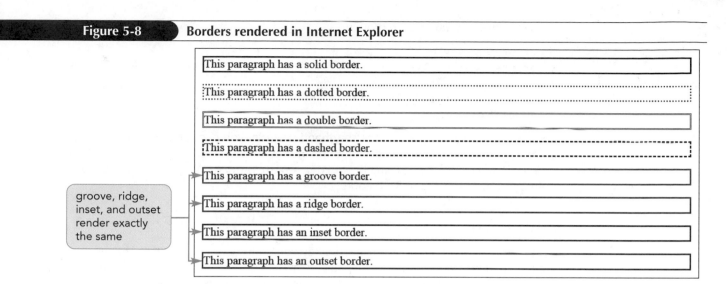

groove, ridge, inset, and outset render exactly the same

This paragraph has a solid border.

This paragraph has a dotted border.

This paragraph has a double border.

This paragraph has a dashed border.

This paragraph has a groove border.

This paragraph has a ridge border.

This paragraph has an inset border.

This paragraph has an outset border.

Figure 5-9 illustrates the border styles as they appear in Chrome.

Figure 5-9   **Borders rendered in Chrome**

This paragraph has a solid border.

This paragraph has a dotted border.

This paragraph has a double border.

This paragraph has a dashed border.

This paragraph has a groove border.

This paragraph has a ridge border.

This paragraph has an inset border.

This paragraph has an outset border.

Figure 5-10 illustrates the border styles as they appear in Safari.

Figure 5-10   **Borders rendered in Safari**

This paragraph has a solid border.

This paragraph has a dotted border.

This paragraph has a double border.

This paragraph has a dashed border.

This paragraph has a groove border.

This paragraph has a ridge border.

This paragraph has an inset border.

This paragraph has an outset border.

There are five `border-style` properties:

* `border-top-style`
* `border-right-style`
* `border-bottom-style`
* `border-left-style`
* `border-style`

The `border-style` property is the shorthand property you can use to set the values for all four border styles with one declaration.

You set the border color using the `border-color` property. You can use the CSS3 color names, or the hex or RGB code.

Setting Border Width

Border width can be expressed using the keywords `thin`, `medium`, and `thick`, as a value in pixels or ems, or as a percentage. Browsers display the thicknesses of the keyword values slightly differently, but in general, a thin border is 1px wide, a medium border is 3px or 4px wide, and a thick border is 4px (or more) wide. When creating page layouts in which elements have borders, it's best to avoid these browser discrepancies, so instead of using keywords, you should rely on pixel values to express border thickness. Figure 5-11 illustrates various border widths.

Figure 5-11	Border thicknesses

There are five `border-width` properties:

* `border-top-width`
* `border-right-width`
* `border-bottom-width`
* `border-left-width`
* `border-width`

The **`border-width` property** is the shorthand property you can use to set the width values for all four borders at once.

Setting Border Color

The border color can be a named color, a hex value, or an RGB value. There are five `border-color` properties:

* `border-top-color`
* `border-right-color`
* `border-bottom-color`
* `border-left-color`
* `border-color`

The **border-color property** is the shorthand property you can use to set the color values for all four borders at once. Figure 5-12 illustrates the border colors.

Figure 5-12   **Border colors**

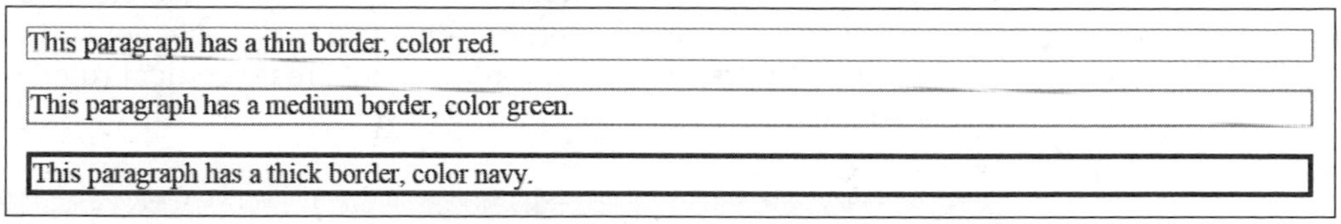

This paragraph has a thin border, color red.

This paragraph has a medium border, color green.

This paragraph has a thick border, color navy.

Using the Border Shorthand Properties

There are eight border shorthand properties. As you saw in the previous section, the following three properties change the border style, width, or color for all four borders:

- border-color
- border-style
- border-width

The following four properties change the border style, width, and color for an individual border:

- border-top
- border-right
- border-bottom
- border-left

Finally, the border property changes the border style, width, and color for all four borders. You must specify a border style when you use the border shorthand property. Use spaces, not commas, to separate values when using the border shorthand properties.

The following border shorthand property sets the border color for all sides to maroon:

```
h1 {
   border-color: maroon;
}
```

The following code sets the top border to be solid, thin, and red:

```
h2 {
   border-top: solid thin red;
}
```

The following code sets all borders to be inset, thick, and orange:

```
h3 {
   border: inset thick orange;
}
```

You can list the border style, thickness, and color in any order, and you do not have to specify three values; however, if you use two values, one of them must be a border style. If you omit a value for color, the border color matches the element's color. For example, to use the border shorthand property to change borders to appear in navy, you would enter the following code:

```
h1 {
   border: dotted navy;
}
```

Note that a border style—in this instance, `dotted`—must be specified. The `border` property is clearly favored over the use of the HTML horizontal rule (`hr`) element, which draws a horizontal line across the screen. Screen readers have trouble interpreting the horizontal rule element, so for accessibility reasons, you should always substitute the border property in place of the horizontal rule element. Another advantage of using the CSS border properties is that you can create vertical ruled lines by changing the border on the left or right. You cannot create vertical ruled lines by using HTML code alone.

REFERENCE

Setting the Appearance of all Four Borders at Once

- To set the border width, use:

  `border-width: width;`

  where *width* is one of the CSS units of measure.
- To set the border color, use:

  `border-color: value;`

  where *value* is a named color, RGB color, or hexadecimal color value.
- To set the border style, use:

  `border-style: style;`

  where *style* is `none`, `solid`, `double`, `dotted`, `dashed`, `outset`, `inset`, `groove`, or `ridge`.
- To use the `border` shorthand property, enter:

  `border: style color width;`
  or
  `border-side: style color width;`

  where *style* is the border style, *color* is the border color, *width* is the border width, and *side* is `top`, `right`, `bottom`, or `left`. Although not all three values need to be specified and values can be entered in any order, at minimum you must specify a border style.

Jackie would like a solid darkkhaki bottom border below the `h3` elements. You'll also use the padding property to create some white space between the bottom border and the `h3` heading text.

To create a bottom border for the `h3` elements:

1. Return to the **elephant.htm** file in your text editor.

2. On a blank line below the style for the `h2` element, type the following code to style the `h3` element, as shown in Figure 5-13:

```
h3  {
    border-bottom: solid thick darkkhaki;
    padding-bottom: 0.5em;
}
```

Be sure to separate each value of the `border-bottom` property with a space only. Do not type a comma separator after each value.

Figure 5-13   **Bottom border and padding for the h3 element**

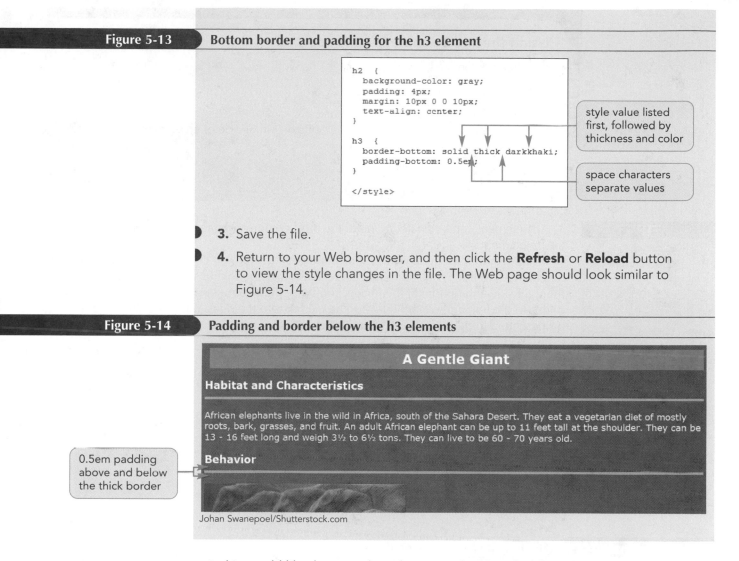

```
h2  {
    background-color: gray;
    padding: 4px;
    margin: 10px 0 0 10px;
    text-align: center;
}

h3  {
    border-bottom: solid thick darkkhaki;
    padding-bottom: 0.5em;
}

</style>
```

style value listed first, followed by thickness and color

space characters separate values

3. Save the file.

4. Return to your Web browser, and then click the **Refresh** or **Reload** button to view the style changes in the file. The Web page should look similar to Figure 5-14.

Figure 5-14   **Padding and border below the h3 elements**

A Gentle Giant

Habitat and Characteristics

African elephants live in the wild in Africa, south of the Sahara Desert. They eat a vegetarian diet of mostly roots, bark, grasses, and fruit. An adult African elephant can be up to 11 feet tall at the shoulder. They can be 13 - 16 feet long and weigh 3½ to 6½ tons. They can live to be 60 - 70 years old.

Behavior

0.5em padding above and below the thick border

Johan Swanepoel/Shutterstock.com

Jackie would like the h1 and h2 elements to be placed to the right of the first image. He would also like the second image to be placed along the right edge of the Web page. You'll create these effects by using the float property.

Using the float Property

Two additional box properties are the float and clear properties. The float property is used to position boxes on the page and to wrap content, such as text, around a box. If the float property for an element has a value of left, the element appears at the left edge of the containing element, which may be the browser window, and the remaining page content wraps to the right of the element. Likewise, if the float property for an element has a value of right, the element appears at the right edge of the browser window and the remaining page content wraps to the left of the element.

The clear property is used to specify whether or not an element can have another floating element beside it. Specifically, the clear property specifies the side or sides where floating elements are not allowed. If the clear property is set to none, floating elements are not allowed on either side. This type of double-negative logic can be difficult to understand, but basically if the clear property for an element is set to none, then floating elements are allowed on all sides of the element. If the clear property for an element is set to both, no floating elements are allowed on either side of the element.

REFERENCE

Using the *float* and *clear* Properties

- To float an element, use the style:

  ```
  float: position;
  ```

  where *position* is left, right, or none.
- To set the restrictions for floating elements on either side of an element use the style:

  ```
  clear: value;
  ```

  where *value* is none or both.

TIP

The float property does not have a value of center or middle. If you want to center an image horizontally, use the text-align property on the element that contains the img element (such as a p element).

Any element can be floated. One of the most common elements to float is the image element.

Jackie would like you to place the first image in the top-left corner, with the h1 and h2 elements to the right of that image. He'd also like you to add some white space on the right side and bottom of the image. You'll use the float property to float the first image to the left, and wrap the h1 and h2 elements to the right. You'll use the margin property to add right and bottom margins of 10px.

To float an image left and add margin space:

1. Return to the **elephant.htm** file in your text editor.

2. On a blank line below the style for the h3 element, type the following code to style the img element, as shown in Figure 5-15:

   ```
   img {
       float: left;
       margin: 0 10px 10px 0;
   }
   ```

Figure 5-15   Floating the first image on the left

```
h3  {
   border-bottom: solid thick darkkhaki;
   padding-bottom: 0.5em;
}

img  {
   float: left;
   margin: 0 10px 10px 0;
}
```

3. Save the file.

4. Return to your Web browser, and then click the **Refresh** or **Reload** button to view the style changes in the file. The Web page should look similar to Figure 5-16.

Figure 5-16	Image floats left and elements wrap to the right of the image

image element floats left

African Elephant

A Gentle Giant

Habitat and Characteristics

African elephants live in the wild in Africa, south of the Sahara Desert. They eat a vegetarian diet of mostly roots, bark, grasses, and fruit. An adult African elephant can be up to 11 feet tall at the shoulder. They can be 13 - 16 feet long and weigh

3½ to 6½ tons. They can live to be 60 - 70 years old.

Behavior

African elephants ... plex society that is ba... approximately 10 ... all elements wrap to the right until the space that spans the entire height of the image is used related females (... ts join together to form a group. After male elephants reach

Johan Swanepoel/Shutterstock.com; Pichugin Dmitry/Shutterstock.com

The second image also floats to the left, and elements wrap to the right of it as well. Jackie would like the second image positioned on the right-hand side of the Web page, with the text wrapping to the left. You can't style the same element two different ways, but you can create a dependent class for the img element. You'll create a dependent class named `right` that will float an image to the right. You'll also use the margin property to create white space on the top, bottom, and left sides of the image. Jackie would also like a border around the second image to make it stand out a bit. You'll use the border property to place a border around the second image.

To create and apply a dependent class to float the second image to the right:

1. Return to the **elephant.htm** file in your text editor.

2. On a blank line below the style for the img element, type the following code to create the dependent class, as shown in Figure 5-17:

```
img.right {
  border: double thick black;
  float: right;
  margin: 10px 0 10px 10px;
}
```

Figure 5-17	Code for the dependent class to float right

```
img {
  float: left;
  margin: 0 10px 10px 0;
}

img.right {
  border: double thick black;
  float: right;
  margin: 10px 0 10px 10px;
}
```

3. In the `<img>` tag below the *Behavior* h3 heading, type the following code to apply the *right* dependent class to the image element as shown in Figure 5-18:

```
class = "right"
```

Figure 5-18   **Apply the class to the image element**

```
<p>
<img src="images/elephants_drinking.jpg" alt="African elephants drinking water" class = "right"/>
</p>
```

4. Save the file.

5. Return to your Web browser, and then click the **Refresh** or **Reload** button to view the style changes in the file. The Web page should look similar to Figure 5-19.

Figure 5-19   **Float right applied to the image**

Behavior

African elephants are very social animals. They have a complex society that is based on a family unit. Each family unit has approximately 10 individual elephants, composed of closely related females (cows) and their calves. Separate family units join together to form a group. After male elephants reach puberty, they tend to form alliances with other males. Elephants are also very nurturing animals. Two elephants will wrap their trunks together to give each other a hug.

African elephants are very intelligent. They communicate with deep growling or rumbling noises. Elephants also communicate using noises that are too low for humans to hear, yet very loud. Their noises can be heard 5 or 6 miles away. Smell is their most highly developed sense.

Tusks

- Elephant tusks are ivory teeth that grow throughout their lives.
- Elephants are right- or left-tusked, using the favored tusk more often, thus shortening it from constant wear.
- Elephants use their tusks to dig up roots and pry bark from trees to find food.

Quick Facts

Here are a few interesting facts:

image floating right with a double thick border

Johan Swanepoel/Shutterstock.com

Jackie is happy with the improvements to the African Elephant Facts Web page. The next improvement he'd like is to move the *Habitat and Characteristics* section below the first image. He'd like the h1 and h2 heading elements to remain on the left side of the image, though. You'll need to use the `clear` property to position the *Habitat and Characteristics* section.

Using the `clear` Property

TIP

If you're not sure which `clear` property value to use, use the value `both`.

You can use the `clear` property to position the contents of an element below another element that has been floated. This is also called **clearing past** an element. The `clear` property takes the following values:

- `left`—content begins below an element floated left
- `right`—content begins below an element floated right
- `both`—content begins below an element floated either left or right

REFERENCE

Using the `clear` Property

- To clear past an element, use the following style:

  `clear: position;`

  where *position* is `left`, `right`, or `both`.

You'll create an independent class called *clear* to apply the `clear` property with a value of `both`. Because different elements on the page might have to use the `clear` property, it's best to create an independent class. The independent class can be applied to other elements as well, rather than creating a dependent class that could be applied only to the `h3` element.

To create and apply an independent class for the `clear` property:

1. Return to the **elephant.htm** file in your text editor.

2. On a blank line below the style for the *img.right* dependent class, type the following code to create the *clear* independent class, as shown in Figure 5-20:

```
.clear {
  clear: both;
}
```

Figure 5-20	Code for the clear independent class

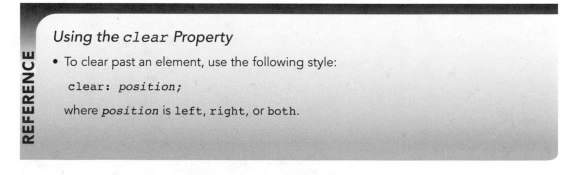

```
img.right {
  border: double thick black;
  float: right;
  margin: 10px 0 10px 10px;
}

.clear   {
  clear: both;
}
```

3. In the start `<h3>` tag for the *Habitat and Characteristics* `h3` element, insert the following code to apply the *clear* independent class:

`class = "clear"`

4. Repeat Step 3 for the start `<h3>` tag for the *Quick Facts* `h3` element. Compare your code to Figure 5-21.

Figure 5-21 **Code for the h3 elements with the clear class applied**

this h3 element is near the top of the Web page

```
<h2>Facts</h2>

<h3 class = "clear">Habitat and Characteristics</h3>

<p>African elephants live in
. . .

</ul>

<h3 class = "clear">Quick Facts</h3>

<p>Here are a few intersting facts:</p>
```

this h3 element is about halfway down the Web page

5. Save the file.

6. Return to your Web browser, and then click the **Refresh** or **Reload** button to view the style changes in the file. The Web page should look similar to Figure 5-22.

Figure 5-22 **Clear class applied to two h3 elements**

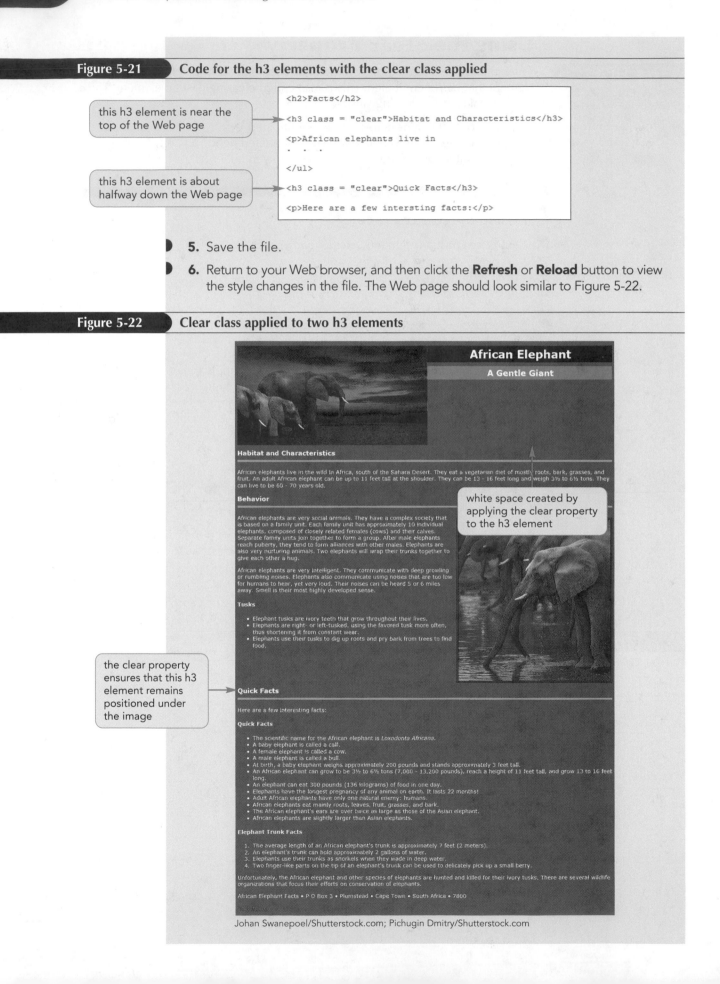

white space created by applying the clear property to the h3 element

the clear property ensures that this h3 element remains positioned under the image

Johan Swanepoel/Shutterstock.com; Pichugin Dmitry/Shutterstock.com

Jackie loves the way the images are staggered on the Web page, adding interest to the design. He'd like you to add a textured background and some background images for other elements on the Web page. You'll look at adding these features in the next session.

PROSKILLS

Problem Solving: Troubleshooting Style Sheet Errors

One of the most frustrating and time-consuming parts of writing any kind of computer code is the troubleshooting phase. Finding and fixing problems in code, known as **debugging** the code, occupies the vast majority of many software developers' time.

If you load or refresh a Web page in a Web browser and then see a problem, what do you do next? Following are some of the most common problems, along with tips for fixing them:

- *Missing semicolons*: Check the end of every style property to ensure there is a semicolon in place. If a semicolon is missing, the style rules that follow will not work.
- *Typo*: The style rule property names and selectors must be typed correctly, including capitalization (uppercase or lowercase).
- *Missing brace bracket*: Be sure there is a brace bracket (also called a curly bracket) at the beginning and end of each style rule to define the block of properties for that rule.

When you find a problem, locate the first instance of the problem, then look for a style associated with that HTML element.

Finally, if you start to become frustrated, take a break! Get up and walk away from your computer for a few minutes. You'll be surprised how many times you find the problem right after you take a break.

You may also want to consider using the CSS validator often while you're developing a Web page. If you make this a habit, you'll save time that would have been spent looking for many errors later!

REVIEW

Session 5.1 Quick Check

1. What is the box model?
2. What is padding?
3. What is the margin?
4. When using the `border` shorthand property, which value must always be specified?
5. What are the possible values for the `float` property?
6. What are the possible values for the `clear` property?

SESSION 5.2 VISUAL OVERVIEW

The link element attaches a CSS external style sheet to the Web page.

```
<link rel = "stylesheet" href = "main_layout.css" type = "text/css" />
```

Use an internal style sheet for styles that apply only to a specific Web page.

```
<style type = "text/css">
ul.facts {
    line-height: 1.4;
    list-style-type: none;
    padding: 0;
    margin-left: 1em;
}
</style>
```

Use an external style sheet for style rules that will be applied to all Web pages in the Web site, such as those that set background and text color and float images.

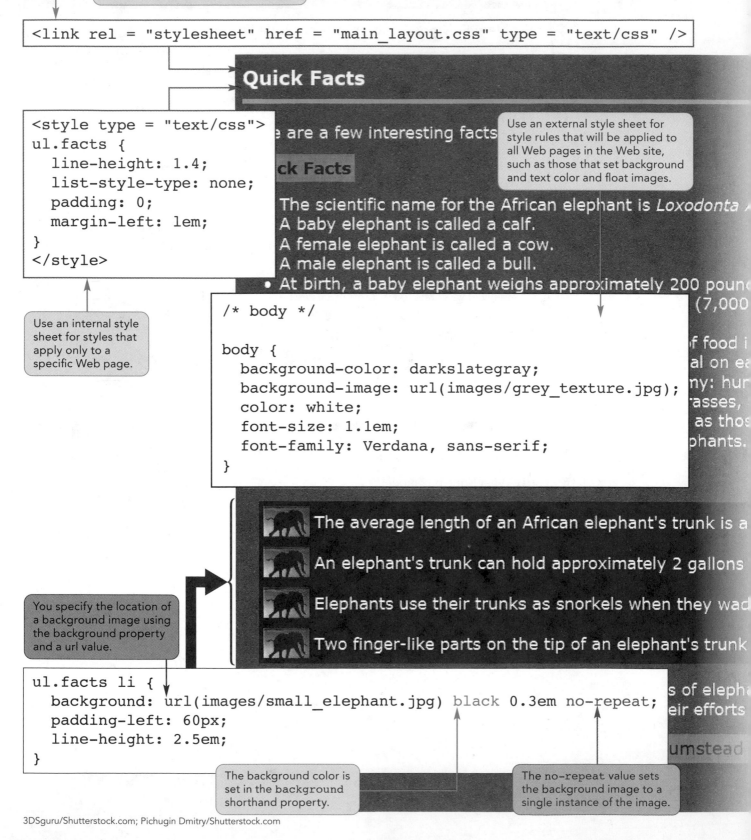

Quick Facts

...e are a few interesting facts...

ck Facts

- The scientific name for the African elephant is *Loxodonta*...
- A baby elephant is called a calf.
- A female elephant is called a cow.
- A male elephant is called a bull.
- At birth, a baby elephant weighs approximately 200 pound... (7,000...

...f food i...
...al on ea...
ny: hur...
...asses,...
...as thos...
...phants.

```
/* body */

body {
    background-color: darkslategray;
    background-image: url(images/grey_texture.jpg);
    color: white;
    font-size: 1.1em;
    font-family: Verdana, sans-serif;
}
```

The average length of an African elephant's trunk is a...

An elephant's trunk can hold approximately 2 gallons...

Elephants use their trunks as snorkels when they wad...

Two finger-like parts on the tip of an elephant's trunk...

You specify the location of a background image using the background property and a url value.

```
ul.facts li {
    background: url(images/small_elephant.jpg) black 0.3em no-repeat;
    padding-left: 60px;
    line-height: 2.5em;
}
```

...s of eleph...
...eir efforts...

...umstead

The background color is set in the background shorthand property.

The no-repeat value sets the background image to a single instance of the image.

USING BACKGROUND IMAGES

Always supply a background color when using a background image in case the image cannot be viewed.

If you specify only a filename for the `background-image` property, the image is automatically tiled to cover the entire element.

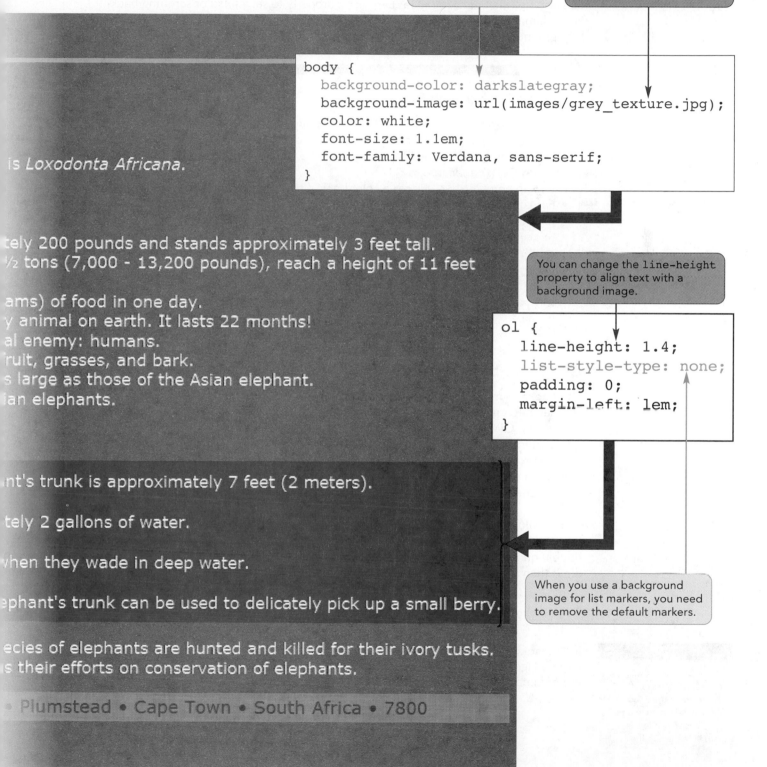

is Loxodonta Africana.

```css
body {
    background-color: darkslategray;
    background-image: url(images/grey_texture.jpg);
    color: white;
    font-size: 1.1em;
    font-family: Verdana, sans-serif;
}
```

tely 200 pounds and stands approximately 3 feet tall.
½ tons (7,000 - 13,200 pounds), reach a height of 11 feet

ams) of food in one day.
y animal on earth. It lasts 22 months!
al enemy: humans.
ruit, grasses, and bark.
s large as those of the Asian elephant.
ian elephants.

You can change the `line-height` property to align text with a background image.

```css
ol {
    line-height: 1.4;
    list-style-type: none;
    padding: 0;
    margin-left: 1em;
}
```

nt's trunk is approximately 7 feet (2 meters).

tely 2 gallons of water.

when they wade in deep water.

ephant's trunk can be used to delicately pick up a small berry.

When you use a background image for list markers, you need to remove the default markers.

ecies of elephants are hunted and killed for their ivory tusks.
s their efforts on conservation of elephants.

Plumstead • Cape Town • South Africa • 7800

Understanding the Background Properties

The **background properties** set the background effects for an element. You've already worked with the `background-color` property to set the background color for an element. To create greater visual interest, you can also use the `background-image` property to use an image as the background for an element. The `background-repeat` property lets you repeat an image vertically, horizontally, or both. To position a background image within an element, you use the `background-position` property. You can also use the `background-attachment` property to set a fixed or scrolling background image. Finally, you can use the `background` shortcut property to set all of the background image properties in one declaration.

REFERENCE

Setting Background Properties

Use the following properties to set the appearance of the background:

- `background-image`—Places an image behind the contents of an element. The image can be any GIF, PNG, or JPEG image, but the filename must be specified using the syntax url(*imagename.gif*).
- `background-color`—Places a color behind an element's contents.
- `background-position`—Positions an image within an element. Use keywords or pixel, em, or percentage values.
- `background-repeat`—Repeats an image horizontally or vertically (or both) to fill the contents of an element.
- `background-attachment`—Sets a background image to scroll with the cursor, or fixes the background, with only the elements on top of the background scrolling.
- `background`—Changes all of the background properties together. Values (if used) must be listed in this order: *image color position repeat attachment*.

Using the `background-image` Property

The `background-image` property is used to fill the background of an element with an image. To create the image, you can use image-editing software such as Adobe Photoshop, GIMP, Microsoft Expression Design, or even Microsoft Paint. Make sure you select an image for the background that preserves the readability of the text. Images such as textures that are almost uniform work well as background images. If an image contains a distinct pattern, ensure the contrast is very light so it truly does fade into the background; a background image should contrast with the text rather than compete with it.

The value for the `background-image` property begins with the word *url*. Although it is not incorrect to enclose the filename for the background image with either single or double quotation marks, most Web developers omit the quotes. The name of the image file is then specified in parentheses, as shown in the following code:

```
body {
    background-image: url(images/tile.jpg);
}
```

TIP

The `url` value is the location and name of the image file. If the image file is stored in an images folder, specify it in the path in the `url` value.

If the `background-image` property is used with the body element as a selector and if the image is repeated both horizontally and vertically (the default), then the background image will repeat to occupy the entire Web page.

Working with Background Color

It's a good coding practice to always use the `background-color` property when you use the `background-image` property, in case the background image is not large enough to cover the entire Web browser window. Select a background color that contrasts with the font color so the font is readable. That way, if the background image is not displayed, the text is still readable. When some browsers have problems displaying an image element, they show a placeholder icon instead of the image to alert you to the problem. However, if the `background-image` code contains an error, an image placeholder icon is not displayed. If you specify a background color for an element, the element's contents still appear against the background color even if there is an error in the image code. Also, specifying a `background-color` property overrides any default setting in the browser for background color, which usually is white. You should always set a background color, even if it is white. If you are using a background image for the `body` element, make sure your body text has a contrasting color, not a similar color.

Setting the `background-position` Property

The `background-position` property allows you to position a background image in different locations within its container element. The container element could be the `body`, `head`, or `footer`. If the container element is the `body` element, the image will be positioned as background for the entire Web page. The values for the `background-position` property can be expressed by using keywords, percent values, or any other CSS measurement units, such as pixels or ems. The keywords are used together to position the image in one of nine regions behind the element, as shown in Figure 5-23. The default value for the `background-position` property is `top left`.

Figure 5-23 Keywords that describe the position of a background image

top left	top center	top right
center left	center center	center right
bottom left	bottom center	bottom right

You can also use percentage pairs instead of keywords. The first percentage describes the horizontal position, and the second percentage describes the vertical position. Figure 5-24 shows values expressed in percentages instead of keywords. The top-left corner is 0% 0%, and the bottom-right corner is 100% 100%. You enter a space, not a comma, between the values.

Figure 5-24 Percentage values that describe the position of a background image

0% 0%	50% 0%	100% 0%
0% 50%	50% 50%	100% 50%
0% 100%	50% 100%	100% 100%

You aren't limited to percentages of 0, 50, and 100%. You can specify any percentage from 0 to 100 for the horizontal and vertical positions, such as 5% 98%. If only one percentage is given, it is assumed to be the horizontal position, and a vertical position of 50% is assigned as a default. Although pixel and em values are less commonly used, you can use them to precisely position the contents of an element within its containing block.

Using the `background-repeat` Property

You use the `background-repeat` property to have copies of an image appear behind an element horizontally, vertically, or in both orientations. Repeating an image is also known as **tiling** an image. The `background-repeat` property accepts the four values shown in Figure 5-25.

| Figure 5-25 | Values for the background-repeat property |

Property	Effect
`repeat`	The image is repeated (tiled) to the right and down to fill the element's contents; this is the default value
`repeat-x`	The image is repeated only horizontally
`repeat-y`	The image is repeated only vertically
`no-repeat`	The image is displayed once and is not repeated

If the `background-repeat` property is not specified, the default setting repeats the image both horizontally and vertically. Figure 5-26 shows a small image tiled as a background image on a Web page.

| Figure 5-26 | Background image is tiled |

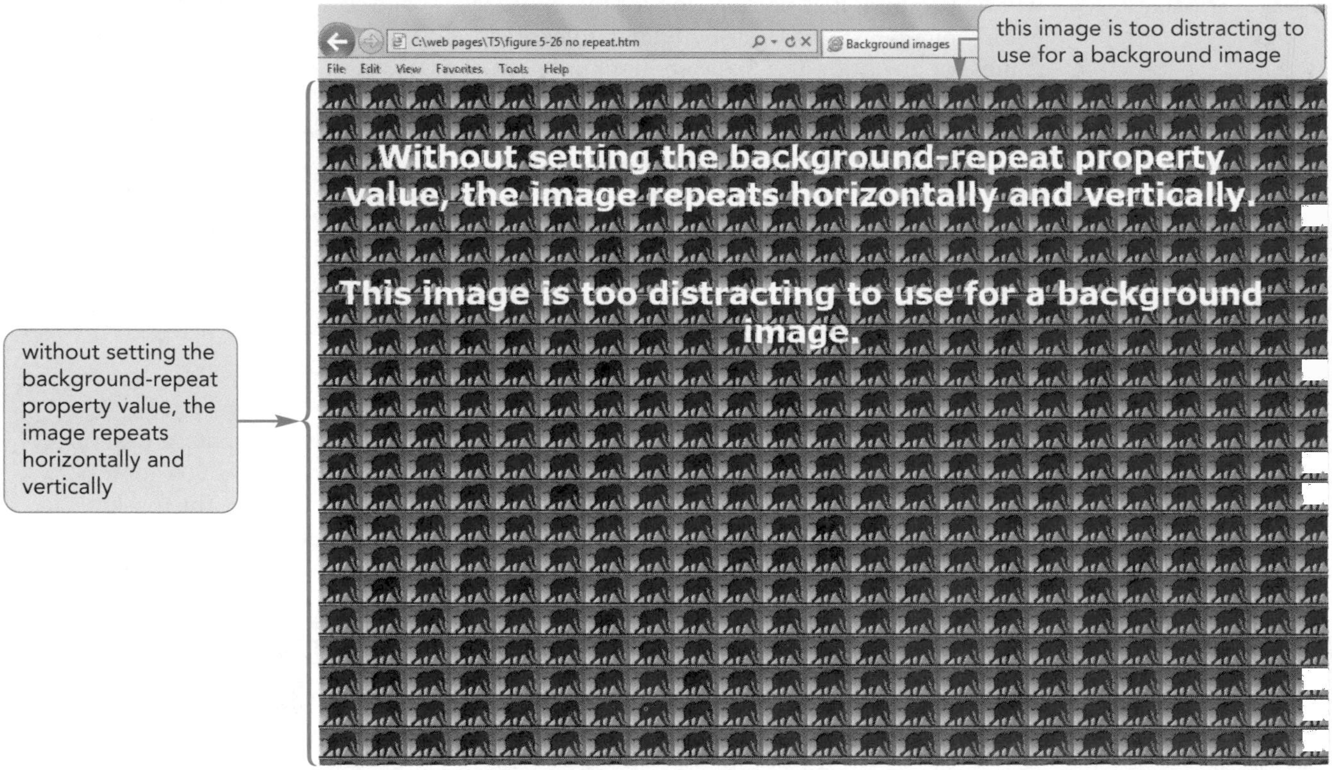

this image is too distracting to use for a background image

without setting the background-repeat property value, the image repeats horizontally and vertically

Pichugin Dmitry/Shutterstock.com

The style used for the body element to achieve this effect is the following:

```
body {
   background-image: url(images/small_elephant.jpg);
}
```

The `repeat-x` value repeats a background image horizontally (along the x-axis, a concept from mathematics). This effect is shown in Figure 5-27.

Figure 5-27   Web page with a horizontally tiled background image

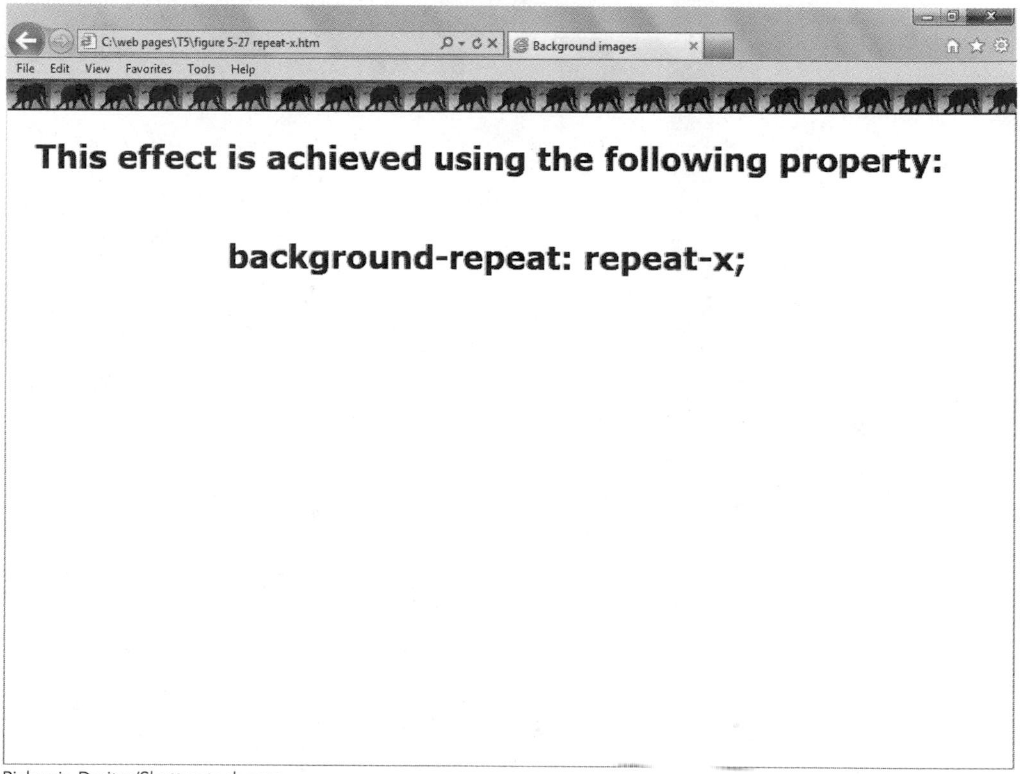

Pichugin Dmitry/Shutterstock.com

Similarly, the `repeat-y` value repeats the image vertically (along the y-axis). This effect is shown in Figure 5-28.

| Figure 5-28 | Web page with a vertically tiled background image |

This effect is achieved using the following property:

background-repeat: repeat-y;

Pichugin Dmitry/Shutterstock.com

Using the *background-attachment* Property

INSIGHT

The background-attachment property allows you to set the behavior of the background image with respect to scrolling. The default behavior is the background image scrolls with the rest of the Web page content. The background-attachment property also allows you to detach the background from the elements so the background stays in place, and the content scrolls on top of the fixed background when you scroll down the page. This effect is only seen when the content is longer than the containing element. This property accepts two values: scroll, the default value, in which the image scrolls down the page; and fixed, in which the image stays in place and text scrolls over the image as the user scrolls down the page. The fixed value would be useful, for example, to ensure that a corporate logo always appears at the top of a page, even as the user scrolls down.

Using the background Shorthand Property

The background property is the shorthand property that lets you specify any or all of the background properties. You can use as few or as many of the properties as you want, but you must specify the properties and their values in the following order:

- background-image
- background-color
- background-position
- background-repeat
- background-attachment

As with the other shorthand properties, you use spaces, not commas, to separate the values, as shown below:

```
body {
    background: url(images/flowers.jpg) yellow top left repeat-y;
}
```

Jackie has found a textured background image that he would like you to use for the African Elephant Facts Web page. The textured background image has been designed so it is seamless, and when it is tiled, you won't be able to tell that the effect was achieved with a lot of smaller images repeating. You'll use the `background-image` property for the `body` element to set the tiled background image. You won't need a `background-repeat` property because the default setting is to repeat, and that's the effect you want.

The background image that Jackie provided is called grey_texture.jpg and is shown in Figure 5-29.

Figure 5-29	Grey texture image

3DSguru/Shutterstock.com

The image has a texture, but not a noticeable repeating pattern. This is an excellent choice for a background because it adds some interest without competing with the text. Also, similar to a solid color, the edges of the image will meet and appear to blend together.

To set a background image for the body element:

1. Return to the **elephant.htm** file in your text editor.

2. Edit the `body` element style rules to include the following code, shown in Figure 5-30:

```
background-image: url(images/grey_texture.jpg);
```

Figure 5-30 **Code to add a background image**

there is no need
to place quotes
around the image
name and path

```
body {
    background-color: darkslategray;
    background-image: url(images/grey_texture.jpg);
    color: white;
    font-size: 1.1em;
    font-family: Verdana, sans-serif;
}
```

3. Save the file.

4. Return to your Web browser, and then click the **Refresh** or **Reload** button to view the style changes in the file. The Web page should look similar to Figure 5-31.

Figure 5-31 **The background image is tiled, appearing as a subtle texture**

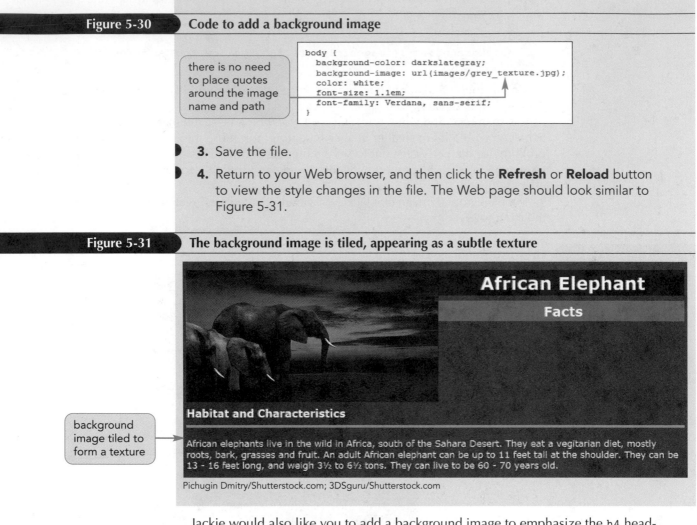

background
image tiled to
form a texture

Pichugin Dmitry/Shutterstock.com; 3DSguru/Shutterstock.com

Jackie would also like you to add a background image to emphasize the h4 headings that precede the unordered lists, and to emphasize the footer section at the bottom of the page. Jackie has provided an image named green_linen.jpg, which creates a textured background. You'll also set the background color to yellow in case a Web browser does not render the background image.

To style the h4 and footer selectors:

1. Return to the **elephant.htm** file in your text editor.

2. After the h3 style rule, insert the following code to style the h4 and footer elements, as shown in Figure 5-32:

```
h4 {
    background-image: url(image/green_linen.jpg);
    background-color: yellow;
    display: inline;
    padding: 4px;
    color: black;
}

footer {
    background-image: url(image/green_linen.jpg);
    background-color: yellow;
    color: black;
    padding: 4px;
    text-align: center;
    font-size: 1.1em;
    display: block;
}
```

Figure 5-32   **Code for the h4 and footer elements**

```
h3   {
   border-bottom: solid thick darkkhaki;
   padding-bottom: 0.5em;
}

h4   {
   background-image: url(images/green_linen.jpg);
   background-color: yellow;
   display: inline;
   padding: 4px;
   color: black;
}

footer  {
   background-image: url(images/green_linen.jpg);
   background-color: yellow;
   color: black;
   padding: 4px;
   text-align: center;
   font-size: 1.1em;
   display: block;
}

img  {
   float: left;
   margin: 0 10px 10px 0;
}
```

3. Save the file.

4. Return to your Web browser, and then click the **Refresh** or **Reload** button to view the style changes in the file. The Web page should look similar to Figure 5-33.

| Figure 5-33 | The h4 and footer elements stylized in the browser |

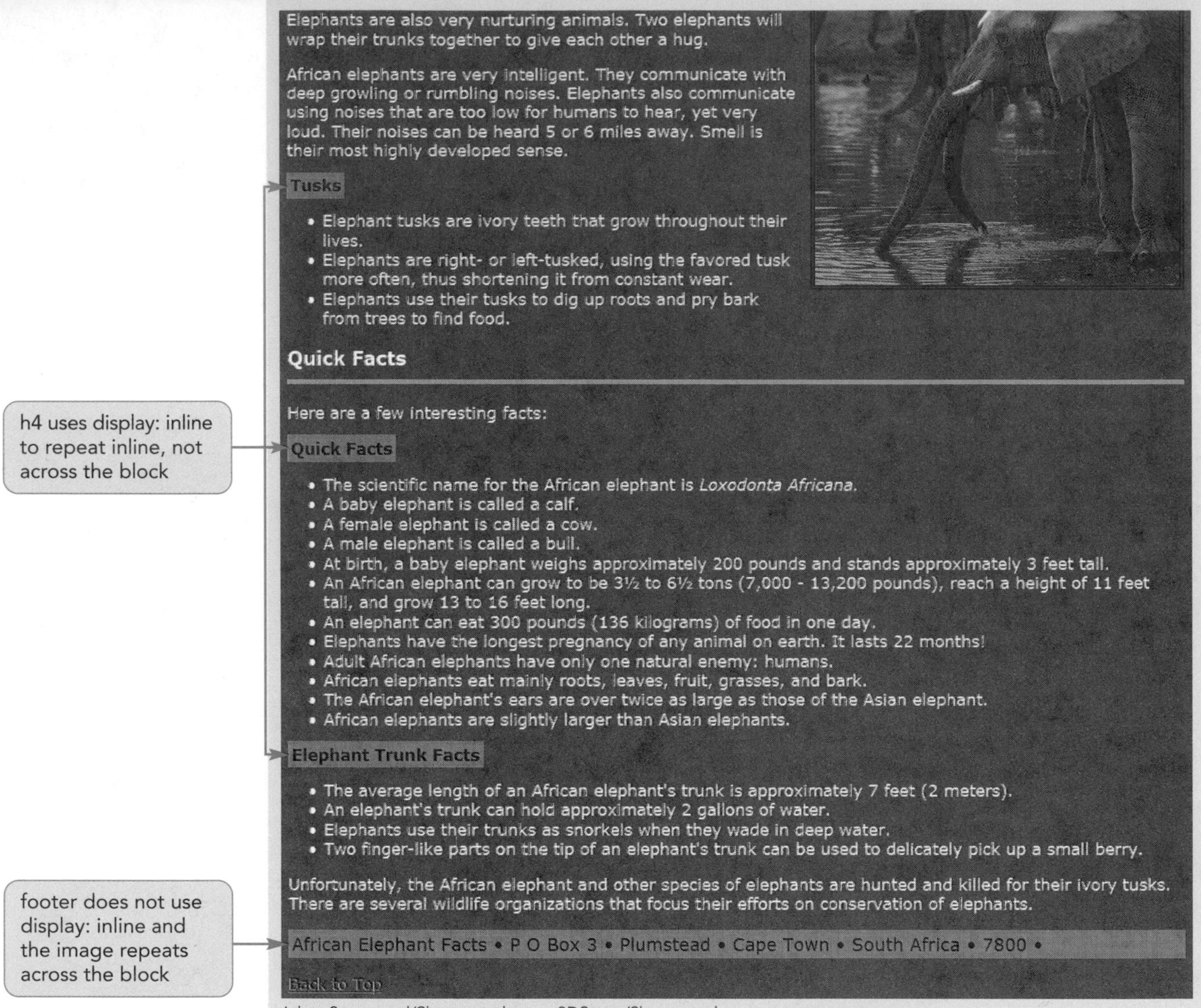

h4 uses display: inline to repeat inline, not across the block

footer does not use display: inline and the image repeats across the block

Johan Swanepoel/Shutterstock.com; 3DSguru/Shutterstock.com

Next, you want to customize the unordered lists. You've already seen a method to use an image as a list marker. You can also use a background image for a list and use the margin and padding properties to position the background image so it looks like a list marker as it tiles. Jackie has provided a small image of an elephant and would like you to use it as a background for the ordered list that describes elephant trunk facts.

Using a Background Image for List Items

Although you can use CSS to change the list style type from solid round bullets to squares, hollow circles, or an image that you specify, CSS does not provide any control over the positioning of list style markers, particularly images used as bullets. Depending on the image used as a marker, the bullet might be either too high or too low in relation to the text to its right in the list item, causing the image and text to look misaligned. Unfortunately, the CSS vertical-align property cannot be used to position bullets in a list. One option is to control the appearance of images used as list markers by using the background-image property to style the list item element.

The position of the list marker and the padding will vary depending on the font size and the size of the image used as a list marker. To accommodate the size of the bullet you choose, you might also have to style the list element to create more (or less) line spacing between the list items. By default, an HTML bullet in an unordered list is about 15px square. If you create an image to be used as a list marker that is larger than 15px, you should also increase the line height to adjust for the size of the image. It is often a process of trial and error to find the correct setting.

Jackie would like to highlight the items in the Elephant Trunk Facts list by using the small elephant image to look like a list item bullet. To do this, you'll remove any list style type, and then you'll change the line height to accommodate the image. Next, you'll specify the padding and a left margin. HTML lists have a certain amount of indentation, but browsers differ on how to create the indent. Some browsers use padding, while others use margins. To compensate for browser differences in the way they render lists, you'll eliminate the padding and set the left margin. With this approach, you'll control the dimensions of the indent yourself, without relying on the browser default setting. One of the ul elements has the *facts* class applied. You'll use the following code for the ul element with the *facts* descendent selector:

```
ul.facts {
   line-height: 1.4em;
   list-style-type: none;
   padding: 0;
   margin-left: 1em;
}
```

Next, you'll set the properties and values for the list item element. In addition to using the elephant image for the bullet, you can provide a background color to highlight the list items. This color will not apply to the image; rather, it will provide a background color for the list item element. Because you want to affect only the appearance of list items within unordered lists, you'll need to create a descendant selector for the unordered list element. You don't want the list marker image to repeat, so the value for the background-repeat property will be no-repeat. The code for the list item will look as follows:

```
ul.facts li {
   background-image: url(images/small_elephant.jpg);
   background-color: black;
   background-repeat: no-repeat;
}
```

Finally, you'll add code to position the image marker. You'll need to create a margin on the left and some padding between the margin and the image marker, and you'll need to position the marker in relation to the list item text to its right. In this instance, you'll use the background-position property to position the image marker 0.3em from the left. You'll add the line-height property to increase the vertical space of list items to 2.5em. Using the background shorthand property, you'll also specify the background-color as black, the background-position at 0.3em, and the background-repeat as no-repeat. The complete code for the list item element is shown below:

```
ul.facts li {
   background: url(images/small_elephant.jpg) black 0.3em no-repeat;
   padding-left: 60px;
   line-height: 2.5em;
}
```

To create the style for the small_elephant.jpg list item marker:

1. Return to the **elephant.htm** file in your text editor.

2. On a blank line below the `.clear` style, type the following code, as shown in Figure 5-34:

```
ul.facts {
   line-height: 1.4em;
   list-style-type: none;
   padding: 0;
   margin-left: 1em;
}

ul.facts li {
   background: url(images/small_elephant.jpg) black 0.3em
no-repeat;
   padding-left: 60px;
   line-height: 2.5em;
}
```

Figure 5-34 Code for the background image to appear as list markers

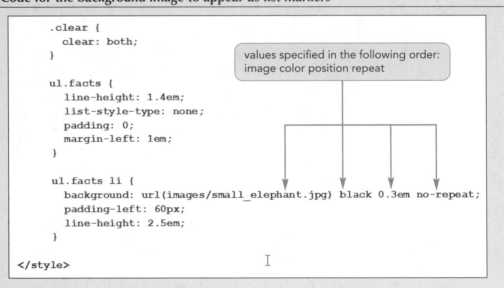

3. Save the file.

4. Return to your Web browser, and then click the **Refresh** or **Reload** button to view the style changes in the file. The Web page should look similar to Figure 5-35.

Figure 5-35   **List stylized with a repeating background image**

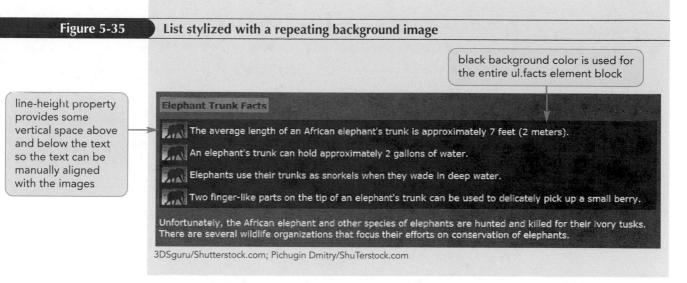

line-height property provides some vertical space above and below the text so the text can be manually aligned with the images

black background color is used for the entire ul.facts element block

3DSguru/Shutterstock.com; Pichugin Dmitry/ShuTerstock.com

Figure 5-36 summarizes the background properties.

Figure 5-36   **The background properties**

Property	What it does	Values
background-image	Places an image behind an element's content	Any GIF, JPEG, or PNG file; for example, url (imagename.gif)
background-color	Places a color behind an element's content	Any named color or RGB or hexadecimal value
background-position	Positions an image within an element's content	Keywords, percentages, or pixel or em values
background-repeat	Repeats an image within an element's content	repeat (the default; the image is copied to the right and down to fill the element)
		no-repeat (the image appears once in the upper-left corner of the element)
		repeat-x (the image is repeated horizontally across the element)
		repeat-y (the image is repeated vertically down the element)
background-attachment	Determines whether an image scrolls with the cursor	fixed
		scroll (the default)
background	Changes some or all of the background properties at once	Not all values must be stated, but if used, they must be stated in this order: image, color, position, repeat, attachment

As you learned in Tutorial 4, pseudo-class selectors can be used to change the appearance of links. The :link pseudo-class selector styles unvisited links, the :visited pseudo-class selector styles visited links, and the :hover pseudo-class selector creates a hover effect when the mouse pointer passes over a link. The :active pseudo-class selector creates a style for the moment when the user clicks a link. The bottom of the African Elephant Facts Web page contains a link back to the page top. Jackie would like to ensure that the link does not go unnoticed, so you'll create styles for the :link, :hover, and :visited pseudo-class selectors.

To create styles for the link to the page top:

1. Return to the **elephant.htm** file in your text editor.

2. On a blank line below the *ul.facts li* descendant selector, type the following code, as shown in Figure 5-37:

```css
/* links */

a:link {
   color: orange;
   text-decoration: none;
}

a:hover {
   color: black;
   background-color: darkkhaki;
   text-decoration: underline;
}

a:visited {
 color: maroon;
 }
```

Figure 5-37	Code for the link styles

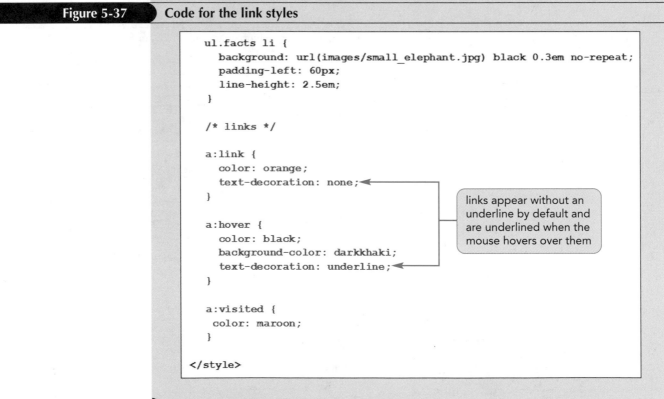

3. Save the file.

4. Return to your Web browser, and then click the **Refresh** or **Reload** button to view the style changes in the file. Hover the mouse pointer over the link to verify the effect of the hover style. The Web page should look similar to Figure 5-38.

Figure 5-38   **Link with the :hover style applied**

link with style applied when the mouse pointer hovers over it

Unfortunately the African elephant and other species of elephants are hunted and killed for their ivory tusks. There are several wildlife organizations that focus their efforts on conservation of elephants.

African Elephant Facts • P O Box 3 • Plumstead • Cape Town • South Africa • 7800

Back to Top

3DSguru/Shutterstock.com

The basic design of the document is now complete. Because Jackie would like to create additional Web pages using many of the same styles, you'll create an external style sheet that he can link to other documents. While you've already worked with external style sheets, this time, you'll create an external style sheet containing only the rules that are likely to be used on all Web pages that Jackie might create. You'll leave the `style` element on the African Elephant Facts Web page and keep styles in it that would be used only for this Web page. To decide which styles belong in each style sheet, you'll need to understand how styles cascade.

Resolving Style Conflicts

You've used external style sheets already, but not in conjunction with internal style sheets. When using external style sheets, you have to be mindful of what happens when you apply different styles to the same element, placing one style in your embedded style sheet and the other in an external style sheet. The term **cascading** in the name Cascading Style Sheets refers to the methods used to determine which style rules apply if more than one rule styles the same element.

Style precedence determines which styles have priority when multiple styles conflict. There are five possible sources for styles. Their order of precedence (from highest precedence to lowest) is as follows:

1. User-defined styles
2. Inline styles
3. Embedded style sheet styles
4. External style sheet styles
5. The browser's style sheet (the browser's default styles)

As this list shows, user styles have precedence over all other styles. **User-defined styles** are set by the person who is using a Web browser, usually to improve Web accessibility; for example, the text size can be increased to compensate for a visual impairment. To change the user styles in Microsoft Internet Explorer, for example, you click Tools on the menu bar, and then click Internet options to open the Internet Options dialog box, which is shown in Figure 5-39. The buttons at the bottom allow a user to change the font and color properties.

Figure 5-39   **Internet Options dialog box for Internet Explorer**

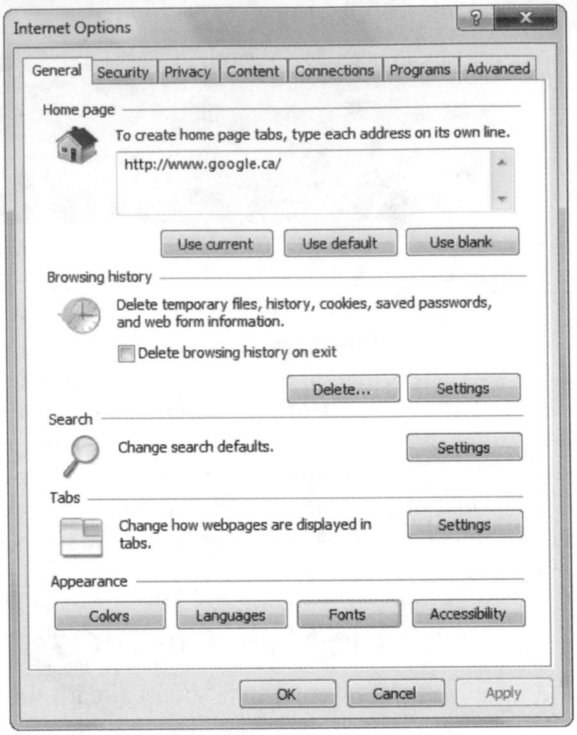

As a Web page designer, you control the three types of styles that follow after user-defined styles in precedence: inline, embedded, and external. Inline styles are written in the document body, and are the next highest in style precedence; therefore, they override all styles other than user styles. The use of inline styles is discouraged because they can become buried in the body of the document. Using inline styles does not allow you to separate the presentation (styles) from the content. Embedded styles are defined in the style element in the document's head section. You define external styles in an external style sheet, which contains CSS style code in a separate file that you then apply to several files or all the files at your Web site.

The browser's default styles have the lowest style precedence. This means that the browser's styles are applied only when styles have not been specified any other way.

Style conflicts can arise accidentally. For instance, what happens if you mistakenly style the same element two different ways in the same embedded or external style sheet? When conflicts occur between two styles in the same location, the style that is lower in the styles list usually takes precedence. For example, the following embedded style sheet styles the h2 element twice with conflicting styles:

```
<style type="text/css">

h2 {
  font-size: 1em;
}

. . . (other styles here). . .

h2 {
  font-size: 2em;
}

</style>
```

The style written last in the style list has the greater precedence, so in this instance, h2 text will appear in a font size of 2em.

What would happen if the first style had other declarations in addition to the font size? For example, what if the first h2 style also had a declaration for the background color, but the second style did not, as in the following code:

```
h2 {
   font-size: 1em;
   background-color: yellow;
}

h2 {
   font-size: 2em;
}
```

In the second h2 style, the intent is to style the h2 heading so the text *only* appears in a font size of 2em. However, because the first style for the h2 heading also has a background color of yellow, all h2 headings would appear in browsers with a background color of yellow. The cascade only resolves style conflicts. Any rules that don't conflict still take effect. Because the second style does not specify a background color, the background color from the first style remains in effect. The result would be the same as if you had entered the following code:

```
h2 {
   font-size: 2em;
   background-color: yellow;
}
```

You'll keep the effects of cascading in mind as you create an external style sheet for Jackie's Web pages.

Understanding External Style Sheets

Many contemporary Web sites consist of hundreds or thousands of pages. If you used embedded style sheets on all of the Web pages for a site of this scale and later decided to change a style or two, you would have to open each file, revise the code for the embedded styles, and then save the file. Imagine doing that a thousand times! When you use an external style sheet, you can make a change to a style simply by editing the external style sheet file. These edits would automatically be reflected in each of the Web documents that use that style sheet—an enormous time saver.

You can type CSS code directly into an external style sheet, but a better method is to begin with an embedded style sheet, as you've done with the African Elephant Fact Web page. It's easier to work with an embedded style sheet while you're developing a file because you don't have to keep switching between the HTML file and the CSS file. After you finish the first draft of the HTML file, you can cut the code you will use for all Web pages in the Web site from the HTML file and paste it into an external style sheet. External style sheet documents follow the same naming conventions as any other file, but the industry convention is to include the extension .css.

Creating and Applying an External Style Sheet

- Create a new file for the external style sheet, and include a CSS comment at the top of the page to document the author name and the creation date. Do not enter any HTML code in this file.
- In the HTML file, cut the CSS styles from the embedded style sheet, and then paste the code into the CSS file. This may take multiple iterations if you need to cut the styles that will be applied to all Web pages, and leave the styles that are specific to the current Web page.
- Save the CSS file with a .css filename extension, and close it.
- In the head section of the HTML file, enter the following code to link to the external CSS file:

```
<link rel="stylesheet" href="filename.css" type="text/css" />
```

where *filename.css* is the name of the external style sheet file.
- To create a link to a CSS file, enter the following code between the <head> </head> tags in an HTML document:

```
<link rel="stylesheet" href="filename.css" type="text/css">
```

where the `rel` attribute and its value specify that the linked file is a style sheet, the `href` attribute and its value identify the path and filename of the CSS file, and the `type` attribute and its value specify that the file is a text file written in CSS.

External style sheets separate presentation (styles) from content. All of the common style rules to be used for the Web pages in a Web site are stored in a separate file that contains *only* CSS code. The following code shows a sample external style sheet:

```
/* Created by Your Name
 All files for this Web site link to this style sheet */

/* body */
body {
  font-size: 1.1em;
  font-family: Arial, Helvetica, sans-serif;
  color: white;
  background-color: #6d6f58;
}
```

TIP

The codes to begin and end CSS comments are often referred to as *slash star* and *star slash*, respectively.

Note that the style sheet began with a CSS comment. The code for a CSS comment is slightly different from the code for an HTML comment. A CSS comment begins with a forward slash and an asterisk, and then the comment text follows. The comment ends with an asterisk and a forward slash.

Creating an External Style Sheet

External style sheets usually begin with a comment that identifies the style sheet, such as its purpose, the author, the last revision date, and so forth. Like an HTML comment, a CSS comment can have as few or as many lines as you want.

To create an external style sheet and add a CSS comment:

1. Return to your text editor, and then create a new document.

2. In the new document, type the following comment code on two lines, as shown in Figure 5-40, using your own name and today's date in the first line:

```
/* Created by Your Name on Today's Date
All files for this Web site link to this style sheet */
```

Figure 5-40   **Comment for the main_layout.css file**

```
/* Created by Your Name on Today's Date

All files for this Web site link to this style sheet */
```

3. Save the file as **main_layout.css** in the tutorial5\tutorial folder included with your Data Files.

Now that you've created the comment, you will cut some of the CSS code from the embedded style sheet in the African Elephant Facts file and paste it into the main_layout.css file. You'll leave the style rules for ul.facts and ul.facts li in the internal stylesheet; these style rules are likely specific to the African Elephant Facts page because they define the background image as the elephant image for the markers for the list. You'll move all other style rules to the external CSS document.

To cut and paste the CSS code:

1. Return to the **elephant.htm** file in your text editor, leaving the main_layout.css file open.

2. In the embedded style sheet of the elephant.htm file, select the style rules for the elements body, h1, h2, h3, h4, footer, img, img.right, and .clear.

3. Press **Ctrl+X** to cut the CSS code.

   Trouble? If you're using a Mac, use command+X to cut the text.

4. Return to the **main_layout.css** document, leaving the elephant.htm file open.

5. In the main_layout.css document, position the insertion point on a blank line below the comment.

6. Press the **Ctrl+V** keys to paste the code, as shown in Figure 5-41 (not all of the code is shown).

   Trouble? If you're using a Mac, use command+V to paste the text.

Figure 5-41   Some of the styles for the main_layout.css external style sheet

```
/* Created by Your Name on Today's Date
All files for this Web site link to this style sheet */

/* body */

body {
  background-color: darkslategray;
  background-image: url(images/grey_texture.jpg);
  color: white;
  font-size: 1.1em;
  font-family: Verdana, sans-serif;
}

/* headings */

h1  {
  background-color: black;
  margin: 0 0 0 10px;
  padding: 4px;
  text-align: center;
}
```

7. Return to the **elephant.htm** file in your text editor, leaving the main_layout.css file open.

8. In the embedded style sheet of the elephant.htm file, select the style rules for the elements a:link, a:hover, and a:visited, and then use the **Ctrl+X** or **command+X** keys to cut the CSS code.

9. Return to the **main_layout.css** document, leaving the elephant.htm file open.

10. In the main_layout.css document, position the insertion point on a blank line below the .*clear* selector.

11. Press the **Ctrl+V** or **command+V** keys to paste the code, as shown in Figure 5-42.

Figure 5-42   Additional styles for the main_layout.css file

```
.clear {
  clear: both;
}

/* links */

a:link {
  color: orange;
  text-decoration: none;
}

a:hover {
  color: black;
  background-color: darkkhaki;
  text-decoration: underline;
}

a:visited {
  color: maroon;
}
```

12. Save the **main_layout.css** file.

13. Return to the **elephant.htm** file, and then ensure the only styles left in the style element are the ul.*facts* and ul.*facts li* styles. Save the **elephant.htm** file.

14. Return to your Web browser, and then click the **Refresh** or **Reload** button to view the style changes in the file. The Web page should look similar to Figure 5-43. The external style sheet isn't linked to the HTML document yet, so the browser shows only the remaining embedded styles combined with the browser's own default styles.

Figure 5-43 **Web page rendered using browser styles and embedded styles**

African Elephant

A Gentle Giant

Habitat and Characteristics

African elephants live in the wild in Africa, south of the Sahara Desert. They eat a vegetarian diet of mostly roots, bark, grasses, and fruit. An adult African elephant can be up to 11 feet tall at the shoulder. They can be 13 - 16 feet long and weigh 3½ to 6½ tons. They can live to be 60 - 70 years old.

Behavior

> black text and white background are based on browser default styles

African elephants are very social animals. They have a complex society that is based on a family unit. Each family unit has approximately 10 individual elephants, composed of closely related females (cows) and their calves. Separate family units join together to form a group. After male elephants reach puberty, they tend to form alliances with other males. Elephants are also very nurturing animals. Two elephants will wrap their trunks together to give each other a hug.

African elephants are very intelligent. They communicate with deep growling or rumbling noises. Elephants also communicate using noises that are too low for humans to hear, yet very loud. Their noises can be heard 5 or 6 miles away. Smell is their most highly developed sense.

Tusks

- Elephant tusks are ivory teeth that grow throughout their lives.
- Elephants are right- or left-tusked, using the favored tusk more often, thus shortening it from constant wear.
- Elephants use their tusks to dig up roots and pry bark from trees to find food.

Quick Facts

Here are a few interesting facts:

Quick Facts

- The scientific name for the African elephant is *Loxodonta Africana*.
- A baby elephant is called a calf.
- A female elephant is called a cow.
- A male elephant is called a bull.
- At birth, a baby elephant weighs approximately 200 pounds and stands approximately 3 feet tall.
- An African elephant can grow to be 3½ to 6½ tons (7,000 - 13,200 pounds), reach a height of 11 feet tall, and grow 13 to 16 feet long.
- An elephant can eat 300 pounds (136 kilograms) of food in one day.
- Elephants have the longest pregnancy of any animal on earth. It lasts 22 months!
- Adult African elephants have only one natural enemy: humans.
- African elephants eat mainly roots, leaves, fruit, grasses, and bark.
- The African elephant's ears are over twice as large as those of the Asian elephant.
- African elephants are slightly larger than Asian elephants.

Elephant Trunk Facts

> black background from the embedded style combines with black text from the browser default to make list items unreadable

Unfortunately, the African elephant and other species of elephants are hunted and killed for their ivory tusks. There are several wildlife organizations that focus their efforts on conservation of elephants.

African Elephant Facts • P O Box 3 • Plumstead • Cape Town • South Africa • 7800

Back to Top

Johan Swanepoel/Shutterstock.com; Pichugin Dmitry/Shutterstock.com

The CSS file now has most of the style rules, but there's still more work to do before the style sheet will work: the HTML file and the CSS file have to be linked. As you saw in an earlier tutorial, the code to create the link is entered in the head section of the HTML file.

Linking an HTML File to an External Style Sheet

The true power of CSS lies in the ability to use an external style sheet to determine the appearance of as many documents as you want. The `link` element is used to link an HTML file to another file, such as a CSS file. An unlimited number of HTML files can link to the same external style sheet file. You enter the code for the `link` element in the head section of each document you want to link to the external style sheet file. For example, the following code links an HTML file to an external style sheet file named paper.css:

```
<link rel = "stylesheet" href="paper.css" type="text/css" />
```

The `link` element accepts the attributes `rel`, `href`, and `type`. The attribute `rel` stands for *relationship*; for a CSS file, its value is always `stylesheet`. The `href` attribute stands for *hypertext reference*, and its value is the name of the CSS file to which you are linking—in this case paper.css. The value for the `type` attribute value is always `text/css`.

You'll create a link in elephant.htm to the external style sheet file main_layout.css.

To link a CSS file to an HTML file:

▶ **1.** Return to the **elephant.htm** file in your text editor.

▶ **2.** After the `title` element, which is inside the `head` element, insert the following code as shown in Figure 5-44:

```
<link rel = "stylesheet" href = "main_layout.css" type = "text/css" />
```

Figure 5-44 **Code for the link element**

```
<title>African Elephant</title>

<link rel = "stylesheet" href = "main_layout.css" type = "text/css" />

<style type = "text/css">

  ul.facts {
    line-height: 1.4em;
    list-style-type: none;
    padding: 0;
    margin-left: 1em;
  }
```

▶ **3.** Save the file.

▶ **4.** Return to your Web browser, and then click the **Refresh** or **Reload** button to view the style changes in the file. The Web page should look similar to Figure 5-45.

Figure 5-45   **Completed African Elephant Facts Web page**

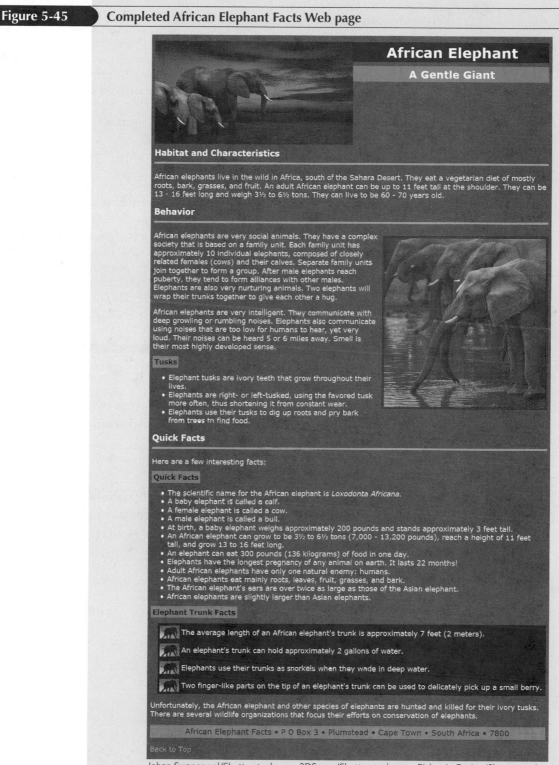

Johan Swanepoel/Shutterstock.com; 3DSguru/Shutterstock.com; Pichugin Dmitry/Shutterstock.com

Jackie is thrilled with the stylized African Elephant Facts Web page. He'll look over the work you've done and will contact you when he's ready to expand his Web site.

PROSKILLS

Written Communication: Creating Buttons and Web Graphics

Many Web pages contain buttons or other graphic elements for navigation. Communicating their functionality to users is very important, and it is more difficult to do when you can only put a small amount of text on a button.

When selecting or creating buttons and icons for your Web sites, consider the following standard conventions:

- **To navigate to the next Web page**—Use the word *next* or an arrow pointing to the right.
- **To navigate to the previous Web page**—Use the word *previous* or an arrow pointing to the left.
- **To navigate to the home page**—If there is a logo on the Web page, place it in the top-left corner, and make it a link that points to the main Web page in the Web site.
- **When using buttons**—Try to use one or two words, and less than 10 characters if possible; if you anticipate translating your Web site into different languages, create buttons that do not have text at all, and use international icon symbols instead.

There are many free resources that you can use to create buttons or small icons. Use your favorite search engine with the key words *Web button generator*, and you'll see dozens of options.

REVIEW

Session 5.2 Quick Check

1. What are the possible values for the `background-repeat` property?
2. If you use the `background` shorthand property, in what order must you list the values?
3. Can you use the `vertical-align` property to align an image used as a list marker?
4. What code should appear at the beginning of every CSS style sheet?
5. True/False: A CSS external style sheet should not contain any HTML code.
6. What element is used to connect a CSS style sheet to an HTML file?

Review Assignments

Data Files needed for the Review Assignments: consult_T5.htm, images/ JackieSelebilogo.jpg

Jackie loves the work you've done stylizing the African Elephant Facts Web page. In addition to his involvement in animal conservation, Jackie also has a small consulting business. He would like you to stylize his business consulting Web page.

Although you will not be instructed to do so after each step, you should do the following after entering the code to create a style in your text editor: Save the file, switch to your browser, refresh or reload the page, verify that you entered the style code correctly, and then switch back to your text editor and complete the next step. A preview of the Web page you will create appears in Figure 5-46.

Figure 5-46	**Consulting Web page**

Jackie Selebi Consulting

We Can Assist You in All of These Areas

PROPOSAL SPECIFICATIONS

We can help you with your proposal specifications. You need to justify your return on investment, and we can provide you with the facts and figures on how we can establish cost savings for your firm. We specify not just the hard numbers, like the savings on hardware and supplies that you no longer have to purchase, but we also factor in the soft savings, such as increased productivity and efficiency. We can give you a payback schedule on your return on investment that will give you the cost justification you are seeking to employ a paperless office solution.

RETURN ON INVESTMENT ANALYSIS

We've got the facts and the figures you need to send to upper management to back your ideas with cost-saving facts. We'll give you not just the numbers, but the charts and the database data you need to support your argument to upper management that a paperless office is the way to go.

ON-SITE SUPERVISION OF HARDWARE

Once you have purchased a hardware or a software solution from us, we won't leave you hanging. We are there to literally stand behind you as you work towards the implementation of a plan to reduce costs in your office. We will work with your to set up a timetable for conversion, and we will have staffing on site when you decide to move towards a new hardware or software solution. Whether you decide to implement on a department-by-department basis or have a move-forward cutoff date established for your entire company, we will be there to ensure that the transition goes smoothly and seamlessly.

SOFTWARE INSTALLATION

We know that our customers are not computer experts and may not have the IT staff to implement a software migration. We will be there to install and debug software. Once we are there, we are in no hurry to leave. We won't leave you with a hit-and-run solution, where software is installed and any problems that might occur are left for you to resolve. We will be on site to install and ensure that the installation of all new software works as planned.

TRAINING

It doesn't take much training to use less paper or shred fewer documents, but if you are stepping up to a more global, system-wide solution, we can provide your IT staff with the business intelligence to maximize the features of any new software solution that we propose for your business. We can arrange for small or large classes. You can come to one of our training sites, or we can come to you to conduct on-site training classes. We have full documentation for all software that we implement.

Jackie Selebi Consulting • P O Box 3 • Plumstead • Cape Town • South Africa • 7800 •

Complete the following:

1. Use your text editor to open the **consult_T5.htm** file, which is provided in your Data Files in the tutorial5\review folder. In the head section and below the page title, enter *your name* and *today's date* in the comment section where noted.

2. Save the file as **consult.htm** in the same folder. Open the file in your browser, and observe the appearance of the original file.

3. Switch back to your text editor. Below the comment and in the head section, insert the start and end tags necessary to create an embedded style sheet.

4. Within the tags for the embedded style sheet, style the body element to have text appear with a line height of **1.5em**, in a font size of **1.1em**, and in the **Georgia** (serif) font.

5. Save the **consult.htm** file. Switch to your browser, and refresh or reload the page. Verify that the body element style appears correctly in your file.

6. Switch back to your text editor. Create a style for the h1 element to have text appear in **navy**; display a bottom border that is **solid**, **thin**, and **gray**; and include padding of **15px** on the bottom.

7. Create a style for the h3 element to have text appear in **teal** and in **uppercase**. (Use a text property to change the case; do not retype the h3 headings in uppercase.)

8. Create a style for the footer element so the text is centered, appears in **navy**, has a text decoration of both **overline** and **underline**, and has a **display** property set to **block**.

9. Create a style for the img element to float the image **right**. Use the margin shorthand property to set margins for the image of **0** on the top and right, and **10px** on the bottom and left.

10. Save the **consult.htm** file. Switch to your browser, and refresh or reload the page. Compare your file to Figure 5-46 to verify that your file is correct.

11. Submit the file to your instructor, in either printed or electronic form, as requested.

Create a Web page for a planetarium.

APPLY

Case Problem 1

Data Files needed for this Case Problem: planetarium_T5.htm, images/planets.jpg, images/planetariumlogo.jpg

Shore River Planetarium   When it is completed next month, the Shore River Planetarium will be one of the largest planetariums in the South. Located in East Landing, about 20 miles northeast of Charleston, South Carolina, this state-of-the-art facility will house a space museum in addition to the planetarium. Edward Ortiz, the director of the facility, has asked you to create a Web page that describes the attractions at the Shore River Planetarium. After you complete a step to create a style (or a set of steps to create and apply a class), verify in your browser that the style code has been entered correctly, and then switch back to your text editor. A preview of the Web page you will create appears in Figure 5-47.

Figure 5-47   Shore River Planetarium

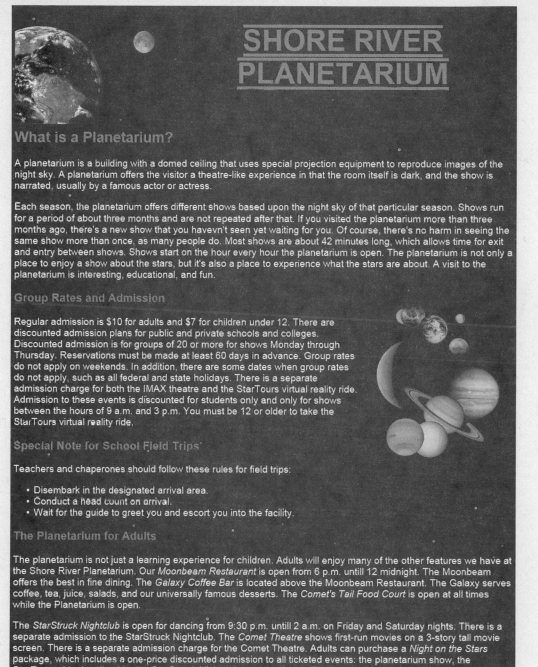

bestimagesevercom/Shutterstock.com; Ronald van der Beek/Shutterstock.com

Complete the following:

1. Use your text editor to open the **planetarium_T5.htm** file, which is provided in your Data Files in the tutorial5\case1 folder. In the head section and below the page title, enter *your name* and *today's date* in the comment section where noted.

2. Save the file as **planetarium.htm** in the same folder. Open the file in your browser, and observe the appearance of the original file.

3. Switch back to your text editor. In the code for the embedded style sheet, style the `body` element to have text appear in **1.2em** and in **Arial**, a sans-serif font. The text should appear as **white** text on a **black** background.

4. Save the **planetarium.htm** file. Switch to your browser, and refresh or reload the page. Verify that the `body` element style appears correctly in your file.

5. Switch back to your text editor. In the embedded style sheet and below the `body` style, create the following styles for the `h1` element:
   - Have the text appear in **uppercase**.
   - Create a text decoration of **underline** and **overline**.
   - Center the `h1` text.
   - Set the color to **goldenrod**.
   - Set the font size to **3em**.

6. Style the `h2` and `h3` elements to also appear in the color **goldenrod**.

7. Create the following styles for the `footer` element:
   - Set the top border so it appears **solid**, **thick**, and with a color value of **goldenrod**.
   - Add padding of **10px** on the top.
   - Center the `footer` text.
   - Set the color to **goldenrod**.
   - Set the display property to **block**.

8. For the image element, create a dependent class named *left* that floats images left. Use the margin shorthand property to set margins of **0** on the top, **15px** on the right, **10px** on the bottom, and **0** on the left.

9. In the image code for the planetariumlogo.jpg image, apply the *left* dependent class to the `img` element.

10. For the image element, create a dependent class named *right* that floats images right and has margins of **10px** on the top, **0** on the right, **10px** on the bottom, and **10px** on the left.

11. In the image code for the planets.jpg image, apply the *right* dependent class to the `img` element.

12. Create an independent class named **clear** that clears an element on both the left and the right.

13. Apply the *clear* independent class to the start `<h2>` tag.

14. Save the **planetarium.htm** file. Switch to your browser, and refresh or reload the page. Compare your file to Figure 5-47 to verify that your file is correct.

15. Submit the file to your instructor, in either printed or electronic form, as requested.

Create and style a Web page about corporate event planning.

APPLY

Case Problem 2

Data Files needed for this Case Problem: eventplanner_T5.htm, images/ eventplannerlogo.jpg, images/parchment.jpg

Corporate Event Planning   Corporate event planning is a multifaceted field that is attracting many people. Event planning can occur on many levels, from planning a simple dinner party for a few people to arranging the details for a convention that may be attended by thousands of people. You've been asked to format a Web page that describes this interesting and growing field. After you complete a step to create a style (or a set of steps to create and apply a class), verify in your browser that the style code has been entered correctly, and then switch back to your text editor. A preview of the Web page you will create appears in Figure 5-48.

Figure 5-48   **Corporate Event Planner Web page**

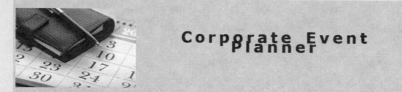

What Is a Corporate Event Planner?

Almost everyone has had some experience at planning an event. It may have been planning a birthday party, a high school or college reunion, or even a wedding. You may not have realized it at the time, but even just going out on a date involves the logistics of where to go, when to arrive and depart, what to do, how much to spend, what to wear, and how to get there. If you've ever gone out on a prom date, you are quite familiar with the planning it took to get you and your date ready for your big night. Ideally it was a lot of fun, but it also involved a great deal of preparation on the part of many individuals.

What Does a Planner Do?

Corporate event planners are needed to plan for ceremonies, such as awards ceremonies, luncheon and dinner parties, and conventions. Of course, on the corporate level, the stakes are higher. You are planning an event that will have dozens or even hundreds of people in attendance. How the event fares has a great deal to do with how the company is perceived. Even though the company may not have planned the event, if the event does not turn out to be an enjoyable one, certainly the company will appear to be the one to be blamed. Mismanaged events have a way of implying that the company itself is mismanaged, so every corporate event has a lot riding on it. The event may be for employees only, but then, again, there may be hundreds of clients — or potential clients — in attendance. Your goal as a corporate event planner is to cast the company in the most favorable light.

Event planning involves a great many business skills. Certainly the accounting side of budgeting is an important one. You won't be given an unlimited amount of cash to stage an event; you will be expected to match or come in under budget. You also can't pick dates at random. You have to choose a date (and perhaps an alternate date), interview people, inspect the event site, and coordinate transportation and parking for those in attendance—in particular, the executives of the company you are planning the event for. Project management skills and a knowledge of project management software are a must. You have to establish a timeline of events, and determine how each of those events impact the other. You have to determine the critical path, which is the timeline of key tasks that will impact the most on the event should a problem occur with any of them over the course of staging the event.

What's Expected of You?

Event planners may also be asked to develop a theme for an event, plan for the decoration of a hall or outdoor area, arrange for speakers to appear, and arrange for their transportation to and from the event. If the event is outdoors, there are a number of critical issues to be confronted that you would not have to worry about if the event will be held indoors; you have to arrange for electricity, heating or cooling, tables, chairs, flowers, tablecloths, a band or DJ, security, portable toilets, signage, and cleanup of the area once the event is over. Event planners also need to know how to delegate work. Most corporate planners delegate the smaller but still important details, such as the food, drinks, guest list, advertising and marketing, and decorations. There is a great deal of preparation in planning the event, and if you try to do too much yourself, you will not do a good job at either the larger aspects of the event or the smaller ones. You need to know whom to trust with both the large and small details of the event. Over time, you will develop a relationship with your staff, so you will know whom to entrust with a particular planning event.

You need a particular disposition to be an event planner. Because there's so much to do, you have to be a take-charge person who likes the challenge of acting on a great many details, often without a great deal of time. You have to respond well to pressure, work efficiently, and be diplomatic. You will be interfacing with a great many people, and you need the cooperation and support of these people. Your appearance does matter. You need to be appropriately dressed to engage in a professional manner with executives and clients. Of course, you need excellent written and verbal skills. Above all, you have to gain the confidence of others because you will be directing a great many other people in the successful planning of each event. Whether you are coordinating a conference, planning a convention, arranging for a special event, or coordinating and managing a meeting, you need to be your professional, competent, and energetic self at all times. You also have to throw away the clock because many events occur during the evening and on weekends. Corporate event planning is a relatively new field, but it can be a lucrative one for a person with the right organizational, management, and communication skills.

The Basics

Corporate event planning involves the following areas:

- Scheduling
- Facility Management
- Budgeting
- Logistics
- Marketing
- Travel and Lodging
- Project management
- Exhibitor management

Top

Complete the following:

1. Use your text editor to open the **eventplanner_T5.htm** file, which is provided in your Data Files in the tutorial5\case2 folder. In the head section and below the page title, enter *your name* and *today's date* in the comment section where noted.

2. Save the file as **eventplanner.htm** in the same folder. Open the file in your browser, and observe the appearance of the original file.

3. Switch back to your text editor. Within the tags for the embedded style sheet, create the following styles for the `body` element:
   - Set the font size to **1.2em**.
   - Set the font to **Verdana** (a sans-serif font).
   - Set the line height to **1.25em**.
   - Add a background color with the value of **blanchedalmond**.
   - Add a background image using the image **parchment.jpg** found in the images folder.

4. Save the **eventplanner.htm** file. Switch to your browser, and refresh or reload the page. Verify that the `body` element style appears correctly in your file.

5. Switch back to your text editor. Below the `body` style, create a style for the image element so images are floated **left**. Use the `margin` shorthand property to create margins of **0** on top, **10px** on the right, **10px** on the bottom, and **0** on the left.

6. Create an independent class named *clear* that clears an element on both the left and the right. Apply the *clear* independent class to the start `<h3>` tag for the *What Is a Corporate Event Planner?* header.

7. Create the following styles for the `h1` element:
   - Set the letter spacing to **0.2em**.
   - Set the word spacing to **0.2em**.
   - Center the text.
   - Add **1.5em** padding on the top.

8. Style the `h3` element to appear with a bottom border that is **solid**, **thick**, and **saddlebrown**. Also style the `h3` element to have **0.5em** padding on the bottom.

9. Style the list item element to display the list marker as a **circle**.

10. Save the **eventplanner.htm** file. Switch to your browser, and refresh or reload the page. Compare your file to Figure 5-48 to verify that your file is correct. Depending on your browser and browser version you may see different letter spacing and word spacing than that shown in Figure 5-48.

11. Submit the file to your instructor if requested.

Use what you've learned and expand your skills to create and style a Web page for a book retailer.

CHALLENGE

Case Problem 3

Data Files needed for this Case Problem: books_T5.htm, bio_teal_button.jpg, grey_texture.jpg, science_teal_button.jpg, spiralbound.jpg, teal_square_bullet.jpg, travel_teal_button.jpg

Wordpendium Books Wordpendium Books, a regional book retailer in Kanihilo, Hawaii, has always relied on print media to promote its new book listings. Now Wordpendium would like to open an online store so it can market its books in other states. You've been asked to create a Web page that will highlight some of Wordpendium's books. After you complete a step to create a style (or a set of steps to create and apply a class), verify in your browser that the style code has been entered correctly, and then switch back to your text editor. A preview of the Web page you will create appears in Figure 5-49.

Figure 5-49 Wordpendium Books Web page

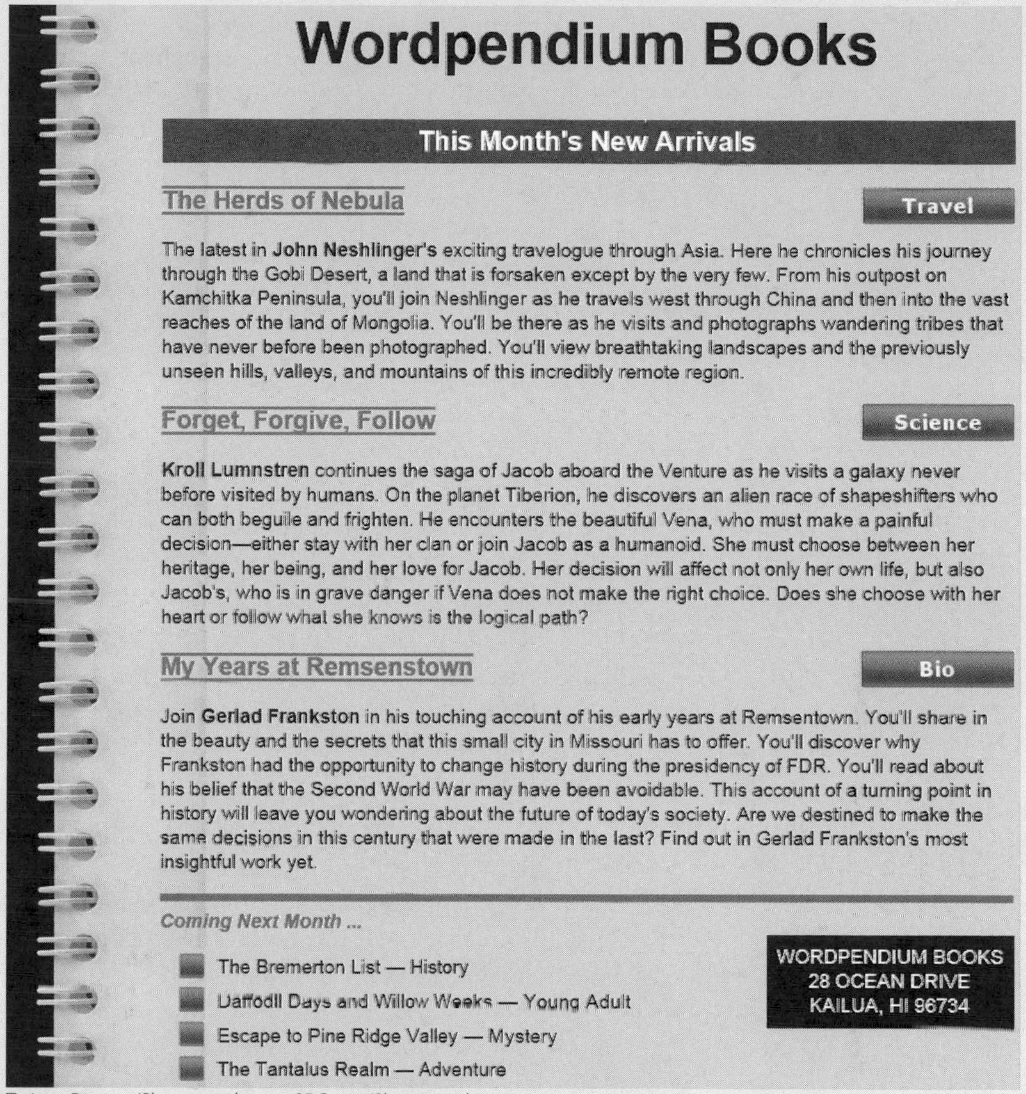

Tatiana Popova/Shutterstock.com; 3DSguru/Shutterstock.com

Complete the following:

1. Use your text editor to open the **books_T5.htm** file, which is provided in your Data Files in the tutorial5\case3 folder. In the head section and below the page title, enter *your name* and *today's date* in the comment section where noted.

2. Save the file as **books.htm** in the same folder. Open the file in your browser, and observe the appearance of the original file.

3. Switch back to your text editor. Within the tags for the embedded style sheet, style the body element to use the image **spiralbound.jpg**, found in the images folder, as the background. Repeat the image vertically. In addition, create the following styles for the body element:

   - Set the background color to **gainsboro**.
   - Set the font size to **1.2em**.
   - Set the font to **Arial** (a sans-serif font).
   - Set the left margin to **8em**.
   - Set the line height to **1.25em**.

4. Save the **books.htm** file. Switch to your browser, and refresh or reload the page. Verify that the `body` element style appears correctly in your file.

5. Switch back to your text editor. In the code for the embedded style sheet and below the `body` element style, style the `img` element to float **right**. Using the `margin` shorthand property, set margins of **0** on the top and right, and **10px** on the bottom and left.

6. Create the following styles for the `h1` element:
   - Set the top margin to **0.5em**.
   - Center the `h1` text.
   - Set the font size to **3em**.
   - Add **25px** of padding on the bottom.

7. Style the `h2` element to use a background image named **grey_texture.jpg**, located in the images folder. In addition, create the following styles for the `h2` element:
   - Center the `h2` text.
   - Set the color to **white**.
   - Set the font size to **1.4em**.
   - Add **10px** of padding on all sides (use the `padding` shorthand property).

8. Create the following styles for the `h3` element:
   - Set the color to **teal**.
   - Set the font size to **1.3em**.
   - Add a text decoration of **overline** and **underline**.

9. Create the following styles for the `footer` element:
   - Center the footer text.
   - Set the color to **white**.
   - Add a background color of **black**.
   - Float the footer text **right**.
   - Add padding of **10px** on all sides (using the `padding` shorthand property).
   - Display text in all capital letters (use a text property for this declaration).

10. Create a dependent class for the `p` element selector named *border*. Create the following styles for the class:
    - Add a top border that is **solid** and **teal**, with a thickness of **0.4em**.
    - Add padding on the top of **0.4em**.
    - Set the font weight to **bold**.
    - Set the font style to **italic**.
    - Set the color to **teal**.
    - Set the bottom margin to **0**.

11. Apply the *border* class to the start <p> tag in the last paragraph (which begins *Coming Next Month* ...).

12. Create the following styles for the unordered list element:
    - Float the element **left**.
    - Set the list style type to **none**.
    - Add padding of **0** on all four sides.
    - Add a top margin of **1em**.
    - Add a left margin of **1em**.

13. Create the following styles for the list item element:
    - Use the teal_square_bullet.jpg file as a background image. Do not repeat the image.
    - Add padding on the left of **2em**, padding on the bottom of **0.25em**, and set a line height of **1.5em**.

14. Save the **books.htm** file. Switch to your browser, and refresh or reload the page. Compare your file to Figure 5-49 to verify that your file is correct.

15. Switch back to your text editor. In the embedded style sheet, delete the start `<style>` tag and the end `</style>` tag. Select all of the remaining CSS code for the embedded style sheet, cut it, and then paste it to the Clipboard.

16. In the head section and on a blank line below the page title, enter the code to link to a CSS file named **bookstyles.css**.

17. Save and then close the **books.htm** file.

18. Open a new document in your text editor. Create a comment section at the top of the document, and enter *your name* and *today's date* in the comment section.

19. On a blank line below the comment code, paste the CSS code that you cut from books.htm.

20. Save the file as **bookstyles.css** in the same folder.

21. Switch to your browser, and refresh or reload the page for the **books.htm** file. Observe the result; the file should look similar to the preview file in Figure 5-49.

22. Submit the file to your instructor, in printed or electronic form, as requested.

Create a Web page for the governance of a new planet.

RESEARCH

Case Problem 4

Data File needed for this Case Problem: hope_T5.htm

Planet Hope   Astronomers have discovered a new planet, which they've tentatively named planet Hope. The planet is similar to Earth in size, land, sea mass, and atmosphere. Assuming you were in charge of colonizing this planet, how would you do it? What government would you choose for its residents? Would you create cities or use the planet for agriculture? What would you do if you learned that the planet had enormous mineral and energy riches, but extracting them would substantially damage the environment? Create a Web page that outlines how you intend to govern the planet and how you will use its land and sea resources.

Complete the following:

1. Use your text editor to open the **hope_T5.htm** file, which is provided in your Data Files in the tutorial5\case4 folder. In the head section, give your page an appropriate title. Below the page title, enter *your name* and *today's date* in the comment section where noted.

2. Save the file as **hope.htm** in the same folder.

3. Within the tags for the embedded style sheet, format the `body` element with the text size, font, color, and background color of your choice. Ensure the text is readable and attractive.

4. Include at least one image that illustrates what life would be like on the new planet. Use the `float` property to style the image, and float the image either left or right.

5. In the styles you create for the hope.htm document, create examples of the following properties:
   * `margin`
   * `padding`
   * `border`
   * `background`
   * `float`
   * `clear`

6. In the body section, enter text for at least five paragraphs that describe how you plan to govern the planet. Use at least two examples of `h1`, `h2`, `h3`, or `h4` headings.

7. Save the **hope.htm** file. Switch to your browser, and refresh or reload the page. Verify that all styles work correctly.

8. Switch back to your text editor. Create a new CSS file containing a comment section with your name and today's date in the comment.

9. Save the file as **hope.css**.

10. Without closing the hope.css file, switch back to the **hope.htm** file. In the head section, use the `link` element to create a link to the **hope.css** file.

11. In the **hope.htm** file, delete the start and end `<style>` tags in the embedded style sheet.

12. Cut and paste the remaining embedded style sheet code from the hope.htm file into the hope.css external style sheet.

13. Save the **hope.css** file and the **hope.htm** file.

14. Submit the file to your instructor, in either printed or electronic form, as requested.

ENDING DATA FILES

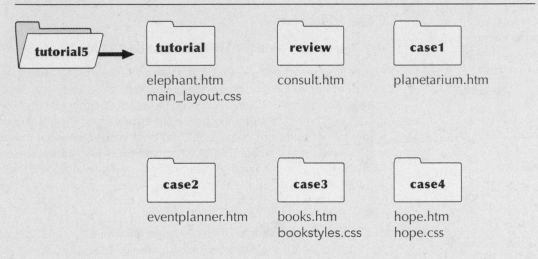

tutorial5 → **tutorial**
elephant.htm
main_layout.css

review
consult.htm

case1
planetarium.htm

case2
eventplanner.htm

case3
books.htm
bookstyles.css

case4
hope.htm
hope.css

Creating Fixed-Width Layouts

Creating a Web Page Layout for an Art Gallery

OBJECTIVES

Session 6.1
- Understand Web page layouts
- Create a two-column layout
- Use universal and id selectors to create styles
- Create page structure with container sections and the `header`, `nav`, `section`, `aside`, and `footer` elements
- Specify fixed column widths using pixels

Session 6.2
- Create a three-column layout
- Create a box shadow around an element
- Add rounded corners to borders
- Create a `figure` element with a caption
- Import CSS styles using the `@import` rule

Case | *Ink Wash Art Gallery*

The Ink Wash Gallery is a small specialty art gallery in Seattle, Washington. The owner is Yan Lin, a Chinese artist who recently moved to Seattle from Gansu province in northwest China. She started painting when she was 5 years old, practicing the traditional ink wash painting techniques that were developed in China during the Tang Dynasty, from 618 CE to 907 CE. Yan has collected ink wash paintings from around the world to showcase and sell in her gallery. She has been working on a basic Web page that provides information about her gallery and would also like to provide some information about ink wash painting techniques. You'll work with Yan to design a layout for her gallery Web site, focusing on the top-level Web page to create a design that can be used for the entire Web site.

STARTING DATA FILES

tutorial

art_T6.htm
bamboo.jpg
inkwashgallery.jpg
modernizr-2.js
ricepaper.jpg

review

direct_T6.htm
inkwashgallery.jpg
modernizr-2.js

case1

biz_T6.htm
bizlogo.jpg
modernizr-2.js
texture.jpg

case2

griff_T6.htm
grifflogo.jpg
links.css
modernizr-2.js
stones.jpg

case3

blacktexture.jpg
footer.css
modernizr-2.js
ziller_T6.htm

case4

modernizr-2.js
travel_T6.htm
triangle.jpg

SESSION 6.1 VISUAL OVERVIEW

A **wrapper** or **container** is a div element created for formatting purposes that contains one or more elements.

```
#container {
    width: 930px;
    border-width: 1px;
    margin: 0 auto;
    background-color: navy;
}
```

```
aside {
  width: 200px;
  margin: 0 10px 10px 0;
  padding: 10px;
  background-color: orange;
  float: left;
  height: 400px;
}
```

The aside element marks content that is not the main content.

A **two-column layout** contains two columns of content.

In a **fixed-width layout**, the column widths don't change when the browser window changes size.

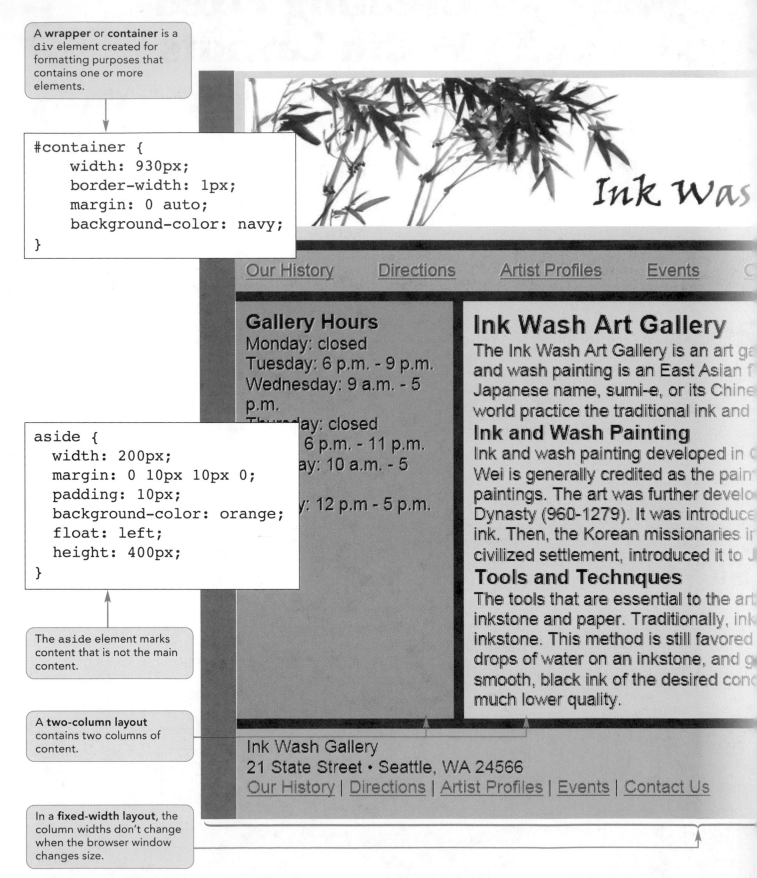

Our History   Directions   Artist Profiles   Events

Gallery Hours
Monday: closed
Tuesday: 6 p.m. - 9 p.m.
Wednesday: 9 a.m. - 5 p.m.
Thursday: closed
6 p.m. - 11 p.m.
ay: 10 a.m. - 5
y: 12 p.m - 5 p.m.

Ink Wash Art Gallery

The Ink Wash Art Gallery is an art ga
and wash painting is an East Asian f
Japanese name, sumi-e, or its Chine
world practice the traditional ink and

Ink and Wash Painting

Ink and wash painting developed in C
Wei is generally credited as the pain
paintings. The art was further develo
Dynasty (960-1279). It was introduce
ink. Then, the Korean missionaries in
civilized settlement, introduced it to J

Tools and Technques

The tools that are essential to the art
inkstone and paper. Traditionally, ink
inkstone. This method is still favored
drops of water on an inkstone, and g
smooth, black ink of the desired cond
much lower quality.

Ink Wash Gallery
21 State Street • Seattle, WA 24566
Our History | Directions | Artist Profiles | Events | Contact Us

A 2-COLUMN FIXED LAYOUT

```
header {
    width: 910px;
    margin: 0 0 10px 0;
    padding: 10px;
    background-color: yellow;
}
```

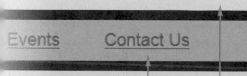
Wash Art Gallery

> The body selector defines the rules for the part of the Web page that surrounds the content section.

```
body {
    font-size: 1.1em;
    font-family: Arial, Helvetica, sans-serif;
    background-color: gray;
```

Events   Contact Us

Gallery

ery is an art gallery specializing in ink and wash paintings. Ink
n East Asian form of brush painting. It is also know by its
-e, or its Chinese name, shui-mo hua. Artists from all over the
itional ink and wash painting techniques.

> In a two-column layout, the header, nav, and footer elements span the full width of the container.

nting

developed in China during the Tang dynasty (618 - 907). Wang
ed as the painter who applied color to existing ink and wash
further developed into a more polished style during the Song
was introduced to Korea shortly after China's discovery of the
missionaries in Japan, in helping the Japanese establish a
troduced it to Japan in the mid-14th century.

ques

ential to the art form are called the four treasures: brush, ink,
raditionally, ink was made by grinding an ink stick on a moist
is still favored by many brush painters today. An artist puts a few
kstone, and grinds the inkstick in a circular motion until a
e desired concentration is made. Prepared inks are usually

> A **gutter** is the margin space between elements.

```
#main {
    width: 680px;
    margin: 0 0 10px 0;
    padding: 10px;
    background-color: aqua;
    float: right;
    height: 400px;
```

ntact Us

Understanding Web Page Layouts

At present, neither HTML nor CSS has a standard method for creating Web page layouts. This is because there are many ways to create a Web page layout; each Web developer eventually settles on a preferred method. Each method involves trade-offs—there are advantages and disadvantages to each. Some methods are flexible and position elements to make the maximum use of the space available in the Web browser. Other methods position elements at fixed locations so the content in the Web page is in the same position regardless of the size of the Web browser window. This tutorial focuses on content that is in fixed positions.

Layouts take planning, and as you design and test your layouts, it's common to encounter problems. The term **broken layout** is used to describe layouts that don't appear on the screen as planned. For example, a column that was intended to appear beside another column may inexplicably appear below that column instead.

A major goal of all the methods for planning the layout of a Web page is to ensure that users can view the page without having to scroll horizontally—something most people find tedious and annoying. Generally, Web page layouts fall into two major categories: fixed width or fluid. In a fixed-width layout, the page and columns are set to certain widths using pixel values. Fixed-width layouts are the most common on the Web today. In contrast, a **fluid layout** expands and contracts so the content fills the entire screen width. This tutorial focuses on fixed-width layouts, and you will learn about fluid layouts in the next tutorial. In a fixed-width layout, a Web page designer chooses how wide the page content should appear in the document window, which is the content area for the Web page.

In the past, the most common screen resolution was 800 by 600 pixels, but with today's larger monitors, it is at least 1024 by 768 pixels. More and more people are also accessing the Internet using handheld devices including smart phones and tablets. Designing Web pages optimized for specific devices is a large topic area, beyond the scope of this textbook, but you should be aware that the Web pages you create may be viewed in Web browsers on handheld devices.

When you design a Web page using a fixed-width layout, you are making an educated guess about the typical resolution your visitors will use to view your Web page. Note that even if you design your Web page for a width of 1024 pixels, you must actually create a design that is somewhat narrower. Some browsers have a 1- or 2-pixel frame on both the left and right sides of the browser document window. Also, some browsers always display a vertical scroll bar (usually about 19 pixels wide), regardless of whether the scroll bar is needed.

Designing Web pages for the maximum screen width can be difficult. For example, some users do not view Web pages with the browser screen maximized. Other viewers may have **widget sidebars**—software add-ons used to enhance a particular browser—that appear vertically on either side of the viewport, reducing the viewing area. Also, several methods can be used to change the appearance of Web page content, such as pressing the Ctrl and plus (+) keys to enlarge the content or the Ctrl and minus (−) keys to shrink the content. If you have a wheel mouse, you can zoom in to the current location of the mouse pointer by holding down the Ctrl key and scrolling the mouse wheel forward. You can also zoom out from the current location of the mouse pointer by holding down the Ctrl key and scrolling the mouse wheel backward. Thus, it can be hard to predict the size of the screen on which users will view your Web pages.

Yan has been looking at a variety of Web pages for layout ideas and has provided you with a sketch of a layout she'd like you to implement, shown in Figure 6-1.

Figure 6-1	Sketch of the Web page layout

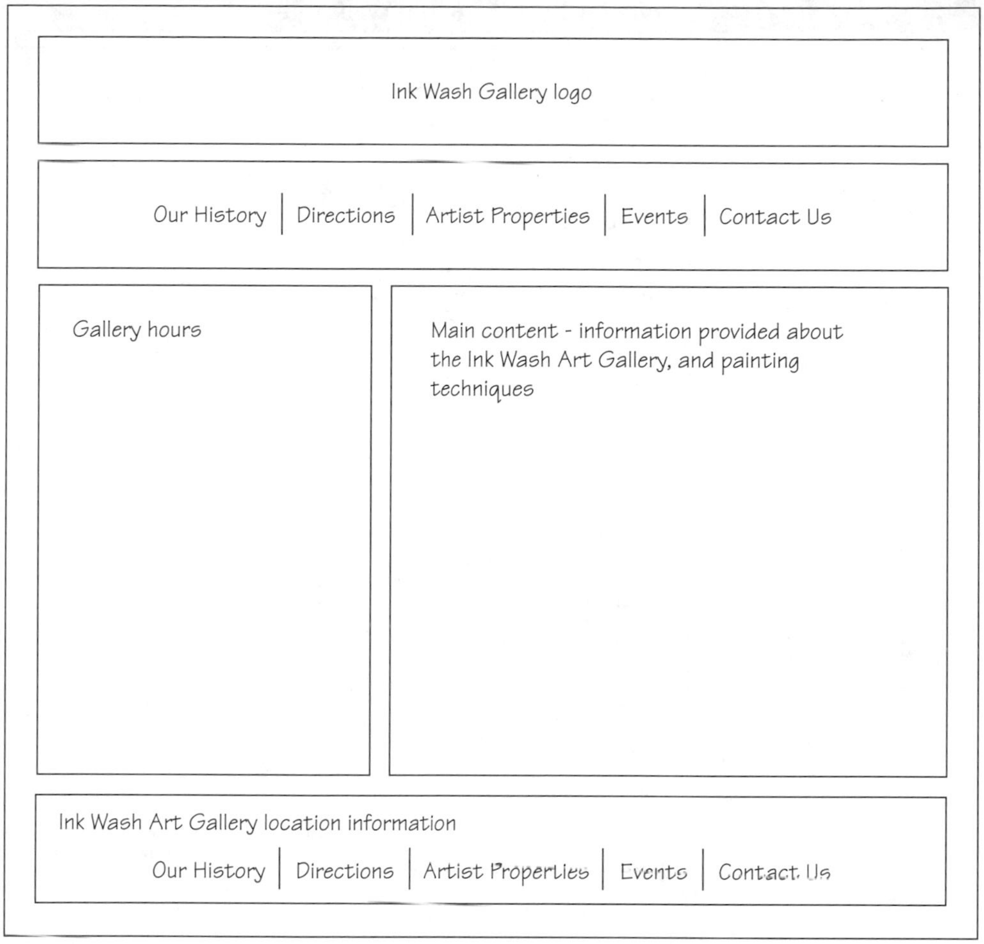

The links on the Web page will use the href value # (which is a placeholder for the link value) during the development of this Web page in order to test the CSS for the links. Once you and Yan are happy with the layout, it can be applied to create other Web pages for the Web site, and the href values for the links could be changed to actual Web page filenames at that time. Yan has created a simple Web page with most of the content and has provided it to you as the file art_T6.htm. You'll open the file, view the contents, and save it.

To open the art_T6.htm file and view it:

1. In your text editor, open the **art_T6.htm** file, which is located in the tutorial6\tutorial folder included with your Data Files. In the head section and below the page title, enter **your name** and **today's date** in the comment section where noted. The code is shown in Figure 6-2. Look through the code and notice it does not contain header, nav, footer, or section elements.

Figure 6-2   **Code for the art_T6.htm Web page**

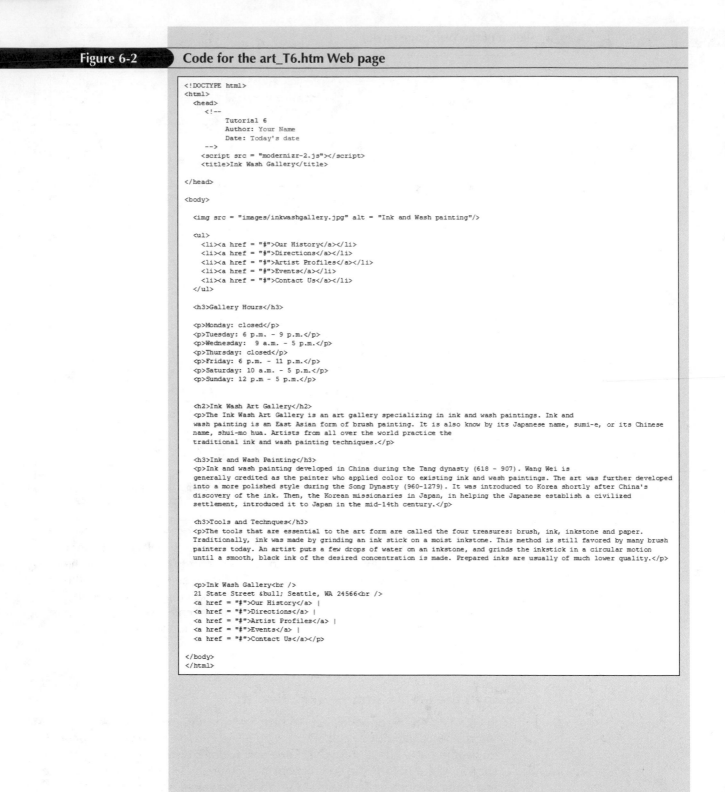

```
<!DOCTYPE html>
<html>
  <head>
    <!--
          Tutorial 6
          Author: Your Name
          Date: Today's date
    -->
    <script src = "modernizr-2.js"></script>
    <title>Ink Wash Gallery</title>

</head>

<body>

  <img src = "images/inkwashgallery.jpg" alt = "Ink and Wash painting"/>

  <ul>
    <li><a href = "#">Our History</a></li>
    <li><a href = "#">Directions</a></li>
    <li><a href = "#">Artist Profiles</a></li>
    <li><a href = "#">Events</a></li>
    <li><a href = "#">Contact Us</a></li>
  </ul>

  <h3>Gallery Hours</h3>

  <p>Monday: closed</p>
  <p>Tuesday: 6 p.m. - 9 p.m.</p>
  <p>Wednesday:  9 a.m. - 5 p.m.</p>
  <p>Thursday: closed</p>
  <p>Friday: 6 p.m. - 11 p.m.</p>
  <p>Saturday: 10 a.m. - 5 p.m.</p>
  <p>Sunday: 12 p.m - 5 p.m.</p>


  <h2>Ink Wash Art Gallery</h2>
  <p>The Ink Wash Art Gallery is an art gallery specializing in ink and wash paintings. Ink and
  wash painting is an East Asian form of brush painting. It is also know by its Japanese name, sumi-e, or its Chinese
  name, shui-mo hua. Artists from all over the world practice the
  traditional ink and wash painting techniques.</p>

  <h3>Ink and Wash Painting</h3>
  <p>Ink and wash painting developed in China during the Tang dynasty (618 - 907). Wang Wei is
  generally credited as the painter who applied color to existing ink and wash paintings. The art was further developed
  into a more polished style during the Song Dynasty (960-1279). It was introduced to Korea shortly after China's
  discovery of the ink. Then, the Korean missionaries in Japan, in helping the Japanese establish a civilized
  settlement, introduced it to Japan in the mid-14th century.</p>

  <h3>Tools and Technques</h3>
  <p>The tools that are essential to the art form are called the four treasures: brush, ink, inkstone and paper.
  Traditionally, ink was made by grinding an ink stick on a moist inkstone. This method is still favored by many brush
  painters today. An artist puts a few drops of water on an inkstone, and grinds the inkstick in a circular motion
  until a smooth, black ink of the desired concentration is made. Prepared inks are usually of much lower quality.</p>


  <p>Ink Wash Gallery<br />
  21 State Street &bull; Seattle, WA 24566<br />
  <a href = "#">Our History</a> |
  <a href = "#">Directions</a> |
  <a href = "#">Artist Profiles</a> |
  <a href = "#">Events</a> |
  <a href = "#">Contact Us</a></p>

</body>
</html>
```

> **2.** Save the file as **art.htm** to the tutorial6\tutorial folder included with your Data Files.

> **3.** Open the **art.htm** file in a Web browser to view the Web page. The page should look similar to Figure 6-3.

Figure 6-3   The art.htm Web page

iBird/Shutterstock.com

In this session, you'll create a two-column fixed-width layout.

Creating a Two-Column Fixed Layout

Web page designers typically use layouts that include one or more of the following design components:

- A horizontal **header** block at the top of the page that usually includes a corporate logo or banner advertising; this will be identified using the `header` element.
- A horizontal navigation bar for links, or **navbar**, which is a row usually placed just below the header; this will be identified using the `nav` element.

- A **sidebar**, which is a narrow column used to display a list of links or content of secondary importance; this will be identified using the `aside` element. In Yan's Web page, this will contain the gallery hours.
- A **main content area**, which is a wide column used to display the primary page content; this will be identified using a `section` element.
- A horizontal **footer** row at the bottom of the page that usually displays contact information for the Web site and sometimes displays links to other Web pages at the site. This will be identified using the `footer` element.

Figure 6-4 identifies the parts of Yan's Web page sketch that correspond to these components.

Figure 6-4 **Components of the Web page layout**

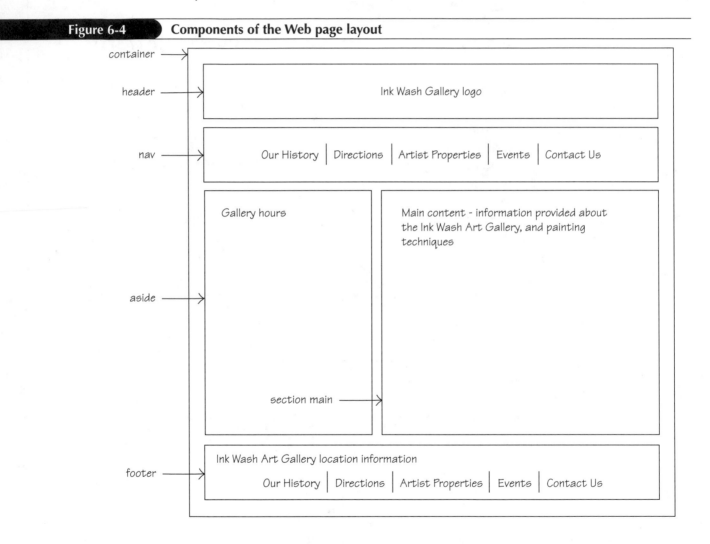

TIP

Before you begin to code a Web page, sketch the layout to identify the main components of the Web page. It gives you a plan from which to work.

HTML elements are used to describe the content of a Web page. You've used the `header`, `footer`, and `nav` elements in previous tutorials to describe Web page content. Content that does not fit the description of `header`, `footer`, `nav`, or one of the other container elements can be described using the `section` element and an id selector. If you need a container solely for formatting, not for marking content, then you'll use a div container. Recall that a div container is a block-level container that does not have any formatting associated with it but is used with an id or class to apply CSS styles.

An **id selector** is a selector used to select a single element on a page. In CSS style sheet code, an id selector name is preceded by the # flag character, as shown in the following code:

```
#main {
  width: 930px;
  background-color: #6e8953;
  margin-bottom: 10px;
}
```

You then apply the `id` attribute to the element you want to select, as shown in the following code:

```
<section id = "main">
```

Unlike a class selector, which can be used to format several elements, an id selector is used to select only one instance of a particular element. Two elements on the same page cannot have the same `id` attribute.

Using the Universal Selector

TIP

Zeroing out the value for a property is also referred to as *initializing* the value.

Each browser has its own styles for determining the margins and padding for the Web browser window and for elements on the Web page. To ensure that your Web pages appear as consistently as possible in all browsers, it's a good coding practice to **zero out**, or cancel, any margins and padding that browsers might add to a Web page by default. This is accomplished by assigning a value of 0 to these properties. Later, you will create styles that selectively add margins and padding to elements. Bear in mind that despite your best efforts, the appearance of your Web pages will vary in different browsers. It's always a good idea to preview your work in the latest and prior versions of each of the contemporary browsers to check the appearance of your Web pages.

The **universal selector** is used to select all of the elements on a Web page. In CSS code, the universal selector is represented by an asterisk. Typically, you use the universal selector to set `margin` and `padding` properties to 0. You'll use the universal selector at the start of your style sheet to set the margins and padding to 0. If you use this after you've set specific margins and paddings, you'll just undo the margins and paddings set previously. So, it's important to place this at the start of the CSS code because it establishes a baseline situation where all margins and padding are 0, and you'll add specific `margin` and `padding` properties in subsequent styles. Entering the following lines of code at the start of your style sheet removes the default browser margins and padding from every element:

```
* {
  margin: 0;
  padding: 0;
}
```

The asterisk (*) applies the styles to all selectors. That includes `body`, headings `h1` through `h6`, `ul`, `ol`, `li`, and all other selectors.

The Universal Selector Controversy

Many Web developers reset properties for all selectors or for specific selectors before adding other selectors. This technique provides a baseline for the properties that are reset. Some Web developers use the universal selector (*) with a simple reset that includes only the `padding` and `margin` properties. Others use a universal selector that also sets the `border` and `outline` properties to 0, in addition to `padding` and `margin`. Using a universal selector to set these properties for all selectors is arguably a sensible idea, but not all Web developers agree with this approach. Following are some arguments in favor of using the universal selector as a reset, as well as some arguments against.

Arguments in favor of using the universal selector:

- Browser defaults can cause issues with layout, so it's best to reset at least `margin` and `padding` to 0 for all selectors.
- It's an easy method that may slow down the rendering of the Web page, but the amount of extra time would not be noticeable to a user.

Arguments against using the universal selector:

- Using the universal selector to reset `margin` and `padding` for all elements is not necessary because a well-designed Web page includes `margin` and `padding` settings for all elements where needed.
- Someone who uses the universal selector habitually could remove the default behavior of an element and forget to restyle it.
- The universal selector slows down the rendering of the Web page, and even though the length of the delay is miniscule, it should be eliminated.

Recall that 0 is one of the few values in CSS code that does not need a unit measurement, because 0 of any measurement is 0. In this layout, you'll express all other measurements in pixel values.

Understanding the box properties is key to planning a Web page layout. Recall that when only one value is used for the `margin` and `padding` shorthand properties, the value is applied to all four sides. When two values are used, the first value is applied to the top and bottom sides equally, and the second value is applied to the left and right sides equally. When four values are used, they are applied individually to each side in this order: top, right, bottom, and left. You'll create code to style the universal selector to set all padding and margin values to 0.

To create a style for the universal selector:

1. Return to the **art.htm** file in your text editor. Position the insertion point on a blank line below the end `</title>` tag, and then type the following embedded style sheet code and CSS, as shown in Figure 6-5:

```
<style type = "text/css">

 * {
    padding: 0;
    margin: 0;
 }

</style>
```

Figure 6-5 The code for the universal selector

```
<title>Ink Wash Gallery</title>

<style type = "text/css">

  * {
      padding: 0;
      margin: 0;
    }

</style>

</head>
```

▶ **2.** Save the file, return to your Web browser, and then click the **Refresh** or **Reload** button to view the changes in the file. The Web page should look similar to Figure 6-6. Notice the padding and margins have been removed and the text seems much more cramped.

Figure 6-6 Web page with margins and padding set to 0

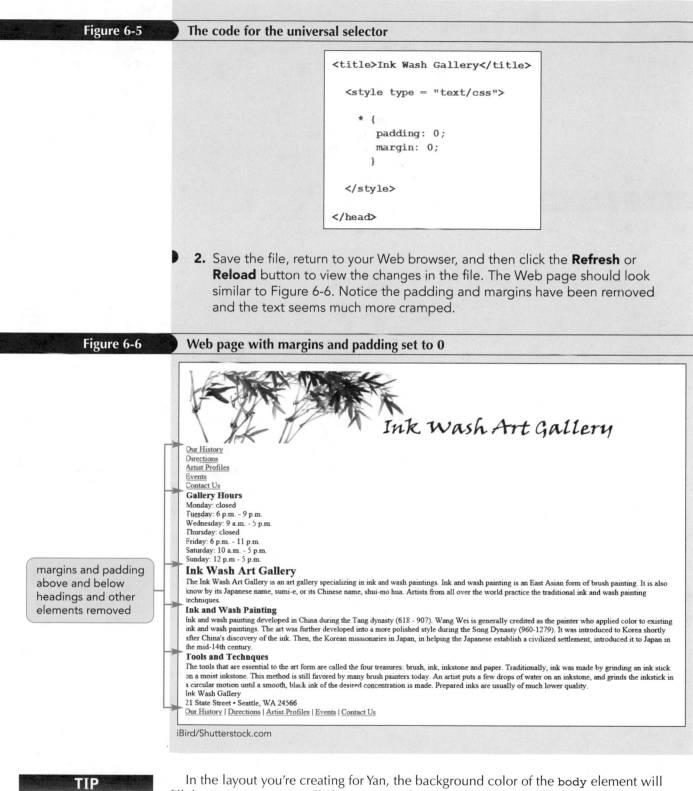

margins and padding above and below headings and other elements removed

iBird/Shutterstock.com

In the layout you're creating for Yan, the background color of the body element will fill the entire screen. You'll also create each section with its own background color to make it easy to tell one section from another.

First, you'll style the body element to create styles for the font size and font family. You'll also apply a background color of gray to the body element.

To style the body element:

1. Return to the **art.htm** file in your text editor. Position the insertion point on a blank line below the universal selector rule and above the close `</style>` tag, and then type the following CSS style rule, as shown in Figure 6-7:

```
body {
  font-size: 1.1em;
  font-family: Arial, Helvetica, sans-serif;
  background-color: gray;
}
```

Figure 6-7	CSS code for the body element

```
<style type = "text/css">

  * {
    padding: 0;
    margin: 0;
  }

  body {
    font-size: 1.1em;
    font-family: Arial, Helvetica, sans-serif;
    background-color: gray;
  }

</style>
```

2. Save the file, return to your Web browser, and then click the **Refresh** or **Reload** button to view the changes in the file. The Web page should look similar to Figure 6-8.

Figure 6-8   **Body styles applied**

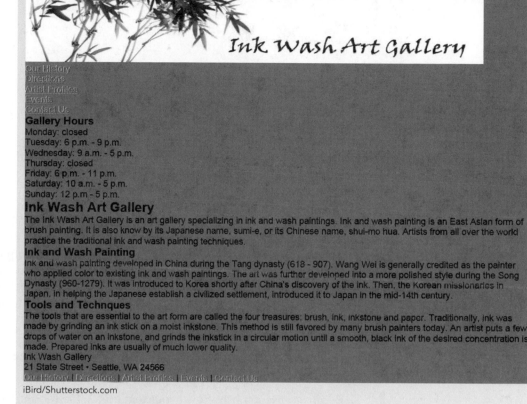

iBird/Shutterstock.com

Creating the Container Section

A container section serves as a large box in which you can place all the other boxes (the smaller content sections and elements). All of the section elements that have content will themselves be contained in a large container section.

Using a container section can offer several advantages and serve several important functions:

- It can determine the width of the page layout.
- It can be used to center the layout horizontally.
- It can have a border applied around it, which serves to unify the page content.
- It can be used to apply a background color or image to contrast the background color or image of the body element.

TIP

The term *wrapper* is also used to describe a container section.

The section element with an id selector is used to style a section in a Web page when there isn't another appropriate element to describe the content such as nav, header, or footer. The id selector name is preceded by the # flag character. For a screen width of 1024 pixels, most Web designers create their layouts to have a width of 900 to 960 pixels. As stated earlier, you don't have the full screen width available for your layout, so the container section cannot be 1024 pixels wide. You must account for each browser's frame (borders) on the left and right, scroll bars, and other inconsistencies among browsers.

Creating an id Selector

- To create an id selector, use the declaration:

```
#id {
   property: value;
}
```

where *id* is the id selector, *property* is any one of the CSS properties, and *value* is any one of the applicable values for that property.

Yan would like the layout to be centered horizontally. To center the layout, you need to apply auto as the value for the left and right margins. The auto value makes the left and right margins expand or contract to fit the container width. Using auto ensures the left and right margins are the same; when the left and right margins are the same, the content is, by definition, centered. You'll use the margin shorthand property to set the top and bottom margins to 0 and the margins on the left and right to auto. The layout will have a width of 930 pixels. A border width of 1px will be added so the document will be centered correctly in the Firefox browser if the user selects the zoom function to make the content larger. You'll set the background color to navy for the container, which will contrast against the background color of gray for the body element. Finally, you'll use the div element to define the container and will apply the *container* class to the div element.

To style the *container* id selector and enter the container section code:

1. Return to the **art.htm** file in your text editor. Position the insertion point on a blank line below the *body* style rule, and then type the following CSS style rule, as shown in Figure 6-9:

```
#container {
   width: 930px;
   border-width: 1px;
   margin: 0 auto;
   background-color: navy;
}
```

Figure 6-9 **Sketch of the Web page layout**

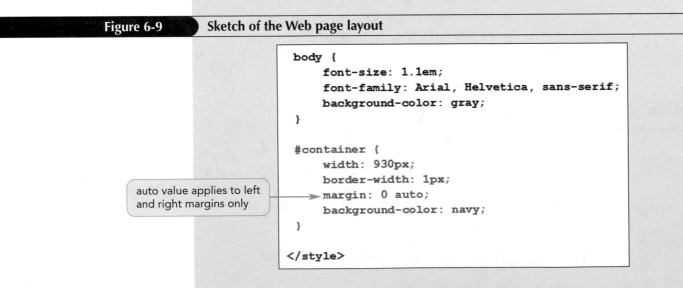

```
body {
    font-size: 1.1em;
    font-family: Arial, Helvetica, sans-serif;
    background-color: gray;
}

#container {
    width: 930px;
    border-width: 1px;
    margin: 0 auto;
    background-color: navy;
}

</style>
```

auto value applies to left and right margins only

2. Position the insertion point on a blank line below the start `<body>` tag, and then type the following HTML code, as shown in Figure 6-10:

```
<div id = "container">
```

Figure 6-10 HTML code for the start container section tag

```
<body>

  <div id = "container">

  <img src="images/inkwashgallery.jpg" alt="Ink and Wash painting"/>
```

3. Position the insertion point on a blank line below the *Contact Us* code and above the end `</body>` tag, and then type the following HTML code, as shown in Figure 6-11:

```
</div> <!-- end container -->
```

Figure 6-11 HTML code for the end container section tag

```
<a href="#">Contact Us</a></p>
</div> <!-- end container -->
</body>
```

4. Save the file, return to your Web browser, and then click the **Refresh** or **Reload** button to view the changes in the file. The Web page should look similar to Figure 6-12.

Figure 6-12   **Web page showing the body and container colors**

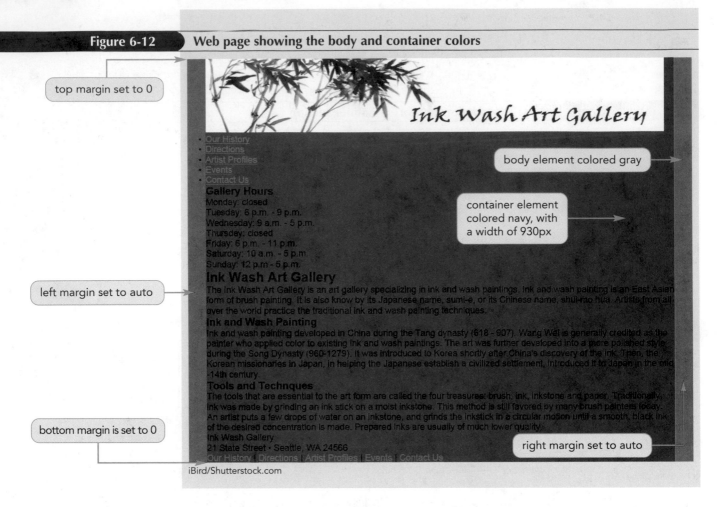

top margin set to 0

body element colored gray

container element colored navy, with a width of 930px

left margin set to auto

bottom margin is set to 0

right margin set to auto

iBird/Shutterstock.com

The *container* div, like other wrapper `div` elements or `section` elements, is a container for other elements. The id selector is applied to the appropriate `div` or `section` tag, so identifying where a `div` or `section` starts is not a problem. The end `</div>` tags and end `</section>` tags pose a problem if there is more than one `div` element or more than one `section` element in a Web page. It's a good coding practice to enter comments that identify each `</div>` and `</section>` tag, rather than having a confusing number of `</section>` and `</div>` tags at the bottom of your page, such as the following:

```
</section>
</section>
</div>
</div>
```

For instance, if a Web page has sections nested within each other where a news section is nested within a main section that is nested within a container section, the well-documented code would look like this:

```
        </section> <!-- end news -->
      </section> <!-- end main  -->
    </div> <!-- end wrapper -->
  </div> <!-- end container -->
```

Determining the Content and Column Widths

Recall that you set the *container* section to have a width of 930px, which means no element that spans the entire page, such as the header or footer element, can have a width greater than 930px. Similarly, side-by-side columns, such as the sidebar and the main column, cannot have a width greater than 930px; otherwise, the layout will break.

To determine the widths of the columns, you first need to determine the width of the entire container. Next, subtract the left and right margins, borders, and padding values from the width of the container to determine the content width. The calculated content width is the maximum number of pixels available for the total width of the columns. Next, determine the number of columns. The column of primary importance should be the widest. All content should fit in the column width. If an image is wider than the column in which you'd like to place it, resize the image; otherwise, the column width increases to fit the image, which overrides the set column width.

REFERENCE

Determining the Content Width

To determine the value for the `width` property of an element to be used for column content:

- If an element such as a `header` or `footer` element spans the entire container, subtract the sum of the left and right margins, borders, and padding values from the width of the parent container to determine the content width.
- For side-by-side columns, choose an appropriate content width for each column. Columns of secondary importance, such as a sidebar, should be narrow. The column of primary importance should be the widest.

Understanding Container, Content, and Column Widths

Determining the `width` property value for the `header` element isn't as easy as it might seem. If the `header` element spans the entire container, the width of the `header` element should be 930px, the same as the *container* section. However, that won't work well.

Elements are boxes, and they make full use of the box properties, such as margins, borders, and padding—all of which take up space on the screen. When you enter the value for the `width` property of an element, class, or an id selector, you need to enter the value for the content width. However, it's important to understand which width measurement you need. The **parent container width** is the width of the containing box. For instance, `body` is the parent container for all elements in the document. The **content width** is the width of the content inside a container. An example of content is an image, table, or text. The **column width** is the sum of the content, left and right padding, left and right border widths, and left and right margins. The sum of the column widths cannot exceed the width of the parent container. These terms are shown in Figure 6-13.

Figure 6-13 **Types of widths**

Width Type	Definition
Parent container width	The size of the containing box. The container section is the parent for elements that span the full width of the screen, such as the header, the nav, and the footer.
Content width	The width of only the box content, which might be text, an image, a table, or any other type of content.
Column width	The sum of the content and its left and right margins, borders, and padding. For side-by-side columns, the sum of the column widths must not exceed the parent container width.

You'll start by calculating the content width for the `header` element. The header will not have a left or a right margin, nor will it have a border. The header will contain an image, and for the purpose of being able to see the placement of the image within the header element you'll add padding of 10px on all sides to create some white space. Figure 6-14 details the calculation of the sum of the padding widths, the border widths, and the margin widths used in the `header` element.

Figure 6-14 **Calculating the sum of left and right margins, borders, and padding**

Pixels	Used For
0	Left margin width
0	Left border width
10	Padding width on the left
10	Padding width on the right
0	Right border width
0	Right margin width
20	Total number of pixels in the margin, border, and padding on the left and right

The parent element for the `header` element is the *container* section, which has a width of 930px. If you subtract the padding (20px) from the width of the parent container section (930px), the result is 910px. In other words, 910px is the content width; you'll enter this value for the `width` property when you enter the code for the *header* selector.

INSIGHT

Keeping Your Code Consistent

When you create a style for an id, class, or element selector, it's a good coding practice to list the properties in this order: `width`, `margin`, `border`, and `padding`. Grouping the properties in this order will help you to locate the pixel values you need to determine the content width. Also, in fixed-width layouts, use a pixel value rather than a keyword for the border width. Browsers interpret keyword values slightly differently and may assign more or less thickness to a keyword value. Miscalculating by even one or two pixels could break your layout. For the remaining style declarations, group the `color` property with the `background-color` and `background-image` properties. Group the font properties, listing them in the specific order required, and list all of the other properties and values for the selector in alphabetic order.

You'll set the background color for the header element as yellow, to clearly identify the header section. Recall that the body element is colored gray and the container section is colored navy.

To style the header selector and add the header element:

1. Return to the **art.htm** file in your text editor. Position the insertion point on a blank line after the *#container* rule and above the end `</style>` tag, and then type the following CSS style rule, as shown in Figure 6-15:

```
header {
    width: 910px;
    margin: 0 0 10px 0;
    padding: 10px;
    background-color: yellow;
}
```

Figure 6-15	CSS code for the header element

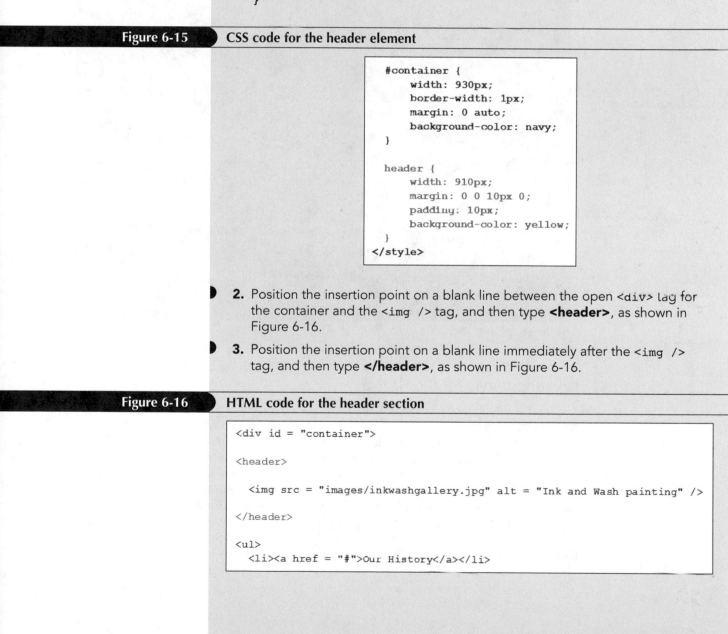

```
#container {
    width: 930px;
    border-width: 1px;
    margin: 0 auto;
    background-color: navy;
}

header {
    width: 910px;
    margin: 0 0 10px 0;
    padding: 10px;
    background-color: yellow;
}
</style>
```

2. Position the insertion point on a blank line between the open `<div>` tag for the container and the `<img />` tag, and then type **<header>**, as shown in Figure 6-16.

3. Position the insertion point on a blank line immediately after the `<img />` tag, and then type **</header>**, as shown in Figure 6-16.

Figure 6-16	HTML code for the header section

```
<div id = "container">

<header>

  <img src = "images/inkwashgallery.jpg" alt = "Ink and Wash painting" />

</header>

<ul>
  <li><a href = "#">Our History</a></li>
```

4. Save the file, return to your Web browser, and then click the **Refresh** or **Reload** button to view the changes in the file. The Web page should look similar to Figure 6-17.

Figure 6-17 | Web page showing the header

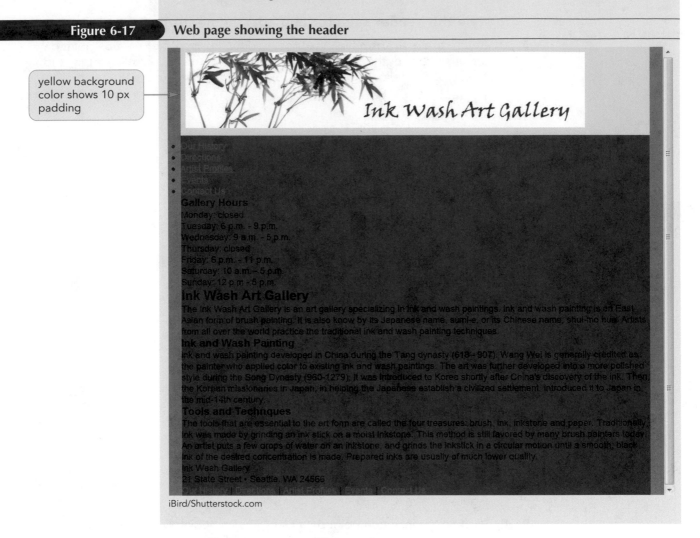

yellow background color shows 10 px padding

iBird/Shutterstock.com

Creating a Style for the Navbar

A navbar is often placed below the header. A Web page could also contain a sidebar column that contains links to other resources in addition to a navbar. Usually the navbar contains only important links, such as those to other content areas on the Web site. As with previous Web pages you've created, the navbar for Yan's Web site will be contained in the nav element. It will also span the entire container width and will be placed below the header, as shown in the sketch in Figure 6-4. The navbar will have 10px of padding on all sides, so the value for the width property of the nav element will be the same as that for the header—910px. You'll also set the nav element background color to silver. Additionally, you'll style the unordered list inside the nav element as an inline list, using the same technique you used in Tutorial 4.

To style the *nav* selector and add the `nav` element:

1. Return to the **art.htm** file in your text editor. Position the insertion point on a blank line after the *header* rule and above the end `</style>` tag, and then type the following CSS style rules, as shown in Figure 6-18:

```
nav {
    width: 910px;
    margin: 0 0 10px 0;
    padding: 10px;
    background-color: silver;
}

nav li  {
    display: inline;
    list-style-type: none;
    padding-right: 40px;
}
```

Figure 6-18	CSS code for the nav element and li elements inside the nav element

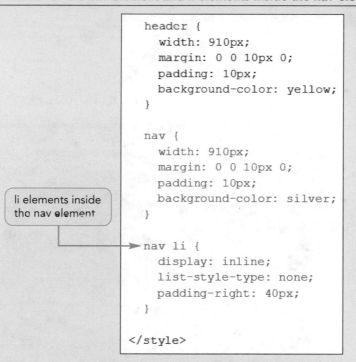

li elements inside the nav element

```
header {
    width: 910px;
    margin: 0 0 10px 0;
    padding: 10px;
    background-color: yellow;
}

nav {
    width: 910px;
    margin: 0 0 10px 0;
    padding: 10px;
    background-color: silver;
}

nav li {
    display: inline;
    list-style-type: none;
    padding-right: 40px;
}

</style>
```

2. Position the insertion point on a blank line between the close `</header>` tag and the open `<ul>` tag, and then type **<nav>**, as shown in Figure 6-19.

3. Position the insertion point on a blank line immediately after the close `</ul>` tag, and then type **</nav>**, as shown in Figure 6-19.

Figure 6-19 **HTML code for the nav element**

```
</header>
<nav>
  <ul>
    <li><a href="#">Our History</a></li>
    <li><a href="#">Directions</a></li>
    <li><a href="#">Artist Profiles</a></li>
    <li><a href="#">Events</a></li>
    <li><a href="#">Contact Us</a></li>
  </ul>
</nav>

<h3>Gallery Hours</h3>
```

▶ **4.** Save the file, return to your Web browser, and then click the **Refresh** or **Reload** button to view the changes in the file. The Web page should look similar to Figure 6-20.

Figure 6-20 **Web page showing the nav element**

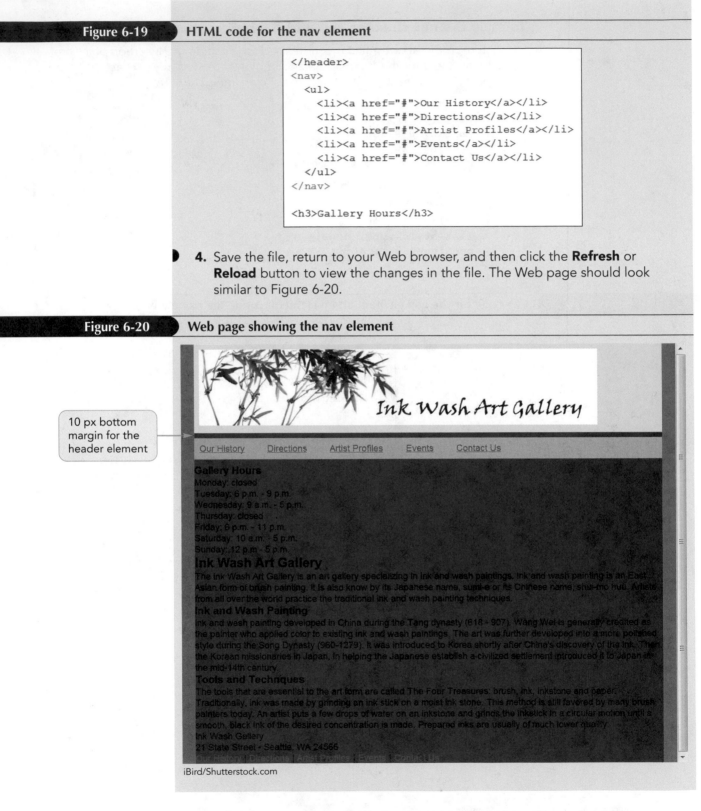

10 px bottom margin for the header element

iBird/Shutterstock.com

Now that the nav element has been created and styled, you'll create a sidebar column to display the gallery hours.

Using the `aside` Element

The `aside` element is an HTML element that marks content that is not the main content but is extra, or tangential content. You can include more than one `aside` element in a Web page, and if you do, it's helpful to use the id selector to identify each `aside` element. You'll use an `aside` element for the gallery hours on Yan's Web page.

The body of the art.htm Web page will have two side-by-side columns—a narrow sidebar column on the left and a larger main column to its right. Recall that the container section, which will be the parent element to the side-by-side columns, has a width of 930px. The content of the sidebar column and the main column, as well as all their margins, borders, and padding, cannot exceed a total of 930px. One of the two side-by-side columns can have a margin to create a gutter, or white space between columns. You could create a right margin for the sidebar column or create a left margin for the main column. For the art.htm Web page, you'll give the sidebar column a right margin of 10px.

Because a sidebar column should be narrow, you'll set its width to 200px. To allow some internal white space, the sidebar column will also have 10px of padding on all sides, but it will not have a border. With this information, you can now determine the column width of the sidebar column—230px. Figure 6-21 illustrates the calculation of this number.

| Figure 6-21 | Calculating the column width for the sidebar column |

Left Margin Width	Left Border Width	Left Padding Width	Content Width	Right Padding Width	Right Border Width	Right Margin Width	Column Width
0	0	10	200	10	0	10	**230**

The top and bottom margins for an element do not figure into the calculation for the column width or the content width, but those margin values are important for the vertical spacing. The bottom margin for the sidebar column will be 10px, which will create some white space below the sidebar column. To make the bottom margins equal for the sidebar column and the main column, both columns need to have the same bottom margin of 10px.

In Tutorial 5, you learned about the `float` property and used it to float an image left or right. The `float` property is also used extensively in page layouts to position elements left or right. In the art.htm Web page, you'll float the sidebar column left. To see the layout better, you'll also assign a background color and a height to the sidebar column.

To style the *aside* selector and add the `aside` element:

1. Return to the **art.htm** file in your text editor. Position the insertion point on a blank line after the *nav li* rule and above the end `</style>` tag, and then type the following CSS style rule, as shown in Figure 6-22:

```
aside {
    width: 200px;
    margin: 0 10px 10px 0;
    padding: 10px;
    background-color: orange;
    float: left;
    height: 400px;
}
```

Figure 6-22	CSS code for the aside selector

```
nav li {
    display: inline;
    list-style-type: none;
    padding-right: 40px;
}

aside {
    width: 200px;
    margin: 0 10px 10px 0;
    padding: 10px;
    background-color: orange;
    float: left;
    height: 400px;
}
</style>
```

2. Position the insertion point on a blank line in the body between the close `</nav>` tag and the open `<h3>` tag, and then type **<aside>**, as shown in Figure 6-23.

3. Position the insertion point on a blank line immediately after the close `</p>` tag that contains the Sunday hours, and then type **</aside>**, as shown in Figure 6-23.

Figure 6-23	HTML code for the aside element

```
      </ul>
</nav>

<aside>
  <h3>Gallery Hours</h3>

  <p>Monday: closed</p>
  <p>Tuesday: 6 p.m. - 9 p.m.</p>
  <p>Wednesday:  9 a.m. - 5 p.m.</p>
  <p>Thursday: closed</p>
  <p>Friday: 6 p.m. - 11 p.m.</p>
  <p>Saturday: 10 a.m. - 5 p.m.</p>
  <p>Sunday: 12 p.m - 5 p.m.</p>
</aside>

<h2>Ink Wash Art Gallery</h2>
```

4. Save the file, return to your Web browser, and then click the **Refresh** or **Reload** button to view the changes in the file. The Web page should look similar to Figure 6-24.

Figure 6-24   Web page showing the aside element

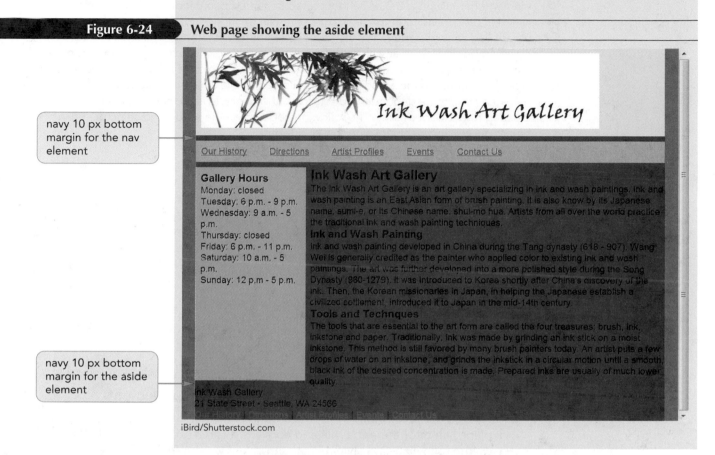

navy 10 px bottom margin for the nav element

navy 10 px bottom margin for the aside element

iBird/Shutterstock.com

Creating a Style for the Main Column

Now that the sidebar column has been established, you need to calculate the width of the main column. Recall that the container `div` is 930px wide. The sidebar column has a width of 230px, so the column width of the main column will be 700px (930 – 230 = 700). The main column for this layout will not have margins or a border, but it will have padding of 10px on all sides. You now have all the data you need to determine the content width for the main column, as shown in Figure 6-25.

Figure 6-25   Determining the content width of the main column

Width	Items
700px	The width of the main column
20px	The margins, borders, and padding (10px of padding on both the left and right)
680px	The content width of the main column (700 – 20)

Using Dependent id Selectors

Recall that a class can be dependent, meaning that it can be applied only to a particular element. For instance, the dependent selector named *p.info* indicates the *info* class can only be applied to a `<p>` tag. Likewise, it can be independent, meaning that it can be applied to any element. For instance a selector named *.center* indicates the *center* class can be applied to any element. You can also make an id selector dependent on an element as well. You have already seen examples in which id selectors have been created by entering the # flag character followed by the id selector name.

When you create dependent id selectors, the principle is the same as that for creating dependent classes. The following code is an independent id selector. It can be applied to any element using the `id` attribute.

```
#highlight {
   background-color: yellow;
}
```

The following code is a dependent id selector. It can be applied only to a `div` element.

```
div#container {
   background-color: teal;
}
```

You've calculated 680px as the value to use for the `width` property of the *main* id selector. You'll now create the section and style it.

To style the *main* id selector and add the `section` element:

▶ 1. Return to the **art.htm** file in your text editor. Position the insertion point on a blank line after the *aside* rule and above the end `</style>` tag, and then type the following CSS style rule, as shown in Figure 6-26:

```
#main {
   width: 680px;
   margin: 0 0 10px 0;
   padding: 10px;
   background-color: aqua;
   float: right;
   height: 400px;
}
```

Figure 6-26	CSS code for the #main selector

```
aside {
    width: 200px;
    margin: 0 10px 10px 0;
    padding: 10px;
    background-color: orange;
    float: left;
    height: 400px;
}

#main {
    width: 680px;
    margin: 0 0 10px 0;
    padding: 10px;
    background-color: aqua;
    float: right;
    height: 400px;
}
</style>
```

2. Position the insertion point on a blank line in the body of the Web page between the close `</aside>` tag and the open `<h2>` tag, and then type the following code, as shown in Figure 6-27:

```
<section id = "main">
```

3. Position the insertion point on a blank line immediately after the close paragraph `</p>` tag at the end of the third paragraph, and then type the following code, as shown in Figure 6-27:

```
</section> <!-- end main section -->
```

Figure 6-27	HTML code for the main section

```
    <p>Sunday: 12 p.m - 5 p.m.</p>
</aside>

<section id = "main">
    <h2>Ink Wash Art Gallery</h2>
    <p>The Ink Wash Art Gallery is an art gallery specializing in ink and wash paintings. Ink and
    wash painting is an East Asian form of brush painting. It is also know by its Japanese name,
    sumi-e or its Chinese name, shui-mo hua. Artists from all over the world practice the
    traditional ink and wash painting techniques.</p>

    <h3>Ink and Wash Painting</h3>
    <p>Ink and wash painting developed in China during the Tang dynasty (618 - 907). Wang Wei is
    generally credited as the painter who applied color to existing ink and wash paintings. The
    art was further developed into a more polished style during the Song Dynasty (960-1279). It was
    introduced to Korea shortly after China's discovery of the ink. Then, the Korean missionaries
    in Japan, in helping the Japanese establish a civilized settlement introduced it to Japan in
    the mid-14th century.</p>

    <h3>Tools and Technques</h3>
    <p>The tools that are essential to the art form are called The Four Treasures: brush, ink,
    inkstone and paper. Traditionally, ink was made by grinding an ink stick on a moist ink stone.
    This method is still favored by many brush painters today. An artist puts a few drops of water
    on an inkstone and grinds the inkstick in a circular motion until a smooth, black ink of the
    desired concentration is made. Prepared inks are usually of much lower quality. </p>
</section> <!-- end main section -->

<p>Ink Wash Gallery<br />
```

4. Save the file, return to your Web browser, and then click the **Refresh** or **Reload** button to view the changes in the file. The Web page should look similar to Figure 6-28.

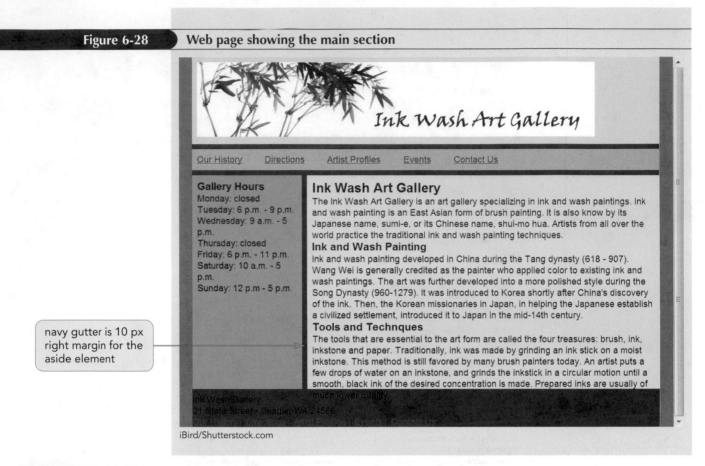

navy gutter is 10 px right margin for the aside element

iBird/Shutterstock.com

Next, you'll create the `footer` element and style it.

Creating a Style for the Footer

In a two-column layout, the footer usually appears below the sidebar and main columns. You'll create a *footer* style similar to the *header* and *nav* styles you created earlier. The footer will not have margins or a border, but it will have 10px of padding on all sides. The width will be 910px, the same as for the *header* and *nav* selectors. However, you will also use the `clear` property to clear past both the sidebar and main columns.

TIP

Use the value of both rather than `left` or `right` for the `clear` property. This way, you won't have to change the `clear` property value should the sidebar later be floated right instead of left.

To style the *footer* selector and add the `footer` element:

1. Return to the **art.htm** file in your text editor. Position the insertion point on a blank line after the #*main* rule and above the end `</style>` tag, and then type the following CSS style rule, as shown in Figure 6-29:

```
footer {
    width: 910px;
    padding: 10px;
    background-color: lime;
    clear: both;
    height: 75px;
}
```

Figure 6-29   CSS code for the footer selector

```
#main {
   width: 680px;
   margin: 0 0 10px 0;
   padding: 10px;
   background-color: aqua;
   float: right;
   height: 400px;
}

footer {
   width: 910px;
   padding: 10px;
   background-color: lime;
   clear: both;
   height: 75px;
}

</style>
```

   2. Position the insertion point in the body of the Web page, on a blank line
   between the comment code **<!-- end main section -->** and the open
   <p> tag, and then type **<footer>**, as shown in Figure 6-30.

   3. Position the insertion point on a blank line immediately after the close **</p>**
   tag at the end of the *Contact Us* link, and then type **</footer>**, as shown in
   Figure 6-30.

Figure 6-30   HTML code for the footer element

```
</section> <!-- end main section -->

<footer>
  <p>Ink Wash Gallery<br />
  21 State Street &bull; Seattle, WA 24566<br />
  <a href="#">Our History</a> |
  <a href="#">Directions</a> |
  <a href="#">Artist Profiles</a> |
  <a href="#">Events</a> |
  <a href="#">Contact Us</a></p>
</footer>

</div> <!-- end container -->
```

   4. Save the file, return to your Web browser, and then click the **Refresh** or
   Reload button to view the changes in the file. The Web page should look
   similar to Figure 6-31.

Figure 6-31   **Web page showing the footer element**

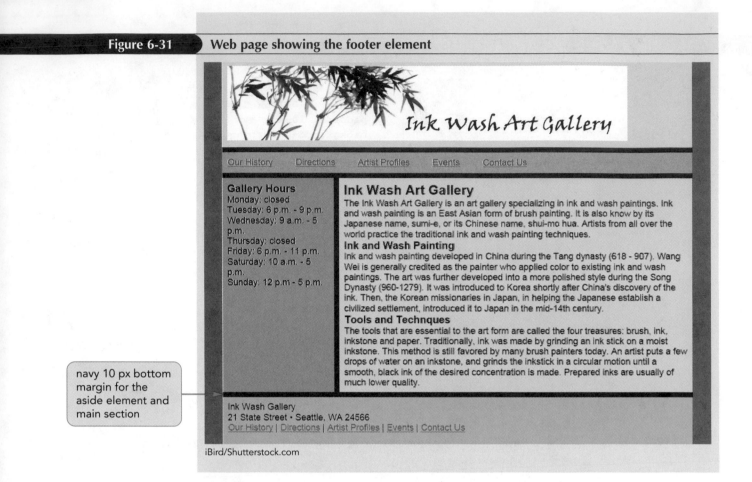

navy 10 px bottom margin for the aside element and main section

iBird/Shutterstock.com

The `footer` element has the bottom margin set at 0 so it is flush with the bottom of the browser window. The fixed pixel sizes mean that as the size of the browser window expands and shrinks, the container section and the elements inside it don't change widths. This method is favored when you want to ensure that elements do not change positions when the browser window size changes.

Using the Positioning Properties

The **document flow** describes how the contents of the page are recognized by the browser. The positioning properties can place any element—images or text—anywhere on the screen regardless of where the element appears in the document flow. When you use **absolute positioning** on an element, the element is displayed in the exact position you specify, no matter what elements surround it. If text or an image already appears in that screen location, the item that has an absolute position may even appear on top of that object. Floated elements are not shifted around absolutely positioned elements. When you use **relative positioning**, by contrast, you shift an element's position from the point where it normally would appear in the document flow.

The `left` property with a positive value positions an element a certain distance from the left edge of the screen, moving the element to the right. The `top` property with a positive value positions an element a certain distance from the top edge of the screen, moving the element down. Although they are not used nearly as often, the `bottom` property and the `right` property function in the same way. The `bottom` property with a positive value moves an element up; the `right` property with a positive value moves an element to the left.

The values for the `top`, `bottom`, `left`, and `right` properties can be expressed in any of the CSS measurements, such as pixels, points, percentages, or em values, as shown below:

```
img.absolute {
   position: absolute;
   top: 40px;
   left: 120px;
}
```

The preceding code positions an image 40 pixels from the top edge of the screen and 120 pixels from the left edge of the screen.

Yan likes the work you've done, but she'd like to see another layout option that has three columns rather than two columns, and colors that are more suitable for an ink wash art Web site. You'll redesign the gallery Web page using a three-column layout in the next session.

PROSKILLS

Problem Solving: Creating a Layout Design Without Content

During the process of designing a Web site, a Web developer or designer is likely to use placeholder text in place of real content during the design of the layout. **Placeholder text** is text used solely to demonstrate the typography or layout in a document, and is also called **dummy text** or **filler text**. Although placeholder text can be any word or short phrase repeated, this may be misleading or distracting during the design phase. For instance, if a client or designer is distracted by reading *this is placeholder text* or a word or phrase that is repeated and used as a placeholder text, then the client or designer is not as focused on the layout and design elements.

Instead, many designers use ***lorem ipsum* text**, which is Latin text that is not distracting because it looks more like natural language, as opposed to using placeholder words that are repeated over and over again. Here's an example of lorem ipusm text:

Lorem ipsum dolor sit amet, consectetuer adipiscing elit. Donec eget nibh. Suspendisse ut ligula ultricies odio rhoncus vestibulum. Curabitur ut magna sed felis bibendum commodo. Vestibulum semper condimentum tortor. Vivamus tellus velit, dapibus at, tincidunt ac, vestibulum quis, lectus. Nunc tempus nisi a lectus. Donec diam libero, convallis sed, commodo eu, rutrum ut, mauris. Ut vulputate, ligula eu vehicula nonummy, augue dolor commodo sem, at eleifend justo lectus vitae odio.

When you glance at this text, it looks like any paragraph. When you start to read it, you notice that the words are Latin. It's not distracting because it has the variety of words, characters, and punctuation that any paragraph has. But it's not content, so it also does not distract a client or designer with a readable message. Many Web sites generate *lorem ipsum* text, and some word-processing applications and Web design tools do as well. You can use as much of the text as you need, with short snippets for links and longer paragraphs for blocks of content. After the layout design is complete, you substitute the real content in place of the *lorem ipsum* text.

The use of *lorem ipsum* text did not begin with Web design. This technique has a long history that goes back to typesetting in the 1500s. The standard *lorem ipsum* text is a long quote from *The Extremes of Good and Evil*, written by Cicero in 45 BCE (http://www.lipsum.com). Today there are many forms of the *lorem ipsum* text widely used as placeholder text.

REVIEW

Session 6.1 Quick Check

1. What term describes layouts that do not function as intended?
2. What are the two major categories of layouts?
3. What element would you use to mark content that will be used as a sidebar?
4. What technique can be used to create a gutter between two columns?
5. What are the usual five components of any layout?

SESSION 6.2 VISUAL OVERVIEW

The box-shadow property sets the values for the drop-shadow around an element.

The *h-shadow* value pushes the shadow to the right.

```
border: 1px solid #888888;
box-shadow: 15px 15px 5px 0 #888888;
border-radius: 25px;
```

The *v-shadow* value pushes the shadow down.

The border-radius property sets the size of the round corners of an element.

The *blur* value specifies the amount of blur around the edges.

In a three-column layout, the header, nav, and footer elements span the full width of the container.

A **three-column layout** contains three columns of content.

```
border-bottom-left-radius: 25px;
border-bottom-right-radius: 25px;
```

Individual corners can be rounded separately using individual border-radius properties.

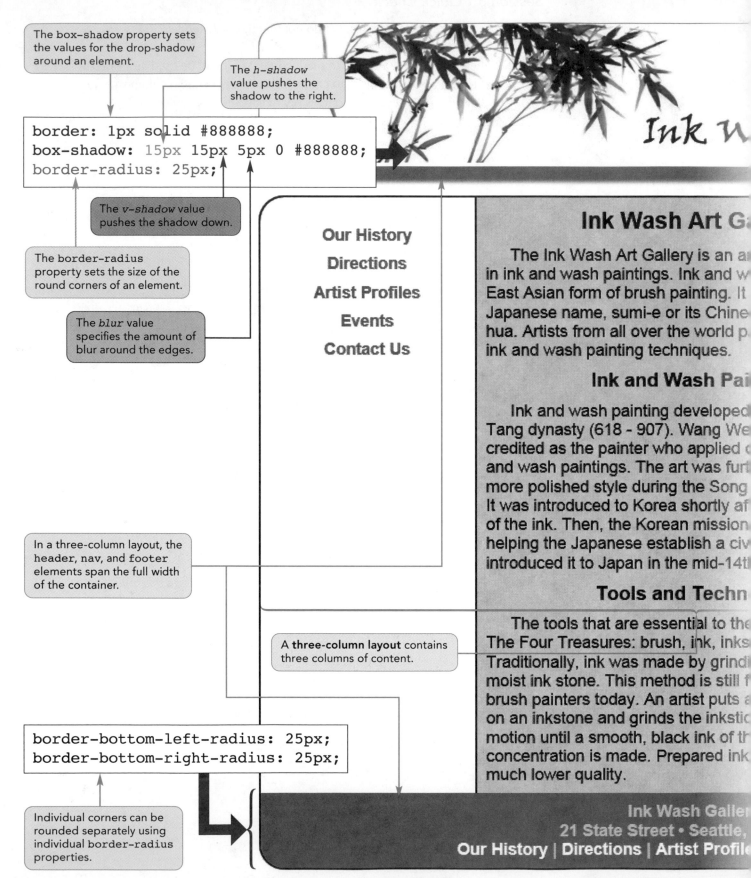

Ink w...

Ink Wash Art Ga...

The Ink Wash Art Gallery is an a... in ink and wash paintings. Ink and w... East Asian form of brush painting. It... Japanese name, sumi-e or its Chine... hua. Artists from all over the world p... ink and wash painting techniques.

Ink and Wash Pai...

Ink and wash painting developed... Tang dynasty (618 - 907). Wang We... credited as the painter who applied ... and wash paintings. The art was fur... more polished style during the Song ... It was introduced to Korea shortly af... of the ink. Then, the Korean mission... helping the Japanese establish a civ... introduced it to Japan in the mid-14th...

Tools and Techn...

The tools that are essential to the... The Four Treasures: brush, ink, inks... Traditionally, ink was made by grindi... moist ink stone. This method is still f... brush painters today. An artist puts a... on an inkstone and grinds the inkstic... motion until a smooth, black ink of th... concentration is made. Prepared ink... much lower quality.

Our History
Directions
Artist Profiles
Events
Contact Us

Ink Wash Galler...
21 State Street • Seattle,...
Our History | Directions | Artist Profile...

A 3-COLUMN FIXED LAYOUT

The wrapper section includes the nav, main article, aside, and footer elements.

```
<section id = "wrapper">
...
</section>
```

Ink Wash Art Gallery

ash Art Gallery

Gallery is an art gallery specializing
ngs. Ink and wash painting is an
ush painting. It is also know by its
i-e or its Chinese name, shui-mo
ver the world practice the traditional
techniques.

d Wash Painting

ting developed in China during the
307). Wang Wei is generally
r who applied color to existing ink
The art was further developed into a
uring the Song Dynasty (960-1279).
orea shortly after China's discovery
orean missionaries in Japan, in
establish a civilized settlement
in the mid-14th century.

and Technques

essential to the art form are called
brush, ink, inkstone and paper.
made by grinding an ink stick on a
method is still favored by many
An artist puts a few drops of water
inds the inkstick in a circular
, black ink of the desired
. Prepared inks are usually of

Gallery Hours

Monday: closed
Tuesday: 6 p.m.
Wednesday: 9
Thursday: clos
Friday: 6 p.m.
Saturday: 10 a.m. - 5 p.m.
Sunday: 12 p.m - 5 p.m.

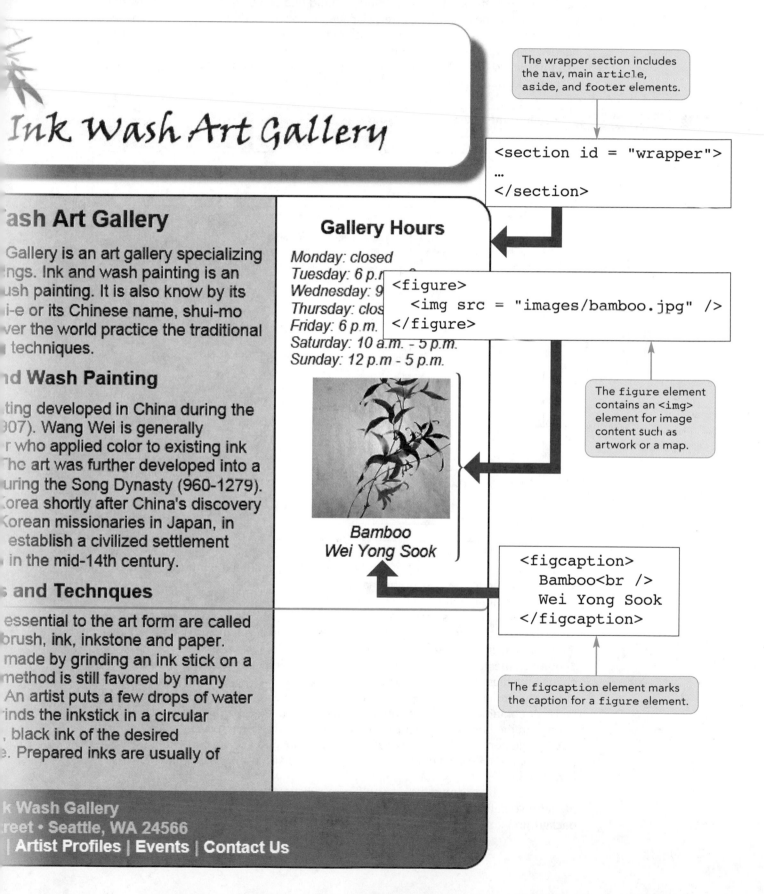

Bamboo
Wei Yong Sook

```
<figure>
    <img src = "images/bamboo.jpg" />
</figure>
```

The figure element contains an <img> element for image content such as artwork or a map.

```
<figcaption>
    Bamboo<br />
    Wei Yong Sook
</figcaption>
```

The figcaption element marks the caption for a figure element.

k Wash Gallery
reet • Seattle, WA 24566
| Artist Profiles | Events | Contact Us

Creating a Three-Column Layout

Yan likes the two-column layout, but she would like you to redesign the Ink Wash Gallery Web page as a three-column layout. She is wondering what the Web page would look like with the navbar in a column instead of placed horizontally below the header. She'd also like to include an image of one of the paintings with a caption. She'd like this placed below the gallery hours in one of the columns. Yan has sketched out a proposed layout for the side-by-side columns, as shown in Figure 6-32.

Figure 6-32 **Sketch of the three-column layout**

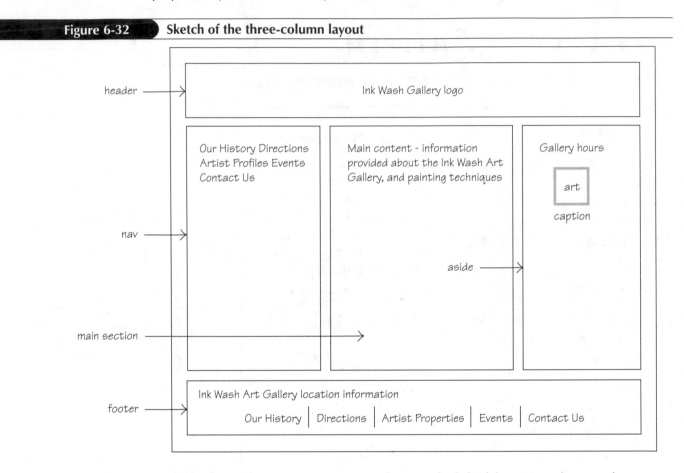

As the figure shows, Yan wants one column to the left of the main column and another column to the right of the main column. Columns that appear to the left and right of the main column are known as **flanking columns**.

You've created styles in your two-column layout that you can still use for the body, the universal selector, and the *container* id selector. In addition, you've already marked the content using a container `div` and `header`, `aside`, `nav`, main `section`, and `footer` elements. Because the HTML tags are marking content, there is no need to change the tags. You'll simply add another `div` called *wrapper* and you'll modify or create style rules that will reposition and style the elements. The wrapper `div` will be an inner container, inside the container `div`. The wrapper `div` will contain all of the content in the body except for the header element. The container `div` will contain the `header` element and the wrapper `div` (which contains all of the content in the body except for the `header` element). The *container* `div` and *wrapper* `div` are shown in Figure 6-32.

You'll start by opening the art.htm file you've already created, saving it with a new filename, deleting the style rules you'll be changing or won't need, and changing the background color to white.

To open the art.htm file, modify it, and save it with a new filename:

1. If you took a break after the previous session, make sure that the **art.htm** file is open in your text editor.

2. Save the file as **art3col.htm**.

3. Delete the CSS style rules code for the selectors *header*, *aside*, *nav*, *nav li*, *#main*, and *footer*, leaving only the style rules for the universal selector, *body*, and *#container*, as shown in Figure 6-33.

Figure 6-33   **CSS code for the style rules**

```
<style type="text/css">

* {
    margin: 0;
    padding: 0;
}

body {
    font-size: 1.1em;
    font-family: Arial, Helvetica, sans-serif;
    background-color: gray;
}

#container {
    width: 930px;
    border-width: 1px;
    margin: 0 auto;
    background-color: navy;
}

</style>
```

all other style rules deleted

4. Edit the `background-color` property values in the *body* and *#container* selector rules to change the color to **white**, as shown in Figure 6-34.

Figure 6-34 CSS code showing color change for background-color properties

```
<style type="text/css">

* {
    margin: 0;
    padding: 0;
}

body {
    font-size: 1.1em;
    font-family: Arial, Helvetica, sans-serif;
    background-color: white;
}

#container {
    width: 930px;
    border-width: 1px;
    margin: 0 auto;
    background-color: white;
}

</style>
```

color changed → background-color: white;

color changed → background-color: white;

▶ **5.** Save the **art3col.htm** file, and then open the file in your Web browser. The Web page should look similar to Figure 6-35.

Figure 6-35 Web page with white background

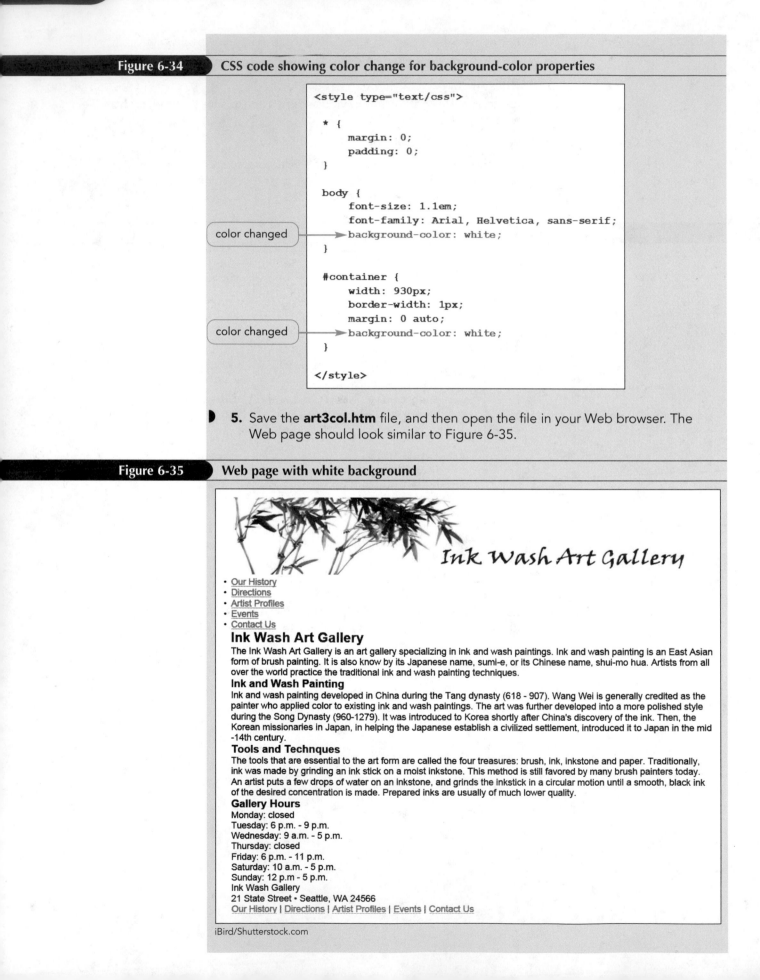

Ink Wash Art Gallery

- Our History
- Directions
- Artist Profiles
- Events
- Contact Us

Ink Wash Art Gallery

The Ink Wash Art Gallery is an art gallery specializing in ink and wash paintings. Ink and wash painting is an East Asian form of brush painting. It is also know by its Japanese name, sumi-e, or its Chinese name, shui-mo hua. Artists from all over the world practice the traditional ink and wash painting techniques.

Ink and Wash Painting

Ink and wash painting developed in China during the Tang dynasty (618 - 907). Wang Wei is generally credited as the painter who applied color to existing ink and wash paintings. The art was further developed into a more polished style during the Song Dynasty (960-1279). It was introduced to Korea shortly after China's discovery of the ink. Then, the Korean missionaries in Japan, in helping the Japanese establish a civilized settlement, introduced it to Japan in the mid -14th century.

Tools and Technques

The tools that are essential to the art form are called the four treasures: brush, ink, inkstone and paper. Traditionally, ink was made by grinding an ink stick on a moist inkstone. This method is still favored by many brush painters today. An artist puts a few drops of water on an inkstone, and grinds the inkstick in a circular motion until a smooth, black ink of the desired concentration is made. Prepared inks are usually of much lower quality.

Gallery Hours

Monday: closed
Tuesday: 6 p.m. - 9 p.m.
Wednesday: 9 a.m. - 5 p.m.
Thursday: closed
Friday: 6 p.m. - 11 p.m.
Saturday: 10 a.m. - 5 p.m.
Sunday: 12 p.m - 5 p.m.
Ink Wash Gallery
21 State Street • Seattle, WA 24566
Our History | Directions | Artist Profiles | Events | Contact Us

When designing a three-column layout, you'll use the `float` property to position elements left or right. Rather than positioning elements from top to bottom and left to right as the Web browser interprets the HTML code, the `float` property interrupts the flow of the document.

Interrupting the Document Flow

The **source order** is the order of page content in the document flow. Normally, a browser reads content from top to bottom and left to right, like a page in a book. However, for columns that are side by side, floated elements must be displayed before nonfloated elements. This can result in elements being rendered in the Web browser out of their original source order. The art.htm file from Session 6.1 is a good example of the source order being interrupted, as the elements do not appear as they would in the normal document flow. The `aside` element is to the left of the main content section, but when you look at the HTML code, the `aside` element is above the main content code, not to the left, as shown in Figure 6-27. Without the float positioning, the `aside` element would be rendered above the main content section, not to the left.

In the art3col.htm document, three elements will be side by side: the `nav` element, the *main* `section` element, and the `aside` element. In the normal document flow, the `nav` element would come first, the *main* `section` element would be second, and the `aside` element would come next. However, if you floated the `nav` element left and the `aside` element right and did not float the *main* `section` element, the elements would have to be arranged like this:

```
<nav>
</nav>

<aside>
</aside>

<section id = "main">
</section><!-- end main section -->
```

The two floated elements would have to appear in the document body before the *main* `section` element, which might be confusing when someone else has to revise the code. Also, screen readers would read the secondary content (the `nav` and `aside` elements) before the main content, which now would come last. To retain the source order, you will float the *main* `section` element as well.

Creating Styles for the Header

For the header selector, you'll use a width value of 930, the full width of the container. You'll also add a 1px solid border to the header so you can see the edges of the header against the white background. Just as in the two-column layout, the only content for the header in the three-column layout will be an image.

To style the *header* selector:

1. Return to the **art3col.htm** file in your text editor. Position the insertion point on a blank line below the *#container* rule and above the end `</style>` tag, and then type the following style rule, as shown in Figure 6-36:

```
header {
  width: 930px;
  margin-bottom: 30px;
  border: 1px solid #888888;
}
```

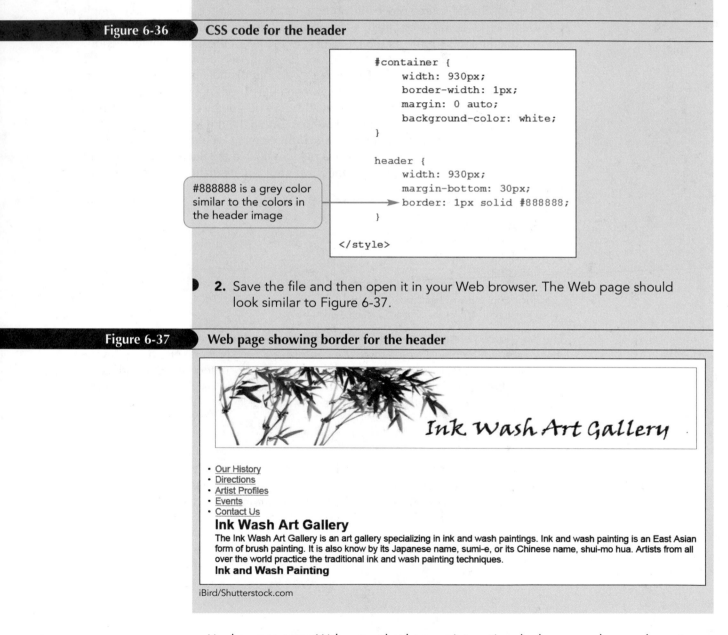

| Figure 6-36 | CSS code for the header |

```
#container {
    width: 930px;
    border-width: 1px;
    margin: 0 auto;
    background-color: white;
}

header {
    width: 930px;
    margin-bottom: 30px;
    border: 1px solid #888888;
}

</style>
```

#888888 is a grey color similar to the colors in the header image

2. Save the file and then open it in your Web browser. The Web page should look similar to Figure 6-37.

| Figure 6-37 | Web page showing border for the header |

Ink Wash Art Gallery

- Our History
- Directions
- Artist Profiles
- Events
- Contact Us

Ink Wash Art Gallery

The Ink Wash Art Gallery is an art gallery specializing in ink and wash paintings. Ink and wash painting is an East Asian form of brush painting. It is also know by its Japanese name, sumi-e, or its Chinese name, shui-mo hua. Artists from all over the world practice the traditional ink and wash painting techniques.

Ink and Wash Painting

iBird/Shutterstock.com

Yan has seen some Web pages that have an interesting shadow around some elements. She'd like you to use that effect around the header.

The box-shadow Property

To apply a shadow to an element you'll use the box-shadow property, which creates a 3D shadow effect. You can specify the size of the shadow, the distance it is offset from the element, the width of the shadow, the width of the blur along the shadow, and the shadow color. Older Web browsers do not support this property reliably, but current browsers support it.

The syntax for the box-shadow property is:

```
box-shadow: h-shadow v-shadow blur spread inset;
```

The *h-shadow* value is the position of the horizontal shadow. It shifts the shadow to the right. The *v-shadow* value is the position of the vertical shadow. It shifts the shadow down, from the top edge of the element. The *blur* value is the blur distance, which is the amount of shadow that will be blurry. It is an optional value. The *spread* value is the spread distance, which is the width of the shadow, and is also optional. The *inset* value is the shadow placement inside the element, rather than outside and is also optional. The value to place the shadow inside the element is *inset*, and the value to place the shadow outside the element is *outset*.

For example, to create a shadow with 10px offset to the right, 15px offset down from the top, 5px blur, 8px spread, and outset shadow, you'd use the following CSS code:

```
box-shadow: 10px 15px 5px 8px outset;
```

REFERENCE

Using the box-shadow Property

To set a box shadow for an element, use the box-shadow property with the following values, in order:

- *h-shadow*—The position of the horizontal shadow; shifts the shadow to the right, offset from the right edge of the element
- *v-shadow*—The position of the vertical shadow; shifts the shadow down, offset from the top edge of the element
- *blur*—The blur distance (optional)
- *spread*—The spread distance (optional)
- *inset*—Shadow placement inside the element, rather than outside (optional)

The values for the drop-shadow property specify how far the shadow will drop (*v-shadow*) and how far the shadow will push to the right (*h-shadow*). The *spread* value specifies the additional width of the shadow, and the *blur* value specifies an additional width that will be blurred. The *spread* and *blur* values are added to the width specified for the *v-shadow* and *h-shadow* measurements, as shown in Figure 6-38.

Figure 6-38 **The values for the box-shadow property**

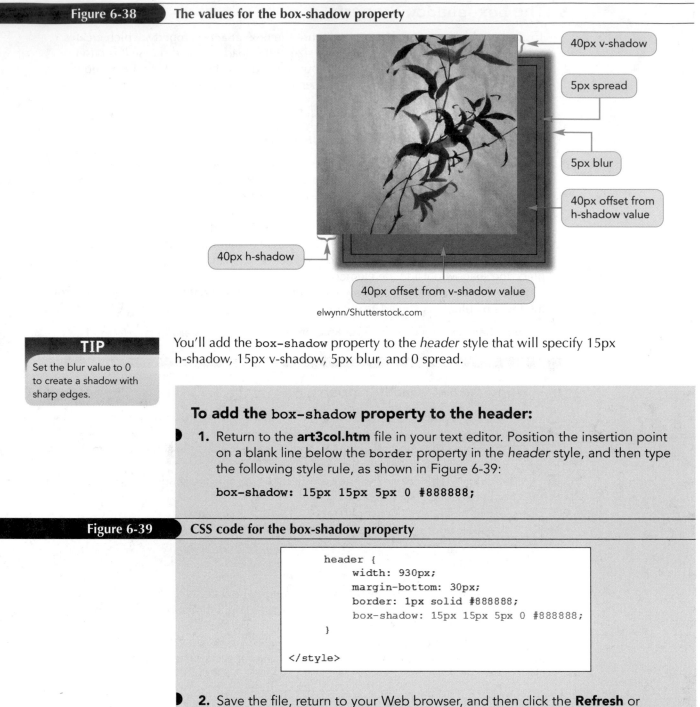

elwynn/Shutterstock.com

TIP

Set the blur value to 0 to create a shadow with sharp edges.

You'll add the `box-shadow` property to the *header* style that will specify 15px h-shadow, 15px v-shadow, 5px blur, and 0 spread.

To add the `box-shadow` **property to the header:**

1. Return to the **art3col.htm** file in your text editor. Position the insertion point on a blank line below the `border` property in the *header* style, and then type the following style rule, as shown in Figure 6-39:

   `box-shadow: 15px 15px 5px 0 #888888;`

Figure 6-39 **CSS code for the box-shadow property**

```
header {
    width: 930px;
    margin-bottom: 30px;
    border: 1px solid #888888;
    box-shadow: 15px 15px 5px 0 #888888;
}

</style>
```

2. Save the file, return to your Web browser, and then click the **Refresh** or **Reload** button to view the changes in the file. The Web page should look similar to Figure 6-40.

Figure 6-40   Web page showing the shadow around the header

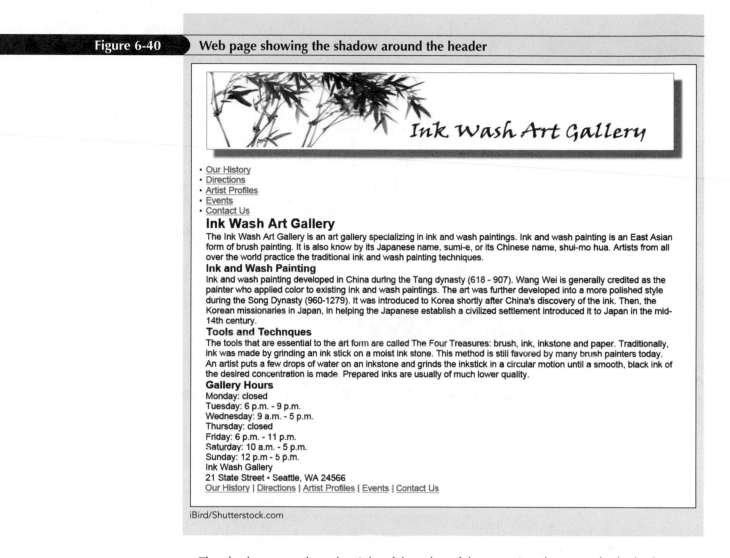

iBird/Shutterstock.com

The shadow extends to the right of the edge of the container because the h-shadow value added 15 pixels of shadow to the right edge of the header and the blur value added 5 px again to the right edge of the header. A total of 20 px has been added to the right edge of the header. To align this edge with the container, you'll subtract 20 pixels from the header width in the *header* style.

To adjust the header width to accommodate the shadow:

1. Return to the **art3col.htm** file in your text editor. Change the value of the width property in the *header* style to **910**, and then add a comment to indicate why this value has been changed, as shown in Figure 6-41.

The CSS code showing the changed width value and comment

```
header {
    width: 910px;   /* reduced by 20px to accommodate shadow */
    margin-bottom: 30px;
    border: 1px solid #888888;
    box-shadow: 15px 15px 5px 0 #888888;
}

</style>
```

2. Save the file, return to your Web browser, and then click the **Refresh** or **Reload** button to view the changes in the file. The Web page should look similar to Figure 6-42.

Figure 6-42 **Web page showing the header and container edges aligned**

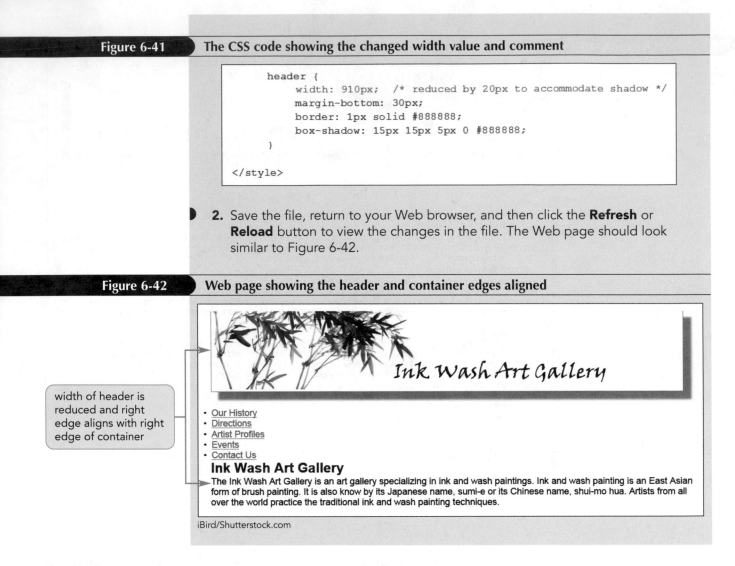

width of header is reduced and right edge aligns with right edge of container

Ink Wash Art Gallery

- Our History
- Directions
- Artist Profiles
- Events
- Contact Us

Ink Wash Art Gallery

The Ink Wash Art Gallery is an art gallery specializing in ink and wash paintings. Ink and wash painting is an East Asian form of brush painting. It is also know by its Japanese name, sumi-e or its Chinese name, shui-mo hua. Artists from all over the world practice the traditional ink and wash painting techniques.

iBird/Shutterstock.com

Yan loves the shadow around the header, but she thinks the square corners do not fit the style of ink wash art. She's seen rounded corners on other Web pages and would like that effect on the header as well. She feels that rounded corners soften the hard edge of straight corners and are more consistent with the free-flowing nature of ink wash art.

Creating Rounded Corners

Rounded corners can be created using the `border-radius` property. The value for the `border-radius` property specifies a radius measurement. To achieve a wider curve, you use a larger number of pixels for the value; to achieve a tighter curve, you use a smaller number of pixels. The value represents the radius of a circle that would fit in the corner, as shown in Figure 6-43.

Figure 6-43   **Part of a circle forms the curve of a rounded corner**

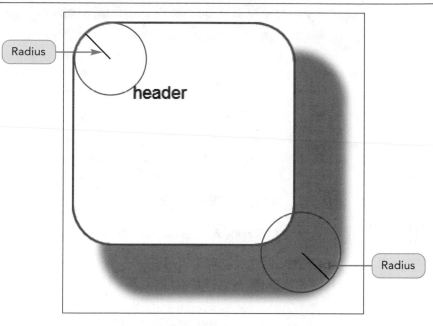

If a rounded corner is applied to an element with a box shadow, it is also applied to the shadow.

The `border-radius` properties can also be set individually. The corners are: `border-top-left-radius`, `border-top-right-radius`, `border-bottom-right-radius`, and `border-bottom-left-radius`. The `border-radius` shorthand property can be used to set all border radius values at once. Like the `margin`, `border`, and other similar properties, the values are set clockwise, starting from the top.

REFERENCE

Using the `border-radius` Properties

The `border-radius` properties can be set individually or using the `border-radius` shortcut property. The individual properties are:

- `border-top-left-radius`
- `border-top-right-radius`
- `border-bottom-right-radius`
- `border-bottom-left-radius`

The values of the `border-radius` properties can be indicated using the standard measurements such as px, em, or percent.

The `border-radius` shorthand property can be used to set all four corners individually or to apply one measurement to all corners. Like margins, borders, and other similar properties, the shorthand property can specify four values in a clockwise direction: top-left, top-right, bottom-right, bottom-left.

You'll apply a `border-radius` property with a value of 25px to the header. You'll also add a top margin of 10px so you can see the top of the `header` element to trouble shoot for potential issues.

To apply the `border-radius` property to the header:

1. Return to the **art3col.htm** file in your text editor.

2. Position the insertion point to the right of the `margin-bottom` property in the *header* style rule, and then press the **Enter** key to add a new line. Type the following CSS code, as shown in Figure 6-44:

   ```
   margin-top: 10px;
   ```

3. Position the insertion point to the right of the `box-shadow` property in the header, and then press the **Enter** key to add a new line. Type the following CSS code, as shown in Figure 6-44:

   ```
   border-radius: 25px;
   ```

Figure 6-44　The CSS code for the border-radius property

```
header {
    width: 910px;   /* reduced by 20px to accommodate shadow */
    margin-bottom: 30px;
    margin-top: 10px;
    border: 1px solid #888888;
    box-shadow: 15px 15px 5px 0 #888888;
    border-radius: 25px;
}

</style>
```

4. Save the file, return to your Web browser, and then click the **Refresh** or **Reload** button to view the changes in the file. The Web page should look similar to Figure 6-45.

Figure 6-45　Web page showing rounded corners applied with a rectangular image

Gaps in border outline

Ink Wash Art Gallery

iBird/Shutterstock.com

Rounded corners reduce the amount of space available for content in an element. In the case of the `header` element, the content is the image. This causes gaps in the border, as shown in Figure 6-45. If the image is too wide, it can overlap the shadow and the top-right corner as well. One remedy would be to reduce the size of the image. In this case, the image is narrower than the width of the header, so a quick fix is to center-align the image in the header. You'll add the `text-align` property to the `header` style.

To apply the `text-align` property to the header:

1. Return to the **art3col.htm** file in your text editor.

2. Position the insertion point to the right of the `margin-top` property in the *header* style rule, and press the **Enter** key to add a blank line. Type the following CSS code, as shown in Figure 6-46:

   `text-align: center;`

Figure 6-46   **Adding the text-align property to the header style**

```
header {
    width: 910px;   /* reduced by 20px to accommodate shadow */
    margin-bottom: 30px;
    margin-top: 10px;
    text-align: center;
    border: 1px solid #888888;
    box-shadow: 15px 15px 5px 0 #888888;
    border-radius: 25px;
}

</style>
```

3. Save the file, return to your Web browser, and then click the **Refresh** or **Reload** button to view the changes in the file. The Web page should look similar to Figure 6-47.

Figure 6-47   **Web page header with image centered**

iBird/Shutterstock.com

Now that the header has been created, you're ready to begin working on the column layout. You'll start by stylizing the navigation column. The `nav` element contains the navbar links and will be positioned as a column on the left.

Creating Styles for the Navigation Column

Yan is pleased with the appearance of the header. The `nav` element contains an unordered list that will contain links to the other pages at the Ink Wash Art Gallery Web site, which she will link to later. Yan would like to make those links stand out. You'll create some descendant selectors for the *nav* selector to style the list items. The navigation column will have a content width of 200px. With margins of 5px on both the left and right and padding of 10px on both the left and right, the full column width will be 230px. You'll also use a top padding of 25px to allow some white space between the top of the menu and the top of the navigation column.

To add styles for the navigation column:

1. Return to the **art3col.htm** file in your text editor. Position the insertion point on a blank line after the *header* style rule, and then type the following CSS code, as shown in Figure 6-48:

```
nav {
    width: 200px;
    margin: 0 5px 0 5px;
    padding: 25px 10px 0 10px;
    float: left;
    text-align: center;
}

nav ul {
    font-weight: bold;
    list-style: none;
}
```

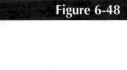 **Figure 6-48**   **The CSS code for the nav and nav ul selectors**

```
header {
    width: 910px;    /* reduced by 20px to accommodate shadow */
    margin-bottom: 30px;
    margin-top: 10px;
    text-align: center;
    border: 1px solid #888888;
    box-shadow: 15px 15px 5px 0 #888888;
    border-radius: 25px;
}

nav {
    width: 200px;
    margin: 0 5px 0 5px;
    padding: 25px 10px 0 10px;
    float: left;
    text-align: center;
}

nav ul {
    font-weight: bold;
    list-style: none;
}

</style>
```

2. Save the file, return to your Web browser, and then click the **Refresh** or **Reload** button to view the changes in the file. The Web page should look similar to Figure 6-49.

Figure 6-49   **Web page showing nav foated left**

nav element floated to the left

iBird/Shutterstock.com

The links are positioned on the left side of the Web page. You'll style the links by removing the underline and adding bold. Yan would also like something a bit more stylish for the hover effect and suggested a gray background with rounded corners. With a gray background, the link text needs to be white in order to stand out.

To style the links in the nav element:

1. Return to the **art3col.htm** file in your text editor. Position the insertion point on a blank line after the *nav ul* style rule, and then type the following CSS code, as shown in Figure 6-50:

```
nav ul li a {
   padding: 5px;
   color: gray;
   text-decoration: none;
   display: block;
}

nav ul li a:hover {
   background: gray;
   border-radius: 10px;
   color: white;
}
```

Figure 6-50 | **CSS code for the nav list links**

```
nav ul {
   font-weight: bold;
   list-style: none;
}

nav ul li a {
   padding: 5px;
   color: gray;
   text-decoration: none;
   display: block;
}

nav ul li a:hover {
   background: gray;
   border-radius: 10px;
   color: white;
}

</style>
```

2. Save the file, return to your Web browser, and then click the **Refresh** or **Reload** button to view the changes in the file. Pass the mouse pointer over the links to see if the hover effect is working correctly. The Web page should look similar to Figure 6-51.

Figure 6-51 | **Web page showing stylized links**

iBird/Shutterstock.com

Yan is really pleased with the navigation column and the hover effect. Next, you'll determine the width of the main and aside columns, and style them.

Creating Styles for the Main Column

To determine the column width and content width for the main column, you need to perform some calculations. The sidebar column currently has a column width of 230px. Yan wants the aside column on the right that contains the gallery hours to have the same width as the navigation column, so the aside column will also have a width of 230px, using the same padding and margins for both the left and the right. Figure 6-52 shows the layout plan so far.

Figure 6-52   The layout plan for the main column

nav	main section	aside
margin-left: 5		margin-left: 5
border-left: 0		border-left: 0
padding-left: 10		padding-left: 10
content: 200		content: 200
padding-right: 10		padding-right: 10
border-right: 0		border-right: 0
margin-right: 5		margin-right: 5
Total: 230px		Total: 230px

Next you need to determine the column width of the main column. The sum of the navigation column plus the aside column is 460px. To determine the column width for the main column, you subtract the sum of the widths for the flanking columns (460px) from the container width (930px), as shown in Figure 6-53.

Figure 6-53   The three column widths

Width	Item
930px	The container width
460px	The sum of the column widths of the two flanking columns
470px	The column width of the main column (930 – 460)

As you can see, the width of the main column will be 470px. To determine the content width for the main column, subtract the combined width of the margins, border, and padding used in the main column from the column width. The main column will have 10px of padding on both the left and the right, no margins, and 2px borders on both the left and the right. The main column, therefore, will have a content width of 446px, as shown in Figure 6-54.

Figure 6-54 Determining the content width for the main section column

Width	Item
470px	The column width of the main column
24px	The sum of the margins, padding, and border for the main column
446px	The content width of the main column (470 – 24)

You'll create the CSS styles for the *main* id selector. In addition to setting the positioning and border properties, you'll add a background image. Yan has provided you with the ricepaper.jpg image. You'll also create a descendant selector for the *main* id selector so paragraph text is indented.

To style the *main* id selector:

1. Return to the **art3col.htm** file in your text editor. Position the insertion point on a blank line after the *nav ul li a:hover* style, and then type the following CSS code, as shown in Figure 6-55:

```
#main {
    width: 446px;
    padding: 10px;
    float: left;
    color: black;
    border-left: 2px solid;
    border-right: 2px solid;
    background-image: url(images/ricepaper.jpg);
}

#main p {
    text-indent: 1.5em;
}
```

Figure 6-55 CSS code for the main id selector

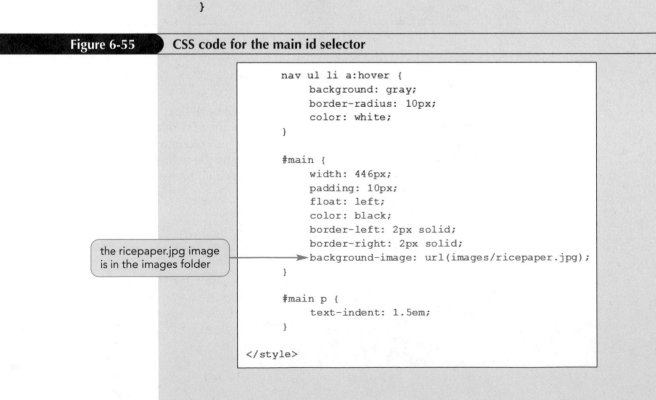

```
nav ul li a:hover {
    background: gray;
    border-radius: 10px;
    color: white;
}

#main {
    width: 446px;
    padding: 10px;
    float: left;
    color: black;
    border-left: 2px solid;
    border-right: 2px solid;
    background-image: url(images/ricepaper.jpg);
}

#main p {
    text-indent: 1.5em;
}

</style>
```

the ricepaper.jpg image is in the images folder

2. Save the file, return to your Web browser, and then click the **Refresh** or **Reload** button to view the changes in the file. The Web page should look similar to Figure 6-56. If you are using an older Web browser, or if the window size of your Web browser is smaller, you may see the aside section above the main section rather than positioned to the right, or you may see elements overlapping each other. If you are using a current Web browser you will see the `aside` element positioned in the right column, as shown in Figure 6-56.

Figure 6-56 | Web page showing main section column

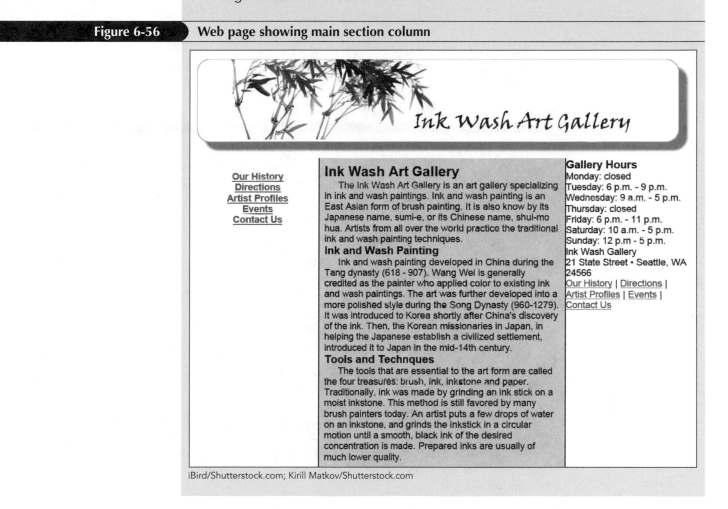

iBird/Shutterstock.com; Kirill Matkov/Shutterstock.com

The footer text will appear to the right of the main column. Later you'll move the footer so it's below all three columns.

Now that you've created the styles for the *main* id selector, you'll create the style for the aside column.

Creating Styles for the Aside Column

The `aside` element contains information about the gallery hours. It will also include an image and a caption of a work of art entitled *Bamboo*, created by Wei Yong Sook. The *aside* selector will be styled to have a width of 230px and to float right. You'll add the image as a `figure` element, and add a caption to it as well. You'll start your work on the aside column by adding the code for the figure.

The `figure` element

You've used images for assorted purposes. An image can be used as a logo, background image, a bullet for a list item, or the basis of an image map. Sometimes an image itself is an important part of the Web page content. Examples of this might be an illustration that shows how to use a product, a photograph of interesting architecture, or a picture of an artifact such as an Egyptian mummy. When an image is provided for informational purposes, it can be marked with the `figure` element rather than a paragraph or another block-level element. The `figure` element can also include a caption, which you mark using the `figcaption` element. For instance, if the image is a photograph of a farm, in the file images/farm.jpg, the code for the `figure` and `figcaption` elements would be as follows:

```
<figure>
   <img src = "images/farm.jpg" alt = "a family farm" />
   <figcaption>A family farm</figcaption>
</figure>
```

REFERENCE

Using the `figure` element

- To mark a figure, enter:

```
<figure>
   <img src = "imagefilename" />
</figure>
```

- To include a caption with a figure, enter:

```
<figure>
   <img src = "imagefilename" />
   <figcaption>caption</figcaption>
</figure>
```

The `figcaption` content appears below the image when it is rendered in a Web browser.

Yan has provided an image file of the artwork (bamboo.jpg) that you'll add to the `aside` element, under the gallery hours. You'll also add a caption that includes the title of the painting and the artist's name. You'll create a *figure* selector style that centers the figure and adds 10px top padding, and you'll add a *figcaption* selector style that styles the caption using italics.

To add the `figure` and `figcaption` HTML and CSS code:

1. Return to the **art3col.htm** file in your text editor. Position the insertion point on a blank line after the close </p> tag for the Sunday hours in the aside element, and then type the following HTML code, as shown in Figure 6-57:

```
<figure>
   <img src = "images/bamboo.jpg" alt = "Bamboo on old grunge
paper" width = "150" height = "150" />

   <figcaption>
     Bamboo<br />
     Wei Yong Sook
   </figcaption>
</figure>
```

Be sure to nest the **figcaption** element inside the **figure** element; the **</figure>** tag must go after the **</figcaption>** tag.

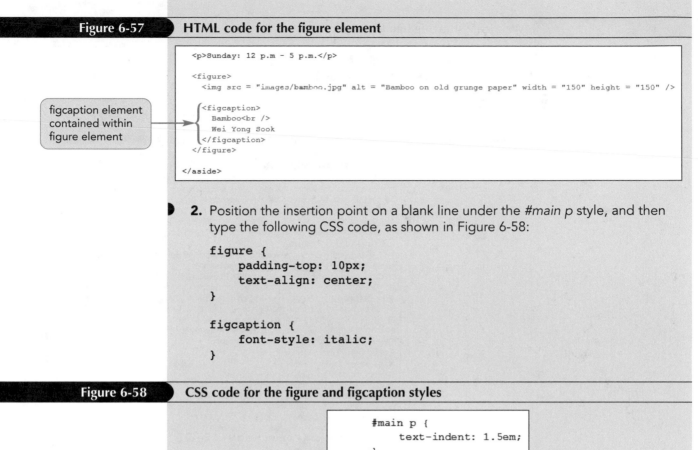

Figure 6-57   **HTML code for the figure element**

```
<p>Sunday: 12 p.m - 5 p.m.</p>

<figure>
  <img src = "images/bamboo.jpg" alt = "Bamboo on old grunge paper" width = "150" height = "150" />

  <figcaption>
    Bamboo<br />
    Wei Yong Sook
  </figcaption>
</figure>

</aside>
```

figcaption element contained within figure element

2. Position the insertion point on a blank line under the *#main p* style, and then type the following CSS code, as shown in Figure 6-58:

```
figure {
    padding-top: 10px;
    text-align: center;
}

figcaption {
    font-style: italic;
}
```

Figure 6-58   **CSS code for the figure and figcaption styles**

```
#main p {
    text-indent: 1.5em;
}

figure {
    padding-top: 10px;
    text-align: center;
}

figcaption {
    font-style: italic;
}

</style>
```

3. Save the file, return to your Web browser, and then click the **Refresh** or **Reload** button to view the changes in the file. The Web page should look similar to Figure 6-59. Again, if you are using an older Web browser, you may see the aside section above the main section rather than positioned to the right. If you are using a current Web browser you will see the `aside` element positioned in the right column, as shown in Figure 6-59.

Figure 6-59   Web page showing figure and caption

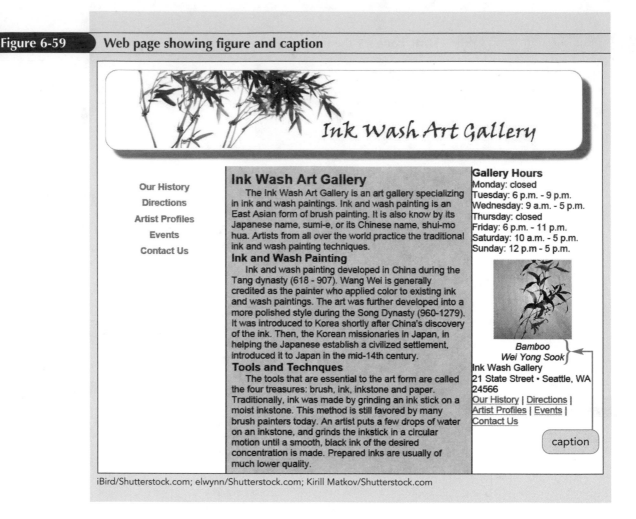

iBird/Shutterstock.com; elwynn/Shutterstock.com; Kirill Matkov/Shutterstock.com

Now that the figure and caption are complete you'll style the *aside* selector. The text for the gallery hours will appear in italic, so you will create a descendant selector to style just the paragraph text that appears within the `aside` element. Yan likes the changes you've made to the Web page, but she would like the gallery hours to be displayed without wrapping to the next line. You'll set the font size to .9em so the text for the gallery hours fits nicely in the column.

To style the *aside* selector:

1. Return to the **art3col.htm** file in your text editor. Position the insertion point on a blank line after the *figcaption* style, and then type the following CSS code, as shown in Figure 6-60:

```
aside {
    width: 200px;
    margin: 0 5px 0 5px;
    padding: 10px;
    float: right;
}

aside p {
    font-style: italic;
    font-size: 0.9em;
}
```

Figure 6-60	CSS code for the aside selectors

```
figcaption {
    font-style: italic;
}

aside {
    width: 200px;
    margin: 0 5px 0 5px;
    padding: 10px;
    float: right;
}

aside p {
    font-style: italic;
    font-size: 0.9em;
}

</style>
```

2. Save the file, return to your Web browser, and then click the **Refresh** or **Reload** button to view the changes in the file. The Web page should look similar to Figure 6-61. The aside column has shifted slightly to the right and down. The footer, however, still appears as though it is in the aside column.

Figure 6-61	Web page with the aside column stylized

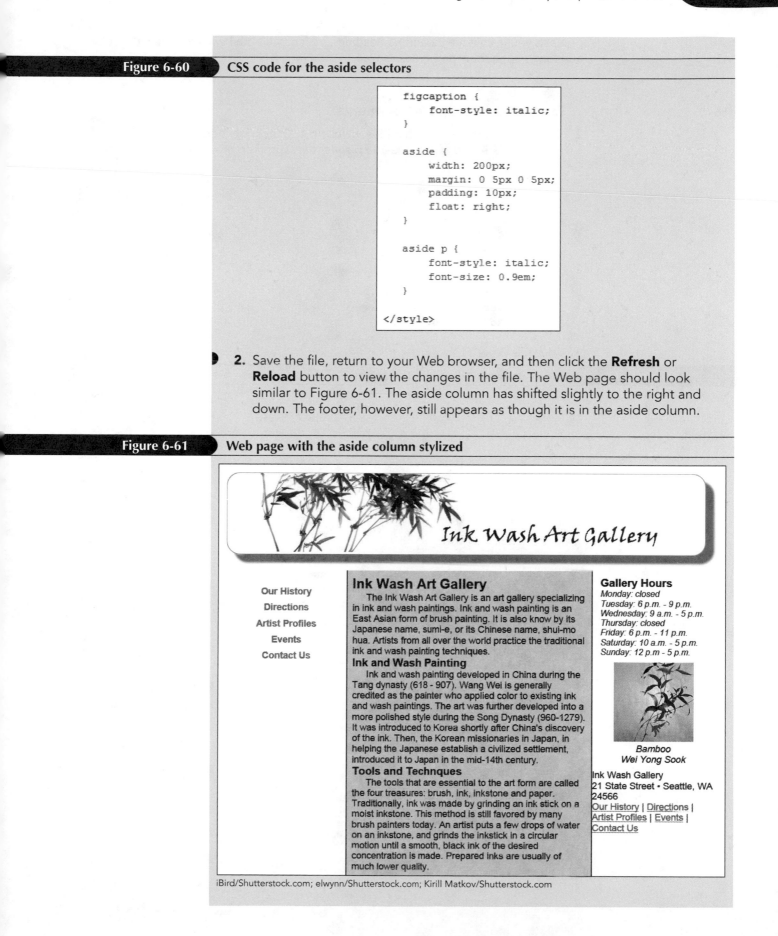

iBird/Shutterstock.com; elwynn/Shutterstock.com; Kirill Matkov/Shutterstock.com

Next, you'll style the h2 and h3 headings, which will both be center-aligned. You'll add font and padding properties as well.

To style the h2 and h3 elements:

1. Return to the **art3col.htm** file in your text editor. Position the insertion point on a blank line after the *aside p* style rule, and then type the following CSS code, as shown in Figure 6-62:

```
h2 {
    font-size: 1.4em;
    text-align: center;
    padding-bottom: 0.5em;
}

h3 {
    text-align: center;
    padding-bottom: 0.5em;
    padding-top: 0.5em;
}
```

Figure 6-62   **CSS code for the h2 and h3 selectors**

```
aside p {
    font-style: italic;
    font-size: 0.9em;
}

h2 {
    font-size: 1.4em;
    text-align: center;
    padding-bottom: 0.5em;
}

h3 {
    text-align: center;
    padding-bottom: 0.5em;
    padding-top: 0.5em;
}

</style>
```

2. Save the file, return to your Web browser, and then click the **Refresh** or **Reload** button to view the changes in the file. The Web page should look similar to Figure 6-63.

Figure 6-63	Web page showing stylized h2 and h3 headings

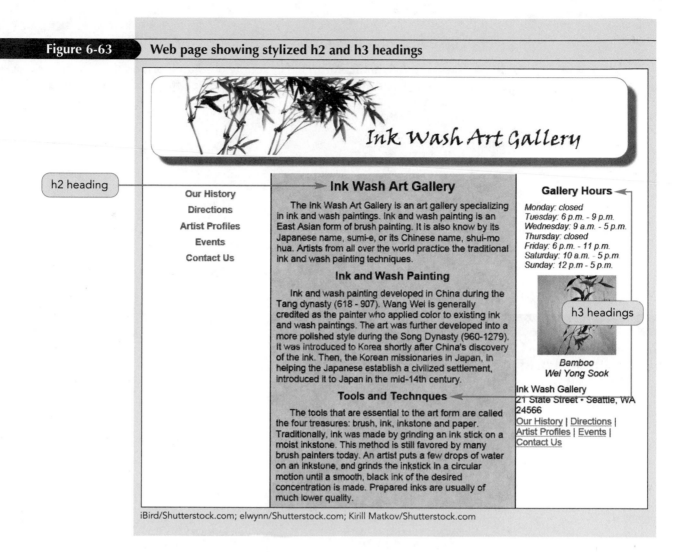

iBird/Shutterstock.com; elwynn/Shutterstock.com; Kirill Matkov/Shutterstock.com

Now that the columns have been styled, you'll create styles for the layout of the footer.

Creating Styles for the Footer

The last section to style is the footer. Because the footer contains text, you'll apply 10px of padding on all sides. As a result of the padding widths on the left and right, the content width will be 910px, not 930px. Currently, the footer appears below the content for the aside, but you want it below all three columns. You'll use the clear property with a value of both to ensure that the footer clears all of the columns. You'll also need rounded corners on only the bottom corners.

To style the `footer` element:

1. Return to the **art3col.htm** file in your text editor. Position the insertion point on a blank line after the *h3* style, and then type the following CSS code, as shown in Figure 6-64:

```
footer {
    width: 910px;
    margin: 0;
    padding: 10px;
    background-color: gray;
    clear: both;
    color: wheat;
    font-weight: bold;
    text-align: center;
    border-bottom-left-radius: 25px;
    border-bottom-right-radius: 25px;
}
```

Figure 6-64   **CSS code for the footer selector**

```
h3 {
    text-align: center;
    padding-bottom: 0.5em;
    padding-top: 0.5em;
}

footer {
    width: 910px;
    margin: 0;
    padding: 10px;
    background-color: gray;
    clear: both;
    color: wheat;
    font-weight: bold;
    text-align: center;
    border-bottom-left-radius: 25px;
    border-bottom-right-radius: 25px;
}

</style>
```

2. Save the file, return to your Web browser, and then click the **Refresh** or **Reload** button to view the changes in the file. The Web page should look similar to Figure 6-65.

Figure 6-65   Web page showing the footer stylized

iBird/Shutterstock.com; elwynn/Shutterstock.com; Kirill Matkov/Shutterstock.com

Yan has a CSS file called navfooter.css that contains the styles for the `footer` element. She would like to use this style sheet for the Web page you are creating. In Tutorial 4, you used the `link` element to link a CSS file to an HTML file. Another method that can be used to include CSS styles from an external CSS file is to import the styles using `@import`. Both `<link>` and `@import` are compliant with current HTML5 standards.

Using `@import`

Over time, you will start to develop a **style sheet library**, which is a collection of frequently used styles. You can create a CSS external style sheet that contains frequently used styles. You can then link to this external style sheet or you can import those styles into either an embedded or external style sheet using the `@import` rule. When you **import** styles, you can use those styles in the Web page where the `@import` rule has been placed. This is similar to using the `link` element to link a CSS file to an HTML file. The `@import` rule imports style rules from other style sheets. The `@import` rule has the following syntax:

```
@import url(stylesheet_filename);
```

The `@import` rule must be placed in the `style` element before any other CSS style rules. For example, the following code would be correct for an embedded style sheet that imports a style sheet named footer.css:

```
<style type = "text/css">

  @import url(footer.css);

  * {
    margin: 0 auto;
    padding: 0;
  }
  . . . (other styles here) . . .

</style>
```

PROSKILLS

Problem Solving: Building a CSS Library

Professional Web developers do not recreate the same CSS for each Web site they build. Instead, they depend on a library of CSS styles. They may have developed some themselves, and they may have also purchased or downloaded free libraries of files and development tools. Here are some common CSS style tools that developers have handy:

- **Reset sheet**—Because browsers handle default margins, padding, and fonts differently, a reset CSS style sheet that specifically resets individual settings helps developers to start with a clean slate.
- **Templates**—Web developers have a collection of various templates, with CSS, for common layouts such as two-column and three-column designs.
- **Browser-specific CSS**—Because browsers handle advanced CSS techniques differently, Web developers will have a collection of CSS code that handles specific style properties for specific Web browsers or versions of Web browsers.

If you'd like to start building your own toolkit, start with a few searches using your favorite search engine. You'll find many reset sheets and templates that are freely available. Similarly, if you use a search term such as *CSS browser compatibility*, you'll find a wealth of information for helpful CSS styles for specific versions of Web browsers.

You'll start building your CSS library by creating a file named navfooter.css that will contain the styles for the footer links. These links will be white with no underline; when a user hovers over a link, the underline will appear. Visited links will be navy. After you've created the navfooter.css file, you'll add the `@import` code to the art3col.htm file to import the footer link styles.

To create the navfooter.css file and add the @import rule:

1. Open a new file in your text editor, leaving the art3col.htm file open. Type the following CSS code:

```
/* navigation for footer */
footer a:link {
    color: white;
    text-decoration: none;
}

footer a:visited {
    color: navy;
    background-color: gray;
    text-decoration: none;
}

footer a:hover {
    text-decoration: underline;
}
```

2. Save the file as **navfooter.css** in the same folder as the art3col.htm file, and then close it.

Be sure the @import rule is the first rule in the embedded style sheet. It must come before all other CSS rules in a style sheet.

3. Return to the **art3col.htm** file. Position the insertion point on a blank line after the open <style> tag, and then insert the following code, as shown in Figure 6-66:

```
@import url(navfooter.css);
```

Figure 6-66	The @import code

```
<style type="text/css">

@import url(navfooter.css);

* {
  margin: 0;
  padding: 0;
}
```

4. Save the file, return to your Web browser, and then click the **Refresh** or **Reload** button to view the changes in the file. The Web page should look similar to Figure 6-67.

Figure 6-67	Web page showing footer links stylized

concentration is made. Prepared inks are usually of much lower quality.

Ink Wash Gallery
21 State Street • Seattle, WA 24566
Our History | Directions | Artist Profiles | Events | Contact Us

Kirill Matkov/Shutterstock.com

5. Pass the mouse pointer over the links in the footer to verify that the hover effect is working correctly.

The @import rule imports the styles from the navfooter.css file to the embedded style sheet in the art3col.htm Web page.

Understanding Specificity

Specificity describes how browsers calculate which style rule prevails if there are conflicting rules in the same source.

If there is a conflict within the same style sheet, generally *the style farthest down in the list prevails for selectors that are the same.* For example, the following embedded style sheet code specifies conflicting colors for h2 elements in two places:

```
h2 {
  color: red;
}
h2 {
  color: blue;
}
```

In this instance, the h2 heading text would appear in blue because that is the color specified furthest down the list. Bear in mind, though, that specificity applies only to conflicts.

To resolve style conflicts among different *types* of selectors, CSS uses specificity. This is a weighting methodology for calculating the specificity of particular selectors. An id selector has a weight of 100, a class selector has a weight of 10, and an element selector (also known as a type selector) has a weight of 1. If two styles conflict in the same source, the rule with the highest weighting will take precedence.

For example, in the following code an id selector (#green), a class selector (h2.yellow), and an element selector (h2) all apply to the same h2 element:

```
<style type = "text/css">
  #green {
    color: green;
  }
  h2.yellow {
    color: yellow;
  }
  h2 {
    color: blue;
  }
</style>
</head>
<body>
<h2 id = "green" class = "yellow">Please be specific.</h2>
```

Even though the #green id selector is at the top of the style list, this style has precedence because it has greater numeric specificity than either the class selector or the element selector. Thus, in this instance, the phrase *Please be specific.* appears in green.

One detail in the art3col.htm layout remains to be completed: the layout could use a border with rounded corners around the three columns. You'll accomplish this by creating another container, which you'll call *wrapper*. You'll use the `div` element and apply a wrapper class to create the *wrapper* container. The *wrapper* section will contain the `nav`, main `section`, `aside`, and `footer` elements. If the content of any of those elements increases the length of a column, the wrapper will lengthen to accommodate the change. The wrapper and containers are shown in Figure 6-68.

Figure 6-68   **The container and wrapper**

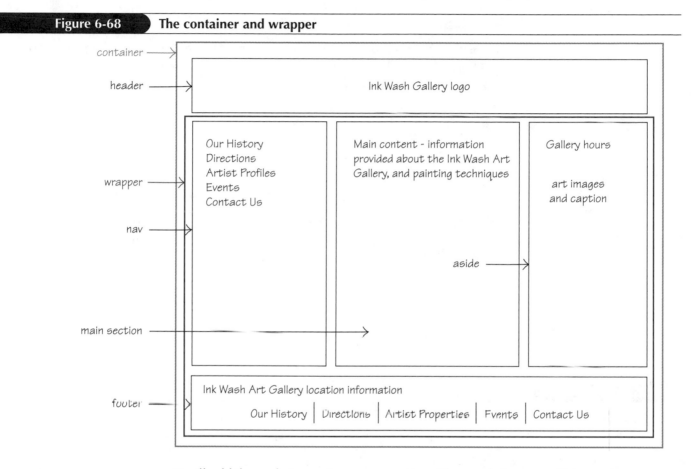

You'll add the code to create a wrapper `div` with rounded corners. The wrapper container will have a 2px border. The additional 2px for the border requires an additional 2px for the border radius, which will result in 27px for the `border-radius` property value.

To create the wrapper section and style it:

1. Return to the **art3col.htm** file in your text editor. Position the insertion point on a blank line after the close `</header>` tag, and then type the following HTML code, as shown in Figure 6-69:

   ```
   <div id = "wrapper">
   ```

Figure 6-69   **HTML code for start section tag for the wrapper**

```
</header>

<div id = "wrapper">

<nav>
```

2. Position the insertion point on a blank line after the close `</footer>` tag, and then type the following HTML code, as shown in Figure 6-70:

```
</div> <!-- end wrapper -->
```

Figure 6-70   **HTML code for the end section tag for the wrapper**

```
</footer>

</div> <!-- end wrapper -->
</div> <!-- end container -->
```

3. Position the insertion point on a blank line after the *footer* style rule, and then type the following HTML code, as shown in Figure 6-71:

```
#wrapper {
    width: 930px;
    margin-bottom: 10px;
    border: 2px solid;
    border-radius: 27px;
}
```

Figure 6-71   **CSS code for the wrapper selector**

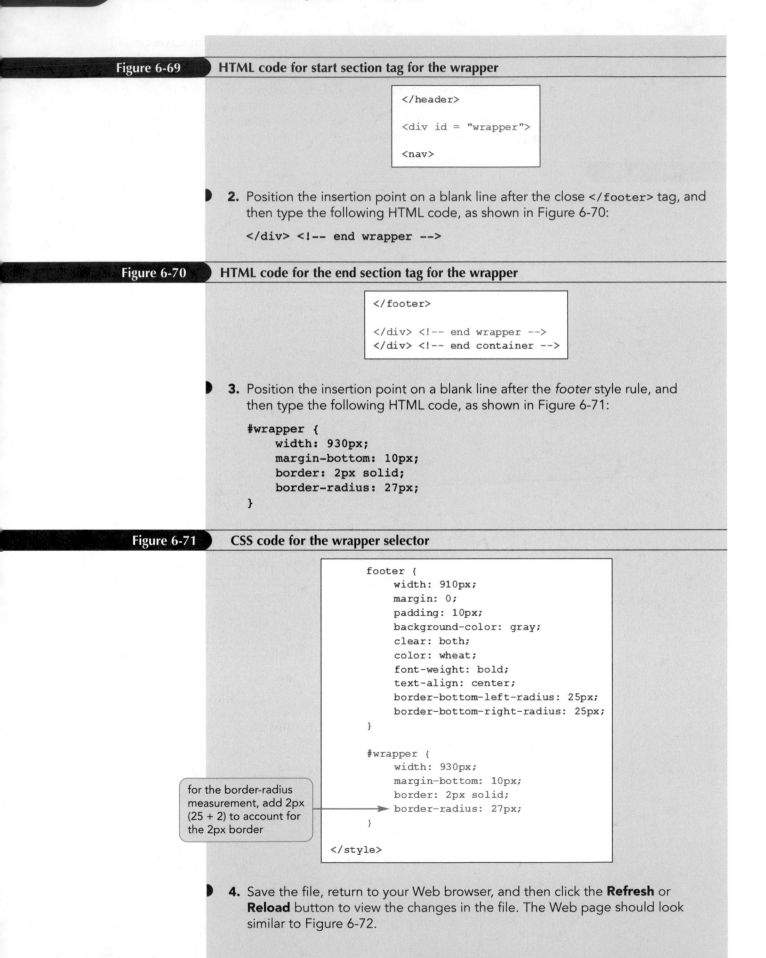

```
footer {
    width: 910px;
    margin: 0;
    padding: 10px;
    background-color: gray;
    clear: both;
    color: wheat;
    font-weight: bold;
    text-align: center;
    border-bottom-left-radius: 25px;
    border-bottom-right-radius: 25px;
}

#wrapper {
    width: 930px;
    margin-bottom: 10px;
    border: 2px solid;
    border-radius: 27px;
}

</style>
```

for the border-radius measurement, add 2px (25 + 2) to account for the 2px border

4. Save the file, return to your Web browser, and then click the **Refresh** or **Reload** button to view the changes in the file. The Web page should look similar to Figure 6-72.

Figure 6-72   **Web page showing the border for the wrapper**

iBird/Shutterstock.com; elwynn/Shutterstock.com; Kirill Matkov/Shutterstock.com

Yan is really pleased with the work you've done on the Ink Wash Gallery Web page. She'll contact you if she has any other work you could do.

Session 6.2 Quick Check

REVIEW

1. When adding an image to a Web page, how do you decide whether to use the `figure` element or some other block-level element?
2. What is the difference between the column width and the content width for a column?
3. What rule is used to import one style sheet into another?
4. What is specificity?
5. In determining specificity, which type of selector has the greatest weight? Which has the lowest?

Practice the skills you learned in the tutorial using the same case scenario.

PRACTICE

Review Assignments

Data Files needed for the Review Assignments: direct_T6.htm, images/ inkwashgallery.jpg

Yan Lin has asked for your assistance in developing more pages at the Ink Wash Art Gallery Web site, including the important page that gives directions to the gallery. She would like you to create an additional layout option. Because of ongoing road construction, the Directions page needs extensive revision so people driving to the gallery will know how to find an alternate route. You have already begun work on the document by styling some selectors and marked sections, including the header and footer in the body of the document. After you create a style in your text editor, save the file, switch to your browser, refresh or reload the page, verify that you entered the style code correctly, and then switch back to your text editor and complete the next step. A preview of the Web page you will create appears in Figure 6-73.

Figure 6-73	Web page for Ink Wash Art Gallery Directions

iBird/Shutterstock.com

Complete the following:

1. Use your text editor to open the **direct_T6.htm** file, which is provided in your Data Files in the tutorial6\review folder. In the head section and below the page title, enter *your name* and *today's date* in the comment section where noted.

2. Save the file as **direct.htm** in the same folder. Open the file in your browser, and then observe the appearance of the original file.

3. Switch back to your text editor. In the embedded style sheet and just below the CSS comment /* add new styles below */, style the **body** element as follows:
   a. Set the font size to **1.1em**.
   b. Have the text appear in **Arial**, **Helvetica**, or a sans-serif font.
   c. Set the text color to **white**.
   d. Set the background color to **white**.

4. Save the **direct.htm** file. Switch back to your browser, and then refresh or reload the page to verify that the **body** element style appears correctly in your file. Note: The white text will not be visible on the white background. You will change the background color in Step 6.

5. Switch back to your text editor. In the embedded style sheet code, below the style for the **body** element, create a style for the universal selector with margin of 0 and padding of 0.

6. Create a style for the **#container** id selector as follows:
   a. Set the width to **930px**.
   b. Set the margin to **10px** on the top and bottom and **auto** on the left and right.
   c. Create a border that's **1px**, **#888888**, and **solid** on all sides.
   d. Set the background color to **#425b5f**.
   e. Add a shadow with an h-shadow value of **20px**, a v-shadow value of **20px**, a blur value of **5px**, and color **#808080**.

7. Create a style for the **header** selector to have a width of **930px**. Set the bottom margin to **10px**. Set the background color to **#6e8953**, and center-align the text.

8. Create a style for the **#banner** id selector to have a border that is **solid**, **5px**, and **teal**. The banner id text should be centered.

9. Create the following styles for the **aside** selector:
   a. Set the width to **200px**.
   b. Set the margin to **0** on the top, **10px** on the right, **10px** on the bottom, and **0** on the left.
   c. Add padding of **10px** on all sides.
   d. Set the value of the float property to **left**.
   e. Set the text indent to **1.4em**.

10. Create the following styles for the **#main** id selector:
   a. Set the width to **670px**.
   b. Set the margins to **0** on the top, **0** on the right, **10px** on the bottom, and **0** on the left.
   c. Add padding of **10px** on all sides.
   d. Set the value of the float property to **right**.

11. Create a descendant selector for the *main* id selector so paragraphs in the *main* div have a text indent of **1.25em**.

12. Save the **direct.htm** file. Switch to your browser, and then refresh or reload the page. Compare your file to Figure 6-73 to verify your file is correct.

13. Submit your completed files to your instructor, in either printed or electronic form, as requested.

Use the skills you learned in the tutorial to create a Web page for a business magazine.

APPLY

Case Problem 1

Data Files needed for this Case Problem: biz_T6.htm, images\bizlogo.jpg, images\ texture.jpg

Biz Blizzard Magazine   Each month, Biz Blizzard Magazine, headquartered in San Antonio, Texas, publishes articles of interest to middle-level managers. Sheryl Jones, an editor at the magazine, has asked for your help in putting one of this month's lead stories on the magazine's Web page. The article focuses on how managers can deal with the thorny issue of employee tardiness. After meeting with Sheryl and creating a layout, you have been asked to further develop the Web page. After you complete a step to create a style, verify in your browser that the style code has been entered correctly, and then switch back to your text editor. A preview of the Web page you'll create appears in Figure 6-74.

Figure 6-74   **Web page for the Biz Blizzard Magazine**

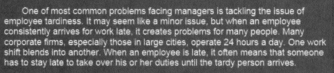

Make Time for Success

One of most common problems facing managers is tackling the issue of employee tardiness. It may seem like a minor issue, but when an employee consistently arrives for work late, it creates problems for many people. Many corporate firms, especially those in large cities, operate 24 hours a day. One work shift blends into another. When an employee is late, it often means that someone has to stay late to take over his or her duties until the tardy person arrives.

Having to wait for someone to arrive to take your place can have lingering effects. If you rely on public transportation, waiting for your coworker to arrive may mean that you're going to miss your bus or your train home, and you may have to wait quite some time for the next bus or train that will take you home. In addition, you've got to greet clients and answer the phone for the tardy person until that person arrives. These issues alone create smoldering resentments and morale issues. They also raise the issue of fairness — why are you expected to arrive to work on time when others aren't? More often than not, callers and clients will blame *you* for not knowing when the tardy person will arrive.

One thing is certain — you, as a manager, can't ignore the problem of employee tardiness. Other workers will be observing how and when you handle the issue and whether you deal with the issue effectively or not. Your reputation as a manager is on the line. In addition, your superiors will take a dim view of your managerial ability if you have a tolerance for lateness. All it takes is one unanswered call; one client who was kept waiting, or one new customer who was treated as though his or her business did not matter, to land you in the managerial dog house — or worse.

In dealing with the problem of employee tardiness, you have to first examine whether the tardiness is short or long. Is the tardy person typically fewer than ten minutes late or does the person come in fifteen or more minutes late? Is the lateness geographical? In many big cities, workers live in the suburbs or exurbs — communities that are more than one hour's travel time to work. Perhaps the problem is physiological — the person lacks the maturity to be counted on to arrive for work on time. Perhaps the problem can be attributed to a bad attitude — the tardy person just doesn't like the job. In examining the pattern of lateness, look beyond the collateral damage of lower office morale, look for what is termed *aggregate tardiness* versus *nonaggregate tardiness*. Aggregate tardiness occurs when the tardy worker compounds the problem by not getting down to work right away. That person may dismiss himself or herself to the cafeteria, the rest room, or make phone calls, surf the Web, send text messages or e-mail or engage in any other activities that compound the tardiness issue.

Document the pattern of lateness and then schedule a counseling session with the employee. If the problem is geographical, perhaps a schedule adjustment is all that is needed. Instead of having the person work 9 to 5, schedule the person's hours for 9:15 to 5:15, or a similar schedule that addresses the employee's child care needs or transportation problems. Rely on progressive discipline for the tough cases. It may be necessary to place the employee on a short-term probation with a written warning that if the tardiness continues, the employee will be discharged.

Biz Blizzard Magazine • 23 Hampton Street • Suite 400 • San Antonio, TX 78221

jocic /Shutterstock.com; Xtremer /Shutterstock.com

Complete the following:

1. Use your text editor to open the **biz_T6.htm** file, which is provided in your Data Files in the tutorial6\case1 folder. In the head section and below the page title, enter *your name* and *today's date* in the comment section where noted.

2. Save the file as **biz.htm** in the same folder. Open the file in your browser, and then observe the appearance of the original file.

3. Switch back to your text editor. In the code for the embedded style sheet, style the body element to have text appear in **white** and in **Arial** or **Helvetica** (sans-serif), size **1.1em**. Use the texture.jpg image as a background image for the body element. The image should repeat.

4. Save the **biz.htm** file. Switch back to your browser, and then refresh or reload the page. Verify that the body element style appears correctly in your file.

5. Switch back to your text editor. In the embedded style sheet and below the body style, create the following styles for the **#container** id selector:
   a. Set the width to **900px**.
   b. Set the margin to **0** on the top and bottom and **auto** on the left and right.
   c. Set the border width to **1px** on all sides.
   d. Set the background color to **#837c63**.

6. Create the following styles for the **aside** selector:
   a. Set the width to **210px**.
   b. Add padding of **10px** on all sides.
   c. Have the text appear in **white**.
   d. Set the background color to **teal**.
   e. Set the value of the float property to **right**.

7. Create a descendant selector for the *aside* selector so images within the aside element have a margin of **0** on the top and bottom and **auto** on the left and right, and are center-aligned.

8. Create the following styles for the **#main** id selector:
   a. Set the width to **640px**.
   b. Set the margin on the right to **10px**.
   c. Add padding of **10px** on all sides.
   d. Set the background color to **teal**.
   e. Set the value of the float property to **left**.
   f. Set the text indent to **2em**.

9. Create a descendant selector for the *#main* id selector so paragraph text within the *main* article has a font size of **1em**.

10. Create a descendant selector for the *#main* id selector so h1 heading text has a border that is **solid**, **thick**, and **orange**. Add padding of **10px** on the bottom. Center the h1 text.

11. Create the following styles for the **footer** selector.
    a. Set the width to **890px**.
    b. Set the border on all four sides to be **solid**, **5px**, and **orange**.
    c. Set the background color to **gray**.
    d. Clear both the left and right margins.
    e. Center the footer text.

12. Save the **biz.htm** file. Switch to your browser, and then refresh or reload the page. Compare your file to Figure 6-74 to verify that your file is correct. Depending on your browser and browser version, you might not see the same amount of padding as shown in Figure 6-74.

13. Submit the results of the preceding steps to your instructor, in either printed or electronic form, as requested.

*Use what you've
learned to create
and style a Web
page for a jewelry
store.*

Case Problem 2

**Data Files needed for this Case Problem: griff_T6.htm, links.css, images\stones.jpg,
images\grifflogo.jpg**

Griff Jewelers   Ernie Griff is the owner of Griff Jewelers in Little Rock, Arkansas. Griff
Jewelers has been in the same location for more than 100 years. The store has built
a loyal clientele looking for gold and silver jewelry at a variety of price points. Griff
Jewelers has a large assortment of engagement and wedding rings at affordable prices,
so the store attracts customers from more than 100 miles away. Ernie seeks your help
in creating a Web page for the store that will highlight the affordability of its jewelry.
You'll create a Web page using a fixed-width design. You'll create an aside column to
call attention to the store's special sale on diamond pendants this month. You'll also
use an existing file named links.css to apply styles for the navigation bar. After you
complete a step to create a style, verify in your browser that the style code has been
entered correctly, and then switch back to your text editor. A preview of the Web page
you will create appears in Figure 6-75.

Figure 6-75	Web page for Grif Jewelers

sniegirova mariia/Shutterstock.com

Complete the following:

1. Use your text editor to open the **griff_T6.htm** file, which is provided in your Data
   Files in the tutorial6\case2 folder. In the head section and below the page title,
   enter *your name* and *today's date* in the comment section where noted.
2. Save the file as **griff.htm** in the same folder. Open the file in your browser, and
   then observe the appearance of the original file.
3. Switch back to your text editor. Within the embedded style sheet code, insert the
   code to import the links.css style sheet, which is provided in your Data Files in the
   tutorial6\case2 folder.

4. Style the **body** element to have text appear in a font size of **1.1em** and in **Arial** or **Helvetica** (sans-serif). The text should have a background color of **#e1d387**.

5. Save the **griff.htm** file. Switch back to your browser, and then refresh or reload the page. Verify that the **body** element style appears correctly in your file.

6. Switch back to your text editor. In the code for the embedded style sheet and below the **body** element style, create a style for the universal selector. Set the margin and padding to **0** on all sides.

7. Create a style for the **#container** id selector. The container should have a width of **930px**, margins on the top and bottom of **0**, and margins on the left and right set to **auto**. Set the border width to **1px** and **solid** on all sides.

8. Create the following styles for the **#wrapper** id selector:

   a. Set the width to **930px**.

   b. Use the stones.jpg file as the background image for the wrapper.

   c. Set the margin on the bottom to **10px**.

   d. Set the overflow to **auto**, and then add the following comment:
      ```
      /* needed for Firefox and IE */
      ```

9. Create the following styles for the **header** selector:

   a. Set the width to **600px**.

   b. Set the left margin to **60px.**

   c. Set the alignment to **center**.

   d. Set the background color to **white**.

   e. Set the border radius to **100px**.

   f. Set the padding on the left and right to **100px**.

10. Create the following styles for the **#main** id selector:

    a. Set the width to **600px**.

    b. Set the margins to **0** on the top, **10px** on the right, **10px** on the bottom, and **0** on the left.

    c. Add padding of **10px** on all sides.

    d. Set the value of the **float** property to **left**.

⊕ **EXPLORE** 11. Create a descendant selector for the *main* id selector so paragraph text has a bottom margin of **10px**.

12. Create the following styles for the **aside** selector:

    a. Set the width to **250px**.

    b. Set the margins to **0** on the top, **0** on the right, **10px** on the bottom, and **0** on the left.

    c. Add padding of **10px** on all sides.

    d. Set the value of the **float** property to **right**.

13. Create a descendant selector for the *aside* selector that creates a style for the unordered list element. The list should have a list style type of **square** and a list style position of **inside**. To the right of the value for the list style position, type the following CSS comment:
    ```
    /* needed for IE */
    ```

14. Create the following styles for the **#special** id selector:

    a. Set the top margin to **5px**.

    b. Add padding of **10px** on all sides.

    c. Set the text color to **white**.

    d. Set the background color to **navy**.

    e. Center the text.

15. Create the following styles for the **#content** id selector:

   a. Set the top margin to **10px**.

   b. Add padding of **10px** on all sides.

   c. Set the text color to **white**.

   d. Set the background color to **olive**.

16. Create the following styles for the **h3** element selector:

   a. Set the bottom margin to **10px**.

   b. Set the bottom border to have values of **solid**, **thick**, and **yellow**.

   c. Center the text.

   d. Set the text to appear in **uppercase**.

17. Create the following styles for the **footer** selector:

   a. Set the width to **910px**.

   b. Set the margin to **0** on all sides.

   c. Add padding of **10px** to all sides.

   d. Set the color to **white**.

   e. Set the background color to **#595959**.

   f. Clear all elements on both the left and the right.

   g. Center the text.

18. Save the **griff.htm** file.

19. Switch to your browser, and then refresh or reload the page. Compare your file to Figure 6-75 to verify that your file is correct.

20. Submit the results of the **griff.htm** file to your instructor, in either printed or electronic form, as requested.

Use the skills you learned in the tutorial, and expand your skills, to create and style a Web page for a financial newsletter.

CHALLENGE

Case Problem 3

Data Files needed for this Case Problem: ziller_T6.htm, footer.css, images\ blacktexture.jpg

The Ziller Financial Group The Ziller Financial Group—or simply the Ziller Group— is an investment firm in Chicago. In the past, the Ziller Group has relied upon a printed publication to address its audience, which is a savvy group of financial investors. The Ziller Group now wants to establish a Web presence. You've been asked to create a Web page that closely matches the format of the firm's printed publication. To do so, you'll create a three-column fixed-width layout. After you complete a step to create a style, verify in your browser that the style code has been entered correctly, and then switch back to your text editor. A preview of the Web page you'll create appears in Figure 6-76.

Figure 6-76 **Web page for The Ziller Financial Group Journal**

Fedorov Oleksiy/Shutterstock.com

Complete the following:

1. Use your text editor to open the **ziller_T6.htm** file, which is provided in your Data Files in the tutorial6\case3 folder. In the head section and below the page title, enter **your name** and **today's date** in the comment section where noted.

2. Save the file as **ziller.htm** in the same folder. Open the file in your browser, and then observe the appearance of the original file.

3. Switch back to your text editor. Just below the start `<style>` tag, enter an `@import` rule to import the footer.css file, which is provided in your Data Files in the tutorial6\case3 folder.

4. Style the `body` element as follows:

   a. Set the font size to **1em**.

   b. Set the font to **Georgia**, a serif font.

   c. Set the top margin to **1em**.

5. Save the **ziller.htm** file. Switch back to your browser, and then refresh or reload the page. Verify that the `body` element style appears correctly in your file.

6. Switch back to your text editor. Below the `body` element style, style the universal selector to have margins of **0** and padding of **0**.

7. Style the **#container** id as follows:

   a. Set the width to **960px**.

   b. Set the margin to **0** on the top and bottom and **auto** on the left and right.

   c. Set the border width to **1px** and **solid** on all sides.

   d. Set the background color to **#f3f6e9**.

8. Style the **header** selector to have a width of **960px**.

9. Style the **#left** id selector as follows:

    a. Enter the `width` property, but leave its value blank for now.

    b. Add padding of **10px** to all sides.

    c. Create a border on the right that is **solid**, **3px**, and **teal**.

    d. Set the value of the `float` property to **left**.

10. Style the **#middle** id selector just as you did the *#left* id selector. (Again, leave the value for the `width` property blank for now.)

11. Style the **#right** id selector just as you styled the *#left* and *#middle* id selectors, but do not create a border.

EXPLORE   12. The three columns should be of equal width. Using the information supplied in the *#container*, *#left*, *#middle*, and *#right* id selectors, determine values for the `width` property for each of the left, middle, and right columns. After you complete your calculations, enter the width value in the code for each of the *#left*, *#middle*, and *#right* id selectors.

13. Style the `h1` heading element as follows:

    a. Add padding of **10px** to all sides.

    b. Have text appear in **white**.

    c. Center the `h1` text.

    d. Using the `background` shorthand property to write one declaration, use the blacktexture.jpg image as a background image. The background color should be **teal**. Repeat the image both horizontally and vertically.

14. Style the `h2` heading element as follows:

    a. Add padding of **10px** to all sides.

    b. Set the bottom margin to **10px**.

    c. Have text appear in **white**.

    d. Set the background color to **navy**.

    e. Center the `h2` text.

15. Style the `p` element to have a text indent of **1em**.

16. Save the **ziller.htm** file. Switch to your browser, and then refresh or reload the page. Compare your file to Figure 6-76 to verify that your file is correct.

17. Switch back to your text editor. In the embedded style sheet, delete the start `<style>` tag. Delete the end `</style>` tag. Select all of the remaining CSS code for the embedded style sheet. Press the Ctrl+X keys to cut the CSS code.

18. Start a new file in your text editor, and then paste the CSS code from the ziller.htm file. Save this file as **zillerstyles.css**.

19. Switch back to the **ziller.htm** file. In the head section and on a blank line below the page title, enter the code to link to a CSS file named zillerstyles.css.

20. Save and then close the **ziller.htm** file.

21. Switch to your browser, and then refresh or reload the **ziller.htm** page. Compare your file to Figure 6-76 to verify that your file is correct.

22. In your browser, go to http://validator.w3.org to open the W3C validator. Validate the ziller.htm file by using the Validate by File Upload method. Note any errors, and then correct them in your file if necessary.

EXPLORE   23. In your browser, navigate to http://jigsaw.w3.org/css-validator. Validate the zillerstyles.css file by using the By file upload method. Note any errors, and then correct them in your file if necessary. Note: If you receive the following warning, you can ignore it: "Imported style sheets are not checked in direct input and file upload modes."

24. Submit the ziller.htm and zillerstyles.css files to your instructor, in either printed or electronic form, as requested.

Create a Web page for a corporate travel agency.

RESEARCH

Case Problem 4

Data Files needed for this Case Problem: travel_T6.htm, images\triangle.jpg

Triangle Travel Planners   Olivia Henry is the owner of Triangle Travel Planners—or Triangle for short—which is a corporate travel agency in Manhattan, New York. Triangle specializes in sending weary executives and their families to exotic locales across the globe. Olivia wants your help in choosing several new travel destinations. She would like you to research new places to travel, and then create a Web page for the Triangle Web site that lists the exciting places you selected based on your research. An image named triangle.jpg has been provided for the banner, and several styles for the *aside* selector have been created for you. In the travel.htm file, use the comments as your guide to structure the Web page.

Complete the following:

1. Use your text editor to open the **travel_T6.htm** file, which is provided in your Data Files in the tutorial6\case4 folder. In the head section, give your page an appropriate title. Below the page title, enter **your name** and **today's date** in the comment section where noted.
2. Save the file as **travel.htm** in the same folder.
3. Within the tags for the embedded style sheet, format the **body** element with the text size, font, color, and background color of your choice.
4. In the body section, enter at least three paragraphs of text that describe the destinations you have chosen.
5. Plan a fixed-width layout for the travel.htm file. The layout should be **900px** wide and have two columns. The layout should have appropriate markup for a header, aside, main section, and footer. The *aside* selector has already been styled, and the **aside** element has already been created for you. Use the triangle.jpg image in the header. Include margins and padding as appropriate in your layout to make it attractive and readable.
6. Create styles for all the id selectors, as well as for the header and footer.
7. In the body section, create sections as necessary. Apply the id selectors to your sections as appropriate.
8. Create a container section for your layout. Create styles for the container section so the page is centered horizontally in the browser.
9. Include at least one descendant selector.
10. Save the **travel.htm** file. Switch to your browser, and then refresh or reload the page. Verify that all styles work correctly.
11. Switch back to the travel.htm file in your text editor.
12. Convert the style sheet to an external style sheet, then link the travel.htm file to the file you created.
13. Open your browser and go to http://validator.w3.org. Use the Validate by File Upload method to check the travel.htm document and ensure the HTML code is correct. If necessary, correct any errors detected by the validation, and then open the file in the browser to confirm the file is correct.

⊕ **EXPLORE**
14. In your browser, go to http://jigsaw.w3.org/css-validator. Use the By file upload method to check the travelstyles.css file and ensure the CSS code is correct. If necessary, correct any errors detected by the validation.
15. Submit the results of the travel.htm and travelstyles.css files to your instructor, in either printed or electronic form, as requested.

ENDING DATA FILES

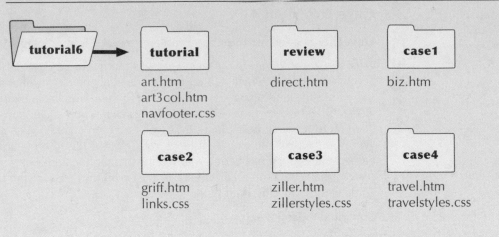

HTML

OBJECTIVES

Session 7.1
- Understand the difference between fixed and liquid layouts
- Create a two-column liquid layout
- Calculate appropriate margin widths using percentages
- Set absolute and relative margins and padding
- Format nested elements

Session 7.2
- Create a three-column liquid layout
- Understand the issues in printing Web pages
- Create print styles

Creating Liquid Layouts

Building a Layout for a Resort

Case | *The Fiji Sunset Spa and Resort*

The Fiji Sunset Spa and Resort—referred to by the locals as simply the Sunset Spa—is located on the tropical island of Denarau, Fiji. Fiji is an island nation of approximately 332 islands in the South Pacific Ocean, located roughly 1,300 miles north east of New Zealand's North Island. The country is an exotic travel destination, and it attracts affluent visitors from all over the world. The Sunset Spa has long been a retreat for people who want to get away from the demands and stresses of city life. Although the stunning beauty of the Fiji islands and beaches are major draws, there is more to the Sunset Spa than fantastic scenery; it offers many activities, including parasailing, game fishing, and hot air ballooning. The owner, Prem Lodhia, is a native Fijian and his family has owned the Sunset Spa for over 50 years. The Sunset Spa has been very popular since the day it opened, but there has been an influx of large chain resorts on Denarau Island, and Prem is concerned that his family-owned business will suffer. He would like to improve the spa's marketing strategy to reach a wider audience. Prem has asked for your assistance in creating a new home page for the Sunset Spa Web site.

STARTING DATA FILES

 tutorial7 →

tutorial

fijispa.jpg
fijisunset.jpg
modernizr-2.js
spa2col_T7.htm
spa3col_T7.htm

review

fijispa.jpg
gift_T7.htm
modernizr-2.js

case1

modernizr-2.js
reddie_T7.htm
reddielogo.jpg
tools.jpg

case2

block.gif
letter_T7.jpg
modblock.gif
modernizr-2.js
printstyles.css

case3

bowlingballs.jpg
lana_T7.htm
lanalogo.jpg
modernizr-2.js
navbar.css

case4

hooks_T7.htm
hookslogo.gif
modernizr-2.js

SESSION 7.1 VISUAL OVERVIEW

A liquid layout uses percentages as values for width, margins, and padding.

Relative margins use percentage, em, or other relative values to change relative to the Web browser size.

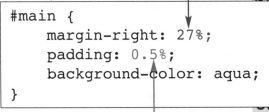

```
#main {
    margin-right: 27%;
    padding: 0.5%;
    background-color: aqua;
}
```

Relative padding changes relative to the Web browser size.

Welcome to the Fiji Sunset Spa and Resort

If you are looking for the perfect getaway, the Fiji Sunset Spa and Resort offer spacious rooms and traditional Fijan huts from small and cozy to [spac]ious. If you are just looking to relax, we have fabulous four-star dinin[g] relaxing day on the beach. If you are the active type, then join the o[ther]g, swimming, parasailing, or game fishing. When you work up an ap[petite] our brunch served in your room or visit any one of our three restaur[ants] Our guest accommodations are the finest at every price point. You will ha[ve] sleep in one of our king-sized beds. Each room has a spa-like tub where [your] troubles away for as long as you wish. You can also visit our sauna or rel[ax] many indoor heated whirlpools. All walls and windows are double-insulat[ed] about the outside world creeping in; you'll be in your own world of peace, [and] relaxation. For a real treat, try an outdoor massage on the beach.
After one visit, you'll see what you have been missing for too long. The F[iji] Resort — let your dreams soar here. We hope to see you soon.

This footer element is styled with the same horizontal margins as the *main* section to create the left column in the layout.

The Sundown Fiji Spa and Resort ✳ Denarau Island North ✳ P.O. Box 9[ ] Directions ▌ Reservations ▌ Lunch Menu ▌ Dinner Menu ▌ Gift Cards

```
margin: 0.5% 27% 0 0;
```

A 2-COLUMN LIQUID LAYOUT

unset

Resort

Dinner Menu   Gift Shop   Contact Us

d Resort

et Spa and Resort is the place to be.
n small and cozy to grand and
lous four-star dining, and beach chairs
pe, then join the other guests for
you work up an appetite, order a
f our three restaurants.
e point. You will have a great night's
spa-like tub where you can relax your
sit our sauna or relax in one of our
are double-insulated, so don't worry
wn world of peace, quiet, and
the beach.
or too long. The Fiji Sunset Spa and
ou soon.

Activities
Scuba
We have some of the best
scuba diving locations in the
world. You'll be amazed at
diversity of sea creatures in
reefs, and the crystal clear
water. Scuba gear can be
rented for a nominal price f
our well-equipped dive sho

Parasailing
Our parasailing activities
include a free lesson, and the
first half hour is free as well.
Enjoy the view of the resort
and beach from above.

Kayaking
Whether you're kayaking for a
leisurely view of the shore or for
fitness, you'll enjoy our large
selection of kayaks. Your first
lesson is complimentary.

Game Fishing
Our fleet of fishing vessels is
rigged with state-of-the-art
equipment suitable for game
fishing.

Hot Air Balloon Flights
What could be more glorious
than watching the Fiji sunset
from above? Enjoy our
champagne sunset balloon ride
for a romantic evening.

orth ✳ P.O. Box 9481 ✳ Nadi, Fiji
Menu ▮ Gift Cards ▮ Contact Us

> The header element is styled with percentage values for padding and margin-bottom.

```
header {
    padding: 0 0.5%;
    margin-bottom: 0.5%;
    background-color: #d7d556;
}
```

> Nested sections are created to style content separately from the containing element.

```
#parasailing, #gamefishing {
    margin-top: 1%;
    border: dashed 1px black;
    padding: 1%;
}
```

> The columns automatically resize when the width of the Web browser window changes.

Creating a Two-Column Liquid Layout

Over the last few years, wide-screen monitors have become quite popular, but such monitors have created a design challenge: whether to design for the traditional **portrait orientation**, in which the page is taller than it is wide, or to design for a **landscape orientation**, in which the page is wider than it is long. In the past, most Web pages were designed based on a screen resolution of 800×600 pixels, but most Web pages today are designed based on a screen resolution of 1024×768 pixels or greater. That said, the larger resolutions are suitable for desktop computers and larger laptops.

As a rule of thumb when designing any Web page, you must ensure the Web page is not only aesthetically pleasing, but readable. Long lines of text are harder to read than short lines of text, which is why newspapers and magazines have several narrow columns of text on a page rather than one wide column. Opinions vary about the optimal line lengths for Web pages; a safe rule is to have columns with line lengths of 60 to 80 characters.

In the previous tutorial, you used fixed-width layouts and calculated how wide you wanted the content to be, based on educated guesses about users' screen resolutions. If a user's screen width is far greater than 1024 pixels, though, your design might waste a lot of space that you could fill with content instead. By designing for a wider page layout, you ensure that such users don't have to scroll down the page to view additional content. The great advantage of fluid layouts is that you don't have to guess about the width of the users' viewports.

The two most common types of fluid layouts are liquid layouts and elastic layouts. A **liquid layout** is a design that expands or contracts in proportion to the size of a user's Web browser window. In a liquid layout, the column widths are determined using percentage values, not pixel values. Just as with fixed layouts, you must consider the widths of the margins, padding, and borders for each column. Then you choose how much of the screen width to use—you can use the entire screen width or restrict the screen width to a certain percentage of the Web browser window. By restricting the screen width, you can center the layout horizontally and have greater assurance that line lengths will not be an issue.

In an **elastic layout**, em values are used instead of percentage values to determine column widths. Elastic layouts work well because ems are relative units, so text becomes larger or smaller based on user preferences set in the browser. The disadvantage to elastic layouts is that you must convert pixels to em units.

In a **hybrid layout**, part of the content (such as the header and navbar) may have a liquid layout and occupy the entire screen width, while the remainder of the content may have a fixed-width layout. Figure 7-1 summarizes the different categories of Web page layouts.

Figure 7-1	The different categories of Web page layouts

Layout	Approach
Elastic	Measurements are in em values. If you want, the layout can use the entire screen width.
Fixed-width	Measurements are in pixels. The layout has a fixed screen width and usually does not occupy the entire screen width.
Hybrid	Attributes of both fixed-width and fluid layouts exist on the same Web page.
Liquid	Measurements are in percentages. If you want, the layout can use the entire screen width.

Prem would like you to use a two-column design. You'll use a two-column liquid layout for his new Web page. He has provided a sketch of the two-column layout, shown in Figure 7-2.

Figure 7-2   **Sketch of the two-column Web page layout**

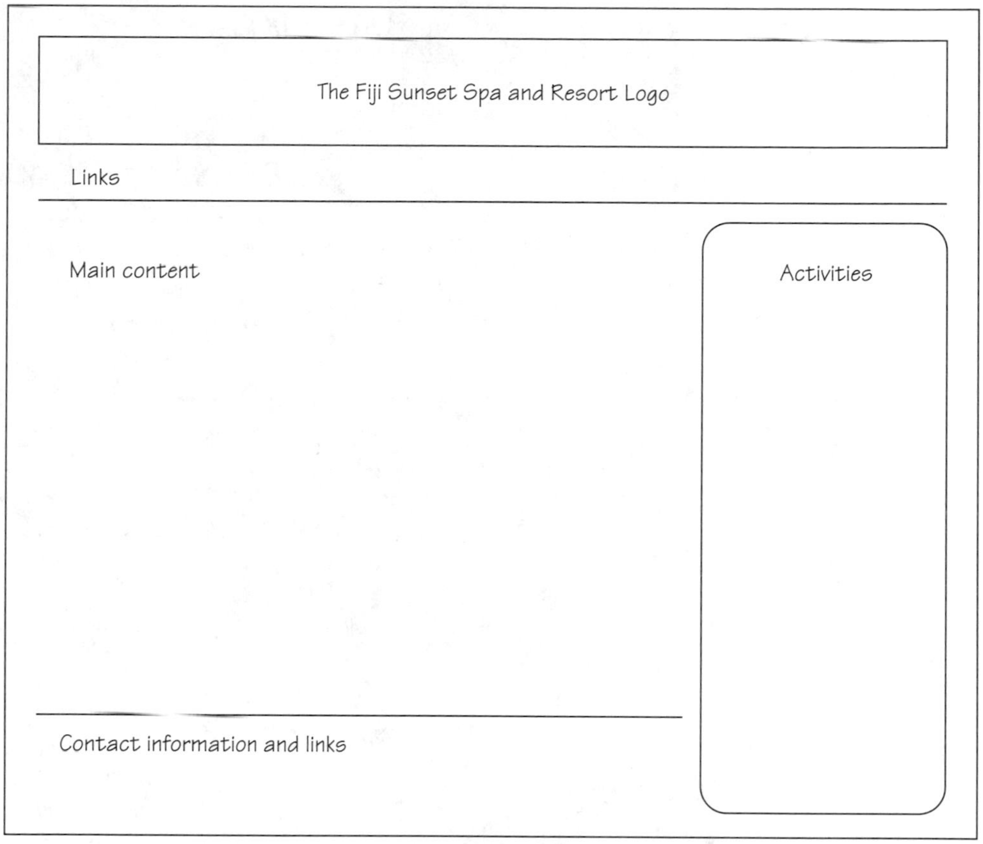

You'll need to create a liquid two-column layout so both the activities section and the main content section expand or contract with the Web browser window. Prem isn't sure whether the activities column should be positioned on the right or the left, so you'll try both. Prem has provided an HTML file that contains `header`, `nav`, `aside`, and `footer` elements, as well as a `section` element with the id *main*. You'll style these elements to create the two-column liquid layout.

To open the HTML file and save it with a new filename:

1. In your text editor, open the **spa2col_T7.htm** file, which is located in the tutorial7\tutorial folder included with your Data Files. In the head section and below the page title, enter *your name* and *today's date* in the comment section where noted.

2. Look through the code to familiarize yourself with it, locate the `header`, `nav`, `aside`, and `footer` elements, and then locate the `section` element with the id *main*.

3. Save the file to the tutorial7\tutorial folder included with your Data Files as **spa2col.htm**.

4. Open the **spa2col.htm** file in a Web browser to view the Web page. The Web page should look similar to Figure 7-3.

Figure 7-3   The Web page showing elements

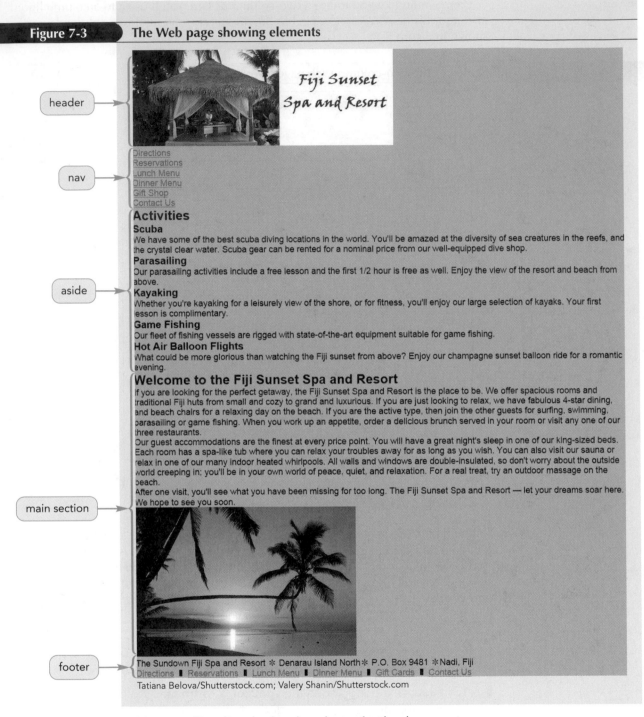

Tatiana Belova/Shutterstock.com; Valery Shanin/Shutterstock.com

Next, you'll stylize the *header* selector for the document.

Stylizing the Header

Unlike a fixed-width layout, you don't specify a width for the `header` element in a liquid layout. If the header contains some text, you specify some padding in the *header* selector. You also give the header a bottom margin to create some white space between the header and the content that follows. As you create these styles, note that the `padding` and `margin` values are expressed in percentages (which are relative values), rather than pixels (which are absolute values).

TIP

For percent values that are less than 1%, some Web developers use a leading 0—for instance, 0.5% rather than .5%.

Be sure to enter the `padding` and `margin-bottom` values as 0.5% (one-half of one percent).

In the spa2col.htm file, the code to style the universal selector to zero out the margins has already been entered. The *body* selector style code is also included in the spa2col.htm file.

You'll enter the code for the *header* selector now.

To style the *header* id selector:

1. Return to the **spa2col.htm** file in your text editor. Position the insertion point on a blank line below the *body* style code, and then type the following CSS, as shown in Figure 7-4:

```
header {
    padding: 0 0.5%;
    margin-bottom: 0.5%;
    background-color: #d7d556;
}
```

Figure 7-4	CSS code for the header element

```
body {
    font-size:1.1em;
    font-family: Arial, Helvetica, sans-serif;
    background-color:darkseagreen;
}

header {
    padding: 0 0.5%;
    margin-bottom: 0.5%;
    background-color: #d7d556;
}

</style>
```

2. Save the file, return to your Web browser, and then click the **Refresh** or **Reload** button to view the changes in the file. The Web page should look similar to Figure 7-5.

Figure 7-5	The stylized header

bottom margin of 0.5% added to the header

background color added to the header

Tatiana Belova/Shutterstock.com

Next, you'll create the layout by planning the sidebar and main columns. In the spa2col.htm file, the sidebar is marked in HTML as an aside element. The main column is marked in HTML as a section element with the id *main*.

Creating the Sidebar and Main Columns

Prem wants you to try a layout with the sidebar column on the left and the main column on the right. A sketch of the layout and elements is shown in Figure 7-6.

Figure 7-6 | Sketch of the Web page layout with the Activities section on the left

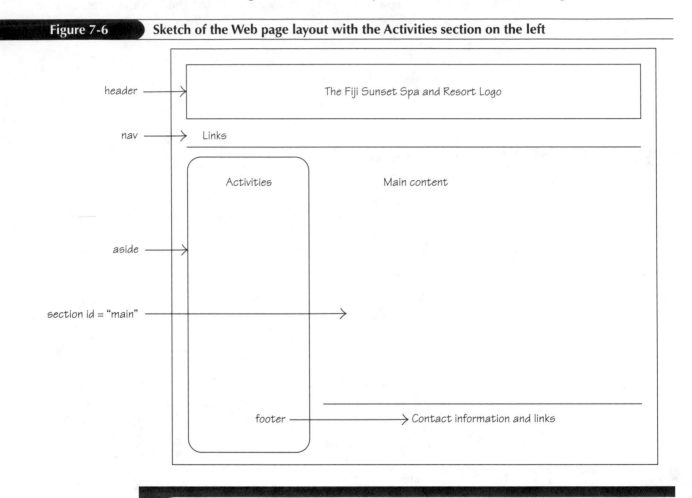

Creating Two-Column Liquid Layouts

To create a two-column liquid layout:
- Decide the width (as a percentage) of the narrower of the two columns. Generally, the sidebar column is narrow and the main column is wide.
- Decide whether you want the sidebar column to appear on the left or the right.
- In the style sheet, enter the code for the sidebar and main id selectors. Assign a width (as a percentage) to the sidebar column. Do not assign a width to the main column.
- In the document body, enter start and end tags for the elements that contain the sidebar and main content.
- If you are not floating all the id selectors, change the source order so the floated content appears before content that is not floated.

Prem wants the `aside` element (the sidebar column) to be floated left. Any element that is floated must have a width, so you will assign a width of 25% for the sidebar column. By establishing a width for the sidebar column, you ensure the column will remain narrow, as intended. The remainder of the screen width will be occupied by the main column. You will not give the main column a width, and you will not float it. You'll create the styles for the selectors for the sidebar and main columns. You'll also give each column a different background color so you can quickly tell if the layout is correct.

To style the *aside* selector and the *main* id selector:

1. Return to the **spa2col.htm** file in your text editor. Position the insertion point on a blank line below the `header` style code, and then type the following CSS, as shown in Figure 7-7:

```
aside {
    width: 25%;
    background-color: orchid;
    float: left;
    border-radius: 20px;
}

#main {
    background-color: aqua;
}
```

Figure 7-7	CSS code for the aside selector and the main id selector

```
header {
    padding: 0 0.5%;
    margin-bottom: 0.5%;
    background-color: #d7d556;

}

aside {
    width: 25%;
    background-color: orchid;
    float: left;
    border-radius:20px;
}

#main {
    background-color: aqua;
}

</style>
```

2. Save the file, return to your Web browser, and then click the **Refresh** or **Reload** button to view the changes in the file. The Web page should look similar to Figure 7-8.

Figure 7-8 **Web page showing stylized sidebar and main columns**

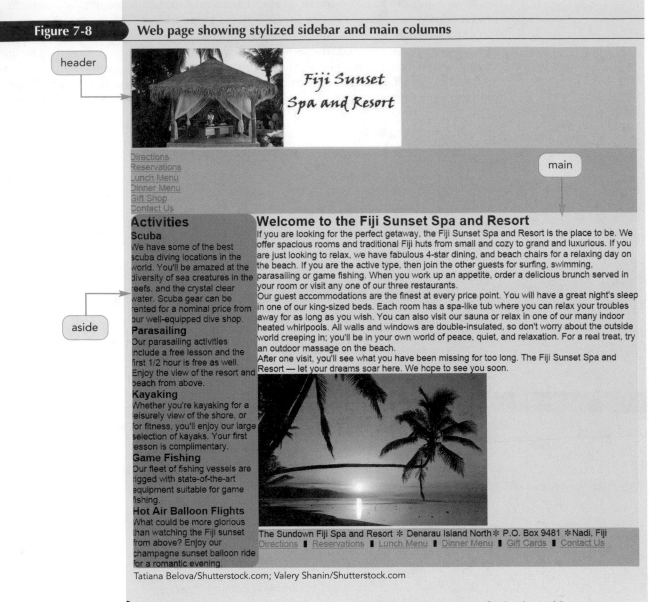

Tatiana Belova/Shutterstock.com; Valery Shanin/Shutterstock.com

3. Change the width of the Web browser window to verify the liquid layout preserves the relative proportions of the columns.

Using the `div` Element

The `div` element is a block-level element. It does not create any formatting of its own. You style the `div` element as you would any other element. To apply the `div` style, you surround inline content with start and end `<div>` tags, as shown in the following code:

```
<div>content</div>
```

Prior to HTML5, the `div` element was used almost exclusively to mark headers, footers, asides, and other named sections. For instance, the following code illustrates marking a header using the `div` element:

```
<div id = "header">
  <p><img src = "logo.jpg">ABC Construction Company</p>
</div> <!-- end header section -->
```

When appropriate, you should use the new elements introduced in HTML5—such as `header`, `footer`, `nav`, `aside`, `article`, and `section`—in place of `div`. However, you'll still see many Web pages where the `div` element is used frequently. If you're talking to Web developers, you'll hear them frequently use the term *div* to refer to `div` elements. They may say something like "I'm using a div to style the main content section."

Although the sidebar column floats to the left and the text for the main column wraps to the right of the sidebar column, just as you planned, there is an obvious problem: neither of these columns looks like a column. To correctly position the main column, you have to establish some distance between it and the sidebar column. To do that, you will create a left margin for the *main* id selector that is at least equal to the width of the *aside* selector. The `aside` element is currently 25% of the screen width, so you'll add a left margin of 25% to the *main* id selector code.

To create a left margin for the main column:

1. Return to the **spa2col.htm** file in your text editor. Position the insertion point on a blank line below the `#main{` code, and then type the following CSS, as shown in Figure 7-9:

   ```
   margin-left: 25%;
   ```

Figure 7-9	Margin-left property added to the main id selector style

```
#main {
    margin-left: 25%;
    background-color: aqua;
}
```

2. Save the file, return to your Web browser, and then click the **Refresh** or **Reload** button to view the changes in the file. The Web page should look similar to Figure 7-10. Confirm that the main column has been repositioned to the right. You may not see a change if your Web browser rendered the main column to the right of the aside column. Change the size of the Web browser window to verify the liquid layout preserves the proportions of the content.

Figure 7-10   **Main column repositioned**

Tatiana Belova/Shutterstock.com; Valery Shanin/Shutterstock.com

Because the margins and padding have been zeroed out in the style for the universal selector, the column text does not have any surrounding white space. The aside column slightly overlaps the main column.

You'll add padding of 0.5% to all sides of both the sidebar and main columns. This will create 0.5% padding on the left and on the right, for a total of 1% of the width of each column.

To add padding to the columns:

1. Return to the **spa2col.htm** file in your text editor. Position the insertion point on a blank line after the `width` property in the *aside* selector code, press the **Enter** key, and then type the following CSS code, as shown in Figure 7-11:

```
padding: 0.5%;
```

Figure 7-11   Padding property for the aside selector

```
aside{
    width: 25%;
    padding: 0.5%;
    background-color: orchid;
    float: left;
    border-radius: 20px;
}
```

2. Position the insertion point after the `margin-left` property in the *main* id selector style. Press the **Enter** key, and then type the following CSS code, as shown in Figure 7-12:

```
padding: 0.5%;
```

Figure 7-12   Padding property for the main id selector

```
#main {
    margin-left: 25%;
    padding: 0.5%;
    background-color: aqua;
}
```

3. Save the file, return to your Web browser, and then click the **Refresh** or **Reload** button to view the changes in the file. The Web page should look similar to Figure 7-13.

Figure 7-13   Sidebar and main columns with padding added

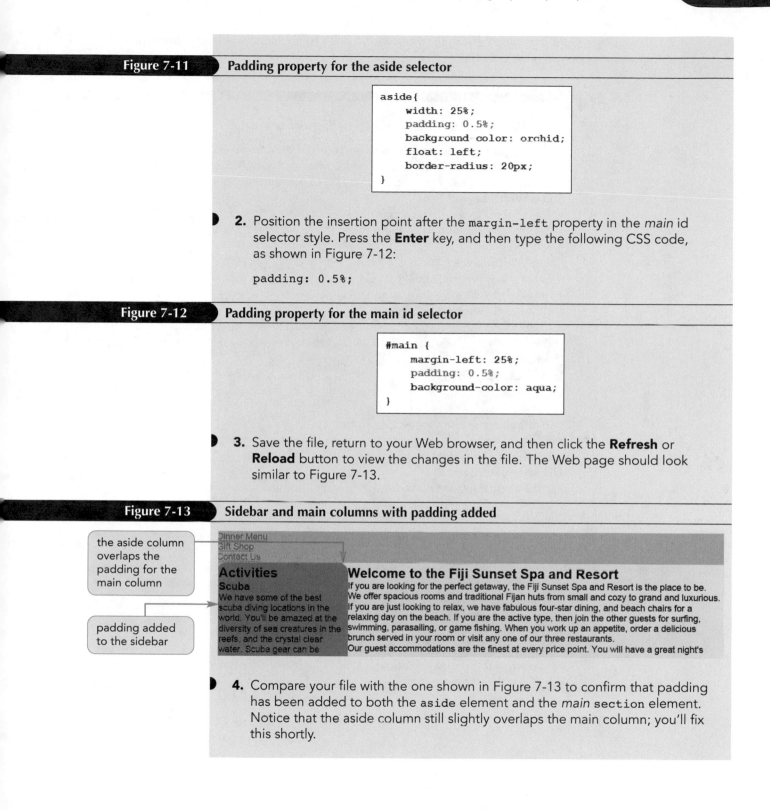

the aside column overlaps the padding for the main column

padding added to the sidebar

4. Compare your file with the one shown in Figure 7-13 to confirm that padding has been added to both the `aside` element and the *main* `section` element. Notice that the aside column still slightly overlaps the main column; you'll fix this shortly.

Prem is pleased with the work you've done so far. Next, you'll add some space between the columns.

Decision Making: Fixed-Width or Liquid Layout?

Web designers will debate the pros and cons of using fixed-width versus liquid layout designs. Each has a favorite, or favorite for a specific purpose. Here are some pros and cons to keep in mind when trying to decide which suits your needs best:

Fixed-Width Layout Pros

- The content looks identical regardless of the resolution of the monitor.
- Widths of columns remain the same regardless of the size of the Web browser window.

Fixed-Width Layout Cons

- Excessive whitespace could be displayed on screens with large resolution.
- Smaller screen resolutions may display horizontal scroll bars depending on the width of the Web page content.
- People who require adaptive technologies such as enlarged displays may have difficulty using a site that is designed with fixed pixel measurements for font and other properties.

Liquid Layout Pros

- Expands and contracts to fill the available space, reducing the amount of vertical scrolling.
- Provides consistency in relative widths.
- Can be used with adaptive technologies to enlarge the display, such as those used by people with visual impairments.

Liquid Layout Cons

- Little or no control over widths of elements, sometimes resulting in elements such as images shifting position.
- If a fixed-width element such as an image is placed inside a liquid element, the element can shrink to the point of not being able to accommodate the image, and columns can droop.
  How do you decide which layout to use? Here are a few considerations:
- If the Web page has a large amount of text, a liquid layout will make better use of the available space in the Web browser.
- If the Web site requires precision in placement of elements for purposes such as branding and consistency, a fixed layout will provide that reliability.

If your Web site is using a three-column design, another option is to use a hybrid approach: you can use a fixed layout for the left and right columns, and use a liquid layout for the middle column.

Although padding has been added, you see a new problem: there isn't any space between the columns, and worse, the sidebar column is overlapping the main column. To create some space between the columns, you'll change the value for the `margin-left` property of the *main* id selector. You added padding totaling 1% to the left and the right of the sidebar column, so you'll change the value for the `margin-left` property for the *main* id selector from 25% to 27%, which will provide enough space to create a gutter between the two columns.

To create gutter space between the columns:

1. Return to the **spa2col.htm** file in your text editor, and then change the value for the `margin-left` property in the *main* id selector from *25%* to **27%**, as shown in Figure 7-14:

   ```
   margin-left: 27%;
   ```

Figure 7-14   **Value for the margin-left property increased to 27%**

```
#main {
    margin-left: 27%;
    padding: 0.5%;
    background-color: aqua;
}
```

2. Save the file, return to your Web browser, and then click the **Refresh** or **Reload** button to view the changes in the file and confirm that gutter space now exists between the sidebar and main columns. The Web page should look similar to Figure 7-15.

   Trouble? If there still is not enough white space between the columns, increase the value for the `margin-left` property by an additional 1% or 2%.

TIP

The `margin-left` value measures from the left side of the browser window. A width of 25% is closer to the left edge of the Web browser window than a width of 27%.

Figure 7-15 | **Main selector id with margin-left of 27%**

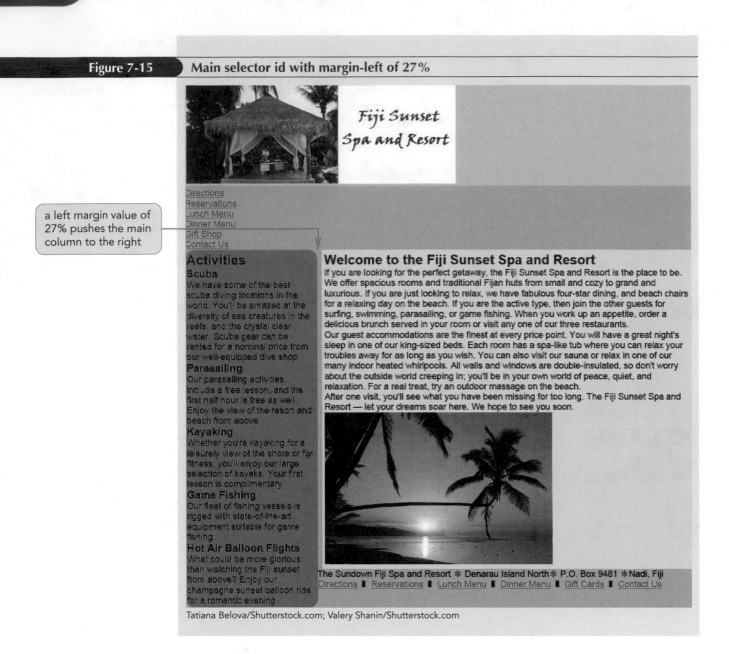

a left margin value of 27% pushes the main column to the right

Tatiana Belova/Shutterstock.com; Valery Shanin/Shutterstock.com

Repositioning a Column

Prem's original sketch showed the sidebar column on the right rather than the left. Figure 7-16 shows his original sketch with the elements marked.

Figure 7-16   Sketch of the Web page layout with elements

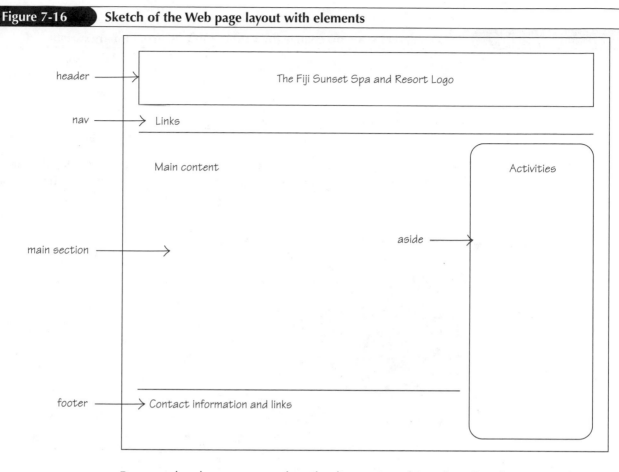

Because the element names describe the content, the code still makes sense when you switch an element to float right rather than float left. Prem would like you to change the layout to switch the column placements. You'll rearrange the columns to match the sketch in Figure 7-16.

It will take just two changes to flip the order of the columns: you'll float the sidebar column right, and you'll give the main column a margin on the right instead of on the left.

To reposition the columns:

1. Return to the **spa2col.htm** file in your text editor. In the *aside* selector code, change the value for the `float` property to **right**, as shown in Figure 7-17:

   ```
   float: right;
   ```

Figure 7-17   Changing the aside float property to right

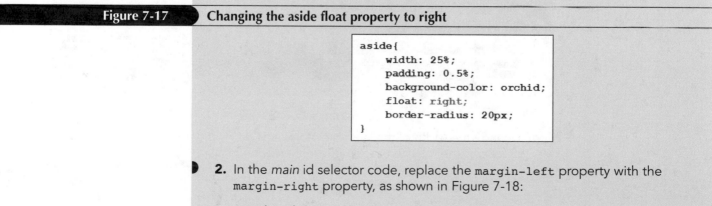

```
aside{
    width: 25%;
    padding: 0.5%;
    background-color: orchid;
    float: right;
    border-radius: 20px;
}
```

2. In the *main* id selector code, replace the `margin-left` property with the `margin-right` property, as shown in Figure 7-18:

   ```
   margin-right: 27%;
   ```

Figure 7-18   **In the main id selector, change the margin-left property to margin-right**

```
#main {
    margin-right: 27%;
    padding: 0.5%;
    background-color: aqua;
}
```

3. Save the file, return to your Web browser, and then click the **Refresh** or **Reload** button to view the changes in the file and confirm that the sidebar is now positioned on the right. The Web page should look similar to Figure 7-19.

Figure 7-19   **Main section on the left and sidebar on the right**

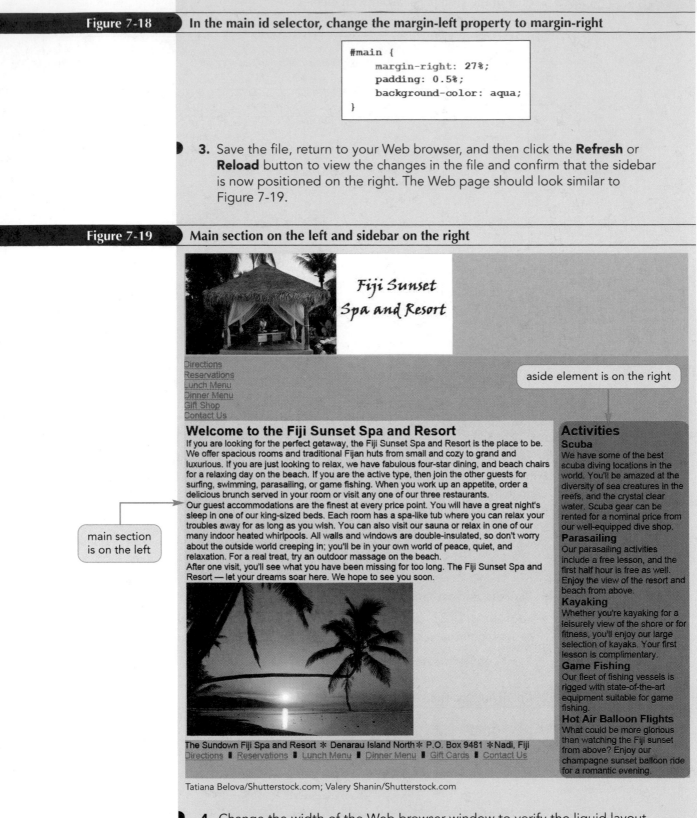

Tatiana Belova/Shutterstock.com; Valery Shanin/Shutterstock.com

4. Change the width of the Web browser window to verify the liquid layout preserves the relative proportions of the content.

Prem likes the sidebar in the new position. Now that the layout has been determined, you'll develop some of the other parts of the page.

Creating a Navigation Bar

Prem likes the look of Web pages with the navigation bar under the header, inline. He'd like you to do the same for this Web page as well. You'll add relevant styles for the nav, ul, and li elements. Note that the navigation bar links are just placeholder links for now, pending further development of the site.

To style the nav element and links:

1. Return to the **spa2col.htm** file in your text editor. Position the insertion point on a blank line below the *main* id selector CSS code, and then type the following code, as shown in Figure 7-20:

```
nav ul li {
    margin-right: 1em;
    display: inline;
    list-style-type: none;
}

nav li a {
    padding: 1em;
    color: white;
    text-decoration: none;
}

nav li a:hover {
    color: yellow;
    text-decoration: underline;
}
```

Figure 7-20 | CSS code for the navigation bar and links

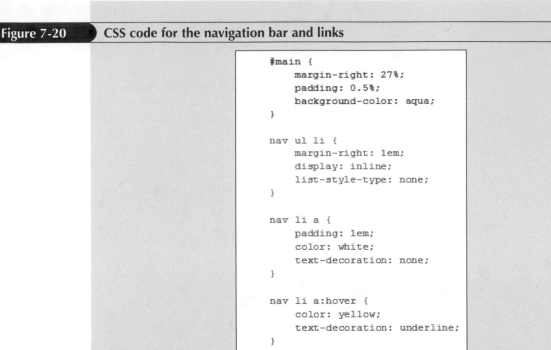

```
#main {
    margin-right: 27%;
    padding: 0.5%;
    background-color: aqua;
}

nav ul li {
    margin-right: 1em;
    display: inline;
    list-style-type: none;
}

nav li a {
    padding: 1em;
    color: white;
    text-decoration: none;
}

nav li a:hover {
    color: yellow;
    text-decoration: underline;
}

</style>
```

2. Save the file, return to your Web browser, and then click the **Refresh** or **Reload** button to view the changes in the file and confirm that the links appear below the header. The Web page should look similar to Figure 7-21.

Figure 7-21 | Web page with links stylized

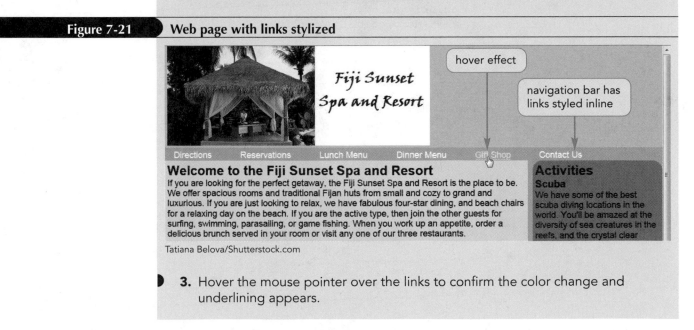

Tatiana Belova/Shutterstock.com

3. Hover the mouse pointer over the links to confirm the color change and underlining appears.

Now that the `nav` element and links have been styled, you're ready to style the `footer` element.

Styling the Footer

As shown in his sketch in Figure 7-16, Prem would like the footer containing contact information and links to appear below the main column only. You'll use the same right margin as the *main* `section` element, which is 27%. Without the right margin set at 27%, the footer would extend the full width of the Web browser window and the `aside` element would overlap because it's longer than the *main* `section` element. You'll also add a top teal-colored border and a background color of lime for the footer.

To insert the code for the *footer* selector:

1. Return to the **spa2col.htm** file in your text editor. Position the insertion point on a blank line below the *nav li a:hover* selector CSS code, and then type the following code, as shown in Figure 7-22:

```
footer {
    margin: 0.5% 27% 0 0;
    border-top: solid thick teal;
    padding: 0.5%;
    background-color: lime;
}
```

Figure 7-22   CSS code for the footer element

```
nav li a:hover {
    color: yellow;
    text-decoration: underline;
}

footer {
    margin: 0.5% 27% 0 0;
    border-top: solid thick teal;
    padding: 0.5%;
    background-color: lime;
}

</style>
```

2. Save the file, return to your Web browser, and then click the **Refresh** or **Reload** button to view the changes in the file. The Web page should look similar to Figure 7-23.

Figure 7-23   Web page with footer stylized

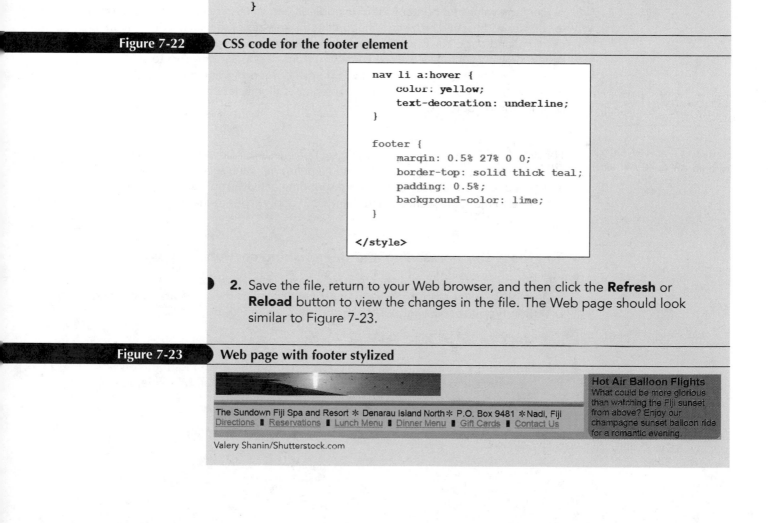

Hot Air Balloon Flights
What could be more glorious than watching the Fiji sunset from above? Enjoy our champagne sunset balloon ride for a romantic evening.

The Sundown Fiji Spa and Resort ✳ Denarau Island North ✳ P.O. Box 9481 ✳ Nadi, Fiji
Directions ▌ Reservations ▌ Lunch Menu ▌ Dinner Menu ▌ Gift Cards ▌ Contact Us

Valery Shanin/Shutterstock.com

Prem sometimes likes to feature specific activities on his Web page. He'd like the featured activities to stand out in the group of activities in the sidebar. You can use a nested `section` element to mark content within another block element.

Creating Nested Elements

TIP

When you use borders to create vertical lines between columns, apply the borders to the left or right sides of the longest columns in the layout.

When creating liquid layouts, it's quite common to create nested `section` elements, where a `section` element is located within another `section` element. In the next session, you'll use a nested `section` element in an `aside` element to group common elements. You created a structure in an earlier tutorial by nesting sections within a named container section. In addition to creating structure, you can use nested sections to group content. For example, in a section of page that describes flowers, you might want to create nested sections that focus on different types of flowers. By including an image or a background image, you could create a gallery of different flowers and a description of each. You could use a background color or border for the main container section to establish that its subsections are part of a larger category. The nested sections could have a similar appearance or look completely different; the choice would be up to you as the designer.

INSIGHT

Issues with Border Widths

Borders can present a problem for liquid layouts because browsers do not recognize percentage values for border widths. In addition, em values are not displayed correctly for border widths, and browsers differ on the thicknesses of the keyword values *thin*, *medium*, and *thick*. You can use keywords or pixel values to set border widths, but you should preview your file in several current versions of popular browsers to see if you need to modify the border widths. If you do use borders in a liquid layout, make sure the total of your column widths (in percentages) is slightly less than 100%. If you don't account for the border widths, your layout might break.

For Prem's Web page, you'll create two sections nested inside the `aside` element. You'll name these sections *parasailing* and *gamefishing*. Each section will contain an `h3` element and text that describe the corresponding activity. You'll start by creating the HTML code to mark the sections, and then you'll apply styles to them.

To create the *parasailing* and *gamefishing* sections:

▶ 1. Return to the **spa2col.htm** file in your text editor. Position the insertion point on a blank line above the `h3` element that contains the text *Parasailing*, and then type the following HTML code, as shown in Figure 7-24:

```
<section id = "parasailing">
```

▶ 2. Position the insertion point on a blank line after the `</p>` tag at the end of the parasailing paragraph, and then type the following HTML code, as shown in Figure 7-24:

```
</section><!-- end parasailing section -->
```

3. Position the insertion point on a blank line above the **h3** element that contains the text *Game Fishing*, and then type the following HTML code, as shown in Figure 7-24:

```
<section id = "gamefishing">
```

4. Position the insertion point on a blank line after the `</p>` tag at the end of the game fishing paragraph, and then type the following HTML code, as shown in Figure 7-24:

```
</section><!-- end gamefishing section -->
```

Figure 7-24 HTML code showing parasailing and gamefishing named sections

```
<h3>Scuba</h3>
<p>We have some of the best scuba diving locations in the world. You'll be amazed at
the diversity of sea creatures in the reefs, and the crystal clear water. Scuba gear
can be rented for a nominal price from our well-equipped dive shop.</p>

<section id = "parasailing">
<h3>Parasailing</h3>
<p>Our parasailing activities include a free lesson, and the first half hour is free
as well. Enjoy the view of the resort and beach from above.</p>
</section><!-- end parasailing section -->

<h3>Kayaking</h3>
<p>Whether you're kayaking for a leisurely view of the shore or for fitness, you'll
enjoy our large selection of kayaks. Your first lesson is complimentary.</p>

<section id = "gamefishing">
<h3>Game Fishing</h3>
<p>Our fleet of fishing vessels is rigged with state-of-the-art equipment suitable
for game fishing.</p>
</section><!-- end gamefishing section -->

<h3>Hot Air Balloon Flights</h3>
<p>What could be more glorious than watching the Fiji sunset from above? Enjoy our
champagne sunset balloon ride for a romantic evening.</p>
</aside>
```

5. Save the file.

Now that you've created the *parasailing* and *gamefishing* ids, you'll style the id selectors. You'll style both of them with a 1% top margin, 1% padding, and a border that is dashed, 1px, and black. In addition, you'll style the *parasailing* id selector to color the text yellow, and you'll style the *gamefishing* id selector to color the text maroon.

To style the *parasailing* and *gamefishing* id selectors:

1. Return to the **spa2col.htm** file in your text editor. Position the insertion point on a blank line below the code for the *footer* selector, and then type the following CSS code, as shown in Figure 7-25:

```
#parasailing, #gamefishing {
    margin-top: 1%;
    border: dashed 1px black;
    padding: 1%;
}

#parasailing {
    color: yellow;
}

#gamefishing {
    color: maroon;
}
```

Figure 7-25	CSS code for the parasailing and gamefishing id selectors

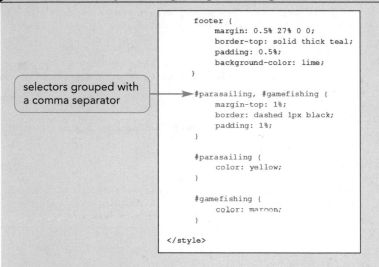

```
footer {
    margin: 0.5% 27% 0 0;
    border-top: solid thick teal;
    padding: 0.5%;
    background-color: lime;
}

#parasailing, #gamefishing {
    margin-top: 1%;
    border: dashed 1px black;
    padding: 1%;
}

#parasailing {
    color: yellow;
}

#gamefishing {
    color: maroon;
}

</style>
```

selectors grouped with a comma separator

2. Save the file, return to your Web browser, and then click the **Refresh** or **Reload** button to view the changes in the file. The Web page should look similar to Figure 7-26.

| **Figure 7-26** | Web page showing the Parasailing and Game Fishing content stylized |

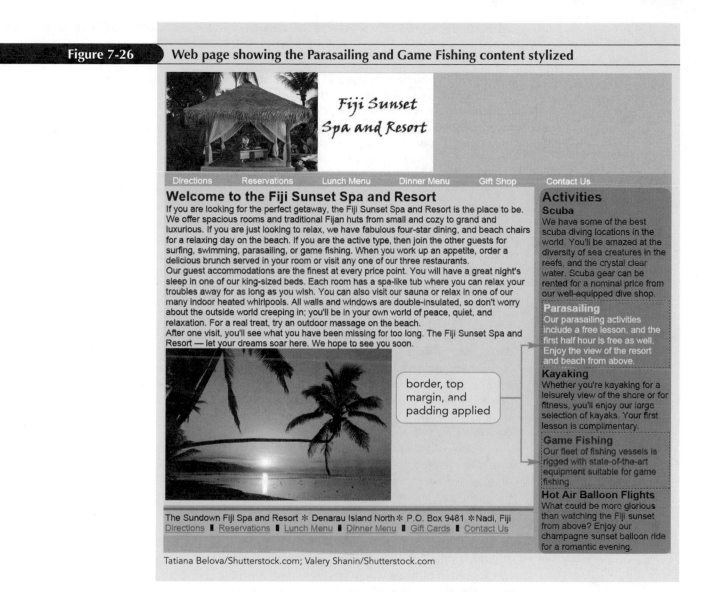

Tatiana Belova/Shutterstock.com; Valery Shanin/Shutterstock.com

The borders around the *parasailing* and *gamefishing* sections separate these sections visually within the aside section. Prem likes the way these activities are featured.

INSIGHT

Floating All Columns

In the layouts you have created so far, one column was floated and the other was not. The advantage to this method is that the layout should not break because not all the columns have a width. The disadvantage is that your HTML code may not be in source order—that is, the content may not be in order in the document flow. In the document flow, floated columns must precede columns that are not floated, so floating all of the columns is one way to preserve their source order.

If you float all of the columns, however, you have to be certain of your math: all of the columns have a specified width, so you must make sure that your layout doesn't break as a result of a browser rounding off the percentage values you have listed for the column widths. Browsers convert percentage widths to pixel values, so some rounding of pixel values is bound to occur as a result. If you haven't left any extra space in your layout between the columns, it takes only one pixel too many to break the layout. Therefore, it's a good idea to accommodate rounding by building a small amount of extra space between the columns. Also, don't forget that subsequent changes to the margin, padding, and border values affect the layout width as well.

The direction that a column floats determines whether any extra space appears to its left or right. For example, if you had a layout with three columns and you floated each column left, any extra space would appear to the right of column 3. On the other hand, if you floated all three columns right, any extra space would appear before column 1. If you floated the columns in different directions, the extra space would be placed where the columns change direction. For example, if you floated column 1 and column 2 left and you floated column 3 right, any extra space would appear between columns 2 and 3.

For accessibility purposes, consider floating all your columns to retain the source order. Some Web designers argue that it's important that a sidebar column with links be displayed on the left; others argue that the most accessible layouts are those with the main column on the left, as it has the most important information to convey to the user, and any sidebar columns should be to the right of the main column.

Prem likes the layout of the two-column design, and he appreciates the variety of colors that help him see where each element is positioned. In the next session, you'll create a three-column version of the design for Prem to compare.

REVIEW

Session 7.1 Quick Check

1. What is a liquid layout?
2. How would you specify margins differently for a liquid layout versus a fixed layout?
3. What is a nested section?
4. What is the purpose of a nested section?

SESSION 7.2 VISUAL OVERVIEW

A three-column liquid layout uses defined percentages for the left and right column widths and no specification for the width of the middle column.

```
#activities {
    width: 20%;
    float: left;
}
```

```
#spa {
    width: 20%;
    float: right;
}
```

A grouped selector with two descendent selectors applies styles to both descendent selectors.

```
#activities h2, #spa h2 {
    margin-bottom: 0.5em;
    color: white;
    background-color: goldenrod;
    text-align: center;
    text-transform: uppercase;
}
```

```
#container {
    width: 90%;
    margin: 10px auto;
    border: 2px solid black;
    border-radius: 20px;
}
```

The container id selector contains all content, and styles applied to it affect all elements inside the container that are not already styled.

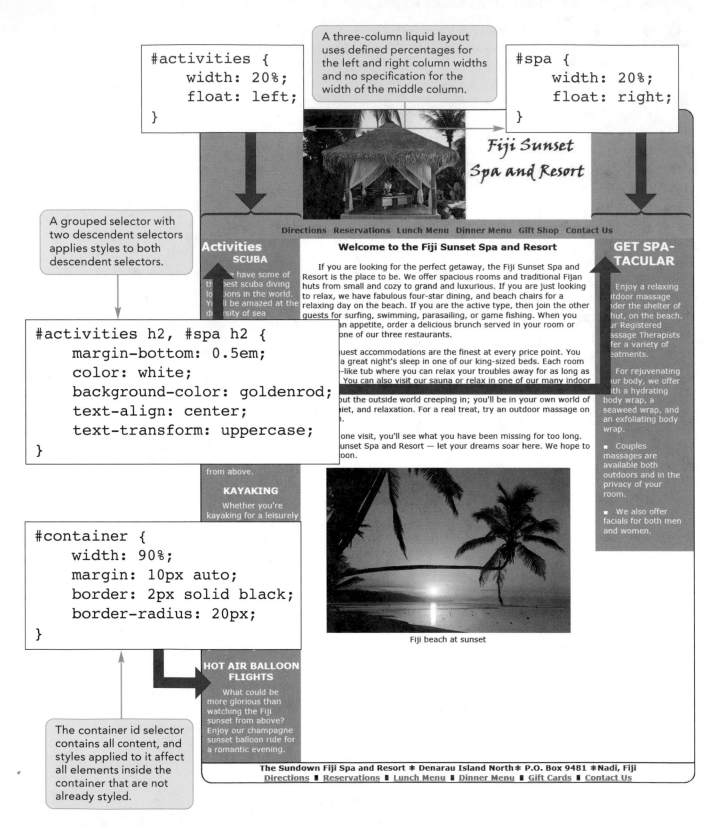

Fiji Sunset Spa and Resort

Directions Reservations Lunch Menu Dinner Menu Gift Shop Contact Us

Activities
SCUBA

...e have some of
th... ...est scuba diving
lo... ...ions in the world.
Y... ...ll be amazed at the
di...rsity of sea

...from above.

KAYAKING

Whether you're
kayaking for a leisurely

HOT AIR BALLOON FLIGHTS

What could be
more glorious than
watching the Fiji
sunset from above?
Enjoy our champagne
sunset balloon ride for
a romantic evening.

Welcome to the Fiji Sunset Spa and Resort

If you are looking for the perfect getaway, the Fiji Sunset Spa and Resort is the place to be. We offer spacious rooms and traditional Fijian huts from small and cozy to grand and luxurious. If you are just looking to relax, we have fabulous four-star dining, and beach chairs for a relaxing day on the beach. If you are the active type, then join the other guests for surfing, swimming, parasailing, or game fishing. When you ...an appetite, order a delicious brunch served in your room or ...ne of our three restaurants.

...uest accommodations are the finest at every price point. You ...a great night's sleep in one of our king-sized beds. Each room ...-like tub where you can relax your troubles away for as long as ... You can also visit our sauna or relax in one of our many indoor

...but the outside world creeping in; you'll be in your own world of ...iet, and relaxation. For a real treat, try an outdoor massage on ...

...one visit, you'll see what you have been missing for too long. ...unset Spa and Resort — let your dreams soar here. We hope to ...oon.

Fiji beach at sunset

GET SPA-TACULAR

Enjoy a relaxing
...tdoor massage
...der the shelter of
...hut, on the beach.
...ur Registered
...assage Therapists
...fer a variety of
...eatments.

For rejuvenating
...ur body, we offer
...th a hydrating
body wrap, a
seaweed wrap, and
an exfoliating body
wrap.

■ Couples
massages are
available both
outdoors and in the
privacy of your
room.

■ We also offer
facials for both men
and women.

The Sundown Fiji Spa and Resort ✱ Denarau Island North ✱ P.O. Box 9481 ✱ Nadi, Fiji
Directions ▮ Reservations ▮ Lunch Menu ▮ Dinner Menu ▮ Gift Cards ▮ Contact Us

A THREE-COLUMN LIQUID LAYOUT

CSS styles can be used to hide some elements when a Web page is printed by setting the display property value to none.

```
nav, header {
    display: none;
}
```

The @page selector has properties for page size and margins.

```
@page {
    size: 8.5in 11in;
    margin: 0.5in;
}
```

Set the font and background colors to colors with high contrast for printing, and remove any background image.

```
/* print designed for accessibility */
body {
    color: black;
    background-color: white;
    background-image: none;
}
```

Fiji Sunset Spa and Resort   Page 1 of 2

Activities

Scuba

We have some of the best scuba diving locations in the world. You'll be amazed at the diversity of sea creatures in the reefs, and the crystal clear water. Scuba gear can be rented for a nominal price from our well-equipped dive shop.

Parasailing

Our parasailing activities include a free lesson, and the first half hour is free as well. Enjoy the view of the resort and beach from above.

Kayaking

Whether you're kayaking for a leisurely view of the shore or for fitness, you'll enjoy our large selection of kayaks. Your first lesson is complimentary.

Game Fishing

Our fleet of fishing vessels is rigged with state-of-the-art equipment suitable for game fishing.

Hot Air Balloon Flights

What could be more glorious than watching the Fiji sunset from above? Enjoy our champagne sunset balloon ride for a romantic evening.

Get Spa-tacular

- Enjoy a relaxing outdoor massage under the shelter of a hut, on the beach. Our Registered Massage Therapists offer a variety of treatments.
- For rejuvenating your body, we offer both a hydrating body wrap, a seaweed wrap, and an exfoliating body wrap.
- Couples massages are available both outdoors and in the privacy of your room.
- We also offer facials for both men and women.

Welcome to the Fiji Sunset Spa and Resort

If you are looking for the perfect getaway, the Fiji Sunset Spa and Resort is the place to be. We offer spacious rooms and traditional Fijian huts from small and cozy to grand and luxurious. If you are just looking to relax, we have fabulous four-star dining, and beach chairs for a relaxing day on the beach. If you are the active type, then join the other guests for surfing, swimming, parasailing, or game fishing. When you work up an appetite, order a delicious brunch served in your room or visit any one of our three restaurants.

Our guest accommodations are the finest at every price point. You will have a great night's sleep in one of our king-sized beds. Each room has a spa-like tub where you can relax your troubles away for as long as you wish. You can also visit our sauna or relax in one of our many indoor heated whirlpools. All walls and windows are double-insulated, so don't worry about the outside world creeping in; you'll be in your own world of peace, quiet, and relaxation. For a real treat, try an outdoor massage on the beach.

file:///C:/Users/Sharon/Documents/publishing/cengage/NPBlendedH

Creating a Three-Column Liquid Layout

Now that Prem has seen the two-column liquid layout design possibility, he'd like to see an option using a three-column liquid layout. He'd like the third column to include some information about the spa services at the Sunset Spa. He wants to include a sidebar column on the left that lists the activities, a main column in the center with the general resort information, and a third column to the right of the main column that highlights some of the spa's services.

You and Prem discuss possible layouts and sketch the one you'll use, shown in Figure 7-27.

Figure 7-27 Sketch of elements and sections for the three-column liquid layout

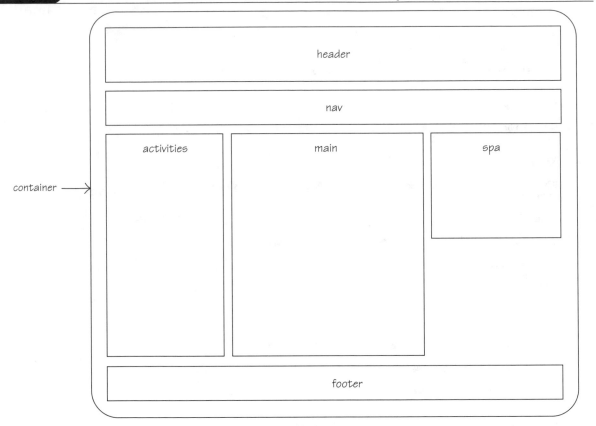

Prem provides a file called spa3col_T7.htm that includes the HTML for the Web page including the new spa services information. You'll open that file now.

To open the file and save it with a new filename:

▶ **1.** In your text editor, open the **spa3col_T7.htm** file, which is located in the tutorial7\tutorial folder included with your Data Files. In the head section and below the page title, enter **your name** and **today's date** in the comment section where noted.

▶ **2.** Look through the code and notice the `header`, `nav`, `section`, and `footer` elements with the ids *activities*, *spa*, and *main*. Notice that because the spa services could also be a sidebar column, the activities content is no longer the only possible `aside` element, and it is marked using the `section` element with the id *activities*. You could mark more than one `aside` element and use ids to differentiate them, or you could use `section` elements as in this example.

3. Save the file to the tutorial7\tutorial folder included with your Data Files as **spa3col.htm**.

4. Open the **spa3col.htm** file in a Web browser to view the Web page. The Web page should look similar to Figure 7-28.

| Figure 7-28 | Web page with spa services information, not stylized |

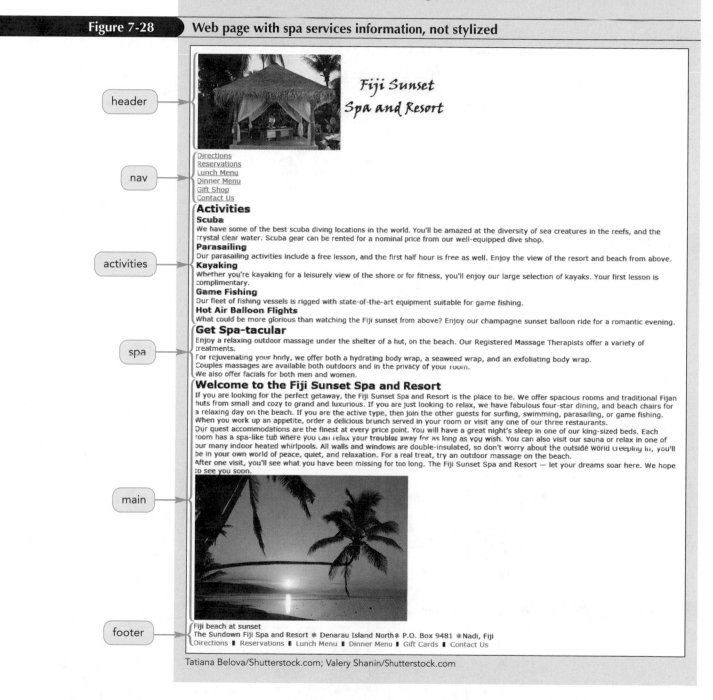

Tatiana Belova/Shutterstock.com; Valery Shanin/Shutterstock.com

The CSS code for the universal selector and body element has already been included in the file. You'll begin by creating the CSS for the *header* selector. The outside corners of the Web page content will be rounded, so you'll need rounded corners at the top left and top right of the header element as well. You won't need rounded corners for the bottom corners of the header, however. You'll also set the background color as *darkkhaki* and center the content.

To style the *header* selector:

1. Return to the **spa3col.htm** file in your text editor. Position the insertion point on a blank line below the *body* selector code, and then type the following CSS code, as shown in Figure 7-29:

```
header {
    background-color: darkkhaki;
    border-top-left-radius: 20px;
    border-top-right-radius: 20px;
    text-align: center;
}
```

Figure 7-29 CSS code for the header selector

```
body {
    background-color: white;
    font-size: 0.9em;
    font-family: Verdana, Arial, Helvetica, sans-serif;
}

header {
    background-color: darkkhaki;
    border-top-left-radius: 20px;
    border-top-right-radius: 20px;
    text-align: center;
}

</style>
```

2. Save the file, return to your Web browser, and then click the **Refresh** or **Reload** button to view the changes in the file. The Web page should look similar to Figure 7-30.

Trouble? If the color doesn't appear in the header, check your spelling; the color *darkkhaki* has a double *kk*.

Figure 7-30 Web page showing stylized header

top corners are rounded with a 20px radius

Fiji Sunset Spa and Resort

Tatiana Belova/Shutterstock.com

Prem would like the navigation bar below the header, but he'd like it to look like it belongs with the header. You'll achieve this by setting the same background color for the nav element as for the header. Prem would also like the hover effect to simply change a link's background color.

To style the *nav* selector and links:

1. Return to the **spa3col.htm** file in your text editor. Position the insertion point on a blank line below the *header* selector code, and then type the following CSS code, as shown in Figure 7-31:

```
nav {
    padding: 0.5em;
    background-color: darkkhaki;
    text-align: center;
}

nav ul li {
    display: inline;
    list-style-type: none;
}

nav a {
    padding: 0.25em;
    color: #5c4033;
    font-weight: bold;
    text-decoration: none;
}

nav a:hover {
    color: black;
    background-color: goldenrod;
}
```

Figure 7-31   **CSS code for the nav selector and links**

```
header {
    background-color: darkkhaki;
    border-top-left-radius: 20px;
    border-top-right-radius: 20px;
    text-align: center;
}

nav {
    padding: 0.5em;
    background-color: darkkhaki;
    text-align: center;
}

nav ul li {
    display: inline;
    list-style-type: none;
}

nav a {
    padding: 0.25em;
    color: #5c4033;
    font-weight: bold;
    text-decoration: none;
}

nav a:hover {
    color: black;
    background-color: goldenrod;
}

</style>
```

2. Save the file, return to your Web browser, and then click the **Refresh** or **Reload** button to view the changes in the file. The Web page should look similar to Figure 7-32. Some Web browsers may show a border around the header.

Figure 7-32   **Web page with stylized nav and links**

Tatiana Belova/Shutterstock.com

3. Pass the mouse pointer over each of the links to confirm that the hover effect appears, as shown in Figure 7-32.

The setup for the header and the navbar is complete. Now you're ready to create the three-column liquid layout for the Sunset Spa home page.

Creating Styles for the Left Column

You first need to determine the column widths for the three columns. The *activities* section will be positioned as the column furthest to the left. The *main* section will be positioned in the middle, and the *spa* section will be positioned as the column furthest to the right. Prem wants the left and right columns to be narrow, so you'll assign each a width of 20%.

Creating Three-Column Liquid Layouts

To create a three-column liquid layout:
- Decide on the width (in percentages) for each of the narrower two sidebar columns.
- Decide how you want each sidebar column to float (left or right).
- In the style sheet, enter the code for the sidebar and main id selectors. Assign widths to both sidebar columns. Do not assign a width to the main column.
- Make sure the left and right column content (sidebars) is marked with `section` elements with ids.
- If necessary, change the source order so the floated content appears before the content that is not floated.

The middle column will not have a set width—its width will expand or collapse based on the screen resolution. The *activities* section will be floated left, and the *spa* section will be floated right. In the `body` element, the sections are currently in the following source order. Note that the *main* section (middle) follows both the *activities* (left) and *spa* (right) sections:

1. `header`
2. `nav`
3. *activities* `section`
4. *spa* `section`
5. *main* `section`
6. `footer`

Recall that when elements appear side by side, floated elements must appear before elements that are not floated, which is why the preceding source order seems incorrect. The elements appear as left (*activities*), right (*spa*), and then middle (*main*). As you've seen, it's easy to change the position of an element by changing the value of the float property. For this reason it would be terribly confusing if you named an element using a position word such as *left, middle, right, top,* or *bottom*.

The left and right columns (*activities* and *spa*) will have the same background color. You'll also create a descendent selector style for the `h2` element to style it as uppercase text only in the *activities* and *spa* sections. You'll start by styling the *activities* section, which will be positioned as the left column.

TIP

Choose an id name for an element that describes something about the content.

To enter the *activity* id selector code:

1. Return to the **spa3col.htm** file in your text editor. Position the insertion point on a blank line below the *nav a:hover* selector code, and then type the following CSS code, as shown in Figure 7-33:

```
#activities {
    width: 20%;
    float: left;
    background-color: goldenrod;
    color: white;
}

#activities h3 {
    margin-bottom: 0.5em;
    color: white;
    background-color: goldenrod;
    text-align: center;
    text-transform: uppercase;
}

#activities p {
    padding: 0 1% 1% 5%;
}
```

Figure 7-33	CSS code for the activities section

```
nav a:hover {
    color: black;
    background-color: white;
}

#activities {
    width: 20%;
    float: left;
    background-color: goldenrod;
    color: white;
}

#activities h3 {
    margin-bottom: 0.5em;
    color: white;
    background-color: goldenrod;
    text-align: center;
    text-transform: uppercase;
}

#activities p {
    padding: 0 1% 1% 5%;
}

</style>
```

2. Save the file, return to your Web browser, and then click the **Refresh** or **Reload** button to view the changes in the file. Some current browsers may not show the bullets; you'll standardize their appearance later in this tutorial. The Web page should look similar to Figure 7-34.

Figure 7-34   **Activities section floating left**

Fiji beach at sunset

Tatiana Belova/Shutterstock.com; Valery Shanin/Shutterstock.com

Now that the *activities* section column has been styled, you'll create styles for the *main* section, which will be positioned as the middle column.

INSIGHT

Controlling Minimum and Maximum Widths

When creating a design with a fluid layout, you must be wary of objects on the Web page that have fixed widths, such as images, tables, forms, or multimedia controls. These types of objects may prevent a column from resizing when a user makes the Web browser window narrower. When designing a fluid Web page that includes fixed-width content, try to place such objects into the widest column and assign these objects a generous amount of white space on the left and right so the columns can be resized to some extent.

You can also use the `min-width` and `max-width` properties to help fluid layouts better adapt to fixed-width content. The `min-width` and `max-width` properties set the minimum and maximum width of an element, respectively. The minimum and maximum widths are for the content only, and do not include the widths of margins, borders, or padding. You can apply the `min-width` or `max-width` property to the container element to keep the layout from expanding or contracting too much. If the document body contains fixed-width content, such as an image, you don't want to have overlapping content if a user has a small screen or resizes the browser window to be smaller. You could set the `min-width` value to the width of an image element in a particular section, for instance. Similarly, you could use the `max-width` property to limit how large a layout could appear. At some point, a layout may contain too much white space. You can set the `max-width` property to the limit at which you want users to maximize the screen. This limit would depend on the number of columns and content in your layout.

Creating Styles for the Middle Column

Recall that the left column and right column will each have a width of 20%. The middle column will occupy the remaining space between those columns. Right now there is no space between the left and main column, so you need to move the contents of the middle column over from the left. You also need to decrease the width of the middle column to create space for the right column. To ensure adequate space between the columns, you'll assign the middle column padding of 0.5%. Prem would also like h1 heading text centered, so you'll create a descendant selector for the h1 element in the *main* id selector. Finally, you'll create some white space below the h1 heading by giving it a bottom margin of 1em. The em measurement is also a relative measurement and will provide some elastic functionality. That is, if a user changes the font size, the proportions will remain the same.

To enter the middle column id selector code:

▶ 1. Return to the **spa3col.htm** file in your text editor. Position the insertion point on a blank line below the *#activities p* selector code, and then type the following CSS code, as shown in Figure 7-35:

```
#main {
    padding: 0.5%;
    margin: 0 20% 0 20%;
}

#main h1 {
    margin-bottom: 1em;
    text-align: center;
}
```

Figure 7-35   CSS code for the main id selector

```
#activities p {
    padding: 0 1% 1% 5%;
}

#main {
    padding: 0.5%;
    margin: 0 20% 0 20%;
}

#main h1 {
    margin-bottom: 1em;
    text-align: center;
}

</style>
```

2. Save the file, return to your Web browser, and then click the **Refresh** or **Reload** button to view the changes in the file. The Web page should look similar to Figure 7-36.

   Trouble? Don't be concerned if the columns appear too close in some sections and the bullets in the main column overlap the sidebar column. You'll address these issues in upcoming steps.

Figure 7-36   Web page showing main section stylized

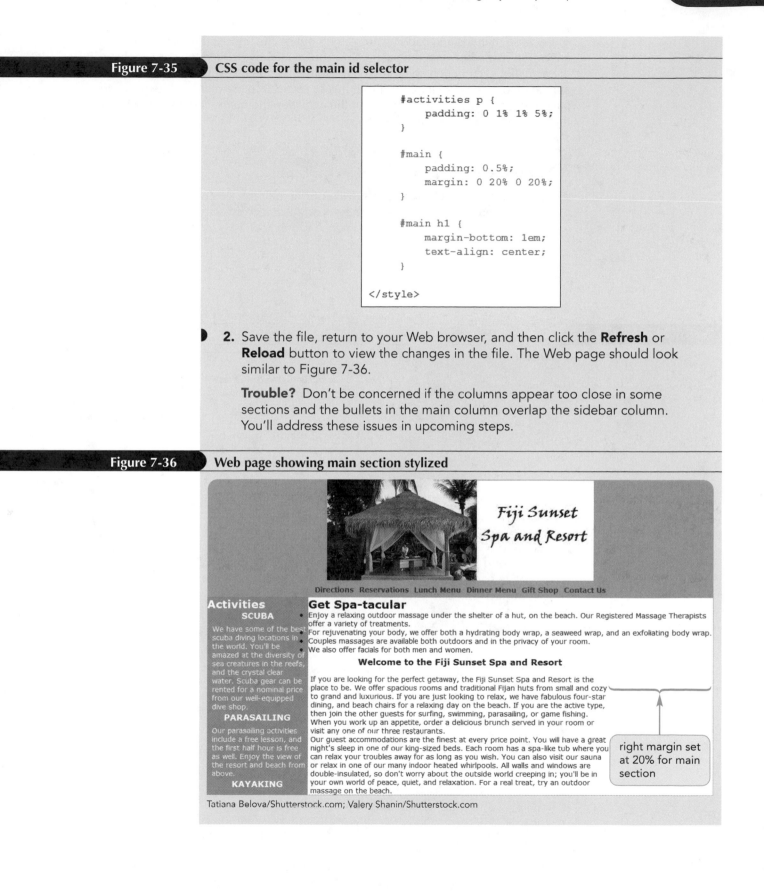

Tatiana Belova/Shutterstock.com; Valery Shanin/Shutterstock.com

Because margins and padding are zeroed out by the universal selector, there isn't any white space between the paragraphs. You've already defined the paragraphs in the *activities* section (left column) to have some padding. Next you'll further refine the appearance of the paragraphs in the *activities* section. To give some white space to the paragraph text, you'll create a style for the *activities* and *main* sections that will indent the text and create a bottom margin.

To refine the appearance of paragraphs:

1. Return to the **spa3col.htm** file in your text editor. Position the insertion point on a blank line below the *#main h1* selector code, and then type the following CSS code, as shown in Figure 7-37:

```
#activities p, #main p {
    margin-bottom: 1em;
    text-indent: 2em;
}
```

Figure 7-37	CSS code for the grouped selectors

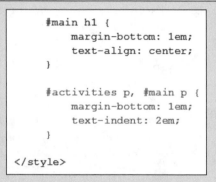

```
#main h1 {
    margin-bottom: 1em;
    text-align: center;
}

#activities p, #main p {
    margin-bottom: 1em;
    text-indent: 2em;
}

</style>
```

2. Save the file, return to your Web browser, and then click the **Refresh** or **Reload** button to view the changes in the file. The paragraphs should now have some space between them, as well as a text indent. The Web page should look similar to Figure 7-38.

Figure 7-38   Web page showing stylized paragraphs in activities and main sections

the text-indent property indents the first line of each paragraph

the margin-bottom property adds white space after each paragraph

Tatiana Belova/Shutterstock.com; Valery Shanin/Shutterstock.com

Now that the left and middle columns have been styled, you're ready to create styles for the right column.

Creating Styles for the Right Column

In a three-column layout, it's visually pleasing to use the same or similar layout features for the columns that flank the center column. You'll stylize the *spa* section element to position it on the right, and you'll use the same styles for `width`, `color`, and `background` as for the *activities* section. This will create balance between the left and right columns.

To stylize the *spa* section element:

1. Return to the **spa3col.htm** file in your text editor. Position the insertion point on a blank line below the *#activities p, #main p* selector code, and then type the following CSS code, as shown in Figure 7-39:

```
#spa {
    width: 20%;
    color: white;
    background-color: goldenrod;
    float: right;
}
```

Figure 7-39 CSS code for the spa id selector

```
#activities p, #main p {
    margin-bottom: 1em;
    text-indent: 2em;
}

#spa {
    width: 20%;
    color: white;
    background-color: goldenrod;
    float: right;
}

</style>
```

2. Save the file, return to your Web browser, and then click the **Refresh** or **Reload** button to view the changes in the file. The Web page should look similar to Figure 7-40.

Trouble? Depending on your browser and browser version, you may not see the bullets for the unordered list in the right column. You will address these problems shortly.

Figure 7-40   Web page showing stylized spa section

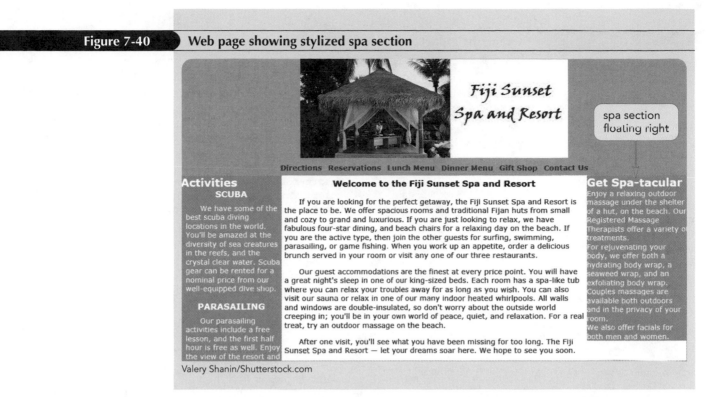

Valery Shanin/Shutterstock.com

The h2 element in the *spa* section is not using the same style as the h3 element in the *activities* section. You'll add the *spa h2* descendent selector as a grouped selector to the *activities h3* selector style to address this.

To add the *spa h2* selector to the *activities h3* style:

1. Return to the **spa3col.htm** file in your text editor. Position the insertion point after the *#activities h3* selector, type a comma, and then type **#spa h2**, as shown in Figure 7-41:

   ```
   #activities h3, #spa h2
   ```

Figure 7-41 | Adding the #spa h2 selector to the #activities h3 style

```
#activities {
    width: 20%;
    float: left;
    background-color: goldenrod;
    color: white;
}

#activities h3, #spa h2 {
    margin-bottom: 0.5em;
    color: white;
    background-color: goldenrod;
    text-align: center;
    text-transform: uppercase;
}

#activities p {
    padding: 0 1% 1% 5%;
}
</style>
```

2. Save the file, return to your Web browser, and then click the **Refresh** or **Reload** button to view the changes in the file. The Web page should look similar to Figure 7-42.

Figure 7-42 | Web page with styled spa h2 dependent selector

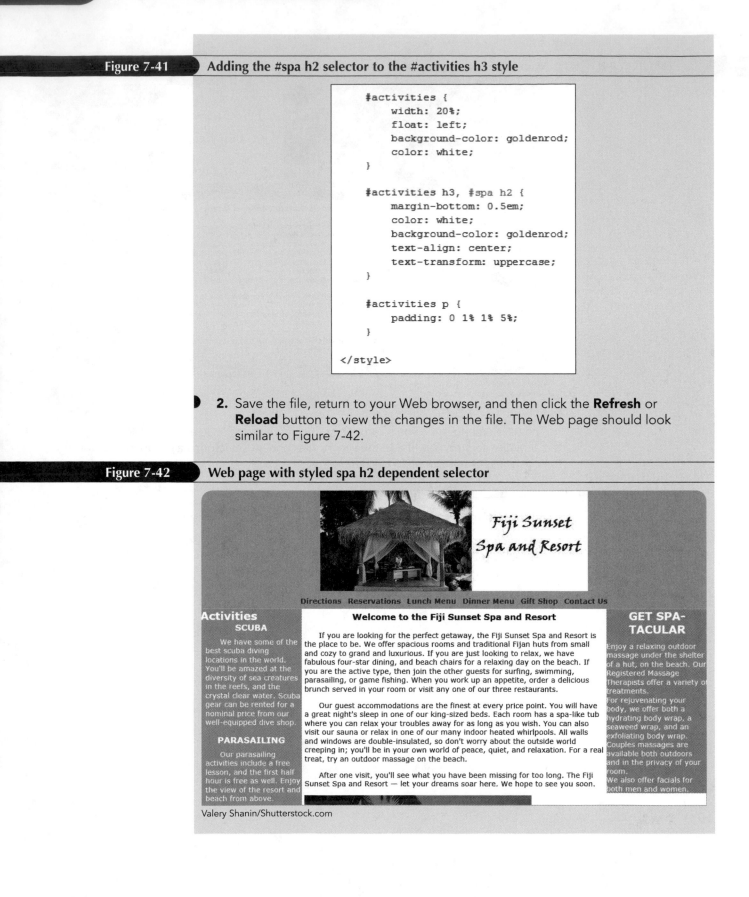

Valery Shanin/Shutterstock.com

You've already styled an unordered list for the `nav` element, and you'll create similar CSS code to style the unordered list in the *spa* section to look different from the unordered list items in the navbar.

To address the problems with the list markers in the right columns, you'll change the list style position to create an indent, and then you'll provide some white space by creating a margin below each list item. In addition, Prem prefers square list markers, so you'll change the list style type as well.

TIP

Different browsers and different versions of the same browser provide different amounts of padding and margin space for list markers, so always view your lists in several browsers and browser versions. Adjust margins or padding as needed.

To style the unordered list in the right column:

1. Return to the **spa3col.htm** file in your text editor. Position the insertion point below the *#spa* selector code, and then type the following CSS code, as shown in Figure 7-43:

```
#spa ul {
    padding: 1em;
    list-style-type: square;
    list-style-position: inside;
}

#spa ul li {
    margin-bottom: 1em;
}
```

Figure 7-43 CSS code for the spa list

```
    #spa {
        width: 20%;
        color: white;
        background-color: goldenrod;
        float: right;
    }

     #spa ul {
         padding: 1em;
         list-style-type: square;
         list-style-position: inside;
     }

     #spa ul li {
         margin-bottom: 1em;
     }

</style>
```

2. Save the file, return to your Web browser, and then click the **Refresh** or **Reload** button to view the changes in the file. The Web page should look similar to Figure 7-44.

Figure 7-44　　Web page with stylized spa section list

Valery Shanin/Shutterstock.com

The list markers should now be visible (if they were not before), and they should appear inside the right column.

The last task is to create styles for the site footer.

Creating Styles for the Footer

The footer must clear all columns, and Prem also wants to center the footer content. You'll give the footer some white space by providing margin space and padding on the top.

To create styles for the footer:

1. Return to the **spa3col.htm** file in your text editor. Position the insertion point after the *#spa ul li* selector code, and then type the following CSS code, as shown in Figure 7-45:

```
footer {
    margin-top: 1em;
    padding: 1em auto;
    border-top: solid 2px black;
    clear: both;
    font-weight: bold;
    text-align: center;
}
```

Figure 7-45	CSS code for the footer selector

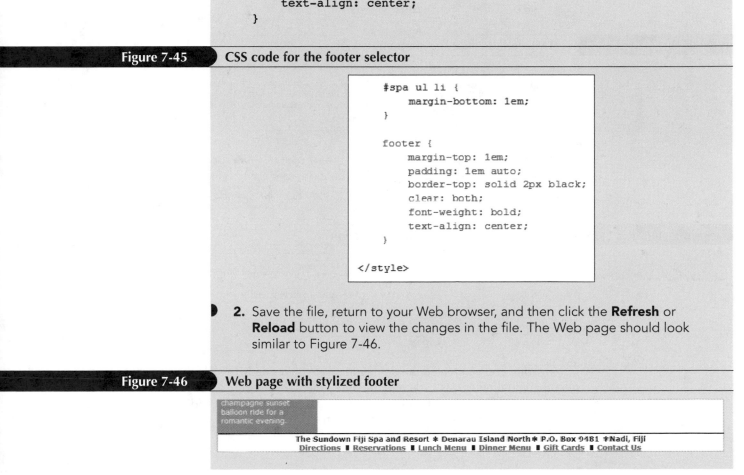

```
#spa ul li {
    margin-bottom: 1em;
}

footer {
    margin-top: 1em;
    padding: 1em auto;
    border-top: solid 2px black;
    clear: both;
    font-weight: bold;
    text-align: center;
}

</style>
```

2. Save the file, return to your Web browser, and then click the **Refresh** or **Reload** button to view the changes in the file. The Web page should look similar to Figure 7-46.

Figure 7-46	Web page with stylized footer

champagne sunset
balloon ride for a
romantic evening.

The Sundown Fiji Spa and Resort ✱ Denarau Island North ✱ P.O. Box 9481 ✱Nadi, Fiji
Directions ❚ Reservations ❚ Lunch Menu ❚ Dinner Menu ❚ Gift Cards ❚ Contact Us

You've completed styling the sections of the Web page and Prem likes the new look. The *activities* and *spa* sections are styled using the same background color, which gives the Web page a balanced look. The header and footer span the width of the Web page, with the content centered.

Modifying the Layout Width

A liquid layout can be constrained so the layout is centered and does not occupy the entire screen width. In the previous tutorial, you used a wrapper to add a border around the content of the Web page. You'll use the same technique for the three-column liquid layout as well.

TIP

It's common to constrain liquid layouts to 70–90% of the screen width.

Prem would like the layout centered horizontally, which will result in shorter, more readable lines in the main column. To limit the layout width, you'll create a container section in the body of the document and then style the *container* selector to 90% of the screen width.

To enter the container section code:

1. Return to the **spa3col.htm** file in your text editor. Position the insertion point after the <body> tag, and then type the following HTML code, as shown in Figure 7-47:

   ```
   <div id = "container">
   ```

Figure 7-47   **HTML code to start the container section**

```
<body>

   <div id = "container">
   <header>
```

2. Position the insertion point after the </footer> tag, before the </body> tag, and then type the following HTML code, as shown in Figure 7-48:

   ```
   </div> <!-- end container -->
   ```

Figure 7-48   **HTML code to end the container section**

```
</footer> <!-- end footer -->

</div> <!-- end container -->

</body>
```

Now that you've created the *container* div, you're ready to style the *container* selector. You'll enter this code after the body element selector style. You'll add a border radius of 22px. The header radius was 20px, but you'll need the additional 2px to accommodate the 2px border for the container.

To style the *container* id selector:

1. Return to the **spa3col.htm** file in your text editor. Position the insertion point after the *body* selector code, and then type the following CSS code, as shown in Figure 7-49:

```
#container {
    width: 90%;
    margin: 10px auto;
    border: 2px solid black;
    border-radius: 22px;
}
```

| Figure 7-49 | CSS code for the container id selector |

```
body {
    background-color: white;
    font-size: 0.9em;
    font-family: Verdana, Arial, Helvetica, sans-serif;
}

#container {
    width: 90%;
    margin: 10px auto;
    border: 2px solid black;
    border-radius: 22px;
}

header {
    background-color: darkkhaki;
    border-top-left-radius: 20px;
    border-top-right-radius: 20px;
    text-align: center;
}
```

2. Save the file, return to your Web browser, and then click the **Refresh** or **Reload** button to view the changes in the file. The Web page should look similar to Figure 7-50.

Figure 7-50 Web page showing stylized container

Directions Reservations Lunch Menu Dinner Menu Gift Shop Contact Us

Activities
SCUBA

We have some of the best scuba diving locations in the world. You'll be amazed at the diversity of sea creatures in the reefs, and the crystal clear water. Scuba gear can be rented for a nominal price from our well-equipped dive shop.

PARASAILING

Our parasailing activities include a free lesson, and the first half hour is free as well. Enjoy the view of the resort and beach from above.

KAYAKING

Whether you're kayaking for a leisurely view of the shore or for fitness, you'll enjoy our large selection of kayaks. Your first lesson is complimentary.

GAME FISHING

Our fleet of fishing vessels is rigged with state-of-the-art equipment suitable for game fishing.

HOT AIR BALLOON FLIGHTS

What could be more glorious than watching the Fiji sunset from above? Enjoy our champagne sunset balloon ride for a romantic evening.

Welcome to the Fiji Sunset Spa and Resort

If you are looking for the perfect getaway, the Fiji Sunset Spa and Resort is the place to be. We offer spacious rooms and traditional Fijan huts from small and cozy to grand and luxurious. If you are just looking to relax, we have fabulous four-star dining, and beach chairs for a relaxing day on the beach. If you are the active type, then join the other guests for surfing, swimming, parasailing, or game fishing. When you work up an appetite, order a delicious brunch served in your room or visit any one of our three restaurants.

Our guest accommodations are the finest at every price point. You will have a great night's sleep in one of our king-sized beds. Each room has a spa-like tub where you can relax your troubles away for as long as you wish. You can also visit our sauna or relax in one of our many indoor heated whirlpools. All walls and windows are double-insulated, so don't worry about the outside world creeping in; you'll be in your own world of peace, quiet, and relaxation. For a real treat, try an outdoor massage on the beach.

After one visit, you'll see what you have been missing for too long. The Fiji Sunset Spa and Resort — let your dreams soar here. We hope to see you soon.

Fiji beach at sunset

GET SPA-TACULAR

- Enjoy a relaxing outdoor massage under the shelter of a hut, on the beach. Our Registered Massage Therapists offer a variety of treatments.

- For rejuvenating your body, we offer both a hydrating body wrap, a seaweed wrap, and an exfoliating body wrap.

- Couples massages are available both outdoors and in the privacy of your room.

- We also offer facials for both men and women.

The Sundown Fiji Spa and Resort ✱ Denarau Island North✱ P.O. Box 9481 ✱Nadi, Fiji
Directions ❚ Reservations ❚ Lunch Menu ❚ Dinner Menu ❚ Gift Cards ❚ Contact Us

Tatiana Belova/Shutterstock.com; Valery Shanin/Shutterstock.com

Prem has noticed that the sunset image is not centered in the middle column. He thinks that centering the image would make the content appear more balanced. You'll style the `figure` element so the image and the caption are centered.

To center the `figure` **element:**

1. Return to the **spa3col.htm** file in your text editor. Position the insertion point after the *footer* selector code, and then type the following CSS code, as shown in Figure 7-51:

```
figure {
    text-align: center;
}
```

Figure 7-51	CSS code for the figure selector

```
footer {
    margin-top: 1em;
    padding: 1em auto;
    border-top: solid 2px black;
    clear: both;
    font-weight: bold;
    text-align: center;
}

figure {
    text-align: center;
}

</style>
```

2. Save the file, return to your Web browser, and then click the **Refresh** or **Reload** button to view the changes in the file. The Web page should look similar to Figure 7-52.

Figure 7-52 Completed Web page showing the stylized figure

figure is centered in the main column

Tatiana Belova/Shutterstock.com; Valery Shanin/Shutterstock.com

Prem would like to know if it's possible to print just the text of the document. He's concerned the layout may be too wide to print. He also thinks it might take too long to print the header and the navbar. You'll next add styles that cause only specified parts of the Web page to print.

Using Print Styles

Printing a three-column or even a two-column layout Web page can be problematic. To make sure a Web page prints correctly for your users, as a Web page designer you need to create a **print style**, which is a style designed to create output for printed copy. For instance, you might not want users to have to print the navbar, the banner, or the images. When you create a print style, you can hide individual elements or even entire page divisions so only the text content is printed.

REFERENCE

Creating an External Print Style Sheet

To create print styles:
- Change the text color to black and the background color to white.
- Specify a font size in points.
- Specify the font family as a serif font.
- Style the navbar, banner, and images to have a `display` property value of `none`.
- Set the line height to 120% or greater.
- Use the `@page` rule to set the page size and margin.

To avoid confusion between which elements you want to print and exclude from printing, it's best to create print styles in an external style sheet rather than adding an additional embedded style sheet. Therefore, you need to use the `link` element to create a link to the external style sheet that contains the print styles. You've already worked with the `link` element to create a link to an external style sheet using the following syntax:

```
<link rel = "stylesheet" href = "printstyles.css" type =
"text/css" />
```

To create a link to a print style sheet, you enter the code for the `link` element and add the `media` attribute and value to the `link` element code. The `media` attribute determines where output will be directed. The `media` attribute has 10 possible values, but the most common (and most browser-supported) are the following:

- `all` (the default choice)—Styles are applied to all devices.
- `screen`—Tells browsers to apply the styles only when displaying the page in a browser window.
- `print`—Tells browsers to apply the assigned set of styles only when the document is printed.

For example, if you wanted to have two style sheets—one for the screen styles and one for the print styles—you would enter code similar to that shown below. Note the two different values for the `media` attribute:

```
<link rel = "stylesheet" href = "mystyles.css" type = "text/css"
media = "screen" />
<link rel = "stylesheet" href = "printstyles.css" type = "text/css"
media = "print" />
```

TIP

With the exception of `print`, `screen`, and `all`, most values for the `media` attribute are not supported by all browsers.

If you didn't want to create a separate style sheet for the CSS screen styles, you could simply add the `media` attribute and its value to the start `<style>` tag for the embedded style sheet, as follows:

```
<style type = "text/css" media = "screen">
```

Whenever you have more than one set of links to external style sheets, it's good coding practice to add the `media` attribute and its value to each of the `link` element codes. You will thus avoid confusion about the purpose of each style sheet. You also must be concerned with the order of the `link` elements in the head section. If you have more than one `link` element, the `link` elements further down the list have greater precedence.

After you create the link to the print style sheet, you must create the style sheet itself. In doing so, you have to choose which parts of the page you don't want to be printed when a user prints the page. For Prem's Web page, you don't want the header and navbar to be printed, so you'll hide those elements by creating grouped selectors and using the `display` property with a value of `none`.

You'll create the printstyles.css file now, which will contain the print styles for the Sunset Spa Web page. You'll then hide the `nav` and `header` elements using a grouped selector to set the `display` property to a value of `none`.

To create the printstyles.css file:

▶ **1.** Open a new document in your text editor, and then type the following CSS code, substituting **your name** and **today's date** where indicated:

```
/* Print styles */
/* Author: your name */
/* Date: today's date */
```

▶ **2.** Save the file as **printstyles.css**.

▶ **3.** Position the insertion point after the last comment code, press the **Enter** key and then type the following CSS code, as shown in Figure 7-53:

```
/* hides elements */

nav, header {
    display: none;
}
```

Figure 7-53	CSS code for grouped nav and header selectors

```
/* Print styles */
/* Author: your name */
/* Date: today's date */

/* hides elements */

nav, header {
    display: none;
}
```

▶ **4.** Save the file.

If you have a sidebar or section containing banner ads or links that you'd want to hide, you would add the corresponding selectors to the grouped selector.

Most people who print a Web page will be using standard 8.5″ by 11″ paper. You can define the size of the paper as well as the print margins.

The **@page rule** is a style rule using the @page selector that sets the size of the print area and the margins for printing. Within an @page rule, you can use the **size property** to set the size of the page. The syntax for the @page rule is as follows:

```
@page {
    size: widthvalue heightvalue;
    margin: marginvalue;
}
```

The *widthvalue* and *heightvalue* define the size of the paper. The values can use inches (in) or centimeters (cm) measurements. The margins can be set using the shorthand `margin` property or the individual margin properties, as usual.

You'll add the @page rule for this print style sheet.

To add the @page selector style to the printstyles.css file:

1. Return to the **printstyles.css** file in your text editor. Position the insertion point after the *nav, header* grouped selectors style, press the **Enter** key and then type the following CSS code, as shown in Figure 7-54:

```
@page {
    size: 8.5in 11in;
    margin: 0.5in;
}
```

Figure 7-54   CSS code for the @page selector

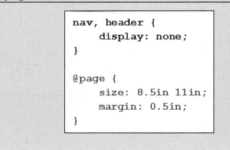

```
nav, header {
    display: none;
}

@page {
    size: 8.5in 11in;
    margin: 0.5in;
}
```

2. Save the file.

TIP

Use points (pt) instead of em values for the print style sheet because printers use point values by default.

Your next task is to create a printer-friendly style for the body element. You'll set the text color to black, the background color to white, and the background-image property to a value of none. You'll also set the font size to the default size, which is 12pt.

In addition, you'll use a serif font, which is easier to read on a printed page, and you'll increase the line height to 120% to create some white space between the lines of text.

To add the *body* selector style to the printstyles.css file:

1. Position the insertion point after the @page selector style, press the **Enter** key and then type the following CSS code, as shown in Figure 7-55:

```
/* formats page for printing */
body {
    color: black;
    background-color: white;
    background-image: none;
    font-size: 12pt;
    font-family: "Times New Roman", Times, serif;
    line-height: 120%;
}
```

Figure 7-55 **CSS code for the body selector**

```
@page {
    size: 8.5in 11in;
    margin: 0.5in;
}

/* formats page for printing */
body {
    color: black;
    background-color: white;
    background-image: none;
    font-size: 12pt;
    font-family: "Times New Roman", Times, serif;
    line-height: 120%;
}
```

2. Save the file.

When printing a Web page, links should be underlined. This is particularly important if the links are embedded in paragraphs or aren't otherwise obvious. Next you'll create a style that will underline links and also color the links blue.

To add the *body* selector style to the printstyles.css file:

▶ **1.** Return to the **printstyles.css** file in your text editor. Position the insertion point after the *body* selector styles, press the **Enter** key and then type the following CSS code, as shown in Figure 7-56:

```
/* sets links to default colors */
a {
    text-decoration: underline;
    color: blue;
}
```

| Figure 7-56 | CSS code for links |

```
body {
    color: black;
    background-color: white;
    background-image: none;
    font-size: 12pt;
    font-family: "Times New Roman", Times, serif;
    line-height: 120%;
}

/* sets links to default colors */
a {
    text-decoration: underline;
    color: blue;
}
```

▶ **2.** Save the file.

Prem doesn't want images to be printed, because he thinks they'll take up too much space on the page. You'll style the img element to have a display property value of none.

To add the *img* selector style to the printstyles.css file:

▶ **1.** Position the insertion point after the *a* selector styles, and then type the following CSS code, as shown in Figure 7-57:

```
/* removes images from printout */
img {
    display: none;
}
```

Figure 7-57	CSS code for the img selector

```
/* sets links to default colors */
a {
     text-decoration: underline;
     color: blue;
}


/* removes images from printout */
img {
     display: none;
}
```

2. Save the file, and then close the printstyles.css file.

Now that you've created a print style sheet, you'll add the code to link the spa3col.htm file to printstyles.css.

To link to the printstyles.css style sheet:

1. Return to the **spa3col.htm** file in your text editor. Position the insertion point after the `</title>` HTML tag, and then type the following HTML code, as shown in Figure 7-58:

```
<link rel = "stylesheet" href = "printstyles.css"
type = "text/css" media = "print" />
```

Figure 7-58	HTML link element for the printstyles.css file

```
<title>Fiji Sunset Spa and Resort</title>

<link rel = "stylesheet" href = "printstyles.css" type = "text/css" media = "print" />

<style type = "text/css" media = "screen">
```

2. Save the **spa3col.htm** file.

You should always verify your print style sheet code by printing pages from several different browsers and browser versions. The print preview feature of most browsers provides a *likeness* of how the page will be printed, which is great, but not always completely accurate. To be certain that your print styles are correct, you should print from several of the most popular browsers, browser versions, and printers, compare the results, and if necessary, adjust your styles accordingly.

Now that the link has been established, you'll use the print preview feature of your browser to see how the page should be printed. The print preview is entirely browser dependent, and browsers can preview pages in significantly different ways.

To use the print preview feature of the browser:

1. Switch to your browser, and then refresh or reload the **spa3col.htm** page.

2. Click **File** on the menu bar, and then click **Print preview**. Some current Web browsers do not have a File menu. If yours does not have a File menu, use the Help feature to determine how to select the Print Preview feature. Compare your print preview to Figure 7-59, which shows a print preview in Internet Explorer. Note that a print preview for the same document in another browser, such as Chrome, Safari, or Firefox, might look different.

   Trouble? Some Web browsers show a preview by default if you select the File on the menu bar and then click Print. Other current Web browsers do not have a File menu. If you have difficulty, consult the documentation for your Web browser.

Figure 7-59	Print preview of the Web page

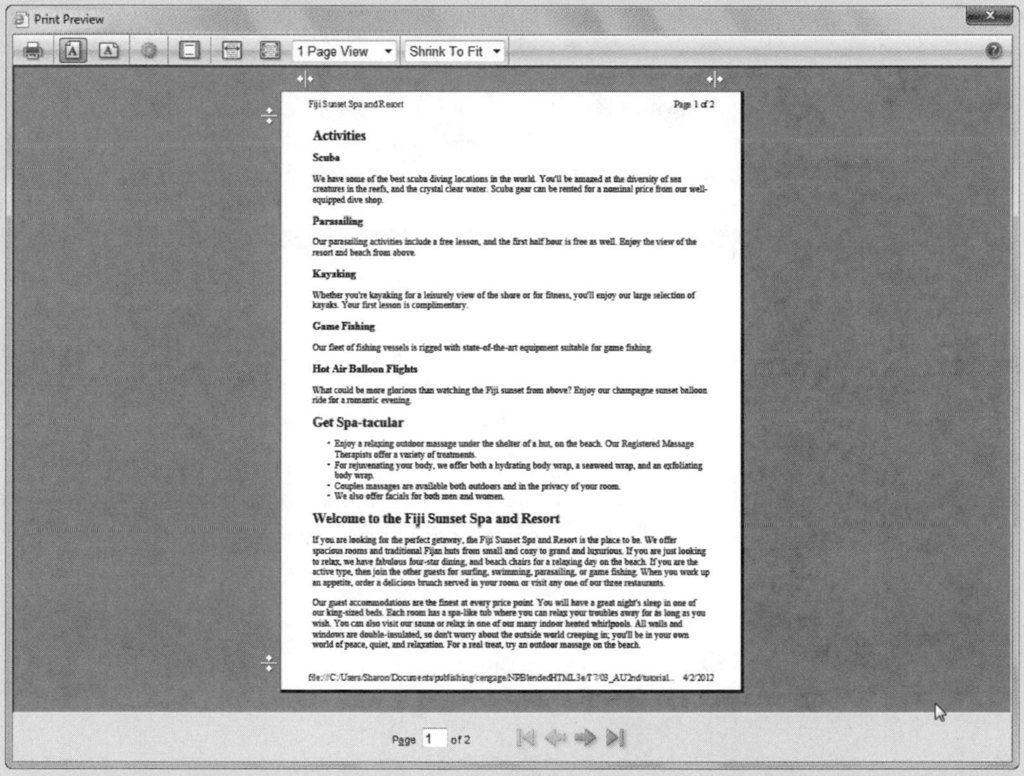

3. Close the print preview without printing the document.

Prem is really pleased with the work you've done on the Sunset Spa Web page. He will contact you if he needs any help with other Web pages.

PROSKILLS

Decision Making: Selecting Screen Resolutions and Window Sizes

In the 1990s, it was easy to decide upon which screen size and resolution you should base a Web page design because the most popular device people used to view Web pages was a desktop computer. Today, the diversity of devices used to view Web pages is enormous. People use cell phones, tablets, e-book readers, netbooks, laptops, desktops, and projectors to view Web pages. As the trends change, it's important to periodically research which Web browsing technologies are the most popular, including which versions of Web browsers people are using. Here are some quick facts that may help you to decide which statistics to consider for your Web site design:

- On desktop computers, most people do not maximize the Web browser to the full screen size.
- Tablet computer screens range in size from 7 inches to 10 inches, measured on the diagonal. As tablets become more popular, consider designing for a smaller screen size.
- Many Web site hosting companies can provide visitor statistics so you can track which Web browser and version your visitors are using to view your Web site.
- Most people do not spend large amounts of time viewing Web pages with their cell phones. They use the cell phone Web browser to quickly find information that is important in that moment. Web pages designed for cell phones should contain small amounts of information.

REVIEW

Session 7.2 Quick Check

1. What's the difference between a liquid layout and a fixed layout?
2. What is the purpose of the container `div` in a liquid layout?
3. What is a print style?
4. In what type of style sheet should print styles be entered?
5. What attribute and value are used in the `<link>` tag to link to a print style sheet?
6. What rule is commonly used only with print style sheets?

Practice the skills you learned in the tutorial using the same case scenario.

PRACTICE

Review Assignments

Data Files needed for the Review Assignments: gift_T7.htm, images\fijispa.jpg

Prem has asked for your assistance in developing other pages at the Fiji Sunset Spa and Resort Web site. He would like to see one more two-column design. One priority is to create a page that features the gift shop. The gift shop stocks all sorts of items, ranging from fashion to food, and it's the primary seller of the resort's gift cards. Prem has provided a file that requires stylizing. After each step, save the file, switch to your browser, refresh or reload the page, verify you entered the style code correctly, and then switch back to your text editor and complete the next step. A preview of the Web page you will create appears in Figure 7-60.

Figure 7-60 Gift Store Web page

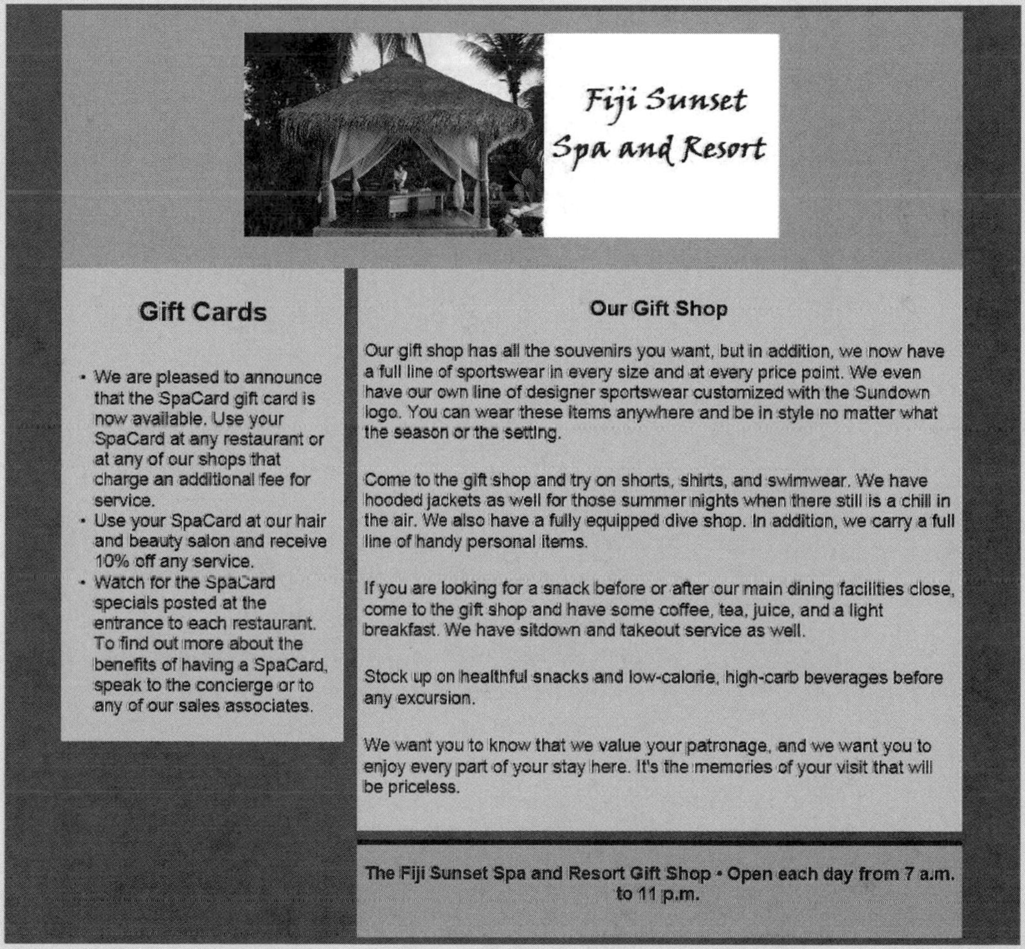

Tatiana Belova/Shutterstock.com

Complete the following:

1. Use your text editor to open the **gift_T7.htm** file, which is provided in your Data Files in the tutorial7\review folder. In the head section and before the page title, enter ***your name*** and ***today's date*** in the comment section where noted.
2. Save the file as **gift.htm** in the same folder. Open the file in your browser, and then observe the appearance of the original file.

3. Switch back to your text editor. In the embedded style sheet and below the comment *add new styles below*, style the body element to have a font size of **1.1em** and appear in **Arial** (sans-serif). The body element should have a dark green background color of **#556b2f**.

4. Save the **gift.htm** file. Switch back to your browser, and then refresh or reload the page. Verify the body element style appears correctly in your file.

5. Switch back to your text editor. In the embedded style sheet code, you'll continue to add styles below the style for the body element. Create a style for the universal selector to have a margin of **0** and padding of **0**.

6. Create a style for the **#container** id selector as follows:
   a. Set the width to **90%**.
   b. Set the margin to **0** on the top and bottom and **auto** on the left and right.

7. Create a style for the **header** selector to add padding of **0.5%** on all sides. Set the background color to **#cbbf8b**.

8. Create a descendant selector for images within the *header* selector so the img element has margins of **0** on the top and bottom, and margins of **auto** on the left and right. Set the display value to **block**.

9. Create the following styles for the **aside** selector:
   a. Set the width to **30%**.
   b. Add padding of **0.75%** on all sides.
   c. Set the background color to **#f3da79**.
   d. Float the aside element **left**.

10. Create the following styles for the **#main** id selector:
   a. Set the margin on the left to **33%**.
   b. Add padding of **0.75%** on all sides.
   c. Set the background color to **#f3da79**.

11. Create the following styles for the **footer** selector:
   a. Set the margins to **1%** on the top, **0** on the right, **1%** on the bottom, and **33%** on the left.
   b. Create a border on the top that is **solid**, **thick**, and **black**.
   c. Add padding of **1%** on the bottom.
   d. Set the background color to **#cbbf8b**.
   e. Clear all elements on both the left and right.
   f. Center the footer text.

12. Save the **gift.htm** file. Switch to your browser, and then refresh or reload the page. Compare your file to Figure 7-60 to verify your file is correct.

13. Submit the results of the preceding steps to your instructor, in either printed or electronic form, as requested.

Use what you've learned to create and style a Web page for an auto repair service.

APPLY

Case Problem 1

Data Files needed for this Case Problem: reddie_T7.htm, images\reddielogo.jpg, images\tools.jpg

Reddie Motors and Repair Reddie Motors and Repair is a small chain of auto repair shops in Mexico City, Mexico. Reddie Motors has built its reputation on being able to service almost any vehicle on the road. Because it has been able to offer car repair as a commodity, the franchise is becoming more popular every day. Jose Acevedo, the general manager of Reddie Motors, has asked you to create a new layout and home page for their Web site. You have decided on a two-column layout. After you complete a step to create a style, verify in your browser the style code has been entered correctly, and then switch back to your text editor. A preview of the Web page you will create appears in Figure 7-61.

Figure 7-61	Reddie Motors and Repair Web page

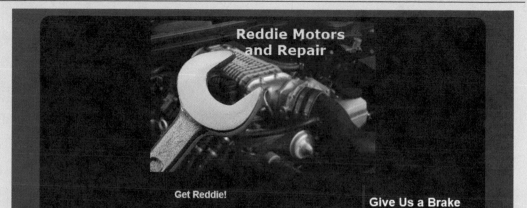

Reddie Motors and Repair

Get Reddie!

Bring Your Car to Reddie Motors and Repair

If you need your engine tuned or repaired, don't wait! Come in to Reddie Motors and Repair. We'll diagnose what ails your car and have it running right in no time. Need brakes? We can have brakes installed in under an hour.

Need an engine tune up? Let Reddie Motors and Repair take care of that, too. Can't get the car out of the driveway? Let Reddie Motors and Repair tow in your car. We offer tow hook and flatbed towing at very reasonable rates. If we can't fix a towed car in the first day, we don't charge for storage. We'll order the parts you need the same day so you can get back on the road in no time.

Professional Tools

There's no time like today to get a tune up. Changing your air filter and getting a tune up can save you a considerable amount of money on gas, and who doesn't want to save money on gas these days? Keeping your car in top shape also pays dividends later when you want to trade in or sell your car. You want your car to last for as long as possible. The only way to do that is to treat your car like one of the family. Be good to your car, and it will be good to you.

We stock every major brand of tire. If you need tires, we've got your brand in your size and at your price. We stock tires for passenger cars, SUVs, vans, and trucks. No matter what tire you need, we've got it in stock or we'll get the tires you need that same day. Come visit the men and women of Reddie Motors. There's a Reddie Motors near you today.

We're celebrating the grand opening of five new Reddie Motors stores this month and next. We have all kinds of specials and discounts on nearly every kind of car care.

Give Us a Brake

How are your brakes? Your brakes are one of the most critical components of your car, and it's important that they always be in top shape. We can check your brakes and brake fluid levels, and make all necessary repairs and replacements. Don't let a brake problem go unrepaired. Come to Reddie Motors and Repair today so we can ensure that you always drive safely.

Get on Our List

Get your name on our mailing list. We're always offering promotional items and service. We have a complete catalog of parts that will save you money on everything you purchase. You can shop for brand names or for off-brand parts — we stock them all. We'll automatically let you know when it's time to bring in your car for service. Qualify for discounts, coupons, and free gifts — all from the men and women at Reddie Motors and Repair.

Reddie Motors and Repair ★ 60 Cuajimalpa ★ Mexico City, Distrito Federal 05000

AlexussK/Shutterstock.com; Christopher Dodge/Shutterstock.com

Complete the following:

1. Use your text editor to open the **reddie_T7.htm** file, which is provided in your Data Files in the tutorial7\case1 folder. In the head section and above the page title, enter *your name* and *today's date* in the comment section where noted.

2. Save the file as **reddie.htm** in the same folder. Open the file in your browser, and then observe the appearance of the original file.

3. Switch back to your text editor. Within the tags for the embedded style sheet, style the **body** element to have text appear in a font size of **1.1em** and in **Arial** (sans-serif). The text should be **white** with a blue background color of **#5d4190**.

4. Save the **reddie.htm** file. Switch back to your browser, and then refresh or reload the page. Verify the body element style appears correctly in your file.

5. Switch back to your text editor. In the code for the embedded style sheet and below the `body` element style, create a style for the **#container** id selector as follows:
   a. Set the width to **90%**.
   b. Create margins on the top and bottom of **0**, and margins on the left and right set to **auto**.
   c. Set the background color to **#38265a**.
   d. Set the border radius to **20px**.

6. Create a descendant style for the **header** selector to align images. Set top and bottom margins to **0** and left and right margins to **auto**. Set the `display` property to **block** and padding on all sides to **1%**.

7. Create the following styles for the **aside** selector:
   a. Set the width to **25%**.
   b. Add padding of **0** on the top, and **1%** on the right, bottom, and left sides.
   c. Float the `aside` element **right**.
   d. Set the text color to **white**.

8. Create a descendant style for the *aside* selector so **h2** text is displayed in **white**.

9. Create the following styles for the **#main** id selector:
   a. Set the margin on the right to **27%**.
   b. Create a border on the right that is **solid**, **5px**, and **purple**.
   c. Add padding of **1%** on all sides.
   d. Set the color to **white**.

10. For the *#main* id selector, create a descendant grouped selector to style both the **h1** and **h2** elements in the *main* section to appear with a margin on the top of **0**. The `h1` and `h2` text should appear in **yellow** and should be centered.

11. Create a descendant style for the *#main* id selector so images within the *main* section have margins of **1%** on all sides and float **left**.

12. Create a style for the **figure** selector so it floats **left**.

13. Create a style for the **figcaption** element so it clears elements both to the left and right, and is centered.

14. Create the following styles for the **footer** selector:
   a. Create a margin on the top of **1%**.
   b. Create a border on the top that is **solid**, **thick**, and **purple**.
   c. Add padding of **1%** on all sides.
   d. Clear elements on both the left and the right.
   e. Set the color to **#ffc800**.
   f. Center the footer text.

15. Save the **reddie.htm** file.

16. Switch to your browser, and then refresh or reload the page. Compare your file to Figure 7-61 to verify your file is correct.

17. Submit the results of the reddie.htm file to your instructor, in either printed or electronic form, as requested.

Case Problem 2

Data Files needed for this Case Problem: letter_T7.htm, printstyles.css, images\block. gif, images\modblock.gif

Writing Effective Business Communications   Professor Janet Shah, chair of the English Department at Canyon Lake College in Davis, Oklahoma, teaches several sections of her English 245 class, Writing Effective Business Communications. She has asked you to create a new Web page for this course. You will create a three-column liquid layout that has nested elements in the center column. After you complete a step to create a style, verify in your browser the style code has been entered correctly, and then switch back to your text editor. A preview of the Web page you'll create appears in Figure 7-62.

Figure 7-62   **Effective Business Communications Web page**

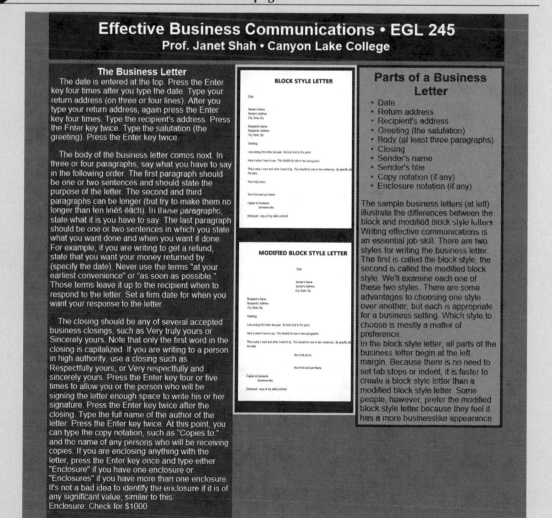

Complete the following:

1. Use your text editor to open the **letter_T7.htm** file, which is provided in your Data Files in the tutorial7\case2 folder. In the head section and above the page title, enter *your name* and *today's date* in the comment section where noted.

2. Save the file as **letter.htm** in the same folder. Open the file in your browser, and then observe the appearance of the original file.

3. Switch back to your text editor. In the code for the embedded style sheet, style the universal selector to have margins of **0** and padding of **0**.

4. Style the **body** element to have text appear with a font size of **1.1em** in **Arial** (a sans-serif font). Set the background color to a green/brown using the value **#818039**.

5. Save the **letter.htm** file. Switch back to your browser, and then refresh or reload the page. Verify the body element style appears correctly in your file.

6. Switch back to your text editor. In the head section and below the page title, use the link element to create a link to the printstyles.css file. Insert the appropriate value for the media attribute in the <link> tag.

7. In the start <style> tag, add the media attribute with a value of **screen** to the right of the *text/css* value.

8. In the embedded style sheet and below the *body* style, create the following styles for the **#container** id selector:

   a. Set the width to **90%**.

   b. Set the margin to **0** on the top and bottom and **auto** on the left and right.

9. Create the following styles for the **header** selector:

   a. Set the margin on the bottom to **0.5em**.

   b. Add padding of **1em** on all sides.

   c. Set the text color to **white**.

   d. Set the background color to **black**.

10. Create the following styles for the **#main** id selector:

    a. Set the width to **40%**.

    b. Add padding of **0.5%** on all sides.

    c. Set the text color to **white**.

    d. Set the background color to **#48332f**.

    e. Float the contents **left**.

11. Create the following styles for the **#samples** id selector:

    a. Set the margin on the left to **41%**.

    b. Set the margin on the right to **32%**.

    c. Add padding of **0.5%** on all sides.

    d. Set the background color to **yellow**.

12. Create the following styles for the **#letterstyles** id selector:

    a. Set the width to **30%**.

    b. Create a border that is **solid**, **thick**, and **black**.

    c. Add padding of **0.5%** on all sides.

    d. Set the background color to **orange**.

    e. Float the contents **right**.

13. Create a grouped descendant selector for the #*main* id selector and the #*samples* id selector so paragraph text appears with a margin of **1em** on the bottom and a text indent of **1em**.

14. Create a grouped selector to style the **#block** id selector and the **#modblock** id selector as follows:

    a. Create a border that is **solid**, **thick**, and **navy**.

    b. Add padding of **0.5%** on all sides.

    c. Set the background color to **black**.

    d. Set the `overflow` property to **hidden**.

15. Create a style for the **img** element to have margins of **0** on the top and bottom and **auto** on the left and right. Set the display value to **block**.

16. Style the **ul** element selector to have a margin on the left of **2em** and a margin on the bottom of **1em**.

17. Create a grouped selector to style both the **h1** and **h2** element selectors so `h1` and `h2` text is centered.

18. Save the **letter.htm** file. Switch to your browser, and then refresh or reload the page. Compare your file to Figure 7-62 to verify your file is correct.

19. From the menu bar, click File, and then click Print preview. Preview the print style that has been created. Exit Print Preview.

20. Submit the results of the preceding steps to your instructor, in either printed or electronic form, as requested.

Use what you've learned and expand your skills to create and style a Web page for a bowling complex.

CHALLENGE

Case Problem 3

Data Files needed for this Case Problem: lana_T7.htm, navbar.css, images/lanalogo.jpg, images/bowlingballs.jpg

Lana Lanes   Lana Lanes is a large bowling and entertainment complex on the outskirts of Fargo, North Dakota. The bowling alley, restaurants, game rooms, and party room are all designed with a 1950s retro-style décor to attract customers. Lana Lanes is opening a new restaurant called the Strike 'n Spare and a new dance club called the Tailfin Lounge. Lana Clark, the owner of Lana Lanes, has asked you to develop a new home page for the company's Web site. You'll create a three-column liquid layout. After you complete a step to create a style, verify in your browser the style code has been entered correctly, and then switch back to your text editor. A preview of the Web page you will create appears in Figure 7-63.

Figure 7-63   Lana Lanes Web page

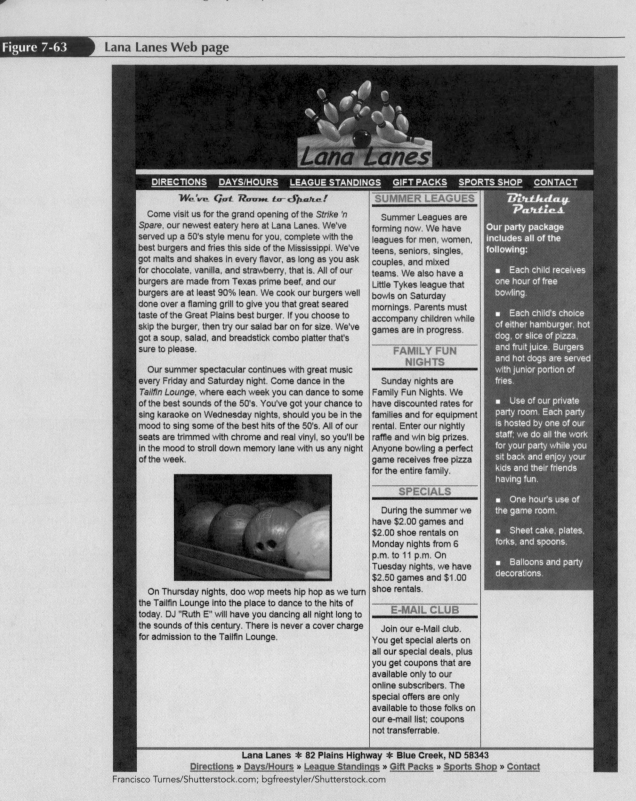

Francisco Turnes/Shutterstock.com; bgfreestyler/Shutterstock.com

Complete the following:

1. Use your text editor to open the **lana_T7.htm** file, which is provided in your Data Files in the tutorial7\case3 folder. In the head section and below the page title, enter **your name** and **today's date** in the comment section where noted.

2. Save the file as **lana.htm** in the same folder. Open the file in your browser, and then observe the appearance of the original file.

3. Switch back to your text editor. Just below the start style tag, enter an **@import** rule to import the navbar.css file, which is provided in your Data Files in the tutorial7\ case3 folder.

4. Style the **body** element as follows:

   a. Set the font size to **1.1em**.

   b. Set the font to **Arial, Helvetica** (sans-serif).

   c. Set the background color to a dark green using the value **#0d4a2c**.

   d. Set the line height to **1.25em**.

5. Save the **lana.htm** file. Switch back to your browser, and then refresh or reload the page. Verify the body element style appears correctly in your file.

6. Switch back to your text editor. Below the body element style, style the universal selector to have margins of **0** and padding of **0**.

7. Style the **#container** id selector as follows:

   a. Set the width to **90%**.

   b. Set the margin to **0** on the top and bottom and **auto** on the left and right.

   c. Set the border to **1px** and **solid** on all sides.

   d. Set the background color to **#c2efd8**.

8. Style the **header** selector to have a background color of **black**.

9. Style the **#info** id selector as follows:

   a. Set the width to **50%**.

   b. Add padding of **0.5%** on all sides.

   c. Float the contents **left**.

10. Create a descendant selector for the *#info* id selector so h1 text appears as follows:

   a. Set the bottom margin to **0.5em**.

   b. Set the font family to **Magneto** (a serif font).

   c. Center the h1 text.

⊕ EXPLORE   11. Create a grouped style for the **#info p** and **#activities p** selectors so paragraph text in both the left and middle columns appears as follows:

   a. Set the margin on the bottom to **1em**.

   b. Set the text indent to **1em**.

12. Style the **#activities** id selector as follows:

   a. Set the width to **23%**.

   b. Set the border on the left to **solid**, **thin**, and **black**.

   c. Set the border on the right to **solid**, **thin**, and **black**.

   d. Add padding of **0.5%** on all sides.

   e. Float the contents **left**.

13. Style the **#parties** id selector as follows:

   a. Set the width to **23%**.

   b. Add padding of **0.5%** on all sides.

   c. Set the text color to **white**.

   d. Set the background color to **green**.

   e. Float the contents **right**.

14. Create a descendant selector for the *#parties* id selector so unordered list items appear as follows:

   a. Set the margin on the left to **1em**.

   b. Set padding on the top to **0**.

   c. Set the list style type to **square**.

   d. Set the list style position to **inside**.

15. Create a descendant selector for the *#parties* id selector so list items within unordered lists have a margin of **1em** on the top and bottom and **0** on the left and right.

16. Style the **footer** selector as follows:

   a. Set the margin on the top to **1em**.

   b. Set the border on the top to **solid**, **thick**, and **green**.

   c. Clear the contents of the footer on both the left and the right.

   d. Set the font weight to **bold**.

   e. Center the contents of the footer.

17. Style the **h2** heading element selector as follows:

   a. Set the margin on the bottom to **0.5em**.

   b. Set the font family to **Magneto** (a serif font).

   c. Center the **h2** text.

18. Style the **h3** heading element selector as follows:

   a. Set the margin on the bottom to **0.5em**.

   b. Set the border on the top to **solid**, **thin**, and **black**.

   c. Set the border on the bottom to **solid**, **thick**, and **black**.

   d. Set the text color to **#68964c**.

   e. Center the **h3** text.

   f. Have the **h3** text appear in uppercase.

19. Style the **img** element selector as follows:

   a. Set margins to **0** on the top, **10px** on the bottom and **auto** on the left and right.

   b. Set the border to **solid**, **thick**, and **black**.

   c. Set the value for the `display` property to **block**.

20. Save the **lana.htm** file. Switch to your browser, and then refresh or reload the page. Compare your file to Figure 7-63 to verify your file is correct.

✦ EXPLORE 21. In your browser, go to http://validator.w3.org to open the W3C validator. Validate the lana.htm file by using the Validate by File Upload method. Note any errors, and then correct them in your file if necessary.

✦ EXPLORE 22. In your browser, navigate to http://jigsaw.w3.org/css-validator. Validate the **lana.htm** file by using the By file upload method, validating for CSS3. Note any errors and correct them in your file if necessary. You can ignore the following warning, which you will see regarding the imported style sheet: *Imported style sheets are not checked in direct input and file upload modes.*

23. Submit the results of the lana.htm file to your instructor, in either printed or electronic form, as requested.

Create a Web page to promote a new snack food.

Case Problem 4

Data Files needed for this Case Problem: hooks_T7.htm, images\hookslogo.gif

Hooks, Wheels, and Ladders   The latest entry into the snack food industry is a health-conscious offering named Hooks, Wheels, and Ladders. Each box mixes several flavors, such as ranch, cheddar, and salsa. The snack is designed to appeal to kids based on the snack shapes; however, the company hopes to appeal to adults as well, based on taste, variety, and ingredients. Maye Hanley, the senior marketing manager, has hired you to create a Web site to promote Hooks, Wheels, and Ladders. She previously gave you some promotional copy that you incorporated into a basic Web page; she now wants you to create an attractive layout for the page.

Complete the following:

1. Use your text editor to open the **hooks_T7.htm** file, which is provided in your Data Files in the tutorial7\case4 folder. In the head section, give your page an appropriate title. Below the page title, enter *your name* and *today's date* in the comment section where noted.

2. Save the file as **hooks.htm** in the same folder.

3. Create the tags for an embedded style sheet. Within these tags, format the body element with the text size, font, color, and background color of your choice.

4. Plan a liquid layout for the hooks.htm file. The layout should have elements for a header, an aside, a main section, and a footer. Use the hookslogo.gif image in the header. Include margins and padding as appropriate in your layout.

5. Create styles for all the id selectors and all other selectors.

6. In the body section, create sections as necessary. Apply the id selectors to your sections as appropriate.

7. Create a container section for your layout. Create styles for the container section so the page is centered horizontally, with rounded corners in the browser.

8. Include at least one descendant selector.

9. Feel free to add other images and text content (as appropriate) to the Web page.

10. Save the **hooks.htm** file. Switch to your browser, and then refresh or reload the page. Verify all styles work correctly.

11. Open your browser, and then go to http://validator.w3.org. Use the Validate by File Upload method to check the hooks.htm document and ensure the HTML code is correct. If necessary, correct any errors detected by the validation.

12. In your browser, go to http://jigsaw.w3.org/css-validator. Use the By file upload method to check the hooks.htm file and ensure that the CSS code is correct. If necessary, correct any errors detected by the validation.

13. Submit the results of the hooks.htm file to your instructor, in either printed or electronic form, as requested.

ENDING DATA FILES

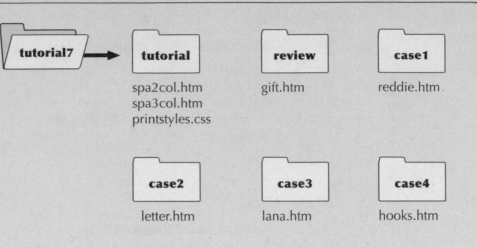

tutorial7 → tutorial

spa2col.htm
spa3col.htm
printstyles.css

review

gift.htm

case1

reddie.htm

case2

letter.htm

case3

lana.htm

case4

hooks.htm

TUTORIAL 8

Creating Data Tables

Using Tables to Display Data

OBJECTIVES

Session 8.1
- Create a table to display and organize data
- Add a caption to a table
- Create table headings
- Merge cells to span multiple rows and columns
- Style a table with collapsed borders

Session 8.2
- Style table elements using CSS styles
- Create styles for alternating rows of a table
- Create a hover effect for table rows
- Adjust the position of content within a table cell
- Work with column groups to style columns of cells

Case | *Banff Busy Seniors*

The Banff Busy Seniors is a community group in the town of Banff, Alberta. Located in the heart of the Canadian Rockies, Banff is a popular year-round tourist location with world-class winter sports facilities, hiking, horseback riding, theater, and museums. The town of Banff has approximately 7,000 residents, and among them is a large population of seniors who are very active. The Banff Busy Seniors are committed to supporting an active lifestyle, particularly among seniors. Their fitness activities include hiking along the shore of Moraine Lake and through the Bow Valley. The activities are currently advertised by word of mouth and via posters at the local grocery store and community center. Sue Casey, a member of the Banff Busy Seniors, would like to advertise their activities on their Web site as well. Sue would like you to create a Web page that contains the weekly schedule of activities, along with some information about the Banff Busy Seniors. This will be the first Web page for the new Banff Busy Seniors Web site, and the group is very excited about being able to access the activity schedule online.

STARTING DATA FILES

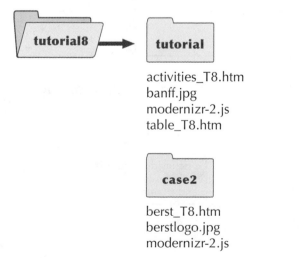

tutorial8 → **tutorial**

activities_T8.htm
banff.jpg
modernizr-2.js
table_T8.htm

review

banff.jpg
lodging_T8.htm
modernizr-2.js

case1

body_T8.htm
fitnessclass.jpg
modernizr-2.js

case2

berst_T8.htm
berstlogo.jpg
modernizr-2.js

case3

admit.htm
baxter_T8.htm
baxterlogo.jpg
modernizr-2.js

case4

modernizr-2.js

SESSION 8.1 VISUAL OVERVIEW

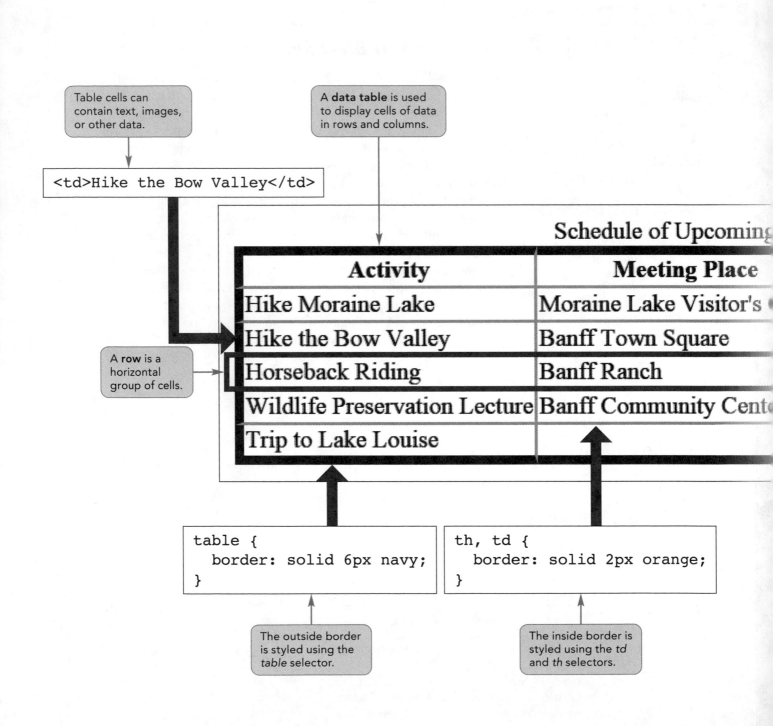

Table cells can contain text, images, or other data.

A **data table** is used to display cells of data in rows and columns.

```
<td>Hike the Bow Valley</td>
```

A **row** is a horizontal group of cells.

Schedule of Upcoming

Activity	Meeting Place
Hike Moraine Lake	Moraine Lake Visitor's
Hike the Bow Valley	Banff Town Square
Horseback Riding	Banff Ranch
Wildlife Preservation Lecture	Banff Community Cent
Trip to Lake Louise	

```
table {
   border: solid 6px navy;
}
```

```
th, td {
   border: solid 2px orange;
}
```

The outside border is styled using the *table* selector.

The inside border is styled using the *td* and *th* selectors.

A TWO-COLUMN LIQUID LAYOUT

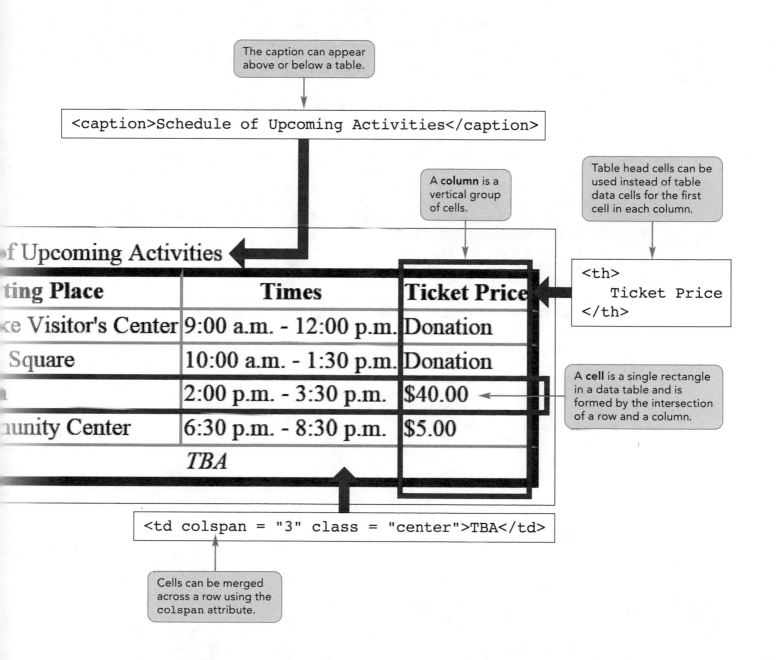

The caption can appear above or below a table.

`<caption>Schedule of Upcoming Activities</caption>`

A **column** is a vertical group of cells.

Table head cells can be used instead of table data cells for the first cell in each column.

```
<th>
    Ticket Price
</th>
```

A **cell** is a single rectangle in a data table and is formed by the intersection of a row and a column.

f Upcoming Activities

ting **Place**	**Times**	**Ticket Price**
ce Visitor's Center	9:00 a.m. - 12:00 p.m.	Donation
Square	10:00 a.m. - 1:30 p.m.	Donation
	2:00 p.m. - 3:30 p.m.	$40.00
nunity Center	6:30 p.m. - 8:30 p.m.	$5.00
	TBA	

`<td colspan = "3" class = "center">TBA</td>`

Cells can be merged across a row using the colspan attribute.

Creating a Table to Display and Organize Data

If you're familiar with the table feature of a word-processing program, you know that you can create tables made up of columns and rows that display data in an organized manner. To organize data for a Web page, you create a data table, which is a table used to align Web content in columns and rows. You might also know how easy it is to create tables using a "quick create" or "table draw" feature in a word-processing program. HTML, however, does not have a quick means to create tables. HTML table columns and rows have to be entered one cell at a time.

You might also be familiar with a spreadsheet program, such as Microsoft Excel, that uses columns and rows of cells to organize data. A spreadsheet program has extensive math, formula creation, and charting features, but HTML does not. HTML also does not have cell addresses.

Until a few years ago, HTML tables were used both as a means for organizing data and creating page layout. A **layout table** is a table in which the code is used for page layout. The use of layout tables has declined dramatically over the past few years for several reasons. For one, tables require a substantial amount of code. Additionally, layout tables can be a barrier to accessibility. Finally, browsers and search engines assume that content marked by table tags is a table of data, rather than Web page elements being positioned. Although HTML tables are still used to organize data, you should no longer use tables for page layout; CSS positioning is now the preferred method instead.

Similarly, until just a few years ago, HTML frames were also commonly used for page layout. **Frames** divide the browser window into sections, with each one displaying a different Web document, but frames pose a significant challenge for screen reader software. The use of frames for page layout has been discouraged by the World Wide Web Consortium (the W3C) for more than a decade, and frames are not supported in HTML5. As a result, today you'll rarely encounter a Web site with a layout created with HTML frames. For accessibility reasons alone, you should convert any existing pages created with frames into pages with layout created by CSS code. Layout tables and frames today are considered **legacy code**—outdated code that should be replaced with more contemporary CSS code.

Sue has typed a draft of the content for the Seniors Activities Web page, as shown in Figure 8-1.

Figure 8-1   **Text for the Banff Busy Seniors Activities Web page**

Schedule of Upcoming Activities

Activity	Meeting Place	Times	Ticket Price
Hike Moraine Lake	Moraine Lake Visitor's Center	9:00 a.m. - 12:00 p.m.	Donation
Hike the Bow Valley	Banff Town Square	10:00 a.m. - 1:30 p.m.	Donation
Horseback Riding	Banff Ranch	2:00 p.m. - 3:30 p.m.	$40.00
Wildlife Preservation Lecture	Banff Community Center	6:30 p.m. - 8:30 p.m.	$5.00
Trip to Lake Louise	TBA		

Banff Busy Seniors Activities

Banff Busy Seniors is a volunteer organization that hosts activities and supports community events. Activities include hiking, golf, trips to Calgary and Lake Louise, horseback riding, and community education with respect to nature and wildlife. We support wildlife preservation and eco-tourism.

Banff National Park

Banff National Park is located in the Canadian Rockies, in south-western Alberta, Canada. It extends eastward, from the continental divide. It is Canada's oldest national park, and encompasses 2,564 square miles of mountainous terrain, with numerous glaciers and ice fields. The town of Banff rests in the Bow Valley, with a population of approximately 7,000 residents.

Banff National Park is home to at least 56 mammal species that include grizzly bears and black bears. Bears are wild animals and can be very dangerous. Hence, hiking trails may be closed when grizzly and black bears are active in the area. Elk and moose are also plentiful. Elk can be seen roaming through the town of Banff, and will generally ignore humans as they graze in front of houses.

In this session, you'll focus on creating the table. In the next session, you'll put the table into the Activities Web page and stylize it. You'll begin by opening a file in which you'll create the data table for the Banff Busy Seniors Activities Web page.

To open the table_T8.htm file and save it with a new filename:

1. In your text editor, open the **table_T8.htm** file, which is located in the tutorial8\tutorial folder included with your Data Files. Add **your name** and the **current date** to the comment in the head element. The contents of this file will be copied and pasted into the activities.htm file in Session 8.2, so you won't create a page title for this file.

2. Save the file as **table.htm** in the same folder.

Next, you'll enter the table tags and give the table a title.

Entering Table Tags and Creating a Table Title

The `table` element is used to create an HTML table. Tables begin with the start `<table>` tag and end with the closing `</table>` tag. Tables can be placed anywhere within the `<body> </body>` tags, as shown in the following code:

```
<body>

   <table>
       . . . table code goes here . . .
   </table>

</body>
```

Similar to an image, you can use the `title` attribute to describe table content. If you do, and the user passes the mouse pointer over the table, a ScreenTip displays the title.

REFERENCE

Creating a Table

- To create a table, enter the following code:

```
<table title = "tabletitle">
    tablecontent
</table>
```

where `tablecontent` is the elements containing the table content.
- To create a table caption, enter the following code:

```
<caption>captiontext</caption>
```

where `captiontext` is the text of the caption.
- To create a table row, enter the following code:

```
<tr>
    rowdata
</tr>
```

where `rowdata` is the elements containing the row data.
- To create a table header cell, enter the following code:

```
<th>
    celldata
</th>
```

where `celldata` is the data for the header cell.
- To create a table cell, enter the following code:

```
<td>
    celldata
</td>
```

where `celldata` is the data for the cell.

TIP

Always enter the
`<table></table>` tags
at the same time so you
don't forget to insert the
end `</table>` tag.

You'll enter code for the start `<table>` tag, the `title` attribute and its value, and the end `</table>` tag.

To enter code for the table tags and the `title` attribute:

1. Return to the **table.htm** file in your text editor. Position the insertion point on a blank line below the start `<body>` tag, and then type the following HTML code, as shown in Figure 8-2:

   ```
   <table title = "Banff Busy Seniors Activities Schedule">
   ```

2. Press the **Enter** key twice, and then type the following code, as shown in Figure 8-2.

   ```
   </table>
   ```

Figure 8-2	HTML code for the table tag

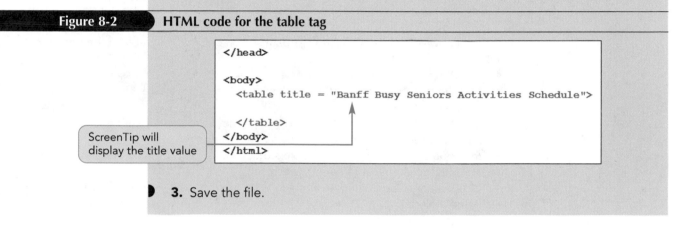

```
</head>

<body>
  <table title = "Banff Busy Seniors Activities Schedule">

  </table>
</body>
</html>
```

ScreenTip will
display the title value

3. Save the file.

Now that you've entered the start and end table tags, you're ready to add a descriptive caption to the table.

INSIGHT

Planning a Table

Because tables involve a considerable amount of code, it can be difficult to debug a problem in your table code. Approaching table creation methodically can help alleviate some problems. The following process can be a useful strategy for creating tables:

- Sketch out the table using a pencil and paper. Give each cell a number, starting with cell 1 in the upper-left corner and continuing from left to right and top to bottom. You might even consider labeling the cells as they would appear in a spreadsheet program, such as A1, B1, C1, and so on for the first row, and A2, B2, C2, and so on for the second row.
- In your text editor, create a style sheet (either embedded or external), and then enter styles to make the table borders visible.
- In the document body, enter the start and end table tags, along with the title attribute and its value.
- Type the code for the first row of the table. Use the same placeholder data in all the cells. (You can type anything in the cell, including the word *placeholder*, as long as each cell has the same placeholder data so you can globally replace the data later.)
- Name and save the file.
- Open the file in the browser. Observe the result. Debug as necessary.
- Copy the table row code and table data code, and then paste it in each row you'll need for the table.
- If you merge cells, perform one merge at a time. Save the file after each merge. View the result in the browser, and debug as necessary.
- When you are satisfied that the table structure is correct, replace the placeholder data with the actual table data for each cell.
- After you enter the table data and verify the table code is correct, create styles for the table elements.

Creating a Caption

A **caption** is a brief description of a table. You've already entered a title to describe a table when the mouse pointer passes over it. Unlike a title, caption text appears as part of the table and remains visible in the browser at all times. The caption text can be as brief as the words "Figure 1" or more descriptive, such as "Profit and Loss Statement for the Last Two Quarters of the Current Fiscal Year." A table caption is optional, but it helps describe the table data, especially if the table is complex and has a great deal of numeric data. You use the caption element to provide a data table with a caption.

If you include a table caption, the caption tags must follow the start `<table>` tag, because the caption is part of the table. As a result, a caption inherits properties applied to the table; for example, if you set the table style to display text in the Arial font, the caption text will also appear in Arial. The end `</caption>` tag does not have to be placed on a separate line; it can follow the caption text, similar to the way you've used the `figcaption` element inside the `figure` element. For instance, the following code creates a table caption containing the text *Fitness Classes Schedule*:

```
<table title = "The York Region Community Center">
  <caption>Fitness Classes Schedule</caption>
</table>
```

By default, the caption text is centered and is placed above the table. If you don't want the caption to be centered, you could create a style for the `caption` element and style the caption to align with the left edge of the table. You could also use the CSS `caption-side` property to position a caption above or below a table. Note, however, that older Web browsers, such as Internet Explorer 7 and earlier, may not display a caption positioned below the table. The `caption-side` property takes the values shown in Figure 8-3.

Figure 8-3		**The caption-side property values**

Value	Purpose
top	The caption is displayed above the table and is centered (the default value)
bottom	The caption is displayed below the table and is centered

Sue thinks the caption should be placed above the table, because the caption will act like a heading for the entire table. You'll add a caption to the table to identify it as the activities schedule.

To enter the table caption:

1. Return to the **table.htm** file in your text editor. Position the insertion point on a blank line below the start `<table>` tag, and then type the following HTML code, as shown in Figure 8-4:

   `<caption>Schedule of Upcoming Activities</caption>`

Figure 8-4	**HTML code for the caption**

```
</head>

<body>
  <table title = "Banff Busy Seniors Activities Schedule">
    <caption>Schedule of Upcoming Activities</caption>
  </table>
</body>
</html>
```

indented one level because it is inside the table element

2. Save the file.

Next, you'll create rows and cells for the table.

Creating Table Rows and Table Cells

TIP

If an ending `</tr>` tag is omitted, data that you wanted to appear in a cell will be displayed outside the table structure, which is usually above the table.

The `tr` (table row) element is used to create table rows. As with other tags—and especially with table-related tags—it's good coding practice to type the start `<tr>` tag and the end `</tr>` tag at the same time so you don't forget to insert the `</tr>` tag after entering the table data into the row. If you fail to enter an end `</tr>` tag, you won't get the structure for the table that you intended.

To make table row code easier to read, enter the code for the table row tags on separate lines, as shown in the following code:

```
<tr>
    table data goes here
</tr>
```

You enter the content for a cell using the `td` (table data) element. The table data element identifies each cell and has a start `<td>` tag and an end `</td>` tag. The contents of the table data cell go between the table data tags. The contents could be text, an image, or even another table nested inside. It's common practice to indent the table data code by at least two spaces to make it easier to see the start and end table row tags that enclose the table data tags.

The data table for the activities schedule initially will consist of six rows, each with four columns—a total of 24 cells. You can use the th (table header) element to format the first row of a table, which often describes the contents of the columns. In most browsers, the table header element centers text and makes text bold. Table header tags can also be placed at the start of each row to create row headings in addition to column headings. If you want to style a header column, use th (table header) elements rather than td (table data) elements for the first cell in each of the remaining rows as well, as shown in the following code:

```
<tr>
  <th>Last Year</th>
  <td>900,000</td>
  <td>500,000</td>
  <td>2,000,000</td>
</tr>

<tr>
  <th>This Year</th>
  <td>1,250,000</td>
  <td>1,600,000</td>
  <td>1,800,000</td>
</tr>
```

You could then create a style for the table header element and a different style for the table data element, such as the following:

```
th {
  color: white;
  background-color: navy;
}

td {
  text-align: right;
}
```

The completed table would then appear as shown in Figure 8-5.

Figure 8-5   **A table with table heading and table data cells**

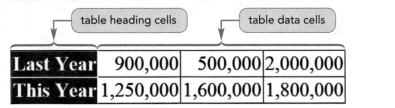

When you create the structure for a table, it's a good idea to enter the table data for the first row, save the file, and then open the file in the browser to see the result. If there are any problems with the table structure, it's much easier to correct code errors early, before you create dozens of rows in the table.

You'll enter the table data now for the header row.

To enter the table header data:

1. Return to the **table.htm** file in your text editor. Position the insertion point on a blank line below the end `</caption>` tag, and then type the following HTML code, as shown in Figure 8-6:

```
<tr>
   <th>Activity</th>
   <th>Meeting Place</th>
   <th>Times</th>
   <th>Ticket Price</th>
</tr>
```

Figure 8-6 HTML code for the table row and table cells

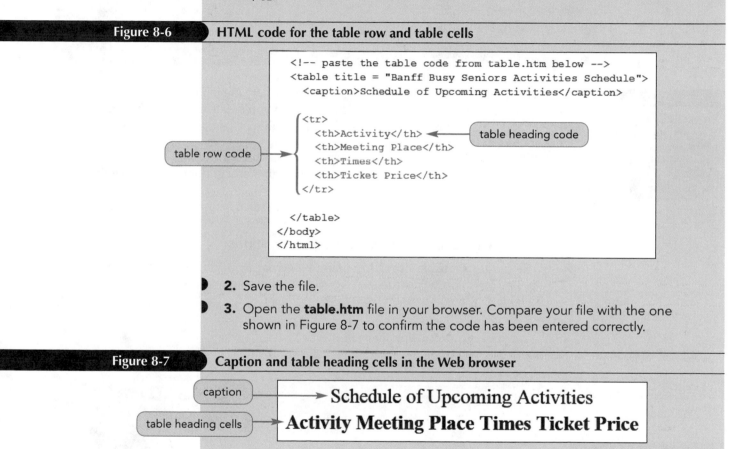

2. Save the file.

3. Open the **table.htm** file in your browser. Compare your file with the one shown in Figure 8-7 to confirm the code has been entered correctly.

Figure 8-7 Caption and table heading cells in the Web browser

caption → **Schedule of Upcoming Activities**

table heading cells → **Activity Meeting Place Times Ticket Price**

TIP

Any element can be placed into a table cell, including an image, a list, or a link.

Although the table has content, it does not have any horizontal or vertical ruled lines, so it's not easy to see the boundaries of the table cells. This is the default rendering for a table. You'll add the ruled lines to the table so you can see where each table cell is located.

Creating Table Borders

Table borders are the horizontal and vertical lines that surround the table. You use the `border` property and a value in pixels to create the table borders. The `table` element is displayed without a table border by default in most browsers, so you must use CSS styles to create it.

When you create a CSS border style for the `table` element, you affect only the appearance of the outer borders. To have horizontal and vertical lines—known as gridlines—appear within a table, you must also add a border style to the table header and table data elements.

REFERENCE

Creating Table Borders

- To create external borders (borders around the outside edge of the entire table), enter the following CSS code:

```
table {
   border: value;
}
```

where *value* is a thickness using any CSS measurement unit.

- To create gridlines, enter the following CSS code:

```
th, td {
   border: value;
}
```

TIP

Use values rather than keywords to specify border widths because browsers interpret the keywords *thin*, *medium*, and *thick* differently.

When you first create a data table, it's useful to display the table borders and gridlines so you can clearly see the table structure. If you create a style for the `table` element and use the `border` property with a pixel value of 1 or greater, you'll see the table borders in the browser.

You'll create styles for the `table` element, the table header element, and the table data element so a border appears around the table and gridlines appear within the table.

To show the table borders and table gridlines:

1. Return to the **table.htm** file in your text editor. Position the insertion point on a blank line below the start `<style>` tag, and then type the following HTML code, as shown in Figure 8-8:

```
table {
   border: solid 6px navy;
}

th, td {
   border: solid 2px orange;
}
```

Figure 8-8 **CSS code to add a border and gridlines**

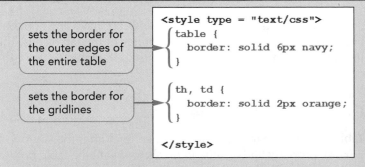

sets the border for the outer edges of the entire table

sets the border for the gridlines

```
<style type = "text/css">
table {
   border: solid 6px navy;
}

th, td {
   border: solid 2px orange;
}

</style>
```

> **2.** Save the file, return to your Web browser, and then click the **Refresh** or **Reload** button to view the changes in the file. Confirm the table borders and gridlines appear as shown in Figure 8-9.

Figure 8-9   Table border and table heading borders in the Web browser

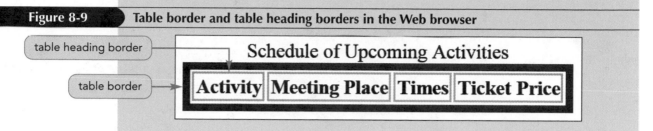

table heading border

table border

Schedule of Upcoming Activities

| Activity | Meeting Place | Times | Ticket Price |

Now that you've confirmed the border and gridlines appear the way you intended, you'll insert the remaining rows of the table.

To enter the table data tags:

Be sure to place the end </tr> tag at the end of the table row.

> **1.** Return to the **table.htm** file in your text editor. Position the insertion point on a blank line below the last end **</tr>** tag, and then type the following HTML code, as shown in Figure 8-10:

```
<tr>
  <td></td>
  <td></td>
  <td></td>
  <td></td>
</tr>
```

Figure 8-10   HTML code for the table row to be copied

```
<!-- paste the table code from table.htm below -->
<table title = "Banff Busy Seniors Activities Schedule">
  <caption>Schedule of Upcoming Activities</caption>

  <tr>
    <th>Activity</th>
    <th>Meeting Place</th>
    <th>Times</th>
    <th>Ticket Price</th>
  </tr>

  <tr>
    <td></td>
    <td></td>
    <td></td>
    <td></td>
  </tr>

  </table>
</body>
</html>
```

2. Save the file.

3. Select the code you just typed.

4. Press the **Ctrl+C** keys to copy the code.

5. On a blank line below the end `</tr>` tag for the table data code you just typed, press the **Ctrl+V** keys to paste the code.

6. Repeat the preceding step three times to make three more copies of the table row and table data tags. Make sure to include a blank line between each set of `<tr>` and `</tr>` tags to separate each group of table row code.

7. Type the following code between the `<td>` and `</td>` tags for each row, as shown in Figure 8-11. Note that there is no content for the last two cells in the last row.

```
Hike Moraine Lake
Moraine Lake Visitor's Center
9:00 a.m. - 12:00 p.m.
Donation

Hike the Bow Valley
Banff Town Square
10:00 a.m. - 1:30 p.m.
Donation

Horseback Riding
Banff Ranch
2:00 p.m. - 3:30 p.m
$40.00

Wildlife Preservation Lecture
Banff Community Center
6:30 p.m. - 8:30 p.m.
$5.00


Trip to Lake Louise
TBA
```

Figure 8-11   Complete table code

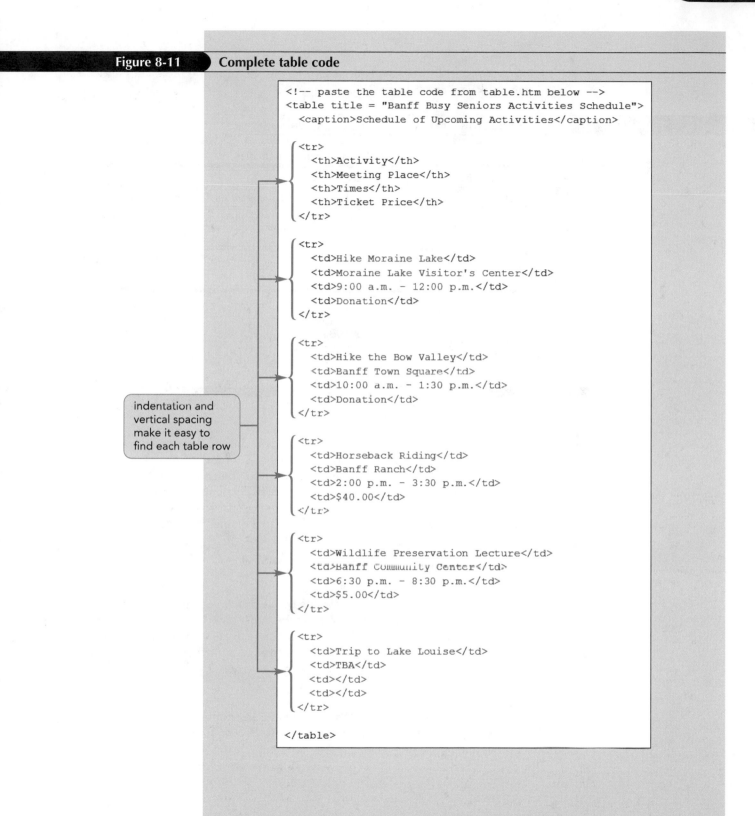

```
<!-- paste the table code from table.htm below -->
<table title = "Banff Busy Seniors Activities Schedule">
  <caption>Schedule of Upcoming Activities</caption>

  <tr>
    <th>Activity</th>
    <th>Meeting Place</th>
    <th>Times</th>
    <th>Ticket Price</th>
  </tr>

  <tr>
    <td>Hike Moraine Lake</td>
    <td>Moraine Lake Visitor's Center</td>
    <td>9:00 a.m. - 12:00 p.m.</td>
    <td>Donation</td>
  </tr>

  <tr>
    <td>Hike the Bow Valley</td>
    <td>Banff Town Square</td>
    <td>10:00 a.m. - 1:30 p.m.</td>
    <td>Donation</td>
  </tr>

  <tr>
    <td>Horseback Riding</td>
    <td>Banff Ranch</td>
    <td>2:00 p.m. - 3:30 p.m.</td>
    <td>$40.00</td>
  </tr>

  <tr>
    <td>Wildlife Preservation Lecture</td>
    <td>Banff Community Center</td>
    <td>6:30 p.m. - 8:30 p.m.</td>
    <td>$5.00</td>
  </tr>

  <tr>
    <td>Trip to Lake Louise</td>
    <td>TBA</td>
    <td></td>
    <td></td>
  </tr>

</table>
```

indentation and vertical spacing make it easy to find each table row

8. Save the file, return to your Web browser, and then click the **Refresh** or **Reload** button to view the changes in the file. Confirm the table cells and data look similar to Figure 8-12.

Figure 8-12	Table in the browser showing border and gridlines

table border →

Schedule of Upcoming Activities			
Activity	**Meeting Place**	**Times**	**Ticket Price**
Hike Moraine Lake	Moraine Lake Visitor's Center	9:00 a.m. - 12:00 p.m.	Donation
Hike the Bow Valley	Banff Town Square	10:00 a.m. - 1:30 p.m.	Donation
Horseback Riding	Banff Ranch	2:00 p.m. - 3:30 p.m.	$40.00
Wildlife Preservation Lecture	Banff Community Center	6:30 p.m. - 8:30 p.m.	$5.00
Trip to Lake Louise	TBA		

gridlines set using the
th and td border property

Displaying Empty Cells

INSIGHT

An **empty cell** is a cell without content. Depending on your browser and browser version, you may not see gridlines around empty cells. CSS has an `empty-cells` property, which can create gridlines around empty cells. The `empty-cells` property takes either the `show` value, in which gridlines are drawn around an empty cell, or `hide`, in which gridlines are not drawn around an empty cell. To always show a border even if a cell is empty, set the following style for the `td` element selector:

```
td {
   empty-cells: show;
}
```

By default, cells without content appear with a border in some contemporary browsers. However, in some versions of Internet Explorer, you must enter the ` ` character entity in order for an empty cell to appear with a border. By using the `empty-cells` property and setting the style for the `td` element to always show borders, you don't have to include the ` ` character entity in each empty cell.

Sue noticed the last two cells of the table don't have any content. She'd like you to combine the cell that contains *TBA* (an acronym for *To Be Announced*) with the cells without content to create a single cell.

Merging Cells in Columns

HTML allows you to combine, or **merge**, adjacent cells using two different attributes: `colspan` and `rowspan`. The `colspan` attribute is used to merge cells across columns. You enter the `colspan` attribute in the start `<td>` tag where you want the column merge to begin.

Figure 8-13 shows an example of a table that could benefit from merged cells: a student's weekly timetable.

Figure 8-13   A table without merged cells

Class timetable					
	Monday	**Tuesday**	**Wednesday**	**Thursday**	**Friday**
9am - 10am	COMP 101		BUSN 210	work	work
10am - 11am	COMP 101		BUSN 210	work	work
11am - 12pm			BUSN 210		
12pm - 1pm	Lunch	Lunch	Lunch	Lunch	Lunch
1pm - 2pm					
2pm - 3pm	COMM 141			COMM 141	

You can see there is a lunch period every day from 12pm–1pm. Rather than creating separate table data cells for each lunch period, you could create only one, then span it across five columns. You'd then delete the `<td>` and `</td>` tags for the number of additional cells the column spans. The `colspan` code for the revised Lunch row would appear as shown below:

```
<tr>
   <td>12pm - 1pm</td>
   <td colspan = "5">Lunch</td>
</tr>
```

Note that because the second cell is now part of five columns, the remaining cells in the row have been deleted. The effect of spanning the Lunch cell across five cells is shown in Figure 8-14.

Figure 8-14   **A table with column spanning**

Class timetable

	Monday	Tuesday	Wednesday	Thursday	Friday
9am - 10am	COMP 101		BUSN 210	work	work
10am - 11am	COMP 101		BUSN 210	work	work
11am - 12pm			BUSN 210		
12pm - 1pm	Lunch				
1pm - 2pm					
2pm - 3pm	COMM 141			COMM 141	

lunch cell spans across five columns, including the original location

Using the `colspan` Attribute

- To span a cell across columns, enter the following code:

  ```
  <td colspan = "value">
  ```

  where *value* is the number of columns that will be spanned. The `colspan` attribute and its value must be placed in the cell in which the column merge should begin. All empty spanned table data cells should be deleted. Be sure the `colspan` value plus the number of unmerged cells in the row equals the number of columns you want in the table.

The `rowspan` attribute is used to merge cells in rows. In the timetable example, the COMP 101 course runs from 9am–11am. In addition, the BUSN 210 course runs from 9am–12pm. Like `colspan`, you enter the `rowspan` attribute in the start `<td>` tag where you want the row merge to begin. You then delete the `<td></td>` tags in the next row and subsequent rows for cells that will be replaced by the spanned cell. The COMP 101 course with row spanning is shown in Figure 8-15.

Figure 8-15   **Table with row spanning**

Class timetable

	Monday	Tuesday	Wednesday	Thursday	Friday
9am - 10am	COMP 101		BUSN 210	work	work
10am - 11am			BUSN 210	work	work
11am - 12pm			BUSN 210		
12pm - 1pm	Lunch				
1pm - 2pm					
2pm - 3pm	COMM 141			COMM 141	

COMP 101 spans two rows

The code that could be used to span the COMP 101 cells is as follows:

```
<tr>
  <td>9am - 10am</td>
  <td rowspan = "2">COMP 101</td>
  <td></td>
  <td>BUSN 210</td>
  <td>work</td>
  <td>work</td>
</tr>

<tr>
  <td>10am - 11am</td>
  <td></td>
  <td>BUSN 210</td>
  <td>work</td>
  <td>work</td>
</tr>
```

Notice that there is one fewer <td></td> table data cell in the code for the second row. Figure 8-16 illustrates an example of a table in which three cells are merged using row spanning, to merge the cells for BUSN 210.

Figure 8-16   Table with cell spanning across three rows

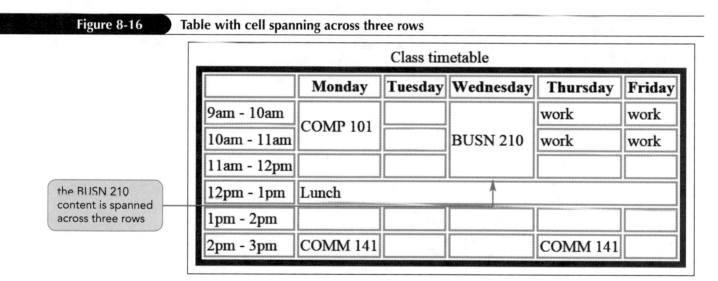

the BUSN 210 content is spanned across three rows

The code that could be used to span the BUSN 210 cells is as follows:

```html
<table>
    <caption>Class timetable</caption>

    <tr>
      <th></th>
      <th>Monday</th>
      <th>Tuesday</th>
      <th>Wednesday</th>
      <th>Thursday</th>
      <th>Friday</th>
    </tr>

    <tr>
      <td>9am - 10am</td>
      <td rowspan = "2">COMP 101</td>
      <td></td>
      <td rowspan = "3">BUSN 210</td>
      <td>work</td>
      <td>work</td>
    </tr>

    <tr>
      <td>10am - 11am</td>
      <td></td>
      <td>work</td>
      <td>work</td>
    </tr>

    <tr>
      <td>11am - 12pm</td>
      <td></td>
      <td></td>
      <td></td>
      <td></td>
    </tr>

    <tr>
      <td>12pm - 1pm</td>
      <td colspan = "5">Lunch</td>
    </tr>

    <tr>
      <td>1pm - 2pm</td>
      <td></td>
      <td></td>
      <td></td>
      <td></td>
      <td></td>
    </tr>
```

```
<tr>
  <td>2pm - 3pm</td>
  <td>COMM 141</td>
  <td></td>
  <td></td>
  <td>COMM 141</td>
  <td></td>
</tr>

</table>
```

You always enter the `colspan` and `rowspan` attributes and their values in the **key cell**, which is the cell where the cells begin to merge. In this instance the key cell is the cell that contains BUSN 210.

You can also combine `rowspan` and `colspan` in the same table data start tag to achieve both effects. Figure 8-17 illustrates an example of a table in which `colspan` and `rowspan` are used to merge four cells together.

Figure 8-17   Table using rowspan and colspan to merge four cells

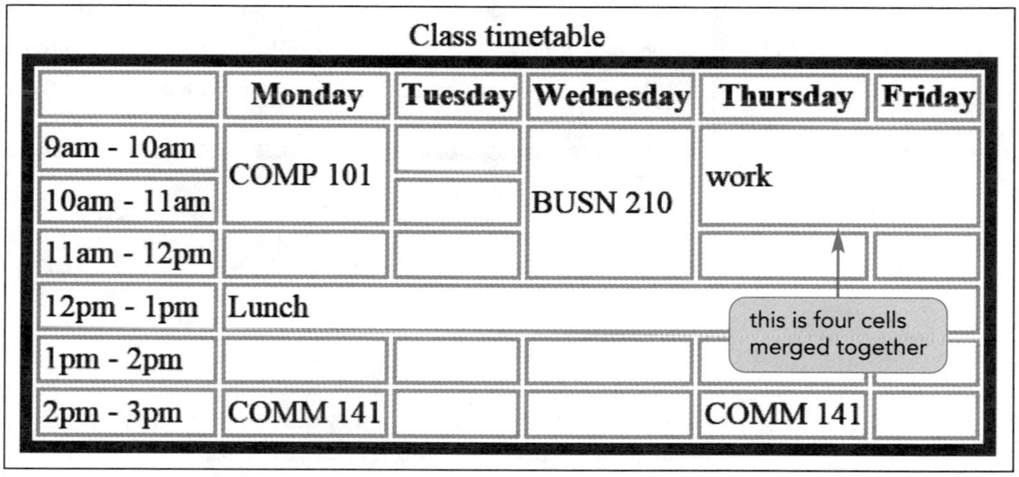

Class timetable

	Monday	Tuesday	Wednesday	Thursday	Friday
9am - 10am	COMP 101			work	
10am - 11am			BUSN 210		
11am - 12pm					
12pm - 1pm	Lunch				
1pm - 2pm					
2pm - 3pm	COMM 141			COMM 141	

this is four cells merged together

It's easier to figure out which cells to merge if you start with table data tags for all cells, add content, then merge and delete content as necessary.

Sue would like you to merge the cell that contains *TBA* with the other two cells to the right. You'll use the `colspan` attribute to accomplish this task.

To merge the cells in the TBA row:

1. Return to the **table.htm** file in your text editor. Position the insertion point in the start `<td>` tag before the right angle bracket in the *TBA* cell.

2. Press **[Spacebar]** once.

3. Type **colspan = "3"**

4. Delete the `<td></td>` tags for the two cells that do not have any content. Your code should look similar to that in Figure 8-18.

Figure 8-18 | **HTML code for column spanning**

table cells were deleted here →

```
<tr>
  <td>Trip to Lake Louise</td>
  <td colspan = "3">TBA</td>
</tr>
```

5. Save the file, return to your Web browser, and then click the **Refresh** or **Reload** button to view the changes in the file. Verify the cell containing *TBA* has been merged with the two cells to its right, as shown in Figure 8-19.

Figure 8-19 | **Cells merged using the colspan attribute**

Schedule of Upcoming Activities

Activity	Meeting Place	Times	Ticket Price
Hike Moraine Lake	Moraine Lake Visitor's Center	9:00 a.m. - 12:00 p.m.	Donation
Hike the Bow Valley	Banff Town Square	10:00 a.m. - 1:30 p.m.	Donation
Horseback Riding	Banff Ranch	2:00 p.m. - 3:30 p.m.	$40.00
Wildlife Preservation Lecture	Banff Community Center	6:30 p.m. - 8:30 p.m.	$5.00
Trip to Lake Louise	TBA		

this cell is a merged cell, combining three cells

By default, the text in merged cells is not formatted. Spanned cells often contain a lot of white space and benefit from formatting. Sue thinks the spanned text would look better if it were centered and appeared in italic. You'll create an independent class to format the text, and then you'll apply the class to the key cell.

To format the data in the merged cells:

1. Return to the **table.htm** file in your text editor. Position the insertion point on a blank line after code for the th, td grouped selector rule, and then type the following CSS code, as shown in Figure 8-20:

```
.center {
  font-style: italic;
  text-align: center;
}
```

Figure 8-20   **CSS code for the center independent class**

```
th, td {
   border: solid 2px orange;
}

.center {
   font-style: italic;
   text-align: center;
}

</style>
```

2. In the document body, position the insertion point to the right of the closing quote in the *colspan = "3"* code.

3. Press **[Spacebar]** once.

4. Type **class = "center"**.

Your code should look similar to that shown in Figure 8-21.

Figure 8-21   **Applying the center class**

```
<tr>
  <td>Trip to Lake Louise</td>
  <td colspan = "3" class = "center">TBA</td>
</tr>
```

5. Save the file, return to your Web browser, and then click the **Refresh** or **Reload** button to view the changes in the file. The *colspan* text should be centered and displayed in italics, as shown in Figure 8-22.

Figure 8-22   **Table with the center class applied**

Schedule of Upcoming Activities			
Activity	**Meeting Place**	**Times**	**Ticket Price**
Hike Moraine Lake	Moraine Lake Visitor's Center	9:00 a.m. - 12:00 p.m.	Donation
Hike the Bow Valley	Banff Town Square	10:00 a.m. - 1:30 p.m.	Donation
Horseback Riding	Banff Ranch	2:00 p.m. - 3:30 p.m.	$40.00
Wildlife Preservation Lecture	Banff Community Center	6:30 p.m. - 8:30 p.m.	$5.00
Trip to Lake Louise	*TBA*		

table data content is centered and in italic

Grouping Rows

Sometimes a table of data is quite long. Although a user can scroll down, what if the user needs to print the table? The table may print on multiple pages, with the table header row on the first page only and the footer row only on the last. To address just this situation, HTML includes elements that make it possible to specify rows that should repeat at the top and bottom of printed pages.

Table rows can be grouped into a table header, a table footer, or into one or more table body sections. The elements used to group table row content are `thead`, `tfoot`, and `tbody`. The `thead` and `tfoot` elements are useful when you expect users will want to print tables that are longer than one page; using these elements, the table header and footer information can be printed on each page that contains table data, similar to a header row in Microsoft Word or Excel. However, if you use all three of these elements in your table code, you must disrupt the source order in the table code, which is why these elements are not often used. If you do use these elements, you must list the `thead` element followed by the `tfoot` element, and then list the code for the `tbody` element, as shown in the following example. Note the source order of the elements:

```
<table>
<caption>caption text here</caption>

<thead>
    ...header row code and content ...
</thead>

<tfoot>
   ...footer row code and content ...
</tfoot>

<tbody>
   ...first row of code and content ...
   ...second row of code and content ...
</tbody>

</table>
```

Although the `tfoot` element does upset the source order, placing the contents of the `tfoot` element before the contents of the `tbody` element has no effect on how the content appears in the browser.

Sue is curious about the appearance of the gridlines. She points out that they don't appear as they would in a word-processing table. They instead look like double lines because each individual table data cell is outlined, and there is a small space between each cell. She'd like a single line between cells instead. You can accomplish this by collapsing the internal borders.

Collapsing Internal Borders

By default, each cell has its own border, so each gridline appears as a double ruled line rather than a single ruled line. The double ruled lines tend to compete for attention with the cell contents. To give the table a cleaner, simpler appearance, you can change the cell borders to single rules by using the `border-collapse` property and assigning a value of `collapse`. The default value, `separate`, creates a double ruled line, as the table currently uses. You'll add the `border-collapse` property to the `table` element style to collapse the table gridlines and simplify the table's appearance. Although the `border-collapse` property is added to the *table* selector, it will collapse the borders around each of the table cells.

To collapse the internal borders:

1. Return to the **table.htm** file in your text editor. In the code for the *table* style rule, create a blank line, and then type the following CSS code, as shown in Figure 8-23:

   ```
   border-collapse: collapse;
   ```

Figure 8-23   CSS for the border-collapse property

```
<style type = "text/css">
   table {
      border: solid 6px navy;
      border-collapse: collapse;
   }

   th, td {
      border: solid 2px orange;
   }
```

2. Save the file.

3. Return to your Web browser, and then click the **Refresh** or **Reload** button to view the changes in the file. As shown in Figure 8-24, the internal table borders should now appear as single rules rather than double rules.

Figure 8-24   Table with collapsed borders

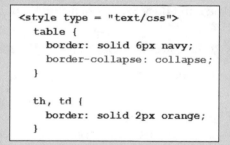

Schedule of Upcoming Activities			
Activity	**Meeting Place**	**Times**	**Ticket Price**
Hike Moraine Lake	Moraine Lake Visitor's Center	9:00 a.m. - 12:00 p.m.	Donation
Hike the Bow Valley	Banff Town Square	10:00 a.m. - 1:30 p.m.	Donation
Horseback Riding	Banff Ranch	2:00 p.m. - 3:30 p.m.	$40.00
Wildlife Preservation Lecture	Banff Community Center	6:30 p.m. - 8:30 p.m.	$5.00
Trip to Lake Louise			TBA

inside borders collapsed to a single line

INSIGHT

Using the `border-spacing` Property

In a table with the `border-collapse` property set to `separate`, you can use the `border-spacing` property to add white space around cells. Border spacing specifies the distance between the borders of adjacent cells. Like the `border-collapse` property, the `border-spacing` property is also a property of the `table` element, and affects each table cell. Values can be expressed in any CSS unit of measurement, but negative values are not allowed. If one value is specified, it sets both the horizontal and vertical spacing. If two length values are specified, the first value sets the horizontal spacing, and the second value sets the vertical spacing. You must use the `border-collapse` property of `separate` for the `border-spacing` property to work, as shown in the following code. In this instance, 5px of border spacing will be added on the top and bottom, and 10px of border spacing will be added on the left and right:

```
table {
   border-spacing: 5px 10px;
   border-collapse: separate;
}
```

Sue is happy with the table you've created. In the next session you'll add this table to the Banff Busy Seniors Activities Web page, and you'll add additional styling.

PROSKILLS

Problem Solving: Page Layout Techniques

Before it was possible to position elements on a Web page using CSS, Web developers used tables as the primary layout technique. A table cell can contain an image, list, paragraph, or other elements. Using column and row spanning, tables with merged cells would be created and elements placed inside the table cells. Most Web developers no longer use tables for layout. Instead, Web developers favor CSS positioning using techniques such as the `float` property. Compared to using CSS positioning, using tables for layouts has the following drawbacks:

- Table layouts can become quite complex, making them difficult to revise. A complex table layout has multiple rows and columns, merged cells, and perhaps nested tables. Imagine table code that involves five or more levels of indents! Commenting the code to identify each row helps a bit, but this is still a cumbersome method for page layout.

- Table layouts require a lot more code than CSS positioning code. This means that sometimes Web browsers can take longer to render the code, because it takes longer for a Web browser to read the code and to calculate where each table cell is displayed.

- HTML tags are meant to describe content. Table tags describe content that is in a tabular format. Using a table for layout rather than for a set of related data goes against the specification of HTML as a markup language that describes content. If the table element is used for layout, its contents are not a table of data. The `table` element should be reserved for tables of data.

REVIEW

Session 8.1 Quick Check

1. What is the purpose of a data table?
2. What is the effect of the `title` attribute when used with a table?
3. What is the purpose of a table caption?
4. What types of data can be placed into a table cell?
5. How does a table header cell differ from a table data cell?
6. What attribute is used to merge cells from different columns?
7. What is a key cell?

SESSION 8.2 VISUAL OVERVIEW

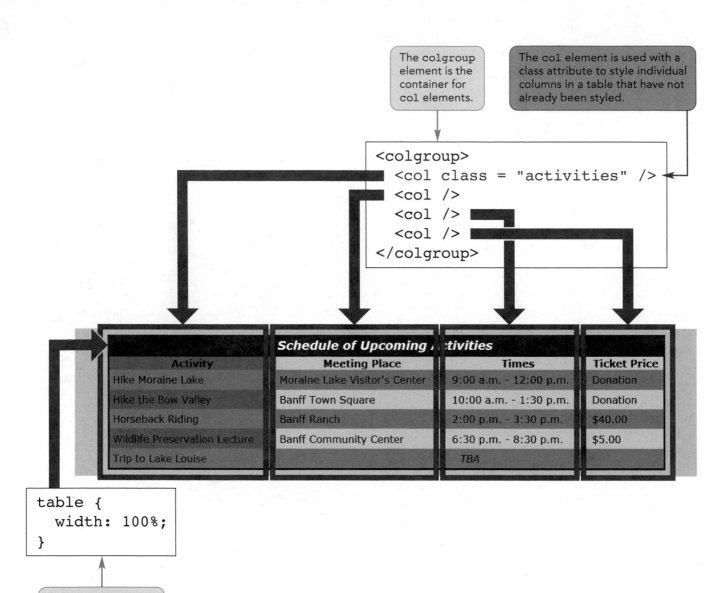

The colgroup element is the container for col elements.

The col element is used with a class attribute to style individual columns in a table that have not already been styled.

```
<colgroup>
  <col class = "activities" />
  <col />
  <col />
  <col />
</colgroup>
```

Schedule of Upcoming Activities

Activity	Meeting Place	Times	Ticket Price
Hike Moraine Lake	Moraine Lake Visitor's Center	9:00 a.m. - 12:00 p.m.	Donation
Hike the Bow Valley	Banff Town Square	10:00 a.m. - 1:30 p.m.	Donation
Horseback Riding	Banff Ranch	2:00 p.m. - 3:30 p.m.	$40.00
Wildlife Preservation Lecture	Banff Community Center	6:30 p.m. - 8:30 p.m.	$5.00
Trip to Lake Louise		*TBA*	

```
table {
  width: 100%;
}
```

The width property is used to set the width of a table within its container.

USING CSS TO FORMAT TABLES

The padding property is used to add white space within a cell.

```
td {
   padding: 6px;
}
```

You can create **row striping** in a table by applying a class with contrasting formatting to alternate tr elements.

```
tr.stripe {
   background-color: dodgerblue;
}
```

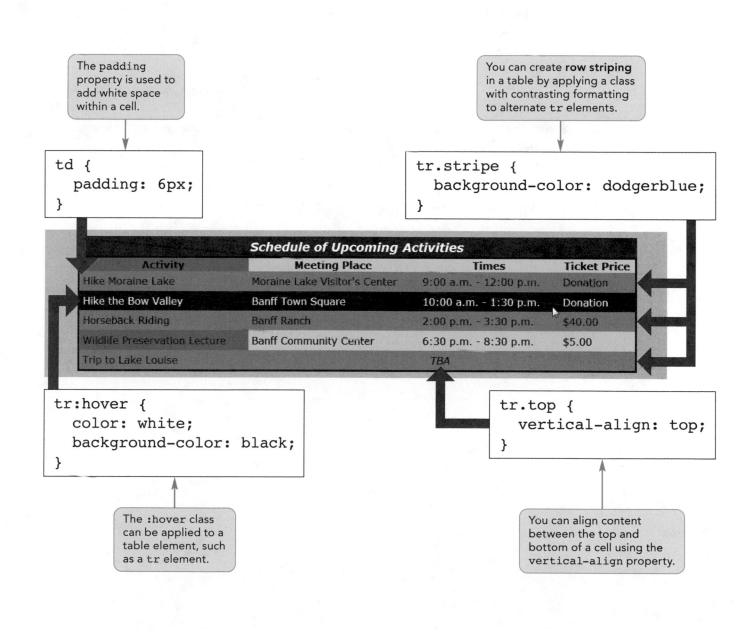

Schedule of Upcoming Activities

Activity	Meeting Place	Times	Ticket Price
Hike Moraine Lake	Moraine Lake Visitor's Center	9:00 a.m. - 12:00 p.m.	Donation
Hike the Bow Valley	Banff Town Square	10:00 a.m. - 1:30 p.m.	Donation
Horseback Riding	Banff Ranch	2:00 p.m. - 3:30 p.m.	$40.00
Wildlife Preservation Lecture	Banff Community Center	6:30 p.m. - 8:30 p.m.	$5.00
Trip to Lake Louise		TBA	

```
tr:hover {
   color: white;
   background-color: black;
}
```

```
tr.top {
   vertical-align: top;
}
```

The :hover class can be applied to a table element, such as a tr element.

You can align content between the top and bottom of a cell using the vertical-align property.

Using CSS to Format Tables

In the past, it was common to format a table using HTML attributes and values. Today, however, most Web designers now use CSS to format tables—this allows designers to separate presentation from the table structure.

You've already created some simple styles for the table to make the table border and the table gridlines visible. Now that you're satisfied with the basic table code, you'll copy and paste the table code into the activities.htm page. Afterward, you'll create additional CSS styles that will improve the overall appearance of the table.

To copy and paste the table code:

▶ **1.** If you took a break after the previous session, make sure that the table.htm file is open in your text editor.

▶ **2.** Leaving the table.htm document open in your text editor, open the **activities_T8.htm** file in your text editor from the tutorial8\tutorial folder included with your Data Files.

▶ **3.** In the head section and below the page title, enter **your name** and **today's date** in the comment section where noted.

▶ **4.** Save the file as **activities.htm**.

▶ **5.** Return to the **table.htm** file, and then select all the table code from the start <table> tag through the end </table> tag. Select only the table code.

▶ **6.** Press the **Ctrl+C** keys to copy all the table code to the clipboard.

▶ **7.** Return to the **activities.htm** file, locate the comment *paste the table code from table.htm below*, and then position the insertion point on a blank line below the comment. Press the **Ctrl+V** keys to paste the table code from the table.htm file, as shown in Figure 8-25.

Figure 8-25   **Table element in the activities Web page**

```
<header>
  <p><img src="images/banff.jpg" alt="Banff Busy Seniors logo"
    width="900" height="250" /></p>
</header>

<!-- paste the table code from table.htm below -->
<table title = "Banff Busy Seniors Activities Schedule">
  <caption>Schedule of Upcoming Activities</caption>

  <tr>
    <th>Activity</th>
    <th>Meeting Place</th>
    <th>Times</th>
    <th>Ticket Price</th>
  </tr>

  <tr>
    <td>Hike Moraine Lake</td>
    <td>Moraine Lake Visitor's Center</td>
    <td>9:00 a.m. - 12:00 p.m.</td>
    <td>Donation</td>
  </tr>

  <tr>
    <td>Hike the Bow Valley</td>
    <td>Banff Town Square</td>
    <td>10:00 a.m. - 1:30 p.m.</td>
    <td>Donation</td>
  </tr>

  <tr>
    <td>Horseback Riding</td>
    <td>Banff Ranch</td>
    <td>2:00 p.m. - 3:30 p.m.</td>
    <td>$40.00</td>
  </tr>

  <tr>
    <td>Wildlife Preservation Lecture</td>
    <td>Banff Community Center</td>
    <td>6:30 p.m. - 8:30 p.m.</td>
    <td>$5.00</td>
  </tr>

  <tr>
    <td>Trip to Lake Louise</td>
    <td colspan="3" class="center">TBA</td>
  </tr>

</table>


<section id="content">
```

8. Save the **activities.htm** file, and open it in your Web browser, as shown in Figure 8-26.

Figure 8-26   **Table added to the Web page**

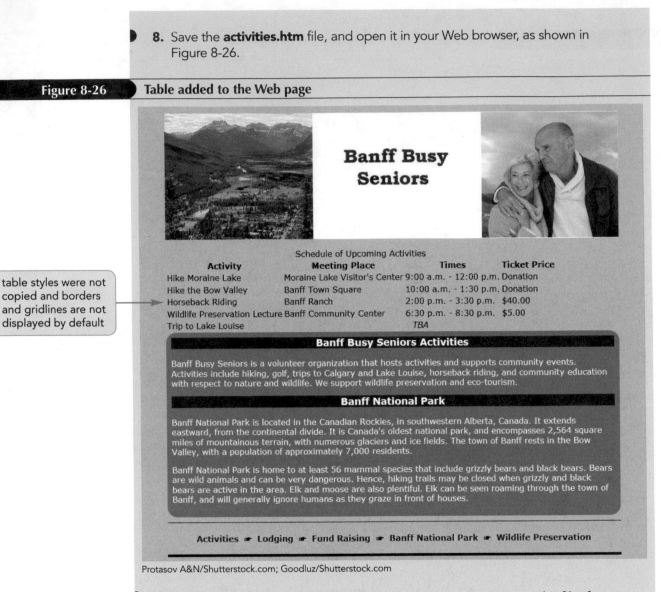

table styles were not copied and borders and gridlines are not displayed by default

Protasov A&N/Shutterstock.com; Goodluz/Shutterstock.com

9. Close the table.htm file *without saving changes*. Do not save the file if you are prompted to do so.

TIP

Like other block elements, tables can be floated left or right.

The activities.htm file already contains several styles to format the document, but it does not include any styles to enhance the appearance of the table. You'll create several styles that will add more visual interest to the table. You'll begin by creating a style for the `table` element.

Styling the `table` Element

The `table` element can be styled to affect the appearance of a table and its contents. Generally, you want to style the `table` element to set the table width and perhaps display the table borders. By default, a table is as wide as the sum of the longest lines in each column. The table expands horizontally until it reaches the full browser width, at which time the text in the cells begins to wrap. Depending on the length of the data in the longest line in each column, the table might appear narrower or wider than you'd like. Tables can also be floated to wrap content around the table. If you are floating a table, or if you just want to control the display width of a table, it's a good idea to give the table an appropriate width.

Setting Table Width

- To set table width, enter the following CSS code:

```
table {
   width: value;
}
```

where *value* is a value for the table width expressed in any of the CSS units of measurement.

- To create row striping, enter the following code:

```
tr.stripe {
   styles
}
```

where `tr` is the table row element, `stripe` is a dependent class name, and *styles* are the styles to change the appearance of an alternate row of the table. Apply the *stripe* class within the start `<tr>` tag for each alternate row in the table.

- To format table columns, enter the following code below the table caption code:

```
<colgroup>
   <col />
   <col />
   ...
</colgroup>
```

where each `col` element can represent one or more columns in the table. The total of stand-alone `col` elements plus `span` values must equal the total number of columns in the table.

You'll use the `width` property when you style the `table` element. The value for the `width` property can be a percentage based on the table's parent container, an absolute value measured in pixels, or one of the other CSS measurement options. A percentage measurement is useful for liquid layouts, and a pixel measurement is useful for fixed-width layouts. The activities.htm page has a container section that sets the page width to 900px. The table will be 100 percent of the container section width, so the table will also be 900px wide, regardless of the length of the longest lines in each column. If necessary, more space will be added between the columns to expand the table width to match that of the container section width. Tables sized using a percentage expand or contract as the parent container is resized. In this case, the container is fixed at 900px, so it will not change size. Tables sized using pixels will not expand or contract. Tables can be contracted only up to a certain point; browsers ignore a width value that is too small to display the table contents. Also, if you include an image in a table cell, the table will not make the image either larger or smaller as it scales.

You'll enter new table styles in the activities.htm file so you can style the table. In addition to setting the table width, you'll create 10px of margin space on the top and the bottom of the table. The margin value of `auto` for the left and right margins will center the table horizontally. You'll give the table a 3px border, and you'll use the `border-collapse` property to collapse the table gridlines. Finally, you'll give the table a background color so it will contrast with the body background color.

To style the `table` element:

1. Return to the **activities.htm** file in your text editor. Position the insertion point on a blank line below the CSS comment *enter the code for table styles below*.

2. Type the following code, as shown in Figure 8-27.

```
table {
    width: 100%;
    margin: 10px auto;
    border: solid 3px black;
    border-collapse: collapse;
    background-color: lightblue;
}
```

CSS code for the table

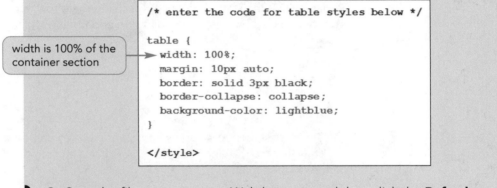

width is 100% of the
container section

```
/* enter the code for table styles below */

table {
    width: 100%;
    margin: 10px auto;
    border: solid 3px black;
    border-collapse: collapse;
    background-color: lightblue;
}

</style>
```

3. Save the file, return to your Web browser, and then click the **Refresh** or **Reload** button to view the changes in the file. Compare your file with the one shown in Figure 8-28 to confirm the table has the correct width, margin, border, and background color.

Figure 8-28   **The table stylized**

outside border
is collapsed, without
a beveled edge

Protasov A&N/Shutterstock.com; Goodluz/Shutterstock.com

Next, you'll create a style for the table caption.

Creating a Style for the Table Caption

Recall that the table caption is part of the table, so any styles created for the `table` element are also applied to the table caption. Also remember that the caption is centered by default. You can, however, style the `caption` element to have a different appearance from that of the table. For example, your table can have a background color of aqua, but your caption can have a background color of maroon. Sue would like the caption to stand out from the rest of the table. You'll accomplish this by specifying font properties and color properties for the caption.

To style the table caption:

▶ 1. Return to the **activities.htm** file in your text editor. Position the insertion point on a blank line below the CSS code for the *table* selector style, and then type the CSS code, as shown in Figure 8-29:

```
caption {
    padding: 4px;
    color: white;
    background-color: midnightblue;
    font-weight: bold;
    font-style: italic;
    font-size: 1.2em;
}
```

Figure 8-29 | **CSS code for the caption**

```
table {
    width: 100%;
    margin: 10px auto;
    border: solid 3px black;
    border-collapse: collapse;
    background-color: lightblue;
}

caption {
    padding: 4px;
    color: white;
    background-color: midnightblue;
    font-weight: bold;
    font-style: italic;
    font-size: 1.2em;
}

</style>
```

▶ 2. Save the file, return to your Web browser, and then click the **Refresh** or **Reload** button to view the changes in the file. The Web page should look similar to Figure 8-30.

   Trouble? Depending on your browser and browser version, you may or may not see space between the caption and the table.

Figure 8-30 Table with stylized caption

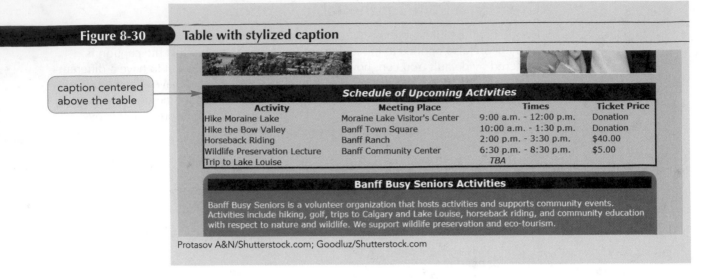

caption centered above the table

Protasov A&N/Shutterstock.com; Goodluz/Shutterstock.com

Next, you'll create a style for the table data.

Creating a Style for Table Data

At this point, the text of the table runs right up against the top, left, and bottom borders, and the cell contents are very close to each other as well. You'll add padding to the table cells, just as you would to any other block element, to give the cell contents some space.

To style the table data:

1. Return to the **activities.htm** file in your text editor. Position the insertion point on a blank line below the CSS code for the *caption* selector style, and then type the following CSS code, as shown in Figure 8-31:

```
td {
   padding: 6px;
}
```

Figure 8-31 CSS code for the td selector

```
caption {
   padding: 4px;
   color: white;
   background-color: midnightblue;
   font-weight: bold;
   font-style: italic;
   font-size: 1.2em;
}

td {
   padding: 6px;
}

</style>
```

2. Save the file, return to your Web browser, and then click the **Refresh** or **Reload** button to view the changes in the file. The Web page should look similar to Figure 8-32.

Figure 8-32   Table with cell padding

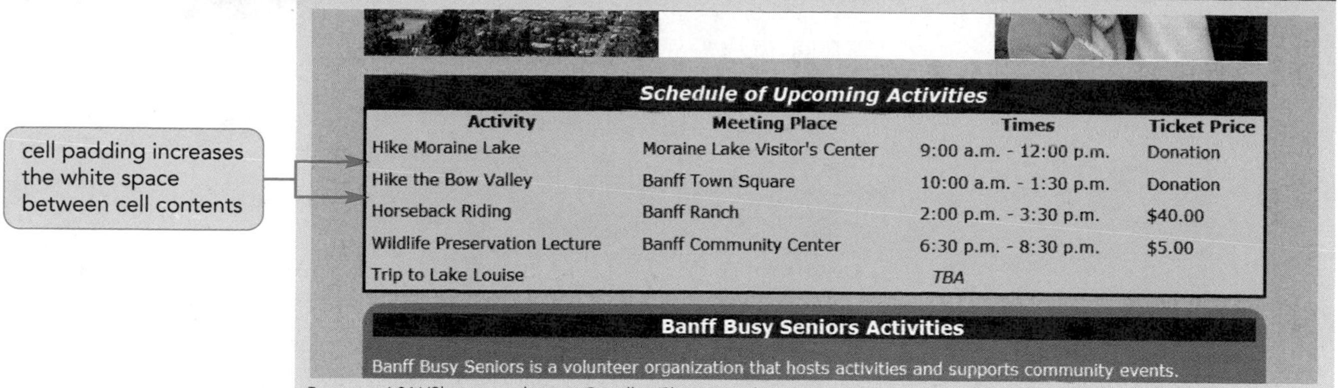

cell padding increases
the white space
between cell contents

Protasov A&N/Shutterstock.com; Goodluz/Shutterstock.com

Instead of using gridlines, Sue would like you to use background colors to differentiate the rows.

Striping Rows

Row striping alternates the background color of the rows in a table, making the rows easier to locate and read. You accomplish row striping by creating a CSS class and applying the class to every other row.

Don't name the class *odd* or *even*. As a table grows in complexity and more rows are added, it becomes more difficult to determine an odd or even row. In this instance, you'll name the class *stripe*.

To create the *stripe* dependent class:

1. Return to the **activities.htm** file in your text editor. Position the insertion point on a blank line below the CSS code for the td selector style, and then type the following CSS code, as shown in Figure 8-33:

```
tr.stripe {
  background-color: dodgerblue;
}
```

Figure 8-33   CSS code for the stripe dependent class

```
td {
  padding: 6px;
}

tr.stripe {
  background-color: dodgerblue;
}

</style>
```

2. Position the insertion point to the left of the end angle bracket of the
   <tr> tag in the second row of the table. Press **[Spacebar]** once.

3. Type the code in bold below, as shown in Figure 8-34:

```
<tr class = "stripe">
     <td>Hike Moraine Lake</td>
     <td>Moraine Lake Visitor's Center</td>
     <td>9:00 a.m. - 12:00 p.m.</td>
     <td>Donation</td>
</tr>
```

Figure 8-34   **Applying the stripe class**

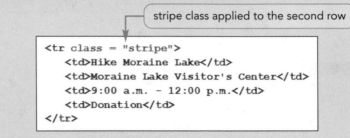

stripe class applied to the second row

```
<tr class = "stripe">
     <td>Hike Moraine Lake</td>
     <td>Moraine Lake Visitor's Center</td>
     <td>9:00 a.m. - 12:00 p.m.</td>
     <td>Donation</td>
</tr>
```

4. Repeat the previous step to apply the *stripe* dependent class to the fourth
   and sixth rows of the table, as shown in Figure 8-35:

Figure 8-35 Table with the stripe class applied to alternate rows

```
<!-- paste the table code from table.htm below -->
<table title = "Banff Busy Seniors Activities Schedule">
  <caption>Schedule of Upcoming Activities</caption>

  <tr>
    <th>Activity</th>
    <th>Meeting Place</th>
    <th>Times</th>
    <th>Ticket Price</th>
  </tr>

  <tr class = "stripe">
    <td>Hike Moraine Lake</td>
    <td>Moraine Lake Visitor's Center</td>
    <td>9:00 a.m. - 12:00 p.m.</td>
    <td>Donation</td>
  </tr>

  <tr>
    <td>Hike the Bow Valley</td>
    <td>Banff Town Square</td>
    <td>10:00 a.m. - 1:30 p.m.</td>
    <td>Donation</td>
  </tr>

  <tr class = "stripe">
    <td>Horseback Riding</td>
    <td>Banff Ranch</td>
    <td>2:00 p.m. - 3:30 p.m.</td>
    <td>$40.00</td>
  </tr>

  <tr>
    <td>Wildlife Preservation Lecture</td>
    <td>Banff Community Center</td>
    <td>6:30 p.m. - 8:30 p.m.</td>
    <td>$5.00</td>
  </tr>

  <tr class = "stripe">
    <td>Trip to Lake Louise</td>
    <td colspan = "3" class = "center">TBA</td>
    <td></td>
    <td></td>
  </tr>

</table>
```

stripe class applied to the 2nd, 4th and 6th rows

5. Save the file, return to your Web browser, and then click the **Refresh** or **Reload** button to view the changes in the file. The Web page should look similar to Figure 8-36.

Figure 8-36 Table with striped rows

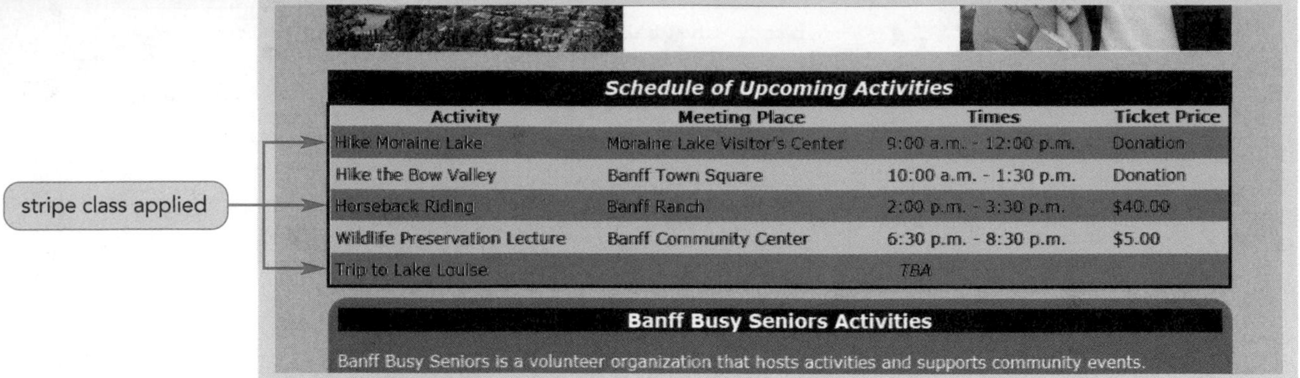

stripe class applied

Protasov A&N/Shutterstock.com; Goodluz/Shutterstock.com

INSIGHT

Keeping Your Tables Accessible

Tables can pose a significant barrier for screen reader software. To make your tables as accessible as possible, follow these tips:

- Don't use tables for layout. Create data tables only.
- Don't nest tables; a table should never be placed within another table.
- Don't use background images for content in a table. Background images can't be used with the `alt` attribute, which a screen reader needs to describe the image. As a result, if you use background images for the content of your table cells, you might be making the data inaccessible.
- Use the `scope` attribute to let the screen reader software know the association between table data and the cells below it or to its right.
- In the start `<table>` tag, include only the `title` attribute and its value. Do not include any other HTML attributes and values.

Now that you have created styles for the table rows and added row striping, you'll create a hover effect for the table rows.

Creating a Hover Effect for Table Rows

In addition to row striping, another common means of calling attention to an individual row is to create a hover effect, so when the mouse pointer passes over a row, the row has different text and background colors compared to the rest of the table. Sue would like the hover effect applied to every row. To create the hover effect, you use the `:hover` pseudo-class selector, just as you did when you created styles for link text. It's important to test a hover effect in several contemporary browsers to confirm it works as intended.

Sue wants the hover effect to display white text on a black background. Because the last row has merged columns, the hover effect may appear differently in the last row in some browsers, and you may not see the hover effect across the entire row. For all other rows, the hover effect will change the appearance of the entire row as you pass the mouse pointer over any cell in that row.

To create the hover effect for the table rows:

1. Return to the **activities.htm** file in your text editor. Position the insertion point on a blank line below the CSS code for the *tr.stripe* dependent selector style, and then type the following CSS code, as shown in Figure 8-37:

```
tr:hover {
   color: white;
   background-color: black;
}
```

Figure 8-37   CSS code for the hover effect

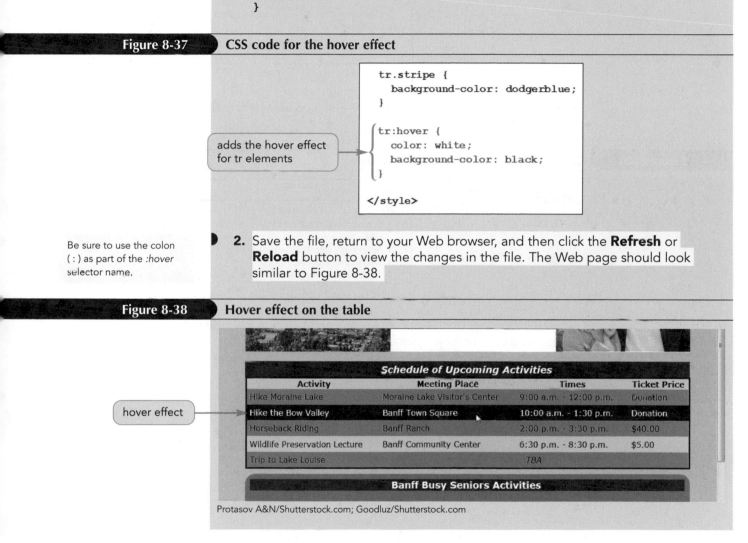

```
tr.stripe {
   background-color: dodgerblue;
}

tr:hover {
   color: white;
   background-color: black;
}

</style>
```

adds the hover effect for tr elements

Be sure to use the colon (:) as part of the *:hover* selector name.

2. Save the file, return to your Web browser, and then click the **Refresh** or **Reload** button to view the changes in the file. The Web page should look similar to Figure 8-38.

Figure 8-38   Hover effect on the table

Schedule of Upcoming Activities			
Activity	**Meeting Place**	**Times**	**Ticket Price**
Hike Moraine Lake	Moraine Lake Visitor's Center	9:00 a.m. - 12:00 p.m.	Donation
Hike the Bow Valley	Banff Town Square	10:00 a.m. - 1:30 p.m.	Donation
Horseback Riding	Banff Ranch	2:00 p.m. - 3:30 p.m.	$40.00
Wildlife Preservation Lecture	Banff Community Center	6:30 p.m. - 8:30 p.m.	$5.00
Trip to Lake Louise		TBA	
Banff Busy Seniors Activities			

hover effect

Protasov A&N/Shutterstock.com; Goodluz/Shutterstock.com

Sometimes the height of a cell is increased because it contains an image or multiple lines of text. Because all cells in a row have the same height, this can add extra white space to other cells in the row with little content. If the text is aligned along the bottom of a long cell, this can look odd. You can set the vertical alignment of contents in a cell to adjust the contents to align at the top, middle, or bottom of a cell.

Positioning Cell Contents

By default, text aligns in the vertical middle of a cell, as shown in Figure 8-39.

Figure 8-39   Default position for a text block

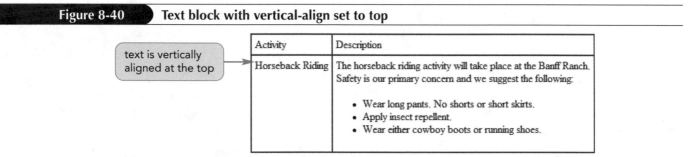

If a cell will contain several lines of text, however, the cell content generally looks better if you align all columns with text positioned at the top of the cell, as shown in Figure 8-40.

Figure 8-40   Text block with vertical-align set to top

You can accomplish this by creating a dependent class and using the `vertical-align` property with a value of `top`, as in the following code:

```
tr.top {
   vertical-align: top;
}
```

You then apply the class to each row in which you want text to have a `vertical-align` value of `top`. If you want all cells in the table to have text with a particular vertical alignment, you can simply create a style for the `tr` element, as shown in the following code:

```
tr {
   vertical-align: top;
}
```

You don't need to change the vertical alignment of the table rows from the default, so you won't apply the `vertical-align` property to the table you've created.

Formatting Table Columns

The column element is used to format one or more columns, and it is represented in HTML code by the `<col />` tag. The column element must be closed by a space followed by a forward slash. You enter the code for column elements directly below the code for the table caption. You should add a `<col />` tag for each column in the table. The column element tags are placed inside a `colgroup` element. The `colgroup` element is a container for the `col` elements. The `colgroup` element has a start `<colgroup>` tag and an end `</colgroup>` tag.

For example, imagine a table that contains information about movies. The first column contains names of movies and the table contains three more columns of information. To apply styles to the columns, you'd begin by entering four column tags in a `colgroup` element below the caption tags, as shown in the following code:

```
<table>
  <caption>Movies</caption>
  <colgroup>
    <col />
    <col />
    <col />
    <col />
  </colgroup>
```

Next, you create one or more independent classes to format the columns. Then, you apply each class to the <col /> tag or tags for the column or columns you wanted to format. If you wanted to create a style named *movie* for the column that contains names of movies, you could enter the following code in your style sheet:

```
.movie {
  background-color: #efebb1;
}
```

You would then apply the class to as many columns as you want. For example, to apply the *movie* class to the first column, you enter the following code:

```
<colgroup>
  <col class = "movie" />
  <col />
  <col />
  <col />
</colgroup>
```

If you wanted, you could create other styles for one or more of the other columns, as shown in the following code:

```
.altborder {
  border: solid 4px navy;
}

.backimage {
  background-image: url(reels.gif);
}
```

You then apply the styles to one or more of the other columns, as shown in the following code. Note that not every column needs to be styled.

```
<colgroup>
  <col class = "movie" />
  <col />
  <col class = "altborder" />
  <col class = "backimage" />
</colgroup>
```

You can also use the `span` attribute to apply the same class to more than one column. The value for the `span` attribute is the number of columns to where you want to apply the style. For example, if you wanted to apply a class named *special* to the second and third columns, you'd enter the following code:

```
<colgroup>
  <col />
  <col class = "special" span = "2" />
  <col />
</colgroup>
```

Note that in the preceding code, the third `<col />` tag formatted by the span attribute has been deleted, leaving only three `<col />` tags.

According to the CSS standard, the only properties you can apply to a column or column group are the `background`, `border`, `width`, and `visibility` properties. Internet Explorer, however, allows you to use other formatting properties, such as the `font`, `color`, and text-related properties.

To enhance the design of Sue's page, you'll create an independent class named *activities* that will change the background color of cells in the first column that do not already have a color. Note, however, that the cells formatted by the *tr.stripe* dependent class will remain unchanged because of specificity. In other words, the *tr.stripe* dependent class is more specific to the table row element than the *.activities* independent class. The order of precedence for Web table styles is shown in Figure 8-41.

Figure 8-41   **Order of precedence for table styles**

Element	Precedence level
Table cell (th or td)	Highest precedence
Table row (tr)	Middle precedence
Table (table)	Lowest precedence

As shown in Figure 8-41, styles applied to a table cell have the highest precedence and override any styles applied to a table row or to the `table` element itself.

You'll create the *activities* class now, and then apply it to the first column using the `col` element.

To create and apply the .activities independent class:

1. Return to the **activities.htm** file in your text editor. Position the insertion point on a blank line below the CSS code for the *tr:hover* dependent selector style, and then type the CSS code, as shown in Figure 8-42:

```
.activities {
  background-color: royalblue;
}
```

Figure 8-42   **CSS code for the activities independent selector**

```
tr:hover {
  color: white;
  background-color: black;
}

.activities {
  background-color: royalblue;
}

</style>
```

2. In the table code, on a blank line below the caption, type the following code, as shown in Figure 8-43:

```
<colgroup>
  <col class = "activities" />
  <col />
  <col />
  <col />
</colgroup>
```

Figure 8-43   **HTML code for the column group**

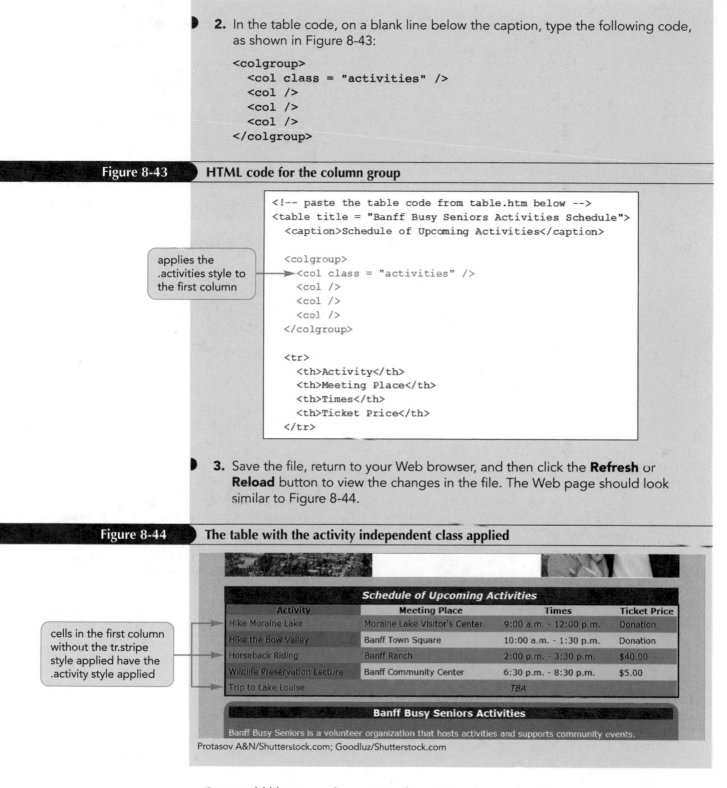

```
<!-- paste the table code from table.htm below -->
<table title = "Banff Busy Seniors Activities Schedule">
  <caption>Schedule of Upcoming Activities</caption>

  <colgroup>
  <col class = "activities" />
    <col />
    <col />
    <col />
  </colgroup>

  <tr>
    <th>Activity</th>
    <th>Meeting Place</th>
    <th>Times</th>
    <th>Ticket Price</th>
  </tr>
```

applies the .activities style to the first column

3. Save the file, return to your Web browser, and then click the **Refresh** or **Reload** button to view the changes in the file. The Web page should look similar to Figure 8-44.

Figure 8-44   **The table with the activity independent class applied**

cells in the first column without the tr.stripe style applied have the .activity style applied

Schedule of Upcoming Activities

Activity	Meeting Place	Times	Ticket Price
Hike Moraine Lake	Moraine Lake Visitor's Center	9:00 a.m. - 12:00 p.m.	Donation
Hike the Bow Valley	Banff Town Square	10:00 a.m. - 1:30 p.m.	Donation
Horseback Riding	Banff Ranch	2:00 p.m. - 3:30 p.m.	$40.00
Wildlife Preservation Lecture	Banff Community Center	6:30 p.m. - 8:30 p.m.	$5.00
Trip to Lake Louise		TBA	

Banff Busy Seniors Activities

Banff Busy Seniors is a volunteer organization that hosts activities and supports community events.

Protasov A&N/Shutterstock.com; Goodluz/Shutterstock.com

Sue would like to use the activities.htm CSS code in other documents that will be created at the Web site, so you'll cut and paste the CSS code from the activities.htm file to create an external style sheet file.

To cut and paste the CSS code and add the `link` element:

1. Return to the **activities.htm** file in your text editor. Position the insertion point on a blank line below the page title, and then type the following code, as shown in Figure 8-45. (Note: You can type the code on a single line and let your text editor wrap it automatically if necessary.)

```
<link rel = "stylesheet" href = "banffstyles.css"
type = "text/css" />
```

Figure 8-45 HTML code for the link element

```
<script src = "modernizr-2.js"></script>
<title>Banff Busy Seniors</title>

<link rel = "stylesheet" href = "banffstyles.css" type = "text/css" />

<style type = "text/css">
```

> link to the external style sheet

2. Leaving the activities.htm file open, create a new document in your text editor, and then save the file as **banffstyles.css**.

3. In the **banffstyles.css** file, type the following code, substituting *your name* and *today's date* where indicated:

```
/*
   Tutorial 8
   Your Name
   Today's Date
*/
```

4. Save the **banffstyles.css** file.

5. Switch to the **activities.htm** file, and then in the embedded style sheet, delete the start `<style type = "text/css">` tag and the end `</style>` tag.

6. Select all of the CSS style code from the embedded style sheet, and then press the **Ctrl+X** keys to cut the code and place it on the Clipboard. Do not cut any HTML code. Figure 8-46 shows the HTML code in the activities.htm file after the CSS code is moved.

Figure 8-46 HTML code in the activities.htm file after CSS code is removed

```
<head>

  <!--
    Tutorial 8, Tutorial
    Your Name: your name
    Today's Date: today's date

  -->

  <script src = "modernizr-2.js"></script>
  <title>Banff Busy Seniors</title>
  <link rel = "stylesheet" href = "banffstyles.css" type = "text/css" />

</head>
```

7. Switch to the **banffstyles.css** file, and then position the insertion point on a blank line below the comment code. Press the **Ctrl+V** keys to paste the code.

8. Save the **banffstyles.css** file.

9. Switch to the **activities.htm** file, and then save the file.

Now that the code has been copied to the external style sheet and a `<link>` tag has been entered in the activities.htm file, you want to test the activities.htm file to verify the link works properly. You'll check that the style sheet works and validate both the HTML file and the CSS file now.

To verify the link code and validate the files:

1. Return to your browser, and then refresh or reload the **activities.htm** page. Compare your file with the one shown in Figure 8-47 to confirm the styles are correct.

| Figure 8-47 | Completed Web page |

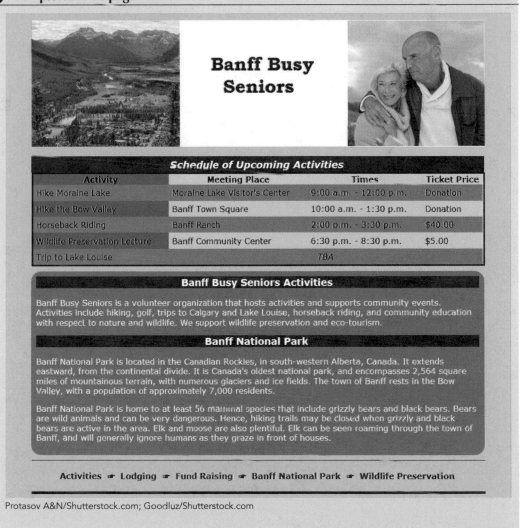

2. In your browser, go to http://validator.w3.org to open the W3C validator. Validate the **activities.htm** file by using the Validate by File Upload method. Note any errors, and then correct them in your file if necessary.

3. In your browser, navigate to http://jigsaw.w3.org/css-validator. Validate the **banffstyles.css** file by using the By file upload method. Be sure to select *More Options* and use the CSS level 3 profile to validate the code.

You've completed the Banff Busy Seniors activities Web page, and Sue is really impressed with your work. She particularly likes the hover effect on the stylized table. She'll review your work and will contact you if she has any other Web design needs.

PROSKILLS

Problem Solving: Tables and Handheld Devices

The popularity of handheld devices such as smartphones and small tablet computers adds an extra dimension to Web page design. Data tables are great for organizing data in a readable format, but what do you do when the usable screen size is very small, and the processing ability is not robust? Here are some considerations:

• Don't use complex tables. Besides the fact that a complex table is likely to be tall or wide, the overhead of processing a lot of table tags means the Web page will load slowly if at all.

• If you're sure the Web page will be displayed on a cell phone, don't use tables at all. Some cell phones do not support tables.

• Convert the table data into lists.

• Rethink the content. Do you really need to display a table of data on the Web page? Perhaps the data could be described some other way through a short text description, or isn't really needed at all.

• If you must use a list, make it a small one.

• Test your Web pages on as many handheld devices as possible. A Web page might look fine on a tablet but not be readable on a smartphone.

Designing Web pages for mobile devices is a complex topic, but it's important to be aware there are some solutions.

REVIEW

Session 8.2 Quick Check

1. What element controls table width?
2. Should table width be set as a percentage or as a pixel value?
3. What is row striping?
4. Why is row striping useful?
5. What HTML element is used for column formatting?
6. What attribute is sometimes used to apply formatting to several columns?

Practice the skills you learned in the tutorial using the same case scenario.

PRACTICE

Review Assignments

Data Files needed for the Review Assignments: lodging_T8.htm, modernizr-2.js, images/banff.jpg

The Banff Busy Seniors have friends and family members who love to visit Banff and enjoy spending time in Banff National Park. So the seniors have made arrangements for bulk rate discounts with four local hotels to provide an all-inclusive package for transportation, food, and lodging. Sue has asked for your help in developing the lodging page at the Banff Busy Seniors Web site. Sue has already begun work on a document that has a banner and several paragraphs of promotional material, but she needs your assistance in creating the table that will be in the document body. After entering the code to create a style in your text editor, save the file, switch to your browser, refresh or reload the page, verify you entered the style code correctly, and then switch back to your text editor and complete the next step. A preview of the Web page you'll create appears in Figure 8-48.

Figure 8-48	Lodging Web page

Banff Busy Seniors
Friends and Family Lodging

Banff has plenty of great accommodations for friends and family of Banff Busy Seniors. Below is a list of the hotels that offer discounts. Mention *Banff Busy Seniors* at the time of reservation

Discounts are available for one through seven days.

Hotel	Type of Lodging	Breakfast	Amenities on Site
The Banff Mountain View Hotel	Luxury	Buffet breakfast included	Pool, Spa, Shopping, Tennis, Golf, Horseback Riding
Blue Sky Hotels	Standard	Continental breakfast included	Pool, Resturant, Exercise Room, Lounge, Night Club
Inn on the Mountain	Economy	Not Included	Pool
Bow River Budget Hotel	Budget	Not Included	Snack Bar

For further information about lodging, call (403) 555-5890

Protasov A&N/Shutterstock.com; Goodluz/Shutterstock.com

Complete the following:

1. Use your text editor to open the **lodging_T8.htm** file, which is provided in your Data Files in the tutorial8\review folder. In the head section and below the page title, enter *your name* and *today's date* in the comment section where noted.

2. Save the file as **lodging.htm** in the same folder. Open the file in your browser, and then observe the appearance of the original file.

3. Switch back to your text editor. In the embedded style sheet, style the **body** element as follows:

    a. Set the width to **910px**.

    b. Set the margins on the top and bottom to **0**; set the margins on the left and right to **auto**.

    c. Set the background color to **#a6c3a8**.

    d. Set the font to **Verdana**, a sans-serif font.

    e. Set the line height to **1.5**.

4. Create a grouped selector to style both the **h2** heading and **footer** elements to appear with a bottom border that is **solid**, **4px**, and **navy**. Center the text.

5. Create a grouped selector for the table, table head, and table data elements to create the following styles:

    a. Set the border to **solid**, **2px**, and **navy**.

    b. Collapse the table borders.

    c. Set the text color to **white**.

    d. Set the background color to **teal**.

    e. Set the table text to appear in **bold**.

    f. Set the padding to **4px** on all sides.

    g. Set the vertical alignment to **top**.

6. Below the comment in the document body, enter the code to create the table shown in Figure 8-49.

Figure 8-49 | **Table of lodging partners**

Hotel	Type of Lodging	Breakfast	Amenities on Site
The Banff Mountain View Hotel	Luxury	Buffet breakfast included	Pool, Spa, Shopping, Tennis, Golf, Horseback Riding
Blue Sky Hotels	Standard	Continental breakfast included	Pool, Restaurant, Exercise Room, Lounge, Night Club
Inn on the Mountain	Economy	Not Included	Pool
Bow River Budget Hotel	Budget	Not Included	Snack Bar

7. Save the **lodging.htm** file. Refresh or reload the file in the browser, and then compare your file to Figure 8-48 to verify your file is correct.

8. Submit the completed file to your instructor in either printed or electronic form, as requested.

Use the skills you learned in the tutorial to create a Web page for a chain of health clubs.

APPLY

Case Problem 1

Data Files needed for this Case Problem: body_T8.htm, modernizr-2.js, images/ fitnessclass.jpg

Body by You   Joan Gardner owns Body by You, a large chain of fitness centers headquartered in Alhambra, California. While most health clubs and fitness centers have adult clienteles, Body by You offers fitness classes for all ages. Each day is devoted to focusing on one particular age group. Joan is keenly interested in helping children and teens maintain proper health and fitness, and she arranges special classes for baby boomers and seniors who want to avoid a sedentary lifestyle. Joan has approached you about creating a table for her Web site. You'll create table styles, and apply them to a table that highlights the weekly activities at Body by You. After you complete a step to create a style, verify in your browser the style code has been entered correctly, and then switch back to your text editor. A preview of the Web page you'll create appears in Figure 8-50.

Figure 8-50   Body by You Web page

Body by You

A Lifetime of Fitness

At *Body by You*, you don't have to be in your 20's to look great. We believe age is just a number. Here at *Body by You*, even 80 is the new 40!

Got an overweight child? *Body by You* will strive to have your child maintain an appropriate weight that will restore your child's confidence and good health. All of our exercises are coupled with classes on making smart, healthful, and nutritional choices for your children.

Had a baby? We can get you back into shape in just a few weeks. We have a nursery service right here at *Body by You*. We'll take care of your baby while you work yourself back into shape.

At *Body by You* we feel your senior days should be spent swimming in our Olympic-size pool, doing low-impact or non-impact exercises, yoga, Pilates, and gentle cardiovascular conditioning. We've designed programs for every age group from 6 to 106. Come join the fun at *Body by You*. It's *your* body; make the most of it.

EACH OF OUR CLUBS HAS THE FOLLOWING

World Class Leader in Facility Design

Body by You has been in business for over 30 years. We have all the equipment you need to stay fit for the rest of your life. We have leading-edge technology and a spacious, attractive, inviting decor.

Your Choice of Classes

We offer our members a wide assortment of classes to choose from. Whatever age and whatever level of fitness, we have a class that will meet your needs.

Certified Instructors

All of our classes are taught by certified instructors. From Pilates to gymnastics, you will get a specialized workout from experienced professionals who know how to design a fitness program.

Every Day Is a Special Day

Mondays	Kids Central (grades K-3)
Tuesdays	Tweens and Teens Time (grades 4-8 and grades 9-12) in separate groups
Wednesdays	Active Adults (ages 19-49)
Thursdays	BoomerVille
Fridays	Senior City (ages 70+)
Saturdays	Boys, Girls, Tweens, and Teens Gymnastics
Sundays	Slimnastics
Holiday Special	Just Announced! Tweens can join for an extra six months and get two months' membership for free!
Super Holiday Special	As an even better holiday offer, any tween who signs up for a full-year membership can get an extra six months free.

BODY BY YOU ◇ 28 SAN PALMETTO WAY ◇ ALHAMBRA, CA 91801 ◇ (555) 744-1230

Kzenon/Shutterstock.com

Complete the following:

1. Use your text editor to open the **body_T8.htm** file, which is provided in your Data Files in the tutorial8\case1 folder. Below the head open tag, enter **your name** and **today's date** in the comment section where noted.

2. Save the file as **body.htm** in the same folder. Open the file in your browser, and then observe the appearance of the original file.

3. Switch back to your text editor. In the embedded style sheet and below the CSS comment *enter table styles below*, style the **#schedule** id selector to have a width of **45%** and to float **right**.

4. Style the **table** element to have the following styles:

   a. Set the margin to **1em**.

   b. Set the table borders to appear as **solid**, **thin**, and **black**.

   c. Collapse the table borders.

5. Style the table data element to have padding of **0.5em**.

6. Style the table header element to have the following styles:

   a. The text should appear in a text color of **#ede568** and a background color of **#626d71**.

   b. The text should appear in **uppercase**.

7. Style the table row element to have text appear in **black** on a background color of **#dff3ef**.

8. Create a dependent class named **stripe** for the table row element. Style the *stripe* dependent class to have text appear in **white** with a background color of **#2a5e73**.

9. In the body of the document and below the comment *enter the table code below*, enter the code to create the table shown in Figure 8-51. The text *Every Day is a Special Day* should be a caption.

Figure 8-51 | **Table data for the fitness schedule**

Every Day is a Special Day	
Mondays	Kids Central (grades K-3)
Tuesdays	Tweens and Teens Time (grades 4-8 and grades 9-12) in separate groups
Wednesdays	Active Adults (ages 19-49)
Thursdays	BoomerVille
Fridays	Senior City (ages 70+)
Saturdays	Boys, Girls, Tweens, and Teens Gymnastics
Sundays	Slimnastics
Holiday Special	Just Announced! Tweens can join for an extra six months and get two months membership for free!
Super Holiday Special	As an even better holiday offer, any tween who signs up for a full-year membership can get an extra six months free.

10. After you have completed the table, apply the *stripe* class to the *Mondays*, *Wednesdays*, *Fridays*, *Sundays*, and *Super Holiday Special* rows.

11. Save the **body.htm** file. Switch to your browser, and then refresh or reload the page. Compare your file to Figure 8-50 to verify your file is correct.

12. Submit the results of the preceding steps to your instructor, in either printed or electronic form, as requested.

Use what you've learned to create and style a Web page for a used car dealership.

APPLY

Case Problem 2

Data Files needed for this Case Problem: berst_T8.htm, modernizr-2.js, images/ berstlogo.jpg

Berst Used Cars   Berst Used Cars is one of the largest used-car dealerships in suburban Milwaukee, Wisconsin. In 50 years, Berst Used Cars has grown from a 10-car lot in downtown Milwaukee to a 500-car lot in the suburbs. Berst sells only late-model, low-mileage cars, and its customers have been quite happy with the cars they have purchased there. Fred Berst, the owner, has approached you about updating the Berst Web site. In particular, he wants a Web site that highlights some of the special cars that are on sale. The berst.htm file already contains several styles that will be used for the home page. You'll now work on creating styles for the table and entering the table data. After you complete a step to create a style, verify in your browser the style code has been entered correctly, and then switch back to your text editor. A preview of the Web page you'll create appears in Figure 8-52.

Figure 8-52	Berst Used Cars Web page

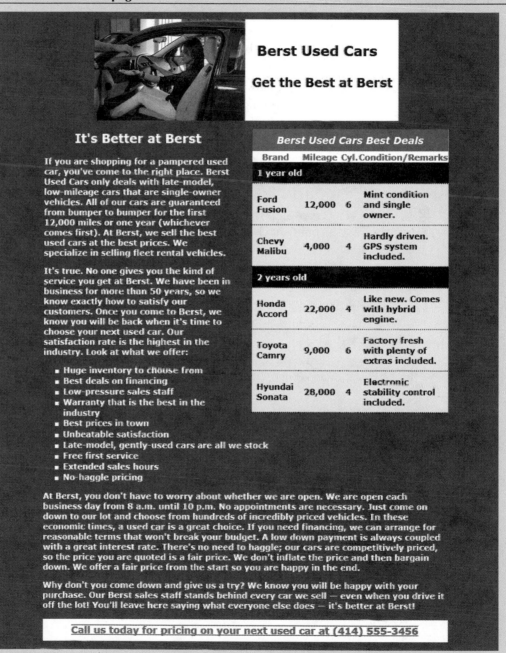

Levent Konuk/Shutterstock.com

Complete the following:

1. Use your text editor to open the **berst_T8.htm** file, which is provided in your Data Files in the tutorial8\case2 folder. Below the `<head>` tag, enter *your name* and *today's date* in the comment section where noted.

2. Save the file as **berst.htm** in the same folder. Open the file in your browser, and then observe the appearance of the original file.

3. Switch back to your text editor. In the code for the embedded style sheet and below the comment *enter table styles below*, style the **table** element as follows:

   a. Set the width to **40%**.

   b. Set the margin on the left to **5%**.

   c. Collapse the table borders.

   d. Float the table **right**.

4. Style the table data element as follows:

   a. Set the bottom border to be **dotted**, **2px**, and **navy**.

   b. Add padding of **10px** on all sides.

   c. Set the text color to **black**.

   d. Set the background color to **#deefce**.

   e. Set the font weight to **bold**.

5. Style the table header element to have a text color of **teal** and a background color of **white**.

6. Create a dependent class named **year** for the table data element. Style this dependent class to have text appear in **white** on a **black** background.

7. Style the **caption** element as follows:

   a. Add padding of **0.5em** on all sides.

   b. Set the text color to **white**.

   c. Set the background color to **teal**.

   d. Set the font weight to **bold**.

   e. Set the font style to **italic**.

   f. Set the font size to **1.2em**.

8. In the document body and below the comment *enter the code for the data table below*, create the data table shown in Figure 8-53, noting the following details:

   a. *Berst Used Cars Best Deals* is the caption text.

   b. Format the first row of the table as a table header row.

   ⊕ **EXPLORE**   c. Merge columns for the *1 year old* and *2 years old* rows.

   d. Apply the *year* class to the start table data tag for the *1 year old* and *2 years old* rows.

   e. Create the rest of the table row and table data elements using the data shown in Figure 8-53.

Figure 8-53   Table data for used cars

Berst Used Cars Best Deals

Brand	Mileage	Cyl.	Condition/Remarks
1 year old			
Ford Fusion	12,000	6	Mint condition and single owner.
Chevy Malibu	4,000	4	Hardly driven. GPS system included.
2 years old			
Honda Accord	22,000	4	Like new. Comes with hybrid engine.
Toyota Camry	9,000	6	Factory fresh with plenty of extras included.
Hyundai Sonata	28,000	4	Electronic stability control included.

9. Save the **berst.htm** file.
10. Switch to your browser, and then refresh or reload the page. Compare your file to Figure 8-52 to verify your file is correct.
11. Submit the results of the berst.htm file to your instructor, in either printed or electronic form, as requested.

Use the skills you learned in the tutorial to create and style a Web page for the Education Department at a community college

APPLY

Case Problem 3

Data Files needed for this Case Problem: admit.htm, baxter_T8.htm, modernizr-2.js, images/baxterlogo.jpg

Baxter Lake Community College   Baxter Lake Community College is a small, public college in eastern Colorado. The college grants a 2-year associate's degree in education; nearly all the graduates transfer to 4-year public or private institutions to obtain a full 4-year bachelor's degree in education. Dr. Anandami Greer, the chair of the Education Department, has approached you about updating the department's home page. Dr. Greer wants the page to focus on the department's philosophy of education. She wants to ensure that Baxter Lake Community College is attracting students who believe in a similar philosophy. After you complete a step to create a style, verify in your browser the style code has been entered correctly, and then switch back to your text editor. A preview of the Web page you'll create appears in Figure 8-54.

Figure 8-54   **Baxter Lake Community College Web page**

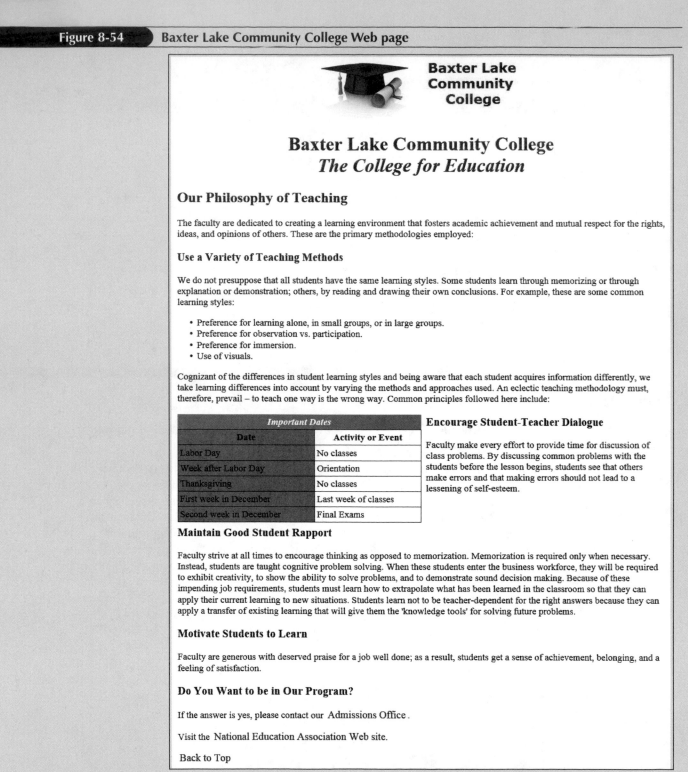

Baxter Lake Community College
The College for Education

Our Philosophy of Teaching

The faculty are dedicated to creating a learning environment that fosters academic achievement and mutual respect for the rights, ideas, and opinions of others. These are the primary methodologies employed:

Use a Variety of Teaching Methods

We do not presuppose that all students have the same learning styles. Some students learn through memorizing or through explanation or demonstration; others, by reading and drawing their own conclusions. For example, these are some common learning styles:

- Preference for learning alone, in small groups, or in large groups.
- Preference for observation vs. participation.
- Preference for immersion.
- Use of visuals.

Cognizant of the differences in student learning styles and being aware that each student acquires information differently, we take learning differences into account by varying the methods and approaches used. An eclectic teaching methodology must, therefore, prevail – to teach one way is the wrong way. Common principles followed here include:

Important Dates	
Date	**Activity or Event**
Labor Day	No classes
Week after Labor Day	Orientation
Thanksgiving	No classes
First week in December	Last week of classes
Second week in December	Final Exams

Encourage Student-Teacher Dialogue

Faculty make every effort to provide time for discussion of class problems. By discussing common problems with the students before the lesson begins, students see that others make errors and that making errors should not lead to a lessening of self-esteem.

Maintain Good Student Rapport

Faculty strive at all times to encourage thinking as opposed to memorization. Memorization is required only when necessary. Instead, students are taught cognitive problem solving. When these students enter the business workforce, they will be required to exhibit creativity, to show the ability to solve problems, and to demonstrate sound decision making. Because of these impending job requirements, students must learn how to extrapolate what has been learned in the classroom so that they can apply their current learning to new situations. Students learn not to be teacher-dependent for the right answers because they can apply a transfer of existing learning that will give them the 'knowledge tools' for solving future problems.

Motivate Students to Learn

Faculty are generous with deserved praise for a job well done; as a result, students get a sense of achievement, belonging, and a feeling of satisfaction.

Do You Want to be in Our Program?

If the answer is yes, please contact our Admissions Office.

Visit the National Education Association Web site.

Back to Top

Sashkin/Shutterstock.com

Complete the following:

1. Use your text editor to open the **baxter_T8.htm** file, which is provided in your Data Files in the tutorial8\case3 folder. Below the `<head>` tag, enter *your name* and *today's date* in the comment section where noted.

2. Save the file as **baxter.htm** in the same folder. Open the file in your browser, and then observe the appearance of the original file.

3. Switch back to your text editor. Style the **body** element as follows:
   a. Set the background color to **#ffffff**.
   b. Set the font size to **1.2em**.
   c. Set the font family to **"Times New Roman"**, **Times** (a serif font).

4. Create a grouped style for the **header** and **h1** selectors so the text is centered.

5. Style the anchor (**a**) element so link text appears in **maroon** and in a font size of **1.1em**, without underlining, and with padding of **4px**.

6. Style the *a:hover* pseudo-class selector so when the mouse passes over a link, the link text appears with underlining and with **4px** of padding.

7. Create an independent class named **clear** that clears elements on both the left and the right.

8. Apply the *clear* class to the start `<h3>` tag before the *Maintain Good Student Rapport* heading.

9. Style the **table** element as follows:
   a. Set the width to **50%**.
   b. Set the margins to **2px** on the top, **10px** on the right, **8px** on the bottom, and **0** on the left.
   c. Create a border that is **solid**, **thin**, and **navy**.
   d. Collapse the table borders.
   e. Float the table **left**.

10. Create a grouped selector for the table data and table header elements. These elements should appear with a border that is **solid**, **thin**, and **black**. Also add padding of **4px** to these elements.

11. Style the **caption** element as follows:
    a. Add padding of **4px** to all sides.
    b. Set the font weight to **bold**.
    c. Set the font style to **italic**.
    d. Set the text color to **white**.
    e. Set the background color to **green**.

12. Create a dependent class named **date** for the **col** element. Style the *date* class as follows:
    a. Set the text color to **white**.
    b. Set the background color to **gray**.

13. Apply the *date* class to the first `col` element. (The `col` element is just below the `caption` element in the table.)

14. In the start `<h1>` tag, enter the code for an id named **top**.

15. In the start `<table>` tag, create the title **Baxter Community College Academic Calendar** for the table.

16. Scroll to the bottom of the page. Using the words *Admissions Office* as the link text, create a link to the **admit.htm** file, which is provided in your Data Files in the tutorial8\case3 folder.

17. Using the words *National Education Association Web site* as the link text, create a link to the National Education Association Web site at **www.nea.org**.

18. Using the words *Back to Top* as the link text, create a link to the id named **top**.

19. Save the **baxter.htm** file. Switch to your browser, and then refresh or reload the page. Compare your file to Figure 8-54 to verify your file is correct.

20. In your browser, test all links.

21. In your browser, go to http://validator.w3.org to open the W3C validator. Validate the baxter.htm file by using the Validate by File Upload method. Note any errors, and then correct them in your file if necessary.

22. In your browser, go to http://jigsaw.w3.org/css-validator. Validate the baxter.htm file using the By file upload method. Note any errors, and then correct them in your file if necessary.

23. Submit the results of the baxter.htm file to your instructor, in either printed or electronic form, as requested.

Create a Web page to list your personal chronology.

RESEARCH

Case Problem 4

Data Files needed for this Case Problem: none

Your Personal Chronology   Use what you've learned about creating and styling tables to create a personal chronology of your life. Create a two-column table. The first column should list important dates in your life—or, alternatively, the age you were at each event—and the second column should list the important events that occurred on those dates. List at least 10 important events.

Complete the following:

1. Create a file with the DOCTYPE, html, head, body, and title elements appropriate for a personal chronology Web page. Save the file as **personal.htm** in the tutorial8\case4 folder.

2. Create the tags for an embedded style sheet, and within them format the body element with the text size, font, color, and background color of your choice.

3. Create styles for the table, td, th, and caption elements. Create a dependent class for the td element to stripe a row with a different format.

4. Create a two-column data table that shows examples of the following:
   a. A caption
   b. A table header
   c. colspan or rowspan
   d. Row striping

5. Save the **personal.htm** file.

6. Open your browser and go to http://validator.w3.org. Use the Validate by File Upload method to check the **personal.htm** document and ensure the HTML code is correct. If necessary, correct any errors detected by the validation.

7. In your browser, go to http://jigsaw.w3.org/css-validator. Use the By file upload method to check the **personal.htm** file and ensure the CSS code is correct. If necessary, correct any errors detected by the validation.

8. Submit the results of the personal.htm file to your instructor, in either printed or electronic form, as requested.

ENDING DATA FILES

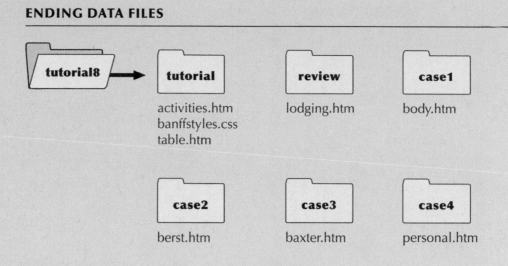

tutorial8 → tutorial
activities.htm
banffstyles.css
table.htm

review
lodging.htm

case1
body.htm

case2
berst.htm

case3
baxter.htm

case4
personal.htm

Creating Forms

Designing a Family Information Form

OBJECTIVES

Session 9.1
- Understand how data is collected and processed
- Construct an HTML form
- Determine input types
- Create and label text boxes for text input
- Use fieldsets to organize form controls
- Use CSS to style form controls
- Set a text box value and placeholder

Session 9.2
- Create option buttons for a single input
- Restrict the number of characters in a text box
- Use check boxes for multiple inputs
- Develop a select list for text input
- Create a text area for long text input
- Create buttons for submitting and clearing form data

Case | *Sullivan Family Reunion*

Patrick Sullivan lives in Dublin, Ireland. His close family members live in counties Kerry and Cork, in the southwest part of the Republic of Ireland. Ireland has a tumultuous history, fraught with war and famine. During the 18th and 19th centuries, many families emigrated from Ireland in search of opportunities and better living conditions. The largest exodus happened in the 1840s during the great potato famine. Potatoes were the main source of food, and a blight destroyed most of the crops. Hundreds of thousands of Irish immigrants left the island, hoping to live in the United States and Canada. Among them were many of Patrick's distant relatives.

In 1921, Ireland was split into two separate countries. Northern Ireland became a country, which is part of the United Kingdom. The rest of the island became the Republic of Ireland, although many people refer to it as simply Ireland.

Patrick is planning a family reunion. He has been doing some ancestry research and would like to reach out to any Sullivans to discover more relatives. He would love to spread the word about the family reunion and his ancestry research. He has begun work on a Web site and has asked for your help in making it possible for his relatives to contact him through the site. In this tutorial, you'll help him add a contact form to his Web site.

STARTING DATA FILES

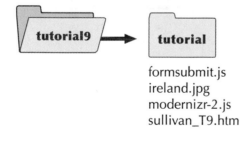

tutorial9 →

tutorial

formsubmit.js
ireland.jpg
modernizr-2.js
sullivan_T9.htm

review

formsubmit.js
ireland.jpg
modernizr-2.js
reunion_T9.htm

case1

awardballot_T9.htm
awardstyles.css
modernizr-2.js
wkzlogo.jpg

case2

food_T9.htm
foodlogo.jpg
foodstyles.css
modernizr-2.js

case3

hall.jpg
hall_T9.jpg
hallstyles.css
modernizr-2.js

case4

modernizr-2.js
survey_T9.htm
surveylogo.gif

SESSION 9.1 VISUAL OVERVIEW

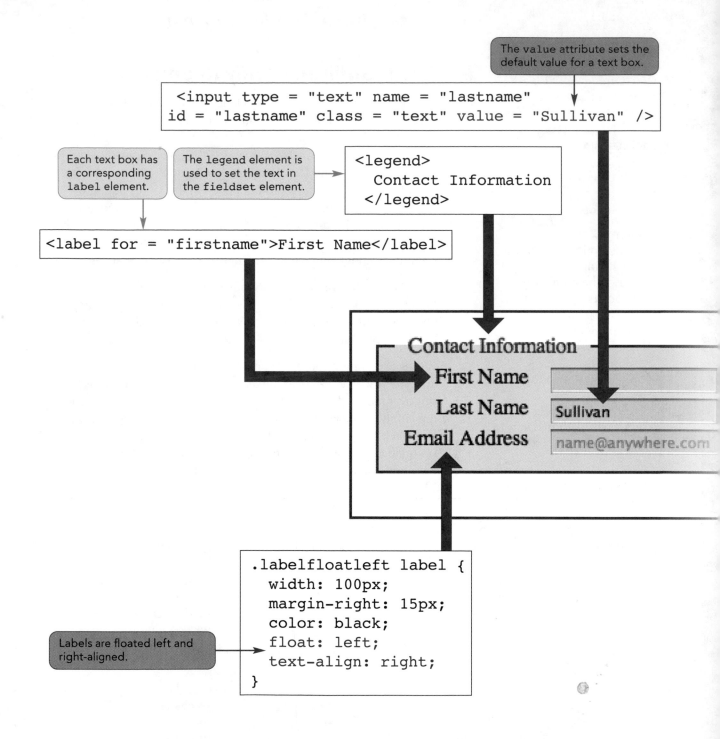

The value attribute sets the default value for a text box.

```
<input type = "text" name = "lastname"
id = "lastname" class = "text" value = "Sullivan" />
```

Each text box has a corresponding label element.

The legend element is used to set the text in the fieldset element.

```
<legend>
    Contact Information
</legend>
```

```
<label for = "firstname">First Name</label>
```

Contact Information
First Name
Last Name   Sullivan
Email Address   name@anywhere.com

Labels are floated left and right-aligned.

```
.labelfloatleft label {
    width: 100px;
    margin-right: 15px;
    color: black;
    float: left;
    text-align: right;
}
```

CREATING AND STYLING TEXT BOXES

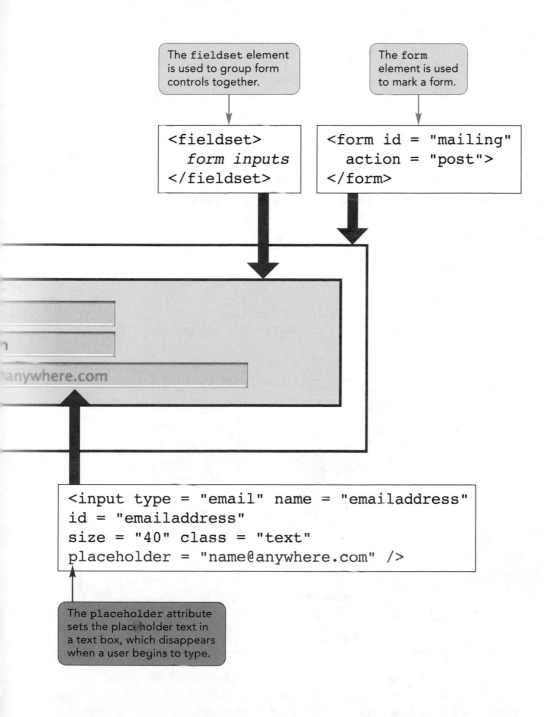

The fieldset element is used to group form controls together.

```
<fieldset>
  form inputs
</fieldset>
```

The form element is used to mark a form.

```
<form id = "mailing"
  action = "post">
</form>
```

```
<input type = "email" name = "emailaddress"
id = "emailaddress"
size = "40" class = "text"
placeholder = "name@anywhere.com" />
```

The placeholder attribute sets the placeholder text in a text box, which disappears when a user begins to type.

Understanding How Data Is Collected and Processed

Prior to taking a course in HTML, you might not have had much experience in creating Web pages, but you certainly have worked with various kinds of forms. You have most likely completed forms—either paper forms or Web forms—to apply for college, financial aid, or a job. In addition, you have probably either shopped or completed a survey online, and you entered and submitted data in your browser to do so. An HTML **form** is a collection of HTML elements used to gather data that a user enters online.

You use HTML to create the form, but the form does not process any of the data. When a user clicks a form's submit button to send the data, the form connects to a **form handler**—software that runs on a Web file server and processes the form. In a simple program, the form handler software may do nothing more than transfer the data to a database on the server, and then send a confirmation Web page back to the Web browser. On the other hand, the form handler software may perform complex data manipulations.

For example, if you fill out a form online to purchase an item, click the Submit button, and then receive a confirmation page in response, here's what happens to make the transaction possible:

1. The Web browser loads the HTML Web form. After you enter data into the form, you click the submit button to send the data.
2. The browser sends the data to a Web server.
3. Form handler software on the server processes the data in the form and then retains the data in a database.
4. The form handler creates a new Web page that contains information—in this case, an order confirmation.
5. The server sends the confirmation page to the browser.
6. The Web browser receives the page and displays it for you to read.

This process is shown in Figure 9-1.

Figure 9-1	Processing a Web form

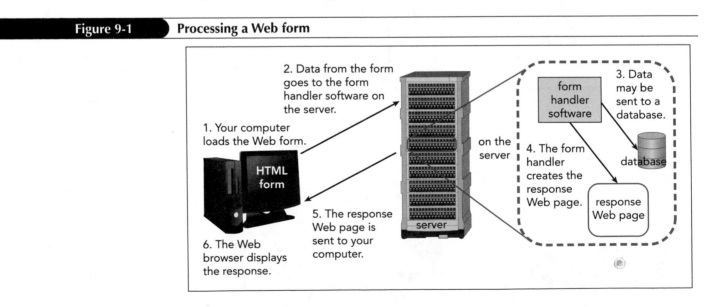

The form handler could be a **script**, which is a short series of programming instructions. Scripts can perform tasks such as transferring data to a database, sending an email message, or creating and sending a response Web page to a browser. Scripting languages commonly used with HTML forms include ASP, PHP, and JavaScript. A scripting language can run on a server or run in a Web browser. For instance, JavaScript is run on Web browsers, and ASP and PHP run on servers.

The data sent to a server could be stored electronically in a **database**, which is an organized collection of data. Database software such as MySQL, MS SQL, Oracle or even Microsoft Access is used to store and manipulate the data. A **field** represents a single kind of data in the database. For example, a field could be people's first names, a date, or invoice numbers. Each field has a name, such as *firstname*, *lastname*, or *date*. When you design your HTML form, you need to know these field names because you'll enter them in the code for your form. An HTML form is used only to collect the data; it does not perform any of the functions of a database program, such as organizing data, sorting data, or searching for and retrieving information. Scripting and databases are not covered in this text. Please ask your instructor about additional courses that cover this content.

The HTML `form` element serves as the container for all of the elements in a form. You use HTML code to create **form controls**, which are elements that allow users to enter text, select options, or click to submit the form. Examples of form controls include text boxes, option buttons, and check boxes. As you create the form for Patrick, you'll learn how to determine which form controls you need and how to organize them on a form.

Patrick has already created a file with some information about Irish immigration and the Sullivan family. You'll open the file, enter a comment, and then save the file with a new filename.

To open the Sullivan file:

▶ **1.** In your text editor, open the **sullivan_T9.htm** file, which is located in the tutorial9\tutorial folder included with your Data Files. In the head section and below the page title, enter *your name* and *today's date* in the comment section where noted.

▶ **2.** Save the file as **sullivan.htm** in the same folder.

▶ **3.** Open the **sullivan.htm** file in your browser. Figure 9-2 shows Patrick's original file.

Figure 9-2   **The Sullivan Web page**

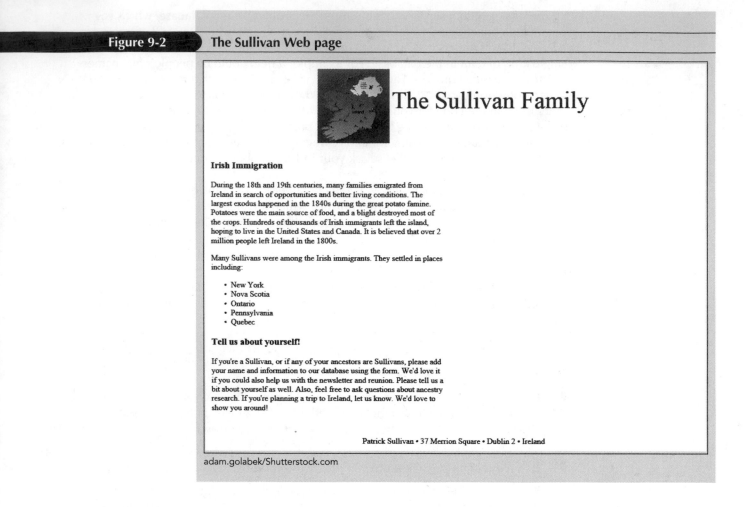

adam.golabek/Shutterstock.com

Creating a Form

Every form begins with the start `<form>` tag and ends with the closing `</form>` tag, which must be within the document `<body></body>` tags. The `<form>` tag has several attributes and values, including a unique id for the form. You can use any value you want for the `id` attribute, but it makes sense to specify a value that describes the information the form gathers or that is similar to the name of the database that will receive the data. In this instance, you'll use an id value of *mailing* because the purpose of the form is to gather family information to create a mailing list and send a message to Patrick.

Creating the *form*, *text*, and *fieldset* Elements

- To create a form, enter the following code:

```
<form id = "idvalue" method = "methodtype" action =
"script_url"></form>
```

where *idvalue* is the name of the form, *methodtype* is either get or post, and *script_url* is the location on the file server where the script will be run when the form is submitted.

- To create a text box, use the following code:

```
<input type = "texttype" name = "name" id = "id" value =
"initialvalue" size = "sizevalue" maxlength = "maxvalue" />
```

where *texttype* is text, password, email, or another valid value; *initialvalue* is the default data that appears in the field; *sizevalue* is the width of the box in characters; and *maxvalue* is the maximum number of characters that a user can type in the field.

- To organize form elements using the fieldset and legend elements, enter the following code:

```
<fieldset><legend>legendtext</legend>
    form elements
</fieldset>
```

where *legendtext* is the text for the legend, and *form elements* is the code for the form controls you want to group together.

TIP

A Web page can include more than one form.

The action attribute in the **form** tag identifies the location on the server where you'll send the data. It also identifies the script that will run when a user clicks the submit button to send the data collected by the form. The method attribute tells the browser how to submit the form information. The two values for the method attribute are get and post. The default get method sends the data in the form directly to the server by appending the data to the URL. A query string using the get method is less secure than the post method because all of the form input values appear in the query string, so anyone can see them. The post method passed the query string to the server behind the scenes. The user never sees the query string and its inputs. Therefore, the post method is used more often to submit form data that requires confidentiality, such as credit card information. Using the post method, the browser contacts the server, and then the data in the form is sent to the server. Using the post method, the code for the start <form> tag would look similar to the following:

```
<form id = "mailing" action =
"http://webserver.com/formhandler.asp" method = "post">
```

Because you don't have access to a form handler, you'll enter just the code for the form in the sullivan.htm file without sending data to any server. You'll enter a value for the method attribute using the post method so the form data does not appear in the URL. You'll enter the form element and its attributes and values now.

To enter the `form` element code:

1. Return to the **sullivan.htm** file in your text editor. Scroll down almost to the bottom of the file, position the insertion point on a blank line below the comment *enter the form code below*, and then type the following HTML code, as shown in Figure 9-3:

```
<form id = "survey" name = "survey" method = "post">

</form>
```

Figure 9-3 **Code for the form container**

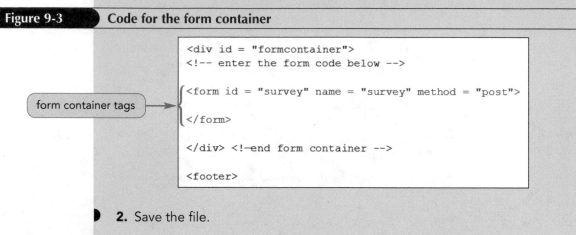

```
<div id = "formcontainer">
<!-- enter the form code below -->

<form id = "survey" name = "survey" method = "post">

</form>

</div> <!--end form container -->

<footer>
```

form container tags

2. Save the file.

You can format a `form` element the same way you format other HTML elements. To see the boundary of a form, you create a border. You can also create styles for margin, padding, and the font size. For Patrick's form, each group of form controls will appear within a `section` container, so you'll create a descendant selector for the `section` element. A form does not require `section` elements, but using them has several advantages. First, you can style the `section` element to clear past other controls in the form, which ensures that no form element is placed on top of another. Also, several form elements must always be inside a block-level element; by using `section` elements, you won't have to populate your form with <p></p> tags to meet this requirement. Finally, you can create a style for a `section` element to call attention to a particular part of the form or to position the `form` element within the form.

You'll add the CSS code that will float the *formcontainer* container `div` element. You'll also add the CSS that will add a border to the form, set padding and margins, and set the size of the font.

To style the `form` and the `section` elements:

1. Return to the **sullivan.htm** file in your text editor. Scroll up to the embedded style sheet, and position the insertion point on a blank line after the comment *enter the form styles below*, and then type the following HTML code, as shown in Figure 9-4:

```
form {
    margin-top: 1em;
    border: solid 2px #305704;
    padding: 1em;
    font-size: 16px;
}

#formcontainer {
    width: 47%;
    float: right;
}
```

CSS code for the form and formcontainer selectors

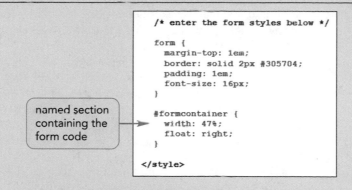

named section containing the form code

```
/* enter the form styles below */

form {
    margin-top: 1em;
    border: solid 2px #305704;
    padding: 1em;
    font-size: 16px;
}

#formcontainer {
    width: 47%;
    float: right;
}

</style>
```

2. Save the file, return to your Web browser, and then click the **Refresh** or **Reload** button to view the changes in the file. The Web page should look similar to Figure 9-5.

Figure 9-5   **form element stylized**

The Sullivan Family

Irish Immigration

During the 18th and 19th centuries, many families emigrated from Ireland in search of opportunities and better living conditions. The largest exodus happened in the 1840s during the great potato famine. Potatoes were the main source of food, and a blight destroyed most of the crops. Hundreds of thousands of Irish immigrants left the island, hoping to live in the United States and Canada. It is believed that over 2 million people left Ireland in the 1800s.

form border

adam.golabek/Shutterstock.com

Now that you've set the style for the form, you're ready to add form controls for collecting form data.

Determining Input Types

Recall that a field represents a single kind of data. A user enters data into each field in a form based on **prompting text**—a short description that suggests what data belongs in a certain field. Examples of prompting text would be *Last Name, Choose an item,* or *Country*. You want data entry to be easy for a user, and you want the user to enter correct data in the form, so the prompting text needs to be clear and specific. For example, prompting text such as *Enter your Name* might be confusing to a user, as it's unclear whether users should enter their full names, first names, last names, or titles, and in what order. The **label element** is used to display prompting text on the screen. You should always use the label element with the `for` attribute because the value of the `for` attribute helps screen readers associate the prompting text with the corresponding form control.

Controlling Label Placement on Forms

When designing your forms, you need to decide where to position the label text. In general, you have three options, each of which has benefits and trade-offs. The first option is to use top alignment, in which you place each label text above its corresponding text field. This option is good for shorter forms because it uses two lines for every field; however, in a very long form, top alignment would require users to scroll down too much.

The second option is to align the labels flush left. Left-aligned labels are the easiest to read because a user's eye naturally views the left edge of the screen first in languages that are normally read from left to right. The disadvantage of left alignment is that it creates some white space between each label and its form element, which might slow down some users as they enter data. If the form control is to the right of the label, it could produce a ragged look, as the lengths of text for each line are likely different. The form controls would not align vertically.

The third option is to right-align the labels, which creates the closest connection between the label text and the form control. The form control would be immediately to the right of the label, which is text. The form controls would align vertically along the left edge. This is the most commonly used option.

The `input` element is used to determine the type of data a control collects. The `label` element is used together with the `input` element. The `label` element uses the `for` attribute, which associates the label with the id value in the input element. The **label text** is the text that appears between the start `<label>` and end `</label>` tags. For instance, in the code below, the label text is *First Name;* a user would see these words next to the field as the prompting text in the browser:

```
<label for = "firstname">First Name</label>
```

The `type` attribute determines the specific type of form object that is created. It could be a text input, a check box, an option button, or another form object. The `input` element is an empty element (it doesn't mark up any content), so its code must be closed with a space and forward slash. As with the `img` element, HTML5 does not require the space and forward slash to close single tag elements, but its use is recommended for XHTML compatibility. You enter the `input` element code below the `label` element code, as shown in the following example:

```
<label for = "firstname">First Name</label>
<input type = "text" name = "firstname" id = "firstname" />
```

Note that the input element uses both the name attribute and the id attribute. Currently, you must still use the name attribute in the input element code so the data can be recognized by older browsers and different computer software platforms. To make it easier to enter data into a database, the name and id attribute should have the same name as the field name in the database that receives the data. If you work as part of a Web development team, the database administrator would provide you with the names of the database fields that must be used.

Creating Text Boxes

You use the **text box** control to gather **alphanumeric data** (letters or numbers) as a single line of text in a form. Later, you'll learn about another form control used when users may need to input more than one line of data. You use the type attribute with a value of text to create a single-line text box.

Another type of single-line text field is a **password field**. This is a text field in which the input is masked on the screen. As a user enters data in a password field, stars or bullets appear in the text box to disguise the characters the user is actually typing. If you want a text field to be a password field, change the value of the type attribute to password.

The size attribute and its value are used to control the text box width. The size attribute value determines the width of the box in characters. A user could continue typing characters beyond the end of a text box, and the field would still accept input as the data scrolled to the right. Also, the width is wide enough to contain the text only if you style the field to accept text in a monospace font, such as Courier or Courier New. To set a limit on the number of characters a user can type in a text box, you use the maxlength attribute. For example, if you set the maxlength attribute to a value of 25, then the text box would not continue to scroll and would stop accepting input after the 25th character had been entered. The following code shows an example of the size and maxlength attributes:

```
<input type = "text" name = "firstname" id = "firstname" size =
"15" maxlength = "15" />
```

If you want a text box to display a value by default, you use the value attribute and assign the value you expect most users to enter. Recall that you want users to complete a form as quickly and easily as possible, so you should use a default value only if you're sure the overwhelming majority of users would otherwise enter it. Otherwise, users will have to delete the value and enter a new one.

Organizing Form Controls

It's important to organize form controls in related groups so users can read them easily. For example, in this tutorial, you'll organize the contact information form elements into one related group, and then organize personal information form elements into another group. Finally, you'll organize the message form elements into another group.

Two elements are used together to organize form controls. The fieldset element groups a series of related form elements. By default, the fieldset element creates a 1px border around the elements you have grouped in the fieldset in most browsers. The legend element creates caption text for a fieldset. The **legend text** is entered between the legend tags and appears in the legend caption in the browser. By default, the caption appears in the upper-left corner of the fieldset border in most browsers. The following code illustrates the use of the fieldset and legend elements:

```
<fieldset><legend>Descriptive Caption</legend>
. . . form code . . .
</fieldset>
```

TIP

Fieldsets are also known as group boxes.

The appearance of fieldset borders and legend text can differ depending on the browser, so you should check them in several contemporary browsers to make sure their appearance is satisfactory. Internet Explorer, for example, places the legend text inside the fieldset, whereas the Firefox browser places the legend outside the fieldset. If necessary, you can style the `fieldset` and the `legend` elements to add padding or create margin space around the legend text.

Now that you've entered the `form` element tags, you're ready to create some form controls. You'll create text box controls to accept a user's first name, last name, and email address. The email input type is an HTML5 element. You'll group these together in a fieldset group for the contact information. You'll start by entering the code for the first text box control and the contact information fieldset.

Do not type a space in *fieldset*.

To enter the code for the first text box and fieldset:

▶ 1. Return to the **sullivan.htm** file in your text editor. Position the insertion point on a blank line after the start `<form>` tag, and then type the following fieldset tags:

```
<fieldset>
</fieldset>
```

▶ 2. Position the insertion point after the start `<fieldset>` tag, and then enter the following legend code:

```
<legend>Contact Information</legend>
```

▶ 3. Position the insertion point on a blank line after the end `</legend>` tag, and then enter the following code for the label and text control, as shown in Figure 9-6:

```
<label for = "firstname">First Name</label>
<input type = "text" name = "firstname" id = "firstname" />
```

HTML code for the fieldset and text box control

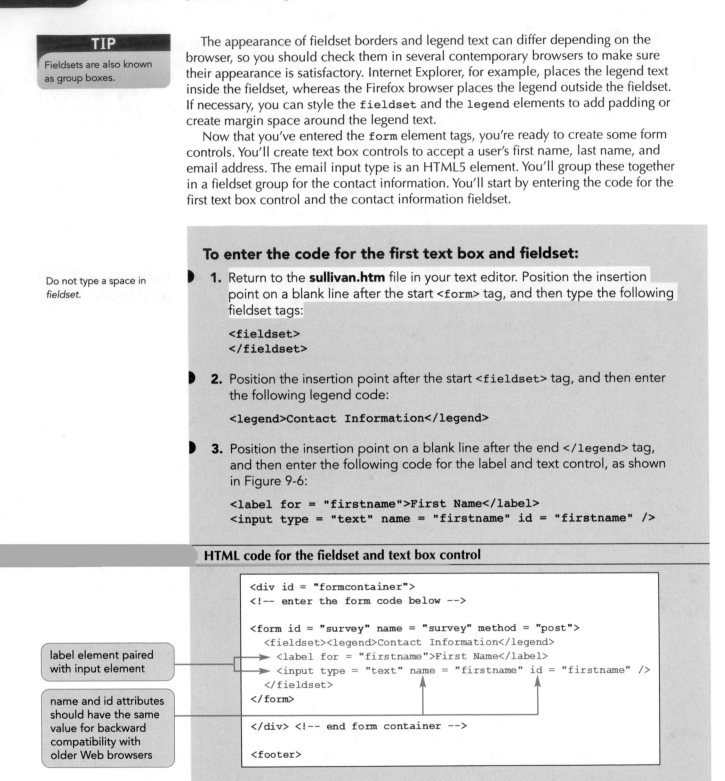

```
<div id = "formcontainer">
<!-- enter the form code below -->

<form id = "survey" name = "survey" method = "post">
   <fieldset><legend>Contact Information</legend>
   <label for = "firstname">First Name</label>
   <input type = "text" name = "firstname" id = "firstname" />
   </fieldset>
</form>

</div> <!-- end form container -->

<footer>
```

label element paired with input element

name and id attributes should have the same value for backward compatibility with older Web browsers

▶ 4. Save the file, return to your Web browser, and then click the **Refresh** or **Reload** button to view the changes in the file. The Web page should look similar to Figure 9-7.

| Figure 9-7 | The fieldset, legend, label, and text box in the Web page |

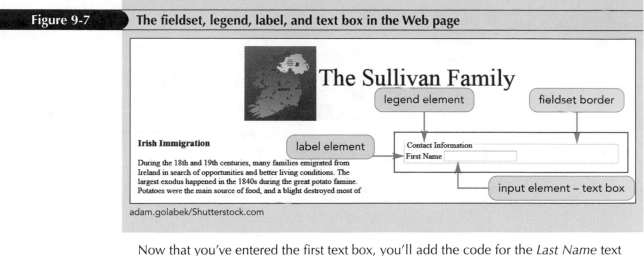

adam.golabek/Shutterstock.com

Now that you've entered the first text box, you'll add the code for the *Last Name* text box and the *Email* text box in this fieldset. Instead of using the value `text` for the type attribute, you'll use the value `email` to identify the content as an email address. The form elements aren't styled yet, so the elements will not be aligned.

To enter the code for the Last Name and Email Address text boxes:

1. Return to the **sullivan.htm** file in your text editor. Position the insertion point on a blank line above the end `</fieldset>` tag, and then type the following HTML code, as shown in Figure 9-8:

```
<label for = "lastname">Last Name</label>
<input type = "text" name = "lastname" id = "lastname" />

<label for = "emailaddress">Email Address</label>
<input type = "email" name = "emailaddress"
id = "emailaddress" />
```

| Figure 9-8 | HTML code for the Last Name and Email Address text boxes |

```
<div id = "formcontainer">
<!-- enter the form code below -->

<form id = "survey" name = "survey" method = "post">
  <fieldset><legend>Contact Information</legend>
    <label for = "firstname">First Name</label>
    <input type = "text" name = "firstname" id = "firstname" />

    <label for = "lastname">Last Name</label>
    <input type = "text" name = "lastname" id = "lastname" />

    <label for = "emailaddress">Email Address</label>
    <input type = "email" name = "emailaddress" id = "emailaddress" />
  </fieldset>
</form>
```

email address uses email as the type value

2. Save the file, return to your Web browser, and then click the **Refresh** or **Reload** button to view the changes in the file. The Web page should look similar to Figure 9-9.

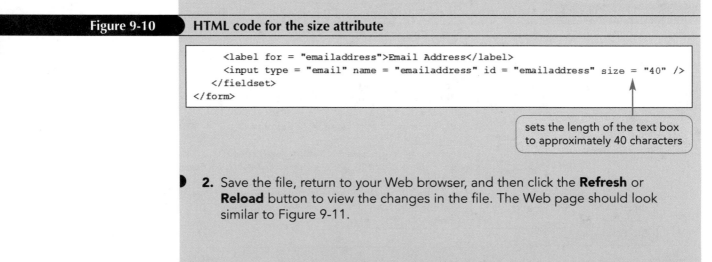

text and email text boxes

The Sullivan Family

email text box looks the same as the text boxes with the text value

Irish Immigration

During the 18th and 19th centuries, many families emigrated from Ireland in search of opportunities and better living conditions. The largest exodus happened in the 1840s during the great potato famine. Potatoes were the main source of food, and a blight destroyed most of the crops. Hundreds of thousands of Irish immigrants left the island,

Contact Information
First Name   Last Name
Email Address

adam.golabek/Shutterstock.com

The text boxes and labels are not yet aligned, and may not even be close to each other. You'll be adding CSS later to align the text boxes with the labels.

Patrick likes the text boxes for the first and last names, but he points out that some email addresses can be quite long. He wonders if the text box for email could be increased in length. The default length for the text boxes is 20 characters; however, you may not always see 20 characters, depending on the font used. Patrick would like the email text box to accommodate at least 40 characters. You can use the `size` attribute to change the length of any text box control. Here, you'll use the `size` attribute to set the length of the Email Address text box to 40 characters.

To set the size of the Email Address text box:

▶ **1.** Return to the **sullivan.htm** file in your text editor. Position the insertion point to the left of the slash (/) at the end of the `<input>` tag for the email address, and then type the following HTML code followed by a space, as shown in Figure 9-10:

```
size = "40"
```

Figure 9-10   HTML code for the size attribute

```
<label for = "emailaddress">Email Address</label>
<input type = "email" name = "emailaddress" id = "emailaddress" size = "40" />
</fieldset>
</form>
```

sets the length of the text box to approximately 40 characters

▶ **2.** Save the file, return to your Web browser, and then click the **Refresh** or **Reload** button to view the changes in the file. The Web page should look similar to Figure 9-11.

Figure 9-11   email text box with the size set to 40

The Sullivan Family

Email Address text box is approximately 40 characters long

Irish Immigration

During the 18th and 19th centuries, many families emigrated from Ireland in search of opportunities and better living conditions. The largest exodus happened in the 1840s during the great potato famine. Potatoes were the main source of food, and a blight destroyed most of the crops. Hundreds of thousands of Irish immigrants left the island, hoping to live in the United States and Canada. It is believed that over 2 million people left Ireland in the 1800s.

Contact Information

First Name   Last Name

Email Address

adam.golabek/Shutterstock.com

Using CSS to Style Form Controls

Now that you've created a few text boxes, Patrick thinks the form looks a little messy. He'd like you to style the text boxes so their left edges are vertically aligned, with each label right-aligned to the left of its corresponding text box. You'll use CSS to accomplish this.

First you'll create a style rule for the descendent selector .*labelfloatleft label*. Then you'll apply the class *labelfloatleft* to the fieldset. You'll be creating other fieldsets later that will not require labels to be aligned on the left side of the text controls, so you'll apply the *labelfloatleft* class only to the current fieldset. By specifying styles for the descendent selector .*labelfloatleft label*, only the labels in the fieldset with the *labelfloatleft* class will be affected. The style for the descendent selector .*labelfloatleft label* will set a width of 100px for the label; float the label to the left, and align it to the right, as well as define the color as black, and the right margin at 15px. You'll also create a style rule for the descendent selector .*labelfloatleft input* that will display the input element as a block element so the next element appears below it. You'll create the styles, and then apply the .*labelfloatleft* style to the fieldset now.

To create the style for the .*labelfloatleft label* descendent selector and apply it to the fieldset:

1. Return to the **sullivan.htm** file in your text editor. Scroll up to the embedded style sheet, position the insertion point on a blank line after the #*formcontainer* style, and then type the following CSS code, as shown in Figure 9-12:

```
.labelfloatleft label {
   width: 100px;
   margin-right: 15px;
   color: black;
   float: left;
   text-align: right;
}

.labelfloatleft input {
   display: block;
}
```

CSS code for the .labelfloatleft label and .labelfloatleft input descendent selectors

```
#formcontainer {
  width: 47%;
  float: right;
}

.labelfloatleft label {
  width: 100px;
  margin-right: 15px;
  color: black;
  float: left;
  text-align: right;
}

.labelfloatleft input {
  display: block;
}

</style>
```

2. Position the insertion point in the start `<fieldset>` tag to the left of the > symbol, type a space, and then type the following HTML code, as shown in Figure 9-13:

```
class = "labelfloatleft"
```

Figure 9-13   **HTML code to apply the labelfloatleft class**

```
<form id = "survey" name = "survey" method = "post">
  <fieldset class = "labelfloatleft"><legend>Contact Information</legend>
    <label for = "firstname">First Name</label>
    <input type = "text" name = "firstname" id = "firstname" />
```

3. Save the file, return to your Web browser, and then click the **Refresh** or **Reload** button to view the changes in the file. The Web page should look similar to Figure 9-14.

Figure 9-14   **Stylized labels and text boxes**

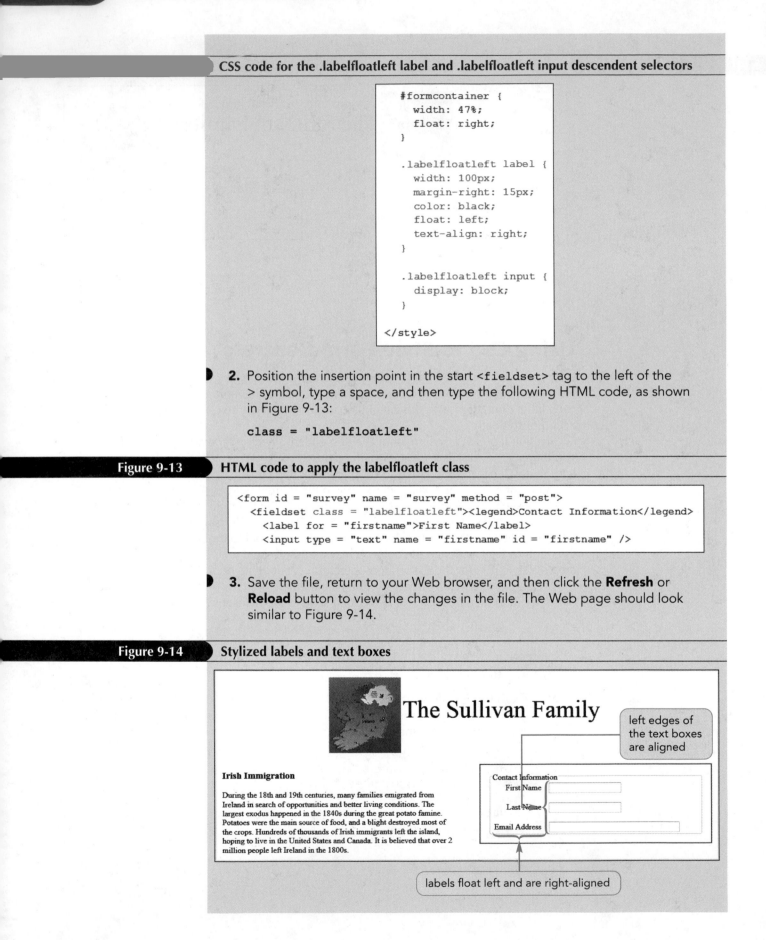

The Sullivan Family

left edges of the text boxes are aligned

Irish Immigration

During the 18th and 19th centuries, many families emigrated from Ireland in search of opportunities and better living conditions. The largest exodus happened in the 1840s during the great potato famine. Potatoes were the main source of food, and a blight destroyed most of the crops. Hundreds of thousands of Irish immigrants left the island, hoping to live in the United States and Canada. It is believed that over 2 million people left Ireland in the 1800s.

Contact Information
First Name
Last Name
Email Address

labels float left and are right-aligned

If you wanted the label elements to appear above the fields, rather than to their left, you would remove the declarations for width, margin, float, and text alignment from the label element style. Instead, you would use the declaration display: block to make each label appear above its corresponding field.

Now that the text boxes and labels are aligned, you'll add color to the fieldset, legend, and labels. Patrick would like an Irish green theme and has chosen some suitable colors for the form. You'll add styles for the *fieldset*, *legend*, and *label* selectors.

To create the styles for the *fieldset*, *legend* and *label* selectors:

▶ **1.** Return to the **sullivan.htm** file in your text editor. Position the insertion point on a blank line after the *.labelfloatleft input* descendent selector style, and then type the following CSS code, as shown in Figure 9-15:

```
fieldset {
   margin-bottom: 1em;
   border: solid 2px #305704;
   background-color: #befca7;
   display: block;
}

legend {
   color: #305704;
   padding: 0 10px;
}

label {
   color: black;
}
```

Figure 9-15   CSS code for the fieldset, legend, and label selectors

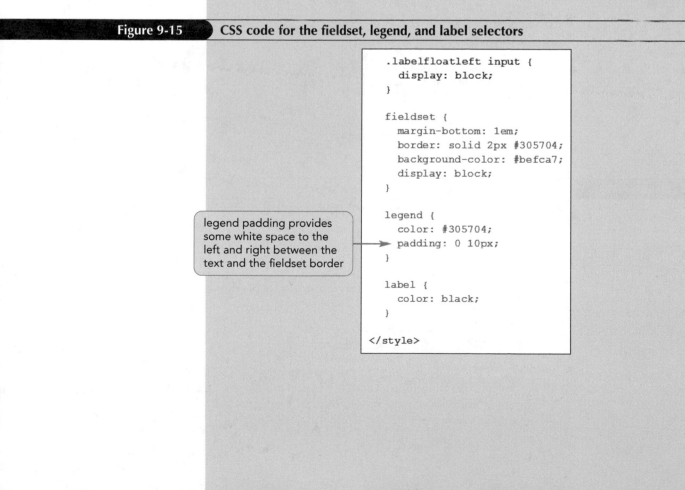

```
.labelfloatleft input {
   display: block;
}

fieldset {
   margin-bottom: 1em;
   border: solid 2px #305704;
   background-color: #befca7;
   display: block;
}

legend {
   color: #305704;
   padding: 0 10px;
}

label {
   color: black;
}

</style>
```

legend padding provides some white space to the left and right between the text and the fieldset border

2. Save the file, return to your Web browser, and then click the **Refresh** or **Reload** button to view the changes in the file. The Web page should look similar to Figure 9-16.

Figure 9-16   **fieldset, legend, and labels stylized**

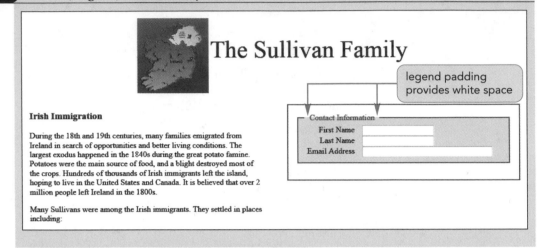

The text boxes themselves can be stylized using the *input* selector. To style the text boxes, you'll create a dependent class called *text* and apply it to the `input` elements in which the value of the `type` attribute is *text*. You'll create the style and apply it to the `input` elements.

TIP

Be sure to choose a contrasting color for the text box so it does not blend into the form background.

To create the style for the input.text dependent selector and apply it to the input elements:

1. Return to the **sullivan.htm** file in your text editor. Position the insertion point on a blank line after the `label` style, and then type the following CSS code, as shown in Figure 9-17:

```
input.text {
   background-color: #f0eea4;
}
```

Figure 9-17   **CSS code for the input.text dependent selector**

```
label {
   color: black;
}

input.text {
   background-color: #f0eea4;
}

</style>
```

2. Position the insertion point in the First Name `<input>` tag to the left of the / symbol, and then type **class = "text"** followed by a space, as shown in Figure 9-18. Repeat this process for the Last Name and Email Address fields, as shown in Figure 9-18.

Figure 9-18   HTML code to apply the text class to each input element

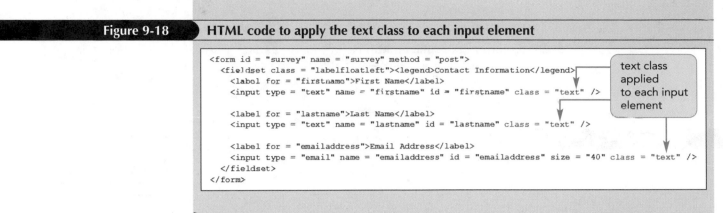

```
<form id = "survey" name = "survey" method = "post">
  <fieldset class = "labelfloatleft"><legend>Contact Information</legend>
    <label for = "firstname">First Name</label>
    <input type = "text" name = "firstname" id = "firstname" class = "text" />

    <label for = "lastname">Last Name</label>
    <input type = "text" name = "lastname" id = "lastname" class = "text" />

    <label for = "emailaddress">Email Address</label>
    <input type = "email" name = "emailaddress" id = "emailaddress" size = "40" class = "text" />
  </fieldset>
</form>
```

text class applied to each input element

3. Save the file, return to your Web browser, and then click the **Refresh** or **Reload** button to view the changes in the file. The Web page should look similar to Figure 9-19.

Figure 9-19   Text boxes stylized in the form

Irish Immigration

During the 18th and 19th centuries, many families emigrated from Ireland in search of opportunities and better living conditions. The largest exodus happened in the 1840s during the great potato famine. Potatoes were the main source of food, and a blight destroyed most of the crops. Hundreds of thousands of Irish immigrants left the island, hoping to live in the United States and Canada. It is believed that over 2 million people left Ireland in the 1800s.

Contact Information
First Name
Last Name
Email Address

color applied to each text box

Patrick likes the work you've done creating the form. He has noticed some forms that have some of the information partially completed and would like to help speed up completing the form for some of his extended family members. He anticipates that most of the people who complete the form will share his last name and would like you to add the name *Sullivan* to the Last Name text box. This way, people whose last name is *Sullivan* will not have to type it in the Last Name text box. Other people will have to delete the name *Sullivan* in the Last Name text box and type their own last name in the text box.

Setting a Value in a Text Box

You set the initial value of a text box control using the `value` attribute. The value of the `value` attribute appears in the text box when the Web page opens. This is useful if the value is the most likely data for a particular text box. If the value already appears in the text box, this saves users time. Users for whom the data is not appropriate would select the text, delete it, and then type the appropriate data.

You'll set the value of the Last Name input box to *Sullivan*.

To set the `value` attribute for the Last Name text box:

1. Return to the **sullivan.htm** file in your text editor. Position the insertion point in the Last Name `input` element to the left of the slash, and then type the following HTML code followed by a space, as shown in Figure 9-20:

   `value = "Sullivan"`

Figure 9-20 **HTML code to set the value of a text box**

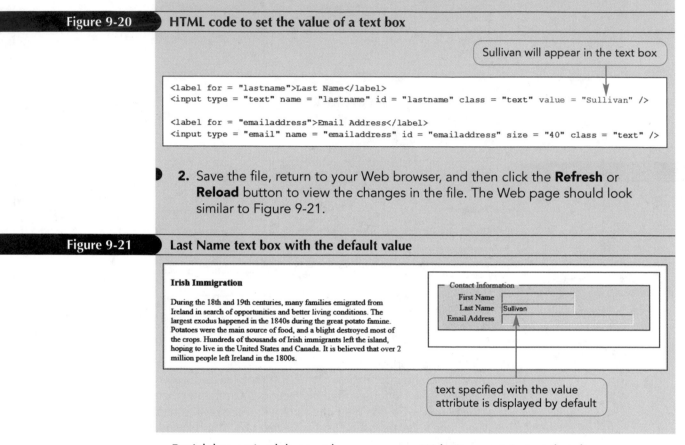

2. Save the file, return to your Web browser, and then click the **Refresh** or **Reload** button to view the changes in the file. The Web page should look similar to Figure 9-21.

Figure 9-21 **Last Name text box with the default value**

Patrick has noticed that text boxes on some Web sites contain text that disappears when a user types a character in the text box. He'd like this feature to be included in the Email Address text box. You can use the `placeholder` attribute to create the feature Patrick wants.

Setting a Placeholder Value

Some Web browsers recognize the `placeholder` attribute and display its value in a light grey color. In these browsers, the placeholder value disappears when the user begins to type in the text box. This is an HTML5 feature. This is useful for providing instructions to users so they're not left wondering what they should type or select. The `placeholder` attribute allows you to display a sample email address in the input box. Internet Explorer versions 9 and earlier do not recognize this attribute and simply ignore the attribute and its value. Safari, Firefox, Opera, and other Web browsers, however, recognize the `placeholder` attribute. You'll add a placeholder value to the Email Address text box. The value will provide a sample email address as guidance for users. Whenever you add features to a Web page that not all browsers will render, it's important to make sure the information the features contain isn't crucial for using or understanding the Web page and its content.

To add a placeholder value to the Email Address text box:

1. Return to the **sullivan.htm** file in your text editor. Position the insertion point in the Email Address input tag to the left of the slash, and then type the following HTML code followed by a space, as shown in Figure 9-22. If necessary, you may have to break up the input tag on separate lines, as shown in Figure 9-22:

   ```
   placeholder = "name@anywhere.com"
   ```

Figure 9-22   **HTML code for the placeholder value**

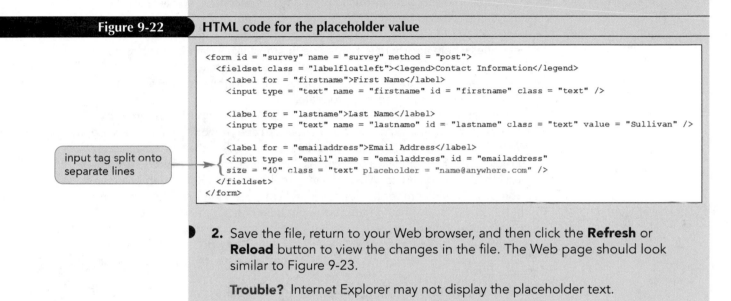

```
<form id = "survey" name = "survey" method = "post">
  <fieldset class = "labelfloatleft"><legend>Contact Information</legend>
    <label for = "firstname">First Name</label>
    <input type = "text" name = "firstname" id = "firstname" class = "text" />

    <label for = "lastname">Last Name</label>
    <input type = "text" name = "lastname" id = "lastname" class = "text" value = "Sullivan" />

    <label for = "emailaddress">Email Address</label>
    <input type = "email" name = "emailaddress" id = "emailaddress"
    size = "40" class = "text" placeholder = "name@anywhere.com" />
  </fieldset>
</form>
```

input tag split onto separate lines

2. Save the file, return to your Web browser, and then click the **Refresh** or **Reload** button to view the changes in the file. The Web page should look similar to Figure 9-23.

   Trouble? Internet Explorer may not display the placeholder text.

Figure 9-23   **Placeholder value in the Email Address text box**

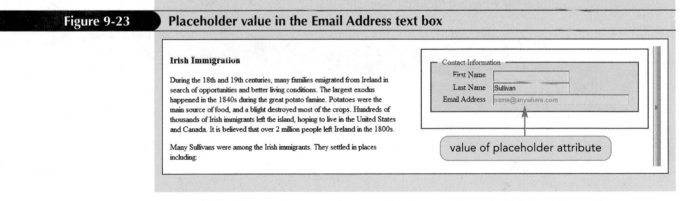

Irish Immigration

During the 18th and 19th centuries, many families emigrated from Ireland in search of opportunities and better living conditions. The largest exodus happened in the 1840s during the great potato famine. Potatoes were the main source of food, and a blight destroyed most of the crops. Hundreds of thousands of Irish immigrants left the island, hoping to live in the United States and Canada. It is believed that over 2 million people left Ireland in the 1800s.

Many Sullivans were among the Irish immigrants. They settled in places including:

Contact Information
First Name
Last Name   Sullivan
Email Address   name@anywhere.com

value of placeholder attribute

Patrick likes the work you've done on the form so far and is looking forward to adding form controls to collect additional information. You expand the form in the next session.

Written Communication: Creating Forms That Are Easy to Use

Forms are the primary method used to collect data from users. Whether it's a simple form for a quick voting poll or a complex form for ordering a product from an online catalogue, a form must be easy to use. This means the instructions must be clear. If users find the form difficult to use, they are more likely to abandon it and move on. Here are a few tips for creating forms that are easy to use:

- Provide simple and clear instructions for each form control. A label such as *First Name* is better than *Please enter your First Name*.
- Indicate any form controls that must be completed.
- Set values where appropriate to provide the most likely data in text box controls.
- Use the `placeholder` attribute to set sample text in a text box.
- Limit the amount of text users must type by using option buttons, check boxes, or other form controls where appropriate.
- Use the `autocomplete` attribute, which is an HTML5 attribute supported by some Web browsers. With the code `autocomplete = "on"` in a text box tag, a Web browser automatically fills in that text box with data that has been completed in previous forms. Typically this includes firstname, lastname, city, country, email, and other common fields. When you're completing a form, the Web browser may prompt you to remember the form values. When the Web browser remembers these values, they will automatically be populated in a form when the names of the text box controls are recognized. It's very frustrating when you enter all the information in the form controls, only to discover after you submit the form that there was an error and all data must be reentered. Instead, use the `autocomplete` attribute to save the user some time.
- Align form controls so text box controls are aligned along their left edges when they are arranged vertically.
- Use `fieldset` elements to group form controls logically.
- Ensure text boxes are sized to accommodate the longest reasonable text input.
- Ask for only essential data. Don't ask for data you won't need.

REVIEW

Session 9.1 Quick Check

1. What tags are used to start and end forms?
2. What input type would you use to create a text box?
3. What does the `size` attribute do?
4. What is the purpose of the `fieldset` element?
5. What element do you use to associate text to a form control?
6. What element do you use to specify a title for a fieldset?

SESSION 9.2 VISUAL OVERVIEW

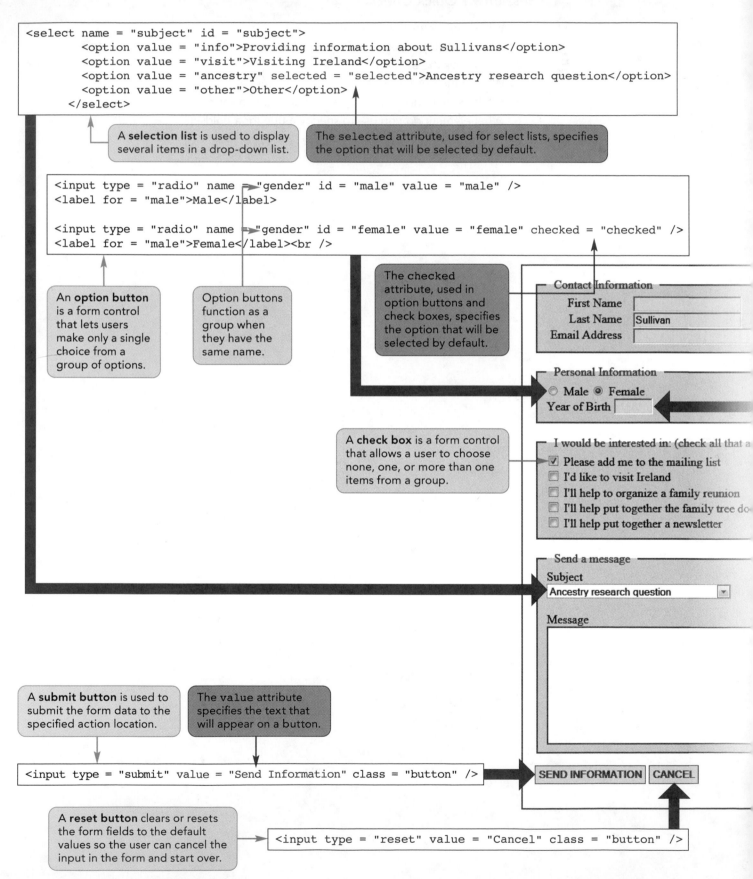

```
<select name = "subject" id = "subject">
      <option value = "info">Providing information about Sullivans</option>
      <option value = "visit">Visiting Ireland</option>
      <option value = "ancestry" selected = "selected">Ancestry research question</option>
      <option value = "other">Other</option>
   </select>
```

A **selection list** is used to display several items in a drop-down list.

The selected attribute, used for select lists, specifies the option that will be selected by default.

```
<input type = "radio" name = "gender" id = "male" value = "male" />
<label for = "male">Male</label>

<input type = "radio" name = "gender" id = "female" value = "female" checked = "checked" />
<label for = "male">Female</label><br />
```

An **option button** is a form control that lets users make only a single choice from a group of options.

Option buttons function as a group when they have the same name.

The checked attribute, used in option buttons and check boxes, specifies the option that will be selected by default.

Contact Information
First Name
Last Name   Sullivan
Email Address

Personal Information
○ Male ● Female
Year of Birth

A **check box** is a form control that allows a user to choose none, one, or more than one items from a group.

I would be interested in: (check all that a
☑ Please add me to the mailing list
☐ I'd like to visit Ireland
☐ I'll help to organize a family reunion
☐ I'll help put together the family tree do
☐ I'll help put together a newsletter

Send a message
Subject
Ancestry research question ▼

Message

A **submit button** is used to submit the form data to the specified action location.

The value attribute specifies the text that will appear on a button.

```
<input type = "submit" value = "Send Information" class = "button" />
```

SEND INFORMATION | CANCEL

A **reset button** clears or resets the form fields to the default values so the user can cancel the input in the form and start over.

```
<input type = "reset" value = "Cancel" class = "button" />
```

CREATING AND STYLING FORM CONTROLS

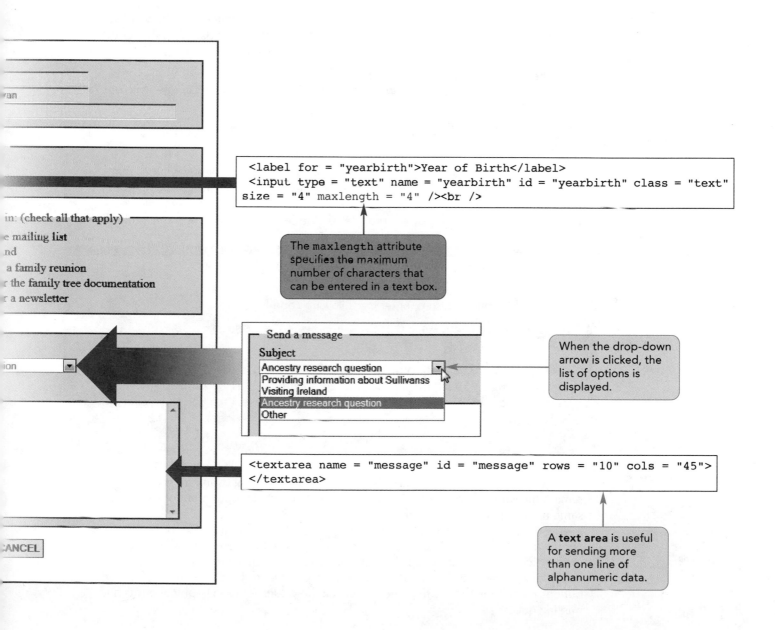

```
<label for = "yearbirth">Year of Birth</label>
<input type = "text" name = "yearbirth" id = "yearbirth" class = "text"
size = "4" maxlength = "4" /><br />
```

The maxlength attribute specifies the maximum number of characters that can be entered in a text box.

When the drop-down arrow is clicked, the list of options is displayed.

```
<textarea name = "message" id = "message" rows = "10" cols = "45">
</textarea>
```

A **text area** is useful for sending more than one line of alphanumeric data.

in: (check all that apply)
e mailing list
nd
a family reunion
r the family tree documentation
r a newsletter

Send a message
Subject
Ancestry research question
Providing information about Sullivanss
Visiting Ireland
Ancestry research question
Other

CANCEL

Creating Option Buttons

The controls you have added to your form so far have all used text boxes to enable users to input alphanumeric text. HTML also allows you to create controls with predefined values from which users can select. One of the most common is the option button, also known as a **radio button**, which lets users make only a single choice from a group of options. A primary advantage of using option buttons in your form is that users don't have to type any data. When a Web form designer can control the input from users, the possibilities for user errors are reduced, making it more likely that users will provide **clean**, or error-free, data. Another big advantage of using option buttons, and other form controls such as check boxes and selection lists, is that they simplify data entry for users. It's good coding practice to limit the possibility of user errors as much as possible. Although you can create any number of options for a particular field, you shouldn't overwhelm users with too many choices.

The input type for an option button is `radio`. Just as with text fields, you name an option button to correspond to the appropriate field name in the database. Remember that the label element precedes the code for each radio button. The id value should always match the value of the `for` attribute in the `label` element code. The value for the `value` attribute is the data sent to the appropriate field in the database. The code for a group of two radio buttons would look similar to the following code:

```
<label for = "male">Male</label>
<input type = "radio" name = "gender" id = "male" value = "male" />

<label for = "female">Female</label>
<input type = "radio" name = "gender" id = "female" value =
"female" />
```

Each option button would appear to the right of each label. The option buttons that form one group all have the same `name` attribute and value. This groups the option buttons so that when one is selected, the others in the same group are not selected. The `value` attribute is used by the program on the server when the form is submitted.

REFERENCE

Creating Option Buttons

- To create option buttons, enter the following code for each one:

  ```
  <input type = "radio" name = "name" id = "id"
  value = "field_data" />
  ```

  where *name* identifies the corresponding field in the database, *id* associates the field with the `for` attribute in the `label` element, and *field_data* is the data that will be sent to the appropriate field in the database if the button is selected.
- To specify that an option button is checked by default, add the attribute and value of `checked = "checked"` to the `<input>` tag code.

TIP

Use option buttons when only one choice of several can be selected, such as for gender or method of payment.

Note that the value for the `name` attribute (in the preceding example, *gender*) must remain the same for each `<input>` tag. The value groups all option buttons with the same name value as one group.

If your group of option buttons is working properly, a user can make only one choice from the group. If you test your form and notice that you can make more than one choice from a group of option buttons, check the accuracy of the values you typed for the `name` attribute. All the values for the `name` attribute in a group of option buttons must be identical. In particular, check the values for typographical errors and missing quotes.

To further ensure clean data, you should add the attribute that checks one of the option buttons by default, so a value is returned even if a user does not make a choice. To establish a default choice, enter the checked attribute with a value of checked. For instance, in the following example, *male* is the default choice:

```
<label for = "male">Male</label>
<input type = "radio" name = "gender" id = "male" value = "male"
checked = "checked" />

<label for = "female">Female</label>
<input type = "radio" name = "gender" id = "female" value =
"female" />
```

You'll create a new fieldset for the Personal Information group of form controls. You'll then enter the option button code for users to indicate their gender in the form. Patrick thinks that most of the people who use genealogy Web sites are female, and thus most people who will fill out his form will be female as well; for this reason, you'll set the female gender option button to be checked by default. The label elements after the input tags display the labels to the right of the option buttons.

To enter the code for the gender option buttons:

1. If you took a break after the previous session, make sure that the **sullivan.htm** file is open in your text editor.

2. Position the insertion point on a blank line after the end </fieldset> tag, and then type the following HTML code, as shown in Figure 9-24:

```
<fieldset><legend>Personal Information</legend>
  <input type = "radio" name = "gender" id = "male" value =
  "male" />
  <label for = "male">Male</label>

  <input type = "radio" name = "gender" id = "female" value =
  "female" checked = "checked" />
  <label for = "female">Female</label>
</fieldset>
```

| Figure 9-24 | HTML code for the option buttons |

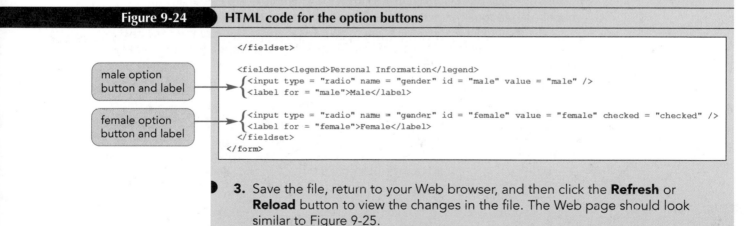

3. Save the file, return to your Web browser, and then click the **Refresh** or **Reload** button to view the changes in the file. The Web page should look similar to Figure 9-25.

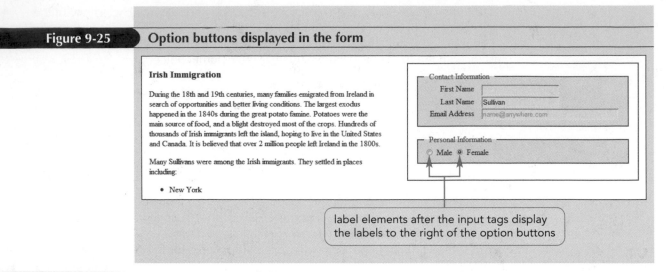

Figure 9-25 **Option buttons displayed in the form**

label elements after the input tags display the labels to the right of the option buttons

TIP

You cannot unselect an option button. You can only select another option button in the group of option buttons.

Patrick likes the option buttons you've created. He'd also like to include a field for each user's year of birth. Because the Sullivan name is common, he anticipates there may be several people who have exactly the same name; indeed, he already knows two other people named Patrick Sullivan! He'd like to use the year of birth to add this information to the family tree documentation he's creating. He'd also like you to restrict the year of birth data to four digits. You'll do this by adding the `maxlength` attribute to the `<input>` tag.

Restricting the Number of Characters in a Text Box

When the data from a form is going to be stored in a database, there are always limits to the number of characters that can be stored in each field. If you're developing a form that will accept data to be stored in a database, the database administrator will provide this information to you. For instance, if the data is a first name, the database may be set for a maximum of 20 characters. The `maxlength` attribute can be used to set the maximum number of characters that are permitted for a specific text box.

You'll use the `maxlength` attribute to restrict the number of characters for the year of birth to four characters. You'll also enter the `label` and text `input` element in a `fieldset` element to group them together as a block. Without the `fieldset` or some other container, the label and text `input` would appear inline to the right of the option buttons. Later, you'll create a style and apply it to this `fieldset` element.

To add the `maxlength` attribute to the Year of Birth field:

1. Return to the **sullivan.htm** file in your text editor. Position the insertion point on a blank line before the end `</fieldset>` tag, and type the following HTML code, as shown in Figure 9-26:

```
<fieldset>
  <label for = "yearbirth">Year of Birth</label>
  <input type = "text" name = "yearbirth" id = "yearbirth"
  class = "text" size = "4" maxlength = "4" />
</fieldset>
```

Figure 9-26	HTML for the Year of Birth text box

```
<fieldset><legend>Personal Information</legend>

  <input type = "radio" name = "gender" id = "male" value = "male" />
  <label for = "male">Male</label>

  <input type = "radio" name = "gender" id = "female" value = "female" checked = "checked" />
  <label for = "female">Female</label>

  <fieldset>
    <label for = "yearbirth">Year of Birth</label>
    <input type = "text" name = "yearbirth" id = "yearbirth" class = "text"
    size = "4" maxlength = "4" />
  </fieldset>

</fieldset>
</form>
```

> number of characters to input is restricted to 4 for the text box

2. Save the file, return to your Web browser, and then click the **Refresh** or **Reload** button to view the changes in the file. The Web page should look similar to Figure 9-27. Type some numbers in the year of birth text box control and notice that you can type only a maximum of four characters.

Figure 9-27	Year of Birth text box in the form

Irish Immigration

During the 18th and 19th centuries, many families emigrated from Ireland in search of opportunities and better living conditions. The largest exodus happened in the 1840s during the great potato famine. Potatoes were the main source of food, and a blight destroyed most of the crops. Hundreds of thousands of Irish immigrants left the island, hoping to live in the United States and Canada. It is believed that over 2 million people left Ireland in the 1800s.

Many Sullivans were among the Irish immigrants. They settled in places including:

- New York
- Nova Scotia
- Ontario
- Pennsylvania

Contact Information
First Name
Last Name   Sullivan
Email Address   name@anywhere.com

Personal Information
○ Male ● Female
Year of Birth

> maxlength attribute restricts the number of characters that can be entered to 4 characters

The year of birth label and text control are in a `fieldset` element. You'll create a style called *group* that eliminates the border, margins, padding, and removes the float. You'll apply the *group* style to the `fieldset` element that contains the year of birth label and input control.

To create and apply the *group* style:

1. Return to the **sullivan.htm** file in your text editor. Position the insertion point on a blank line after the end `input.text` style, and then type the following CSS code, as shown in Figure 9-28.

```
fieldset.group {
  float: none;
  border: 0;
  margin: 0;
  padding: 0;
}
```

Figure 9-28 | CSS code for the group descendent selector and the class applied to the fieldset

```
input.text {
    background-color: #f0eea4;
}

fieldset.group {
    float: none;
    border: 0;
    margin: 0;
    padding: 0;
}

</style>
```

2. Position the insertion point before the end > in the open fieldset tag before the Year of Birth label, type a space character, and then enter the HTML code below, as shown in Figure 9-29:

```
class = "group"
```

Figure 9-29 | Applying the group class to the fieldset element

```
<input type = "radio" name = "gender" id = "female" value = "female" checked = "checked" />
<label for = "female">Female</label>

<fieldset class = "group">
    <label for = "yearbirth">Year of Birth</label>
    <input type = "text" name = "yearbirth" id = "yearbirth"
    class = "text" size = "4" maxlength = "4" />
</fieldset>

</fieldset>
```

3. Save the file, return to your Web browser, and then click the **Refresh** or **Reload** button to view the changes in the file. The Web page should look similar to Figure 9-30.

Figure 9-30 | Fieldset with the group style applied

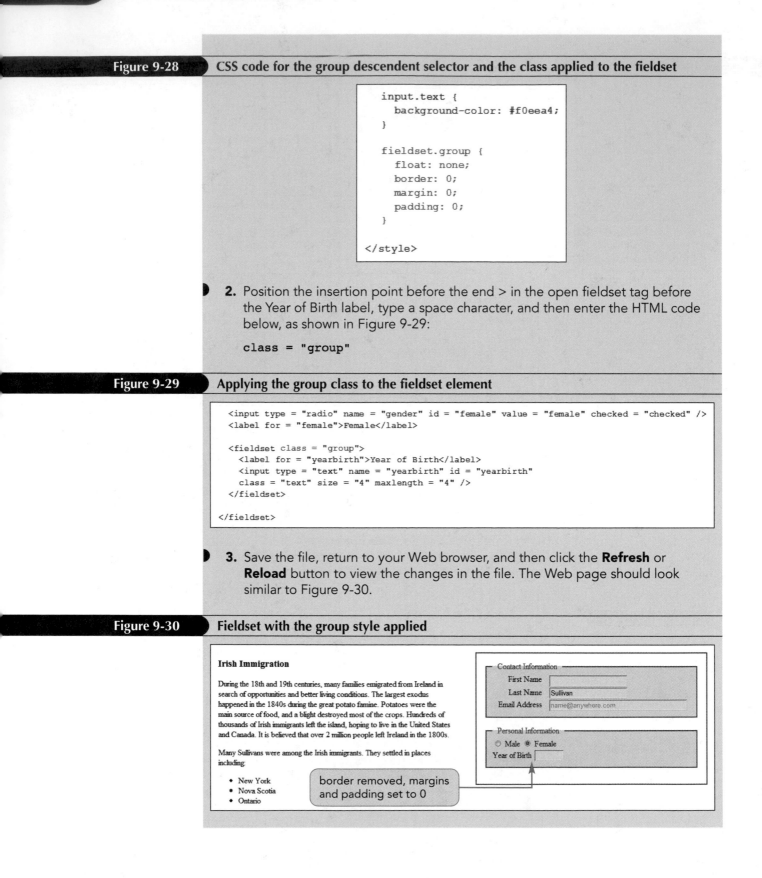

Patrick would like people who use his form to be able to choose from a list of activities and interests. For instance, he'd like them to be able to sign up for the mailing list, volunteer to help with the newsletter, or indicate their interest in visiting Ireland. The users should be able to choose none, one, or more than one of the choices. You'll use check boxes to achieve this functionality.

Creating Check Boxes

A check box is a form control that allows a user to choose none, one, or more than one items from a group. The input type for a check box is `checkbox`. You can include any number of check boxes in a group.

Creating Check Boxes

- To create check boxes, enter the following code:

```
<input type = "checkbox" name = "name" id = "id" value = "data" />
```

where *name* identifies the check box field with a field in the database, *id* associates the field with the `for` attribute in the `label` element, and *data* is the data that will be sent to the database if the check box is selected.
- To specify that a check box is checked by default, add the attribute and value of `checked = "checked"` to the tag.

You name a check box to correspond to the field name in the database that receives the data when a user selects that check box. This is different from the option button name, which functions to group the option buttons together. Rather, the `name` attribute for a check box should be different for each check box. The following is an example of code to create a check box:

```
<label for = "sportswear">Sportswear</label>
<input type = "checkbox" name = "special" id = "sportswear" value = "sportswear" />
```

Recall that you can have an option button selected by default. Similarly, you can have a check box checked by default, using the same `checked` attribute with a value of `checked`, as shown in the following code:

```
<label for = "sportswear">Sportswear</label>
<input type = "checkbox" name = "special" id = "sportswear" value = "sportswear" checked = "checked" /><br />
```

As with radio buttons, the `name` attribute must have the same value for each check box in the group.

Patrick has provided a list of activities he'd like the users to be able to identify. You'll now enter code to list these options as check boxes. Patrick would like everyone to be added to the mailing list, so he wants that option checked by default. You'll put each label to the right of its corresponding check box, so the `label` element follows the `input` tag for each text box control. You'll also create a separate fieldset for each checkbox and `label` element pair, and then you'll apply the *group* class to these fieldsets.

To enter the code for the check boxes:

1. Return to the **sullivan.htm** file in your text editor. Position the insertion point on a blank line before the last end `</fieldset>` tag, and then type the following HTML code, as shown in Figure 9-31:

```
<fieldset><legend>I would be interested in: (check all that
apply)</legend>

  <fieldset class = "group">
    <input type = "checkbox" name = "interested" id =
    "mailinglist" value = "mailinglist" checked = "checked" />
    <label for = "mailinglist">Please add me to the mailing
    list</label>
  </fieldset>

  <fieldset class = "group">
    <input type = "checkbox" name = "interested" id = "ireland"
    value = "ireland" />
    <label for = "ireland">I'd like to visit Ireland</label>
  </fieldset>

  <fieldset class = "group">
    <input type = "checkbox" name = "interested" id =
    "volunteer" value = "reunion" />
    <label for = "reunion">I'll help to organize a family
    reunion</label>
  </fieldset>

  <fieldset class = "group">
    <input type = "checkbox" name = "interested" id =
    "volunteer" value = "familytree" />
    <label for = "familytree">I'll help put together the family
    tree documentation</label>
  </fieldset>

  <fieldset class = "group">
    <input type = "checkbox" name = "interested" id =
    "volunteer" value = "newsletter" />
    <label for = "newsletter">I'll help put together a
    newsletter</label>
  </fieldset>

</fieldset>
```

Figure 9-31   HTML code for the check boxes

```
      <fieldset class = "group">
        <label for = "yearbirth">Year of Birth</label>
        <input type = "text" name = "yearbirth" id = "yearbirth" class = "text" size = "4" maxlength = "4" />
      </fieldset>

    </fieldset>

    <fieldset><legend>I would be interested in: (check all that apply)</legend>

      <fieldset class = "group">
        <input  type = "checkbox" name = "interested" id = "mailinglist"
        value = "mailinglist" checked = "checked" />
        <label for = "mailinglist">Please add me to the mailing list</label>
      </fieldset>

      <fieldset class = "group">
        <input type = "checkbox" name = "interested" id = "ireland" value = "ireland" />
        <label for = "ireland">I'd like to visit Ireland</label>
      </fieldset>

      <fieldset class = "group">
        <input type = "checkbox" name = "interested" id = "volunteer" value = "reunion" />
        <label for = "reunion">I'll help to organize a family reunion</label>
      </fieldset>

      <fieldset class = "group">
        <input type = "checkbox" name = "interested" id = "volunteer" value = "familytree" />
        <label for = "familytree">I'll help put together the family tree documentation</label>
      </fieldset>

      <fieldset class = "group">
        <input type = "checkbox" name = "interested" id = "volunteer" value = "newsletter" />
        <label for = "newsletter">I'll help put together a newsletter</label>
      </fieldset>

    </fieldset>

  </form>
```

2. Save the file, return to your Web browser, and then click the **Refresh** or **Reload** button to view the changes in the file. The Web page should look similar to Figure 9-32.

Figure 9-32   Check boxes in a fieldset in the form

Irish Immigration

During the 18th and 19th centuries, many families emigrated from Ireland in search of opportunities and better living conditions. The largest exodus happened in the 1840s during the great potato famine. Potatoes were the main source of food, and a blight destroyed most of the crops. Hundreds of thousands of Irish immigrants left the island, hoping to live in the United States and Canada. It is believed that over 2 million people left Ireland in the 1800s.

Many Sullivans were among the Irish immigrants. They settled in places including:

- New York
- Nova Scotia
- Ontario
- Pennsylvania
- Quebec

Tell us about yourself!

If you're a Sullivan, or if any of your ancestors are Sullivans, please add your name and information to our database using the form. We'd love it if you

first check box is checked by default

Patrick would like anyone who uses his Web site to be able to send him a message. He'd like each user to be able to select a subject heading by selecting an option in a list. Then users should be able to type a message in another control and send the message with the form data. You'll start by creating a fieldset for the message controls, and then you'll add the controls for the message subject and text.

Creating a Selection List

A selection list is a form control that displays all the items in a list and allows a user to choose from the list. A **drop-down list box** displays only one item in a selection list; the user clicks a list arrow to display the remaining contents of the list and to make a selection. Drop-down list boxes are useful when you want to conserve screen space; for example, if you needed a list box that contained the names of the 50 states, you'd probably want users to see that list only after clicking the list arrow.

REFERENCE

Creating a Selection List

- To create a selection list, enter the following code:

```
<select name = "name" id = "id">
  <option value = "value1">optiontext1</option>
  <option value = "value2">optiontext2</option>
  ...
</select>
```

where *name* identifies a field in the database, *id* identifies the value for the `for` attribute in the `label` element, *optiontext1* and *optiontext2* are choices in the option list, and *value1* and *value2* are the values sent to the program on the server when the form is submitted.

- To allow more than one item in the list to appear in the browser, use `size = "number"`, where *number* is the number of items you want to display in the selection list. The default size value of 1 creates a drop-down list in which only one choice is visible.
- To allow each user to select more than one choice, use `multiple = "multiple"` in the `<select>` tag code.
- To make an option the default choice, use `selected = "selected"` in the `<option>` tag code.

You use the `select` element to create a selection list, and enter an `option` element to define each menu choice within a selection list. An `option` element's `value` attribute and its value determine the data that is sent to the form handler. The **option text** is the text that appears in the browser as a choice in the selection list. You enter the option text between the start `<option>` and end `</option>` tags. The following code shows a sample selection list:

```
<label for = "country">Country</label><br />
<select name = "country" id = "country" size = "1">
  <option value = "Australia">Australia</option>
  <option value = "Belgium">Belgium</option>
  <option value = "Canada">Canada</option>
  <option value = "China">China</option>
  <option value = "Sierra Leone">Sierra Leone</option>
  <option value = "United States">United States</option>
</select>
```

TIP

Use a selection list to provide common options for the user to select rather than typing the values in a text box.

You've already used the `size` attribute with text boxes. For selection lists, the `size` attribute indicates the number of items that are initially shown in the selection box. By default, the `size` attribute has a value of 1, so only one item appears, which creates a drop-down list box.

You've already used the `checked` attribute with option buttons and check boxes. In the same way, you can make an option in a selection list selected by default by adding the `selected` attribute with a value of `selected`, as shown in the following code:

```
<option value = "China" selected = "selected">China</option>
```

The `multiple` attribute and its value of `multiple` allows a user to select nonadjacent items in a list by pressing Ctrl and clicking each item, or to choose adjacent options in the list by clicking the first option, pressing Shift, and then clicking the last option. The `multiple` attribute and value are entered in the start `<select>` tag, as shown in the following code:

```
<select name = "country" id = "country" multiple = "multiple">
```

INSIGHT

Creating Option Groups

Sometimes when creating a list it's useful to group items together. You can do this using an **option group**. An option group is a set of options within a selection list. You use the `optgroup` element and the `<optgroup></optgroup>` tags to create option groups. The `label` attribute serves as the heading for an option group; the value you assign to the attribute appears in bold when the selection list is displayed in a browser. The following code creates a selection list containing two option groups:

```
<select name = "purchase" id = "purchase">
  <optgroup label = "Petites">
    <option value = "4p">4P</option>
    <option value = "6p">6P</option>
    <option value = "8p">8P</option>
  </optgroup>

  <optgroup label = "Misses">
    <option value = "6">6</option>
    <option value = "8">8</option>
    <option value = "10">10</option>
  </optgroup>
</select>
```

An optgroup label is not selectable and is used only as a heading in a drop-down box.

People who fill out Patrick's form may wish to send a message. Patrick has provided the following list of possible subject headings:

• Providing information about Sullivans
• Visiting Ireland
• Ancestry research question
• Other

You'll use these subject headings as the options for the selection list. Patrick would like the option *Ancestry research question* selected by default. You'll create a `fieldset` element, and inside it you'll add the selection list for the subject options for the message.

To create the selection list:

1. Return to the **sullivan.htm** file in your text editor. Position the insertion point on a blank line after the last end `</fieldset>` tag, and type the following HTML code, as shown in Figure 9-33.

```
<fieldset><legend>Send a message</legend>
  <label for = "subject">Subject</label>
  <select name = "subject" id = "subject">
    <option value = "info">Providing information about
    Sullivans</option>
    <option value = "visit">Visiting Ireland</option>
    <option value = "ancestry" selected = "selected">Ancestry
    research question</option>
    <option value = "other">Other</option>
  </select>
</fieldset>
```

Figure 9-33	Code for the selection list

```
  </fieldset>

<fieldset><legend>Send a message</legend>
  <label for = "subject">Subject</label>
  <select name = "subject" id = "subject">
    <option value = "info">Providing information about Sullivans</option>
    <option value = "visit">Visiting Ireland</option>
    <option value = "ancestry" selected = "selected">Ancestry research question</option>
    <option value = "other">Other</option>
  </select>
</fieldset>
</form>
```

selection list code contains the option elements

2. Save the file, return to your Web browser, and then click the **Refresh** or **Reload** button to view the changes in the file. The Web page should look similar to Figure 9-34. Click the drop-down button to display the selection list options.

Figure 9-34	Selection list in the form

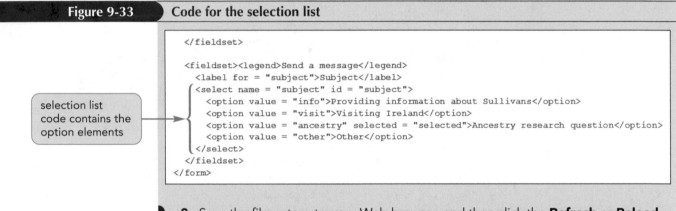

Irish Immigration

During the 18th and 19th centuries, many families emigrated from Ireland in search of opportunities and better living conditions. The largest exodus happened in the 1840s during the great potato famine. Potatoes were the main source of food, and a blight destroyed most of the crops. Hundreds of thousands of Irish immigrants left the island, hoping to live in the United States and Canada. It is believed that over 2 million people left Ireland in the 1800s.

Many Sullivans were among the Irish immigrants. They settled in places including:

- New York
- Nova Scotia
- Ontario
- Pennsylvania
- Quebec

Tell us about yourself!

If you're a Sullivan, or if any of your ancestors are Sullivans, please add your name and information to our database using the form. We'd love it if you could also help us with the newsletter and reunion. Please tell us a bit about yourself as well. Also, feel free to ask questions about ancestry research. If you're planning a trip to Ireland, let us know. We'd love to show you around!

Contact Information
First Name
Last Name   Sullivan
Email Address   name@anywhere.com

Personal Information
Male   Female
Year of Birth

I would be interested in: (check all that apply)
☑ Please add me to the mailing list
☐ I'd like to visit Ireland
☐ I'll help to organize a family reunion
☐ I'll help put together the family tree documentation
☐ I'll help put together a newsletter

selection list with the selected value displayed

Send a message
Subject   Ancestry research question

Now that you've created the selection list for the subject of the message, you'll create a form control for the message itself.

Creating a Text Area

Recall that you used a text box to create a single-line field for alphanumeric input. A **text area** is a control that allows users to enter more than one line of alphanumeric input. The `textarea` element is used to create a multiline text field. Patrick wants to add a text area so people who use his Web page can type a message to be sent with the form data.

Creating a Text Area

- To create a text area, enter the following code:

```
<textarea name = "name" id = "id" rows = "height_value" cols =
"width_value"></textarea>
```

where *name* identifies the field in the database associated with the text area, *id* associates this field with the `for` attribute value in the `label` element, *height_value* is the number of rows, and *width_value* is the character width of the text area expressed as a number.

A text area allows users to enter comments that suggest how to improve a particular service or the form itself, or to provide other feedback. You must specify a width and a height for a text area using the `cols` attribute and the `rows` attribute, respectively. By default, a text area has a width of 19 characters and a height of 2 rows. The actual number of characters that would fit into the default text area depends on each browser's default font, and thus varies slightly.

Text area form controls are often used to gather comments from a user. The code in the following example would create a text area with a width of 40 characters and a height of 6 rows, using the name and id value *comments*:

```
<textarea name = "comments" id = "comments" cols = "40" rows = "6">
</textarea>
```

Optionally, you can include some default text in a text area. You enter the default text between the start `<textarea>` and end `</textarea>` tags, as shown in the following example:

```
<textarea name = "comments" id = "comments" cols = "40"
rows = "6">Your comments, please.</textarea>
```

You'll now create a text area so users can enter the text for a message in Patrick's form.

To enter the code for the text area:

1. Return to the **sullivan.htm** file in your text editor. Position the insertion point on a blank line before the last end `</fieldset>` tag, and then type the following HTML code, as shown in Figure 9-35:

```
<label for = "message">Message</label>
<textarea name = "message" id = "message" rows = "10" cols =
"45"></textarea>
```

Figure 9-35 Code for the textarea element

```
</select>

<label for = "message">Message</label>
<textarea name = "message" id = "message" rows = "10" cols = "45"></textarea>
</fieldset>
```

rows attribute
defines the height

cols attribute
defines the width

2. Save the file, return to your Web browser, and then click the **Refresh** or **Reload** button to view the changes in the file. The Web page should look similar to Figure 9-36.

Figure 9-36 Text area in the form

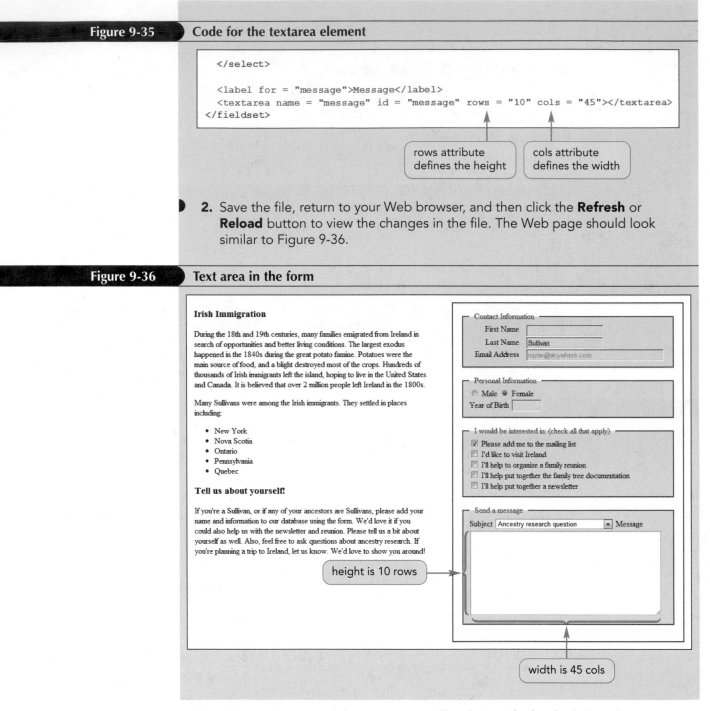

Irish Immigration

During the 18th and 19th centuries, many families emigrated from Ireland in search of opportunities and better living conditions. The largest exodus happened in the 1840s during the great potato famine. Potatoes were the main source of food, and a blight destroyed most of the crops. Hundreds of thousands of Irish immigrants left the island, hoping to live in the United States and Canada. It is believed that over 2 million people left Ireland in the 1800s.

Many Sullivans were among the Irish immigrants. They settled in places including:

- New York
- Nova Scotia
- Ontario
- Pennsylvania
- Quebec

Tell us about yourself!

If you're a Sullivan, or if any of your ancestors are Sullivans, please add your name and information to our database using the form. We'd love it if you could also help us with the newsletter and reunion. Please tell us a bit about yourself as well. Also, feel free to ask questions about ancestry research. If you're planning a trip to Ireland, let us know. We'd love to show you around!

height is 10 rows

width is 45 cols

Now that you've created the text area, you'll style it so the border is 2px, the same color as the `fieldset` border color, with block display. You'll also style the `select` element with block display, which will position the label and text area below the `select` element.

To style the `textarea` **and** `select` **elements:**

1. Return to the **sullivan.htm** file in your text editor. Position the insertion point on a blank below the `fieldset.group` dependent selector style, and then type the following CSS code, as shown in Figure 9-37:

```
textarea {
  border: solid 2px #305704;
  display: block;
}

select {
  display: block;
}
```

Figure 9-37   **CSS code for the textarea and select style**

```
fieldset.group {
  float: none;
  border: 0;
  margin: 0;
  padding: 0;
}

textarea {
  border: solid 2px #305704;
  display: block;
}

select {
  display: block;
}

</style>
```

2. Save the file, return to your Web browser, and then click the **Refresh** or **Reload** button to view the changes in the file. The Web page should look similar to Figure 9-38.

Figure 9-38 | **Styled text area and select elements in the form**

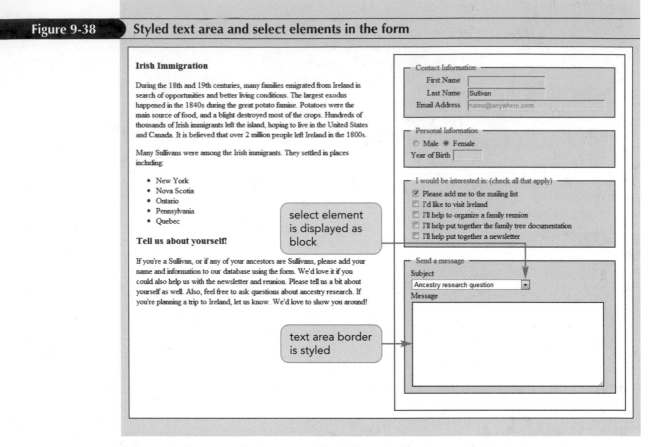

To complete Patrick's form, you'll add buttons that let users submit data to the form handler.

Submitting Data

After a user enters all the data in the form, the data must be submitted to the form handler. You also might want to give the user the option to clear the data and cancel the operation. A **command button** is a form control that lets a user execute or cancel an action. A submit button is used to submit the form data to the specified action location; a reset button clears or resets the form fields to the default values so the user can cancel the input in the form and start over.

You use the `input` element to create a submit or reset button. In the code for a submit or reset button, the `value` attribute determines what text appears on the button in the browser. For instance, the button created by the following code would be displayed in a browser with the words *Send Information* on it:

```
<input type = "submit" value = "Send Information" />
```

Likewise, the following code would create a reset button with the word *Cancel* on it:

```
<input type = "reset" value = "Cancel" />
```

Creating a Submit or Reset Button

- To create a submit button, enter the following code:

```
<input type = "submit" value = "buttontext">
```

  where *buttontext* is the text that appears on the button.
- To create a reset button, enter the following code:

```
<input type = "reset" value = "buttontext">
```

Creating a Custom Button

Although you can style a submit button or reset button, you can't add a background image to it. The button element is used to create a button control, which can be used to run a JavaScript program in your Web page. The JavaScript program can also submit the form, or it could run a program that performs other tasks. Unlike the submit or reset command buttons, if you use the button element you can place an image on the button or use an image as a background for the button. With the button element, you can set a button to submit data, clear a form, create a link, or execute a script. When using an image with the button, you should create a dependent class for the image element selector, include margin space around the image, and position the image vertically.

TIP

Submit buttons and reset buttons don't require label elements because their descriptions are contained in their value attributes

You'll add a submit button to send the data to the form handler. You'll also add a reset button to reset the form controls. You'll add a class called *button*, which you'll use as a dependent selector for a CSS style.

To enter the code for the submit and reset buttons:

1. Return to the **sullivan.htm** file in your text editor. Position the insertion point on a blank line after the last end `</fieldset>` tag, and then type the following HTML code, as shown in Figure 9-39:

```
<input type = "submit" value = "Send Information" class = "button" />
<input type = "reset" value = "Reset" class = "button" />
```

Figure 9-39   **Code for the submit and reset buttons**

```
    <label for = "message">Message</label>
    <textarea name = "message" id="message" rows="10" cols="45"></textarea>
</fieldset>

<input type = "submit" value = "Send Information" class = "button" />
<input type = "reset" value = "Reset" class = "button" />
</form>
```

value will appear as text on the button

2. Save the file, return to your Web browser, and then click the **Refresh** or **Reload** button to view the changes in the file. The Web page should look similar to Figure 9-40.

Trouble? Depending on your browser and browser version, the size, shape, and background color of the buttons may appear differently.

Figure 9-40	Submit and reset buttons in the form

TIP

Unlike a link, the mouse pointer does not change to a hand symbol when it hovers over a button.

If you're a Sullivan, or if any of your ancestors are Sullivans, please add your name and information to our database using the form. We'd love it if you could also help us with the newsletter and reunion. Please tell us a bit about yourself as well. Also, feel free to ask questions about ancestry research. If you're planning a trip to Ireland, let us know. We'd love to show you around!

Send a message
Subject
Ancestry research question
Message

submit button → Send Information Reset ← reset button

Next you'll create a style for the buttons.

To style the submit button:

1. Return to the **sullivan.htm** file in your text editor. Position the insertion point on a blank line below the *select* selector style, and then type the following CSS code, as shown in Figure 9-41:

```
input.button {
  color: #305704;
  text-transform: uppercase;
  font-weight: bold;
  padding: 4px;
  background-color: #f0eea4;
  border: 1px solid #305704;
  display: inline;
}
```

Figure 9-41	CSS code for the input.button descendent selector

```
select {
  display: block;
}

input.button {
  color: #305704;
  text-transform: uppercase;
  font-weight: bold;
  padding: 4px;
  background-color: #f0eea4;
  border: 1px solid #305704;
  display: inline;
}

</style>
```

padding may increase the size of the button

2. Save the file, return to your Web browser, and then click the **Refresh** or **Reload** button to view the changes in the file. The Web page should look similar to Figure 9-42.

Completed form including the stylized buttons

The Sullivan Family

Irish Immigration

During the 18th and 19th centuries, many families emigrated from Ireland in search of opportunities and better living conditions. The largest exodus happened in the 1840s during the great potato famine. Potatoes were the main source of food, and a blight destroyed most of the crops. Hundreds of thousands of Irish immigrants left the island, hoping to live in the United States and Canada. It is believed that over 2 million people left Ireland in the 1800s.

Many Sullivans were among the Irish immigrants. They settled in places including:

- New York
- Nova Scotia
- Ontario
- Pennsylvania
- Quebec

Tell us about yourself!

If you're a Sullivan, or if any of your ancestors are Sullivans, please add your name and information to our database using the form. We'd love it if you could also help us with the newsletter and reunion. Please tell us a bit about yourself as well. Also, feel free to ask questions about ancestry research. If you're planning a trip to Ireland, let us know. We'd love to show you around!

Patrick Sullivan • 37 Merrion Square • Dublin 2 • Ireland

adam.golabek/Shutterstock.com

Currently, when you click the Send Information button on Patrick's form, nothing happens. To get an idea of what it might be like to really submit the form data to a form handler, a JavaScript file has been provided called formsubmit.js. This JavaScript file lets you simulate form submission and see something happen on your screen when you click the submit button. The sullivan.htm file already contains a `script` element that includes this file. You'll use the JavaScript file as the action in the `form` element.

To set the form action to use the script:

Be sure to type a colon symbol after *javascript*, with no spaces.

1. Return to the **sullivan.htm** file in your text editor. Position the insertion point in the form tag to the left of the >, type a space, and then type the following `action` attribute code, as shown in Figure 9-43:

```
action = "javascript:submitform();"
```

Figure 9-43 **Form tag with the action value set**

```
<div id = "formcontainer">
<!-- enter the form code below -->

  <form id = "survey" name = "survey"  method = "post" action = "javascript:submitform();">
    <fieldset class = "labelfloatleft"><legend>Contact Information</legend>
```

2. Save the file, return to your Web browser, and then click the **Refresh** or
   Reload button.

3. Type some values in each of the form controls, making selections for the
   option buttons, check boxes, and selection list. Click the Submit button.
   The JavaScript will display an alert message box, similar to Figure 9-44.
   If you're using a browser other than Internet Explorer, you may instead
   see the message "No invalid data detected. Will retain for further testing."

Figure 9-44 **Submitted data is shown in the alert box**

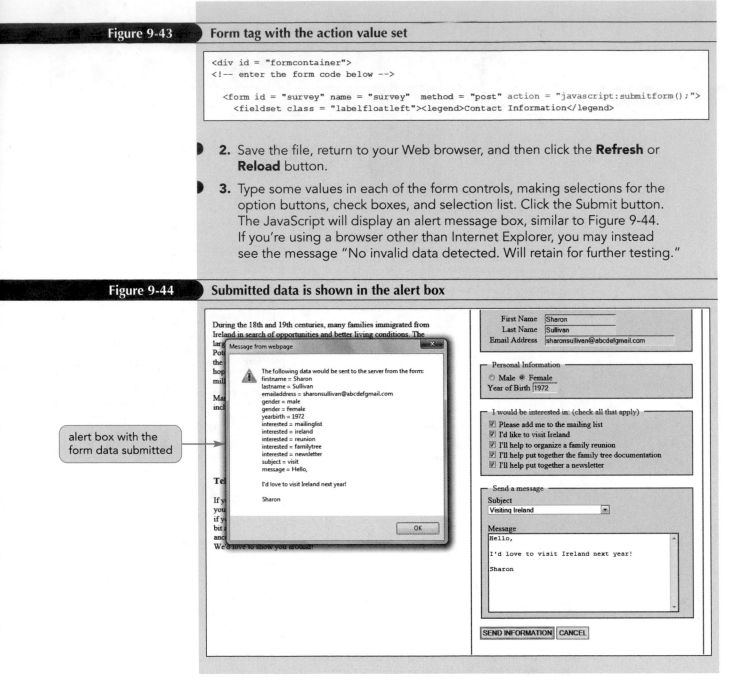

alert box with the
form data submitted

Patrick is thrilled with the work you've done on his Web site and is excited about
receiving messages from his distant relatives all over the world. He'll work with a
software developer to set up a database and the server program that will be required
to collect data. He'll contact you if he has other work for you to do.

PROSKILLS

Written Communication: Considering Accessibility in Form Design

Many people use assistive devices to access the Internet. This might include special keyboards and mice that are designed for people with dexterity issues and screen readers for people who are visually impaired. In addition, some people who do not use assistive devices have conditions that need to be considered in Web page design. For instance, content that flashes can cause a seizure, and people with the most common types of color blindness cannot distinguish between red and green.

The World Wide Web Consortium (W3C) has published strategies and guidelines for designing Web pages that are accessible. This information can be found at http://www.w3.org/WAI/. There is also an accessibility validator, so you can see if your Web page conforms to accessibility standards.

There is a long list of guidelines available, but the bottom line is that Web sites should be easy to use and content should be available to everyone regardless of their abilities. Here are just a few of the WAI guidelines that apply to Web design in general, but are particularly important for designing forms:

- Users must be able to easily find content. Form elements must be visible and well labeled.
- Content should operate in predictable ways. The usage of form controls should make sense. For instance, if you want users to choose from a group of items where only one choice can be made, use option buttons or a selection list rather than check boxes.
- Users should be helped to avoid and correct mistakes. If the content of a text box should contain only a few characters, set the `maxlength` appropriately. Use form controls such as option buttons and check boxes rather than text boxes whenever possible.

REVIEW

Session 9.2 Quick Check

1. How many options can a user choose from a selection list?
2. What attribute and value sets the default choice in a group of options for either option buttons or check boxes?
3. What element is used to create a list of options?
4. What form control creates a button that sends form data to a form handler?
5. What form control creates a button that sets the form controls back to their default values?

Practice the skills you learned in the tutorial using the same case scenario.

PRACTICE

Review Assignments

Data Files needed for the Review Assignments: formsubmit.js, modernizr-2.js, reunion_T9.htm, images/ireland.jpg

Patrick has asked for your help in creating a new page at the Sullivan Family Web site, where people could fill out a form to indicate they will attend the family reunion. The form would consist of text fields, a text area, and command buttons. After each step, save the file, switch to your browser, refresh or reload the page, and then switch back to your text editor and complete the next step. A preview of the Web page you'll create appears in Figure 9-45.

Figure 9-45   **Sullivan Reunion Web page**

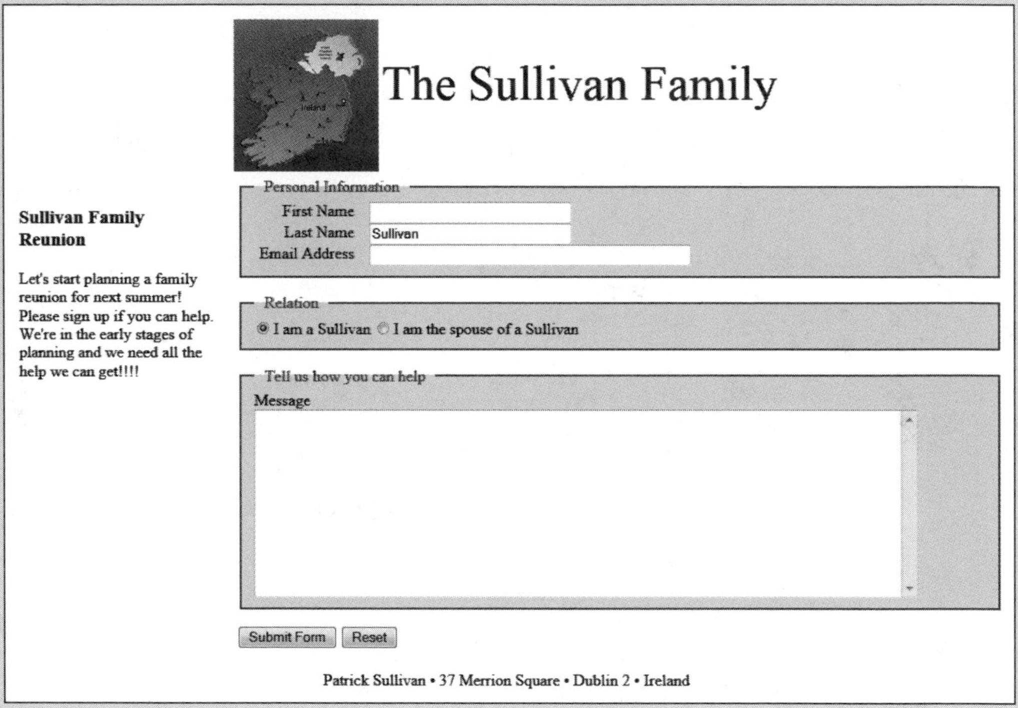

adam.golabek/Shutterstock.com

Complete the following:

1. Use your text editor to open the **reunion_T9.htm** file, which is provided in your Data Files in the tutorial9\review folder. In the head section and below the start `<head>` tag, enter *your name* and *today's date* in the comment section where noted.

2. Save the file as **reunion.htm** in the same folder. Open the file in your browser, and then observe the appearance of the original file.

3. Switch back to your text editor. In the body of the document and below the comment *enter the form code below*, enter the start `<form>` tag and the end `</form>` tag. Within the start `<form>` tag, enter the code for the `id` attribute with a value of **reunionhelp**. Enter the `action` attribute with an empty value, as follows: `action = ""`.

4. Enter a start `<fieldset>` tag and end `</fieldset>` tag within the `form` element. Apply the class *labelfloatleft* to the start `<fieldset>` tag. Add a legend for the fieldset using **Personal Information** as the legend text.

5. Create three **\<input>** tags, and then enter the code for three text fields using the data shown in Figure 9-46. Enter the corresponding label tag for each input element and value where indicated. For the last name set a value of **Sullivan**. For the email address, set a placeholder of **name@anywhere.com**.

Figure 9-46   Table of values for the input text tags

Label for value	Label text	Input type	name attribute value	id attribute value	Size
firstname	First Name	text	firstname	firstname	30
lastname	Last Name	text	lastname	lastname	30
email	Email Address	email	emailaddress	email	50

6. On a blank line below the end **\</fieldset>** tag for the text fields, enter the code for another start **\<fieldset>** tag. Apply the class *group* to the start **\<fieldset>** tag. After the start **\<fieldset>** tag, create a legend for the fieldset. Use **Relation** as the legend text.

7. Enter the code for an option button with the following attributes:
   a. Set the **name** as **sullivan**.
   b. Set the **value** as **iamsullivan**.
   c. Set the **id** as **iamsullivan**.
   d. Set **checked** to **checked**.

8. Enter the text **I am a Sullivan**.

9. Enter the code for an option button with the following attributes:
   a. Set the **name** as **sullivan**.
   b. Set the **value** as **spouse**.
   c. Set the **id** as **spouse**.

10. Enter the text **I am the spouse of a Sullivan**.

11. Enter an end **\</fieldset>** tag on a blank line.

12. On a blank line below the end **\</fieldset>** tag for the option buttons, enter another start **\<fieldset>** tag. After the start **\<fieldset>** tag, create a legend for the fieldset. Use **Tell us how you can help** as the legend text.

13. Enter the code for a text area that meets the following criteria:
    a. The text area **name** and **id** values are both **message**.
    b. The text area has 12 rows and 80 columns.
    c. The label text is **Message**.

14. Enter the end **\</fieldset>** tag.

15. On a new line, enter the code for a submit button. The value for the submit button is **Submit Form**.

16. On a new line, enter the code for a reset button. The value of the reset button is **Reset**.

17. Save the **reunion.htm** file. Switch to your browser, and then refresh or reload the page. Compare your file to Figure 9-45 to verify your file is correct.

18. Submit the results of the preceding steps to your instructor, in either printed or electronic form, as requested.

Use what you've learned to create and style a Web page for a cable television station.

APPLY

Case Problem 1

Data Files needed for this Case Problem: awardballot_T9.htm, awardstyles.css, modernizr-2.js, images/wkzlogo.jpg

WKZ Hollywood   WKZ is a cable television station broadcasting from Hollywood, California. WKZ prides itself as being the best source for news about pop culture and the world of entertainment. The Academy Awards will be presented next week, and Brett Michaels, station manager at WKZ, has asked you to create a form to collect users' opinions about which actors and movies should win the top five Oscars. You'll create a form with a series of option buttons and command buttons. A preview of the Web page you'll create appears in Figure 9-47.

Figure 9-47   WKZ Hollywood Web page

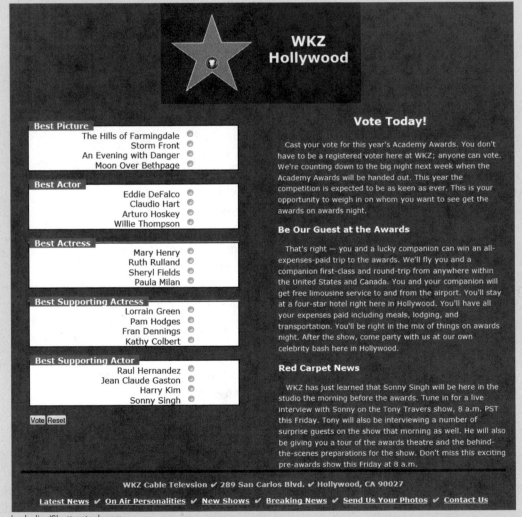

barbaliss/Shutterstock.com

Complete the following:

1. Use your text editor to open the **awardballot_T9.htm** file, which is provided in your Data Files in the tutorial9\case1 folder. In the head section, below the start `<head>` tag, enter *your name* and *today's date* in the comment section where noted.

2. Save the file as **awardballot.htm** in the same folder. Open the file in your browser, and then observe the appearance of the original file.

3. Switch back to your text editor. On a blank line in the document body and below the open `<fieldset>` tag for *Best Picture*, enter the start and end `<label>` tags with the following attributes:

   a. The value for the `for` attribute is **hills**.

   b. The label text is **The Hills of Farmingdale**.

   Note: Do not follow the end `</label>` tag with a `<br />` tag.

4. On a blank line below the `<label>` tags, complete the following:

   a. Enter an `input` element with an appropriate `type` value to create an option button.

   b. Set the value for the `name` attribute to **picture**.

   c. Set the values for the `id` and `value` attributes to **hills**.

5. On a blank line before the end `</style>` tag, create a style for the `input` element as follows:

   a. Set the value for the display to **block**.

   b. Set the float value to **left**.

6. Save the file. Switch to your browser, and then refresh or reload the **awardballot.htm** file. Verify the option button appears correctly in the browser.

7. Copy the two lines of code you have entered so far, along with the blank line following the code. On a blank line below the existing radio button code, paste a copy of the code and the blank line.

8. In the copied code, create code with placeholder values (`""`) so you can make a template from which you can repeatedly copy the code to create more radio buttons. Complete the following:

   a. Delete the existing value for the `for` attribute (*hills*) so the code appears as placeholder code, as follows: `for = ""`

   b. Delete the label text, *The Hills of Farmingdale*, between the start and end `<label>` tags.

   c. Delete the values for the `id`, and `value` attributes, so the code appears as placeholder code, like this: `id = "" value = ""`

   d. Select the two lines of `<label>` tag and `<input>` tag code that hold the placeholder values. Copy the code.

   e. On a blank line below the placeholder code you just created, paste two copies of the placeholder code.

   f. Insert the values shown in Figure 9-48 into the placeholder code as indicated.

Figure 9-48   **Values for the Best Picture nominees**

Label `for` value	Label text	Input type	name value	id value	value value
storm	Storm Front	radio	picture	storm	storm
danger	An Evening with Danger	radio	picture	danger	danger
moon	Moon Over Bethpage	radio	picture	moon	moon

   g. Save the file. Switch to your browser, and then refresh or reload the awardballot.htm file. Verify that the radio buttons for Best Picture appear correctly in the browser.

9. Complete the following steps for each of the remaining four fieldsets:

   a. Select all code for the Best Picture fieldset including the `<label>` and `<input>` elements. Copy the code and then paste it four times.

   b. Replace the values in the new fieldsets, as shown in Figure 9-49, replacing the `name` attribute values for each of the four remaining fieldset groups of option buttons.

Figure 9-49   Movie categories

Fieldset	Value for the `name` Attribute
Best Actor	actor
Best Actress	actress
Best Supporting Actress	suppactress
Best Supporting Actor	suppactor

   c. For the `for`, `id`, and `value` attributes, use the last names of the nominees shown in Figure 9-47.

   d. As text for each label, use the first and last names of the nominees shown in Figure 9-47.

10. Save the **awardballot.htm** file.

11. Switch to your browser, and then refresh or reload the page. Compare your file to Figure 9-47 to verify that your file is correct.

12. Submit the results of the **awardballot.htm** file to your instructor, in either printed or electronic form, as requested.

Use the skills you learned in the tutorial to create a Web page for a food supplier.

APPLY

Case Problem 2

Data Files needed for this Case Problem: food_T9.htm, foodstyles.css, modernizr-2.js, images/foodlogo.jpg

OnLoin Meat and Poultry Foods   OnLoin Meat and Poultry Foods supplies many of the nation's finest restaurants with top-quality meats and poultry. The company also has begun selling its products to individual customers on the Web. The company uses its national distribution channels to ship its products within hours after receiving orders. Gus Tyrell, the chief marketing manager, has asked you to create a new form for ordering OnLoin products. A preview of the Web page you'll create appears in Figure 9-50.

Figure 9-50   **OnLoin Meat and Poultry Foods Web page**

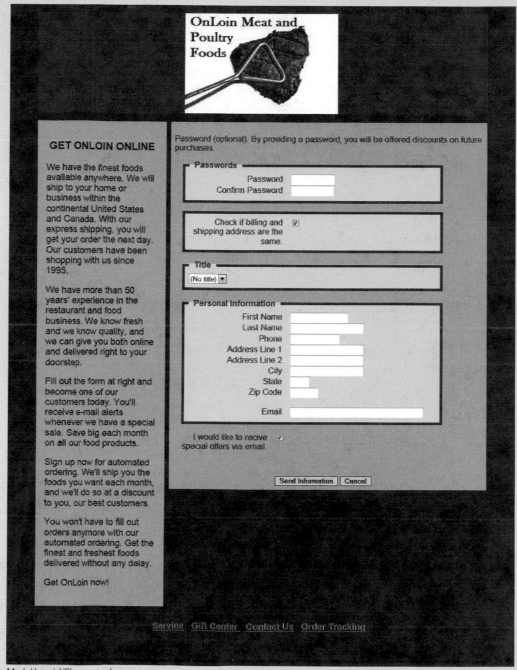

Mark Herreid/Shutterstock.com

Complete the following:

1. Use your text editor to open the **food_T9.htm** file, which is provided in your Data Files in the tutorial9\case2 folder. In the head section and below the start `<head>` tag, enter *your name* and *today's date* in the comment section where noted.
2. Save the file as **food.htm** in the same folder. Open the file in your browser, and then observe the appearance of the original file.

3. Switch back to your text editor. In the embedded style sheet, style the `form` element as follows:
   a. Set the margin on the bottom to **1em**.
   b. Add padding of **0.5em** on all sides.
   c. Set the background color to **#c9c3b5**.
   d. Set the font size to **16px**.
4. Create a dependent style for the `form` element with the following styles:
   a. Set the margin to **0** on all sides.
   b. Add padding of **0.5em**.
   c. Set the `clear` property to have a value of **both**.
5. Create a style for the `label` element as follows:
   a. Set the width to **180px**.
   b. Set the margin to **0** on the top, **15px** on the right, **0** on the bottom, and **4px** on the left.
   c. Set the text color to **black**.
   d. Set the `float` property to have a value of **left**.
   e. Align the label text **right**.
6. Create a style for the `legend` element as follows:
   a. Add padding of **0** on the top and bottom and **10px** on the left and right.
   b. Set the text color to **#354660**.
   c. Make the legend text **bold**.
7. Create a style for the `fieldset` element as follows:
   a. Set the width to **80%**.
   b. Set the margins to **1em**.
   c. Create a border that is **solid**, **5px**, and **#354660**.
   d. Add padding of **0.5em** on all sides.
   e. Set the background color to **#e9edda**.
8. Create a style for the *input.button* selector as follows:
   a. Set the top margin to **5em**.
   b. Create a border that is **solid**, **thin**, and **black**.
   c. Set the text color to **black**.
   d. Set the background color to **yellow**.
   e. Make the button text **bold**.
   f. Set the display to **inline**.
9. Create a style for the `input` element that sets the display to **inline**.
10. In the body of the document and below the comment *password fields are below* use the table in Figure 9-51 to create two password fields.

Figure 9-51 Table of input elements

Label for value	Label text	Input type	name **attribute** value	id **attribute** value	size value	m value
password	Password	password	password	password	10	1
password2	Confirm Password	password	password2	password2	10	1

11. On a blank line in the body of the document and below the comment *first checkbox is below*, enter the start and end `<label>` tags. The value for the `for` attribute is **shipping**. The label text is **Check if billing and shipping address are the same**.

12. On a blank line below the `<label>` tags, enter the code for a check box. The value for both the `name` and `id` attributes is **shipping**. Make this check box checked by default.

13. On a blank line below the comment *selection list is below*, enter the code to create a selection list with four options. The `<select>` tag `name` and `id` attribute values are both **title**. Refer to Figure 9-52 for the `option` element values and the option text.

Figure 9-52   Values for the option elements

option **element value**	**Option text**
no	(No title)
mr	Mr.
mrs	Mrs.
ms	Ms.

14. Below the comment *text boxes are below*, enter the code for nine text boxes. Refer to Figure 9-53 for the label values and input values.

Figure 9-53   Table of values for the text boxes

Label for value	Label text	Input type	name attribute value	id attribute value	size attribute value	maxlength attribute value
firstname	First Name	text	firstname	firstname	15	-
lastname	Last Name	text	lastname	lastname	20	-
phone	Phone	text	phone	phone	12	12
address1	Address Line 1	text	address1	address1	20	-
address2	Address Line 2	text	address2	address2	20	-
city	City	text	city	city	20	-
state	State	text	state	state	2	2
zip	Zip Code	text	zip	zip	5	5
email	Email	email	email	email	40	40

15. Below the comment *second check box is below*, enter start and end `<label>` tags on a blank line. For the `for` attribute use the value **offers**. As the label text, use **I would like to receive special offers via email**. On a blank line below the `<label>` tags, enter the code for a check box. Use the value **offers** for both the `name` and `id` attributes. Make this check box checked by default.

16. Below the comment *buttons are below*, enter the code for two `input` elements. The first `input` element is a submit button that submits the data, and the second `input` element is a reset button to clear the form. Apply the class **button** to each input button.

17. Save the **food.htm** file. Switch to your browser, and then refresh or reload the page. Compare your file to Figure 9-50 to verify that your file is correct.

18. Submit the results of the preceding steps to your instructor, in either printed or electronic form, as requested.

Use the skills you learned in the tutorial to create and style a Web page for a catering service.

APPLY

Case Problem 3

Data Files needed for this Case Problem: hall_T9.htm, hallstyles.css, modernizr-2.js, images/hall.jpg

LaFleur Caterers   LaFleur Caterers is a large catering hall in Benson Falls, Montana, that specializes in arranging events for 50 to 500 people. LaFleur makes all the arrangements for invitations, flowers, limousines, portrait photography, videography, live or recorded music, and tuxedo and gown rentals. LaFleur also arranges weddings, including honeymoon plans, wait staff, personal bridal attendants, directional cards, coat checks, and gazebo garden ceremonies. Brenda McNair, the new manager of LaFleur Caterers, has asked you to create a Web-based form that allows customers to choose from the services available. A preview of the Web page you'll create appears in Figure 9-54.

Figure 9-54   LeFleur Caterers Web page

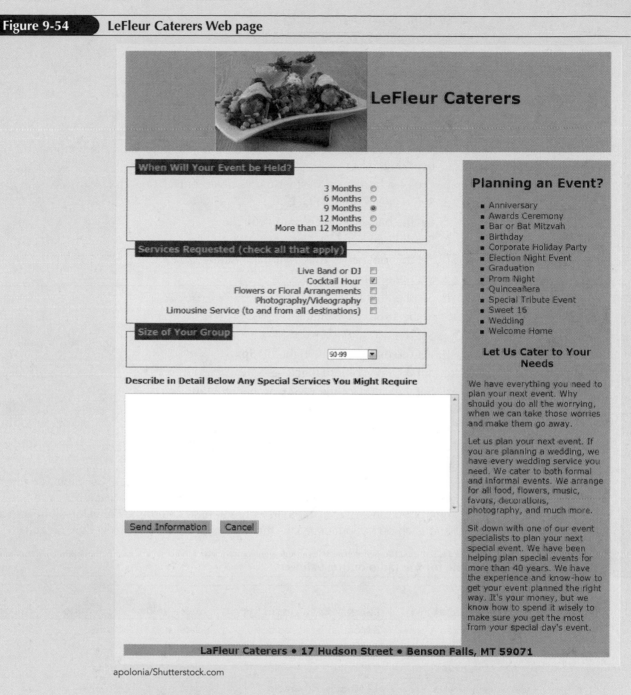

apolonia/Shutterstock.com

Complete the following:

1. Use your text editor to open the **hall_T9.htm** file, which is provided in your Data Files in the tutorial9\case3 folder. In the head section below the start <head> tag, enter **your name** and **today's date** in the comment section where noted.

2. Save the file as **hall.htm** in the same folder. Open the file in your browser, and then observe the appearance of the original file.

3. Switch back to your text editor. In the embedded style sheet, style the fieldset element to have a border that is color **#6c3705**, **solid**, and **1px**. Add padding of **1em** to all sides.

4. Style the `legend` element as follows:
   a. Add padding of **5px** on all sides.
   b. Set the text color to **#e5bf5a**.
   c. Set the background color to **#6c3705**.
   d. Set the font weight to **bold**.
   e. Set the font size to **1.1em**.
5. Style the *input.button* selector as follows:
   a. Set the margin to **1em** on the top, **1em** on the right, **0** on the bottom, and **0em** on the left.
   b. Create a border on all sides that is **silver**, **outset**, and **1px**.
   c. Set the text color to **black**.
   d. Set the background color to **#e5bf5a**.
   e. Set the font size to **1.1em**.
   f. Set the font family to the **Verdana** (sans-serif) font.
   g. Set the display to **block**.
   h. Set the float to **left**.
6. Style the `label` element as follows:
   a. Set the width to **450px**.
   b. Set the margin on the right to **15px**.
   c. Set the text color to **black**.
   d. Set the value for the `float` property to **left**.
   e. Align the text to the **right**.
7. Style the `select` element to have a left margin of **385px**.
8. Style the `input` element to set the `display` property to **block** and the `float` property to **left**.
9. In the body of the document and within the first set of `<fieldset>` tags with the legend *When Will Your Event be Held?*, enter the code for five labels and five option buttons. Use the table in Figure 9-55 to determine the values for each label and each option button. Make the choice for *9 Months* checked by default.

Figure 9-55   Table for the radio button values

Label `for`	Label text	Input type	name **value**	id **value**	value **value**
three	3 Months	radio	date	three	3
six	6 Months	radio	date	six	6
nine	9 Months	radio	date	nine	9
twelve	12 Months	radio	date	twelve	12
greater	More than 12 Months	radio	date	greater	13

10. Within the fieldset with the legend *Services Requested (check all that apply),* enter code for five check boxes. Use the table in Figure 9-56 to determine the values for each label and each check box. Make the choice for *Cocktail Hour* checked by default.

Figure 9-56   Table of values for the check boxes

Label for	Label text	Input type	name value	id value	value value
band	Live Band or DJ	checkbox	service	band	band
cocktail	Cocktail Hour	checkbox	service	cocktail	cocktail
flowers	Flowers or Floral Arrangements	checkbox	service	flowers	flowers
photo	Photography/ Videography	checkbox	service	photo	photo
limo	Limousine Service (to and from all destinations)	checkbox	service	limo	limo

11. On a blank line within the fieldset with the legend *Size of Your Group*, enter the code for a selection list. In the start **<select>** tag, enter **size** as the value for both the **name** and **id** attributes. Use Figure 9-57 to determine the values for each option. Make the option for *50-99* selected by default.

Figure 9-57   Table of values for the selection list

Option value	Option text
10	10-19
20	20-29
30	30-49
50	50-99
100	100-249
250	250-499
500	500 or more

12. Position the insertion point below the sentence that begins *Describe in Detail Below any Special ....* On a blank line, enter the code for a text area that has **15** rows and **80** columns, using **comments** as the name and id.

13. Use the **input** element to create two buttons. The first should be a submit button with **Send Information** as the button text. The second should be a reset button with **Cancel** as the button text.

14. Save the **hall.htm** file. Switch to your browser, and then refresh or reload the page. Compare your file to Figure 9-54 to verify your file is correct.

15. In your browser, go to http://validator.w3.org to open the W3C validator. Validate the **hall.htm** file by using the Validate by File Upload method. Note any errors, and then correct them in your file if necessary. Recall that color names may not validate.

16. In your browser, navigate to http://jigsaw.w3.org/css-validator. Validate the **hall.htm** file by using the By file upload method. Note any errors, and then correct them in your file if necessary. Note any errors in the code for the embedded style sheet. You can ignore the warning "File not found: import file://localhost/hallstyles.css: Operation not permitted," which pertains to the linked style sheet.

17. Submit the results of the **hall.htm** file to your instructor, in either printed or electronic form, as requested.

Create a Web page to query students about life on campus.

Case Problem 4

Data Files needed for this Case Problem: modernizr-2.js, survey_T9.htm, images/ surveylogo.gif

Student Life Survey Brad Tillman, the director of campus life at Sterling College, has asked you to design an online form that surveys students about their college experience. Possible survey topics include the following:

- Appearance and availability of campus housing
- Classroom and student center facilities
- Course availability
- Course relevance to major
- Parking issues
- Registration issues
- Satisfaction with and availability of campus activities
- Satisfaction with campus services such as admissions, the bursar, and the registrar
- Satisfaction with courses
- Scholarship availability
- Tuition costs

Complete the following:

1. Use your text editor to open the **survey_T9.htm** file, which is provided in your Data Files in the tutorial9\case4 folder. In the head section, give your page an appropriate title. Below the start `<head>` tag, enter *your name* and *today's date* in the comment section where noted.

2. Save the file as **survey.htm** in the same folder.

3. Within the embedded style sheet, in addition to the existing styles, format the `body` element with a text size, font, color, and background color of your choice.

4. In the document body and within the `form` element tags, enter code for your survey that includes examples of each of the following:

   a. Three or more text fields

   b. One password field

   c. At least one group of option buttons (make one of the radio buttons selected by default)

   d. At least one group of check boxes (make one of the boxes checked by default)

   e. A fieldset (set a style for this element)

   f. A legend (set a style for this element)

   g. A selection list (make one of the options selected by default)

   h. A text area

   i. Submit and reset buttons

5. Also make appropriate use of the `label` element and the `for` attribute.

6. Save the **survey.htm** file. Switch to your browser, and then refresh or reload the page. Verify all styles work correctly.

7. Open your browser, and then go to http://validator.w3.org. Use the Validate by File Upload method to check the survey.htm document and ensure that the HTML code is correct. If necessary, correct any errors detected by the validation.

8. In your browser, go to http://jigsaw.w3.org/css-validator. Use the By file upload method to check the survey.htm file and ensure that the CSS code is correct. If necessary, correct any errors detected by the validation.

9. Submit the results of the survey.htm file to your instructor, in either printed or electronic form, as requested.

ENDING DATA FILES

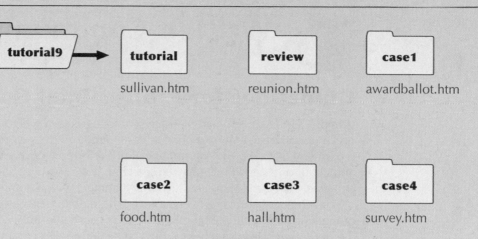

tutorial9 → tutorial
sullivan.htm

review
reunion.htm

case1
awardballot.htm

case2
food.htm

case3
hall.htm

case4
survey.htm

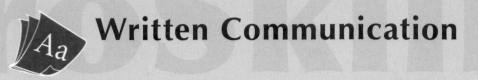

Written Communication

Guidelines for Professional Communication

Whether it's a simple email message sent to a group, a memo to provide information on an upcoming event, or a press release introducing a new product to the market, the quality of your written communications tells the world how prepared, informed, and detail oriented you are. When searching for a job, an ability to write clearly and effectively is essential. After all, your first contact with a company is often a cover letter and resume. For a prospective employer, these documents provide the first indicators of the kind of employee you might be. To make the best possible impression, follow the important rules listed below in all types of business communication.

Rule One: Identify Your Audience

Who will read your document? What do they already know about your subject? For starters, you can assume your audience is made up of busy people who will only take the time to read what is important and relevant to them. They don't want to be entertained. They just want to read the information you have to present as quickly as possible. In the case of a resume and cover letter, your audience is typically one or more professional people who don't know you. The goal of your resume and cover letter, then, should be to introduce yourself quickly and efficiently.

Rule Two: Do Your Research

Provide all the information the reader will need to make a decision or take action. Be absolutely certain the facts you present are correct. Don't assume something is true just because a friend told you it was, or because you read it on the Web. Verify all your facts using reputable sources. Remember, your goal as a writer is to make the reader trust you. Nothing alienates a reader faster than errors or misleading statements. When applying for a job, make sure you are knowledgeable about the company, so you can mention relevant and accurate details in your cover letter.

Rule Three: State Your Purpose

At the beginning of the document, explain why you are writing. The reader shouldn't have to wonder. Are you writing to inform, or do you want action to be taken? Do you hope to change a belief or simply state your position? In a cover letter accompanying your resume, state clearly that you are writing to apply for a job, and then explain exactly for what job you are applying. That might sound obvious, but many job applicants forget about directness in their efforts to come across as clever or interesting. This only hurts their chances, because prospective employers typically have many cover letters to read, with no time to spare for sorting through irrelevant information.

Rule Four: Write Succinctly

Use as few words as possible. Don't indulge in long, complicated words and sentences because you think they make you sound smart. The most intelligent writing is often short and to the point. Keep in mind that hiring a new employee is a very time-consuming process.

In small companies, people in charge of hiring often have to do it while performing their regular duties. Thus, the more succinct your resume and cover letter, the greater the chances that a potential employer will actually read both documents.

ProSkills

Rule Five: Use the Right Tone

Be professional and courteous. In the case of writing to a prospective employer, don't make the mistake of being overly friendly, as it might indicate to the reader that you are not taking the job application process seriously.

Rule Six: Revise, Revise, Revise

After you finish a document, set it aside for a while, and then proof it when it's no longer fresh in your mind. Even a small grammar or punctuation error can cause a potential employer to set aside your resume in favor of a more polished one with no errors. Remember, the best writers in the world seek out readers who can provide constructive suggestions, so consider having a friend or colleague read it and provide feedback. If someone points out an unclear passage, make every attempt to improve it.

Following these basic rules will help to ensure that you develop strong, professional written communication skills.

Creating a Resume

Now that you have learned how to create Web pages, you'll create some for your personal use. Today, most job applicants submit resumes to companies using the Web. To differentiate yourself from other job candidates who might be submitting their resumes as word-processing documents, you can send your resume as an HTML file.

In this exercise, the Web site for the resume should consist of at least two pages. One should contain the resume, and the other should contain an image file, other supplementary material, or a cover page. Your Web pages do not have to be about yourself—they can describe any person, living or dead, or even a fictional character. You might create a resume to help Mark Twain apply for a job as a newspaper columnist, to help Thomas Edison apply for a job as an inventor, or to help Eleanor Roosevelt apply for a job in government. The job can be at a real or fictional company.

The contents of your Web pages must be original work—something that you create specifically for this project. Your Web pages should meet the requirements of your campus acceptable computer use policy and should not be offensive. The home page file can have either a fixed or liquid layout, but the layout should illustrate the design principles you learned in this text.

ProSkills

Note: Be sure *not* to include sensitive information about yourself in the Web pages you create and submit to your instructor for this exercise. Later, you can update the Web pages with more personal information.

Complete the following:

1. Using an embedded style sheet to format your home page, create a Web page that has the following components:

   - An anchor at the top of the page (used for a link to the bottom of the page)
   - A link at the bottom of the page back to the anchor at the top
   - At least two section headings of different sizes (such as `<h1>` and `<h2>`)
   - Examples of bold text and italic text
   - At least five paragraphs of text
   - At least one image that is not a link
   - At least one image that is a link
   - A link to another page
   - At least three external links to appropriate Web sites
   - An ordered or unordered list (change the list style type or use a list style image)
   - The `<div> </div>` tags and a class applied to the `<div>` tag
   - A table with a minimum of three columns and three rows, including a `colspan` or a `rowspan`
   - An independent class that changes the appearance of text to 1.2em, italic, and red. Apply this independent class to several words on your resume.

2. Style and use the following elements in your Web pages:

   - `<h1>`, `<h2>`, or `<h3>`
   - `<em>`
   - `<strong>`
   - `<p>`
   - `a:link`
   - `a:visited`
   - `a:hover`

3. Save your file with a name of ***yourlastname_resume.htm***. Save all other files using a similar naming convention.

4. Submit your completed files to your instructor, in either printed or electronic form, as requested.

Multimedia and Accessibility

The term **multimedia** describes anything that includes sound, video, or animation. Multimedia is used extensively on the Web, particularly at news and information sites. Clearly, the popularity of sites such as *www.youtube.com* shows that anyone can use multimedia on the Web.

Although HTML and image files are usually small, multimedia files tend to be very large. Downloading these files also requires a lot of **bandwidth**—a measurement of the amount of data that can be sent over communications lines at once. During the early days of the Internet, most users went online using a **dial-up connection** via standard phone lines. Dial-up access is still common in rural areas or parts of the world where Internet access is not as prevalent, or when people are looking for a less expensive Internet connection option. Dial-up connections are slow to transmit data and have a low bandwidth, so to make their Web sites load quickly, most Web designers do not include a lot of multimedia on their sites, or they do so in a way that gives users the option to download multimedia or not. To download a multimedia file rapidly, your computer needs to have a **broadband** connection—a high-bandwidth communication line, such as a cable or fiber-optic line. Today, the majority of Internet users in developed countries have a broadband connection, whether at work or at home.

The difference between dial-up and broadband connections is crucial when it comes to **streaming media**, which are multimedia files that can begin playing without first having to be downloaded in their entirety. Internet users who still have dial-up phone connections can use only **nonstreaming media**—multimedia files that are downloaded completely before they can be played. If you're responsible for a Web site that depends on streaming media files, you should probably sign up for a **hosted streaming media plan** with a company that has dedicated servers used solely for high-volume streaming media.

If you have a high-speed broadband connection, you can enjoy many multimedia features of the Internet. For example, **podcasting** is the use of sound files to record and then play audio and video commentary. You can find podcasts everywhere on the Web, but particularly on news and information sites. **Blogs** (Web logs) are personal diaries or commentaries posted on the Web. **Video blogs** are sites whose content is presented with video files.

STARTING DATA FILES

There are no starting Data Files needed for this Appendix.

Understanding Plug-Ins and Players

As a Web page designer, you obviously want all visitors to your Web site to be able to view its multimedia content. In the past, Web browser support for audio and video was unreliable. However, audio and video support is built into most current Web browsers. To play multimedia content using older standards, a browser needs a **plug-in** (or **add-on**), which is any software that adds functionality to a program. A **player** is a plug-in program designed to play multimedia files. The most popular players are Adobe Flash, Apple QuickTime, Microsoft Silverlight, Real Media, and Windows Media. Your Web browser likely already has plug-ins installed, but you might be prompted to install upgrades periodically.

To assist the visitors to your Web site, use the following guidelines when selecting multimedia formats:

- Don't make the visitor guess; show what file format your multimedia file uses.
- Offer several versions of the same multimedia file. For example, offer the file in both the Apple QuickTime and Adobe Flash player formats.
- Provide links to download the player.

Understanding Multimedia File Formats

Multimedia files are created in several different types of file formats, as there is no universally accepted format for audio, video, or animation. The filename extension, such as .swf or .avi, identifies the file format. Some of the formats were designed for personal computers, and others were created for the Apple computer. **Cross-platform** formats run on both types of computers. There are several popular audio file formats:

- The **WAVE** format was developed together by IBM and Microsoft, and is supported by all computers running the Windows operating system. WAVE sound files have the extension .wav.
- The **MP3** file format was developed by the Moving Pictures Experts Group (MPEG). This file format also supports video. Today, MP3 is perhaps the most popular sound format for recorded music. MP3 files have the extension .mp3.
- The **Ogg** format (audio and video) is an open source format maintained by the Xiph.Org Foundation. Files have the extension .ogv, .oga, .ogx, .ogg, or .spx. The format is supported by Firefox and Safari but may not be supported by other browsers.

Similarly, video files can be stored in a variety of file formats. Video formats include those that involve animation, such as Adobe Flash. There are several popular video file formats:

- The **MPEG** (Moving Pictures Expert Group) format is one of the most popular on the Internet. MPEG is supported cross-platform and by all contemporary browsers. Videos stored in the MPEG format have the extension .mpg or .mpeg. Most videos posted on the Internet today are in the MPEG-4 format or a subset of it.
- The **QuickTime** format was developed by Apple. To play QuickTime movies, you need the QuickTime player and the appropriate plug-in. QuickTime video files have the extension .mov.
- The **Shockwave/Flash** format was developed by Adobe. The Flash player is installed when you install most contemporary browsers, such as Firefox or Internet Explorer. Videos stored in the Shockwave/Flash format have the extension .swf. Note that, currently, the iPhone and iPad cannot play Flash files.

Placing Multimedia on Your Web Pages

You have three options for placing multimedia on your Web pages. You can use the HTML `object` element, use the nonstandard `embed` element, or combine the two methods. Many video sharing sites use the `embed` element, even though it is nonstandard.

Using the `object` Element

The `object` element was designed to embed a variety of data types, images, and other file types (such as PDF documents). The `type` attribute and its value describe the data type. The value for the `type` attribute is often a **MIME** (Multipurpose Internet Extension) value. For example, the MIME type for a WAV sound file is audio/wav. The `width` and `height` attributes determine the width and height of the object in the browser.

```
<object
    data = "moviename.swf"
    type = "application/x-shockwave-flash"
    width = "400"
    height = "400">
</object>
```

Besides the `type` attribute, several attributes and values should always be included in the start `<object>` tag regardless of the player. For example, the `classid` attribute identifies which plug-in should be loaded. The class id is a combination of letters, numbers, and hyphens that identifies a system registry entry and assigns a unique number for each player. The class id tells the operating system which player to use to access the multimedia file. All class ids begin with *clsid:* and are followed by a series of alphanumeric characters grouped in the following five quantities of digits: 8 – 4 – 4 – 4 – 12.

The values for the `classid` attribute for several popular players are shown in Figure A-1.

| Figure A-1 | Values for the classid attribute for several players |

Player	classid
Windows Media	clsid:22D6F312-B0F6-11D0-94AB-0080C74C7E95
Real Media	clsid:CFCDAA03-8BE4-11CF-B84B-0020AFBBCCFA
Apple Quick Time	clsid:02BF25D5-8C17-4B23-BC80-D3488ABDDC6B
Flash	clsid:D27CDB6E-AE6D-11CF-96B8-444553540000

The class id code would be entered as shown in the following example:

```
<object
    data = "moviename.swf"
    type = "application/x-shockwave-flash"
    classid = "clsid:D27CDB6E-AE6D-11CF-96B8-444553540000"
    width = "400"
    height = "400">
      <param name = "src" value="moviename.swf" />
</object>
```

The `codebase` attribute identifies the URL where you can download the plug-in if it is not already installed on the computer. (The `pluginspage` attribute performs the same function when you use the `embed` element.) Generally, these installation files have the filename extension of .cab, as in the following example, where the URL points to the location of the most recent version of the Flash player:

```
<object
    data = "moviename.swf"
    type = "application/x-shockwave-flash"
    classid = "clsid:D27CDB6E-AE6D-11CF-96B8-444553540000"
    codebase = "http://fpdownload.adobe.com/pub/shockwave/
cabs/flash/swflash.cab#version=9,0,0,0"
    width = "400"
    height = "400">
</object>
```

Figure A-2 lists the attributes and descriptions for the `object` element.

Figure A-2	Attributes and descriptions for the object element

object **Attribute**	**Description**
data	The source of the multimedia file
type	The type of multimedia and the filename extension
autostart	A value of true plays the multimedia file automatically and a value of false does not
controller	Determines whether the play, pause, stop, and rewind buttons appear on the player
height	The height of the element in pixels or as a percentage
width	The width of the element in pixels or as a percentage
standby	The text displayed while the object is loading

Using the Parameter Element

The `object` element works together with the `param` (parameter) element, which uses both the `name` and `value` attributes. **Parameters** define the characteristics of the object; an object can have multiple parameters. The parameter element can be used only within the start and end `object` tags. The parameter element is an empty element and should be ended with a space and forward slash. Besides the `src` parameter, which identifies the file to be played, you should always include the `autoplay` and `controller` parameters. The `autoplay` parameter determines when the media file starts to play. Set the value to `true` to make the media file play automatically or `false` to make the user click a control to start the media file. Generally, you should set the `autoplay` value to `false` so that visitors to your Web site have the option of playing the multimedia file or not. Not everyone has a broadband connection, and few people enjoy having their browsing interrupted while a media file plays. The `controller` parameter determines whether the player controls are visible. Set the value to `false` or true depending on whether you want to display the control buttons. Generally, you should set the value to `true` so that the user can control the playback of the media. The `width` attribute determines how many of the controls you can view. The code to embed a Flash video using the `object` and `param` elements would be similar to the following example, where *moviename.swf* is the filename. Indenting the code is optional, but it helps readability.

```
<object
    data = "moviename.swf"
    type = "application/x-shockwave-flash"
    classid = "clsid:D27CDB6E-AE6D-11CF-96B8-444553540000"
    codebase = "http://fpdownload.adobe.com/pub/shockwave/
cabs/flash/swflash.cab#version=9,0,0,0"
    width = "400"
    height = "400">
      <param name = "src" value="moviename.swf" />
      <param name = "autoplay" value="false" />
      <param name = "controller" value="true" />
</object>
```

Each player has its own long list of parameters, some of which are required. When using the object element, check the list of parameters available for the particular player you're using by going to the Web site for that player.

Using the embed Element

Not all contemporary browsers use the object element in the same manner, so the embed element can be nested within the object element. If a browser has trouble interpreting the object element code, it will read and execute the code within the embed element. The <embed> tag uses the src attribute to identify the multimedia file that will play when the user clicks the file link. The src, width, and height attributes are required for the embed element. Figure A-3 lists the attributes and descriptions for the embed element.

| Figure A-3 | Attributes and descriptions for the embed element |

Attribute	Description
autoplay	Determines whether a multimedia file starts automatically; value can be either true or false
controller	Determines whether the play, pause, stop, and rewind buttons appear on the player
loop	Determines whether the multimedia file should play more than once
src	Specifies the source of the multimedia file
width	Specifies the width of the element in pixels or as a percentage
height	Specifies the height of the element in pixels or as a percentage

The following example shows how the embed element code can be nested within the object element code. The values for the autoplay and controller attributes should be the same as those in the object element.

```
<object width = "400" height="400"
classid = "clsid:02BF25D5-8C17-4B23-BC80-D3488ABDDC6B"
codebase = "http://www.apple.com/qtactivex/qtplugin.cab">

  <param name = "src" value="build.mov" />
  <param name = "autoplay" value="false" />
  <param name = "controller" value="true" />

  <embed src = "build.mov" width="400" height="400" autoplay =
"false" controller="true" pluginspage =
"http://www.apple.com/quicktime/download/">
  </embed>

</object>
```

Using HTML5 for Multimedia

The use of audio and video on the Web is thriving, but the formats are almost all proprietary. For example, the Adobe Flash and Apple QuickTime players play only their own files. Other formats, such as MPEG, are restricted by patents. Currently, markup that successfully embeds content in one browser might not work in another. For instance, the iPhone and iPad currently do not play Adobe Flash files.

HTML5 includes the `video` element and the `audio` element. Most current Web browsers support these elements. The goal is to make embedding video and audio as easy as embedding an image on a Web page. The following code uses the `video` element to embed a video on a Web page; note the similarity between this code and the code you used earlier in the book to insert an image on a Web page:

```
<video src = "http://www.cafeaulait.org/birds/sora.mov" />
```

For accessibility purposes, the `audio` and `video` elements can contain additional markup that describes the audio and video content. For even greater accessibility, some browser vendors, such as Firefox, are trying to add closed captioning for video.

Currently, all contemporary browsers, except Internet Explorer 8 and earlier versions, support the new HTML5 `audio` and `video` elements. The `video` and `audio` elements replace the `object` and `embed` elements and all of their attributes and values. The new elements are designed to be cross-browser compatible, but an industry-standard format does not yet exist for video and audio encodings. Most of the issues involved are not technical—the technology already exists. The issues are primarily legal, involving patents, royalties, and restrictions.

Note that text can be placed within the `<video>` tag so that users are alerted if their browsers do not support the `video` element, as in the following example:

```
<video src = "http://www.somebodyswebsite.com/videos/myvideo.wmv">
    Your browser does not support the video tag.
</video>
```

The `video` element takes the attributes and values shown in Figure A-4.

Figure A-4	Video element attributes and values

Attribute	Value	Purpose
autoplay	true | false	The value of `true` causes a video to play automatically.
controls	true | false	The value of `true` shows users some controls, such as a play button.
end	a number	By default, the video plays until the end. However, you can define where the video stream should stop playing; this feature is useful if you want to show a brief clip of a video.
height	a number	Specifies the height of the video player in pixels or as a percentage.
width	a number	Specifies the width of the video player in pixels or as a percentage.
src	a URL	Specifies the location of the video to play (similar to the src attribute for an image file).
loop	a number	Specifies the number of times to repeat the video.
poster	a URL	Specifies the location of an image to show before the video is ready to play (useful for users with low bandwidth).

The following code uses the audio tag to add a sound file to a Web page; note that for accessibility purposes, you should place the text for the audio between the start and end audio tags, in case the user's browser does not support the audio element, as shown below:

```
<audio src = "http://www.somebodyswebsite.com/audios/myaudio.mp3">
  <p>The transcript for the audio file would be placed here,
  encapsulating each paragraph in the paragraph element</p>
</audio>
```

The audio element takes the attributes and values shown in Figure A-5.

Figure A-5   **Audio element attributes and values**

Attribute	Value	Purpose
autoplay	true | false	The value of true causes the audio to play automatically.
controls	true | false	The value of true shows users some controls, such as a Play button.
src	a URL	Specifies the location of the audio to play (similar to the src attribute for an image file).
loop	a number	Specifies the number of times to repeat the audio.

Creating Accessible Web Pages

Many people who use the Web have physical challenges. Therefore, it's important to ensure that Web pages are as accessible as possible to all people, regardless of their abilities. Consider what content would be missed if a user had a vision impairment, hearing impairment, or difficulty with fine motor skills. That is, would a user miss content on your Web page if he or she couldn't move the mouse pointer easily, or only used a keyboard? Would a user miss content on the Web page if he or she had a hearing or visual impairment?

The Web Accessibility Initiative (WAI), part of the W3 group, creates guidelines that are widely regarded as the international standard for Web accessibility. The group prides itself on creating guidelines that make the Web accessible to people with disabilities. The guidelines and more information can be found at http://www.w3.org/WAI. There are also free WAI conformance validators available.

Below are some of the WAI recommendations for Web design:

- Make sure text can be enlarged to at least 200% without loss of functionality (use relative font sizes).
- Do not use color as the only visual means of conveying information.
- Use a high contrast between the background and the foreground (text).
- When audio is provided, also include a text transcript.
- When a movie is provided, also include text descriptions of the visuals.
- Make the purpose of a link clear and describe it in the link text.
- Provide a site map of a large Web site when possible to aid in navigation.
- Highlight a link or control when a user's mouse pointer hovers over it.
- Use label elements to associate form controls with labels.
- Use the alt attribute for every image.
- Ensure that the Web page is operable using only a keyboard.
- Make sure that blinking content blinks no more than three times per second.
- If blinking content is used, include a mechanism to pause or stop it.

The WAI Web site also contains some excellent examples of Web sites that were not accessible, and were then redesigned for accessibility.

Accessible Web page design is more than a consideration for access. Many countries also have legislation in place to require WAI conformance for organizations that receive funding or do business with the government, and recommendations for accessibility design. In the United States, this is covered by the Americans with Disabilities Act (1990) and other legislation. In Canada, this is covered by the Canadian Human Rights Act (1977). In Europe, this is covered by the Council of the European Union, Accessibility of Public Websites – Accessibility for People with Disabilities Council Resolution (2002). More information can be found through WAI at http://www.w3.org/WAI/Policy/.

HTML Character Entities

HTML

You can use character entities when you need to display characters that are not on the standard keyboard.

Figures B-1 through B-3 list the character entities.

STARTING DATA FILES

There are no starting Data Files needed for this Appendix.

Figure B-1   **Punctuation and special characters**

Named Reference	Displays As	Number Reference	Description
&acute;	´	&#180;	acute accent
&amp;	&	&#38;	ampersand
&brvbar;	¦	&#166;	piping symbol
&bull;	•	&#8226;	bullet
&cedil;	¸	&#184;	cedilla
&cent;	¢	&#162;	cent sign
&circ;	ˆ	&#710;	modifier letter circumflex accent
&clubs;	♣	&#9827;	black club suit = shamrock
&copy;	©	&#169;	copyright sign
&curren;	¤	&#164;	currency sign
&dagger;	†	&#8224;	dagger
&Dagger;	‡	&#8225;	double dagger
&diams;	♦	&#9830;	black diamond suit
&euro;	€	&#8364;	euro sign
&frasl;	⁄	&#8260;	fraction slash
&gt;	>	&#62;	greater-than sign
&hearts;	♥	&#9829;	black heart suit = valentine
&hellip;	…	&#8230;	horizontal ellipsis
&iexcl;	¡	&#161;	inverted exclamation mark
&iquest;	¿	&#191;	inverted question mark
&laquo;	«	&#171;	left-pointing double angle quotation mark
&ldquo;	"	&#8220;	left double quotation mark
&loz;	◊	&#9674;	lozenge
&lsaquo;	‹	&#8249;	single left-pointing angle quotation mark
&lsquo;	'	&#8216;	left single quotation mark
&lt;	<	&#60;	less-than sign
&macr;	¯	&#175;	macron
&mdash;	—	&#8212;	em dash
&middot;	·	&#183;	middle dot
&ndash;	–	&#8211;	en dash
&not;	¬	&#172;	not sign
&oline;	‾	&#8254;	overline
&ordf;	ª	&#170;	feminine ordinal indicator
&ordm;	º	&#186;	masculine ordinal indicator
&para;	¶	&#182;	paragraph sign
&permil;	‰	&#8240;	per mille sign
&pound;	£	&#163;	pound sign
&prime;	′	&#8242;	feet
&Prime;	″	&#8243;	inches
&quot;	"	&#34;	quotation mark

Figure B-1　　**Punctuation and special characters (continued)**

Named Reference	Displays As	Number Reference	Description
&raquo;	»	&#187;	right-pointing double angle quotation mark
&rdquo;	"	&#8221;	right double quotation mark
&reg;	®	&#174;	registered trademark sign
&rsaquo;	›	&#8250;	single right-pointing angle quotation mark
&rsquo;	'	&#8217;	right single quotation mark
&sbquo;	‚	&#8218;	single low-9 quotation mark
&sect;	§	&#167;	section sign
&spades;	♠	&#9824;	black spade suit
&sup1;	¹	&#185;	superscript one
&tilde;	˜	&#732;	small tilde
&trade;	™	&#8482;	trademark sign
&yen;	¥	&#165;	yen sign

Figure B-2　　**Math and scientific characters**

Named Reference	Displays As	Number Reference	Description
&and;	∧	&#8743;	logical wedge
&ang;	∠	&#8736;	angle
&asymp;	≈	&#8776;	almost equal to
&cap;	∩	&#8745;	intersection
&cong;	≅	&#8773;	approximately equal to
&cup;	∪	&#8746;	union
&deg;	°	&#176;	degree sign
&divide;	÷	&#247;	division sign
&empty;	∅	&#8709;	empty set
&equiv;	≡	&#8801;	identical to
&exist;	∃	&#8707;	there exists
&fnof;	ƒ	&#402;	latin small f with hook
&forall;	∀	&#8704;	for all
&frac12;	½	&#189;	fraction one half
&frac14;	¼	&#188;	fraction one quarter
&frac34;	¾	&#190;	fraction three quarters
&ge;	≥	&#8805;	greater-than or equal to
&infin;	∞	&#8734;	infinity
&int;	∫	&#8747;	integral
&isin;	∈	&#8712;	element of
&lang;	⟨	&#9001;	left-pointing angle bracket

Figure B-2   Math and scientific characters (continued)

Named Reference	Displays As	Number Reference	Description
&lceil;	⌈	&#8968;	left ceiling
&le;	≤	&#8804;	less-than or equal to
&lfloor;	⌊	&#8970;	left floor
&micro;	μ	&#181;	micro sign
&minus;	−	&#8722;	minus sign
&nabla;	∇	&#8711;	backward difference
&ne;	≠	&#8800;	not equal to
&ni;	∋	&#8715;	contains as member
&notin;	∉	&#8713;	not an element of
&nsub;	⊄	&#8836;	not a subset of
&oplus;	⊕	&#8853;	circled plus
&or;	∨	&#8744;	logical
&otimes;	⊗	&#8855;	circled times
&part;	∂	&#8706;	partial differential
&perp;	⊥	&#8869;	perpendicular to
&plusmn;	±	&#177;	plus or minus sign
&prop;	∝	&#8733;	proportional to
&radic;	√	&#8730;	square root (radical sign)
&rang;	〉	&#9002;	right-pointing angle bracket
&rceil;	⌉	&#8969;	right ceiling
&rfloor;	⌋	&#8971;	right floor
&sdot;	⋅	&#8901;	dot operator
&sim;	~	&#8764;	tilde operator
&sub;	⊂	&#8834;	subset of
&sube;	⊆	&#8838;	subset of or equal to
&sum;	Σ	&#8721;	n-ary summation
&sup;	⊃	&#8835;	superset of
&sup2;	^{2}	&#178;	superscripted two
&sup3;	^{3}	&#179;	superscripted three
&supe;	⊇	&#8839;	superset of or equal to
&there4;	∴	&#8756;	therefore
&times;	×	&#215;	multiplication sign

Figure B-3   **Arrow shapes**

Named Reference	Displays As	Number Reference	Description
&crarr;	↵	&#8629;	downward arrow with corner leftward
&darr;	↓	&#8595;	downward arrow
&dArr;	⇓	&#8659;	downward double arrow
&harr;	↔	&#8596;	left right arrow
&hArr;	⇔	&#8660;	left right double arrow
&larr;	←	&#8592;	leftward arrow
&lArr;	⇐	&#8656;	leftward double arrow
&rarr;	→	&#8594;	rightward arrow
&rArr;	⇒	&#8658;	rightward double arrow
&uarr;	↑	&#8593;	upward arrow
&uArr;	⇑	&#8657;	upward double arrow

HTML5 Elements

The following table lists the HTML5 elements by name and provides a description of each. This list is limited to the elements used in this text and is not a comprehensive list of HTML5 elements.

STARTING DATA FILES

There are no starting Data Files needed for this Appendix.

Name	Description
a	Anchor
area	Client-side image map area
article	Identifies content that is information contained in an article
aside	Identifies content that is in a sidebar
body	Document body
br	Forced line break
button	Button
caption	Table caption
col	Table column
colgroup	Table column group
dd	Description list description
div	Generic block-style container
dl	Description list
dt	Description term
em	Emphasis
fieldset	Form control group
figcaption	Identifies content as the caption for a figure
figure	Identifies content as a figure
footer	Identifies footer content
form	Interactive form
h1	Heading level 1
h2	Heading level 2
h3	Heading level 3
h4	Heading level 4
h5	Heading level 5
h6	Heading level 6
head	Document head
header	Identifies header content
hr	Horizontal rule
html	Document root element
img	Embedded image
input	Form control
label	Form field label text
legend	Fieldset legend
li	List item
link	A media-independent link
map	Client-side image map
meta	Generic meta information
nav	Identifies navigation bar content
object	Generic embedded object
ol	Ordered list
optgroup	Option group
option	Selectable choice
p	Paragraph

Name	Description
section	Identifies a section of the content
select	Option selector
span	Generic inline container
strong	Strong emphasis (bold)
style	Style information
table	Document table
tbody	Table body
td	Table data cell
textarea	Multiline text field
tfoot	Table footer
th	Table header cell
thead	Table header
title	Document title
tr	Table row
ul	Unordered list

CSS3 Properties and Values

The following table lists the CSS3 properties and the values available for each property. In the Values column, the default value is shown in bold. The Group column lists the group to which the property belongs. This list is not comprehensive; it includes only the properties that are used in this text.

STARTING DATA FILES

There are no starting Data Files needed for this Appendix.

Property	Description	Values	Group
background	Shorthand property for setting all background properties	*background-attachment* *background-color* *background-image* *background-position* *background-repeat*	background
background-attachment	Sets the position of a background image as fixed or scrolling with the page	fixed **scroll**	background
background-color	Sets the background color of an element	*rgb value* *hex value* *short hex value* *named value* **transparent**	background
background-image	Sets an image as the background	url *(filename)* **none**	background
background-position	Sets the position of a background image	top left top center top right center left **center center** center right bottom left bottom center bottom right *x% y%*	background
background-repeat	Determines whether a background image is repeated	**repeat** repeat-x repeat-y no-repeat	background
border	The shorthand property for setting all of the border properties	*border-width* *border-color* *border-style*	border
border-bottom	The shorthand property for setting all of the properties for the bottom border	*border-bottom-width* *border-bottom-style* *border-bottom-color*	border
border-bottom-color	Sets the color of the bottom border	*color*	border
border-bottom-left-radius	Sets the bottom left radius of the border for an element	*horizontal radius* *vertical radius*	border-radius
border-bottom-right-radius	Sets the bottom right radius of the border for an element	*horizontal radius* *vertical radius*	border-radius
border-bottom-style	Sets the style for the bottom border	*style*	border
border-bottom-width	Sets the width for the bottom border	thin **medium** thick *length* (in ems)	border
border-collapse	Determines whether a table border has a single or double rule	collapse **separate**	table

Property	Description	Values	Group
border-color	Sets the color for all four borders	*rgb value* *hex value* *short hex value* *named value*	border
border-left	The shorthand property for setting all of the properties for the left border	*border-left-width* *border-left-style* *border-left-color*	border
border-left-color	Sets the color for the left border	*color*	border
border-left-style	Sets the style for the left border	*style*	border
border-left-width	Sets the width for the left border	thin **medium** thick *length* (in ems)	border
border-radius	The shorthand property for setting the border-radius properties	*border-top-right-radius* *border-top-left-radius* *border-bottom-right-radius* *border-bottom-left-radius*	border-radius
border-right	The shorthand property for setting all of the properties for the right border	*border-right-width* *border-style* *border-color*	border
border-right-color	Sets the color for the right border	*color*	border
border-right-style	Sets the style for the right border	*style*	border
border-right-width	Sets the width for the right border	thin **medium** thick *length* (in ems)	border
border-style	Sets the style of the four borders	**none** hidden dotted dashed double groove inset outset ridge solid	border
border-top	The shorthand property for setting all of the properties for the top border	*border-top-width* *border-top-style* *border-top-color*	border
border-top-color	Sets the color for the top border	*color*	border
border-top-left-radius	Sets the top left radius of the border for an element	*horizontal radius* *vertical radius*	border-radius
border-top-right-radius	Sets the top right radius of the border for an element	*horizontal radius* *vertical radius*	border-radius

Property	Description	Values	Group
border-top-style	Sets the style for the top border	*style*	border
border-top-width	Sets the width for the top border	thin **medium** thick *length* (in ems)	border
border-width	A shorthand property for setting the width of the four borders in one declaration; can have from one to four values	thin **medium** thick *length* (in ems)	border
bottom	Determines how far from the bottom edge an element is from its parent element	**auto** *length* (in ems or %)	positioning
box-shadow	Attaches one or more drop-shadows to a box, provided by a list of values	*h-shadow* *v-shadow* *blur* *spread* *color*	box-shadow
caption-side	Determines the position of the table caption	**top** bottom left right	table
clear	Positions an element below another element	left right both none	classification
color	Determines text color	*color* in RGB, hex, or short hex, or as a named value	text
display	Sets how and if an element is to be displayed	block inline list-item **none**	classification
empty-cells	Determines whether to show a cell without content in a table	**hide** show	table
float	Positions an element in relation to another element	left right **none**	classification
font	The shorthand property for setting all of the properties for a font	*font-style* *font-variant* *font-weight* *font-size/line-height* *font-family*	font
font-family	A list of font family names from specific to generic	*font family name* *generic family name*	font
font-size	Sets the size for the font	xx-small x-small small medium large x-large xx-large smaller *value* (in pt or em)	font

Property	Description	Values	Group
font-style	Sets the style for the font	**normal** italic oblique	font
font-variant	Displays text in small caps or in a normal font	**normal** small-caps	font
font-weight	Sets the weight of a font	**normal** bold bolder lighter 100 200 300 400 500 600 700 800 900	font
height	Sets the height of an element	**auto** *length* (in ems or %)	dimension
left	Determines how far from the left edge an element is from its parent element	**auto** *length* (in ems or %)	positioning
letter-spacing	Increases or decreases the space between characters	**normal** *length* (in ems)	text
line-height	Determines the white space between lines	**normal** *number* *length* (in ems or %)	text
list-style	The shorthand property for setting all of the list-style properties	*list-style-type* *list-style-position* *list-style-image*	list
list-style-image	Sets an image to be used as a list-style marker	**none** url *(filename)*	list
list-style-position	Determines where the list-item marker will be positioned	inside **outside**	list
list-style-type	Determines the type of the list-item marker	armenian circle decimal decimal-leading-zero **disc** georgian hebrew lower-alpha lower-greek lower-roman none square upper-alpha upper-roman	list
margin	The shorthand property for setting the margin properties	*margin-top* *margin-right* *margin-bottom* *margin-left*	margin

Property	Description	Values	Group
margin-bottom	Sets the bottom margin for an element	auto *length* (in ems or %)	margin
margin-left	Sets the left margin for an element	auto *length* (in ems or %)	margin
margin-right	Sets the right margin for an element	auto *length* (in ems or %)	margin
margin-top	Sets the top margin for an element	auto *length* (in ems or %)	margin
overflow	Determines the visibility of an element should content not fit into its container	auto hidden scroll **visible**	positioning
padding	The shorthand property for setting all of the padding properties	*padding-top* *padding-right* *padding-bottom* *padding-left*	padding
padding-bottom	Sets the bottom padding for an element	*length* (in ems or %)	padding
padding-left	Sets the left padding for an element	*length* (in ems or %)	padding
padding-right	Sets the right padding for an element	*length* (in ems or %)	padding
padding-top	Sets the top padding for an element	*length* (in ems or %)	padding
position	Positions an element	absolute fixed relative **static**	positioning
right	Determines how far from the right edge an element is from its parent element	**auto** *length* (in ems or %)	positioning
text-align	Aligns the text in an element horizontally	center justify **left** right	text
text-decoration	Adds a line above, through, or under text	line-through overline **none** underline	text
text-indent	Indents the first line of text in an element	*length* (in ems or %)	text
text-transform	Determines the capitalization of text	capitalize lowercase **none** uppercase	text
top	Determines how far from the top edge an element is from its parent element	**auto** *length* (in ems or %)	positioning

Property	Description	Values	Group
vertical-align	Sets the vertical alignment of an element	**baseline** bottom middle sub super text-bottom text-top top *length* (in ems or %)	positioning
visibility	Determines whether an element is visible	collapse hidden **visible**	classification
width	Sets the width of an element	**auto** *length* (in ems or %)	dimension
word-spacing	Increases or decreases the space between words	**normal** *length* (in ems)	text
z-index	Determines the stacking order of an element (the greater the number, the higher the element is in the stack)	**auto** *number*	positioning

Pseudo-Classes

Pseudo-Class	Purpose
:active	Determines the style when a link is clicked
:focus	Determines the style when a link has the focus
:hover	Determines the style for mouse-over effect
:link	Determines the style for links that have not been visited
:visited	Determines the style for links that have been visited

Pseudo-Elements

Pseudo-Element	Purpose
:first-letter	Formats just the first letter of a word
:first-line	Formats just the first line of a paragraph
:before	Inserts text, an image, or white space before an element
:after	Inserts text, an image, or white space after an element

GLOSSARY/INDEX